C.F.A. Readings in Financial Analysis

The Institute of Chartered Financial Analysts

Fifth Edition
1981

Richard D. Irwin, Inc.
Homewood, Illinois

ISBN 0-256-02583-5

Printed in the United States of America.

1 2 3 4 5 6 7 8 9 0 ML 8 7 6 5 4 3 2 1

C. F. A. READINGS IN FINANCIAL ANALYSIS

TABLE OF CONTENTS

* * * * *

FOREWORD

This new Edition of *C.F.A. Readings in Financial Analysis* is being published with a threefold purpose. First, it is an up-to-date source of articles to all having a serious interest in the field of financial analysis, with particular emphasis upon securities research analysis and investment management. Second, it serves as a major addition to the I.C.F.A. Continuing Education Program, with a complimentary copy of this book being sent to all members of the I.C.F.A. Third, this book represents an integral part of the readings assignments in the C.F.A. Candidate Study and Examination Program. This Fifth Edition follows the Fourth published in 1977, with the official First Edition sent to members in 1966 (all editions published by Richard D. Irwin, Homewood).

In brief review, The Institute of Chartered Financial Analysts is an autonomous professional self-regulatory organization. Members are called *Chartered Financial Analysts* and have successfully completed a widely recognized three-year study and examination program. A college degree or equivalent is required to enter the program but no experience per se is now required to take any of the three examinations. For Level II and Level III, a candidate should be a member of a constituent Society of The Financial Analysts Federation. For the award of the Charter, a candidate must have had at least four years of experience in financial analysis as related to investments and subscribe to the highest ethical standards of practice. Since the first examination in 1963, financial analysts have taken nearly 30,000 examinations. A total of 6,400 individuals have been awarded the C.F.A. professional designation.

This Fifth Edition covers the spectrum of the seven topic areas in the C.F.A. Program. These areas are described in the lead article, "The C.F.A. Program's Body of Knowledge," by Dr. O. Whitfield Broome, Jr., Executive Director. Half (15) of the remaining 30 articles are new to the C.F.A. Program. Of the balance of the articles, five were in the Fourth Edition, five were included in the 1980 Study Guides, and five are also included in the new book, *C.F.A. Readings in Portfolio Management*. The sequence of articles follows our "tree of knowledge": four in Ethical and Professional Standards, a total of three generalized articles in Financial Accounting and Quantitative Techniques, five in Economics, three in Fixed Income Securities Analysis, four in Equity Securities Analysis, and seven in the broad area of Portfolio Management. The final four articles in this volume cut across the C.F.A. topic areas.

As a novel addition to the articles and a bridge to the past, this book begins with a selected group of *The C.F.A. Digest* abstracts of historical articles. Eight of these abstracts are on articles published in the 1950's, four in the 1960's, and one in the early 1970's. Writers, in order of abstracts herein, are: Markowitz, Sharpe, Treynor, Modigliani, Miller, Lintner, Walter, Molodovsky, Fama, Durand, Osborne, and Black. Readers interested in the complete article are referred to the original publication detailed at the beginning of the respective abstract.

We are indebted to a number of people for suggestions of articles to be included in this Fifth Edition. We necessarily had to prune the list to a manageable proportion and, thus, could not include some excellent articles. The editors of three leading investment publications were a great help—Jack L. Treynor, *Financial Analysts Journal*, Peter L. Bernstein, *The Journal of Portfolio Management*, and Edmund A. Mennis, C.F.A., *The C.F.A. Digest*. The comments and suggestions of Marshall D. Ketchum, C.F.A., (University of Chicago) were, as always, most helpful. A number of articles reflect recommendations of members of the C.F.A. Research and Publications Committee, including Robert W. Morrison, C.F.A. (Chairman), M. H. Earp, C.F.A., Arthur E. Rockwell, C.F.A., George W. Noyes, C.F.A., Stanley D. Ryals, C.F.A., and Harold A. Schwind, C.F.A.

We are most grateful for the advice and counsel of the I.C.F.A. Trustees, including Alfred C. Morley, C.F.A., President, and James R. Vertin, C.F.A., Vice President. For all such projects we are indebted to the I.C.F.A. staff, including the work of Mary Shelton in preparing this manuscript for publication. Special thanks is given to individual authors and their respective publications for allowing the I.C.F.A. to reproduce their articles in this Fifth Edition of *C.F.A. Readings in Financial Analysis*.

Hartman L. Butler, Jr., C.F.A.
Operations Director
January 1981
The Institute of Chartered Financial Analysts

Portfolio Selection, by Harry Markowitz, *The Journal of Finance,* **Vol. 7, No. 1, March 1952.** *(The C.F.A. Digest,* **9-2).**

This 1952 basic article deals with the choosing of a portfolio as opposed to estimating returns on individual securities. Markowitz rejects the strategy of maximizing discounted returns, because such a rule never implies the superiority of diversified portfolios. He also rejects the strategy of diversifying among all those securities that give maximum expected returns, because such a portfolio is not necessarily the minimum variance portfolio. A possible strategy that does emerge is the Expected-Return-Variance (E-V) rule, i.e., maximum expected return for a given level of risk, or minimum risk for a given level of expected return. Risk is defined as the variability, or "spread," in the set of possible returns for the portfolio in the next time period and is measured by the variance.

Expected return for a portfolio is a weighted average of the individual securities' expected returns. To obtain the portfolio variance, however, both variances and covariances must be considered. Covariances express the relationships among securities. Portfolio variance is then calculated as the weighted sum of the individual securities' variances and twice their covariances. The percent of the portfolio placed in each security (the weights) determines the expected return and variance of the selected portfolio. The variance measures the portfolio's risk, and different optimal return-risk tradeoffs produce different portfolios on the efficient frontier (the E-V rule later called the mean-variance approach).

Markowitz presents the E-V rule geometrically for various security cases. Attainable and efficient E-V combinations are shown graphically. The efficient set of portfolios is a series of connected line segments, with the point of minimum variance at one end and the point of maximum expected return at the other. The E-V rule creates diversified portfolios for a wide range of expected returns and variance of returns. Furthermore, the E-V criterion implies diversification for the "right reason"—not because of investing in many securities, but because of the need to invest in stocks that do not have high covariances among themselves.

This pioneering article concludes with two uses for the E-V principle. The first is in theoretical analyses, for example, to investigate a general change in preference as to expected return versus variance. The second is in the actual selection of portfolios. To do this, procedures for finding reasonable expected returns and variances are needed. Markowitz states that such procedures should combine "statistical techniques and the judgement of practical men."

Capital Asset Prices: A Theory of Market Equilibrium Under Conditions of Risk, by William F. Sharpe, *The Journal of Finance,* **Vol. 19, No. 3, September 1964.** *(The C.F.A. Digest, 9-2).*

This 1964 article seeks to construct a market equilibrium theory of asset prices under conditions of risk. The Markowitz article (12 years ago) dealt with investor behavior. Sharpe extends this work to a market equilibrium theory of how asset prices behave when risk is present. He first develops a model of individual investor behavior based on expected returns and risk (standard deviation). The investor chooses from a set of opportunities to maximize utility. To do this, the best set of investment plans must be determined from all those attainable; then, the plan chosen is that lying on the indifference curve representing the highest utility.

Investors also may invest in riskless assets that yield the pure interest rate. Portfolios involving risky assets and the riskless asset have expected returns and risk levels that lie along a straight line connecting the two components. Allowing the investor to borrow at the pure interest rate extends this straight line beyond the point of tangency. This straight line showing attractive portfolios is called the capital market line. Thus, investors choose the optimum combination of risky assets and, by borrowing or lending, achieve a particular point on the capital market line at which an indifference curve is tangent. Based on the assumptions of a pure interest rate for all investors and homogeneous investor expectations, Sharpe derives the conditions for equilibrium in the capital market. Investors seeking their preferred positions of return and risk will cause revisions in the prices of all assets, which in turn cause revisions in investor actions. In equilibrium, a simple linear relationship will exist between expected return and risk (standard deviation) for efficient combinations of risky assets.

While single assets are inefficient and do not fall on the capital market line, a consistent relationship exists between their expected returns and their systematic risk (i.e., that part of their total risk attributable to general market behavior). That part of the risk uncorrelated with the market is the unsystematic component. Prices will adjust so that assets that are more responsive to changes in the market will have higher expected returns. The measure of the risk of market effect should be directly related to expected return.

In summary, capital market theory implies that rates of return from all efficient combinations will be perfectly correlated. Diversification permits the investor to avoid all risk except that of swings in economic activity. Therefore, only the responsiveness of an asset to economic activity is relevant in assessing its risk. Prices adjust until a linear relationship is reached between the magnitude of responsiveness and expected return; if no relation exists to economic activity, an asset would return the pure interest rate.

How to Rate Management of Investment Funds, by Jack L. Treynor, *Harvard Business Review,* **Vol. 43, No. 1, January/February 1965.** *(The C.F.A. Digest,* **9-3).**

This 1965 article provides a new way to rate the management of investment funds. To measure the quality of investment management, it is necessary to analyze the various types of risk. One type, fluctuations in the general market, usually dominates the effect of management on investment returns in any one period. Another type of risk results from fluctuations in the individual securities held. Diversification is important in this regard. A meaningful measure of management performance must treat effectively both of these risks.

Treynor first develops the characteristic line, which graphically relates the expected rate of return on an investment fund (vertical axis) to the rate of return on a market index (horizontal axis). The characteristic line is the straight line drawn through the points on the graph representing the respective returns for each investment period. Excessive deviations indicate either that the fund is not sufficiently diversified to minimize non-market risk or that the management has consciously or unconsciously altered the volatility of the fund during the time period under study in order to adjust for anticipated market fluctuations. The characteristic line also allows comparisons between the management of two funds that have the same volatility.

A second line for performance measurement (called the portfolio-possibility line) relates the expected return of a portfolio containing a given fund to the portfolio owner's risk preferences. The slope of this line, which connects the rate on money-fixed claims to the rate of the equity assets of a particular investment fund, attempts to measure fund performance regardless of differences in investors' attitudes toward risk. Thus, the steepness of a fund's portfolio-possibility line is a direct measure of the fund's desirability to a risk-averse investor.

To implement the performance ratings, both the expected return and an appropriate measure of risk are needed. The slope of the characteristic line provides a measure of risk. The expected rate of return for a fund depends upon an assumed rate-of-return value for the market. The relative rankings of the funds, however, are not affected by the level of market return assumed. A numerical measure of this relative ranking can be obtained by extending a vertical line downward to the market rate of return axis at the point of intersection between a fund's characteristic line and a horizontal line representing the rate of return on money-fixed claims.

In summary, Treynor develops a new method for reviewing the performance of fund management. The differences detected by these procedures can be significant for individual investors regardless of their attitudes toward risk; furthermore, these differences are independent of market fluctuations.

The Cost of Capital, Corporation Finance and the Theory of Investment, by Franco Modigliani and Merton H. Miller, *The American Economic Review,* **Vol. 48, No. 3, June 1958.** *(The C.F.A. Digest,1-2).*

Modigliani and Miller in this 1958 article pose the question "What is the cost of capital?" as a means of delving into the process of valuing a firm's shares. The first part defines a relationship between capital structure and cost of capital (defined as cost to a firm, stated as a percentage, of its permanent financing), and provides an objective measurement of the cost of capital using available financial data. The second part applies the cost of capital to investment decision-making, using it as the cut-off criterion for the selection of proposed projects. Assuming the objective of a manager is to maximize the market value of a firm's shares, only those projects that return more than the cost of their financing are accepted.

Proposition I states that: ". . . the market value of any firm is independent of its capital structure and is given by capitalizing its expected return at the rate appropriate to its [risk] class." Restating this in terms of cost of capital, it becomes: ". . . the average cost of capital to any firm is completely independent of its capital structure and is equal to the capitalization rate of a pure equity stream of its [risk] class."

Proposition II states that: "The expected yield of a share of stock is equal to the appropriate capitalization rate for a pure equity stream in the [risk] class, plus a premium related to financial risk equal to the debt-to-equity times the spread between the [capitalization rate and the risk-free rate.]"

Proposition III states that: ". . . the cut-off point for investment in the firm will in all cases be [the capitalization rate which is cost of capital] and will be completely unaffected by the type of security used to finance the investment."

This means that the average cost of capital, the cost of additional financing, and the capitalization rate are equivalent to one another. It provides a cut-off criterion that serves to test the desirability of a proposed project in terms of its ability to increase the market value of the company's stock.

In concluding, M & M warn financial planners that Proposition III should not be interpreted to mean that capital structure is a matter of indifference and that optimal capital structure is no problem. The proposition refers only to investment decision-making, and does not mean that a manager would have no reason to prefer one type of capital structure over another.

Dividend Policy, Growth, and the Valuation of Shares, by Merton H. Miller and Franco Modigliani, *The Journal of Business,* **Vol. 34, No. 4 October, 1961.** *(The C.F.A. Digest,* 1-2).

Miller and Modigliani in this 1961 article assume that dividends play no role in the process of valuing securities. Management faces what is called "the dividend policy problem," because dividend payout affects the amount of retained earnings available for reinvestment in the company. Dividend payout can be low, providing greater retention of earnings, or it can be high with additional financing provided from external sources. Management faces a problem in setting a dividend policy, interrelated with financing policy, which will maximize the market value of the firm's stock.

In Parts I and II, M & M first assume perfect markets, and rational behavior and perfect certainty on the part of investors, thus postulating a theoretically ideal market. Under these conditions they find that dividends have no impact on the market price of a firm's stock. Therefore, it follows that dividend policy is not a problem at all, and that no optimal level of dividends exists. M & M believe that the controversy over dividends is fruitless, that it is caused by a misunderstanding about what investors capitalize when they buy stocks. Asking the question, "What does the market 'really' capitalize?," they show that four commonly used approaches to share valuation (discounted cash flow, current earnings plus future investment opportunities, stream of dividends, stream of earnings) are equivalent both to each other and to the fundamental principle of valuation.

Part III of the article, examining earnings, dividends, and growth rates, finds that a change in dividend policy affects only the distribution of earnings between dividends and capital gains. M & M conclude that: "If investors behave rationally [according to the M & M definition], such a change cannot affect market valuations."

Parts IV and V relax some of the constraints of a theoretically ideal environment, with no change in the results of the analysis: "For even without a full-fledged theory of what *does* determine market value under uncertainty we can show that dividend policy at least is *not* one of the determinants." M & M note in closing that as capital gains carry favorable tax treatment, stocks with low dividend payouts should command a premium. This is in contrast to the traditional view that such shares sell at a discount. Miller and Modigliani, therefore, attribute some degree of irrationality to the actions of investors.

Distribution of Incomes of Corporations Among Dividends, Retained Earnings, and Taxes, by John Lintner, *The American Economic Review,* **Vol. 46, No. 2, May 1956.** *(The C.F.A. Digest, 2-4).*

This 1956 paper explains the principal results of studies made on corporate dividend policy by the author and others. A basic conclusion is that dividends are an active variable within corporate decision-making, and retained earnings and savings are basically a residual resulting from established dividend policies. Some 600 large industrials were screened for available information and, out of these, 28 were selected for detailed examination. Diversity was sought and the author therefore attaches some significance to the uniform policies found. Fifteen characteristics or factors concerning dividend policy were drawn up. Factors expected to affect dividend policy include size, price-earnings ratio, payout, and stability of earnings.

General findings about the dividend policies of these 28 companies were the following:

1. The question of what to pay in dividends hinged most importantly of all on whether to change the existing rate.

2. Dividends therefore adjust with a lag to changes in earnings, providing stable dividend distributions.

3. Earnings is the most important variable in determining dividend changes and policies.

4. Two-thirds of the companies had formed ideas about a target or ideal payout ratio toward which they moved, but not by any set formula (a payout ratio of 50 percent was the most common).

5. Once the decisions have been made regarding dividend policy, the companies consider them to be active decision variables.

6. The remaining one-third of the companies had no formal policies on target payout and speed of adjustment, but informally most were following the same kind of policy *ad hoc* as the other two-thirds.

Using the results of this study, the author constructs a theoretical model to explain dividend decisions and changes. The equation presented is a regression equation with the change in dividend payments for any year as the dependent variable. The independent variable is the difference between (1) what the company would have paid in dividends this period if it adjusted its payout immediately to current profits and (2) what it actually did pay last period.

The conclusion is that managements evaluate their past experience related to outlays for investment and incorporate this knowledge into their dividend decisions in such a way that they can consistently pay the implied dividends year after year with little strain. Lintner's final conclusion is that the "dividends-profits-retained earnings subsystem is internally very stable though in continuous disequilibrium."

Divided Policies and Common Stock Prices, by James E. Walter, *The Journal of Finance,* **Vol. 11, No. 1, March 1956.** *(The C.F.A. Digest,* **2-4).**

This 1956 article develops a theoretical model that shows the relationship between dividend policies and stock prices. The author begins by referring to a statistical analysis that stock price appreciation is directly associated with the proportion of earnings retained. Retained earnings affect stock prices primarily through effect on expected dividends, laying the groundwork for a model depicting the relation between prices and dividends. Capitalization rates are employed to discount the future dividends rather than using P/E ratios, and these capitalization rates are determined by the pure rate of interest plus the required risk premiums. Walter devises three groups of stocks for consideration—growth, intermediate, and creditor. Each group has its own supposed characteristics, but the payout ratio is not a prime determinant of the three categories. Rather, the rate of return on additional investment is crucial.

To qualify as a growth stock, the prime consideration is the rate of return on additional investment. But to transform a stock into the growth category, the high rate of return must persist and the capitalization rate must not be increased. The author develops his model in equation form, where the present value of a stock is expressed as a function of the dividends, the earnings, the rate of return on additional investment, and the market capitalization rate. The formula focuses on the dividend payout ratio and the relation between the rate of return on additional investment and the market capitalization rate. Many factors can lead the market astray on growth stocks, or they can deceive the analyst into thinking that the market's evaluation is wrong when it is not.

The intermediate stock group includes most listed stocks. This group has a payout greater than 50 percent, an average P/E ratio, and prices that increase slowly. Stockholders prefer high payouts because other reinvestment is more favorable to them. If the rate of return adjusted for the preferential treatment of capital gains is less than the capitalization rate, but greater than zero, it is an intermediate stock. This leads to the conclusion a positive relationship exists between the payout ratio and the stock price. Even if the rate of return is less than the capitalization rate, expansion may still be desirable because part of the financing can come from debt funds. The company has to maintain its competitive position, or its profit rate will definitely decline. Some retained earnings are therefore necessary.

The third group is the creditor group, which is somewhat similar to debt securities. Almost exclusive emphasis is placed on the prevailing level of dividends, and average yields are somewhat higher than bonds. Retained earnings do not affect prices of creditor group stocks over time. If management and/or regulatory commissions regard shareholders as creditors and the economic environment permits this, these stocks will appear to be like credit instruments. Utilities are good examples. The market must be willing to accept a stock as a creditor stock.

In summary, the author develops a model of dividend policy that makes the payout a function of the rate of return on investment. Profitability affects the payout, and retained earnings affect stock prices by affecting expected dividends.

A Theory of Price-Earnings Ratios, by Nicholas Molodovsky, *The Analysts Journal,* **Vol. 9, No. 5, November 1953.** *(The C.F.A. Digest, 2-2).*

This very early article establishes price-earnings ratios as a link between current earnings and estimated earning power, for the purpose of estimating the value of common stocks. A basic set of truths is laid out as background for the development of a theory of price-earnings ratios: (1) Stocks will fluctuate, but they move around a computable value. "They remain bound by gravitational force to that sun of the economic system." (2) Dividends form the hard core of stock values, supported by the expectation of future payments. (3) The "size of the future," is limited by present worth (sometimes called present value). It narrows down the problem of evaluating a never-ending dividend stream because, beyond a certain point, further increments are no longer economically attractive. At the same time, though, present worth introduces the complication of selecting the proper interest rate to be used as the discounting factor.

"The theoretical content of the true investment value of a common stock cannot change; it must always be determined by future dividends and interest rates." As dividends flow out of earnings, it is necessary, first, to estimate future earnings. Then, by capitalizing the future earnings, investors obtain a measure of value. The Molodovsky approach is based on hypothetical price-earnings ratios as capitalization multipliers, and the use of capitalized earning power as a measure of the value of common stocks.

A hypothetical principle of the behavior of price-earnings ratios is developed and submitted to statistical testing with historical data. The essence of the concept is "the compensating principle" and the "rule of opposite movements." When current earnings fall below earning power, they must be compensated. Conversely, when current earnings rise above earning power, they must be discounted. The price-earnings ratio increases (to compensate) when current earnings fall below expectations, and also the price-earnings ratio declines (to discount) when current earnings rise above expectations. Accordingly, current earnings and price-earnings ratios move in opposite directions (opposite movements). To illustrate the concept diagramatically, a line, called the "price orbit," is developed by capitalizing earning power. This line is "the central stem around which stocks will fluctuate . . . the operational value of investors."

The article concludes with a discussion of factors unrelated to capitalization of earning power, such as investors' impressions about structural changes and psychological changes and psychological influences. The author suggests how these influences can be handled by the analyst, within the framework of the theoretical system, by using historical and projected price and earnings data to detect and measure these forces.

Stock Prices and Current Earnings, by Nicholas Molodovsky, *The Analysts Journal,* Vol. 11, No. 4, August 1955. *(The C.F.A. Digest, 2-2).*

This 1955 article continues the distinction between current earnings and earning power, and indicates that stock prices are related to long-run earning power rather than to current earnings. Molodovsky uses correlation analysis to show, for the period 1871-1951, that (with one exception) current earnings and stock prices change at different rates. Their correlation ". . . is so low as to preclude the existence of any significant causal link . . . ." In examining the influence of dividends, trend momentum (cumulative influence of the price trend), and current earnings on stock prices, the author found that all three factors together accounted for slightly more than one-half of the total influence on stock prices, with current earnings showing the smallest influence. The exception occurred during a period (1894-1914) where a basic reappraisal of earning power was underway; investors identified current earnings with earning power, capitalizing stocks on that basis, because of the industrial changes taking place at that time and their projected impact on long-term earnings.

The author warns against the use of yardsticks based on current earnings: "When individual ratios of prices to current earnings are computed for quick ready reference, they carry a clear meaning. But, when they are used as capitalization multipliers and are confronted with one another, strange things begin to happen . . . ." Because the price-earnings ratios fluctuate so much, they are not true capitalizers. They must adjust for departures between volatile current earnings and the slow-to-change earning power.

Price-earnings ratios, by reflecting the action of both prices and earnings, provide a tool for examining their interaction. Changes in prices, earnings, and price-earnings ratios fall into 13 combinations: five that cause price-earnings ratios to rise, five that cause them to decline, and three where no change occurs. A classification of all combinations based on data for the period 1871-1951 revealed that in the majority of historical cases, current earnings and price-earnings ratios moved in opposite directions. Earnings moves are more volatile than price moves. "Stock prices tend to discount the rises of current earnings and to compensate for their declines."

Molodovsky lists capitalized earning power and economic momentum as two principal forces behind the stock market, and sets forth the phases of the market during a typical economic expansion (the scheme is reversed for a period of contraction): (1) Beginning with declines in price-earnings ratios, current earnings begin to rise faster than stock prices. (2) The advance of stock prices catches up to earnings. Price-earnings ratios continue to decline, but more slowly. (3) As both stock prices and current earnings increase, the price-earnings ratios move sideways. (4) Price-earnings ratios begin to move in the same direction as current earnings, amplifying the rate of price increase. This is the phase of over-speculation. The action of the price-earnings ratio indicates a change of trend.

The Behavior of Stock-Market Prices, by Eugene F. Fama, *The Journal of Business,* **Vol. 38, No. 1, January 1965.** *(The C.F.A. Digest,* **9-3).**

This 1965 paper is concerned with the extent to which past stock prices can be usefully utilized to predict future stock prices. Or, how valid is the theory of random walks, which states that past price changes cannot meaningfully be used to predict future price changes? Two separate hypotheses are examined: (1) successive price changes are independent, and (2) price changes conform to some probability distribution.

The independence hypothesis, which is the more important of the two, involves first of all defining what is meant by independence. A random-walk market has implications for security analysis because it implies that prices at any point in time are good estimates of intrinsic values. The distribution of prices need not be specified in the general theory of random walks. The form of the distribution of prices changes, however, is important information. Various forms have been specified, beginning with Bachelier at the turn of the century. Mandelbrot has asserted that the distribution is stable Paretian, which implies the variances of the distributions behave as if they are infinite (which obviously presents problems for typical statistical tests).

Most of this paper is devoted to reporting the results of empirical tests of the random walk theory of stock prices—daily prices for the 30 Dow Jones Industrials from roughly the end of 1957 to September of 1962. The initial investigation involved a basic examination of the distributions of daily stock-price changes. Techniques included the examination of frequency distributions and normal probability graphs. Departures from the normal distribution are found, which upon special examination are in the direction predicted by the Mandelbrot hypothesis. Additional tests involved the stability of the distributions of price changes. Fama next tests for independence or dependence in price changes from both the statistician's and the investor's viewpoints. The first tests are statistical and involve serial correlations and runs tests, neither of which indicated any substantial dependence in price changes. Then a filter technique was used to test a trading rule. Finally, some evidence is found to support the Mandelbrot suggestion that large price changes tend to be followed by similar changes of either sign (although this dependence seems weak). No evidence at all suggests any stock price dependence that would be important for investment purposes.

In summary, this paper tested empirically the random-walk model of stock price behavior. One conclusion supports Mandelbrot's hypothesis that stock price changes are not normally distributed. A second conclusion is that the independence assumption of the random-walk model describes reality, implying that past price changes cannot assist in predicting future price changes.

Growth Stocks and the Petersburg Paradox, by David Durand, *Journal of Finance,* **Vol. 12, No. 3, September 1957.** *(The C.F.A. Digest,* **3-4).**

This 1957 article examines the factors affecting growth stocks, including the Petersburg Paradox and the problem of remote dividends. The author begins by considering the difficulties of appraising growth stocks and finds that most problems fall into two categories: (1) forecasting earnings or dividends; and (2) discounting to present value. Doubts have been raised about the proposition that one could take the sum of all expected payments in the future, discount them at a uniform rate, and assume this to be the present value of a forecasted dividend stream.

Problems such as these lead the author into a discussion of the Petersburg Paradox, which concerns the value of expectations of a game. The value of the game outlined by Bernoulli in 1738 can be shown mathematically to the infinite, but hardly anyone will accept the implication that one should pay an infinite price to enter this game. It is noted that several explanations have been offered to show why the value would usually be only a small finite amount, and that all these explanations are relevant to growth stock appraisal. Modifications of the original Petersburg Paradox are also considered to allow for a series of increasing payments.

The second section of the paper discusses attempts to resolve the Petersburg Paradox. Various writers on the subject, such as Cramer and Bernoulli, are briefly discussed. Whitworth considered the risk of gamblers' ruin, which brings out the need for diversification. It is concluded that all the approaches discussed involve changing the problem in some way, and all aid in explaining why the price paid to play the game is less than the mathematical expectation, which is infinite. The Petersburg solutions for growth-stock appraisal center on two points: (1) the assumptions about indefinitely increasing dividends; and (2) the value of a stock to a buyer versus its theoretical discounted value.

Another important limitation on the evaluation of a growth stock is the remoteness of the later dividend payments. The point considered here is the manner in which one evaluates the discounted value of dividends to be received many years in the future. For example, it is argued that there is no theoretical limit to the valuation of a stock with dividends growing in accordance with the conventional formulations used in analyses of this type. The author notes that Clendenin and Van Cleave have suggested a way to allow for uncertainty in evaluating dividends in the very remote future; namely, to increase the discount rate applicable to the more remote dividends.

The paper concludes with a summary and implications for security appraisal in general. The reasons why an investor would pay less than an infinite price for a growth stock are outlined from the point of view of the writers discussed earlier (Williams, Cramer, Bernoulli, Whitworth, and Clendenin and Van Cleave). The author argues that with so many methods of adjusting for the paradox of an infinite price, no one valuation can be clearly accepted. Even bonds and preferred stocks can present difficulties in evaluation. Durand concludes that growth-stock valuation remains a difficult problem, as shown by the fact that "the Petersburg Paradox has not yielded a unique and generally acceptable solution to more than 200 years of attack by some of the world's great intellects."

Brownian Motion in the Stock Market, by M. F. M. Osborne, *Operations Research,* **Vol. 7, March-April 1959.** *(The C.F.A. Digest, 6-1).*

This 1959 paper shows that common stock prices (more particularly the logarithms of the prices) have just the properties of the position of a dust particle in Brownian motion. The method of analysis (afterwards alternatively referred to as a "random walk") follows closely the method used by the French physicist Perrin, who observed the successive positions of particles in a fluid by following them with a microscope. The basic property of Brownian motion is that the standard deviation (equals square root of variance) of changes of position with time increases as the square root of the time interval of the change. For example, the standard deviation of price changes over 100 days would be 10 times that for price changes for one day. The standard deviation for four-days price change would be twice that for one day. By contrast, for ordinary or Newtonian motion, the standard deviation increases proportional to the time interval, at least for short intervals, rather than as the square root of the time interval. Four-day interval price changes would have a standard approximately four times that for one day.

The evidence indicates that this square root of time interval holds for intervals of one day to 10 years. It does not hold for intervals as short as a few minutes, i.e., between individual transactions. Data for intervals greater than 10 years have not been examined. Bacterial particles also show Brownian motion, but these have a finite lifetime of unambiguous identity. So also do stocks and the associated corporation. The statement that Brownian motion, unlike ordinary motion, lacks the identifiable property of rate of change of position, or velocity, translates in the case of stock prices to the non-existence of an identifiable, unambiguous trend in prices with time; positive if up, negative if down.

One can regard a stock market as a place where people either (a) buy and sell stock certificates with a single or common type of paper (money), or (b) they buy and sell money with different types of stock certificates. Brownian motion is demonstrated equally by either the price of individual stocks, or the price of money that is measured by a stock average. The fact that the Brownian motion occurs in the logarithm of prices rather than directly in the prices can be used to explain the long-term "growth" (3.75 percent per year ignoring dividends) of stock prices as measured by an arithmetic average such as the Dow Jones Industrial Average. This growth rate was first demonstrated by Edgar L. Smith in the 1920's using random samples of stock prices.

This long-term "positive trend" has nothing to do with long-term inflation or the growth of assets in a capitalistic economy. Exactly the same probability structure of prices that leads you to expect with time an increasing number of dollars from the sale of a constant number of shares will also lead you to expect that, with a constant number of dollars, you can buy in the future with time an increasing number of shares. This paradoxical and seemingly contradictory state of affairs is a statistical artifact consequent to a random walk, or Brownian motion in the logarithm of prices.

How to Use Security Analysis to Improve Portfolio Selection, by Jack L. Treynor and Fischer Black, *The Journal of Business,* **Vol. 46, No. 1, January 1973.** *(The C.F.A. Digest,* 10-2).

The purpose of this 1973 paper is to find the best ways to use the information provided by security analysts. Using Sharpe's Diagonal Model, the authors develop a series of questions describing portfolio mean and variance and the optimum position of both a security and the market portfolio. From this analysis, the authors derive the concept of the appraisal premium, defined as the expected return on a security independent of the market. They also develop the idea of an "active" portfolio, which is a portfolio that emphasizes the analysts' estimates of the independent returns of specific securities. The active portfolio is unaffected by changes in the investor's attitude toward risk or the investor's market expectations or the degree of market risk. The "passive" portfolio is designed to approximate the market, adjusted so that the total portfolio can be expected to achieve a specified level of market risk.

On a practical basis, this approach to portfolio selection is a three-stage process: select an active portfolio to maximize the appraisal ratio; combine the active portfolio with a replica of the market portfolio to maximize the ratio of expected excess return to variance of return; scale the positions in the combined portfolio up or down through lending or borrowing (while preserving the proportions).

In summary, Treynor and Black make the following points:

1. In balancing portfolios, it is useful to distinguish between market (systematic) risk and appraisal (insurable) risk. Optimal balancing may not reduce either to negligible levels.

2. A portfolio can be thought of as having three parts: a riskless part, a highly diversified part (no specific risk), and an active part containing both specific risk and market risk.

3. The rate at which a portfolio earns riskless interest depends only upon the current market value of the investor's equity. The rate at which a portfolio earns risk premium (the premium for risk bearing) depends only upon the amount of market risk undertaken and not on the composition of the active portfolio.

4. Optimal selection in the active portfolio depends upon appraisal risk and appraisal premiums.

5. The appraisal ratio depends upon the quality of security analysis and how efficiently the active portfolio is balanced.

6. Over time, a security analyst's potential contribution to overall portfolio performance depends only upon how well the forecasts of future independent returns correlate with the actual independent returns, and not on the magnitude.

by O. Whitfield Broome, Jr.

The C.F.A. Program's Body of Knowledge

In the interests of developing and maintaining professional standards of investment management, The Institute of Chartered Financial Analysts administers a three-level examination program. At each progressive level, the C.F.A. candidate takes a six-hour examination covering seven basic areas—ethical and professional standards, accounting, quantitative techniques, economics, fixed income security analysis, equity security analysis, and portfolio management.

The topic outline describing the program's coverage at each of the three levels is prepared by the Institute's Research and Publications Committee—27 C.F.A.s drawn from brokerage firms, investment banks, investment companies, investment counselors, trust companies, insurance companies, financial consulting companies, and universities. The topic outline provides guidance not only to the candidates studying for the examinations, but also to the 14 C.F.A.s on the Institute's Council of Examiners who develop the three examinations.

The C.F.A. study program is continually modified to reflect changes in the body of professional knowledge. Although abrupt changes are rare—and present a challenge to a program having a continuous stream of candidates taking examinations over three or four years—the defined body of knowledge has undergone several major revisions since its inception. Continuing refinements help to assure the investing public, employers and fellow analysts that the recipient of the C.F.A. designation possesses the knowledge fundamental to the practice of investment management.

T HE primary purpose of The Institute of Chartered Financial Analysts (I.C.F.A.) is to develop and maintain high standards of professional investment management. Towards this end, the Institute administers a study and examination program that guides candidates in mastering a body of professional knowledge and analytical skills and rewards analysts who demonstrate a reasonable level of competency in its examinations with the C.F.A. designation. The investing public, employers and fellow analysts

O. Whitfield Broome, Jr., Ph.D., CPA, is Executive Director of The Institute of Chartered Financial Analysts and Associate Professor at the McIntire School of Commerce of the University of Virginia.

Based upon an article in the Financial Analysts Journal, March/April 1980.

may be assured that the successful candidate possesses the fundamental knowledge necessary to practice his or her profession. Further, the Institute encourages ethical professional practice by both candidates and C.F.A.s through its Code of Ethics and Standards of Professional Conduct.[1] (Footnotes appear at end of article.)

C.F.A. Examination Program

The C.F.A. examination program consists of three separate and progressive levels. To be eligible for Level I, a candidate must hold a bachelor's degree from an accredited academic institution or have the equivalent in investment experience; there are no other other requirements for enrollment, either occupational or experiential. The eligibility requirements for Level II are successful completion of Level I and membership in a constituent society of The Financial Analysts Federation (F.A.F.).[2] To qualify for Level III, a candidate must have successfully completed Level II, and be a member of a constituent society of the F.A.F. Upon successful completion of Level III, and having at least four years of experience in financial analysis related to investments, the candidate is awarded the C.F.A. charter by the Institute's Board of Trustees.

At each level of the program, the candidate studies and then takes a 6 hour examination on seven basic subject matter areas — ethical and professional standards, financial accounting, quantitative techniques, economics, fixed income securities analysis, equity securities analysis and portfolio management. As the candidate moves from Level I to Level II to Level III, he or she covers the seven topic areas in more breadth and depth. Exhibit I outlines the program's body of knowledge and indicates the topic coverage at each of the three levels.

The body of knowledge represented by the general topic outline includes those areas considered relevant to the practice of financial analysis. The outline is prepared by the Institute's Research and Publications Committee and is revised periodically to reflect changes and developments in the practice of financial analysis. The Research and Publications Committee consists of 27 C.F.A.s drawn from many areas of practice—including brokerage firms and investment banks, investment companies, investment counselors, trust companies and departments, insurance companies, financial consulting firms and universities—each possessing expertise in one or more of the seven topic areas.

The general topic outline serves three important roles in the C.F.A. program. First, it provides guidance in the selection of study materials to be assigned to candidates at each level. (The identification of appropriate study materials is also the responsibility of the Research and Publications Committee.) Second, it furnishes guidance to the Institute's Council of Examiners, which is responsible for the development of the three examinations. This group consists of 14 C.F.A.s holding a wide variety of positions in financial analysis. Third, the outline serves as a guide to candidates in their study and professional development. As a candidate studies the assigned materials, he or she may determine that additional study is needed in certain areas.

At each level in the C.F.A. program, candidates receive a Study Guide containing specific assignments for each topic area, past examinations and guideline answers, and comments on the level of understanding required for each examination level. The following summary of these comments will facilitate comprehension of the general topic outline shown in Exhibit I.

Level I

Ethical and Professional Standards: The candidate should be familiar with the general purpose and content of the basic securities laws and regulations pertaining to the investment field, including the structure of the principal regulatory bodies (the Securities and Exchange Commission, the National Association of Securities Dealers and the New York Stock Exchange, for example) that administer these regulations. He or she should be familiar with the purpose and administrative organization of the I.C.F.A./F.A.F. self-regulation programs and aware of the general content of the Code of Ethics, Standards of Professional Conduct, Rules of Procedure and Article VIII (Sections 4,5 and 6) of the I.C.F.A. By-Laws. Candidates must be familiar with the professional obligations and associated sanctions to which members are subject.

Financial Accounting: The candidate should bring to Level I of the program an understanding of the principles of accounting equivalent to at least a one-year course in accounting. The candidate should be able to apply accounting principles and techniques to financial analysis. Emphasis is placed on skill in using published accounting data, including corporate financial statements and reports, in a meaningful analysis of companies.

Quantitative Techniques: The candidate should already have some knowledge of elementary statistics and basic mathematics. He or she is expected to be able to apply this knowledge to basic problems in finance and financial analysis.

Economics: Before beginning the program, the candidates should be familiar with the basic principles of microeconomics, macroeconomics and the workings of the money and capital markets. Minimum knowledge equivalent to a one-year course in principles of economics is assumed. At Level I, the candidate should become familiar with the tools of economic analysis and forecasting, gain a historical perspective of economic trends and the business cycle and obtain an understanding of the way money is created in the banking system and the difference

EXHIBIT I General Topic Outline, 1981

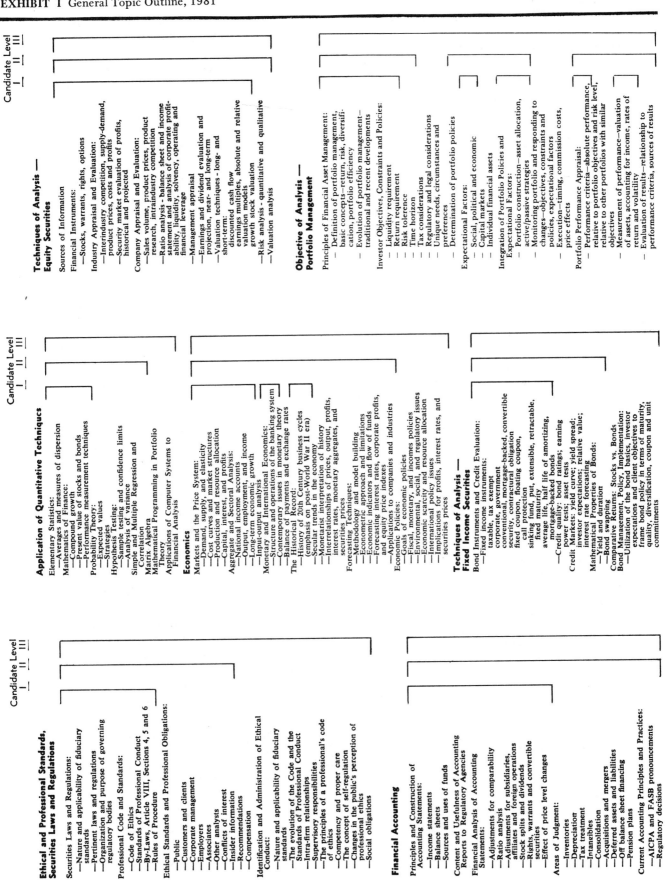

between money and credit. Primary emphasis is placed on ability to apply economic reasoning in the investment analysis of a company, its industry and its investment securities.

Fixed Income Securities Analysis: The candidate should have the equivalent of two years of college study in business administration—including business finance, corporate financial analysis and money and capital markets. For Level I, the candidate is expected to understand and be able to analyze the basic characteristics (coupon, maturity, call, conversion, sinking fund, etc.) of fixed income instruments, including corporate bonds, national and local government bonds, straight preferred stocks and convertible debentures and preferreds. He or she should understand the various contractual forms (mortgage, debenture, pass-through, income bonds, etc.) and be able to determine the basic investment quality of fixed income securities given the borrower's risks of illiquidity or insolvency. The candidate should understand the basic concepts of yield and bond price determination and the price risks attendant on interest rate and purchasing power changes.

Equity Securities Analysis: The program assumes the candidate has had the equivalent of two years of college study in business administration. For Level I, he or she should be able to appraise industries and companies logically within a financial and investment framework. The candidate should be able to understand ordinary types of financial data and to relate this understanding to the important issues of value and risk of common stocks.

Portfolio Management: Portfolio and investment management involves the integration of economics, financial accounting, quantitative techniques, and fixed income and equity securities analysis. The candidate is expected to understand the principles of financial asset management, the theory of risk and return, the financial needs of individual and institutional investors, and be able to suggest suitable investments for their portfolios.

Level II

Ethical and Professional Standards: The candidate should acquire the ability to recognize unprofessional practices and violations of standards in areas where issues are less clear cut, including conflicts of interest and use of inside information, and to understand his or her responsibilities under the I.C.F.A./F.A.F. Rules of Procedure.

Financial Accounting: The candidate should gain a sufficiently thorough understanding of financial accounting—including such areas as mergers and acquisitions, inventory and plant valuation, foreign exchange gains and losses, pension plans and leases—to interpret financial statements for the proper evaluation and assessment of company fundamentals. Candidates are expected to be familiar with the statements and interpretations of the Financial Accounting Standards Board and its predecessor, the Accounting Principles Board, as well as the opinions and decisions of regulatory authorities.

Quantitative Techniques: In addition to the knowledge gained at Level I, the candidate is expected to become familiar with the more advanced statistical techniques—such as probability theory, hypothesis testing and simple and multiple regression and correlation analysis—and to be able to apply these techniques to problems of financial projections, portfolio analysis and risk analysis.

Economics: The candidate should be able to apply basic microeconomic reasoning in the analysis of specific companies and industries. He or she should be familiar with the historical record of key macroeconomic variables—output, prices, interest rates, security prices, corporate profits and the balance of payments—and be able to apply and interpret modern techniques used in forecasting economic trends.

Fixed Income Securities Analysis: In addition to the understanding of the characteristics of fixed income securities gained at Level I, the candidate should understand the implications of the interest rate structure for various types of fixed contracts.

Equity Securities Analysis: Level II emphasizes ability to perform a complete appraisal and evaluation of industries and companies, including the position and outlook for common stocks and other equities. The candidate should be able to apply the techniques of securities analysis, including measures for valuation and risk, to individual companies and also to a group of companies within the same industry.

Portfolio Management: The candidate should be able to formulate portfolio strategies and select securities relative to the current outlook for the economy and conditions in the securities markets. This requires an understanding of how return and risk for individual securities are related to underlying economic and market factors, as well as how the risks of individual securities and their expected returns combine at the portfolio level.

Level III

Ethical and Professional Standards: At Level III, the candidate should be able to administer a program of professional and ethical standards within an organization. Emphasis is placed on internal disciplinary controls as well as compliance with securities laws, regulations and I.C.F.A. standards and rules. The candidate should demonstrate an awareness of current ethical issues, the importance of the public interest and the implications of professionalism in financial analysis.

Financial Accounting: In addition to the knowledge of accounting procedures and techniques gained at Levels I and II, the candidate is expected to be able to relate accounting data to securities valuation and to the investment decision-making process.

Quantitative Techniques: The candidate is expected to have broad familiarity with the application of mathematical and statistical techniques to problems in financial analysis, capital markets and portfolio management.

Economics: At Level III, the candidate should be able to evaluate current economic conditions in light of the historical record and have a basic understanding of various options in regard to fiscal, monetary, incomes, international, regulatory and national resource policies. He or she should be able to formulate investment policy strategies based on a probability assessment of alternative economic scenarios.

Fixed Income Securities Analysis: Level III emphasizes the management of fixed income securities in a portfolio and their suitability given both objectives and constraints of different investors under changing economic and market conditions. The candidate should be able to understand the mechanics of bond management, including analysis of bond swaps and the evaluation of performance.

Equity Securities Analysis: At Level III, emphasis is placed on the analysis of common stocks under conditions of changing economic and market environments.

Portfolio Management: Based on knowledge gained at the preceding levels and in the other topic areas, the candidate is expected to be able: (1) to interrelate economic and market conditions, securities analysis, analysis of the requirements of individual and institutional investors, and efficient portfolio concepts; (2) to develop suitable investment policies; (3) to construct portfolios that meet investors' requirements and circumstances; and (4) to

monitor the portfolio by responding to change. The candidate should have an understanding of the investment process, including how to organize and implement the portfolio management process and how to evaluate the results.

Development of the Program

The practice of investment analysis and management is not static. The investment practitioner faces the challenge of staying abreast of continuing developments in the field. New types of investment opportunities become available. New laws, such as the Employee Retirement Income Security Act, affect the analyst's practice. New theories and techniques, such as Modern Portfolio Theory, come into practice. Changes in accounting and disclosure rules change financial reporting.

The C.F.A. study program and examinations are continually modified to reflect changes in professional practice and commensurate changes in the body of professional knowledge. The importance of exposing candidates to current facts, theories and techniques is obvious. Although the view is occasionally expressed that the C.F.A. program (particularly the examinations) is becoming increasingly difficult, no major shifts in rates of success on C.F.A. examinations have occurred during the past decade.

As the practice of financial analysis develops and changes, the C.F.A. program's general topic outline is modified. Sometimes a special task

Exhibit II The C.F.A. Program, 1968

Examination I—Investment Principles

Financial Accounting
Basic Quantitative Analysis
Basic Economic Analysis
Principles of Financial Analysis
Financial Instruments and Institutions
Ethics

Examination II—Applied Security Analysis

Practical Applications of Financial Analysis
Economic Growth and Business Fluctuations
Ethics

Examination III—Investment Management Decision-Making

Portfolio Management
Organization and Administration of Investment Activities
Common Stock Policy
Fixed Income Securities Policy
Security Selections
Economic Issues
Ethics

EXHIBIT III General Topic Outline, 1969

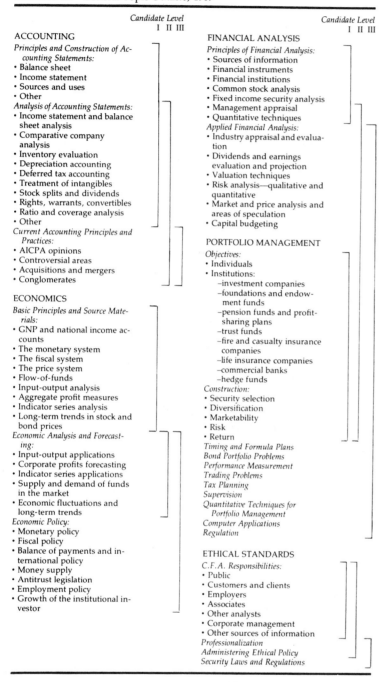

	Candidate Level I II III
ACCOUNTING	
Principles and Construction of Accounting Statements:	
• Balance sheet	
• Income statement	
• Sources and uses	
• Other	
Analysis of Accounting Statements:	
• Income statement and balance sheet analysis	
• Comparative company analysis	
• Inventory evaluation	
• Depreciation accounting	
• Deferred tax accounting	
• Treatment of intangibles	
• Stock splits and dividends	
• Rights, warrants, convertibles	
• Ratio and coverage analysis	
• Other	
Current Accounting Principles and Practices:	
• AICPA opinions	
• Controversial areas	
• Acquisitions and mergers	
• Conglomerates	

ECONOMICS

Basic Principles and Source Materials:
• GNP and national income accounts
• The monetary system
• The fiscal system
• The price system
• Flow-of-funds
• Input-output analysis
• Aggregate profit measures
• Indicator series analysis
• Long-term trends in stock and bond prices

Economic Analysis and Forecasting:
• Input-output applications
• Corporate profits forecasting
• Indicator series applications
• Supply and demand of funds in the market
• Economic fluctuations and long-term trends

Economic Policy:
• Monetary policy
• Fiscal policy
• Balance of payments and international policy
• Money supply
• Antitrust legislation
• Employment policy
• Growth of the institutional investor

	Candidate Level I II III
FINANCIAL ANALYSIS	
Principles of Financial Analysis:	
• Sources of information	
• Financial instruments	
• Financial institutions	
• Common stock analysis	
• Fixed income security analysis	
• Management appraisal	
• Quantitative techniques	
Applied Financial Analysis:	
• Industry appraisal and evaluation	
• Dividends and earnings evaluation and projection	
• Valuation techniques	
• Risk analysis—qualitative and quantitative	
• Market and price analysis and areas of speculation	
• Capital budgeting	

PORTFOLIO MANAGEMENT

Objectives:
• Individuals
• Institutions:
 –investment companies
 –foundations and endowment funds
 –pension funds and profit-sharing plans
 –trust funds
 –fire and casualty insurance companies
 –life insurance companies
 –commercial banks
 –hedge funds

Construction:
• Security selection
• Diversification
• Marketability
• Risk
• Return

Timing and Formula Plans
Bond Portfolio Problems
Performance Measurement
Trading Problems
Tax Planning
Supervision
Quantitative Techniques for Portfolio Management
Computer Applications
Regulation

ETHICAL STANDARDS

C.F.A. Responsibilities:
• Public
• Customers and clients
• Employers
• Associates
• Other analysts
• Corporate management
• Other sources of information
Professionalization
Administering Ethical Policy
Security Laws and Regulations

topic outline reflects its activity to date.

Modifications in the general topic outline are typically made gradually, from year to year, as required to keep the C.F.A. program current. Obviously, abrupt changes in the defined body of knowledge are highly unusual and present a challenge to a program that has a continuous stream of candidates taking examinations over three or more years. Nevertheless, the program has undergone several major revisions since its inception. Prior to 1969, for example, the body of knowledge was classified by examination levels, as shown in Exhibit II. A revision in 1969, involving the classification of the body of knowledge by topic areas, resulted in the general topic outline shown in Exhibit III. Among other changes, the new outline showed five subject groupings—accounting, economics, financial analysis, portfolio management and ethical standards—and their coverage at each examination level.

The general topic outline underwent another major revision in 1975. The resulting changes are shown in Exhibit IV. The five topic areas were expanded to seven, with the addition of application of quantitative techniques and the subdivision of financial analysis into techniques of analysis—fixed income securities and techniques of analysis—equity securities. The 1981 general topic outline in Exhibit I reflects the continuing refinement of the basic body of knowledge, revealing changes in the economics, fixed income securities, portfolio management and ethical and professional standards sections. The fundamental importance of ethical and professional standards has been recognized by placing this topic first in the outline.

The current general topic outline for the C.F.A. program summarizes the knowledge candidates are expected to have or to obtain. The first topic—ethical and professional standards—stresses the analyst's professional and ethical responsibilities. The next three topics—financial accounting, quantitative techniques and economics—provide the tools for his or her work. The three functional subjects—fixed income securities analysis, equity securities analysis and portfolio management—represent the areas of practice in which these tools are applied. This body of knowledge is broad, reflecting as it does the breadth of the profession of financial analysis.

The Institute of Chartered Financial Analysts is dedicated to a study and examination program that assists candidates in increasing their level of professional competence and encourages the

force is formed to work on a particular area. For instance, in 1979 a highly qualified committee of seven practicing C.F.A.s was organized to review the portfolio management subject area. This committee has re-examined the scope of this area and the skills needed by the practitioner and has recommended changes in the general topic outline. It is also reviewing the current literature on the subject in order to augment or replace the study materials currently used. Although the work of this committee is continuing, the 1981 general

EXHIBIT IV General Topic Outline, 1975

Candidate Level
I II III

ECONOMICS

Tools of Analysis and Forecasting:
- National income accounts
- Flow of funds and money supply indicators
- Input-output analysis
- Leading indicators

Historical and Structural Perspective:
- Economic trends and cycles
- Flow of funds and relationship to national income accounts
- Economic price indexes
- Aggregate profit trends by types
- Trends and cycles in stock prices and interest rates

Forecasting Broad Economic Forces:
- Quantitative and qualitative aspects of forecasts
- Implications for forecasts of:
  - interest rates and the structure of interest rates
  - corporate profits and earnings of stock price indexes
  - aggregate equity price indexes
  - industry and company prospects

Economic Policy:
- Government policies and actions regarding:
  - growth, inflation and employment
  - monetary and fiscal policies
  - social goals
  - antitrust and industry regulation
  - international policy, including balance of payments
- Implications of policy decisions for:
  - profit outlook
  - interest rates
  - equity prices
  - industry and company analysis

FINANCIAL ACCOUNTING

Principles and Construction of Accounting Statements:
- Income statements
- Balance sheets
- Sources and uses of funds

Contents and Usefulness of Accounting Reports to Regulatory Agencies

Financial Analysis of Accounting Statements:
- Adjustments for comparability
- Ratio analysis
- Adjustments for subsidiaries, affiliates and foreign operations
- Stock splits and dividends
- Rights, warrants and convertible securities
- Effect of price level changes

Areas of Judgment:
- Inventories
- Depreciation
- Tax treatment
- Intangibles
- Consolidation
- Acquisitions and mergers
- Deferred assets and liabilities
- Off balance sheet financing
- Pension plans

Current Accounting Principles and Practices:
- AICPA and FASB opinions
- Regulatory decisions

Candidate Level
I II III

APPLICATION OF QUANTITATIVE TECHNIQUES

Elementary Statistics:
- Averages and measures of dispersion

Mathematics of Finance:
- Compound growth
- Present value of stocks and bonds
- Performance measurement techniques

Probability Theory:
- Expected values
- Strategies

Hypothesis Testing:
- Sample testing and confidence limits
- Analysis of variance

Simple and Multiple Regression and Correlation

Matrix Algebra

Mathematical Programming in Portfolio Theory

Applications of Computer Systems to Financial Analysis

TECHNIQUES OF ANALYSIS— FIXED INCOME SECURITIES

Classification of Fixed Income Securities:
- By issuer
- By maturity, if any
- By security
- By contractual obligation
- By tax status
- Convertible features, if any

Special Characteristics:
- Call features
- Sinking fund provisions
- Security
- Protective covenants
- Taxable features

Fixed Income Security Selection and Management:
- Quality ratings
- Interest or preferred dividend coverage, past and future
- Coupon and maturity
- New issues, discount and premium bonds
- The yield curve and interest rate structure
- Marketability
- Bond swaps

TECHNIQUES OF ANALYSIS— EQUITY SECURITIES

Sources of Information Financial Instruments:
- Stocks, warrants, rights, options

Industry Appraisal and Evaluation:
- Interindustry competition, supply-demand, product prices, costs and profits
- Security market evaluation of profits, historical and projected

Company Appraisal and Evaluation:
- Sales volume, product prices, product research, intraindustry competition
- Ratio analysis—balance sheet and income statement and analysis of corporate profitability, liquidity, solvency, operating and financial leverage
- Management appraisal
- Earnings and dividend evaluation and projection, near and long-term
- Valuation techniques—long and short-term:
  - discounted cash flow
  - earnings multiples, absolute and relative
  - valuation models
  - growth stock valuation
- Risk analysis—quantitative and qualitative
- Efficient capital market hypothesis

Candidate Level
I II III

OBJECTIVE OF ANALYSIS— PORTFOLIO MANAGEMENT

Investor Objectives and Constraints:
- Individuals
- Institutions:
  - investment companies
  - foundations and endowment funds
  - pension funds and profit-sharing plans
  - trust funds
  - property and liability insurance companies
  - life insurance companies
  - commercial banks

Portfolio Strategy and Construction
- Policy inputs:
  - assumptions regarding the short and long-term outlook for the economy and the securities markets
  - types of investments to be used regarding quality, liquidity, risk and other characteristics
  - portfolio diversification by type of investment and diversification by industry
- Account objectives and constraints:
  - specific definition of objectives, e.g., risk and return, liquidity requirements, legal and regulatory constraints
  - the time horizon for the investment
  - aggressive and speculative properties
- Investment selection:
  - selection of specific investments suitable for objectives
  - comparative evaluation of alternative investments
- Modern portfolio theory and the construction of "efficient portfolios"
- Tax planning
- Execution of purchases and sales
- Evaluation of account performance

CONDUCT OF ANALYSIS— ETHICAL AND PROFESSIONAL STANDARDS, SECURITIES LAWS AND REGULATIONS

Ethical Standards and Professional Responsibilities:
- Public
- Customers and clients
- Employers
- Associates
- Other analysts
- Corporate management
- Other sources of information

Treatment of Ethical Issues:
- Identification of ethical problems
- Administration of ethical policies
- Changing structure of financial markets and the participants therein and the consequent development of new ethical issues

Security Laws and Regulations:
- Nature and applicability of fiduciary standards
- Pertinent laws and regulations
- Treatment of insider information

best practice of financial analysis. In order to achieve these goals, the body of knowlege on which that program is based must be continually reviewed to keep it in tune with a dynamic profession. Although the 1981 general topic outline presents that body of knowledge as it is currently covered in the C.F.A. program, coming years will see further refinements. ■

Footnotes

1. A detailed description of the C.F.A. Candidate Program is published in *The C.F.A. Announcement*, which is available on request from The Institute of Chartered Financial Analysts, University of Virginia, Post Office Box 3668, Charlottesville, VA 22903.

2. Since January 1, 1976, The Financial Analysts Federation has required that applicants for fellow membership in the F.A.F. successfully complete Level I of the C.F.A. program. For one who is considering F.A.F. membership and/or plans to become a C.F.A., the body of knowledge covered in the program is important.

THE EVOLUTION OF FINANCIAL ANALYSTS'
PROFESSIONAL STANDARDS

RICHARD W. LAMBOURNE, C.F.A.

Clearly we have to examine first the evolution of a profession before we can analyze the development of its ethical standards.

Any type of evolution must have a starting point, a history, and a continuing future. No one knows for sure when the profession of financial analysis began. The rudiments of credit analysis have existed for ages, as shown by Babylonian clay tablets, and economic history is replete with examples of people who understood the elements of financial opportunity and risk. The "Boston trustees" of the previous century and the original Prudent Man Rule are manifestations. Someone has said that perhaps Bernard Baruch was the first financial analyst in modern times, or Benjamin Graham*, although a little study will reveal that there were at least a few earlier practitioners worthy of the name.

Other students will maintain that we grew out of the old American Statistical Association in this country, which seems to be the case in some areas. But for the Federation, the beginnings go back about fifty years to the first known group with the appellation of "analyst"–the *Investment Analysts Club of Chicago,* organized in 1925 (the word *Club* was not changed to *Society* until 1953). Then came California with the *Financial Statisticians of San Francisco* in 1929, right at the top of the stock market, followed by *Los Angeles* with a similar title in 1931. It is fortunate that all three of these forerunners survived the perils of the Great Depression. We should note, too, that the present *Toronto* Society dates back to 1936 through a predecessor group.

A landmark, in terms of size and influence, was surely the formation of the *New York Society of Security Analysts* in 1937. The *Financial Analysts of Philadelphia* arrived on the scene in 1943, and the *Boston Security Analysts Society* came in 1946. These three, plus Chicago, were the nucleus of the original NATIONAL FEDERATION OF FINANCIAL ANALYSTS SOCIETIES, organized on June 11, 1947, with a total constituency of 1,580 members, of which 1,200 were in New York. Soon the California groups were brought in along with other societies which formed rather rapidly in the late forties and early fifties, so that the Federation could point to an aggregate membership of 3,300 by the time of the Fifth Annual Convention (in San Francisco) in 1952. Of course, now the total is close to 15,000 with 48 constituent societies in the United States and Canada.

The starting outlines of development in professional standards are hazy at best. One searches for evidence in written documents, such as society constitutions, but none is to be found for the earliest analyst groups. It appears that Chicago went along without a formal constitution until one was hastily devised upon its entrance as a charter member of the National Federation in 1947. In New York, however, we find the first extant *Code of Ethics,* printed in a 1945 edition of *The Analysts Journal,* then published by the New York Society:

> At the recent annual meeting of the Society, members voted to adopt the following code of ethics:

---

*See "Benjamin Graham, The Father of Financial Analysis," by Irving Kahn, C.F.A., and Robert D. Milne, C.F.A., The Financial Analysts Research Foundation Occasional Paper Number 5, Charlottesville, Virginia. 1977.

Paper presented at an October 1976 Symposium co-sponsored by The Financial Analysts Research Foundation, The Financial Analysts Federation, and The Institute of Chartered Financial Analysts.

1. THE SECURITY ANALYST WILL BE INDEPENDENT AND UNPREJUDICED. His first and final obligation is to discover the truth and to state it as he sees it.

2. THE SECURITY ANALYST WILL BE CAREFUL, THOROUGH AND JUDICIOUS IN HIS WORK. In analyzing a situation he will seek to discover all the significant elements, to attach proper relative weight to each, and to present fairly both sides of the picture.

3. THE SECURITY ANALYST WILL BE MODEST AND SELF-CRITICAL. He will recognize that security analysis is both an art and a science, that it has important limitations as well as great possibilities. He will constantly re-examine his own work, in order to learn from his mistakes and improve his techniques.

4. THE SECURITY ANALYST WILL BE CO-OPERATIVE, PUBLIC-SPIRITED AND PROGRESSIVE. To the extent compatible with sound business he will make his studies available to his fellow-analysts, and he will be generous in aid and counsel to his juniors. He will give freely of his time to non-profit activities for the benefit of his profession and the public interest. He will view security analysis as a developing discipline, to the advancement of which he must make his best contribution. He will act always in the realization that the dignity and honor of his calling depends upon the integrity of the individual Security Analyst.

It is certain that New York had a constitution and a Code some years before. The worthy scriveners of that Code are at present unknown, but you will recognize that they produced in short form the main essentialities of professional conduct, with final emphasis on the key ingredient—integrity. These principles stand the test of time.

It is interesting to see the original (1947) constitution of the National Federation. It was quite brief, probably reflecting the common law views of the founding members from New England who disliked elaborate legal codes and preferred to keep matters simple. The purposes of the new Federation were stated to be: "(1) exchange ideas and information and discuss mutual problems; and (2) promote the welfare of the profession and its members." There is not a word in the text about ethics or standards, but a Committee on Professional Ethics and Standards was immediately established. Meanwhile, the New York Society, operating in a "code" state, specifically set as its first constitutional object, "To establish and maintain a high standard of professional ethics among financial analysts." The New York Code of Ethics, cited previously, was maintained as a separate document. While obviously the Boston Society grew and prospered under high internal standards, there was no code for several years after its formation. The Canadian letters patent, establishing the then *Montreal Institute of Financial Analysts* in 1950, listed among its purposes, "To establish and promote the adoption by investment analysts of standards of professional ethics." Most of the societies in the Federation later included similar provisions in their constitutions or by-laws.

But in the National Federation itself, nothing was done in this regard for several years except through voluntary committee work. The Federation had no staff or office and dues were ten cents per member, with a maximum of $100 per Society and $25 minimum. Thus, the treasury was usually bare.

A primary event occurred, however, in the Annual Convention of the Federation held in Philadelphia in 1953. There the Committee on Professional Ethics and Standards, headed by A. Moyer Kulp of Philadelphia, noted the growth and rise in stature of the analyst societies and the need for further progress in *establishing, improving,* and *maintaining high professional standards* in order to measure up to increasing responsibilities. Also, the first overt move in the Federation towards what is now the Chartered Financial Analyst designation (C.F.A.) was made by the

Sub-Committee, chaired by Shelby Cullom Davis of New York, recommending a program for granting "Certified Security Analyst" status. The full Committee then proposed creating a National Federation Board which would set standards as well as methods for determining a professional designation. Throughout these reports and long hearings, one matter continued to plague the participants, as typified by the following excerpt:

> Probably the most basic of all is the question: What precisely are the standards? Until there is a meeting of the minds on this point, very little can be done to implement the idea on a national scale . . . a definition of standards is the question.

Coming six years after the Federation was formed, no one really seemed to know. Some thought of standards in terms of sound analytical procedures (or techniques); others gave emphasis to years of experience as a qualification for practice; while still others got closer to the ethical track by denouncing plagiarism, misleading advice and failing to differentiate between security analysis and sales literature.

Out of all this came, with the passage of another nine years, the first Code of Ethics of the Federation in 1962. Finances had improved with a sizeable increase in dues and considerable profits from conventions. A small initial staff was set in place, and funds were provided for more intensive committee work. The original Code, prepared by the then Professional Ethics and Education Committee (under David G. Watterson of Cleveland as Chairman, with a distinguished group of ten others) consisted of four fundamental standards of conduct which are presented here in outline form:

1. Responsibility to the Public

    Honesty

    Integrity

    Avoid exaggeration, misrepresentation and flamboyant advertising

    Avoid high pressure sales

2. Responsibility to Customers, Clients and Employees

    Fidelity and loyalty

    Divulge sources of compensation

    Full disclosure of any conflict of interest

3. Responsibility to Corporate Management and Sources of Information

    Report the facts accurately

    Do not take unfair personal advantage

4. Responsibility to Associates and Fellow Analysts

    Maintain high standards of professional conduct

    Uphold the dignity and honor of the profession

In 1964 the Constitution was amended to include a specific reference to the Code as a separate document, and the following "Guidelines and Interpretations" of the Code were approved (again paraphrased):

1. Cooperate with regulation by government agencies, stock exchanges, and industry groups.

2. Give meticulous attention to both the letter and spirit of the law.

3. Transactions for clients have priority over personal transactions. Full disclosure.

4. Do not undertake private practice without employer's knowledge and approval.

5. Do not pay fees or commissions to others for recommending your services (unless disclosed).

6. Avoid plagiarism.

A milestone on the road to professionalism was, of course, the founding at long last of The Institute of Chartered Financial Analysts in 1962 under the aegis of the Federation, but with a deliberate degree of autonomy. The first C.F.A. designations were awarded in 1963—285 in all, and now there are over 4,500. After the I.C.F.A. adopted the F.A.F. Code in 1964, in essentially the same form, questions on ethical conduct began to appear in the annual C.F.A. examinations and Study Guides, and they have continued to receive emphasis in all three of the required candidate exams.

In ensuing years it became evident that revisions were necessary in both the form and substance of the Code and Guidelines, in light of changes in the investment environment and the law. Accordingly, the chairmanship of both the F.A.F. and I.C.F.A. Professional Ethics Committees was given to Carl L. A. Beckers of St. Louis, and a major redrafting task was accomplished under his direction. The Committees proceeded with the view that: (1) the Code of Ethics itself should be quite short and express only the basic precepts; and (2) the conduct guidelines should also not be lengthy and not unduly specific; i.e., interpretations should develop mainly by the case method over time. In any event, the revised Code of Ethics and Standards of Professional Conduct adopted in 1969 by the F.A.F. and I.C.F.A. restated the sections on Responsibility in the 1964 version, cited earlier, and substituted the following:

A (Chartered) Financial Analyst should conduct himself with integrity and dignity and encourage such conduct by others in the profession.

A (Chartered) Financial Analyst should act with competence and strive to maintain and improve his competence and that of others in the profession.

A (Chartered) Financial Analyst should use proper care and exercise independent professional judgment.

The previous "Guidelines" were eliminated as such.

In their stead, Standards of Professional Conduct were set for the first time—nine in number. These were couched in language intended to eliminate subjective words that might cause interpretive trouble, such as "exaggeration" and "flamboyant," which disappeared. At the same time, the Standards were written to be reasonably specific but without detailed enumeration of all of the ethical possibilities considered. The nine Standards of the F.A.F. were as follows (the most significant sections are again in outline form):

1. Maintain knowledge of the law and comply with all rules and regulations of government agencies and of the stock exchanges and N.A.S.D., if subject to them.

2. Inform your employer of the existence and content of the Code and Standards (new).

3. Transactions for clients, customers and employer have priority over personal transactions.

4. Disclose any material conflicts of interest which might reasonably be expected to impair ability to render unbiased or objective advice.

5. Be objective in opinions and be accurate and complete in reporting facts.

6. Disclose any additional compensation for services to customers, clients, or employer.

7. Do not pay consideration to others for recommending your services, unless disclosed.

8. Do not undertake independent practice for compensation without written consent from your employer and the person for whom the services are rendered.

9. No plagiarism; identification of the source is required along with acknowledgment.

The I.C.F.A. adopted all of the above in 1969 and added a tenth Standard pertaining to the specific use of the C.F.A. designation. Both the F.A.F. and the I.C.F.A. had earlier provided rules of procedure for their member societies. These were subsequently expanded and clarified, including amplification of the enforcement process.

Thus was the situation in 1969. No further changes were made in the Standards until April, 1974, coincident with approval of the Federation's private self-regulation program by the delegates to the Los Angeles Conference. This necessitated numerous amendments to the F.A.F. Articles of Incorporation and By-laws, including establishment of the Investment Analysis Standards Board and Professional Conduct Committee. A major accomplishment was approval of the concept that the F.A.F., not the member societies, had primary responsibility for enforcement of the Code and Standards and discipline of violators. Society and individual members were encouraged to participate in this program, and all have elected to do so (see Editor's note). Moreover, after a transition period, all new members must pass C.F.A. Examination I.

The Code of Ethics was not altered at the Conference in 1974. However, the Standards were set forth in reorganized form with lettered sectional groupings and numbered sub-sections, together with important restatements and additions. Here most of the credit for improvement was due to the efforts of Robert E. Blixt of St. Paul and, as before, the guidance of counsel, John G. Gillis of Boston. The new substantive changes or amplifications in the Standards adopted in 1974 were as follows (paraphrased):

(A-3)   Not knowingly participate in any acts which violate the Code and Standards or any statute or regulation governing securities matters.

(B-1)   Have a reasonable and objective basis for investment opinions and maintain appropriate supportive records; distinguish between fact and opinion.

(B-2)   Exercise diligence and thoroughness in the analysis of relative investment risks and the valuation of or expected return from investment securities.

(B-3)   Analysts may use without acknowledgment recognized statistical services for factual data.

(B-4)   Avoid statements which guarantee any investment.

(B-5)   Make reasonable efforts to be aware of and consider appropriateness and suitability in making investment recommendations or taking investment action.

(E-2)   Analysts shall not communicate or act on information if to do so would violate the laws and regulations relating to the use of material inside information.

(E-3)   Analysts are encouraged to report evidence of illegal acts to appropriate authorities if encountered in the course of practice.

The duties of the F.A.F. Investment Analysis Standards Board, which supplanted the previous Professional Ethics Committee in 1974, specifically include the following:

To review on a continuing basis the Code of Ethics, Standards of Professional Conduct, standards of practice and requirements for membership of the corporation, to develop and maintain a high level of ethics, standards and competence in the field of financial and security analysis . . . .

Consistent with this charge, the I.A.S.B. in the Spring of 1975 proposed a number of revisions in the Standards which were approved by the delegates at the New York Conference, as noted below:

1. Moved the standard relating to material inside information to Section A and added a caveat that the financial analyst is not obligated to use reasonable effort in achieving public dissemination of such information if he is in a special or confidential relationship with the company.

2. Added a new standard (Section F) on Relationships With Others. Considering its multi-faceted importance, this is reproduced here in full:

The financial analyst shall act in a highly ethical and professional manner in his dealings with the public, his clients, his employees, his associates and fellow analysts. The financial analyst shall conduct himself in a fair and businesslike manner in all competitive business situations and shall adhere to the high standards of business conduct expected of all financial analysts. The financial analyst shall not use his business position to influence fellow analysts improperly on matters relating to their professional analysts organizations and shall respect the right of individual analysts to hold varying viewpoints.

Continuing its process of review, the I.A.S.B. made further recommendations which were approved at the 1975 Fall Conference in Atlanta. The substantive changes in the standards are briefly outlined below:

1. Added a new standard (A-4) providing that a financial analyst having supervisory responsibility shall exercise reasonable supervision of subordinates to prevent violation of statutes, regulations, and the Code of Ethics and Standards.

2. Changed the word "company" to "issuer" in A-5 (to include non-corporate entities in matters of material inside information).

3. Added the words "or similar sources" to B-3 regarding recognized financial or statistical reporting services.

4. Added to Section B (Investment Recommendations and Actions) a new Standard, B-6, providing that the financial analyst shall act in a manner consistent with his obligation to deal fairly with customers and clients in disseminating investment recommendations or material changes in prior investment advice, and in taking investment action.

5. Reworded B-1 and B-5 in the interest of clarification (in the case of B-5, restricting its application to clients as opposed to all those who might receive broadly descriptive materials).

6. Revised Section D (Disclosure of Conflicts) for clarification—particularly the legal requirement that mere disclosure does not absolve the analyst from the necessity to comply with the law.

This brings the chronology of the Code and Standards down to the present. No changes were effected in 1976, but studies were of course continued in certain areas, particularly Standard B-5 and the implications of suitability in terms of total portfolio as against a single investment asset.

The Investment Analysis Standards Board also has been occupied with needed revisions of membership requirements in the Federation and redefinition of "financial analysis" in further implementation of the Federation's self-regulation program approved in 1974. After much debate and research, final recommendations were made to the delegates at San Diego in September, 1976, and amendments to the By-laws were adopted. The thrust of these changes was to focus on participation in the *investment decision-making process* as the primary ingredient for qualification—thereby broadening eligibility for individual membership in the Federation and in the constituent Societies. The implication of this basic change is that further strengthening of the Standards will probably be desirable—the more the universe of membership is broadened, the more necessary become ethical standards of even higher order and coverage. Thus, the Code and Standards are not inscribed in stone, but rather, form a living thing, subject to change in a deliberative process like the Constitution itself. That word *exaggeration* may yet reappear! And more definity is likely in the area of conflicts-of-interest.

It is of historical interest to note that the original Code of Ethics of the New York Society was expanded and strengthened over the years. In May, 1975, the Society adopted a set of Canons of Ethics and Standards of Practice in connection with its effort to obtain separate professional certification under state law. These Canons and Standards contained various provisions similar in intent to those included in the Federation Code of Ethics and Standards of Professional Conduct, which are now a requirement of all member societies of the Federation (see Editor's note).

From the very beginnings of the Societies, the programs of the Federation—in advancement of analytical knowledge, expertise and education—have had strong ethical overtones. The great Beloit (now Rockford) Seminars, the Harvard Investment Workshops, *The Financial Analysts Journal,* The Institute of Chartered Financial Analysts, the twenty-nine Conferences, Fall Conferences, the series of seminars, the thousands of meetings of individual societies with corporations and otherwise, the expanding network of Federation committees, the Canadian Council and Investment Seminars, the self-regulation program, the C.F.A. Examination I requirement for admission to regular membership after July 1, 1976, and now the impetus for a major stride forward in education on a national scale are examples. All of these facets of professional growth and stature have reinforced the ethical structure of the Federation, the Societies, the Institute, and increased the quality and integrity of the individual members.

These remarks demonstrate that our history is still evolving and changing in the right directions in terms of the standards by which the profession must live. The future is bright.

Securities Law and Regulation

By John G. Gillis and M. H. Earp

Interpretations of Professional Conduct

Through their private self-regulation programs, the Financial Analysts Federation and the Institute of Chartered Financial Analysts have now accumulated sufficient experience to reach general agreement on the interpretation of many sections of their Codes of Ethics and Standards of Professional Conduct. A large number of individual cases have been considered by numerous member groups. The principles emerging from their discussions are summarized below for the guidance of members in applying the Codes and Standards to their own behavior.

The Review Procedure

The Codes and Standards of the FAF and ICFA are identical except for an additional ICFA standard regarding use of the Chartered Financial Analyst designation. Although the Code of Ethics contains only four brief paragraphs, it embodies the essential elements required for analysts to achieve and maintain public confidence. The Standards of Professional Conduct are in reality an elaboration of the elements stated in the Code. The Standards serve to provide more specific statements of the conduct implicit in ethical behavior.*

Article VIII of the ICFA and Article XII of the FAF By-Laws, and both Rules of Procedure, set forth the procedures to be followed in processing complaints or other information in-

---

* For a more comprehensive discussion of the Code and Standards, see *Professional Standards of Practice*, John G. Gillis, ed. (Charlottesville, VA: Financial Analysts Research Foundation, 1978).

John G. Gillis is a member of the law firm of Hill & Barlow, Boston, general counsel of The Financial Analysts Federation.
M. H. Earp is Chairman and President of J.W. Davis & Company, Dallas, Vice-Chairman of the FAF's Professional Conduct Committee and an Associate Editor of this journal.

volving members' conduct. Each case may include investigations and recommendations by the staff of either the FAF or the ICFA, by the appropriate regional Professional Conduct Committee and by either a hearing panel or a review committee of the Professional Conduct Committee before submission to the ICFA Board of Trustees or FAF Board of Directors.

Matters involving members of both the FAF and the ICFA are coordinated, with one or the other organizations being the primary communicator with the member in the investigation. If the staff finds that a matter involves violations, they may reach a stipulation (i.e., mutual agreement) for sanction with the member. A review committee of the Professional Conduct Committee advises the Board on stipulations at the time of their referral.

If a member is not satisfied with the stipulation proposed by the staff, the matter is submitted to the regional Professional Conduct Committee consisting of the member's peers in the geographical area in which the member resides. After independent investigation, the regional committee may either recommend that the matter be dismissed or submit a statement of charges to the chairman of the Professional Conduct Committee, who will appoint a hearing panel to consider the testimony, evidence and arguments presented by the member and a representative of the regional committee. If a violation is found, the hearing panel's findings and recommendations are submitted for final disposition to the Board (or both Boards in instances of joint FAF and ICFA membership). However, in no case can the Board's sanction be more severe than the sanction recommended by the hearing panel.

Of the hundreds of matters involving members' conduct reviewed by the FAF and ICFA, only a small percentage were found to involve potential violations and ultimately presented to the

respective Boards. There have been surprisingly few violations and even fewer serious violations, considering the large membership of the FAF and ICFA. (Of the 15,000 members of the FAF, about 5,000 are also ICFA members.)

The most frequent violations thus far considered by the Professional Conduct Committee (the last stage before presentation to the Boards) involved conflicts of interest. While many of these violations were obvious, some required interpretation in the light of special circumstances. Failure to use proper care in exercising "reasonable supervision over subordinate employees" has also been the subject of several cases. Findings have varied widely, depending on particulars. Contrary to expectations, violations relating to "priority of transactions" have primarily concerned inappropriate discrimination between clients, rather than preference given to a member's personal account. Members should give particular attention to these important but sometimes complex areas of responsibility.

It has been the policy of the Professional Conduct Committee to write a "commentary" on the application of the Code and the Standards in each case being considered by either a hearing panel or a stipulation review subcommittee. The following hypothetical cases have been selected to illustrate the care members must exercise in the conduct of their professional practice.

Case A

A member is an executive of a brokerage firm in charge of research and a "supervisory analyst" as defined by the New York Stock Exchange. He decides to change his recommendation from buy to sell on a company he has been following and, following his firm's procedure, advises certain other firm executives of his proposed action.

Anticipating rapid deterioration in the company's operations, one executive sells the stock from his and certain other accounts. Some institutional customers are informed of the change by the firm's research and other personnel before the changed recommendation is disseminated to others. The dissemination process takes 10 days.

The member himself does not personally own stock in the company. But he mentions to a trustee of a trust, of which his children are beneficiaries, that he is making a change in his recommendation. The trustee decides to sell and the member effects the transaction.

Commentary

The above conduct would violate three standards. Standard B-6, requiring fair-dealing with all customers, and Standard A-4, requiring the exercise of reasonable supervision of subordinate employees, would be violated because, respectively, (1) the change was first communicated by the firm on a selected basis to certain preferred customers and not on a timely basis to others who held the stock, and (2) the member failed to supervise employees adequately in that timely and complete dissemination of the change in recommendation was not achieved. Standard E, requiring that client transactions take priority over personal transactions, would also have been violated by the member when he privately communicated his change in recommendation to the trustee before disseminating it to firm clients.

Case B

A member is a trust officer of a bank in charge of a recently established investment advisory subsidiary designed to advise smaller investors on an individual basis. Although the subsidiary is understaffed (a situation not in the member's control), an aggressive new business effort is undertaken. Literature describes extensive individualized services to be offered to clients.

As the service progresses, the member knows the clients are not receiving the services represented and, in fact, are not receiving adequate attention in other respects. Because of understaffing and the large number of accounts, complete information about the needs and circumstances of individual clients is not obtained. The bank pays referral fees to brokers, which are not disclosed to clients.

The SEC finds applicable regulations have been violated. The member contends that he has relied on the senior officers of the bank without adequate advice of counsel.

Commentary

Standard B-5 would be violated in that a member is required, when making recommendations to a client, "to be aware of and consider the appropriateness and suitability of such recommendation or action for such client." Sufficient attention was not paid to these matters. The member would also have violated Standard C-2 (disclosure of consideration paid to others for recommending his services) in not disclosing to clients the fee-referral arrangement with brokers.

Standards A-3 (participation in statutory or regulatory violations) and A-4 (supervisory responsibility) are also relevant since the member was the bank's officer with supervisory responsibility for the new subsidiary. Under these circumstances, the bank's legal counsel responsible for SEC matters was the "proper authority," not the bank's senior officers.

The member contravenes the Code by not conducting himself "in a manner that would reflect credit on himself and on the profession" by his failure to communicate clearly the limited nature of the services being provided by the bank. Unless specifically advised to the contrary, clients should be able to assume that a member engaged in individual investment counseling will render complete individual service.

Case C

A member is the owner-manager of a broker-dealer firm specializing in the sale of mutual fund shares. The firm belongs to an exchange and conducts business through several branches. Through an employee, the member meets an inventor and decides to finance a new venture by placing bonds with 50 of his firm's individual customers as a "private placement," relying solely on his personal knowledge of the applicable securities laws and regulations with respect to public offerings of securities.

In addition to this, the member assists one of his best salesmen in the restitution of funds previously "inad-

vertently" misappropriated by that salesman from two accounts of the firm. But he institutes no new safeguards of client funds. The salesman subsequently misappropriates more funds and disappears.

In another instance, the firm is the subject of SEC sanctions arising from violations of regulations occurring in a branch office managed by relatively inexperienced personnel.

Commentary

The member would have violated Standard A-1 by participating in a public offering of securities without SEC registration. Moreover, the member would have failed to "use proper care and exercise independent professional judgment," in accordance with Paragraph 4 of the Code of Ethics. "Proper care" means, among other things, recognizing and seeking competent counsel. The member is responsible for choosing and relying on the source of the information.

The first paragraph of the Code requires conduct consistent with "integrity and dignity." These principles clearly take precedence over loyalties to employers, associates and employees. Furthermore, Standard A-4 requires that adequate supervision be given to subordinate employees. Placing inexperienced personnel in supervisory positions, or not establishing sufficient safeguards against aberrant employees, is inconsistent with "reasonable supervision."

A distinction should be made between employees under the member's direct supervision and employees only indirectly under a member's control. In the latter instance, the member should be deemed to have discharged his obligation if he has established adequate policies and procedures, and has taken reasonable steps to assure that these policies and procedures are being followed and has no reason to believe that they are not. Such was not the case here.

Case D

In charge of research for a brokerage firm, a member is qualified as a "supervisory analyst" with the New York Stock Exchange. Although he has been given prior written warning by the Exchange that the firm had been guilty of past infractions relating to the required disclosure of market-making activities in its publicly disseminated research reports, the member fails to make certain that several research reports published under his supervision properly carried this notation.

Commentary

The FAF and ICFA have held that the New York Stock Exchange rule relating to the disclosure of possible conflicts of interest is an "applicable rule" as defined under Standard A-1 (compliance with applicable laws and self-regulatory organization rules). In addition, Standard D (disclosure of conflicts) states this obligation specifically.

The Professional Conduct Committee has further suggested that all members be cautioned regarding the importance of disclosing potential conflicts of interest. For instance, many institutions share common directors and banking or other connections with other organizations, which connections should in some circumstances be disclosed to clients and customers.

Case E

This case is similar to Case C above, with the exception that the specific violation involves an "administrative oversight" concerning an "internal office memorandum" that receives limited distribution (about 100 copies) to customers.

A member gives the report to a subordinate for final preparation, and the market-making legend is omitted. Despite the firm's procedure of checking before dissemination to prevent such omissions, over the preceding two weeks several other reports have been distributed without the disclosure. The member knows this, but asserts ignorance of the violation in the internal office memorandum in question.

Commentary

The member would have violated Standards A-1 and D and Standard A-3. While supervisors should not be held accountable for all of their employees' actions, the responsibility for establishing and applying procedures lies with the supervisor. Moreover, the supervisor cannot rely on procedures he knows to be ineffective. He has a clear duty to monitor performance of procedures.

The Committee has noted that supervisory responsibilities are not novel to the brokerage area, but are applicable to all institutions.

Case F

A member is a portfolio manager of a large institution. He inherits an account with a major holding in a manufacturing company in which there is a significant loss. He attempts over several months to analyze the company's status, but finds top management unresponsive to his requests for information.

During his investigation, a middle-level executive indicates at lunch that a significant contract is a "disaster" because of pricing deficiencies and production cost over-runs. Despite the fact that this information is not public, the member immediately relays it to an associate who is responsible for another portfolio containing the company's securities. They both liquidate their positions the next morning.

When the company releases the information about the disastrous contract two weeks later, the stock price falls 15 per cent in two days. The member's defense against the charge of improper use of inside information as a "tippee" is that (1) his general observation and analysis dictated the conclusion to sell, (2) management's failure to communicate was the reason for his decision and (3) the information he received was not sought and only incidental to the timing of the sales.

Commentary

The relation between the time the non-public information was received and the time of the sales suggests that paramount weight was given to this information. The "mosaic" defense of using only non-material information (whether or not public) is not persuasive, since the member knew, or should have known, the extraordinary nature of the information and the expected impact on the market price of the stock. The member would have violated Standard A-5, which prohibits the communication of, or action on, "material inside information."

Case G

A member recommends to a wealthy and "sophisticated" client the purchase of a stock. He recommends the purchase because he has received "third-hand," from a friend at a bank, knowledge of a proposed favorable acquisition (which has not been announced publicly), including the price at which shares will be exchanged. The client agrees to make large purchases. The potential acquisition does not materialize and, in fact, is never publicly announced. The company eventually goes bankrupt and the entire investment is lost.

Commentary

The member would have violated Standard B-1 by failing to have a reasonable and adequate basis for investment recommendations and by failing to "distinguish between facts and opinions in the presentation of investment recommendations." That the member (1) believed that the "rumor" was "public knowledge" and (2) used several sources of information cannot be supported.

To the extent that the member utilized material, non-public information from company sources in making his recommendation, he would also have violated Standard A-5 prohibiting the use of inside information.

Case H

The member is an officer and portfolio manager of an investment advisory firm. Assets of discretionary clients' accounts are invested in convertible debentures of a small publicly held company. Because of the continued disappointing performance of the company, the member liquidates most of the client holdings of the debentures. However, before the debentures of the three last clients can be sold, the company experiences a substantial decline in market price and further deterioration of its financial condition.

The member uses the funds from another discretionary account to purchase a guaranteed note of the company. The company uses the proceeds from this guaranteed note to redeem the convertible debentures held by the three other clients.

Commentary

The member would have violated Standard B-6(c) (obligation to deal fairly with clients) and Standard D (disclosure of conflicts) by indirectly using the funds of one account to effect the liquidation of other accounts without disclosing the transaction to the client for whose account the guaranteed note was purchased.

Experience to Date

The Board of Directors of the FAF and the Board of Trustees of the ICFA are empowered under their respective By-Laws and under Section VI of the Rules of Procedure to impose any one of five sanctions against their members. In increasing order of severity, these sanctions are: (a) private admonishment, (b) private censure, (c) public censure, (d) suspension and (e) expulsion or revocation.

The actions taken in cases to date suggest a definite pattern in the assessment of sanctions. In general, the most severe penalties have been assessed to violations of public trust. These include matters involving (1) "Priority of Transactions" (Standard E), (2) "Disclosure of Conflicts" (Standard D), (3) the "obligation to deal fairly" (Standard B-6) and (4) the requirements relating to diligence in selecting suitable investments (Standards B-1, B-2 and B-5).

Less severe sanctions have been imposed for violations of business practices, such as recordkeeping, and minor incidents of failure to supervise. Even lesser penalties have been imposed with respect to violations of conduct between members, and between members and employers.

Although frequently cited in findings, alleged failure to comply with industry regulations has been only a supplemental factor in most instances. Evaluation of conduct concentrated on the application of professional ethical standards, rather than the added application of legal requirements. Furthermore, consideration has been given to the "intent" and "effects" of actions, especially in technical disclosure matters not involving important conflicts of interest. At the same time, illegal actions have been unanimously considered to be inconsistent with the member's obligations to "conduct himself with integrity and dignity" (Code, first paragraph) and, specifically, to comply with applicable laws and regulations (Standard A-1).

Although often less serious in terms of the sanctions applied, failure to "exercise reasonable supervision over subordinate employees" (Standard A-4) has received strongly worded comment by review committees and hearing panels. We will probably see more cases questioning the actions of members in positions of executive and administrative responsibility.

The benefits accruing to professionalism can be achieved only by conduct worthy of the public's trust. Strict adherence to the spirit and to the stated requirements of the Code and the Standards is the most certain method of gaining this confidence. Consequently, it is the obligation of each member to be both knowledgeable and continually vigilant with respect to his responsibilities. ■

THE INTERPRETATION AND APPLICATION OF
PROFESSIONAL STANDARDS OF CONDUCT

M. H. EARP, C.F.A.

The evolution of an occupation into a profession requires at least five necessary conditions: First, a social justification for the services performed and the establishment of public trust. Second, a common body of knowledge, both definable and subject to being acquired by education or experience. Third, a codification of the ethical principles and standards of practice on which the public may rely in its contacts with members of the profession. Fourth, a recognized institutional organization, which assures the public that members of the profession have at least a minimal mastery of the common body of knowledge and which has the authority to remedy grievances arising from ethical violations. Finally, practitioners must have some degree of idealism, a sense of social responsibility, and a desire to be of public service.

SOCIAL FUNCTION

In the field of financial analysis, the critical social function is the appraisal of business enterprises within the economic sector. Regardless of whether capital is allocated by the market mechanism or arbitrarily by political direction, as long as capital remains a scarce resource, financial analysis must be performed to determine the relative risk-return or cost-benefit relationships between competing investment possibilities.

In a capitalistic system dependent upon private savings as its principal source of funds, this function acquires a fiduciary responsibility to the investors whose investment decisions are being directed by the financial analyst's recommendations. Given the increased complexity of social, economic, and technological factors to be considered, it is unrealistic to assume that the layman's knowledge is generally adequate to make independent judgments even with "full disclosure" of the "relevant" facts.

BODY OF COMMON KNOWLEDGE

The requirement that a profession must have a definable body of knowledge that may be taught to and acquired by others has been met relatively recently. Although the threads of basic investment principles can be traced back to at least the mid-sixteenth century essays of Joseph de la Vega,[1] the eighteenth century publication of Thomas Mortimer,[2] and several nineteenth

---

[1] Joseph de la Vega, Confusion de Confusiones, pub. 1688, translated by Arthur H. Cole, (Boston: The Kress Library of Business and Economics, 1957).

[2] Thomas Mortimer, *Everyone His Own Broker*, (London: S. Hooper, 1769), 7th edition.

Paper presented at an October 1976 Symposium co-sponsored by The Financial Analysts Research Foundation, The Financial Analysts Federation, and The Institute of Chartered Financial Analysts.

century writers,[3] the landmark works of Graham[4] and Williams[5] were not published until the 1930's when rigorous application of scientific methodology became the accepted basis for analysis. Nevertheless, due to the magnitude of the economic and financial data subject to examination, only the development of computer technology has permitted widespread investigations of a large number of analytical concepts and the completion of an established theoretical foundation.

ETHICAL PRINCIPLES

Although some member societies had earlier codes, the first Code of Ethics of The Financial Analysts Federation was approved in 1962. The Code of Ethics of The Institute of Chartered Financial Analysts was approved in 1964. Through experience, interpretation, and amendment, each has evolved into more responsive statements of the profession's responsibilities. Essentially, the present Codes of Ethics and Standards of Conduct cover three subject areas: personal conduct, business relationships, and legal obligations.

For the most part, the legal obligations simply forbid the member to violate existing statutes and regulations. This serves a twofold purpose. Obviously, it is appropriate for members to comply with legal requirements that are often minimally acceptable conduct. This section is used also, however, to circumscribe those specific regulations of other jurisdictions, such as the National Association of Security Dealers, which are administrative in nature and, therefore, not applicable to professional conduct. The major "legal" obligations of financial analysts as presently stated in the Code and Standards require that members:

(A) must know and comply with all applicable laws, rules and regulations (Std. of Prof. Conduct, Section A-1),

(B) must not knowingly participate in, assist or condone acts of violation of any applicable law, rule, or regulation (Std. of Prof. Conduct, Section A-3),

(C) must not violate the laws and regulations related to the use of material inside information (Std. of Prof. Conduct, Section A-5),

(D) must carefully avoid plagiarism (Std. of Prof. Conduct, Section B-3),

(E) must avoid either oral or written statements which guarantee any investment (Std. of Prof. Conduct, Section B-4),

(F) must comply with laws, rules, and regulations governing the disclosure of conflicts of interest (Std. of Prof. Conduct, Section D).

The sections in the Codes and related Standards of Conduct concerning business relationships are primarily directed at intra-professional responsibilities between the members and the members' employers. These state the most important rules of conduct considered essential,

---

[3] See especially John Frances, *Chronicles and Characters of the Stock Exchange,* (London: Willoughby and Co., 1851); William M. Grosvenor, *American Securities,* (New York: Daily Commercial Bulletin, 1885); S. A. Nelson, *The ABC of Stock Speculation,* V (New York: 1903); George Garr Henry, *How to Invest Money,* (New York: Funk & Wagnalls Company, 1908).

[4] Benjamin Graham and Davis L. Dodd, *Security Analysis,* (New York: McGraw Hill Book Company, 1934).

[5] John Burr Williams, *The Theory of Investment Value,* (Amsterdam: North-Holland Publishing Company, 1938).

given the broad diversity of the profession's membership and services. In addition, these sections constitute the framework for an understanding with, or for regulation by, political bodies charged with the oversight of the profession. The financial analyst is obligated to:

(A) encourage the practice of financial analysis in a manner that would reflect credit on the member and/or the profession (Code of Ethics, second paragraph),

(B) be fair and businesslike in all competitive business situations (Std. of Prof. Conduct, Section F),

(C) exercise reasonable supervision over subordinate employees who are subject to a member's control to prevent violations of either applicable laws and regulations or of the Code of Ethics and Standards of Professional Conduct (Std. of Prof. Conduct, Section A-4),

(D) when making investment recommendations,

    (a) distinguish between facts and opinions (Std. of Prof. Conduct, Section B-11),

    (b) make a determination of the relevant investment risks and a valuation of, or the expected return from, investment securities (Std. of Prof. Conduct, Section B-2),

    (c) be aware of and consider the suitability of investments for clients (Std. of Prof. Conduct, Section B-5),

    (d) deal fairly when disseminating recommendations or material changes in prior advice and when taking investment actions (Std. of Prof. Conduct, Section B-6),

    (e) give customers, clients, and employer adequate opportunity to act before initiating personal transactions (Std. of Prof. Conduct, Section E),

    (f) maintain appropriate records to support the reasonableness of the recommendation (Std. of Prof. Conduct, Section B-1).

(E) unless the member is in a special or confidential relationship with an issuer, and receives inside information acting in that capacity, make reasonable effort to achieve public dissemination of such information (Std. of Prof. Conduct, Section A-5),

(F) not take compensation for services in competition with an employer without written consent from both employer and clients (Std. of Prof. Conduct, Section C-3),

(G) respect the right of fellow analysts to hold varying viewpoints, and not use business position to attempt improperly to exert undue influence on matters pertaining to the activities of professional organizations (Std. of Prof. Conduct, Section F),

(H) limit the use of professional designations to those circumstances proscribed by the Standards of Professional Conduct (Std. of Prof. Conduct, Section G).

The ultimate purpose of codes of ethics and other statements of principles should be to establish standards of personal conduct of members in their contact with clients. The standards enunciated should indicate the extent to which the public (to whom the services are offered) can have confidence in members of the profession. Financial analysts are pledged to:

(A) conduct themselves with integrity and dignity, and to encourage other members to act accordingly (Code of Ethics, first paragraph),

(B) act in an ethical and professional manner in relationships with the public, clients, associates, fellow members, and employees (Std. of Prof. Conduct, Section F),

(C) act impartially both between customers and clients (Std. of Prof. Conduct, Section E),

(D) give priority to customers, clients, and employers over personal transactions (Std. of Prof. Conduct, Section E), and not permit personal transactions to affect adversely the interests of customers, clients, and employers (Std. of Prof. Conduct, Section E),

(E) disclose all possible material conflicts of interest and beneficial ownership of assets, which could reasonably be expected to influence recommendations and counsel (Std. of Prof. Conduct, Section D),

(F) inform clients if compensation in addition to compensation from them is being received (Std. of Prof. Conduct, Section C-1), or if the member has paid consideration to others for recommending the member's services to them (Std. of Prof. Conduct, Section C-2),

(G) use proper care and exercise independent professional judgment (Code of Ethics, fourth paragraph), and support all actions by appropriate research and investigation (Std. of Prof. Conduct, Section B-2),

(H) strive to maintain and to improve the ability to perform competently, and to encourage others in the profession to do likewise (Code of Ethics, third paragraph),

(I) assure that employers are aware of the existence and content of the Code of Ethics and Standards of Professional Conduct (Code of Ethics, Section A-2),

(J) upon encountering evidence of illegal acts, be encouraged to report such evidence to proper authority (Std. of Prof. Conduct, Section A-6).

It should be noted that several interesting subjects are *not* included in the above listing. First, no mention is made of any obligation to provide the profession's services to society at large. Second, while employers are required to be advised of the Code and Standards, no similar requirement exists that clients be notified of either the Code, the Standards, or the grievance procedures available to aggrieved clients. Third, although members are obligated to encourage others in the profession to improve their ability to perform competently, nothing is suggested with respect to encouraging the entrance of new members.

All professions must have some organized body recognized by the public and with the responsibility of setting minimum levels of competency and enforcing adherence to the promised standards of conduct. This regulation may be either politically or self imposed. In the older professions, the regulation is a combination of licensing by some governmental jurisdiction and of supervision by a professional association that establishes and enforces higher standards upon its members.

For self-regulation to be meaningful, it is essential that membership in the disciplining organization be considered significant. Otherwise, enforcement would be largely ineffective since the threat of sanctions or of expulsion would be ignored. In the field of securities investment, an extraordinary degree of interdependence between professionals exists both locally and nationally. Access to information and to the trading markets is vital for successful practice. Therefore, a high value is placed on a member's rights and privileges.

INSTITUTIONAL ORGANIZATION

Virtually all practicing financial analysts are members of The Financial Analysts Federation (FAF). In addition, a large group also has attained membership in The Institute of Chartered Financial Analysts (ICFA). These organizations have similar Codes of Ethics, Standards of Professional Conduct, and Professional Conduct Committees to hear grievances and to discipline violators of their codes.

Structurally, continuing surveillance and initial investigatory responsibilities are delegated to the staff personnel by the governing board of each organization. If a possible violation is found, the member is initially contacted by staff personnel to provide further information and explanation. Should the President of the F.A.F. or the Executive Director of the I.C.F.A. determine that sufficient evidence of a violation does not exist, the matter is closed.

If the staff of either organization finds sufficient evidence for prosecution, the case is submitted to the appropriate Regional Professional Conduct Committees, for further investigation and resolution. If these committees conclude that further action is justified, a statement of charges is filed with the Professional Conduct Committee Chairman, who then appoints a Hearing Panel, consisting of members of the Professional Conduct Committee, to hear formally the complaint and to make recommendations to the governing boards for final disposition. If the Regional Committees find that action is not justified, the case is closed.

The grievance procedure described above has two exceptions. First, the staff may enter into a "stipulation" with the accused member, whereby the member voluntarily agrees to findings and a recommended sanction. Under this process, the staff submits its recommendation to the chairman of its Professional Conduct Committee and to its governing board. Thereafter, the Professional Conduct Committee Chairman appoints a Review Committee that will (1) consider the proposed stipulation, and (2) submit its recommendations to the respective governing board. The board then makes the final determination based on both the staff's and the Review Committee's recommendations.

The other exception involves complaints brought against a member by the public. In this instance, a complaint cannot be dismissed without the concurrence of both the staff and the Regional Conduct Committee.

NECESSARY CONDITIONS

To be effective, any statute, regulation, or disciplinary proceeding must have the support of its constituency (i.e., the public that is the recipient of the services) and of the members of the profession who are potentially subject to enforcement actions. This requires that the rules and procedures be considered reasonable and fair. Offended parties must feel that grievances will be remedied. At the same time, the accused must have confidence that the right to due process will be protected, and that the judging tribunal will be a body of peers capable of understanding the circumstances and the defense.

The administration of disciplinary proceedings is often made especially difficult due to rapid and significant changes in economic and financial conditions. For example, reconstruction of circumstances prevailing in prior years is necessary to understand properly the action taken within the context of that environment. Well-reasoned analytical recommendations, based on information and circumstances then existing, may appear almost frivolous in the light of subsequent knowledge. Therefore, every effort is made not to prejudice the conclusions by the inequitable benefit of hindsight.

Nevertheless, disciplinary actions inevitably involve judgments about what should have been known as well as what apparently was known, and what should have been done as well as what was done. This introduces into the considerations the element of competency and care, in addition to questions of conduct. For this reason, it is essential to have the basic standards of professional practice adequately defined. This definition is provided for analysts by the Investment Analysis Standards Board.

Fidelity to clients, other members of the profession, employers, and associates is, unfortunately, far from obvious in many specific instances. The analyst may act in various capacities depending upon particular circumstances. Section A-5 of the Standards of Professional Conduct recognizes one of these roles in distinguishing the analyst acting on behalf of an issuer. A more difficult, but equally important, distinction in roles is the difference in the analyst's obligation for public recommendations contained in broadly distributed publications and in the obligation for recommendations made to specific clients.

In all cases of disputes, a heavy responsibility must rest on the profession's staff and conduct committees. Unlike the codes of Hammurabi, "an eye for an eye,"[6] interpretations of modern codes and standards of conduct often are subtle and possible violations are shaded by many considerations. The obligations to the public and the profession must be weighed carefully against the individual member's rights.

It is apparent that judgmental errors injurious to an individual member are far more devastating than the effect of any such single error on the profession. Thus, the administrative actions of staff and of conduct committees must be marked by an unusual degree of circumspection. In professions such as investment analysis in which personal reputation is vital, accusation may be comparable to conviction. The objective must be diligence in prosecution with discretion in execution.

Another major problem is public identity and recognition of financial analysts. Unlike members of many other professional groups, the financial analyst is still widely thought to be merely a part of the securities industry rather than to be a member of a separate and distinctive profession. Unfortunately, the historical relationship with the securities business has often led to the presumption that the "security analysis" and stock market literature published by brokers are representative of a financial analyst's abilities and scope of activities.

The "professional" unquestionably accepts, implicitly and expressly, the responsibility of being judged by a higher standard than one who makes no representations of superior training and experience. This is a well-established precept particularly familiar to trustees.

For this reason, it is clearly as important to define the limitations of a profession's services as it is to enunciate the range of competency. Otherwise, the public cannot be blamed for believing the profession is accountable for levels of performance that are realistically unattainable. Ex post facto disclaimers can be expected to have little value as a defense.

Almost all professions today have less respect from their clients than formerly.[7] The dominant reason for this decline in public confidence is an increasing emphasis on personal

---

6 Robert Francis Harper, *The Code of Hammurabi*, (Chicago: University of Chicago Press, 1904).

7 *The Troubled Professions*, Business Week, August 16, 1976, p. 126 ff.

opportunity at the expense of public service. Without the dedication to serve, professional trappings become ludicrous. Idealism must be a major factor in professional conduct.

When students desire to become doctors because medicine is a lucrative field rather than because of their desire to help others, or when lawyers wish to practice law primarily because of pecuniary rewards rather than the achievement of justice, loss of professional stature is inevitable. When a professional body becomes a significant influence in either maintaining fees (prices), protecting the members at the expense of the interests of clients, or attaining some other selfish purpose, it may surely anticipate being stripped of its respective professional stature by the political process.

The concept of Adam Smith's "invisible hand," which suggested that each individual following his own self-interest somehow automatically assures the best public good, has, unhappily, not been proven pragmatically.[8] A theory that promises long-run benefits at the expense of short-run abuses is socially intolerable. Consequently, constraints of various forms have been created to limit this self-interest. One response is notably obvious in the more recent revisions of many codes of ethics and standards of conduct that deal almost exclusively with "thou shall not" clauses, instead of more affirmative statements of ideals.[9]

The danger in this approach is the appearance of less emphasis on the positive obligations of a profession to respond properly to the implied responsibilities generally contained in its code of ethics. The concepts of "fairness," "loyalty," "just," and "proper care" should not be misinterpreted as mere homilies.

In a capitalistic, democratic society, the function of the financial analyst in relation to the capital markets should be similiar to the news media's social function in relation to the political system. The attainment of this public trust should be ample stimulation for members to strive for exceptional performance of their respective duties.

This article is based in part on a paper presented at the Symposium on Professional Standards of Practice, October 1976, sponsored by The Financial Analysts Research Foundation in cooperation with The Financial Analysts Federation and The Institute of Chartered Financial Analysts.

---

8 Adam Smith, *The Wealth of Nations*, (New York: Random House, Inc., 1937 p. 423).

9 Ray Patterson, *Wanted: A New Code of Professional Responsibility*, **American Bar Association** Journal; May 1977, Vol. 63, pp. 639-642.

RESEARCH REPORT ETHICS*

Louis J. Zitnik, C.F.A.

The public image of the securities analyst is influenced to a greater extent by the research reports of broker-dealer firms than by all other means of communications. While it is obviously impossible to list precise topics that should be included in a research report and their precise method of treatment, it seems desirable to discuss general areas where guidelines can be established in order to improve the calibre of the reports.

THE CRITICS

Among the critics of the average quality of research reports are the Securities and Exchange Commission and Graham, Dodd and Cottle.[1] The Report of Special Study of the Secrurities Markets of the Securities and Exchange Commission[2] states:

The preparation and dissemination of printed advisory matter has become an ordinary part of conducting a successful retail securities business today and plays an important part in sales promotion. The most common forms taken by broker-dealer published material are the market letter, sent daily or weekly; the research report, devoted to recommending a specific company or group of companies and sent regularly or occasionally; a monthly report and special securities reports, often in finished magazine form. Some of this material contains detailed and extensive evaluations of the merits, risks, and prospects of the securities considered. Far more of it does not purport to make any detailed analysis to support the recommendations. It generally classifies the securities in terms of investment goals, but omits any consideration of adverse data or uncertainties. Overwhelmingly the recommendations are to purchase; recommendations to sell securities are few, and for the most part deliberately avoided, even with respect to securities previously recommended whose prospects may have changed. The core of the recommendation is generally a projection, which often is in the form of an estimate of future earnings but which sometimes involves an outright prediction of a future market price well in excess of the present market. Ordinarily, little information is given concerning the ex-

---

* Reprinted by permisssion of the *Financial Analysts Journal*,
   (January/February 1966).

[1] Graham, Dodd and Cottle, *Security Analysis*, 4th Ed. (McGraw-Hill Book Company, Inc., 1962), pp. 106–7.

[2] Report of Special Study of Securities Markets of the Securities and Exchange Commission, Part 5, (U.S. Government Printing Office, 1963), pp. 56–60.

tent or method of research and about the person responsible for the recommendation. Moreover, usually there is no indication of any interest in or intentions as to the securities recommended on the part of the distributing broker-dealer firm, since few disclosures of these facts go further than an unrevealing boilerplate hedge clause.

By its very nature, the market letter is primarily confined to capsule comments and summaries on particular industries and companies. Such letters should contain the statement that additional information is available upon request. The discussion herein will be confined to the research report prepared for the average investor. The so-called institutional report is designed for a sophisticated analyst or investor who should be entirely competent to appraise incompleteness or shoddy work.

PRESENT REGULATION

The New York Stock Exchange,[3] the National Association of Securities Dealers, Inc.,[4] and the State of California, Division of Corporations[5] have established rules concerning research reports and other advertising for those firms coming under their respective jurisdictions. Such rules are usually quite general, but basic in nature, and are recommended reading for all students of this topic.

Rules of the regulatory bodies prohibit statements which are "promissory, exaggerated, flamboyant, or contain unwarranted superlatives." They are particularly thorough in covering the matter of disclosures of special interests of a broker-dealer regarding such matters as trading markets, securities held (including options), and participation in recent underwritings of the subject company's securities. The regulatory authorities cited all require that the date of issuance of the research report be clearly stated, as well as the market price on the release date. Yet some firms presently do not include the date (or if so, in code) in order that the report may be used for a longer length of time. This is obviously a flagrant violation.

There are other areas that are not covered by specific rules where the policy of reasonable prudence requires proper treatment. The quality of an issue should be clearly stated in terms which the layman will understand. Admittedly, research reports are used for sales purposes, but it would be as wrong to leave the impression that Communication Satellite common stock has the stability of American Telephone & Telegraph common as it would be to represent by indirection that a Volkswagen was comparable to a Cadillac.

There are three separate and distinct meanings for the word invest-

---

[3] *New York Stock Exchange Guide,* Vol. 2 (Commerce Clearing House, Inc., Nov. 1964), pp. 4025–4031.

[4] National Association of Securities Dealers, Inc., Manual, 1965. Advertising Interpretations, G-19–G-22.

[5] State of California, California Administrative Code, Title 10, Investment, Article 24, Advertising 92.10–94.1, Published by Office of Administrative Procedure, Department of Finance, State of California.

ment: (1) investment meaning purchase, (2) investment meaning securities or equities, and (3) investment meaning high quality as opposed to speculation. It is suggested that the first two meanings be avoided in research reports in order that there can be no misinterpretation by the reader.

SINS OF OMISSION

Perhaps the greatest abuses in research reports occur in failure to discuss adequately the negatives in a situation (the sins of omission). It is all too easy to gloss over a marginal trade position and the financial size and resources of competitors in fields with changing technologies. The cyclical nature of an industry should be explained. The thinness of trading markets for certain securities and their volatile nature should be fully discussed, where appropriate.

EARNINGS

The summary of the profit and loss statement for a number of years is regarded as standard in virtually all research reports. A 10-year summary would seem to be desirable, since any recent 10-year period will cover at least two recessions. The latest five-year period—1960–1964—has an optimistic bias, since 1960 was a recessionary period and each subsequent year was one of prosperity. However, it cannot be denied that the SEC requires only five years' results (plus interim periods) in a prospectus which can probably be considered as meeting the minimum requirement for a research report. Obviously, nonrecurring gains should be excluded from the earnings tabulation (though they can be covered by footnotes) and any marked changes in a corporation's tax rate from year to year should be explained.

The proper use of the term "cash flow" has been fully delineated by a committee of the Financial Analyst Federation, and its report has been reproduced in the *Financial Analysts Journal*. The use of the term "cash earnings" in place of "cash flow" is highly misleading to the average investor, and in the writer's opinion should never be used in a research report.

Compound growth rates or absolute rates of increase can also be quite misleading, depending upon the period chosen. It is not easy to suggest a precise formula to use in this regard but common sense should be the rule. A small growth company, for example, could have an average 40 percent compound growth rate for a five-year period because of the small base used, whereas the growth in the last year or two could be 10 percent or less. Using a depressed base for a cyclical company also gives a highly erroneous impression.

BALANCE SHEET

Balance sheet statements should be included in a research report, at least in abbreviated form or in text. The summary of current assets and current liabilities is usually sufficient for a well-established company, but a low cash and account receivable position should be mentioned, if appropriate. The long-term debt and preferred should be enumerated. All potential dilution to the common stock from convertibles, warrants, and options should be clearly indicated. Employee stock options should be commented upon if the quantity is material. It is worth noting that several securities firms are adjusting current year earnings per share estimates for potential dilution rather than merely stating that conversion of senior securities and/or exercise of warrants would result in a dilution of "x" percent.

PROJECTIONS

The use of earnings projections could be the topic of a separate paper as there seems to be a wide divergence of opinion on the matter. It is interesting to observe that the rule of the California commissioner of corporations states: "Estimated earnings, dividends, and profits will ordinarily not be allowed unless based upon a past earnings record and are for a reasonable period in the future. Such estimates must be supported by data filed with the commissioner upon which the reasonableness of the estimate may be determined."

A limited but increasing number of corporate executives are forecasting earnings for their respective companies for as much as one to five years into the future, while others are publicly stating their earnings goals. When such statements are available, the analyst should reveal the source in order to give authority to the report as well as proper credit to the spokesman. On the other hand, the analyst has a responsibility to evaluate independently the prospects for attaining such performances and should avoid inclusion of unrealistic goals in his report regardless of the source.

While a five- or even a ten-year earnings forecast for utility common stock might come close to eventual results, the margin of error in forecasting earnings more than a year ahead for companies with rapid past growth is so great that the use of such projections is to be questioned without considerable qualifications. Many of the enthusiastic growth stock analysts are indeed continuing to be embarrassed by many of their projections of 1961.

COMPARISONS

Comparison of one company with another in the same field is another area of potential abuse unless the differences between the two companies and their equity issues are fully described. On this point, the California commissioner of corporations has ruled that "comparisons with alleged analogous situations and the use of statistics of successful companies ordinarily will be disapproved unless the comparison is supported by a record of operating history sufficient to justify the comparison."

A PROBLEM?

Many research reports are short in nature, being purposely so tailored for the busy individual who wants the salient points without involved details. Nevertheless, this "busy individual" deserves and requires the minimum coverage of the facts, both positive and negative, in the general manner discussed above. This minimum basic information can be covered in two standard size pages which should be short enough for even the busiest individual who will take savings and purchase a security on the basis of the information.

It does not seem practical to include a biography of the report writer (even a short one), though his name should be listed at the conclusion of the study followed by the designation C.F.A., if appropriate. If the writer is truly an industry specialist (closely following one or two groups rather than twenty), this could also be stated.

The regulatory agencies have been diligent in pointing out that many organizations have consistently maintained high standards in research reports. Undoubtedly, there are many research department executives who have devoted considerable time and effort to upgrading the printed output of their respective organizations from an ethical standpoint. It would seem desirable to obtain the benefit of the conclusions of such experts on this matter in general and on specific areas where improvements can be achieved.

by Leopold A. Bernstein and Joel G. Siegel

The Concept of Earnings Quality

▶ The professional investor knows that reported earnings numbers are often the product of deliberate choices between various accounting treatments and business options. In order to assess true earning power, the analyst must make some determination of the quality of earnings.

The quality of a reported earnings figure can be lowered if management recognizes revenues or expenditures either prematurely or belatedly, or chooses a liberal accounting treatment over a more conservative one. The analyst should be particularly wary of changes in accounting policy, taking note of any termination of auditor contracts resulting from disagreements over proposed accounting changes.

But earnings quality is affected by business, as well as by accounting, decisions. Management can manipulate the level of reported net income by raising or lowering discretionary expenses — e.g., increasing income by failing to replace obsolete fixed assets or by neglecting necessary repairs or, in certain cases, by cutting advertising costs. If the company is deferring such outlays merely to increase current earnings, it is degrading earnings quality.

Development costs can also be discretionary, and are particularly worthy of analysis since they often represent the key to a company's future success or failure. Finally, outlays for the development of human resources — the costs of training operating, sales and managerial talent — can have long-term significance. ◀

BECAUSE it seems to be the product of various objective, mathematical operations, a company's reported earnings figure is often taken by the unsophisticated user of financial statements as the quantitative measure of the firm's well-being. Of course, any professional knows that earnings numbers are in large part the product of conscious and often subjective choices between various accounting treatments and business options, as well as of various external economic factors. Two firms in a given industry may report identical earnings but experience completely different operating performance. If he wants to assess the true earning power of each company, the financial statement user must make some determination of the "quality" of its earnings.

The concept of "earnings quality" has gained wide usage in security analysis in recent years. There is at least one service almost exclusively devoted to monitoring earnings quality,[1] and many institutional research houses allude to the concept in their evaluations of reported earnings.[2] The Securities and Exchange Commission has referred to earnings quality on a number of occasions. In Accounting Series Release (ASR) No. 151, it said that "disclosure of the impact of inventory profits on reported earnings is important information for investors assessing the quality of earnings." ASR No. 159 states that "the purpose of the explanation of the Summary of Earnings is to enable investors to assess the source and probability of recurrence of net income, and thus of earnings quality." Release No. 33-5427 requires that "if a company's accounting principles are at variance with prevailing accounting practices within the industry, the dollar effect on earnings should be disclosed for there to be a proper assessment of the quality of earnings of the registrant."

Despite its general utilization, widespread confusion and disagreement remain over what the concept of earnings quality should properly include. Since the concept does have considerable usefulness, particularly as a communications device, it is important that this confusion be dispelled. To that end, this article proposes to consider the elements, as well as the limitations, of this concept.

1. Footnotes appear at end of article.

Leopold Bernstein is Professor of Accounting at Baruch College of the City University of New York and author of Financial Statement Analysis—Theory, Application and Interpretation, *revised edition (Homewood, IL: Richard D. Irwin, Inc., 1978). Joel Siegel is Assistant Professor of Accounting at Queens College of the City University of New York.*

The Elements of Earnings Quality

Earnings figures are affected by managements' and accountants' choices between generally accepted accounting principles (GAAP) and by managements' business choices. Sometimes managements make accounting and business choices in order to manipulate earnings figures and make them deliberately misleading. Sometimes managements make decisions that affect earnings components in such a way that the reported earnings figure is lowered in quality because, although it might reflect current economic reality, it does not give a good indication of future earning power. Sometimes the components of earnings are subject to external economic conditions that make them unreliable indicators of future earnings.

Earnings figures should have integrity—that is, they should not be the product of manipulations designed purely to increase the reported income of the company. Earnings figures should also be reliable, in the sense that they provide a good indication of the firm's earning power. But it is important to keep in mind that the notion of "quality," in the context of earnings evaluation, is one of *comparative* integrity, reliability and predictability. There are no absolute elements of earnings quality.

Liberal vs. Conservative Accounting Policy

One major influence on the quality of earnings is management's and the attesting accountant's discretion in choosing and using accounting policies.[3] Accounting choices can be liberal—that is, they can assume the most optimistic view of the future—or they can be conservative. Generally, conservatively determined earnings are of higher quality than those determined in a "liberal" fashion because they are less likely to prove overstated in the light of future developments. On the other hand, unwarranted or excessive conservatism, while it may contribute to the temporary quality of earnings, actually results in a lack of reporting integrity over the long run and cannot be considered a desirable factor.

Overstatement or understatement of earnings can result from numerous sources. For example, a lessor's failure to provide an allowance for typical maintenance services on leased equipment may result in an underaccrual of expenses and subsequent overstatement of earnings. A company that depreciates a given machine over a period that substantially exceeds the period used by its competitors or the technological life normally expected for that machinery is also likely to report overoptimistic earnings.

Analysts should be particularly wary of changes in accounting policy. They should feel obliged to ask whether the change was made to enhance economic reality or merely to enhance the financial statement numbers at the expense of economic reality. For example, a decision to reduce the bad debt provision as a percentage of sales, despite an increase in shipments to more marginal customers, or a nominal increase in the sales allowance account, even though sales and corresponding returns have increased significantly, may increase reported earnings, but not actual income. Inconsistent application of accounting policies, especially when changes are made to bolster earnings, render earnings numbers less meaningful and less reliable as indicators of future income.

Analysts should take note of any disclosure of termination of auditor contracts resulting from disagreements over proposed accounting changes. If the new auditors agree to the desired change, the company must disclose what the effect on net income would have been if the "old" method had been retained. If the reported results are substantially greater as a result of the accounting change, the earnings increment may be suspect.

Integrity of the Reporting Period

The degree to which current earnings benefit from past earnings or borrow from future earnings affects earnings quality. Unwarranted deferral of expenditures overstates earnings since it relieves reported results of appropriate charges. For example, a public utility that capitalizes increased fuel costs when it is highly unlikely that the regulatory body will allow such costs to be passed on to consumers is merely increasing current earnings at the expense of future income. Boeing capitalized into inventory $24.1 million in general and administrative expenses relating to long-term U.S. government contracts at the end of 1976. This represented a $0.27 per share increase over the 1975 year-end amount of $12.5 million. Capitalized G&A expenses increased, in spite of a substantial decline in inventories from $777.7 million at year-end 1975 to $435.1 million at year-end 1976.

Companies that provide for expense provisions (e.g., warranties) or losses in the current period because they failed to make adequate provisions in previous years usually end up understating current year earnings. Conversely, improper recognition of revenue, either prematurely or belatedly, overstates earnings and lowers their quality. The recognition of revenue before it is reasonably assured to be collectible may result in the reporting of earnings in one year and a resultant loss in a subsequent year. REITs that continue to recognize interest and rental income on bankrupt and foreclosed properties, for example, lower the quality of their reported earnings. On the other hand, immediate recognition of income may be undesirable when substantial services are yet to be performed. Health spas, which often recognize as income the advance cash payment for membership dues, might be wiser to apportion these dues over the membership period, as magazine publishers do.

In evaluating the appropriateness of a firm's accounting policies—whether the deferral of an expense item, a change in accounting policy or choice between GAAP—analysts should compare the policies used with the typical accounting policies employed in the industry. In general, the more liberal the firm's policies, the lower the quality of its earnings. But conformity does not necessarily imply higher quality earnings. Quality exists when the policies used reflect economic reality and when the earnings figure reported gives a true picture of the firm's earning power.[4]

Business Choices—Discretionary Costs

The quality of earnings is related to the degree to which adequate provision has been made for the maintenance of assets and for the maintenance and enhancement of present and future earning power. Management can use its control over discretionary costs—repairs and maintenance, advertising and research and development costs—to manipulate the level of reported net income (or loss). For example, in fiscal 1974, Colgate Palmolive reduced its marketing expenditures as a percentage of sales, thereby increasing its 1974 incremental comparisons by $0.79 a share.

In addition, if management decides to increase its income by failing to replace obsolete fixed assets with new, more efficient equipment, or by not performing the necessary repairs on existing equipment, the company will ultimately experience decreased operating efficiency, with a negative effect on its earning power. (This strategy may also have implications for the reliability of the asset lives underlying the firm's depreciation policies.) In 1970, International Paper had to establish a $39.6 million reserve for expected closedowns of obsolete, 88-year-old facilities because of new pollution control requirements. It is the analyst's task to identify the existence of such practices and to assess their impact on the reported results of operations.

Analysts must pay particular attention to whether the level of reported discretionary expenses is in keeping with the company's past trends and with its current and future requirements. For instance, the analyst should relate maintenance and repair costs to the level of such activity. In comparing repair and maintenance levels from year to year, the analyst can either compare the level of such costs for a period to the level of sales over the period, or to the firm's net property, plant and equipment (exclusive of land).

The latter method relates repair and maintenance costs to the assets for which these costs are incurred and, depending on the amount of information available to him, the analyst can develop specific ratios of repair and maintenance costs to specific categories of assets. Translating the firm's absolute trend in repair and maintenance costs from year to year into index numbers will enable the analyst to compare the resulting numbers with those of related accounts. The basic purpose of all these measures is to determine whether the repair and maintenance programs of the enterprise have been kept at normal and necessary levels, or changed in a way that affects the quality of income and its projection into the future.

In evaluating the degree of a company's maintenance of capital, the analyst must consider the rate of return being earned on its assets. If the company is earning an acceptable return, if the industry return is high, or if the company or industry is growing, the company should be acquiring new equipment. Under these circumstances, a firm's failure to keep its plant and equipment up to date would detract from its competitive position. On the other hand, if the rate of return being earned on corporate assets is unsatisfactory, or if the industry is in a state of decline, the company would be justified in not maintaining capital—for example, in not improving production facilities at branch locations that are being phased out.

Analysts should also determine whether a company's policy of not maintaining capital is of a short or long-term nature. If it's temporary, the firm may be currently short of cash or trying to maintain current profit levels. A permanent decision, however, has serious implications: It means that management does not want to invest further in the business, since it views the company as being in a state of liquidation.

Other Discretionary Costs

Since a significant portion of advertising outlays has an effect beyond the period in which it is incurred, the relation between advertising outlays and short-term results is a tenuous one. Management can, in certain cases, cut advertising costs with no commensurate immediate effects on sales, although the analyst (and management) can assume that, over the longer term, sales will suffer. The analyst should examine year to year variations in the level of advertising expenses with the objective of assessing the impact of such variations on the quality of current earnings and the level of future sales.

Research and development costs (most of which must now be expensed as incurred) can also be discretionary in nature, and the analyst must pay careful attention to year to year changes in their level. In many enterprises, research and development represent substantial costs, much of them fixed in nature, which can be the key to the firm's future success or failure. But the analyst must distinguish between those costs that can be quantified and those that cannot. Of primary concern in this evaluation is whether the enterprise is currently devoting the same portion of its earnings to the preservation and enhancement of earning power as in the past. Any proportionate reduction in investment in research and development effort can affect the quality of reported earnings.

In addition to advertising and research and development, there are other types of future-directed outlays, including the costs of training operating, sales and managerial talent. Although outlays for the development of human resources are usually expensed in the year incurred, they may have future utility, and the analyst may want to recognize this in his evaluation of earnings quality.

External Factors—Variability

Another factor to consider in assessing the quality of earnings is their variability. Earnings that vary considerably are generally less desirable than those that don't, hence the latter are usually thought to be of higher quality than the former. This is because a stable earnings trend provides greater accuracy in predicting future earnings levels. (However, stability should not be gained by artificial smoothing.)

Earnings variability can result from management business decisions. For example, a decision to lever the capital structure by introducing a relatively large amount of debt subjects the enterprise to large fixed interest charges, which in turn contribute to earnings variability and reduced quality. But the primary sources of earnings variability are external. Although skillful management can modify their effects, they are largely beyond management control.

For instance, a great deal of earnings instability can result from the ebb and flow of the economic cycle. A firm that derives revenue from industries affected in contrasting ways by cyclical factors has greater protection from the business cycle. Also, a firm that has countercyclical lines of business and a well diversified product mix will usually have greater earnings stability. Weyerhauser's lumber operations relate both to the fabrication and to the sale of raw materials. Since the cycles associated with these markets differ, this combination provides a degree of overall earnings stability.

Multinational corporations have a particular problem in that the quality of their foreign earnings is affected by difficulties and uncertainties regarding the repatriation of funds, currency fluctuations, the political and social climate and local customs and regulations. For example, the inability to dismiss personnel in some countries in effect converts labor costs into fixed costs. Regulated industries constitute another special problem area. An unsympathetic or even hostile regulatory environment can cause serious lags in obtaining rate relief.

The nature of their source can have a big impact on the quality of earnings. Defense-related expenditures can be regarded as non-recurring in wartime and affected by political uncertainties in peacetime. Analysts should consider income arising from recurring transactions related to normal business activities to be of higher quality than income arising from isolated transactions.

Balance Sheet Analysis as a Check on Earnings Quality

Analysis of the riskiness of the assets and liabilities carried on a company's balance sheet is an important complement to the other approaches to earnings quality evaluation. For example, the future realization of accounts receivable generally has a higher degree of probability than has the realization of, say, unrecovered tool and die or inventory costs. On the other hand, the future realization of inventory costs can generally be predicted with greater certainty than the future realization of goodwill or deferred start-up costs. If a company defers expensing outlays that are unlikely to have realizable value in the future, then the quality of the resulting income is reduced.

The analyst should be on the lookout for overstated assets. Companies in the extractive industry that use the full cost method may overstate assets when the total amounts capitalized as costs of reserves substantially exceed the value of such reserves; furthermore, some oil and gas companies continue to retain capitalized costs on their books even though exploration activity has ceased. A decline in the trend of income generated by a company's securities portfolio in comparison to its carrying value may indicate a failure to recognize declining market values.

Limitations on the Quality of Earnings Concept

The quality of earnings concept is a practical tool for the evaluation of earnings. In fact, it is often a necessary tool for the analyst who wants to compare one company's reported earnings with another's. Moreover, as a measure of the degree of uncertainty and risk inherent in a given earnings figure, earnings quality can be useful in securities evaluation procedures and in the rating of debt instruments.

On the other hand, the analysis of earnings quality does not represent the totality of income statement analysis, but rather a very important aspect of it. Thus the evaluation of unusual, erratic or extraordinary elements of gain or loss in earnings does not necessarily lie within the province of quality measurement. Similarly, period to period changes in effective tax rates do not necessarily affect earnings quality.

Adjusting a company's reported earnings figure is only one method of recognizing the increased risk implicit in earnings of relatively lower quality. Adjustments to a company's price-earnings ratio,[5] or to its discount rate in the security valuation formula, might be more appropriate for certain purposes. ■

Footnotes

1. T. O'glove and R. Olstein, *Quality of Earnings Report* (New Jersey: Reporting Research Company).
2. For example, see D. Hawkins, *Accounting Bulletins* (New York: Drexel Burnham) and L. Seidler, *Accounting Issues* (New York: Bear Stearns).
3. For additional references, see M. Backer, "Financial Reporting for Security Investment and Credit Decisions," *The CPA Journal,* November 1970, p. 885 and D. Hawkins, "Accounting Dodos and Red Flags," *Financial Executive,* May 1974, pp. 89-90.
4. For additional reference, see *Economic Reality* (New York: Touche Ross & Co., 1976), p. 10; Study Group on the Objectives of Financial Statements, *Objectives of Financial Statements* (New York: AICPA, 1973), p. 57; and W. Norby and F. Stone, "Objectives of Financial Accounting and Reporting from the Viewpoint of the Financial Analyst," *Financial Analysts Journal,* July/August 1972, p. 41.
5. See, for example, FASB Discussion Memorandum, *Criteria for Determining Materiality* (Stamford, CT: Financial Accounting Standards Board, March 21, 1975), p. 121.

by William Beaver and Dale Morse

What Determines Price-Earnings Ratios?

► Recent studies on the behavior of earnings growth over time raise doubt about the ability of past growth to explain differences in price-earnings ratios. Either future growth is difficult to predict, or investors are basing their predictions on information other than past growth.

Grouping common stocks into portfolios on the basis of price-earnings ratios, the authors find that the initial P/E differences among the portfolios persist up to 14 years. Growth appears to explain little of the persisting P/E differences, however. Price-earnings ratios correlate negatively with earnings growth in the year of the portfolio's formation, but positively with earnings growth in the subsequent year, suggesting that investors are forecasting only short-lived earnings distortions.

Nor does risk supply the explanation for these differences. Although price-earnings ratios can vary either positively or negatively with market risk, depending on the market conditions in a given year, market risk is of little assistance in explaining the observed persistence in price-earnings ratios over periods longer than two or three years.

The authors conclude that the most likely explanation of the evident persistence in price-earnings ratios is not growth or risk, but differences in accounting method. ►

T HE PRICE-EARNINGS ratio (hereafter P/E ratio) is of considerable interest, yet little is known about how it behaves over time or about the relative importance of the factors believed to influence its behavior. Differences in expected growth are commonly offered as a major explanation for differences in P/E ratios. Yet recent research raises doubt about this interpretation; past growth and analysts' forecasts appear to have little ability to explain subsequent growth.[1] Using a portfolio ap-

proach, we examine the behavior of P/E ratios and explore the ability of earnings growth (hereafter growth) and risk to explain P/E ratio differences across stocks. We find that, although differences in P/E ratios persist for up to 14 years, growth and risk appear to explain little of this persistency. In particular, growth appears to have virtually no effect beyond two years.[2]

Valuation Theory

Under perfect markets and certainty, the price of a security is equal to the present value of the future cash flows. Over an infinite horizon, the current price will reflect the stream of dividends. Under the further assumptions of (1) a constant dividend payout ratio (K), (2) constant growth in earnings per share (g) and (3) a constant riskless rate (r), P/E is given by the Gordon-Shapiro valuation equation:

$$P/E = \frac{K}{r - g} \qquad (1)$$

In a certainty world, earnings per share (E) can be defined as that constant cash flow whose present value is equivalent to the present value of the cash flows generated from current equity investment. Where the investment involves assets with finite lives, this definition implicitly reflects the fact that the value of the assets will depreciate over their lives.[3] We adopt this definition, which is often referred to as permanent earnings. Absent further investment, or if the earnings rate on future investment

---

1. Footnotes appear at end of article.

William Beaver is Thomas D. Dee, II Professor of Accounting at the Graduate School of Business, Stanford University. Dale Morse is a Ph.D. candidate at the Graduate School of Business, Stanford. Financial support for their research was provided by the Stanford Program in Professional Accounting, the major sponsors of which are Arthur Andersen & Co., Arthur Young & Co., Coopers & Lybrand, Ernst & Ernst, Peat, Marwick, Mitchell & Co. and Price Waterhouse.

is r, the P/E ratio is simply the reciprocal of the riskless rate (1/r). The P/E ratio will reflect a growth "premium" (or discount) only when the rate of return on future investment exceeds (or falls below) the riskless rate, r.[4]

When the world is no longer certain, it is no longer clear what the "earnings term" in Equation 1 is intended to represent. The earnings concept underlying market prices is future-oriented, hence is defined in terms of the expectations of market participants. As such, it is not directly observable, but presumably represents some form of *expected* permanent earnings per share attributable to the current equity investment.

A second consequence of uncertainty is that, along with E, the actual values of the variables r, g and K are also unknown. Each symbol in Equation 1 is often interpreted as the expected value of the corresponding variable. When Equation 1 is used to analyze the behavior of current prices, these variables are commonly interpreted as a "consensus" expectation across investors.[5] While there are problems in using Equation 1 in this manner, it may still be a reasonable approximation of a more complex valuation process.

A third consequence of uncertainty is that the expected return is no longer the riskless rate, but rather a risky rate. Since stocks will differ with respect to risk, the expected risky rate for stock i will be denoted r_i. In the one-period capital asset pricing model (CAPM), differences in the expected risky rate of return are due solely to differences in beta—the sensitivity of the stock to return on the general market r_m. In particular:

$$r_i = r_f + b_i(r_m - r_f), \qquad (2)$$

where r_i is the *expected* rate of return on security i, r_f the riskless rate, r_m the *expected* rate of return on the market portfolio and b_i security i's sensitivity to market risk, or beta.

Moreover, actual earnings per share (EPS) will vary from year to year because of transitory (i.e., temporary) factors peculiar to a particular year. Therefore, actual earnings may differ from the expected earnings upon which market prices are based. This leads to the distinction between the transitory versus the permanent component of EPS. This distinction will become crucial in interpreting our results.[6]

Research Design

A portfolio approach potentially diversifies out some of the "noise" at the individual stock level.[7] We selected stocks that satisfied the following criteria: (1) five consecutive years of data on the Compustat and CRSP tapes (the latter implies New York Stock Exchange membership) and (2) a fiscal year ending on December 31.

For each year from 1956 through 1974 we computed the P/E for each stock with data available in

TABLE 1: Median Values of Variables

Year	No. of Stocks	Median P/E	Median Percentage Growth in EPS	Median Beta*
1956	270	11.55	—	0.981
1957	279	10.08	−3.63	0.952
1958	284	17.61	−8.94	0.959
1959	295	15.75	20.73	0.954
1960	354	15.29	−4.83	0.964
1961	373	19.68	1.56	0.959
1962	398	14.98	8.39	1.007
1963	409	15.46	9.00	0.981
1964	435	14.45	19.42	0.960
1965	464	15.18	18.19	0.952
1966	493	11.60	13.01	0.975
1967	514	16.91	−0.69	0.967
1968	548	19.43	7.52	0.991
1969	581	14.04	5.31	0.998
1970	600	15.58	−10.16	0.939
1971	600	17.06	9.92	—
1972	600	14.07	20.46	—
1973	600	7.45	23.10	—
1974	600	5.01	12.37	—
1975	600	8.04	−1.21	—

*A stock's beta for 1956 is computed over the 60-month period following December 1956 (January 1957 through December 1961), according to the method described in Footnote 8.

that year. We defined P/E as price per share on December 31 divided by earnings per share for the year, computed on a pre-extraordinary item basis. Using data from the Compustat tape, we defined earnings growth as the percentage change in the year's earnings per share relative to the previous year and measured risk as the stock's beta, computed from monthly stock price return data available on the CRSP tape.[8]

We then ranked each year's stocks according to P/E and formed 25 portfolios, with Portfolio One comprising those four per cent with the highest P/E's and Portfolio 25 comprising the stocks with the lowest P/E's. We then compared the median P/E for each portfolio in its base year (year of formation) with the median P/E, median realized growth and median risk for the portfolio in subsequent years.[9] Note that, in all cases, once formed the portfolio's composition was fixed (i.e., a buy and hold strategy was used).[10]

Table 1 reports some summary statistics.[11] Once a stock appears on the tape in a given year, its data are available from that year onward. The similarity of stocks appearing later relative to those appearing earlier is supported by the median beta, which shows no trend over time and is close to one. When we correlated the median P/E for each year with the aggregate P/E ratio for Standard & Poor's Composite stocks for the years 1956 through 1975, we obtained a positive rank correlation of 0.85, which is reasonable, given the differences in the stocks and the methods used to compute the average P/E for a given year. Furthermore, the rank correlation between the median annual growth rates reported in Table 1 and the growth in aggregate EPS for S&P Industrials yielded a positive correlation of 0.89.[12]

How Do P/E Ratios Behave Over Time?

Table 2 reports the rank correlation between P/E ratios in the year of formation and P/E ratios in subsequent years.[13] The first row of Table 2 displays the correlations between the P/E ratios of portfolios formed in 1956 and the P/E ratios of the same portfolios in subsequent years. The second row displays results for portfolios formed in 1957 and the final row the correlation between the P/E ratios of the portfolios formed in 1974 and the P/E ratios of those same portfolios in 1975. For example, for the portfolios formed at the end of 1956, the correlation between portfolio P/E ratios in 1956 (the year of formation) and 1957 (one year later) is 0.96. The rank correlation between the P/E ratios in 1956 and 1966 (10 years later) is 0.74.

The median correlation of each column is reported at the bottom of the table. The median correlations are not strictly comparable for several reasons. First, the group of calendar years over which the median is computed gradually changes as one moves across the columns: One year after formation includes calendar years 1957 through 1975, while 14 years after formation includes only calendar years 1970 through 1975. Then, too, the median P/E ratio varies considerably by calendar years, as Table 1 indicates, dropping sharply in 1973, 1974 and 1975. Table 1 also shows that the average number of stocks per portfolio differs; in 1956 the number of

TABLE 2: Rank Correlations of Portfolios Formed By P/E Ratios With P/E Ratios in Subsequent Years

Base Year	1	2	3	4	5	6	7	8	9	10	11	12	13	14
1956	0.96	0.87	0.88	0.65	0.78	0.70	0.82	0.85	0.69	0.74	0.62	0.36	0.41	0.59
1957	0.85	0.91	0.83	0.84	0.89	0.89	0.90	0.81	0.86	0.72	0.51	0.67	0.78	0.44
1958	0.95	0.73	0.64	0.52	0.43	0.55	0.49	0.30	0.60	0.22	0.24	0.49	0.41	0.18
1959	0.96	0.91	0.91	0.73	0.57	0.88	0.74	0.69	0.33	0.46	0.69	0.56	0.40	0.56
1960	0.94	0.94	0.93	0.89	0.88	0.79	0.70	0.63	0.80	0.73	0.61	0.61	0.50	0.24
1961	0.98	0.96	0.86	0.89	0.85	0.76	0.74	0.87	0.83	0.87	0.76	0.72	0.55	0.64
1962	0.92	0.89	0.93	0.94	0.87	0.69	0.86	0.73	0.78	0.76	0.87	0.78	0.77	
1963	0.99	0.98	0.95	0.89	0.71	0.77	0.75	0.61	0.79	0.93	0.77	0.76		
1964	0.95	0.96	0.94	0.72	0.88	0.89	0.72	0.88	0.90	0.81	0.82			
1965	0.99	0.93	0.83	0.83	0.77	0.86	0.93	0.91	0.80	0.71				
1966	0.96	0.89	0.95	0.96	0.84	0.95	0.89	0.80	0.79					
1967	0.98	0.98	0.94	0.89	0.85	0.58	0.57	0.69						
1968	0.98	0.95	0.88	0.84	0.63	0.53	0.35							
1969	0.89	0.92	0.95	0.74	0.80	0.82								
1970	0.95	0.79	0.63	0.72	0.73									
1971	0.96	0.80	0.70	0.67										
1972	0.96	0.96	0.96											
1973	0.99	0.97												
1974	0.97													
Median Correlation	0.96	0.92	0.91	0.83	0.80	0.78	0.74	0.76	0.79	0.73	0.69	0.64	0.50	0.44

stocks is 10, while the base years 1970 through 1974 average 24 per portfolio. On purely statistical grounds, the correlation coefficient should rise as the number of stocks per portfolio increases. However, Table 2 does not display any obvious tendency for the correlations to increase systematically in the later base years.[14]

With these caveats in mind, we interpret the correlations in Table 2 as supporting a long-term persistency in the portfolios' P/E ratios. With only two minor disruptions, the median correlation declines steadily with the number of years since portfolio formation. Five years after formation the median correlation is 0.80, while 10 years after formation the median correlation is 0.73. Fourteen years after formation, the median is 0.44. We tentatively conclude that, although much of the effect of the factors that determine P/E ratios dissipates over the 14 years, a portion still clearly remains after five, 10 or perhaps even 14 years.

This conclusion is supported by Table 3, which displays a composite picture of six of the 25 portfolios.[15] We averaged the P/E ratios across the base years, weighting each year by the number of stocks in that year.[16] The striking feature of Table 3 is the shrinkage over time in the P/E differences among the portfolios. Not surprisingly, this tendency is most evident in the extreme portfolios (i.e., Portfolios One and 25). The P/E of Portfolio One is less than half its value one year after formation, and less than one-third its value two years after formation. Portfolio 25 shows a similar reversion toward a central value, as do other portfolios, for which the pattern is, however, less pronounced.

As a convenient summary, Table 3 reports the ratio of the P/E values for Portfolio One relative to those for Portfolio 25. In the year of formation, Portfolio One's P/E is over eight times that of Portfolio 25's, while in the next year it has shrunk to slightly over three times and by three years after formation it is less than twice Portfolio 25's P/E. Apart from this dramatic convergence of the P/E ratios, their most striking feature is the stability of the relative difference from the third year through the eleventh year after formation. After the eleventh year, further convergence occurs until, in the fourteenth year, Portfolio 25 has a P/E greater than that of Portfolio One's.

We take this to mean that the effect of the factors determining P/E ratios in the year of formation dissipates dramatically by the third year after formation. On the other hand, the fact that the convergence of P/E ratios is by no means complete implies that certain factors are still causing differences in P/E ratios through at least the eleventh year after formation.

The pattern of reversion toward a central value is a common phenomenon among economic variables. Research on the behavior of beta indicates a similar pattern. Two factors explain such behavior: (1) The variable being ranked normally contains a transitory component; in our context, this means that earnings in a given year result in part from factors peculiar to that year whose effects will either not persist beyond that year or will dissipate in subsequent years. (2) The underlying, permanent value is reverting toward the average. Such a reversion in the ratio of price to expected earnings per share could be caused by a change in expected earnings growth or by a change in risk.

Examining the time series behavior of the P/E ratio provides some insight into the nature of the factors that influence it. Apparently, some of these factors dissipate substantially within the first three years after formation. On the other hand, some continue effective through at least the eleventh year after formation. We will consider three potential factors—growth, risk and accounting method.

Does Growth Explain Differences in P/E Ratios?

Table 4 displays correlations between median P/E ratios in the year of formation and median earnings growth in the year of and in the years subsequent to formation.[17] Column zero indicates the correlation between the P/E ratio and growth in the year of formation. The correlation of earnings growth in 1957 with the P/E ratio computed at the end of 1957 is

TABLE 3: Price-Earnings Ratios

Portfolio	Years After Formation														
	0	1	2	3	4	5	6	7	8	9	10	11	12	13	14
1	50.0	22.7	16.4	13.8	12.3	13.2	13.5	13.2	17.2	14.9	13.0	13.2	10.5	9.3	8.3
5	20.8	17.5	16.9	15.9	15.9	13.7	13.0	12.8	12.5	11.8	11.9	10.9	10.1	10.2	8.4
10	14.3	11.9	11.5	11.1	10.3	10.1	9.4	9.0	10.0	10.0	9.9	11.0	10.6	9.5	8.3
15	11.1	10.8	10.4	10.8	10.0	10.0	9.4	9.7	9.3	9.5	8.6	9.2	8.3	8.6	7.1
20	8.9	9.1	9.6	9.3	9.4	9.3	9.3	9.0	8.8	8.8	9.0	8.2	7.6	7.0	7.7
25	5.8	6.9	8.0	7.8	7.9	7.9	8.2	8.8	8.3	8.5	7.8	7.5	7.5	7.5	8.9
Port. 1 / Port. 25	8.6	3.3	2.1	1.8	1.6	1.7	1.6	1.5	2.1	1.8	1.7	1.8	1.4	1.2	0.9

negative 0.28. The median correlation over the 19 years from 1957 through 1975 is also negative 0.28, and 16 of the 19 correlations are negative.

The negative correlation implies that stocks with relatively low earnings growth during the year tend to have relatively high P/E ratios. This is consistent with the contention that market participants perceive that earnings contain transitory components and price stocks accordingly.[18] Since we formed portfolios on the basis of the ratio of price to *realized* earnings, we expect that the ranking will systematically group together stocks with transitory earnings of the same sign. In other words, the portfolio with the highest P/E ratio will tend to include firms with negative transitory components (i.e., realized earnings below expected earnings) and conversely for the portfolio with the lowest P/E ratio.

Table 4 displays a strong correlation between P/E and earnings growth in the year subsequent to portfolio formation. The median correlation for base years 1957 through 1975 is 0.53, and all 19 correlations are positive. Market participants' perceptions of the transitory nature of earnings were confirmed by actual earnings behavior. While, in the year of formation, current earnings were abnormally low relative to expected permanent earnings, in the subsequent year earnings tended to "catch up" to investors' expectations about permanent earnings.[19]

In the second year after formation, the median correlation is 0.25 and, from there on, growth is essentially uncorrelated with P/E in the year of formation. The rapid dissipation in subsequent growth

rates is similar to the pattern for P/E ratios observed in Table 2. In general, the pattern behaves as if market participants, in determining prices, cannot forecast differential growth beyond two years.[20]

One may ask what this tells us about the ability of market participants to isolate and detect transitory elements in current earnings versus their ability to forecast unusual earnings situations with respect to additional investment. Although the distinction may seem arbitrary, the implications can differ substantially. The first process concerns unusual factors due to events of this year that will not persist (e.g., an abnormally high rate of inflation or abnormally high interest rates), while the second asks questions related to future unusual earnings opportunities.[21]

As far as we can tell, the data provide no basis for assessing how much of the observed growth differential is due to each factor (although the introduction of other evidence may permit such a basis).[22] As a result, we cannot preclude the possibility that the results may be entirely due to the detection of transitory components that take more than one year to disappear from reported earnings. It is not our intention to be unduly pessimistic, but rather to caution against interpreting the figures as solely the result of market participants' ability to forecast unusual earnings opportunities on future investments.

Magnitude of Differential Growth

Table 4's correlation matrix does not provide information on the magnitude of differential earnings growth. Table 5 displays this information for the

TABLE 4: Rank Correlations of Portfolios Formed By P/E Ratios With Earnings Growth in Subsequent Years

Base Year	0	1	2	3	4	5	6	7	8	9	10	11	12	13	14	15
1956		0.12	0.13	−0.30	0.48	0.00	−0.12	−0.62	−0.17	−0.19	−0.32	−0.08	−0.31	0.07	0.05	−0.48
1957	−0.28	0.53	−0.23	0.51	−0.07	0.02	−0.73	−0.26	0.26	−0.23	−0.01	−0.14	0.22	0.21	−0.33	−0.03
1958	−0.28	0.52	0.32	0.03	0.18	−0.15	0.19	0.29	0.11	−0.54	0.16	0.32	−0.20	−0.40	0.39	0.23
1959	−0.37	0.62	0.40	−0.12	−0.16	0.27	0.15	0.30	0.04	−0.22	0.32	0.04	−0.48	0.17	0.21	0.36
1960	−0.10	0.49	−0.15	−0.04	−0.04	0.04	−0.01	0.26	0.29	0.26	0.06	−0.13	0.09	−0.05	−0.45	0.10
1961	−0.45	0.53	0.13	0.07	−0.05	−0.03	0.27	−0.11	0.22	0.40	0.08	0.36	−0.16	−0.51	0.27	
1962	−0.35	0.17	0.12	0.05	−0.26	−0.40	0.20	−0.39	0.49	−0.17	−0.19	−0.44	−0.46	0.31		
1963	−0.42	0.26	0.24	0.13	0.35	0.08	0.13	0.56	−0.03	−0.27	−0.12	−0.47	0.28			
1964	−0.43	0.11	−0.14	0.68	0.08	0.44	0.71	0.06	−0.21	−0.30	−0.31	0.04				
1965	0.12	0.47	0.55	0.04	0.22	0.61	−0.16	−0.14	−0.15	−0.26	0.26					
1966	−0.02	0.77	0.02	0.30	0.66	−0.35	−0.14	−0.38	−0.16	0.35						
1967	0.18	0.74	0.41	0.12	0.05	0.39	0.01	−0.31	−0.07							
1968	−0.02	0.77	0.74	0.54	0.42	−0.14	0.15	0.32								
1969	0.15	0.75	0.48	0.05	−0.17	−0.42	0.58									
1970	−0.19	0.90	0.58	−0.09	−0.63	0.34										
1971	−0.22	0.71	0.27	−0.02	0.32											
1972	−0.18	0.45	−0.09	0.39												
1973	−0.31	0.52	0.51													
1974	−0.66	0.89														
1975	−0.66															
Median Correlation	−0.28	0.53	0.25	0.05	0.06	0.02	0.14	−0.11	0.01	−0.22	0.02	−0.08	−0.18	0.07	0.24	0.10

same six composite portfolios reported in Table 3, using the same composite process. The results support the contentions made earlier. Portfolio One (the highest P/E portfolio) experienced a median *drop* in earnings of 4.1 per cent, while Portfolio 25 experienced a median earnings *increase* of 26.4 per cent. In simplest terms, the prices of the stocks in Portfolio One did not change proportionately with their earnings; as a result, their P/E ratios were relatively high. Similarly, the stocks in Portfolio 25 experienced a price change that, on average, was less than 26 per cent, and their P/E ratios were relatively low. Again, this implies a price formation process whereby participants view changes in earnings as containing a transitory element.

In Table 5, Portfolio One shows a median earnings growth of 95.3 per cent in the first year after formation, while Portfolio 25 shows a drop in earnings of 3.3 per cent. This is consistent with the results reported in Table 4: The perceptions of market participants regarding the transitory element in earnings were confirmed by subsequent earnings behavior.

The results in Table 5 differ from those in Table 4 in one major respect—the highest P/E portfolio maintains its distinctive earnings growth behavior for seven years after formation. This is neither contradictory nor surprising. Whereas correlations in Table 4 reflect the strength of the relationship for all 25 portfolios, where growth and P/E are essentially unrelated after two years, the comparison described above involves only one of those portfolios. For that one "extreme" portfolio we would expect non-normal growth to be larger and to last longer.

The results in Table 5 can be deceptive in at least two respects. First, they reflect the average effect across a number of base years and do not reveal variation from one base year to another. A more detailed examination, not reported here, revealed considerable variation across base years. Second, while it is intuitively appealing to focus solely on the high P/E portfolio, it constitutes only four per cent of the observations. It is important to remember that, with the remaining portfolios included, there is little or no apparent relation beyond the second year.

Comparing the P/E analysis with the growth analysis, we conclude that some of the initial dissipation of the P/E ratio in the first three years after formation can be explained by differential growth in earnings. Beyond that, however, there clearly exists a P/E differential that cannot be explained by differential earnings growth.

Before leaving growth analysis, we'd like to comment on one aspect of the data. In contrast to P/E ratios, which exhibit a high degree of correlation over time, previous evidence indicates that earnings growth rates possess near-zero correlation over time. To ensure that the same behavior held for the stocks in our sample, we constructed a portfolio strategy based on earnings growth in the year of formation and then observed subsequent growth. Our results confirmed previous findings of near-zero correlation of earnings growth rates. While a mechanical process relying on past growth rates is largely unsuccessful in predicting future differential growth, the P/E ratio is successful because price reflects a process whereby market participants rely on more information than past earnings in distinguishing the transitory and permanent components of earnings.

Risk Analysis

The expected sign of the correlation between P/E and beta may be either positive or negative. The argument is developed in greater detail in the appendix, but it essentially proceeds as follows: Stocks' earnings move together because of economy-wide factors. In years of transitorily low earnings, the market-wide P/E will tend to be high, but stocks with high betas will tend to have even higher P/E ratios because their earnings are most sensitive to economy-wide events. Conversely, in years of transitorily high earnings, high beta stocks will have even lower P/E ratios than most. Therefore we expect a positive correlation in "high" P/E years and a negative correlation in "low" years.

Table 6 reports the rank correlations between P/E and beta. We compared beta for a given base year over the 60 months subsequent to formation; thus the beta for 1956 was computed over the years 1957

TABLE 5: Earnings Growth

Portfolio	Years After Formation														
	0	1	2	3	4	5	6	7	8	9	10	11	12	13	14
1	−4.1	95.3	37.2	28.2	16.4	18.9	18.1	19.7	13.1	14.8	15.3	10.8	10.9	10.2	11.8
5	10.7	14.9	12.1	13.1	14.2	10.9	10.4	11.8	10.5	11.6	8.0	11.9	8.3	13.3	18.1
10	9.6	12.9	11.5	12.3	12.6	9.2	10.1	10.8	12.8	8.3	12.9	22.2	16.6	20.6	29.6
15	10.0	8.8	8.5	8.1	8.2	14.3	11.6	5.4	13.3	10.3	11.0	10.8	11.9	12.8	33.4
20	10.8	5.2	9.3	12.6	12.4	6.0	8.4	13.0	10.2	11.3	11.1	25.0	12.9	17.7	18.0
25	26.4	−3.3	7.5	10.8	8.3	12.9	17.1	13.6	18.0	12.8	16.7	14.2	10.9	12.4	10.1
Port. 1 / Port. 25	−0.155	*	5.0	2.61	1.98	1.47	1.06	1.45	0.73	1.16	0.92	0.76	1.00	0.82	1.17

*Not meaningful because of negative growth in denominator.

TABLE 6: Rank Correlations of Portfolio Median P/E Ratios and Median Beta

Year	Rank Correlation	Rank of Median P/E[a]	Predicted Sign of Correlation
1956	−0.34	14	−
1957	−0.23	15	−
1958	0.22	3	+
1959	0.41	5	+
1960	0.50	8	+
1961	0.55	1	+
1962	−0.48	10	−
1963	−0.42	7	+[b]
1964	−0.63	11	−
1965	−0.26	9	−
1966	−0.44	13	−
1967	0.50	4	+
1968	0.53	2	+
1969	0.58	12	−[b]
1970	0.28	6	+
Median Adjusted for Predicted Sign	0.41		

[a] Computed from Table 1.

[b] 1963 and 1969 are the two years incorrectly predicted.

through 1961.

To predict the sign of the correlation in a given base year, we ranked the market-wide P/E ratios (as reported in Table 1) from high to low.[23] We hypothesized that the years with the eight highest values of market-wide P/E ratios would have a positive correlation between P/E and beta, while the years with the seven lowest values of market-wide P/E would have a negative correlation. Over the 15 base years 1956 through 1970, the actual correlations are positive eight times and negative seven times. We correctly predicted the sign of the correlation for 13 of the 15 years. This is impressive, given the crudeness of the test. (The test's limitations are discussed in the appendix.)

Table 7 reports the magnitude of the betas for the six portfolios presented in Tables 3 and 5. Because the relation between P/E and beta can be either positive or negative, we averaged results over two sets of years—those in which the correlation was positive

Table 7: Relation of P/E and Beta

Portfolio	Average Beta in All Years	Average Beta in Years of Positive Correlation	Average Beta in Years of Negative Correlation
1	1.22	1.28	1.13
5	1.01	1.03	0.98
10	1.05	1.09	1.00
15	0.96	0.94	1.00
20	1.03	0.96	1.11
25	1.04	0.95	1.14

and those in which the correlation was negative. The third column reports the beta differences for the years of positive correlation. The differences are small for Portfolios Five through 25, where beta ranges from 1.09 to 0.94. The largest difference occurs in the highest P/E portfolio, with its beta of 1.28. In the fourth column, negative correlation is evident for Portfolios Five through 25, with a pronounced aberrant behavior for Portfolio One. For this set of stocks, a "U-shaped" relationship is present. Given the consistently high betas of the highest P/E portfolio, it is imperative that some form of risk-adjusted performance standard be introduced to avoid spuriously inferring superior stock price performance.

While beta clearly holds some explanatory power, the crucial issue is, to what extent does it explain the P/E ratio behavior reported in Tables 2 and 3? We think it explains little: If beta were an important explanatory variable, then the predicted behavior of P/E over time would be much different from what Tables 2 and 3 report. Stocks in Portfolio One during years of high market-wide P/E would tend to move to Portfolio 25 (or its neighbors) in years of low market-wide P/E. Looking across a row of Table 2, we would expect to see a pattern of positive and negative correlations similar to that reported in the last column of Table 6. Instead, we observe a strong positive serial correlation throughout.[24] Furthermore, the relative differences in betas are not of the same magnitude as the relative differences in P/E ratios. Before considering another source of P/E differences, however, we report the results of a regression analysis that combines both growth and risk analysis.

Regression Analysis

Table 8 displays the results of a simple linear regression that included beta and earnings growth as independent variables. We used the E/P, rather than P/E, ratio because the Litzenberger and Rao model posits linearity in E/P (not in P/E).[25] The expected sign of the E/P and beta relationship is thus the reverse of that shown in the final column of Table 6. The actual regression coefficients have the predicted sign in 13 of the 15 years; again, 1963 and 1969 are exceptions.

The predicted signs of the growth coefficients are also negative, since we're using E/P as the dependent variable. For growth in the year subsequent to portfolio formation (g_1), all 15 coefficients have the predicted sign. Growth two years subsequent to formation (g_2) has the predicted sign in 12 years. By the third year (g_3), however, the signs of the coefficients are evenly divided. Table 4 suggests there is little merit to introducing additional growth variables.

TABLE 8: E/P Regression Results

Base Year	Constant	Beta	g_1	g_2	g_3	Adjusted R^2	F Statistic
		Regression Coefficients (t-Statistic)					
1956	0.070	0.030 (0.71)	−0.046 (−1.38)	−0.035 (−0.73)	0.053 (0.93)	0.185	2.36
1957	0.348	0.086* (1.74)	−0.142* (−4.13)	−0.066 (−1.57)	−0.123* (−2.29)	0.581	9.30*
1958	0.136	0.000 (0)	−0.019* (−2.57)	−0.070 (−1.69)	0.013 (0.26)	0.270	3.96
1959	0.076	−0.053* (−1.76)	−0.157* (−4.45)	0.098 (1.29)	0.086 (1.62)	0.505	7.13*
1960	0.155	−0.075* (−2.83)	−0.161* (−3.55)	0.046 (0.71)	0.092 (1.17)	0.502	7.06*
1961	0.077	−0.054* (−1.89)	−0.063 (−1.25)	0.064 (0.93)	0.023 (0.57)	0.289	3.44*
1962	0.119	0.116* (4.68)	−0.055* (−2.10)	−0.026 (−0.50)	−0.064 (−1.02)	0.524	7.61*
1963	0.239	0.097* (3.10)	−0.106* (−1.93)	−0.089* (−1.84)	−0.034 (−0.62)	0.370	4.52*
1964	0.260	0.076* (2.36)	−0.085 (−1.26)	−0.045 (−0.67)	−0.114* (−2.24)	0.572	9.03*
1965	0.300	0.071* (2.00)	−0.167* (−2.54)	−0.091* (−1.73)	−0.022 (−0.32)	0.475	6.44*
1966	0.501	0.112* (3.53)	−0.304* (−7.06)	−0.068 (−0.96)	−0.138* (−1.80)	0.783	22.63*
1967	0.447	−0.065* (−2.15)	−0.164* (−2.87)	−0.106 (−1.67)	−0.034 (−0.94)	0.575	9.10*
1968	0.285	−0.031 (−1.71)	−0.033 (−1.71)	−0.108* (−5.23)	−0.060 (−1.62)	0.738	17.91*
1969	0.380	−0.054 (−1.40)	−0.159* (−4.64)	−0.134* (−2.09)	0.030 (0.57)	0.658	12.56*
1970	0.185	−0.029 (−0.71)	−0.003 (−0.28)	−0.167* (−2.58)	0.089 (1.42)	0.391	4.86*

* Significant at five per cent level (one-tail test on regression coefficients).

The R^2 (proportion of variance explained) adjusted for degrees of freedom ranges from 18.5 per cent to 78.3 per cent, with a median of 50.5 per cent. The F-statistic, which tests the null hypothesis that all of the coefficients are zero, is significant at the five per cent level in 13 of the 15 years.[26]

While risk and growth on the average explain approximately 50 per cent of the variance of the E/P ratio, they obviously leave an equal proportion unexplained. Thus the regression results presented in Table 8 provide only the crude beginnings of an attempt to explain cross-sectional P/E differences. We suggest further research in a number of areas: (1) Even if the realized values of beta and growth are unbiased estimates of expectations, they may still measure those expectations with error; better specification could lead to higher R^2, which is under-stated when measurement error is present. (2) Better specification of the denominator of the P/E ratio might yield better results.[27] (3) Accounting rules could be creating P/E differences; our final comments are devoted to this area.

Accounting Method

The finding that P/E ratio differences persist well beyond three years after portfolio formation suggests the influence of some factor other than risk or growth. Accounting effects are obvious candidates. Accounting method effects are of two types—use of different rules (e.g., depreciation methods) by different firms for essentially the same or similar circumstances and errors introduced by applying a uniform accounting rule (e.g., historical cost) to differing economic circumstances (e.g., current value of assets).

The P/E ratio will be influenced by the effect on earnings of differing accounting methods. Assuming prices are not dependent on the accounting method used in annual reports, firms that use conservative accounting methods (e.g., accelerated depreciation or LIFO inventory valuation) would tend to have higher P/E ratios than firms that use less conservative methods, holding constant the effects of risk and growth.[28] For example, Beaver and Dukes found the P/E ratios of a portfolio of firms using accelerated depreciation were greater than the P/E ratios of a portfolio of firms using straight-line depreciation.[29] The two portfolios were essentially the same with respect to risk (beta) and growth. Moreover, when the earnings of the straight-line portfolio were converted according to the accelerated method, the P/E ratios were essentially the same for both portfolios. In other words, the P/E differences in the two portfolios disappeared when earnings were computed on a uniform depreciation method. We suggest an extension of this type of analysis to other accounting methods as an obvious candidate for future research.[30] ∎

APPENDIX

If the EPS used to compute P/E ratios contained no transitory elements, we would expect a positive relation between E/P and beta and a negative relation between P/E and beta. However, the evidence suggests that transitory elements in EPS are present. How does this affect the analysis of risk?

Previous empirical research indicates that a stock's E/P ratio can be characterized by the following (linear) process:

$$E/P_t = \hat{a} + \hat{b} M_t + u_t ,\qquad (a)$$

where E/P_t = earnings-price ratio for a stock in year t,

M_t = a market-wide E/P ratio for year t,

u_t = a non-market residual for a stock in year t and

$\left.\begin{array}{r}\hat{a}\\[1ex]\hat{b}\end{array}\right\}$ = the intercept and slope of the linear relationship.

Moreover, this research has shown that, at the portfolio level, $\hat{b}$ (the earnings-price "beta") is highly correlated with beta.

In a given year where the actual, realized earnings may differ from the expected earnings, what relation can we expect between E/P and beta? Rearranging

(a) we have:

$$(E/P_t - \overline{E}/P) = \hat{b}(M_t - \overline{M}) + u_t ,\qquad (b)$$

where $\overline{E}/P$ = expected value of E/P_t and
$\overline{M}$ = expected value of M_t

Ignoring u_t and taking $\hat{b}$ equal to b, we have:

$$(E/P_t - \overline{E}/P) = b(M_t - \overline{M})\qquad (c)$$

When the realized M_t is above its expected value, stocks with higher betas will have higher E/P's (expressed as a deviation from the expected value). However, when the realized M_t is below its expected value, stocks with higher betas will have lower E/P's (expressed in terms of a deviation from its mean).

Limitations of the Empirical Test

One obvious limitation is the failure to express P/E (or E/P) as a deviation from its expected value, as indicated by Equation (c). This test implicitly assumes that inter-stock P/E differences are zero. This is obviously not the case, as Tables 2 and 3 indicate. However, we did not take this latter step since our concern throughout has been with the risk differences of a simple, P/E-oriented portfolio strategy, not a strategy that expresses P/E as a deviation from its expected value. A second limitation is the assumption that 15 years taken as a whole contain approximately an equal number of realizations above and below the expected value, which in turn is assumed to be a constant over 15 years.

In the absence of any other evidence, this assumption seems as reasonable as any other. However, the assumption of a constant expected value cannot be strictly true. Factors such as changing interest rates would lead us to expect that market-wide P/E ratios change over time. Third, the test ignores the influence of u_t (the unsystematic component) as expressed in Equation (b).

Further Analysis of Table 7

Evidence in our article supports the contention that transitory elements in earnings exist. We would expect high P/E stocks to have greater earnings variability to the extent that transitory elements account for P/E differences. Research by Beaver and Manegold, among others, confirms that stocks with greater earnings variability have higher betas. However, the argument is not complete: If earnings volatility were exclusively systematic, we would have observed no U-shaped behavior in the years with negative correlation. If unsystematic earnings volatility (the variance of u_t from Equation (a)) is positively correlated with beta, and if high P/E stocks have greater unsystematic volatility, the result would be a consistently higher beta for the highest P/E portfolio. However, a similar argument could be offered for the lowest P/E portfolio. Yet consistently higher betas are not observed here. We offer no explanation for this result.

Footnotes

1. See I. Little, "Higgledy Piggledy Growth" (Institute of Statistics, Oxford, November 1962), the seminal work. See also R. Ball and R. Watts, "Some Time Series Properties of Accounting Earnings Numbers," *Journal of Finance* (June 1972), pp. 663-682; J. Cragg and B. Malkiel, "The Consensus and Accuracy of Some Predictions of the Growth of Corporate Earnings," *Journal of Finance* (March 1968), pp. 67-84; I. Little and Raynor, *Higgledy Piggledy Growth Again* (Oxford: Basil Blackwell, 1966); and J. Murphy, "Relative Growth in Earnings Per Share—Past and Future," *Financial Analysts Journal* (November/December 1966), pp. 73-76. Excellent summaries appear in R. Brealey, *An Introduction to Risk and Return from Common Stocks* (Cambridge: MIT Press, 1969) and in J. Lorie and M. Hamilton, *The Stock Market: Theories and Evidence* (Homewood, Illinois: Irwin, 1973).

2. Previous studies have attempted to use the P/E ratio itself as a growth predictor—with little success. Two examples are Cragg and Malkiel, "Consensus and Accuracy" and J. Murphy and H. Stevenson, "Price/Earnings Ratios and Future Growth of Earnings and Dividends," *Financial Analysts Journal* (November/December 1967), pp. 111-114. The portfolio strategy adopted in our study provides an opportunity to uncover relations that may have been undetected by previous research.

3. Let CF_t equal the cash flow generated t periods from now from current equity investment. Assuming r is constant:

$$\frac{E}{r} \equiv \sum_{t=1}^{\infty} CF_t (1 + r)^{-t} = \text{Present Value of Current Equity Investment,}$$

$$E \equiv r \left[\sum_{t=1}^{\infty} CF_t (1 + r)^{-t} \right] = \text{Permanent Earnings}$$

4 It appears to us that a basic inconsistency may exist when perfect markets are invoked to motivate present value formulas and yet abnormal returns in productive opportunities are posited to explain growth premiums or discounts in P/E ratios. However, this is a puzzle we are not prepared to resolve. Stocks may still be priced "as if" a discounted cash flow model were applied even in the presence of abnormal returns in the productive sector (i.e., the product and factor markets).

5. Consensus expectations in general depend on the wealth, risk preferences and beliefs of market participants. ("Market participants" is a generic term intended to include individuals whose expectations directly or indirectly influence market prices—i.e., analysts as well as investors.) In a one-period setting, expressing price as a function of expected values is an arbitrary, although innocuous, way to view valuation. In a multi-period setting, however, such a valuation scheme will not necessarily hold.

6. Previous attempts by researchers to remove transitory elements from earnings vary from subjective adjustments of the components of earnings to statistical data fitting via Box-Jenkins techniques. For an example of the latter, see P. Griffin, "The Time Series Behavior of Quarterly Earnings," *Journal of Accounting Research* (Spring 1977), 71-83.

   We would like to be able to say a portfolio approach will permit us to diversify out the transitory earnings components. Clearly we cannot make such a statement. To the contrary, since the portfolios will be formed on the basis of the ratio of price to *realized* earnings, we expect the ranking will systematically group together stocks with transitory earnings of the same sign. In other words, the portfolio with the highest P/E ratios will tend to include firms where the transitory component is negative (i.e., realized earnings are below expected earnings) and conversely for the portfolio with the lowest P/E ratios. Our evidence will support these contentions, and it is a major point to keep in mind in interpreting the results.

7. For a more detailed discussion of the effects of aggregation into portfolios see W. Beaver and J. Manegold, "The Association Between Market-Determined and Accounting-Determined Risk Measures," *Journal of Financial and Quantitative Analysis* (June 1975), pp. 231-284. In this context, "noise" refers to the fact that our growth and risk measures may differ from the growth and risk expected at the time of portfolio formation.

8. Beta was estimated as the slope of a linear regression of the form:

$$R_{it} = a_i + b_i R_{mt} + e_{it} \quad , \quad t = 1,60$$

where R_{it} equals monthly percentage change in price (adjusted for dividends) for security i in month t and R_{mt} equals monthly percentage change in a market index of price changes (adjusted for dividends) of all NYSE firms (provided as part of CRSP tape).

9. The median was used because it was a nonparametric measure that would place less demands on the data. Various weighting schemes (e.g., weighting by market value) were also applied with essentially the same results as reported here. Since it is unclear how to define growth off of negative earnings, the portfolios were formed only over those stocks with positive earnings in the base year. However, the sign of earnings was unrestricted in the years subsequent to formation. Hence earnings could be negative in later years.

10. The Compustat tape contains those firms that have survived mergers and bankruptcy. We would expect that this could induce a potential bias in the levels of the variables to be studied. However, the study focuses on differences in these variables across portfolios of stocks. It is not obvious to what extent survivorship imparts a bias for this purpose. This would require knowledge of how non-surviving firms sys-

tematically differ from surviving ones. In any event, because of the survivorship criteria, the portfolio strategies described here could not have been literally followed by an investor.

11. The number of stocks increases over time because of availability on the Compustat tape. In virtually all instances, the firms with incomplete histories on Compustat existed throughout the 1956-75 period but were picked up at some later date by Compustat. In other words, the firms being added do not tend to be new firms.

12. These aggregate statistics were obtained from S&P's *Trade and Securities Statistics, 1976*.

13. It is important to realize that a correlation matrix like that of Table 2 invariably leaves out certain information. For example, does a correlation coefficient of one mean the P/E difference between portfolios remains approximately the same as it was in the year of formation? Not necessarily. We can draw no inference about the magnitude of portfolio differences; the rank correlation coefficient merely indicates a similarity in the rankings of the portfolios. A coefficient of one indicates that the rankings of two portfolios remain the same, but it does not tell us anything about the spread between the portfolios. The spread between the portfolios may have shrunk or grown. However, we do know that, even if the spread has changed, at least the relative positions remained unaltered.

14. Since the P/E ratios are highly correlated, we cannot view elements in one cell as unrelated to the other cells; the results in two adjacent rows should be highly related. In other words, the results for the base year 1957 are, not surprisingly, similar to the results for the base year 1956. Because the results are not perfectly correlated, however, some additional information is conveyed by repeating the portfolio strategy for different base years.

15. Table 3 is subject to the same caveats as Table 2. For example, the years 1971 through 1975 play a relatively more important role in the later years after formation, so the P/E ratios exhibit a downward drift. The real focal point of the table is the difference in P/E ratios across portfolios, rather than the common movement by all portfolios. Moreover, the results of a more extensive examination of the data, which held constant the calendar year composition of each year, did not differ from the findings shown in Table 3. We chose Table 3's composite because it was the most comprehensive and the simplest method of presentation.

16. For example, for Year 0 (the year of formation), the average P/E ratio for Portfolio One was computed by taking a weighted average of each of the median P/E ratios for Portfolio One for the years 1956-74 inclusive. The weights were determined by the number of securities in that portfolio in that year. 1956, with 10 securities per portfolio, carried a weight of 0.029, while 1970-74 carried weights of 0.070 each with the sum of the weights over the 1956-74 period equalling one.

17. Since earnings could be negative in any subsequent year, a problem rose as to how to define growth when the denominator is negative. When earnings changed from negative to positive, the growth was defined to be greater than the median (i.e., "very large"). When earnings remained negative in both years, the observation was deleted. Typically, this caused a deletion of less than two per cent of the observations, with the exception of Portfolio One, where deletions ranged from two to three per cent of the observations.

18. We regard the transitory earnings argument as one, but by no means the only, interpretation to place on the results.

19. Suppose expected earnings per share are $1.00. For convenience, assume that realized earnings per share were $1.00 and $0.75 in 19x1 and 19x2. The actual growth rate of 19x2 is -25 per cent, while the expected growth in 19x3 is 33 per cent. Assuming price remains essentially unchanged (because permanent earnings are unchanged) at $10.00, the P/E ratio would be 10 and 13.3 for 19x1 and 19x2, while the expected P/E in 19x3 would be 10. Note that in 19x2 there was an abnormal low earnings growth associated with a high P/E (negative correlation) and that a high P/E in 19x2 was followed by abnormal high growth in 19x3 (positive correlation). This is discussed in more detail in W. Beaver, "The Information Content of the Magnitude of Unexpected Earnings" (Stanford Research Seminar, 1974).

20. This conclusion is contingent upon the way we chose to measure the variables and to rank the portfolios. For example, a longer term measure of growth (i.e., five or 10 years) might produce different results.

21. By unusual earnings opportunities we essentially mean opportunities to earn a return on future investments greater than the cost of capital. Valuation theory tells us that this form of future earnings growth will induce a growth premium in the P/E. Note that it is crucial to distinguish between unusual earnings opportunities on *future*, rather than current, investment. To the extent there are abnormal returns earned on the current investment, this will not affect the P/E ratio, although the ratio of market price to book value per share would be affected.

22. For example, if one believes that product and factor markets are reasonably competitive, then there exist little or no unusual earnings opportunities and the observed growth differences are almost entirely due to transitory factors.

23. Operationally, the market-wide P/E was defined to be the median P/E as reported in Table 1.

24. Although not reported here, the analysis of the serial correlation in P/E behavior was augmented by an analysis of a transition matrix. This analysis also confirmed the lack of any material tendency to move from one extreme portfolio to extreme portfolios at the other end of the P/E spectrum.

25. Since our study is concerned with differences across P/E ratios at a given point in time, beta (b_i) will be the sole determinant of differences in P/E resulting from differences in r_i. Assuming a finite growth horizon, Litzenberger and Rao ("Estimates of the Marginal Rate of Time Preference and Average Risk Aversion

of Investors in Electric Utility Shares: 1960-66," *The Bell Journal of Economics and Management Science* (Spring 1971), pp. 265-277) have shown the E/P ratio (the reciprocal of P/E) is a simple linear function of beta and a growth variable, with the following form:

$$\frac{E_i}{P_i} = \gamma_0 + \gamma_1 b_1 = \gamma_2 f(g)$$

The sign of γ_1 is expected to vary, $f(g)$ is some function of growth and γ_2 is expected to be negative.

26. An analysis of the residuals indicated that they are well approximated by normality. This is not surprising in the sense that each observation is an "average" for a portfolio of stocks. By the Central Limit Theorem, we would expect the sampling distributions of averages to approach normality. Note, however, that the results from any one year's regression are not independent of those of other years.

27. Two approaches immediately come to mind—the application of Box-Jenkins techniques to the past earnings series or the use of analysts' forecasts of earnings. Either method might produce better assessments of expected earnings per share.

28. This ordinal statement holds for both depreciation and inventory, even though inventory also implies a "real" difference due to taxes. Obviously, the specific adjustments to be made would have to distinguish between accounting differences that imply tax differences versus those that do not.

29. W. Beaver and R. Dukes, "Delta-Depreciation Methods: Some Empirical Results," *Accounting Review* (April 1972), pp. 320-332. In this study, all sample firms were using an accelerated method for tax purposes. Therefore the difference was solely due to the depreciation method used for annual report purposes.

30. Another approach would be to introduce variables related to the accounting effect. Recent works by Watts and Zimmerman ("Toward a Positive Theory of the Determination of Accounting Standards," *Accounting Review* (April 1978)) suggest that conservativeness of accounting method varies positively with firm size. Van Breda ("The Prediction of Corporate Earnings" (Stanford University, 1976)) indicates that average age of assets is one of the variables that explains cross-sectional differences in return on equity (i.e., earnings available to common dividend by the book value of common equity).

by Harry M. Markowitz

Markowitz Revisited

◀ When the tendency for the returns on a portfolio's individual holdings to move together is strong, the dispersion in portfolio returns will be wide, no matter how many holdings it has. The "law of the average covariance" tells us how any reduction in dispersion that diversification can achieve is limited by this tendency.

Are risk and (expected) return adequate measures of a portfolio's utility to its owner? Many academics have argued that they aren't, insisting instead on a more complex measure they call "expected utility." If so-called mean-variance analysis is not adequate, it merely gives us the wrong answer at low cost. But when the investor's expected utility can be closely approximated by some function of his portfolio's mean and variance, he loses little by picking his portfolio on the basis of risk and return. ▶

WE WERE sitting at a council meeting of the Computer Applications Committee of the NYSSA, discussing possible speakers, when Martin Leibowitz said, "What we need is a talk entitled 'Markowitz Revisited'—any volunteers?" Before I knew it I had volunteered.

The "visit" that resulted was to my 1959 book, *Portfolio Selection: Efficient Diversification of Investments.*[1] Some of the audience for the talk were quite familiar with the contents of this book and preferred advanced technical comments. Others had little knowledge of the contents of the book beyond the rumor that it might have something to do with real investing, and preferred a nontechnical introduction to the subject.

In order to provide something for everyone, I presented two topics. The first topic is a favorite formula of mine—a formula of value in practice as well as in theory. It expresses a "law" worth understanding and remembering even if one knows nothing else about portfolio theory. The second topic is concerned with a fundamental question of portfolio theory—namely, the question when it is

proper to use the analysis techniques presented in my book. My views on this topic, as the reader of this article will see, differ somewhat from views held by many current writers.

To understand the formula (the subject of Topic 1) consider a hypothetical investor who bets on a wheel with several rings (as illustrated in Figure 1). The first ring of the wheel represents the returns on Security 1; the second ring represents the returns on Security 2; and so on—except for the innermost ring, which serves a different function. Thus if the wheel stops in the position shown in Figure 1, the investor wins 10 per cent per dollar bet on Security 1, loses five per cent per dollar bet on Security 2, and so on.

The innermost ring indicates which wheel is to be spun next. If the wheel stops as indicated in the figure, for example, then wheel #33 will be spun next, after the player once again places his bets. Different wheels may have different returns, and even different numbers of rings.

Thus the investor divides his money between, say, Securities 1, 2 and 3. The wheel is spun. The investor collects his gains or losses, perhaps uses some of his assets for consumption, and once again divides his assets among the various securities represented by the rings of the new wheel to be spun.

The returns written on the current wheel, together with the way the investor divides his assets among the different securities, determine the play's probability of returns per dollar invested in the *portfolio*

1. Footnotes appear at end of article.

Currently associated with the Thomas J. Watson Research Center of IBM, Dr. Harry Markowitz is author of what is probably the single most influential work in modern finance: Portfolio Selection: Efficient Diversification of Investments *(John Wiley and Sons, New York, 1959). His seminal ideas on portfolio diversification first appeared in* "Portfolio Selection," The Journal of Finance, *March 1952. This article is based on an address to the Computer Applications Symposium of the New York Society of Security Analysts.*

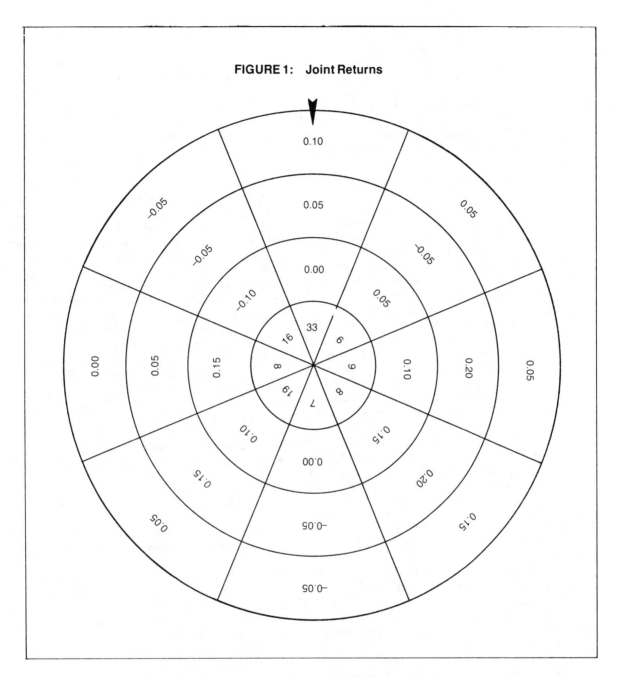

FIGURE 1: Joint Returns

as a whole. Our general concern is with how this investor should distribute his investment dollar for the forthcoming spin of the wheel so as to achieve a good probability distribution of return on the portfolio as a whole.

What do I mean by a *good* probability distribution of returns on the portfolio? For this section of the article, I assume that a probability distribution of returns (on the portfolio as a whole) is not good—or at least not as good as it could be—if some other available distribution has higher expected return with no higher variability (specifically, standard deviation) of return; nor can a distribution be optimal if some other available distribution has less standard deviation of return with no less expected return. (Under Topic 2 I will consider the circumstances under which this is a reasonable assumption.)

To calculate the expected return on the portfolio as a whole, the only data needed are the expected returns on each security and the amounts invested in each security (I won't give the proof here). In fact, the expected return on the portfolio as a whole, per dollar invested, is simply a weighted average of the expected returns of the individual securities, with the amounts invested as the weights. This is true whether or not one assumes normal distributions, and whether or not returns are independent. In fact, there is no way one could draw a wheel such as the one in Figure 1 and choose a portfolio without the expected return on that portfolio as a whole being this weighted sum of the expected returns of the individual securities.

Unfortunately, the standard deviation of the portfolio as a whole is a more complicated matter. It involves a concept that, while not new to the statistician, was rare or nonexistent in the financial literature two decades ago—the notion of "covariance." It is absolutely crucial to an understanding of portfolio risk. In particular, the law expressed by the formula of Topic 1 may be called "the law of the average covariance." I won't give the formal definition of covariance; rather, I will attempt to describe it in terms of concepts already familiar to the reader.

The standard deviation is, of course, a measure of how widely spread a distribution is about its mean; most of any distribution is within plus or minus two standard deviations of its mean. If the distribution were normal—please note, I am not asserting that returns are normal—but if a distribution were normal, then about 95 per cent of the distribution would be within plus or minus two standard deviations of the distribution's mean. For every distribution with a mean and standard deviation—for every possible wheel one could draw—at least 75 per cent of the distribution would be within two standard deviations of the mean.

So standard deviation is a measure of the variability or dispersion of a distribution and, roughly speaking, most of the distribution is contained between the mean minus two standard deviations and the mean plus two standard deviations.

A correlation coefficient relates a pair of random variables, such as a pair of rings on the wheel in Figure 1, or the height and weight of a man drawn at random from the U.S. population. It is a measure of the extent to which the variables tend to go up and down together. The coefficient can be as low as minus one or as high as plus one. For example, if one random variable is always three times another random variable, their correlation coefficient is plus one, and we say that they are perfectly correlated. If two random variables are drawn independently of each other, like two flips of a coin, then their correlation coefficient is zero. If one random variable is usually higher than its mean when the other variable is lower, then the two have a negative correlation. The greater the correlation coefficient, the greater the tendency for the two random variables to move

in the same direction.

The covariance between two random variable may be described in terms of their two standard deviations and their correlation coefficient. Specifically,

COVARIANCE = (the correlation between the two)
times
(the standard deviation of the first)
times
(the standard deviation of the second).

Since the correlation coefficient between a random variable and itself is plus one, the above definition implies that the covariance between a random variable and itself equals the square of its standard deviation (also known as the variance of the random variable).

In general, then, the sign of the covariance is the same (positive or negative) as the sign of the correlation coefficient, while the magnitude of the covariance equals the product of the two standard deviations and the magnitude of the correlation coefficient.

The covariances among securities play a critical role in determining the standard deviation (or variance) of the portfolio as a whole. Suppose, for example, that our hypothetical investor divides his funds equally among 25 securities before the spin of a wheel. It may be shown (omitting the proof here) that—for any possible wheel—the variance on the portfolio as a whole must be

$$V_p = \frac{\text{average variance}}{25} + \frac{24}{25}(\text{average covariance}),$$

where V_p stands for the variance of return on the portfolio as a whole; "average variance" refers to the sum of the variances of the 25 securities divided by 25 (note that this average variance is divided again by 25 in the above formula); and average covariance is the sum of all distinct covariances (not including the covariance between the security and itself) divided by the number of such covariances. More generally, if the investor divides his money equally among N securities, then:

$$(1) \qquad V_p = \frac{\text{average variance}}{N}$$
$$+ \frac{N-1}{N}(\text{average covariance}).$$

As N increases, the right-hand side of the equation simply approaches the average covariance. In symbols,

$$(2) \qquad V_p \rightarrow \text{average covariance}.$$

Since the standard deviation is the square root of the variance, we also have

(3) $\qquad S_p \to \sqrt{\overline{\text{average covariance}}}$

The simple Formula 2, or its equivalent, Formula 3, comprises my law of the average covariance.

Let me emphasize the generality of Formulas 1, 2 and 3. They do not assume that returns are normally distributed, although they apply in such a case. Nor do they assume that returns are uncorrelated; in fact, they take into account the correlations among returns. Their results hold whether or not covariances accord with Sharpe's "beta model" of covariance.[2] In fact, there is no way of drawing a wheel such as that in Figure 1 so that Equation 1 does not hold when equal amounts are invested. For moderate to large size portfolios, Formula 2 gives approximately the same result as Equation 1.

At first glance Formula 2 seems dull and harmless. Yet it confronts the portfolio manager with one of the most difficult problems he faces. To understand its significance, consider an investor who invests equal amounts in a large number of similar securities. Specifically, suppose for this example that each of these securities has the same standard deviation (S_s) as every other, and each pair of securities has the same correlation (cor) as every other pair. Then the covariance between any pair of securities will be

$$\text{cov} = \text{cor} \cdot S_s \cdot S_s = \text{cor} \cdot S_s^2 .$$

Since this is the covariance between each pair, it is also the average of all such covariances. Hence, Formula 3 implies that the standard deviation on the portfolio as a whole (S_p) approaches:

$$S_p \to \sqrt{\text{cor} \cdot S_s} .$$

Suppose that the correlation coefficient is between 0.25 and 0.36. (These figures are in the range of values of observed average correlation coefficients—and I know their square roots.) If cor = 0.25, then $S_p = 0.5 \cdot S_s$; if cor = 0.36, then $S_p = 0.6 \cdot S_s$.

Realize what this is saying! Even if the investor could diversify among unlimited numbers of these securities—even if he could spread his money across 100 or 200 or even 1,000 equally good securities—if there is a 0.25 correlation between their returns, then the standard deviation on the portfolio as a whole is only half as great as that of one single security. Unlimited diversification has reduced standard deviation by only 50 per cent as compared to buying only one security. If the correlation coefficient is 0.36, then an unlimited diversification reduces standard deviation by only 40 per cent as compared to investing everything in one security.

This hardly seems fair. In the life insurance business, assuming policies are written on uncorrelated risks, unlimited diversification would make the variability in mortality approach zero. But our risks are not uncorrelated. As a consequence, the returns on the portfolio as a whole exhibit a disturbingly large variability no matter how many equally good securities are purchased.

Table 1 illustrates how many securities the portfolio must acquire before Formula 2 begins to approximate Equation 1. The table shows, for various numbers of securities, the ratio of the standard deviation of the portfolio as a whole to the standard deviation of one security, assuming that each pair of securities has a correlation of 0.25. Much of the reduction in standard deviation that diversification will yield is already provided by 20 securities. (I am assuming throughout this discussion that the hypothetical investor does not significantly affect prices by his own buying and selling actions. If he did, still greater diversification might be needed because of liquidity and marketability considerations.) Ignoring marketability considerations, 20 securities will cancel out random fluctuations almost as well as (or should I say little worse than) a million equally good securities (if such existed)—if each pair had a correlation coefficient of 0.25.

Table 1
Effect of Diversification (Cor = 0.25)

Number of Securities in Portfolio	Standard Deviation of Portfolio ÷ Standard Deviation of One Security
1	1.000
5	0.632
10	0.570
20	0.536
30	0.524
40	0.518
50	0.515
100	0.507
200	0.504
∞	0.500

Throughout the discussion thus far I have used the standard deviation (or, equivalently, the variance) of return as a measure of the risk involved in the portfolio. The use of this measure has such far-reaching consequences as the law of the average covariance discussed here, the principles of rational investing in the face of correlated risks, and the works of Sharpe, Lintner, Mossin and others on how markets would behave if all investors acted according to these principles.

This brings us to Topic 2: Are the expected value and the standard deviation (or variance) of return reasonable measures of the desirability of a portfolio? Must we look at more than just mean and variance—perhaps at something completely different—or are these two criteria "good enough"?

Validity of Mean-Variance Analysis

I will assume in this section that the investor would really like to maximize the expected value of some utility function $[U = U(R)]$ as of any spin of the wheel. This utility function may change from one spin to another as the investor grows older, or as his wealth or other circumstances change; but as of any spin he would like to maximize the expected value of some such function.[3]

Now, if the investor really wants to maximize the expected value of some utility curve, why should he even consider just looking at the mean and variance of the portfolio? In the first place, the problem of finding portfolios that minimize standard deviation of return for various expected returns is usually computationally much simpler than that of finding the portfolio that exactly maximizes the expected value of most utility functions. Secondly, the inputs required for the mean-variance analysis are usually simpler than the inputs required to find the maximum expected utility (unless special assumptions are made concerning the forms of joint distributions). Finally, real investors these days usually seem more comfortable with the idea of examining risk-return tradeoffs than with psychoanalyzing their utility function and letting the computer pick a portfolio that maximizes its expected value.

In short, it is usually much more convenient and economical to do a mean-variance analysis than to compute the actual portfolio with maximum expected utility. But if the answer supplied by a mean-variance analysis is not almost as good as the answer supplied by a high-priced utility analysis, little is gained. We merely have the wrong answer at low cost.

It is frequently asserted that mean-variance analysis can yield a portfolio with maximum expected utility only if returns are normally distributed or if the utility function is quadratic. I am not concerned here with conditions under which mean-variance analysis will maximize expected utility precisely, but with conditions under which it will yield a portfolio with almost maximum utility. A presumed (though rarely stated) corollary of the previously mentioned position states that mean-variance analysis cannot be expected to give almost maximum utility unless distributions are almost normal or utility functions almost quadratic.

I would like to challenge this corollary. To begin with, consider the case of the logarithmic utility function:

$$U = \log (1 + R).$$

If, for the probability distributions with which investors are concerned—namely, those of the returns on certain portfolios—there were a function of mean

and variance only, such that expected utility was approximately equal to this function,

$$EU \approx f(E,V),$$

then the investor could find a portfolio that almost maximizes EU by picking the one that does maximize $f(E,V)$.

One formula for approximating expected $\log (1 + \text{return})$ when one knows only the mean (E) and variance (V) of a probability distribution is:

$$(4) \qquad EU \approx \log (1+E) - V / (1+E)^2.$$

Chapter VI of *Portfolio Selection* contains a table and a graph of the relationship between the historical average log of $(1 + \text{return})$ on one hand and the above approximation, using the historical E and V, on the other.[4] I believe the reader will find the relationship quite satisfactory if he inspects this table and graph. Similar conclusions were reached by Young and Trent using a larger sample of securities and random portfolios of various sizes.[5]

For probability distributions with means, variances and expected $\log (1 + \text{return})$ observed in these historical experiments, the investor can do a good job of guessing the portfolio's expected log if he knows its E and V. This is true even though I did not assume that the investor's utility is quadratic (for the moment, I am assuming it to be logarithmic) and even though the distribution of returns is not assumed to be normal. (A discrete distribution, the historical sample, was assumed for the experiment. Such a distribution cannot be precisely normal, and some analysts have argued that similarly derived samples do not appear to be even samples from a normal distribution.)

Formula 4 is not the result of fitting many functions to data to see which would fit best. Rather, it is one of two approximations suggested on purely theoretical grounds. The same argument that yielded Formula 4 as an approximation to expect $\log (1 + \text{return})$ also suggests approximations for a wide range of concave (i.e., risk-averse) utility functions. The argument suggests that the approximations will be good unless the distributions are "too wild." The analysis of what makes a distribution too wild for such an approximation is to be found in Chapters VI and XIII of *Portfolio Selection*.[6]

In sum, if a function of E and V only exists such that

$$EU \approx f(E,V)$$

for the distributions he actually faces, the investor loses little by picking his portfolio on the basis of E and V, rather than engaging in the usually much less convenient utility analysis. In this case he may think in terms of the risk and return (variance and mean) of portfolios. The strategic role of covariance, illustrated earlier in terms of the law of the average co-variance, is then one of the consequences of the use of variance as a measure of portfolio risk. ∎

Footnotes

1. Harry M. Markowitz, *Portfolio Selection: Efficient Diversification of Investments* (New York: John Wiley & Sons, Inc., 1959).
2. William F. Sharpe, "A Simplified Model for Portfolio Analysis," *Management Science* (January 1963), 277-93.
3. Many readers will remember that this assumption comes from the theory of rational behavior under risk and uncertainty developed in part by Von Neuman and Morgenstern and in part by Leonard J. Savage. (See Von Neuman and Morgenstern, *Theory of Games and Economic Behavior* (Princeton: Princeton University Press, 1947) and Savage, *The Foundations of Statistics* (New York: John Wiley & Sons, Inc., 1954).) There is, of course, a simplifying assumption already made here when I write utility as a function of return only, rather than as a function of return and "the next wheel to be spun." This more general assumption was explored briefly in my work and at greater length in recent works by Professor Robert Merton. See "Optimum Consumption and Portfolio Rules in a Continuous-Time Model," *Journal of Economic Theory* (III, 1971) 373-413 and "An Intertemporal Capital Asset Pricing Model," *Econometrica* (September 1973), 867-887.
4. Markowitz, *Portfolio Selection,* 123-24.
5. W.E. Young and R.H. Trent, "Geometric Mean Approximations of Individual Security and Portfolio Performance," *Journal of Financial and Quantitative Analysis* (June 1969).
6. Until recently, surprisingly little work has been done on testing whether formulas based on E and V alone can approximate well various utility functions for distributions of return provided by real-world portfolios. Some work is currently being done in this area at the Hebrew University, Jerusalem. I understand from Professor Haim Levy that, thus far at least, this new work is consistent with the work cited above.

NEW TOOLS FOR PROFITS ANALYSIS*

Edmund A. Mennis, C.F.A.

Financial analysis cannot be done in a vacuum. An analyst spends the bulk of his time working on companies and industries, but his conclusions must be affected by the economic environment in which industries or companies operate. The portfolio manager must set investment policy and make security selections in the same economic environment. As a result, the analyst tries to follow changing business conditions, constantly asking the critical question of what these developments will mean for the profits of the companies in which he is interested. His tools are crude and not well organized, however, and the link between the economic environment and the profits outlook is an elusive one.

Fortunately, new material recently published and updated regularly by the Department of Commerce has improved and deepened our under-standing of the important economic variables affecting corporate profits. With this information, our ability to follow profit performance is en-hanced, and our tools for forecasting the implications of changes in the economy on profits is better than it has been heretofore. This new information was published originally in the May 1967 *Survey of Current Business* and is updated regularly in each monthly *Survey* as Table 9, Corporate Gross Product, in the National Income and Product Tables. The purpose of this article is to describe and chart some of the new information made available, to indicate its usefulness for the analysis of historical profit performance, and to suggest a method of using the data to prepare an estimate of future corporate profits.

DEFINITIONS

At the outset, it should be understood that the profits described herein are those reported as a part of the national income and product accounts published regularly by the Department of Commerce. In this series corpo-rate profits are *not* an aggregate of the profits reported to shareholders by the corporations in the United States. In national income terminology, corporate profits represent the accrual to the account of the residents of

---

* N.B. This pioneering article on corporate profits together with the companion article by Grace Wickersham constitute a useful review and analysis of the relevant data on corporate profits contained in the National Income and Product Accounts published by the U.S. Department of Commerce. The intent of publishing these two articles is purely methodological as the specific forecasts contained herein are obviously dated.

the nation of the earnings of domestic and foreign corporations, which are a portion of the aggregate earnings of labor and property arising out of current production. As a part of national income, profits are viewed as measured by the recipient rather than the originator. These profits arise from current production, so that inventory profits and capital gains and losses are excluded. This profit series is statistically based on profits as reported for tax purposes, which, as any financial analyst knows, may well differ in several respects from profits reported to shareholders.[1] Nevertheless, this profit series does have a relationship to shareholder profits in that their broad, general moves and cyclical turning points, over a period of years, are quite similar. Moreover, the new data permit a better analysis of the economic factors affecting profits than any information elsewhere.

The new data provided by the Commerce Department cover gross corporate product quarterly since 1948 and also gross corporate product originating in the nonfinancial sector of the economy (NFGCP). In addition to NFGCP in current dollars, the series provides a price deflator, which enables NFGCP to be stated in constant 1958 dollars. NFGCP is further divided into its components of costs and profits and also unit costs and unit profits. The most effective way of utilizing this series is to concentrate on the NFGCP sector and treat the financial sector separately.

Most of the terms used are not familiar and require some clarification. The first question, therefore, is what is NFGCP? This series reflects the contribution of the domestic operations of nonfinancial corporations to gross national product. Excluded from the nonfinancial area are the results of financial corporations: commercial banks, mutual savings banks, savings and loan associations, credit unions, financial companies, securities and commodity brokers, regulated investment companies, and insurance carriers.

NFGCP can be considered in two ways. Just as the national income accounts have both an income and product side, NFGCP has both a sales or product side and a balancing income or factor cost side. On one hand it can be looked upon as the sale of nonfinancial firms to other businesses, consumers, government and foreigners, plus inventory change, less purchases from other firms, both domestic and foreign. NFGCP can also be defined as the sum of incomes and charges to this gross product. From this latter viewpoint, it is therefore the sum of: (1) capital consumption allowances; (2) indirect business taxes less subsidies plus business transfer

---

[1] For a further discussion of these measures, see "Different Measures of Corporate Profits," by Edmund A. Mennis, *Financial Analysts Journal*, September-October 1962; "Corporate Profits Data—Tax Returns vs. Company Books" by Vito Natrella (see p. 136) and "Profit Measures Published by the Department of Commerce" by John A. Gorman, two papers given at the Federal Statistical Users Conference in Cleveland, Ohio on June 12, 1968.

payments; (3) compensation of employees; (4) net interest; and (5) corporate profits before taxes and inventory valuation adjustment. Capital consumption allowances in national income terminology include depreciation and accidental damage to fixed capital. Indirect business taxes represent primarily sales, excise, and property taxes. Business transfer payments would include gifts to nonprofit organizations and consumer bad debts. Employee compensation includes monetary remuneration plus supplements, such as contributions to social insurance, pension, health, welfare and unemployment funds and compensation for injuries.

In addition to the figures for NFGCP and its factor cost components in current dollars, Commerce also provides data for NFGCP in 1958 prices together with implicit price deflators. The price deflator for NFGCP reflects the current cost per unit of 1958 dollar NFGCP, that is, the costs incurred and the profits earned in producing one 1958 dollar's worth of output in the current period. The current factor costs of capital consumption allowances, indirect business taxes, net interest, employee compensation, and profits have also been related to NFGCP in 1958 dollars, so that we have not only the dollar costs but also unit labor costs, unit nonlabor costs, and unit profits. This additional information is a significant contribution to the field of profits analysis.

HISTORICAL ANALYSIS

Several charts have been prepared that show the historical record of a number of the series described above, arranged in a way that facilitates their use for profits analysis. Chart I plots NFGCP in current dollars against gross national product (GNP) and also shows the implicit price deflators for both series. The data are plotted on a semilogarithmic grid, so that rates of change, rather than absolute values, are stressed. In addition, the cyclical peaks and troughs of the postwar period as defined by the National Bureau of Economic Research are shown on the chart to assist in the analysis.

As the two lines toward the top of the chart indicate, NFGCP, which accounts for about 55 percent of GNP, follows the pattern of GNP fairly closely, although it is more volatile. Its peaks and troughs have in almost all instances coincided with peaks and troughs in GNP. With respect to price changes, the movement of the price deflator of both GNP and NFGCP were quite similar until 1958. Since that time, the price deflator for GNP has moved up more rapidly than for NFGCP, presumably reflecting the more rapid price increases in the service component and government sectors of GNP.

Chart II plots NFGCP in current dollars and nonfinancial corporate profits before taxes and inventory valuation adjustment. (The tax factor and the adjustment for inventory profits will be discussed later.) These two series represent the sales and the pretax profits emerging from those sales in the nonfinancial sector of the economy. At the bottom of the chart we have shown profits per unit of real NFGCP, which is a measure of profit margins. However, this measure is not exactly comparable with pretax margins as ordinarily computed by the financial analyst. Pretax margins normally reflect the proportion of pretax dollars to sales dollars. Unit profits represent the percent that current dollar pretax profits are of

CHART I

GROSS NATIONAL PRODUCT, NONFINANCIAL GROSS CORPORATE PRODUCT
AND PRICE DEFLATORS
(1948–1968)

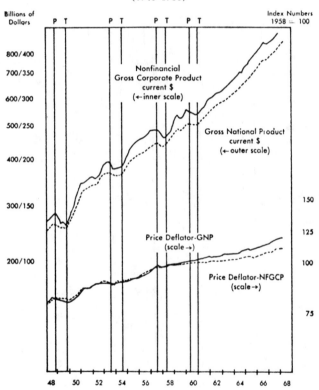

current output measured in 1958 prices. In other words, unit profits relate to profits per unit of real output rather than current dollar sales.

Examining the lines at the top of the chart, the strong growth trend in NFGCP is clearly evident. Moreover, this growth trend accelerated and has been much smoother beginning in 1961. The impact of this sales pattern on profits is seen in the second line. The cyclical fluctuations in corporate profits are quite pronounced and the general growth trend from 1948 to 1961 is substantially slower than the growth in NFGCP. As shown in the third line on the chart, unit profits were in a declining trend and also had substantial cyclical fluctuations in the period 1948 through 1960.

A major change occurred in profits beginning in 1961. Not only was their recovery from the 1960–61 business decline pronounced, but the growth through 1966 was the longest in the postwar period. This can be

CHART II

NONFINANCIAL GROSS CORPORATE PRODUCT, PRETAX PROFITS
AND UNIT PROFITS
(1948–1968)

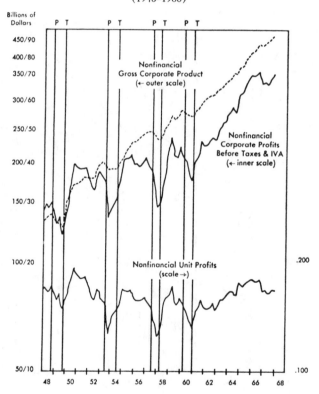

attributable, in part, to the sustained volume rise uninterrupted by cyclical fluctuations from 1961 to 1966. A good portion of the profits improvement was due not just to rising sales volume but also to a significant change in the trend of unit profits. It is also interesting to note that the 1967 decline in profits was quite pronounced considering the brief and moderate decline in sales volume. In fact, unit profits in 1966–67 have reacted more than the sales decline would suggest. The new data supplied by the Commerce Department can be helpful in understanding the behavior of unit profits and the cost factors associated with them.

Cost Analysis

A breakdown of 1967 costs and profits for nonfinancial corporations is contained in the table below:

	Billions of Dollars	Percent
Nonlabor costs:		
Capital consumption allowances................	$ 42.2	9.7%
Indirect business taxes, etc.....................	38.8	9.0
Interest....................................	8.5	2.0
Total nonlabor costs.....................	$ 89.5	20.7%
Labor costs................................	277.0	64.0
Total costs........................	$366.5	84.7%
Corporate profits before tax and IVA.............	66.4	15.3
Nonfinancial gross corporate product.............	$432.9	100.0%

As indicated in the table, nonlabor costs (capital consumption allowances, indirect business taxes and interest) accounted for about 21 percent of NFGCP in 1967, labor costs accounted for 64 percent and profits, which is the remaining factor cost, about 15 percent. A substantial portion of the nonlabor costs are relatively inflexible, while other costs will vary with sales volume.

Chart III plots unit nonlabor costs and unit labor costs quarterly from 1948 through the second quarter of 1968. If we can get a better understanding of these two components of cost, we shall be able to understand the movement of the total unit cost line.

As indicated on the chart, unit labor costs moved up fairly steadily from 1948 to 1961, although a reduction in unit labor costs was fairly characteristic of the periods shortly after a business cycle peak until early in the recovery after the cyclical trough. The experience after the 1961 cyclical trough was unusual, however, because unit labor costs trended downward until 1965. The rise from 1966 to mid-1968 was quite marked.[2]

Unit nonlabor costs moved up even more steeply than unit labor costs, reaching a peak in 1962. Thereafter, unit nonlabor costs flattened out, actually declined in 1965 and 1966, but rose sharply in 1967. Thus, the sharp rise in unit profits in 1961–1966 shown in Chart II was accounted for by the changed direction of both unit labor costs and unit nonlabor costs beginning in 1961.

Chart IV takes the analysis one step further by examining both the numerator and the denominator of each unit cost line. NFGCP is plotted in 1938 dollars, which provide a stable unit of measurement for the

---

[2] This series is similar to the monthly unit labor cost ratio in manufacturing, which is published regularly as Series 62 in the Department of Commerce publication, *Business Cycle Developments*. However, this series covers the entire nonfinancial area and thus includes a broader sector of the corporate universe.

denominator of each of the two unit cost ratios. Then labor costs and nonlabor costs are plotted in current dollars.

As the chart indicates, nonlabor costs have moved up rather steadily during the entire postwar period, and from 1948 to 1961 the rate of increase was more rapid than NFGCP. Consequently, unit nonlabor costs

CHART III

EMPLOYEE COMPENSATION AND NONLABOR COSTS PER UNIT
OF 1958 NFGCP
(1948–1968)

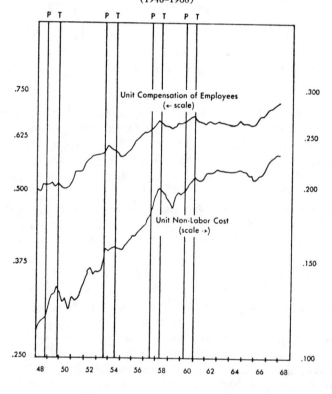

increased. From 1961 to 1965, the two lines moved in parallel, and the unit nonlabor cost ratio flattened out. A slowing in the gain in NFGCP since 1966, however, has resulted once more in an upward movement of the unit nonlabor cost line.

The relationship of labor costs and NFGCP is similar to that of nonlabor costs and NFGCP. Labor costs moved up more rapidly prior to 1961, paralleled the growth in real output from 1961 to 1965, and moved upward more rapidly since. For a better understanding of unit labor costs, however, a deeper analysis of its components is necessary.

Labor costs per unit of output are calculated as the ratio of employee compensation (in current dollars) to NFGCP (in constant 1958 dollars). In order to provide a more useful analytical framework, both the numerator and denominator of this ratio can be divided by manhours, making unit labor costs equal to the ratio of compensation per manhour and output per manhour. Thus, changes in unit labor costs can be analyzed

CHART IV

NONFINANCIAL GROSS CORPORATE PRODUCT IN 1958 DOLLARS
LABOR AND NONLABOR COSTS IN CURRENT DOLLARS
(1948-1968)

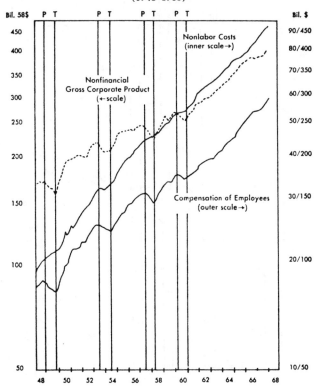

from the interaction of two key factors: hourly wage rates (including salaries and fringe benefits) and labor productivity. When wages advance more rapidly than output per manhour, unit labor costs increase. When productivity gains exceed increases in wage rates, unit labor costs decline. Violating arithmetic principles only slightly, the present change in unit labor costs can be calculated as the difference between the percent changes in hourly compensation and output per manhour. For example, a 4 percent increase in wage rates and a 3 percent advance in productivity result in a rise of 1 percent in unit labor costs.

Unfortunately, the Commerce data on NFGCP do not provide information on manhours and compensation per manhour, and therefore output per manhour cannot be calculated. However, an acceptable substitute for this information is published quarterly by the Bureau of Labor Statistics in their quarterly release "Wages, Prices and Productivity in the

CHART V

INDEXES OF OUTPUT, MANHOURS AND OUTPUT PER MANHOUR
PRIVATE NONFARM SECTOR 1947–1968
(1957–1959 = 100)

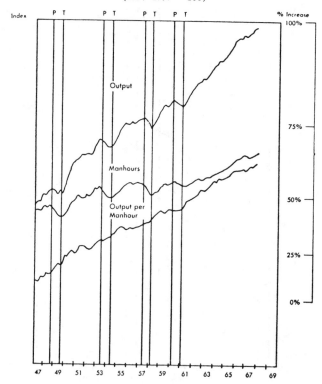

Private Nonfarm Sector." Although not precisely comparable, the movement of unit labor costs in the BLS series and in the Commerce series has been quite similar. Charts V and VI plot the various components of unit labor costs in the BLS series.

As Chart V indicates, output has increased faster than manhours in the postwar period and, consequently, output per manhour has moved upward. The gain in output relative to manhours was particularly pronounced in the 1961–1965 period, partly due to unused resources and available labor supply. In 1966–1967, the rate of gain in output slowed as the economy moved to full utilization of its labor force, and demand also slackened. Consequently, productivity gains slowed and only recently have begun to pick up again.

Chart VI repeats the line showing output per manhour, shows employee compensation per manhour, and finally shows the result of those two forces in the unit labor cost line. One interesting fact shown on the chart is the fairly steady increase in employee compensation, with the trend accelerating beginning in 1965. The rate of gain also shows some-

CHART VI

INDEXES OF OUTPUT PER MANHOUR, HOURLY COMPENSATION AND
UNIT LABOR COSTS PRIVATE NONFARM SECTOR 1947–1968
(1957–1959 = 100)

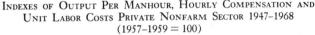
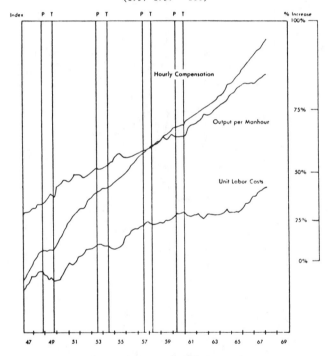

what during periods of cyclical contraction. The slower rate of growth in output per manhour relative to hourly labor costs from 1947 to 1961 accounted for the rising unit labor cost line during that period. The faster rise in productivity, which roughly paralleled hourly compensation from 1961 to 1965, resulted in the leveling of unit labor costs. Since 1966, the acceleration in employee compensation and the slowing in productivity gains have resulted in one of the sharpest rises in unit labor costs in the postwar period.

DOMESTIC CORPORATE PROFITS

Thus far we have examined domestic corporate profits in the nonfinancial sector and the underlying component costs. The profits squeeze of the past three years has been identified as caused by some slowing in the growth of output, a consequent rise in unit nonlabor costs, and also a combination of accelerated hourly compensation and slower productivity gains, which together caused unit labor costs to advance. Price increases,

CHART VII

DOMESTIC CORPORATE PROFITS BEFORE TAXES AND IVA TOTAL, NONFINANCIAL AND FINANCIAL
(1948–1968)

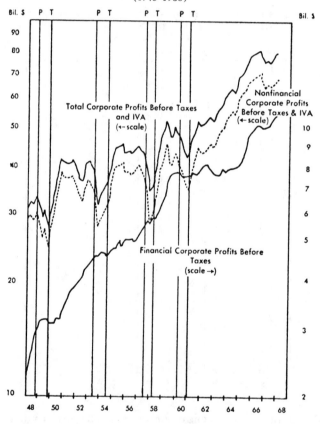

which are the offsetting factor to rising costs, have been sufficient to hold unit profits about level after a sharp drop in the first quarter of 1967.

The last three charts summarize the remaining components that must be included to get a picture of total corporate profits. Chart VII plots total domestic corporate profits before taxes and inventory valuation adjustment and its two components, nonfinancial and financial profits. Nonfinancial corporate profits have been analyzed in some detail because, as the chart indicates, their path closely parallels the path of total domestic profits. The pattern of financial profits is much different, but it has less influence on the total because it represents only about 12 percent of total domestic profits.

The financial component of profits is heavily weighted by the banks, which in the past five years have accounted for from 58 percent to 62 percent of total financial profits. The remainder is accounted for by insurance carriers, security and commodity brokers, and credit agencies and regulated investment companies. The trend in bank earnings has been upward since 1948, although a sharp decline was experienced in 1961 and the growth rate since that time has been slower than the 1948–1960 rate due to higher interest charges and a growing proportion of time deposits. Insurance carriers account for about 17 percent of financial pretax profits, but their impact on changes in financial profits is significant because of their volatility. The fluctuations are due to the wide swings in the profits of nonlife insurance carriers, accounted for by their insurance operations rather than their investment results.[3] The leveling of financial profits in 1961–1964 was due to the decline in bank profits in 1961 and to the decline in insurance carrier profits in the other years. In 1967 the decline was centered in the insurance carriers.

Total Corporate Profits

Two other adjustments are necessary to the domestic corporate profit figures in order to obtain the aggregate measures of corporate profits provided by the Commerce Department. These two adjustments reflect the inventory valuation adjustment and the adjustment for the "rest of the world."

Chart VIII shows the pattern of the inventory valuation adjustment and the rest of the world adjustment on a quarterly basis since 1948. The inventory valuation adjustment is necessary because inventory profits are not considered a part of the profits arising from current production and, consequently, are excluded in the national income account profits component. The IVA measures the excess of the change of the physical volume of nonfinancial inventories valued at the average prices during the period over the change in book value as recorded by corporate accountants. As the chart indicates, the inventory valuation adjustment has fluctuated from positive to negative and has ranged from as much as \$−9 billion to as much as \$+4 billion. (A negative figure means that inventory profits have been included in book profits for a period.) It is interesting to note that, during the period 1958 through 1964, inventory valuation adjustments were rather modest, reflecting the price stability of that period. Inventory valuation adjustments have increased considerably since then and by the first quarter of 1968 they had reached the large sum of \$5.1

---

[3] I am grateful to John Gorman, Associate Chief, National Income Division, Office of Business Economics, Department of Commerce for unpublished data and comments on the profit trends of financial companies.

billion at a seasonally adjusted annual rate. In only two quarters since 1948, during the Korean War, have inventory profits been so large.

The rest of the world adjustment is an allowance for the net receipt of dividends and branch profits from abroad. These receipts may be by either corporations or individuals in the United States. As can be seen, this has been a plus figure since the end of World War II and has been growing fairly significantly, particularly since 1961.

CHART VIII

REST OF WORLD AND INVENTORY VALUATION ADJUSTMENT
(1948-1968)

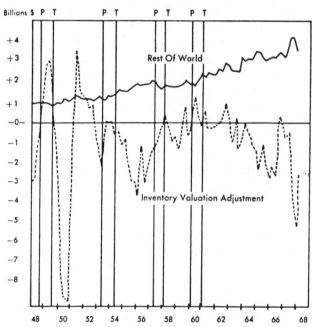

Chart IX plots the usually reported and more familiar profits figures: corporate profits before taxes (including inventory profits), the tax liability, and corporate profits after taxes. These are the figures regularly reported in the financial press.

ESTIMATING FUTURE PROFITS

Thus far we have analyzed in some detail the new profits data recently made available, which consider profits as the difference between receipts and costs. Receipts are treated as the product of prices times output, and costs are apportioned among nonlabor costs and labor costs. Costs have been examined on a unit cost basis, with unit labor costs the result of the

CHART IX

TOTAL CORPORATE PROFITS BEFORE TAXES AND AFTER TAXES AND
TAX LIABILITY

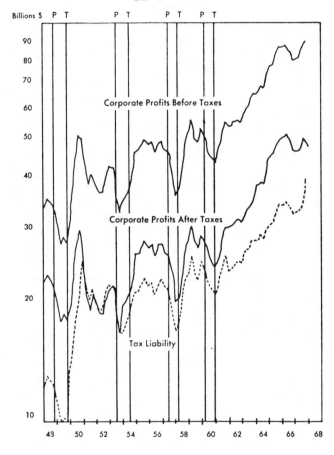

interaction of hourly wage rates and output per manhour.[4] It may be helpful now to organize this information in a form that will facilitate either estimating the profits implications of certain economic assumptions or analyzing the quarterly pattern of profits.

The purpose here is to provide a relatively simple and consistent framework for analysis and the preparation of future estimates. Of course, forecasting the future of the economy and of profits is not a simple task. Relatively elaborate and sophisticated econometric models

[4] For a further discussion of this analytical approach, an excellent reference is *Profits, Profit Markups and Productivity*, by Edwin Kuh, Study Paper No. 15, Study of Employment, Growth and Price Levels, Joint Economic Committee, Congress of the United States (Washington, D.C.: U.S. Government Printing Office, January 25, 1960).

TABLE I

Actual and Estimates of Corporate Profits
Department of Commerce Basis
(Dollars in Billions)

	1966 A	1967 A	1968 E
1. Gross National Product.......................	$747.6	$789.7	$859.0
Gross Corporate Product—nonfinancial			
2. Actual...............................	413.8	433.0	
3. Computed*............................			473.1
4. Price deflator NFGCP.....................	107.4	110.4	113.8
5. Gross Corporate Product—			
nonfinancial—1958 $....................	385.5	392.3	415.7
Unit costs and profits—nonfinancial:			
6. Capital consumption allowances................	.100	.108	.111
7. Indirect business taxes, etc.....................	.095	.099	.102
8. Interest....................................	.019	.022	.022
9. Employee compensation......................	.677	.706	.729
10. Corporate profits + IVA....................	.183	.169	.173
11. Total (= Line 4 ÷ 100)................	1.074	1.104	#1.138
12. Corporate profits—nonfinancial			
+ IVA (10 × 5).......................	70.4	66.4	71.9
13. Inventory valuation adjustment................	−1.7	−1.2	−3.4
14. Corporate profits—nonfinancial...............	72.2	67.6	75.3
15. Corporate profits—financial..................	10.2	10.4	11.4
16. Tax rate—corp. profits, nonfinancial...........	42.1%	42.6%	46.3%
17. Tax rate—corp. profits, financial..............	41.2%	45.2%	48.2%
18. Taxes—corp. profits, nonfinancial..............	30.4	28.8	34.9
19. Taxes—corp. profits, financial.................	4.2	4.7	5.5
20. Taxes—total................................	34.6	33.3	40.4
21. Corp. profits after tax—nonfinancial...........	41.8	38.8	40.4
22. Corp. profits after tax—financial..............	6.0	5.7	5.9
23. Rest of world..............................	3.2	3.6	3.5
24. Total corp. profits after tax..................	51.0	48.1	49.8
Recap:			
25. Total corp. profits after tax (line 24)...........	51.0	48.1	49.8
26. Plus tax (line 20)...........................	34.6	33.5	40.4
27. Corp. profits before tax......................	85.6	81.6	90.2
28. Plus or minus inv. val. adj. (line 13)............	−1.7	−1.2	−3.4
29. Corp. profits before tax + IVA................	83.9	80.4	86.8

*NFGCP = $ −10.04 billion + .562 GNP; r² = .998, Sy = $3.26 billion.
#Does not add due to rounding.

have been constructed for this purpose[5] and a variety of other forecasting techniques are used. However, for the analyst who lacks the time or the

---

[5] An excellent example of an econometric model that includes a profits equation has been prepared by the Department of Commerce and is described in the May 1966 *Survey of Current Business*. In the model, pretax corporate profits excluding inventory profits are made to vary positively with corporate sales and negatively with the ratio of money wage rates to the overall price deflator, manhours per unit of output, and the ratio of capacity to actual output.

desire to engage in the more complex aspects of forecasting, the approaching discussed below may be useful.

Table I provides the actual data for 1966 and 1967 and the writer's estimate for 1968 of corporate profits on a national income basis. Although analysis and preparation of future estimates are usually facilitated by working with the quarterly figures, the annual data are more familiar and the procedures used are the same.

The starting point in any profits estimate is some assumption about overall economic activity or GNP. Such an estimate can be prepared by the analyst himself or estimates by both private and government economists are often available. From this GNP estimate, an estimate of NFGCP is derived. As indicated in the table, using an estimate of $859 billion of GNP for 1968 results in an estimate of $473.1 billion of NFGCP, using the correlation equation given in the footnote of the table. This equation reflects the relationship between these two variables that has prevailed for the 1948–67 period. The r^2 is relatively high at .998 and the deviations of the actual from the computed figure fall within $3.26 billion about two-thirds of the time.[6]

The second step in the analysis is to make an assumption about the movement of prices in the NFGCP area. In this connection the forecaster can be materially helped by either plotting the price deflator on a semilogarithmic grid, as in Chart I, or alternatively by analyzing the quarter-to-quarter changes in this time series and combining this analysis with a general consideration of the pricing environment.

Line 5 is derived by dividing the current dollar NFGCP figure in line 3 by the price deflator in line 4, thereby obtaining NFGCP in constant 1958 dollars.

The next step in the analysis is to determine unit costs. Lines 6, 7, and 8 reflect the nonlabor costs and are relatively easy to estimate, assuming no changes in either depreciation practices or in excise tax laws. If capital consumption allowances, indirect business taxes, and interest in current dollars are plotted on a semilogarithmic grid, it will be seen that they fluctuate relatively little. Consequently, the analyst can, with a fair degree of safety, merely extrapolate recent trends over the forecast period. Having derived the dollar amounts for each factor, they can be divided into NFGCP on line 5 in order to derive the respective unit costs.

The unit employee compensation figure is somewhat more difficult to estimate and also is a more critical figure because of its size. The easiest procedure for the analyst is to make his own independent judgment of

---

[6] As Chart I indicates, NFGCP is more volatile than GNP and thus the equation, which is linear, tends to be less accurate at turning points. However, the regression was run on a percentage change basis and a first difference basis, but the percentage of variance explained and the standard error were inferior to the equation being used. Other unsuccessful attempts to improve the regression include removing from GNP certain components which may not be related to NFGCP.

what increases in productivity and hourly labor costs he anticipates for the forecast period. For example, an increase of 6 percent in hourly compensation and 3 percent in productivity would result roughly in a 3 percent increase in unit labor costs. As an alternative, the BLS data referred to earlier show quarter-to-quarter increases in output, manhours, output per manhour, hourly compensation, and unit labor costs. These data coupled with knowledge of the current labor scene should enable the forecaster to come up with a reasonable estimate of unit labor cost.

When these four computations are completed, corporate profits plus inventory valuation adjustment (line 10) can be derived by subtracting the total of these four unit costs from the price deflator, with the decimal point moved two places to the left. The corporate profits per unit can then be multiplied by real NFGCP (line 5) in order to derive the dollar corporate profits in the nonfinancial sector plus inventory valuation adjustment (line 12).

To this figure must be added an estimate of the inventory valuation adjustment, which can be done most simply by a rough approximation based on recent wholesale price changes and also the recent pattern of the IVA as shown in Chart VIII. The addition or subtraction of the inventory valuation adjustment produces an estimate of nonfinancial corporate profits (line 14), to which can then be added an estimate of corporate profits in financial sector (line 15). This figure can be estimated either by a rough approximation of recent profit trends in banks and other major financial institutions, or, alternatively, by extrapolating recent quarter-to-quarter increases in these profits as published by the Commerce Department. Unfortunately, the uncertainty of future underwriting losses in the nonlife insurance carriers referred to earlier introduces an element of unpredictability in this estimate, but the relatively small size of their contribution to total profits minimizes their impact on the total estimate.

With respect to taxes, the tax rate in the nonfinancial and financial areas should be treated separately because the implicit tax rates are different. The usual procedure is to extrapolate the implicit tax rate used by Commerce in the quarterly profits reports. For 1968 the rate reflects the surcharge of 10 percent, effective January 1. Having computed the appropriate taxes for the nonfinancial and financial area, corporate profits after taxes are derived for each of these sectors. To this computation must be added an estimate of rest of the world profits, which then gives the answer of total corporate profits after tax. This rest of the world estimate can best be made by extrapolating recent trends, although consideration must be given to such developments as the impact of government programs to improve the balance of payments.

The last five lines of Table I indicate a way to derive the usual published estimates of corporate profits. To total corporate profits after tax (line 25) must be added the tax on domestic profits (line 20), which gives total corporate profits before tax; from this total can be added or subtracted the inventory valuation adjustment (line 13). The result will be total corporate profits before taxes and inventory valuation adjustment.

ADDITIONAL USES OF NEW PROFITS DATA

The foregoing description indicates a method of forecasting corporate profits that insures the inclusion of all pertinent factors and also simplifies the judgments that must be made. The most critical factors are the estimates for GNP, the price deflator for NFGCP, and the estimate of unit labor costs. Most of the other variables perform in a relatively predictable fashion over the short term and can be readily estimated from a chart plotting their quarterly movements.

A second advantage of the suggested analysis is that it facilitates testing profits results for various assumptions about GNP, price changes, or unit labor costs. The nonlabor costs and other profits components would not be materially affected. For example, if the price deflator assumed for NFGCP in 1968 were 4 percent above that of 1967 instead of the 3.1 percent increase assumed in Table I, line 4 on the table would be 114.8 and NFGCP in 1958 dollars (line 5) would be $412.1 billion. Unit profits (line 10) would rise to .184 and nonfinancial corporate profits plus IVA (line 12) would be $75.8 billion. The IVA (line 13) would be somewhat larger and working the figures down to profits after taxes (line 24), profits would be about $2.5 billion higher, or 5 percent, more than the $49.8 billion estimated for 1968. Similarly, if unit labor costs (line 9) were up 4 percent in 1968 compared with 1967 instead of the 3.3 percent increase estimated on the table, unit profits (line 10) would be .169 and profits after taxes (line 24) would be about $800 million less. As a result of the availability of the new data and the procedure outlined in the table, it is relatively easy now to experiment with the impact of various economic assumptions on profits.

A third advantage of the suggested analysis is that, using the tabular format provided, an analyst can readily follow the quarterly changes in factors affecting profits. For example, an examination of recent quarterly profits data reveals that, beginning in the fourth quarter of 1967, inventory profits have once again become a significant contributor to total profits. As another example, unit profits in the second quarter of 1968 rose 4.7 percent from the first quarter, after five quarters of relative stability. This improvement was caused by the stability of unit labor costs coupled with an 0.9 percent price increase. An examination of the BLS data indicates that the rise in hourly compensation in the second quarter was offset by a comparable increase in productivity. A continuation of this trend is by no means certain, but the evidence is worth following because it is contrary to the generally accepted opinions of what is occurring in the profits area.

For the financial analyst, this information does not readily translate into forecasts for individual companies, which are affected not only by the economic environment but also by competitive factors, material costs, and other developments of a more particular nature. The analyst must extend his analysis to industries and companies and determine whether their sales and costs patterns differ from the economic environment in which they operate. However, the approach described above does give the analyst a better understanding of the broad economic forces that influence profits, thus helping to bridge that elusive gap between economics and investment management.

THE LATEST TOOLS FOR PROFIT ANALYSIS *

GRACE WICKERSHAM

Vice President and Economist
Security Pacific National Bank

Corporate profits must rank near interest rates and inventories as one of the more volatile economic statistics to project. During the turning points of a business cycle, the volatility in profits becomes even more pronounced, and the ability to project profits accurately becomes impaired. Nonetheless, profits are a critical factor influencing capital spending, pricing, and employment requirements. Thus, projections of earnings may provide an insight into the future path of business activity—an insight that is especially opportune during a recessionary period. Recognizing the difficulties of accurately forecasting corporate profits, especially in the current recessionary framework, this analysis brazenly forges ahead to discuss the outlook for profits through 1980 and some of the factors affecting profitability.

This projection of corporate earnings is based upon the likely impact that the economy will have on nonfinancial corporate (NFC) production and costs through 1980. Thus, the starting point for the profit outlook is a brief description of the 1980 outlook for the total economy. That description will be followed by an analysis of the trends in NFC income and costs. Nonfinancial corporations are highlighted since their book profits typically account for about 80 to 85 percent of total reported profits. Additionally, these corporations generally bear the brunt of the cyclical influences on profitability.

1980 Economic Outlook

The economic outlook that underlies the corporate earnings projections includes a recession that will persist for five quarters—from the second quarter of 1979 through the first half of 1980—and that will result in an estimated 3 percent decline in peak-to-trough output. This recession is expected to be consumer-led, with significant cutbacks in spending for durable goods, notably cars. High rates of inflation, especially in the area of food and fuel prices, should cut into the volume of spending for other consumer goods and services. Record short-term interest rates and a likely slowdown in the growth of the money supply should produce a marked contraction in homebuilding activity. The decline in housing starts, however, may be limited, as the tax/inflation advantages of homeownership act to support the demand for homes. Although capital spending should be adversely affected by slumping retail sales and declining factory operating rates, the expected downturn in capital spending may be the mildest of the postwar period. Inventory investment should be a drag on economic activity, holding down real growth through the third quarter of 1980.

As summarized in Table I, real growth is projected to decline 1.5 percent in 1980, following a 1.3 percent advance in 1979. Inflationary pressures should remain intense even with the business downturn. The pass-through of the higher cost of imported oil will continue to push up prices, and a catch up in wage demands to compensate for losses in real wages should temper the lowering in the inflation rate. Thus, the GNP price deflator is projected to average 9.1 percent higher for both 1979 and 1980. On a year-end to year-end comparison, consumer prices are likely to be 12 percent higher this year and 9 percent higher next year.

---

*Based on the paper, "The Outlook for Corporate Earnings through 1980," presented at the 21st annual meeting of the National Association of Business Economists, <u>October, 1979,</u> New York City.

TABLE I

Corporate Profits Outlook
(Billions of Dollars)

	1977A	1978A	% Change	1979F	% Change	1980F	% Change
1. Gross National Product (current $)	1899.5	2127.6	12.0	2351.1	10.5	2526.4	7.6
2. Gross National Product (1972 $)	1340.5	1399.2	4.4	1417.2	1.3	1395.8	-1.5
3. GNP Price Deflator	141.7	152.1	7.3	165.9	9.1	181.0	9.1
4. Corporate Profits Before Taxes with CCA and IVA Adjustment	150.0	167.7	11.8	175.2	4.5	159.4	-9.0
5. CCA Adjustment	-12.0	-13.1	--	-14.8	--	-15.8	--
6. IVA Adjustment	-15.2	-25.2	--	-35.9	--	-29.5	--
7. Corporate Profits Before Taxes	177.1	206.0	16.3	225.8	9.6	204.6	-9.4
8. Corporate Profits After Taxes	104.5	121.5	16.3	137.0	12.8	123.5	-9.9
9. CCA per Corporate Books	109.3	119.8	9.6	132.2	10.4	149.0	12.7
10. CPAT plus CCA	213.8	241.3	12.9	269.2	11.6	272.5	1.2
11. Dividends	42.1	47.2	12.1	52.6	11.4	55.1	4.8
12. Cash Flow After Dividends	171.7	194.1	13.0	216.6	11.6	217.4	0.4
13. Capital Expenditures	135.8	153.8	13.3	172.9	12.4	184.4	6.7
14. Line 13 as % of Line 12	79.1	79.2	--	79.8	--	84.8	--
15. Compensation per hour worked (NFC)	8.2	9.2	--	9.5	--	9.9	--
16. Output per hour worked (NFC)	1.3	1.8	--	-0.8	--	-0.5	--
17. Unit Labor Costs (NFC)	6.8	7.3	--	9.8	--	10.4	--

A = Actual
F = Forecast
NFC = Nonfinancial Corporation

Security Pacific Corporation
September 19, 1979

NFC Income

The corporate profit forecasting method used at Security Pacific Bank emphasizes the likely trends in the nonfinancial corporate (NFC) sector. Gross domestic product of nonfinancial corporations accounts for approximately 55 to 60 percent of total GNP. Since the late 1950's, this relatively stable share of nominal income resulted from a steady rise in real NFC output as a share of real GNP and from a declining ratio between the NFC and GNP price deflators. During recession years, however, the opposite pattern developed, and real NFC product declined relative to real GNP, and the NFC inflation rate outpaced the overall rate of inflation.

In looking at the outlook for nonfinancial corporations, it may be important to isolate those spending and pricing developments that are outside the NFC sector and, thus, ascertain the possible influences on the ratio between the NFC segment and the total economy. Generally, nonfinancial corporations are affected by consumer spending on goods, business investment activity, nonagricultural exports, and homebuilding activity. Government transfer and wage payouts, the imputed rental value of housing, most financial costs, and U.S. imports are major sectors that are not part of the NFC income stream. Pricing by the farm and imports sectors typically leads NFC pricing trends.

In early 1979 the rapid run-up in the price of imported oil and farm products caused the NFC deflator to slip as a share of the GNP price deflator. Meanwhile, NFC growth in the first quarter rose faster than total real growth, reflecting, in part, consumer efforts to cut spending on sharply higher priced items. In the second quarter the pattern of these ratios reversed slightly, with NFC prices increasing faster than the GNP deflator, due to the pass-through of higher imported oil costs into higher domestic prices for petroleum-based products. Additionally, farm prices moderated, while prices of industrial commodities accelerated. NFC real output slipped modestly as a share of total output, due in large measure to the marked downturn in consumer goods spending, capital spending and U.S. export shipments.

During the second half of 1979 NFC prices should rise at a slightly faster rate than the overall rate of inflation, mainly from the filtering of the higher prices for imported oil through the domestic pricing system. Over the course of 1980 NFC inflation may advance at a slightly lower rate than the rate of inflation, as sluggish sales activity gradually slows price increases in the private economy.

During the second half of this year, real NFC income should decline as a share of real GNP, with higher prices curbing the demand for NFC products. The expected decline in auto sales and capital spending during the fourth quarter of this year should be a major factor in the slippage in the growth share. For all of 1980, as indicated in Table I real output in the NFC sector is projected to decline 1.7 percent compared with the 1.5 percent drop estimated for the total economy. Sluggishness in spending for consumer and business durable goods plus countercyclical support from the government will account for much of the disparity between the NFC and total growth rates.

NFC Cost Trends

Many of the costs measured by the GNP accounting of the NFC sector are fixed and not directly tied to the pace of current production. Fixed costs include the depreciation of the existing capital stock. Interest payments on long-term debt are a fixed cost, while short-term financing of inventories is considered a variable cost. Indirect business taxes are tied to current business activity through the sales and excise taxes, but indirect business taxes also include the fixed charge of property taxes. Employee compensation costs are variable, reflecting changes in employment caused by fluctuations in sales. The increased number of nonproduction-related workers, however, may be lessening the cyclical influences in employee compensation. Table II details the income and cost trends for nonfinancial corporations expected through 1980. The following comments highlight some of the factors influencing NFC costs over the next year.

TABLE II

Corporate Profits, 1978-1980
(Billions of Dollars)

	1978A	% Change	1979F	% Change	1980F	% Change
Gross National Product	2127.6	12.0	2351.1	10.5	2526.4	7.6
NFC Product	1246.9	12.7	1378.6	10.6	1476.8	7.1
% of GNP	58.6	--	58.6	--	58.5	--
GNP Price Deflator	152.1	7.3	165.9	9.1	181.0	9.1
NFC Price Deflator	152.3	6.1	165.0	8.3	179.9	9.0
% of GNP Price Deflator	100.1	--	99.5	--	99.4	--
GNP 1972 $	1399.2	4.4	1417.2	1.3	1395.8	-1.5
NFC Product 1972 $	818.7	6.2	835.5	2.1	821.0	-1.7
% of GNP 1972 $	58.5	--	59.0	--	58.8	--
NFC Costs:						
Capital Consumption Allowance	126.9	9.4	139.9	10.2	159.0	13.7
Indirect Business Taxes	117.2	8.7	124.8	6.5	134.9	8.1
Net Interest	39.7	18.9	46.4	16.9	51.0	9.9
Employee Compensation	834.7	13.9	935.8	12.1	1014.8	8.4
Profits, Adjusted	128.3	10.1	132.9	3.6	117.5	-11.6
NFC Unit Costs:						
Capital Consumption Allowance	.155	2.7	.167	7.7	.194	16.2
Indirect Business Taxes	.143	2.1	.149	4.2	.164	10.1
Net Interest	.048	11.6	.056	16.7	.062	10.7
Employee Compensation	1.020	7.3	1.119	9.7	1.236	10.4
Profits, Adjusted	.157	4.0	.159	1.3	.143	-10.1
NFC Inventory Valuation Adjustment	-25.2	--	-35.9	--	-29.5	--
Capital Consumption Adjustment	-12.6	--	-13.9	--	-14.8	--
Profits Before Taxes	166.1	15.8	182.6	9.9	162.0	-11.4
Taxes	68.8	15.4	72.3	5.1	64.4	-10.9
Profits After Taxes	97.4	16.2	110.3	13.2	97.6	-11.5
Financial Corporations						
Profits Before Taxes	29.7	24.8	31.7	6.7	32.0	0.9
Taxes	15.7	20.8	16.5	5.1	16.8	1.8
Profits After Taxes	14.0	29.6	15.2	8.6	15.2	NC
Rest of the World Profits	10.2	4.1	11.5	12.8	10.9	-5.2
Total Profits Before Taxes	206.0	16.3	225.8	9.6	204.6	-9.4
Taxes	84.5	16.4	88.8	5.1	81.1	-8.7
Profits After Taxes	121.5	16.3	137.0	12.8	123.5	-9.9

NFC = Nonfinancial Corporate
A = Actual
F = Forecast

Capital consumption allowances, according to the GNP accounting, are based upon the replacement cost of plant and equipment, not necessarily the depreciation allowed under the tax schedules. These charges should increase rapidly through 1980, due to an expected high rate of inflation in the capital goods sector.

Net interest charges should continue to grow markedly in 1979 reflecting the sharp rise in business loans, the increase in the corporate bond calendar, and the high short- and long-term interest rates—all of which have already occurred this year. The rise in net interest costs should moderate during 1980 due to a projected lowering in interest rates—notably, short-term rates—and to a slowdown in business borrowing.

The growth in indirect business taxes slowed during the second half of 1978 and again in early 1979. This slowdown largely reflected the drop in California business property taxes that resulted from the passage of Proposition 13. During 1980, the projected slowing in sales growth should produce a corresponding moderation in the growth of business sales receipts. The likely absence of major new business property tax relief, however, will mean that the growth in indirect business taxes in 1980 should outpace the rise projected for 1979.

Employee compensation costs account for about 60 to 70 percent of total unit costs and profits in the NFC sector, and, consequently, increases in the wage bill represent a major factor determining NFC pricing and profitability. Employee compensation costs should be affected by the declines in employment expected through the first half of 1980 and the generally sluggish job gains expected in the final quarters of next year. The employee wage bill, however, will be boosted by the impact of the legislated increase in social security taxes, as well as by increased wage rates. The pushing up of wage rates will play a major role in boosting employee compensation costs. Although the 6.9 percent—or 20¢/hour—rise in the minimum wage rate scheduled for January 1, 1980, is less than the 9.4 percent increase of this year, the increase in the minimum wage rate acts to scale up the wage rates for jobs classified above the minimum wage. The pattern recently set in major union bargaining sessions should become the basis for sizable increases in wage rates during upcoming labor contract bargaining. Both the unionized and nonunionized segments of the work force are likely to demand substantial wage boosts to make up for prior losses in real earnings caused by the rapid acceleration in prices.

Wage costs, therefore, should exert a considerable force upon NFC profitability next year. Rising compensation costs, declining hours worked, and declining output should translate into a substantial rise in unit labor costs over the next year. Hourly compensation costs are projected to increase 9.9 percent in 1980, compared with the 9.5 percent rate estimated for 1979. Productivity is projected to decline, on average, in 1979 and 1980, although gains should be recorded in the second half of next year due to the expected mild recovery in output. Unit labor costs should increase 9.8 percent this year and 10.4 percent during 1980, thus representing a sizable addition to NFC costs and a drain on corporate profitability.

With corporate output declining and costs continuing to advance, unit profits should decline in the second half of 1979 and in the first half of 1980. Unit labor costs are projected to comprise 67.8 percent of total NFC costs and profits during 1979, up 0.8 percentage points from the 1978 share, while the unit labor costs share should rise to 68.7 percent in 1980. Unit nonlabor costs should increase as a share of total costs and profits next year, representing 23.3 percent of the toal compared with 22.5 percent in 1979. These cost increases will place a squeeze on unit profits and the profit share will drop from 10.3 percent of the total in 1978 to 9.6 percent in 1979 and 7.9 percent in 1980. This 7.9 percent share would represent the lowest level since 1974, thus indicating the recession's adverse impact on corporate earning potential. Table III summarizes NFC unit cost and profit activity since 1966, highlighting the growth and share trends affecting NFC pricing.

TABLE III

Cost Per Unit of Real Output-Nonfinancial Sector
(1972=100)

Year	Total Unit Costs and Profits	CCA	IBT	Net Int.	Total UNLC	Labor Costs	Unit Profits
1966	.808	.067	.080	.014	.161	.513	.134
1967	.830	.072	.084	.016	.172	.535	.123
1968	.857	.074	.089	.017	.180	.553	.124
1969	.892	.079	.094	.022	.195	.589	.109
1970	.933	.088	.103	.028	.219	.628	.086
1971	.973	.094	.110	.029	.233	.645	.095
1972	1.000	.093	.110	.028	.231	.661	.107
1973	1.044	.095	.112	.032	.239	.699	.105
1974	1.164	.116	.123	.043	.282	.796	.086
1975	1.285	.142	.136	.045	.323	.848	.113
1976	1.353	.146	.137	.042	.325	.890	.138
1977	1.436	.151	.140	.043	.334	.951	.151
1978	1.523	.155	.143	.048	.347	1.020	.157
1979F	1.650	.167	.149	.056	.372	1.119	.159
1980F	1.799	.194	.164	.062	.420	1.236	.143

Compound Annual Rates of Change

Year	Total Unit Costs and Profits	CCA	IBT	Net Int.	Total UNLC	Labor Costs	Unit Profits
1966 - 1980	5.88	7.89	5.26	11.21	7.1	6.48	0.47
1966 - 1970	3.66	7.05	6.52	18.92	8.00	5.19	-10.49
1970 - 1980	6.79	7.22	4.76	8.27	6.73	7.01	5.22
1966 - 1974	4.67	7.10	5.52	15.06	7.26	5.65	- 5.39
1974 - 1980	7.53	8.95	4.91	6.29	6.86	7.61	8.84

Percentage Analysis of Unit Costs & Profits-Nonfinancial Sector

Year	CCA	IBT	Net Int.	Total UNLC	Labor Costs	Unit Profits
1966	8.3	9.9	1.7	19.9	63.5	16.6
1967	8.7	10.1	1.9	20.7	64.5	14.8
1968	8.6	10.4	2.0	21.0	64.5	14.5
1969	8.9	10.5	2.5	21.9	66.0	9.6
1970	9.4	11.0	3.0	23.5	67.3	9.2
1971	9.7	11.3	3.0	23.9	66.3	9.8
1972	9.3	11.0	2.8	23.1	66.1	10.7
1973	9.1	10.7	3.1	22.9	67.0	10.1
1974	10.0	10.6	3.7	24.2	68.4	7.4
1975	11.0	10.6	3.5	25.1	66.0	8.8
1976	10.8	10.0	3.1	23.9	65.8	10.3
1977	10.5	9.7	3.1	23.9	66.2	10.5
1978	10.2	9.4	3.2	22.8	67.0	10.3
1979F	10.1	9.0	3.4	22.5	67.8	9.6
1980F	10.8	9.1	3.4	23.3	68.7	7.9

F = Forecast

Unit profits multiplied by real NFC yields an estimate of operating profits. During 1979, operating profits of nonfinancial corporations are projected to advance 3.6 percent. Most of that gain occurred in the first quarter, with operating profits in the final three quarters of this year remaining below the first quarter's level. In 1980, the cost squeeze on unit profits will produce an 11.6 percent decline in operating profits.

Adjustment to Profits

Inventory profits and the adjustment for the under-depreciation of capital assets allowed under the tax laws have become a significant portion of reported book profits over the past ten years, as can be noted in Table IV. Notably, during the inflationary environment that has persisted since 1973, the share of the combined totals of the inventory valuation and the capital consumption allowance adjustments has ranged from a low of 14.4 percent of pretax book profits to a high of 34.1 percent—a marked contrast to earlier in the postwar period when these adjustments were an insignificant or negative influence on book profits. The July revisions of the GNP accounts revealed that tax depreciation was a greater proportion of the replacement costs of capital than had been reported earlier. Thus, the capital consumption adjustment was revised down by an average of $2.9 billion for the 1976-78 period, causing the inflation adjustments to profits to represent a smaller share of book profits than had previously been reported.

The rapid acceleration in wholesale price inflation in the first of this year boosted inventory profits to the $40 billion realm. Some easing in wholesale price inflation expected over the second half of 1979 and through 1980 should gradually lower inventory profits. Efforts to trim inventory holdings will also reduce the level of inventory profits during 1980. Thus, inventory profits are likely to decline as a share of book profits, from an estimated 15.9 percent ratio in 1979 to 14.4 percent during 1980.

The behavior of the capital consumption adjustment is closely tied to changes in tax law. Although it is likely that some liberalizations in tax depreciation treatment may be approved during 1980, concern over the inflationary implications of a tax cut and an increased federal budget deficit may cause any tax changes to be delayed until late in 1980. High rates of inflation in the capital spending area and a delay in the passage of liberalized depreciation will cause the CCA adjustment to continue to widen in 1980, equalling 7.7 percent of reported profits next year.

Profit Recap

Total pretax book profits are projected to increase 9.6 percent in 1979, while the recession squeeze on sales and a continued rapid increase in costs—notably, labor costs—will produce a 9.5 percent decline in reported 1980 earnings. Book profits of nonfinancial corporations will register an 11.3 percent decline in 1980 following a 10 percent advance this year. A softening in credit demand will limit the growth in financial corporate profits, with these earnings projected to advance 0.9 percent in 1980 after a 6.8 percent gain in 1979. Remissions of foreign branch profits may suffer from an expected slowing in worldwide business activity, with a 5.2 percent drop forecast for 1980.

Assuming no major cut in corporate tax rates, aftertax earnings should fall during 1980 at a slightly faster rate than pretax profits. Following a 12.8 percent advance in 1979, aftertax profits are projected to be 9.9 percent lower next year. Total profits should decline on a quarter-over-quarter basis through the second quarter of 1980, causing a 15.5 percent peak-to-trough drop in reported earnings. During the 1973-75 recession, this same comparison showed a 27 percent profit decline. Although profits are projected to turn up by the third quarter of next year, earnings should be lower, on a year-over-year basis, throughout the four quarters of 1980.

Total corporate profits will decline as a share of GNP during the recession year. For all of 1980 pretax profits will represent 8.1 percent of GNP (see Table V), down 1.5 percentage points from the 1979 estimated share. Aftertax earnings should sink to 4.9 percent of GNP, following a 5.8 percent margin this year. Although the profit comparison may appear mild relative to the 1973-75 experience, the downturn in earnings—especially on an inflation-adjusted basis—may act as an added deterrent to capital investment.

TABLE IV

IVA and CCA Adjustments as a Percent of Corporate Profits Before Tax

Year	Corporate Profits Before Tax	IVA	IVA as a % of CPBT	CCA Adjustment	CCA Adj. as a % of CPBT	Total Adjustments as a % of CPBT
1966	80.7	- 2.7	2.6	3.9	- 4.8	- 2.2
1967	77.3	- 1.7	2.2	3.7	- 4.8	- 2.6
1968	85.6	- 3.4	4.0	3.7	- 4.3	- 0.3
1969	83.4	- 5.5	6.6	3.5	- 4.2	2.4
1970	71.5	- 5.1	7.1	1.5	- 2.1	5.0
1971	82.0	- 5.0	6.1	0.3	- 0.4	5.7
1972	96.2	- 6.6	6.9	2.5	- 2.6	4.3
1973	115.8	-18.6	16.1	1.9	- 1.6	14.4
1974	126.9	-40.4	31.8	- 2.9	2.3	34.1
1975	120.4	-12.4	10.3	-12.0	10.0	20.3
1976	156.0	-14.6	9.4	-14.5	9.3	18.7
1977	177.1	-15.2	8.6	-12.0	6.8	15.4
1978	206.0	-25.2	12.2	-13.1	6.4	18.6
1979F	225.8	-35.9	15.9	-14.8	6.6	22.5
1980F	204.6	-29.5	14.4	-15.8	7.7	22.1

F = Forecast

TABLE V

Corporate Profits as a Percent of GNP
(Billions of Dollars)

Year	GNP	Profits Before Tax	Profits After Tax	Profits as a % of GNP Before Tax	Profits as a % of GNP After Tax
1966	753.0	80.7	47.1	10.7	6.3
1967	796.3	77.3	44.9	9.7	5.6
1968	868.5	85.6	46.2	9.9	5.3
1969	935.5	83.4	43.8	8.9	4.7
1970	982.4	71.5	37.0	7.3	3.8
1971	1063.4	82.0	44.3	7.7	4.2
1972	1171.1	96.2	54.6	8.2	4.7
1973	1306.6	115.8	67.1	8.9	5.1
1974	1412.9	126.9	74.5	9.0	5.3
1975	1528.8	120.4	70.6	7.9	4.6
1976	1702.2	156.0	92.2	9.2	5.4
1977	1899.5	177.1	104.5	9.3	5.5
1978	2127.6	206.0	121.5	9.7	5.7
1979F	2351.1	225.8	137.0	9.6	5.8
1980F	2526.4	204.6	123.5	8.1	4.9

F = Forecast

Stock prices and the business cycle*

Profits, interest rates, stock prices, and business activity weave complex patterns, but they do give meaningful signals for investors and forecasters.

Geoffrey H. Moore

To what extent has the changing character of the business cycle since World War II affected the behavior of stock prices and the traditional relationships between stock prices and swings in business activity? Or, to put the question somewhat differently, do stock prices behave during the milder fluctuations now referred to as "growth cycles" as they do during the wider fluctuations that typify the term "business cycles"? Indeed, what patterns have emerged from an analysis of the relationships among stock prices, bond prices, corporate profits, and business activity during the postwar years?

In a recent study for the National Bureau of Economic Research, Isle Mintz identified eight growth cycles during 1948-70.[1] Five of the periods of slowdown overlap the business cycle recessions of 1949, 1954, 1958, 1961, and 1970, beginning one or two quarters earlier but ending at about the same time. These five, of course, were the more serious episodes. The other three milder slowdowns occurred in 1951-52, 1962-63, and 1966-67, interrupting the business cycle expansions of 1949-53 and of 1961-69. A ninth slowdown began in the spring of 1973 and remained moderate in severity until the autumn of 1974. It is now clear that this slowdown will encompass a recession, making it the sixth one to do so since 1948.

During the five previous slowdowns that overlapped business cycle recessions, Gross National Product in constant dollars declined, though not in every quarter, at average rates ranging from a minus 1/2% per year in the mildest to minus 2½% per year in the sharpest. In the other three slowdowns, real GNP continued to grow, in most quarters, at rates that averaged about 2½% per year in 1951-52, 3½% in 1962-63, and 3% in 1966-67. During the eight intervening upswings, on the other hand, growth rates ranged from 4% to nearly 12% and averaged 6% per year.

As will be seen, significant changes in stock prices have been associated with even the milder slowdowns in economic growth.

STOCK BEHAVIOR AND BUSINESS ACTIVITY

First let us consider the question whether stock prices are higher at the end of an upswing in economic growth than at the beginning. The answer, as column 5 of Table 1 shows, at least for the period since 1948, is "invariably." The answer to the alternative question, are stock prices lower at the end of the downswing in growth than at the beginning, is less clear-cut. On three occasions they were lower (the current downswing may make it four, but it has not yet ended), but on four occasions they were higher. Nevertheless, the difference in the size of the advances during upswings in growth compared with downswings is substantial. The average rise in Standard and Poor's index of 500 common stock prices during the eight upswings was 24%; the average for the eight downswings was 4%. Expressed as annual rates, the gain during upswings was 11% per year; during downswings, less than 4% per year. Clearly it is of importance from the investor's point of view to know when the turns in the growth cycle occur.

The reason why stock prices were not always lower at the end of a slowdown in economic growth than at the beginning is not that stocks were not depressed by developments associated with the slowdown, but rather that they began to decline sooner and to recover earlier than economic activity as a

---

* This paper is an adaptation and extension of the article on "Security Markets and Business Cycles," published in the *Financial Analyst's Handbook*, Dow Jones-Irwin, Inc., 1975; excerpts are used with the permission of the publisher.

1. Footnotes appear at the end of the article.

© Spring 1975 by *The Journal of Portfolio Management*

Table 1

Changes in Standard & Poor's Index of Common Stock Prices during Cycles in Economic Growth, 1948-73

Date of Growth Cycle[a]		Level of Index at Growth Cycle		Change during Growth Cycle		Length of Growth Cycle		Change per Year during Growth Cycle	
High (1)	Low (2)	High (3) (1941-43=10)	Low (4)	Up-swing (5) (percent)	Down-swing (6)	Up-swing (7) (months)	Down-swing (8)	Up-swing (9) (percent)	Down-swing (10)
7/48		16.4							
	10/49		15.9		-3		15		-2.4
6/51		21.6		+35		20		+20.2	
	6/52		24.4		+13		12		+13.0
3/53		26.0		+7		9		+9.4	
	8/54		30.7		+18		17		+12.5
2/57		43.5		+42		30		+15.1	
	5/58		43.7		0		15		0
2/60		55.8		+28		21		+11.2	
	2/61		62.2		+11		12		+11.0
4/62		68.0		+9		14		+7.7	
	3/63		65.7		-3		11		-3.3
6/66		86.1		+31		39		+8.7	
	10/67		95.7		+11		16		+8.1
3/69		99.3		+4		17		+2.8	
	11/70		84.3		-15		20		-9.3
3/73		112.4		+33		28		+13.0	
Average				+24	+4	22	15	+11.0	+3.7

a   Ilse Mintz, Dating United States Growth Cycles, Explorations in Economic Research, National Bureau of Economic Research, Vol. 1, No. 1, Summer 1974, p. 60.

whole. For example, in 1953-54, Standard and Poor's index reached its highest monthly average in January, 1953, two months before the growth cycle high in March. The decline in the index continued until September, 1953. From then on it rose vigorously so that by the time the August, 1954 trough in the growth cycle had arrived, the index was 18% higher than its level at the previous business cycle peak. The January-September, 1953 decline in the index was evidently associated with the economic slowdown but occurred earlier.

Table 2 shows that this tendency for stock prices to "lead" the growth cycle is highly characteristic. It has happened at every high and low in the growth cycle since 1948 except in 1951-52, when no decline in stock prices occurred. The average lead is around five months, but there have been wide variations around the average, ranging from one month to twelve. Since Table 2 records all the cyclical peaks and troughs in the stock price index, it is clear that no cyclical swing in the market occurred without an accompanying swing in the growth cycle. Only one growth cycle downswing occurred, that of 1951-52, without a cyclical decline in the market.

STOCKS, PROFITS, AND INTEREST RATES

Does the systematic lead in stock prices mean that the stock market predicts turns in the growth cycle? Or does it mean that it is reacting to other developments that also lead? Possibly there are elements of both, but it is worth examining the behavior of two factors bearing on stock prices that may help to account for the lead: profits and interest rates.

Table 3 pulls together some relevant information on profits. Although the turning points in profits and in stock prices do not occur at precisely the same time (the leads would be identical if they did), the tendency is clearly in that direction.[2] Chart 1 shows

Table 2

Leads and Lags of Standard & Poor's Common Stock Price Index
at Growth Cycle Highs and Lows, 1948-73

Date of Growth Cycle		Date of Stock Price Index		Lead (-) or Lag (+) in Months, at Growth Cycle	
High	Low	High	Low	High	Low
7/48		6/48		-1	
	10/49		6/49		-4
6/51		n.s.		n.t.	
	6/52		n.s.		n.t.
3/53		1/53		-2	
	8/54		9/53		-11
2/57		7/56		-7	
	5/58		12/57		-5
2/60		7/59		-7	
	2/61		10/60		-4
4/62		12/61		-4	
	3/63		6/62		-9
6/66		1/66		-5	
	10/67		10/66		-12
3/69		12/68		-3	
	11/70		6/70		-5
3/73		1/73		-2	
Median Lead or Lag					
at highs				-3.5	
at lows					-5
at all turns					-5

n.s. = no specific cycle
n.t. = no timing comparison

the relationship, from which it appears that long leads in profits are associated with long leads in stock prices, at both highs and lows in the growth cycle. It seems reasonable to suppose that promptly available information and astute guesses about profit trends would

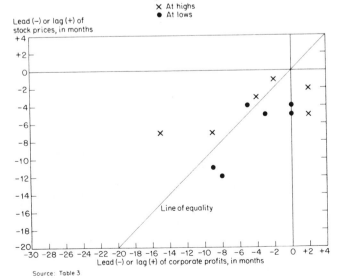

Chart 1
Leads or Lags of Profits and Stock Prices
at Growth Cycle Highs and Lows

× At highs
● At lows

Lead (−) or lag (+) of stock prices, in months

Lead (−) or lag (+) of corporate profits, in months

Source: Table 3

influence the market and help to account for its propensity to lead the growth cycle and occasionally to lead profits. Since other leading indicators such as new orders, housing starts, defense contracts, and construction contracts also have a bearing upon profit prospects, they too influence the thinking of investors about the value of equities and contribute to the lead of stock prices. Unit costs of production, which markedly affect the cyclical movements of unit profits, help to explain the lead in profits and hence the lead in stock prices.[3]

Although increases in profits are likely to have a favorable effect on stock prices, increases in interest rates are likely to have an unfavorable effect. The higher the discount rate applied to future earnings, the lower the capital value of the equity. The higher the yield on bonds, the more attractive they become as an alternative to holding common stocks. Higher interest rates and the accompanying reduced availability of credit may diminish the propensity of investors to borrow in order to buy stocks. Higher interest rates increase the cost of doing business, notably the cost of holding inventory and of accounts receivable, and hence may adversely affect profit margins in certain trades. Thus increases in interest rates tend to depress stock prices, and the sharper the rise the greater this effect is likely to be.

Now interest rates often don't begin to rise, or don't begin to rise rapidly, for some months after an upswing in the growth cycle gets underway. Often they rise fastest in the late stages of the upswing as a result of restrictions on the supply of money and credit. Such a development can depress the stock market even though business activity itself is still expanding rapidly. If this surge in interest rates is coupled with a profit squeeze that also antedates the downturn in growth, as frequently happens, stock prices can drop sharply even while business is good and getting better.

A similar sequence of events during a growth cycle contraction could help to account for upturns in stock prices prior to the upturn in business. The fall in interest rates boosts the market for stocks, and if the customary early upturn in profits also occurs, optimism among investors in common stocks is doubly justified even though business activity is still depressed and sliding downwards.

INTEREST RATE LEADS AND LAGS

If this reasoning is correct, one would expect that upturns in interest rates would lead downturns in stock prices and downturns in interest rates would lead upturns in stock prices, and that variations in the length of the lead of interest rates (treated invertedly)

Table 3

Leads and Lags of Corporate Profits and Stock Prices
at Growth Cycle Highs and Lows, 1948-73

Date of Growth Cycle		Date of Corporate Profits		Lead (−) or Lag (+), in Months					
				of Corporate Profits at Growth Cycle		of Stock Prices at Growth Cycle		of Profits at Stock Price	
High	Low	High[a]	Low[a]	High	Low	High	Low	High	Low
7/48		5/48		−2		−1		−1	
	10/49		5/49		−5		−4		−1
6/51		11/50		−7		n.t.		n.t.	
	6/52		8/52		+2		n.t.		n.t.
3/53		5/53		+2		−2		+4	
	8/54		11/53		−9		−11		+2
2/57		11/55		−15		−7		−8	
	5/58		2/58		−3		−5		+2
2/60		5/59		−9		−7		−2	
	2/61		2/61		0		−4		+4
4/62		n.s.		n.t.		−4		n.t.	
	3/63		n.s.		n.t.		−9		n.t.
6/66		8/66		+2		−5		+7	
	10/67		2/67		−8		−12		+4
3/69		11/68		−4		−3		−1	
	11/70		11/70		0		−5		+5
3/73		n.s.		n.t.		−2		n.t.	
Median Lead or Lag									
at highs				−4		−3.5		−1	
at lows					−3		−5		+3
at all turns				−3.5		−5		+2	

a Mid-month of quarter. Data are for corporate profits after taxes, from U.S. Department of Commerce.
n.s. = no specific cycle   n.t. = no timing comparison

vis-a-vis growth cycles would help to explain variations in the leads of stock prices. Since interest rates on different types of obligations behave differently, there is some question about which interest rates are most relevant to the stock market — short-term rates or long-term rates, rates on government or on corporate issues, etc. Without presuming to decide this matter, we have selected yields on seasoned corporate bonds rated Aaa by Moody's as a widely known rate on traded securities. For simplicity, in order to compare like turns rather than opposite turns, we refer to bond prices instead of yields (Table 4).

The tendency for bond prices to lead growth cycle turns and by long intervals is evident. In most instances the lead is virtually as long as the entire growth cycle upswing or downswing and in four instances even longer. This is, of course, a consequence of a prompt positive reaction of interest rates to the corresponding turn in the growth cycle. Bond prices lead stock prices also, as the table shows, and again by long and variable intervals. The leads at stock price highs are typically much longer than at lows; the most recent episode, the lead of one month at the stock price high in January, 1973, was a notable exception to this rule.

PUTTING IT ALL TOGETHER

These results are consistent with the idea of an inverse relationship running from interest rates to stock prices. But Table 4 and Chart 2 also show there is no consistent relationship between the length of leads in bond prices and in stock prices vis-a-vis the growth cycle. An early downturn in bond prices does not necessarily mean an early downturn in stock prices, or

Table 4

Leads and Lags of Corporate Bond Prices (Moody's Aaa) and
Stock Prices at Growth Cycle Highs and Lows, 1948-73

Growth Cycle		Date of Corporate Bond Price		Lead (−) or Lag (+), in months					
				of Bond Prices at Growth Cycle		of Stock Prices at Growth Cycle		of Bond Prices at Stock Price	
High	Low	High	Low	High	Low	High	Low	High	Low
7/48		4/46		−27		−1		−26	
	10/49		2/48		−20a		−4		−16
6/51		6/50		−12		n.t.		n.t.	
	6/52		n.s.		n.t.		n.t.		n.t.
3/53		n.s.		n.t.		−2		n.t.	
	8/54		6/53		−14		−11		−3
2/57		9/54		−29		−7		−22	
	5/58		8/57		−9		−5		−4
2/60		6/58		−20		−7		−13	
	2/61		1/60		−13a		−4		−9
4/62		n.s.		n.t.		−4		n.t.	
	3/63		n.s.		n.t.		−9		n.t.
6/66		1/63		−41a		−5		−36	
	10/67		9/66		−13		−12		−1
3/69		2/67		−25a		−3		−22	
	11/70		6/70		− 5		−5		0
3/73		12/72		−3		−2		−1	
Median Lead or Lag									
at highs				−25		−3.5		−22	
at lows					−13		−5		−3.5
at all turns				−14		−5		−11	

a   Longer than the corresponding growth cycle phase.

n.s. = no specific cycle   n.t. = no timing comparison

vice versa. In fact, the relationship between the leads in profits and stock prices is much closer than that between bond prices and stock prices. When both factors are taken into account simultaneously, profits contribute more than bond prices to an explanation of the variation in the leads of stock prices.[4]

Putting together the information on the sequences among turns in bond prices, profits, and stock prices contained in Tables 3 and 4, we find the typical sequence at highs is:

	Months before (−) or after (+) Growth Cycle High								
	7/48	6/51	3/53	2/57	2/60	4/62	6/66	3/69	3/73
Bond price high	−27	−12	n.t.	−29	−20	n.t.	−41	−25	−3
Profits high	− 2	− 7	+2[a]	−15	− 9	n.t.	+2[a]	− 4	n.t.
Stock price high	− 1	n.t.	−2[a]	− 7	− 7	− 4	−5[a]	− 3	−2

[a] Stock price high leads profits high.

At lows the usual sequence is somewhat different:

	Months before (−) or after (+) Growth Cycle Low							
	10/49	6/52	8/54	5/58	2/61	3/63	10/67	11/70
Bond price low	−20	n.t.	−14	−9	−13	n.t.	−13	−5
Stock price low	− 4[b]	n.t.	−11	−5	− 4	−9	−12	−5
Profits low	− 5	+2	− 9	−3	0	n.t.	− 8	0

[b] Profits low leads stock price low.

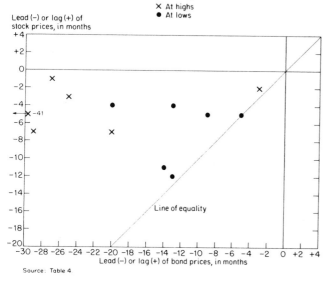

Chart 2
Leads of Bond and Stock Prices
at Growth Cycle Highs and Lows
× At highs
● At lows

Lead (−) or lag (+) of stock prices, in months

Line of equality

Lead (−) or lag (+) of bond prices, in months

Source: Table 4

It appears that at upturns (lows), stock prices are pulled by the upturns in bond prices before the upturn in profits materializes, whereas at downturns (highs), the much earlier decline in bond prices fails to push stock prices down before the decline in profits materializes. In other words, profits seem to have a bigger influence on stock prices at downturns while bond prices seem to have a bigger influence at upturns.

Despite the fact that the evidence we have examined to explain the tendency for stock prices to lead the growth cycles does not provide a full explanation for the variation in the length of lead, the results do support the conclusion that the cyclical behavior of interest rates and profits contributes substantially to the explanation of this persistent phenomenon.

[1] Ilse Mintz, "Dating United States Growth Cycles," *Explorations in Economic Research*, National Bureau of Economic Research, Summer 1974, pp. 1-113.

[2] The correlation between the length of lead in stock prices and in profits, based on the figures in Table 3, is +0.6. This means that about a third of the variation in the length of leads in stock prices is accounted for by corresponding variations in the length of leads in profits.

[3] Although unit costs are ordinarily classified as a lagging indicator, their effect on profits is inverse. Hence, for this purpose, it is appropriate to compare the turns in unit costs with the opposite turns in profits, in which case the lags become leads. For further discussion of this relationship, see "Tested Knowledge of Business Cycles," *Forty-second Annual Report*, National Bureau of Economic Research, June, 1962, pp. 9-15.

[4] A regression analysis yields the following equation:

$$S = .57P + .11B ,$$
$$(.22) \quad (.07)$$

where S, P, and B are the leads in stock prices, profits, and bond prices, respectively, and the parenthetic entries are the standard errors. The regression coefficient for profits is significant, but not that for bond prices. The regression is based on the eleven instances in which observations for all three variables are available and is constrained so that the constant term is zero. The multiple correlation coefficient is +.43, and the partial correlation coefficients for profits and bond prices, respectively, are .66 and .47. According to the regression estimates, the leads in stock prices at growth cycle highs are characteristically longer than those in profits but shorter than those in bond prices, whereas at growth cycle lows the leads in stock prices tend to be shorter than those in profits and in bond prices. That is, the sequence of turns at highs is: bond prices, stock prices, profits. At lows it is: bond prices, profits, stock prices. These results compare closely with those reported by Michael W. Keran in the preceding issue of this journal ("Forecasting Stock Prices," pp. 52-60), especially since his structural stock price equation uses the same variable we have used.

ARTHUR M. OKUN

The Invisible Handshake and the Inflationary Process

Implicit contracts between employers and workers are an important component of the wage-price spiral. They help to explain inflation when conditions of excess supply prevail.

Inflation has plagued the American economy and the economics profession throughout the decade of the seventies. Although the prospects for the economy over the near term are grim, I believe that developments within the profession are encouraging, and that they provide significant new insights into the inflationary process.

The new experience of chronic inflation

The economy's problems with persistent inflation date back to the mid sixties. But economists had no trouble explaining the inflation of the Vietnam period, which was clearly associated with excess demand. That experience fitted all our models, whether we were Keynesian, monetarist, eclectic, or erratic. We explained simply and succinctly that the price level rose because demand in the aggregate exceeded overall supply, just as the price of apples rose when the demand for apples exceeded their supply. The problems for economists emerged in 1970-71 when inflation persisted in the face of excess supply and survived a recession for the first time in the annals of U.S. business-cycle history. And they intensified with a vengeance in 1975-77, when after a severe recession, prices rose at a rate of nearly 6 percent a year while supply in the aggregate exceeded demand by all recognized criteria.

ARTHUR M. OKUN is a Senior Fellow of The Brookings Institution. This article is taken from his speech in acceptance of the Frank E. Seidman Distinguished Award in Political Economy at Southwestern University at Memphis last fall. The views expressed are the author's and are not necessarily those of the officers, trustees, or other staff members of The Brookings Institution.

Chronic inflation that persisted in the face of excess supply confronted economists with many problems of interpretation and explanation. Let me focus on one particular puzzle, which I regard as the critical observation of behavior in the inflationary era of the seventies. In millions of instances, we have observed nonunion employers with no contractual obligations granting general pay increases when they had abundant applicants, no vacancies, and negligible quit rates. Profit-seeking employers presumably try to minimize the payroll costs of obtaining the quantity and quality of workers they wish to hire. Why would those employers *raise* pay when their wage and salary scales were already evoking an excess supply of labor? How can that action at such a time make sense—regardless of how employers perceived monetary and fiscal policy or what rates of unemployment or inflation they expected for the future?

I submit that their behavior is sensible. The employers are in fact striving to minimize payroll costs, *reckoned over a substantial time-horizon.* They know that experienced workers deciding whether to stick with or quit their jobs in periods of prosperity evaluate those jobs in terms of the way the employer has treated them during periods of both tight and weak labor markets. Any management that holds down the wages it pays when most wages are rising must expect to be penalized when opportunities for good jobs become abundant. And so the calculations of firms are sensibly focused on quit rates and hiring requirements, not merely for today or tomorrow, but over a longer period, including intervals of prosperity and boom.

The firm finds it worthwhile to make an investment in personnel relationships; it seeks a reputation as a good employer to maintain an experienced and reliable work force for the long run. Thus the employer opts to treat the worker "fairly," invoking standards of relative wages (how other employers are adjusting pay) and real wages (how the cost of living is affecting the purchasing power of workers' incomes). And once the employer adopts and announces such a personnel policy, the workers are led to expect that their pay will reflect those criteria.

Implicit contracts

This line of reasoning is called the theory of "implicit contracts": firms with no explicit contractual obligations nonetheless act, in the pursuit of long-term profitability, to fulfill certain general commitments to their employees. They are guided by an invisible handshake, as well as by Adam Smith's invisible hand.

This theory, which provides important insights that I will discuss, has had many fathers within the economics profession during the seventies. Had I been asked a decade ago to account for general wage increases in recession, I am not certain exactly how I would have responded. But I am quite certain that my answer would have deserved a failing grade. Of course, all economists recognized that overall pay increases in a very weak economy had occurred in the United States in the mid-thirties and in Brazil on many occasions. But such episodes were explained by special factors rather than by an appeal to sensible strategies of employers and workers.

In retrospect, I can see the theory of implicit contracts foreshadowed in some earlier writings—mainly by labor economists but also by some macroeconomists. But I must confess that I first became impressed with the phenomenon in 1970-71 as a result of some informal conversations with a number of owners and executives of small businesses. I remember one who had experienced declines in sales and profits, had cut back employment, and yet had raised the pay of his workers by 7 percent. He faced no union, saw no threat of unionization, had no need to recruit employees, and was not concerned about current quits. In response to my probing, he explained articulately that, as a conscious policy, he did not "take advantage" of his workers while he had the "upper hand" in the labor market and that he could count on their remembering his actions when the job market tightened. Others echoed the same theme. Some managers mentioned current morale and productivity as well as future labor supply. Whenever I have discussed these issues with business executives, I have been struck by their straightforward, matter-of-fact emphasis on their reputations as employers. Economic theorists have taken a little longer to recognize these considerations. But, after all, we have never met a payroll.

The implicit contract view embraces as a special case the Keynesian assumption of a floor under money wages. Clearly the firm that hires a worker with a career job in mind must lead him to believe that his position will gradually improve, not worsen. Once the firm paints a bright future in order to recruit the worker, any subsequent cut in wages would be a disappointment and a source of antagonism. Hence the firm is inhibited from reducing wages, as Keynes posited. In fact, in an economy where wages normally rise over time, the same inhibitions can also apply to hold-downs or even slowdowns in wages for employees who had been led to expect fairly steady raises.

The same insights also help to resolve puzzles about behavior in many product markets. In periods of boom, many firms that experience excess demand lengthen their backlogs of unfilled orders and some even place their customers on allocation quotas, clearly eschewing price increases that would enhance their current profitability. Their decisions not to exploit fully the potential short-term benefits of tight markets are the understandable result of a longer-run view of their relationships with customers. By foregoing king-size markups in tight markets, the sellers build a clientele and establish a reputation that helps to retain customers when markets ease.

In many industries, firms feel obliged to justify price increases to their customers in terms of cost increases; they want to convince their customers that they are not exploiting a tight market to capture a larger share of the benefits from continuing relationships. And as the mirror image of that behavior in tight markets, these firms adjust prices in line with costs during periods of recession and slack, allowing percentage markups over standard costs to narrow only slightly. During recent recessions, prices in customer markets have not fallen; nor have they even been rigid or sticky. Rather they have kept rising, responding to the push of higher costs but resisting the pull of lower demands.

The cost-oriented pricing in product markets geared to customer relationships offers a dramatic contrast with the behavior of prices for products traded on auction markets. For the latter group, the traditional supply-demand model is confirmed beautifully. The prices of industrial raw materials, which are generally traded in organized commodity markets, fall in periods of recession. For example, they declined on average by 15 percent from a peak in May 1974 to a trough in March 1975. During that same ten-month interval, producers' prices of finished consumer goods other than food and fuel *rose* by 10 percent. Sellers in nonauction and auction markets alike experienced weak demand; they had essentially the same information about their costs and markets; the two groups presumably had similar expectations about the future course of the general price level and economic activity. Their prices behaved differently because they are set differently—one by an impersonal mechanism that equates supply and demand continuously and the other by a managerial strategy oriented strongly toward long-term customer relationships.

The microeconomic aspects

The theory of implicit contracts was developed by macroeconomists investigating various aspects of unemployment and inflation in the overall economy. But the theory has important microeconomic aspects, amending many traditional concepts of market efficiency. To be an effective mechanism, an auction market must have a large number of buyers and sellers competing for a standardized product that can be readily defined in terms of quantity and quality. Those requirements are met by products like soybeans, cotton, hides, and lumber, as well as by many financial instruments ranging from common stocks to foreign exchange. And those items are indeed traded through brokers or auctioneers who find the price that equates demand and supply. But that mechanism for making transactions would be abysmally inefficient for neckties, restaurant meals, haircuts, machine tools to produce bicycles, or blue Chevrolets with standard transmission and stereo but without air conditioning. Most important, the labor market cannot rely on an impersonal auction system, because jobs are specialized and the quality of workers cannot be objectively graded. The isolated cases in which hiring decisions are, in effect, made through brokers—for example, for office temporaries and snow shovelers—underline the nearly universal preference for the face-to-face, personalized transaction.

In the absence of the auctioneer, buyers and sellers must make transactions by search and shopping, which are costly activities. Pursuing rational strategies, they will not play at do-it-yourself auctioneering, but will aim to hold down those costs. Because of the high costs of finding a job and of obtaining a productive worker, continuing relationships in career jobs become worthwhile to both workers and employers in most industries. Because sellers in many product markets depend on sales efforts by employees or on shopping by buyers, the firms promote patterns of recurrent purchases, seeking to convert buyers into regular customers by establishing the reliability, predictability, and generally satisfactory character of pricing and services. Even when purchases are not recurrent, sellers strive to build a reputation whereby the satisfied buyer of the past passes a good word along to the potential buyer of the future. While the sellers are serving their own interests with such a strategy, they also improve the efficiency of the economy by reducing transactions costs. These customer and career relationships are efficient adaptations to the realities of a complex, interdependent economy; they should not be interpreted as evidence of some evil monopoly power.

In some cases, the relationships between buyers and sellers are expressed in written formal contracts that specify the obligations of the two participants to each other. But such explicit contracts have a limited scope because of the expenses of negotiating, formulating, and enforcing them, and because of the rigidity that they can impose on the parties. And thus, in many areas, the efficient way to do business is through understandings and conventions involving fair play and good faith. The participants act to facilitate recurrent transactions, but they do not assume legal contractual obligations. Each has an incentive to satisfy the other in order to maintain the relationship that is mutually beneficial.

The arrangements that people make for such continuing relationships take diverse and sometimes contrasting forms, which cannot be precisely predicted or, at this point, fully explained. For example, under the widely recognized implicit contract between large Japanese firms and their employees, the firm is expected to provide a steady job throughout the careers of the workers, regardless of the state of the business cycle. The employers thereby assume the risk of excessive payrolls during recessions but may obtain compensating benefits through greater loyalty or more moderate wage demands by their workers. In contrast, implicit and explicit contracts in the United States give the employer substantially more discretion over the amount of employment, with the result that mass layoffs are a standard feature of our recessions. Much research lies ahead to explain the

rationale and the consequences of different types of implicit contracts.

Another challenging area of investigation concerns the issues of equity that implicit contracts bring into the workings of the private marketplace. Implicit contracts can be effective only in a social atmosphere that incorporates a sense of mutual respect and a consensus on principles of fair play and good faith. Equity is thus not an extraneous irritant imposed upon the market by political institutions, but rather a vital lubricant of market processes.

Implicit contracts and inflation

The implicit contracts governing wages and prices in many areas are a key reason why any sudden change in total spending has only a small initial impact on inflation and a correspondingly large initial impact on output and employment. Thus an overheated economy initially has a rosy glow from low unemployment rates, ebullient capital formation, and strong productivity growth. For example, during the boom of the late sixties, workers and firms in many sectors gladly supplied more labor input and more output with only moderate deviations of wages and markups above the path regarded as customary and satisfactory. The implicit contracts were in effect shaded, but they were not scrapped. And thus inflation was slow-starting in that prolonged period of excess demand. But for the same reasons, inflation was slow-stopping when demand weakened. In the recession as well as in the boom, output and employment were affected a great deal, but wages and prices only a little.

The slow-starting, slow-stopping nature of inflation has been evident to some degree throughout the era since World War II. Wages and industrial prices responded less sensitively to the business cycle than was the case earlier in our history, reflecting in part the growing role of implicit and explicit contracts. Indeed, the mildness of the postwar business cycle encouraged a longer-run emphasis in wage and markup decisions. During the fifties and sixties, most private behavior was adapted to a modest upward creep in the price level that yielded a secular average inflation rate of 1 or 2 percent, with recurrent cyclical bumps and dents around the trend.

In the seventies, that underlying belief in the long-term stability of the price trend was severely

shaken by prolonged experience with rapid infla-tion. The notion of par-for-the-course on wage in-creases shifted upward. Thus a pay raise of 4 per-cent, which seemed decent and fair to a career worker in 1965, was inadequate and insulting in 1970 and has remained so ever since. Similarly, prices in customer markets became depressed rela-tive to prices in auction markets, and have been subject to recurrent upward pressures. Business and labor practices were altered to depend less heavily on the stability of the dollar. Those changes have sped the transmission of cost increases into price increases through the system—with the institution of cost-of-living escalators; the abandonment or shortening of fixed periods for price-setting like the model-year pricing of automobiles; and the erosion of the willingness of sellers to accept orders with guaranteed prices at delivery.

In general, as people adapt to an inflationary world, they make inflation more rapid and more persistent. Any prolonged experience with an infla-tion rate well above the secular average to which the system has become adapted alters implicit and

explicit contracts in ways that make the inflation feed upon itself. And that has been the continuing experience of the seventies in periods of weak de-mand as well as of strong demand.

Yet even today, Americans continue to depend heavily on the dollar as a yardstick and a standard. Our economy is not adapted to double-digit, or even to 6 percent, rates of increase in prices. If in-flation is not brought under control in the near fu-ture, the eighties will be marked by even more in-dexing, further shortening of the lags in transmission of cost increases, and a continuing shift away from dependence on money in implicit and explicit con-tracts. And such adaptations would further intensify our inflationary woes.

The costs of inflation

Implicit contracts introduce new dimensions in the reckoning of the costs of inflation to society. First, even when added inflation stems from a general, economy-wide cause like an excessively stimulative monetary policy and even when it is reasonably predictable, various types of wages and prices respond differently. Auction prices outrun customer prices; escalated wages outpace other wages in career jobs; wages of workers in casual jobs are likely to rise more rapidly than most wages and salaries in career jobs. These changes in relative prices and wages serve no useful function as rewards or market signals; yet they reshuffle income among families. The redistribution is not primarily from rich to poor or from poor to rich; rather it takes the form of a lottery that renders prizes and penalties arbitrarily and inequitably.

Second, because inflation can feed on itself, an acceleration of inflation must increase uncertainty about the future course of inflation. The record over time and across nations makes clear that, when and where the average rate of inflation is higher, the rate for any year is more variable and more volatile. And uncertain inflation generates a crawl away from money. In asset markets, deposits, bonds, and other fixed-dollar assets become less attractive relative to the time-honored inflation hedges like real estate, precious metals, and art objects. Yet these investments are inherently less liquid than monetary assets and subject to large transactions costs for buyers and sellers.

Finally, in job and product markets, the crawl away from money impairs the most important yardstick and means of communication in the economy. A nation that has learned to keep score in dollars on the fairness of implicit contracts, on balance-sheets and income-statements, and in planning for the future, gradually finds that its training has become obsolete. These developments impair significantly the sense of security and well-being of a society, even when they do not show up as a subtraction from real GNP.

The fiscal-monetary arena

This view of the inflationary process highlights the dangers of excessively stimulative fiscal and monetary policies that permit inflation to become established in the system and feed upon itself. Moreover, it suggests the need for a consistent and determined strategy to slow the growth of aggregate spending —that is, the dollar total of GNP. But it also underlines the high cost of a cure for inflation based solely on monetary and budgetary restraint. Unquestionably, such a cure is available: inflation can

be halted by a policy of tight money and tight budgets maintained intensively enough and long enough. But the costs are extremely high. Because of implicit (and explicit) contracts, a restrictive policy will, for a considerable period, push down output and employment drastically in an effort to slow prices and wages. According to past experience, the current recession, or a deepening of that recession engineered by restrictive monetary and fiscal policies, will sacrifice roughly $200 billion of production for each point that it reduces the basic inflation rate.

A $1 trillion cure for chronic inflation is unthinkable. It would resurrect the dark days of the thirties and jeopardize the political and social viability of our market institutions. To be sure, some economists argue persuasively that a credible and consistent policy of demand restraint would reduce that cost. But it is impossible to predict with any confidence whether the resulting "discount" from the trillion-dollar figure would be 20 percent or 80 percent. If an anti-inflationary strategy relying solely on demand restraint is adopted on the basis of exceedingly optimistic estimates of its costs, subsequent disappointments could readily discredit and reverse the effort. An undiversified anti-inflationary program is an inefficient, high-risk strategy. Fortunately, there are ample opportunities for diversification.

Prices and the price level

In an economy with a significant network of implicit contracts, a jump in the price of any major product raises the price level, and indeed the inflation rate. That connection between particular prices and the price level does not exist in a world of universal auction markets, and that may be the most fundamental difference between the two worlds.

The jump in petroleum prices imposed by the Organization of Petroleum Exporting Countries this year offers a timely example of this distinction. Suppose that the budgetary and monetary dials are controlled in such a way that the dollar total of GNP is not altered by the OPEC action. In an auction world, the consequence of higher fuel prices would then be lower prices for most other things. In particular, the auctioneer in the labor market would ensure that money wages fell enough to keep supply and demand in balance, thus preventing the emergence of unemployment.

It can be true as well in the real world that, if more dollars are spent on petroleum, fewer will be spent on most other items. But the reduced spending on those other items, and particularly on labor, will reduce output and employment——not merely hold down wages and prices. At a given unemployment rate, there is no mechanism to slow wages. Indeed, they will speed up via the chain reaction from fuel prices to the consumer price index to cost-of-living escalators. Given a jump in fuel prices, a policy strategy of stabilizing dollar GNP must put people out of work, waste productive capacity, and discourage investment——including even investment in energy-saving projects and alternative energy sources. It pushes the economy in an inflationary and a recessionary direction at the same time.

The recessionary effects can be avoided if total spending is stimulated by monetary and fiscal policies. But then the inflationary consequences are exacerbated. In addition to the rise in the price level from higher oil prices, the nation is subjected to a prolonged increase in inflation operating through cost-of-living escalation of wages and higher import costs from a likely devaluation of the dollar. The dilemma is genuine. And, incidentally, the more that wages (and other contracts) are indexed to the cost of living, the worse that dilemma is.

The adverse effects of OPEC actions can teach us how to take actions for ourselves with favorable effects. The OPEC price increase is the equivalent of an excise tax imposed on the American consumer, and that quasi-tax can be neutralized by reductions in actual excise taxes——by cuts in state sales taxes or in federal payroll taxes on employers, which act in part as hidden sales taxes on consumers. Although it cannot repeal the higher real cost of oil, that neutralizing strategy can avoid the grim alternatives of accepting a recession or adding to inflation.

The lowering of indirect taxes can also help to counter the inflationary inertia that is now built into our implicit contracts. It can push down on consumer prices and have favorable secondary effects on wages. Various other cost-reducing measures can be used similarly to counter inflation without courting recession. For example, subsidies for low-income workers could substitute for the minimum wage; and acreage controls on farm products could be eliminated. In fact, in recent years,

the nation has suffered self-inflicted wounds in the form of higher payroll taxes, much higher minimum wages, and renewed acreage controls. These have inflationary consequences in the real world of the American economy, although not in the hypothetical world of universal auction markets.

The linkage of prices and the price level applies even more broadly. Indeed, the discretionary price and wage decisions made by major American firms (and unions) affect the entire economy. By opting for the top of the relevant range in setting prices or wages, the private decision-maker acts as a mini-OPEC with the same inflationary-recessionary consequence. On the other hand, a decision on the low end of the range bestows upon society the benefit of less inflation and the opportunity for more growth. And so the whole nation is an affected third party when such private decisions are made.

These are macroeconomic examples of what economists have traditionally identified as "externalities"——effects on other parties stemming from a transaction between a buyer and a seller. Wherever important externalities exist, the market can generate an efficient outcome only if the costs or benefits of the bystanders are somehow incorporated into the reckonings of the decision-makers. To reflect the social benefits of certain private actions, we grant tax credits for the purchase of productive machinery and the employment of unskilled workers. The same reasoning establishes the social desirability in principle of tax-based incomes policies, which apply tax penalties or rewards to encourage restraint in wage and price decisions by reflecting the social benefits of such restraint.

Circumstances in the months ahead may provide a neat opportunity to institute a tax-based incentive for price and wage moderation. As one part of a tax reduction, which will probably be appropriate in 1980, investors in plant and equipment are likely to be granted the opportunity to depreciate their assets more rapidly for tax purposes. Such a stimulus to investment would brighten the outlook for productivity growth. But any anti-inflationary benefits it can provide are clearly limited and long delayed. Prompt and substantial anti-inflationary benefits could be obtained by linking major tax benefits of accelerated depreciation to compliance with the price and wage guidelines. Large firms should be required to exercise price and wage restraint as a condition for obtaining the full benefits of the faster writeoffs. The task of enforcing such a provision could be kept simple by imposing the requirement only on firms obtaining a tax reduction in excess of, say, $100,000. These large firms would file certificates of compliance with the Council on Wage and Price Stability, and that agency would be authorized to deny the validity of any certificate, subject to appeal in the courts. Such a measure would test in practice the ability of a tax incentive to help curb inflation, and it would couple the nation's urgent short-term need for price and wage restraint with its longer-term need for strengthened capital formation and improved productivity performance.

The invisible handshake

The recognition of the invisible handshake and of its role in the inflationary process highlights the many sources of inflation that go beyond excess demand and the many costs of inflation that go beyond short-term surprises. It reveals the inflationary consequences of value-added and sales taxes, and the dangers of the emerging general trend toward cost-of-living escalators and indexing. It corrects the fundamental errors of economic policy and economic analysis that stem from the assumption of universal auction markets. The hawks and the doves on inflation policy make the same mistake of modeling the American economy as a giant soybean market. The hawks then prove that price stability can be achieved readily by monetary policy alone; and, based on the same "soybean illusion," the doves proclaim that inflation, once it becomes anticipated, is not costly.

Implicit contracts help to explain why inflation is costly and why it is difficult to eliminate once it has become entrenched. But those institutions also create the opportunity for cost-reducing measures and tax-based incomes policies to help curb inflation, along with a consistent fiscal-monetary strategy to slow the growth of total dollar spending. Fundamentally, our economy is more efficient because it is guided by the invisible handshake as well as the invisible hand. And it will work even better when policy-makers and theorists recognize the implications for the cure of chronic inflation—in short, when they choose to act as wise owls rather than fierce hawks or passive doves.

A RATIONAL VIEW OF RATIONAL EXPECTATIONS

BY NEIL G. BERKMAN*

ECONOMIC policy in the postwar period may be broadly characterized as "activist" in the sense that changes in the setting of the instruments of monetary and fiscal policy have frequently been undertaken with the expressed intention of offsetting instability in the private sector. For example, evidence that the economy is in recession has often resulted in such activist policy responses as a tax cut or an increase in government spending. Activist policy thus stands in contrast to "built-in stabilizers" like the progressive income tax system that automatically causes tax receipts to rise in booms (and hence moderates consumption spending) and decline in recessions (and hence stimulates consumption spending) without any overt response by the monetary or fiscal authorities.

The government's willingness to pursue activist stabilization policies reflects a long-standing belief in the proposition that monetary and fiscal actions through their influence on aggregate demand and supply have predictable effects on real income and employment, at least in the short run, a proposition that virtually all economists would have agreed to in principle until recently. The theoretical foundation for activist policy is usually attributed to J. M. Keynes, although monetarists such as Milton Friedman have advanced equally compelling alternative arguments — with quite different policy implications — which also indicate that monetary and fiscal actions "matter."[1] Since both groups agree that policy actions can have real effects, the ongoing debate between monetarists and Keynesians over what constitutes the most appropriate ("optimal") policy involves not so much the questions whether money matters or if only money matters as the questions whether a stable money growth rule will produce less volatility in real GNP than a rule that allows the monetary authority to "lean against the wind" or whether stimulative monetary or fiscal policy can be expected to permanently reduce unemployment at the expense of a higher rate of inflation. In other words, economists debated whether the economy is inherently stable, and so over the underlying *need* for activist policy, not over whether the available tools *could* in principle achieve the stabilization goal.[2]

* Economist, Federal Reserve Bank of Boston. The author thanks William Poole for helpful comments on earlier drafts of this paper.

[1] See John Maynard Keynes, *The General Theory of Employment, Interest and Money,* New York, 1935 and Milton Friedman, "The Role of Monetary Policy," *American Economic Review* 58, March 1968, pp. 1-17.
[2] This interpretation is stressed by Franco Modigliani, "The Monetarist Controversy or, Should We Forsake

Theoretical developments in the past few years have shifted the focus of this debate. Building on earlier models of the economy, economists have shown that under certain assumptions concerning the formation of expectations and the effects of expectations on economic decisions, systematic and predictable changes in monetary and fiscal policy will have no effect whatsoever on the behavior of real income and employment, even in the short run.[3] In this so-called *rational expectations* view, attempts to stabilize the economy through activist policies are doomed to failure; indeed, rather than reducing the magnitude of fluctuations in the system, activist monetary and fiscal policies, in so far as policy adjustments are unsystematic and unpredictable, will actually contribute to economic instability.

The argument that activist policies should be abandoned has achieved widespread acceptance in the popular financial press, although the message appears to have been adopted far too uncritically by many in this group, and to a more limited extent in the economics profession.[4] But professional opinion is far from unanimous on the validity of the "policy impotence" view. Much current macroeconomic research attempts

to specify precisely those circumstances in which the traditional conclusions regarding the efficacy of activist policy still hold, and to determine if these circumstances more accurately describe the real world than do those underlying the rational expectations results. The purpose of this paper is to review these important theoretical developments.

This paper is organized as follows. Part I describes the theory underlying the conventional activist view, and explains the mechanisms through which stabilization policy was believed to influence the real economy (for good or ill) prior to the intellectual ascendancy of rational expectations. Part II presents the rational expectations model itself, and discusses the conditions under which policy actions will be completely ineffective in controlling real economic activity. Part III summarizes the various criticisms of the rational expectations model that have recently been developed, and discusses the extent to which they succeed in resurrecting the theoretical foundations of activist policy. Some concluding observations are presented in Part IV.

I. Preliminaries: The Conventional View

The theoretical rationale for activist stabilization policy can be understood most easily by means of an example. Consider the reaction of a fully employed economy to an activist policy designed to increase real output and employment above the prevailing levels. Such a maneuver could take various forms, but for simplicity only two general cases will be considered here: first, a pure fiscal policy, where a tax cut or

---

Stabilization Policies?" *American Economic Review,* March 1977, pp. 1-19. On a *practical* level there was also disagreement over whether economists had enough knowledge to pursue a successful stabilization policy. Milton Friedman, emphasizing long and variable lags, argued that knowledge was too incomplete to permit a successful countercyclical policy. Others, especially those involved in the construction of econometric macro models, reached the opposite conclusion.

[3] See, for example, Robert E. Lucas, Jr., "Some International Evidence on Output-Inflation Tradeoffs," *American Economic Review* 63, June 1973, pp. 326-34; Thomas J. Sargent and Neil Wallace, " 'Rational' Expectations, the Optimal Monetary Instrument, and the Optimal Money Supply Rule," *Journal of Political Economy* 83, April 1975, pp. 241-54; Robert J. Barro, "Rational Expectations and the Role of Monetary Policy," *Journal of Monetary Economics,* 2, January 1976, pp. 1-32. For a sophisticated nontechnical discussion of these issues see Robert E. Lucas, Jr., "Understanding Business Cycles," in Karl Brunner and Allan H. Meltzer, eds., *Stabilization of the Domestic and International Economy,* Carnegie-Rochester Conference Series on Public Policy, Vol. 5, 1977, pp. 7-30.

[4] For example, in the article "The People Can't be Fooled" (*Wall Street Journal,* June 25, 1979, p. 20), Charles I. Plosser and Clifford W. Smith, Jr. argue that, "the idea of rational expectations says people watch what policymakers do and attempt to guess what the future course of policy will be . . . a sound economic policy is one that is as stable and predictable as possible."

an increase in government expenditures leaves the money stock unchanged; second, a pure monetary policy, where the increase in the money stock leaves tax rates and government spending unchanged. How will the economy react to these disturbances? The answer depends primarily on the period over which the reaction is measured — a consideration that is relevant because adjustments that occur in the short run may differ from those that occur in the long run.

In the short run, a tax cut or a government spending increase financed by borrowing from the public will tend initially to increase aggregate demand, and so employment and production will rise in those industries that produce the goods demanded by government (in the case of an increase in government spending) or in those that produce the goods demanded by households (in the case of a tax cut). But rising demand immediately initiates forces that offset the activist fiscal policy stimulus. Assuming prices respond to shifts in demand or supply, prices and wages will tend to increase as aggregate demand rises. The resulting higher nominal value of output encourages individuals to increase their nominal money holdings, since the assumed fixed total amount of money held in cash and in checking accounts will be insufficient to accommodate conveniently the higher nominal value of transactions. With the nominal money stock unchanged, not everyone can accumulate higher money balances, but people will nevertheless attempt to do so by reducing their purchases of goods, services, and financial assets. In addition, the rise in interest rates caused by the fall in the public's demand for financial assets and by the increased supply of these assets due to increased government borrowing will tend to discourage investment spending by business, so that the debt-financed fiscal stimulus "crowds out" some private investment spending. Thus, while employment and production initially rise in response to the fiscal policy,

the accompanying increase in prices and interest rates gradually causes aggregate demand to return to its original level. Although the *composition* of output is altered by the fiscal stimulus, these price and interest rate adjustments insure that neither total employment nor total production can be permanently driven above their full employment levels by activist fiscal policy.

The ability of fiscal policy to alter real output and employment in the short run but not in the long run arises because people do not realize instantaneously the price and wage implications of every shock that affects the economy. Rather, as far as many individual producers and workers are concerned, the only impact of a policy stimulus that is readily observed is an increase in demand at the local level — and not everyone will notice even this much right away. Experience teaches that shifts in the demand for particular products and factor services will occur from time to time and from place to place even when the overall economy is in long-run equilibrium — that is, even when the current price level, wage rate, and rate of interest are consistent with the maintenance of full employment output — and that producers and workers are aware that wage, price, and output adjustments are costly and so not always justified by every transitory shift in demand. Therefore, the rise in wages and prices that is warranted by the assumed policy action and that is ultimately responsible for the return to the original equilibrium may take place slowly and probably not uniformly across different sectors of the economy. The policy-induced "boom" will be shorter the more quickly the public perceives that a permanent and general and not simply a temporary relative demand shift has taken place — that is, it will be shorter if the policy stimulus was expected and hence at least partly reflected in people's action by the time it takes effect than if it comes as a complete surprise — but as long as prices are flexible, the economy is bound to return to its initial levels of employment and output even if this information is slow to disseminate throughout the system.

Now consider the effects of monetary policy. Suppose the monetary authority attempts to reduce unemployment below the level achieved in long-run equilibrium by increasing the money stock. Aggregate demand will rise at first because of the increase in nominal money balances, and producers will respond by scheduling longer production runs and preparing to hire more labor. But if both the supply of and the demand for labor depend on the real wage, additional workers will be forthcoming only at a real wage higher than that which prevailed before the monetary stimulus, and additional jobs will be offered only at a real wage lower than that which prevailed before the stimulus. If everyone knows that both wages and prices are rising because of the increased money supply — leaving the real wage unchanged — then no extra labor will be available, nor will the number of workers demanded rise above the number hired previously. Thus, production plans will return to their original levels and prices will increase until desired money holdings rise to match the larger nominal money supply. As long as the implications for prices and wages of the increased money supply are grasped immediately by all producers and workers, the policy will cause a rapid burst of inflation but will have no lasting effects on any real variables.

Evidently activist policy can affect employment and production in the short run only if information about the impact of an anticipated policy stimulus on wages and prices spreads through the system gradually and unevenly or if the policy stimulus is unexpected. In either case the activist policy causes people to be "fooled" temporarily about the actual values of the real variables that guide their decision making. For example, if workers learn of the higher nominal wages offered by employers before they become aware that prices have also risen in response to an unanticipated increase in the money supply, they will mistakenly believe that real wages have increased and be willing to provide the additional labor services demanded by producers. On the other side of the market, producers will demand more labor because from their perspective the real wage has fallen: labor is paid at discrete intervals —once a month, for example — but goods are sold more or less continuously; thus, producers can raise output prices and so increase nominal revenues before the higher wage bill must be paid. An omniscient observer would know that real wages have neither risen nor fallen in response to the monetary stimulus, that the activist monetary policy has simply increased both wages and prices. These facts are not immediately evident to everyone, however, so labor may believe that real wages have risen while management simultaneously believes that real wages have fallen, permitting output and employment to rise temporarily above their initial levels.

How long this situation will last depends primarily on the speed with which workers revise their expectations of the rate of price inflation, but in any event false expectations will not persist indefinitely. When the full extent of the price inflation induced by the increased money supply finally becomes incorporated in expectations, workers will realize that the real wage they are actually receiving is not as high as the real wage they thought they were receiving; indeed, since it is now understood that the real wage has in fact not risen at all, the supply of labor will return to its prestimulus level. For their part, employers will eventually have to pay the higher nominal wage bill that resulted from the monetary stimulus. Assuming that the price inflation comes to an end once prices have reached the level consistent with the higher money stock, the gap between the rate of growth of nominal receipts for goods sold and the rate of growth of the nominal wage bill that allowed employers to hire more labor in the first place will close, the real wage perceived by employers will rise, and the demand for labor will also return to its pre-stimulus level. To prevent this sequence of adjustments from offsetting the initial drop in unemployment, the monetary authority must increase the money supply yet again. This second injection of money will presumably have to be larger than the previous one, since labor will be fooled into believing that the real wage has risen only if the rate of price inflation is greater than that experienced — and so built into expectations and labor contracts — after the initial stimulus. Unless the monetary authority is willing to accept a continuously accelerating inflation, or unless labor can be expected to underestimate continuously a constant rate of inflation, monetary policy is no more capable than fiscal policy of maintaining employment and production permanently above the levels the economy naturally reaches in an environment free of activist policy shocks.

The ability of activist policies to increase employment and production beyond their long-run equilibrium levels for any but the briefest short-run adjustment interval depends on the assumption that a policy-induced increase in the rate of inflation — and, more importantly, its recognition — takes time. Since the behavior of the inflation rate is to a large extent governed by the behavior of wages, and since wage rates themselves are powerfully influenced by workers' *expectations* of future price increases, in an inflationary environment the case for or against activist policies thus rests on the responsiveness of price expectations to exogenous economic shocks on the one hand and to the various possible policy responses on the other. Whether there exists a stable "Phillips curve" tradeoff between inflation and unemployment that can be exploited at will by monetary or fiscal policy ultimately depends on how rapidly and

how accurately expectations adjust to changes in the economic environment and on how rapidly changes in expectations affect actual wages and prices, some of which may be importantly affected by contracts signed in the past.[5]

II. Rational Expectations

Systematic monetary or fiscal actions will have a predictable impact on real output and employment in the short run only if people follow a certain pattern of behavior in response to the policy maneuver. In particular, people's expectations about the inflationary consequences of a policy change must be systematically incorrect — more specifically, people must systematically *underpredict* the inflation induced by the stimulus for at least a short period of time — if the policy is to produce the intended result. By contrast, the essential argument of the rational expectations school is that people's expectations about the impact on prices and wages of a given change in policy are not systematically incorrect *even in the short run*. Because firms' profits and losses, and households' real wages and real consumption depend in part on realized wages and prices, people have a strong incentive to form their expectations as accurately as possible; expectations should depend on all available information, including information about the likely course of monetary and fiscal policy. If expectations are rational in this sense, then systematic, and therefore predictable, activist policies can have no predictable real effects.

An example will help to clarify the reasoning behind this conclusion. Suppose the monetary authority announces its intention to increase the money stock in the months just ahead, that

---

[5] These issues are explored empirically in Stephen K. McNees, "The Phillips Curve: Forward- or Backward-Looking?" *New England Economic Review,* July/August 1979.

everyone is convinced the authority will actually do so, and that the money stock increases as announced. In a world in which expectations are rational, people will react to this information by increasing their price and wage expectations to match the price increases most likely to result from the monetary stimulus. Employment and production plans will be adjusted as well to reflect the revised inflation outlook. If everyone forecasts correctly the wage and price implications of the policy move — the assumption that expectations are rational requires that this be the case on average — then, as explained in the previous section, the increase in the money supply will cause an inflation without changing the real wage, the expected real profitability of production, employment or output.

The rational expectations view recognizes that the revision of expectations induced by an anticipated policy change will not be precisely correct in every case. Although on average people will accurately predict the impacts of an expected policy action, sometimes the revision of expectations will be in error. If people should by chance underestimate inflation, then employers may for a time mistakenly believe that the increased price of their product reflects not only the anticipated economy-wide inflation but also a relative demand shift in their favor. For similar reasons, workers may mistakenly believe that the observed increase in nominal wages reflects not only the anticipated economy-wide inflation but also an increase in the real wage caused by a relative increase in the demand for their services. As a result, employment and output will tend to rise until the expectational error — the difference between the actual and the expected inflation rate — is recognized and incorporated into everyone's behavior.

A policy-maker who is willing to use activist tools on the chance that the public will underestimate their inflationary impact should recognize the symmetry of expectational errors

implied by the rational expectations hypothesis: when surprises occur, they are as likely to be positive as they are to be negative. Should people generally *overestimate* the inflationary impact of the policy action, then producers may for a time believe the relative price of their product has fallen and workers may for a time perceive a decline in the real wage. In this case, employment and production may actually *decline* as a result of the preannounced monetary stimulus. When expectations are rational, activist policies are most likely to have no real effects, but on those occasions when real effects are produced, they may or may not be in the intended direction.

The crucial distinction between the traditional activist view and the rational expectations view involves first, the formation of expectations and, second, the speed of adjustment of actual wages and prices to changes in expectations. The traditional view contends that the inflationary effects of a policy are eventually fully and accurately reflected in expectations and in actual wages and prices. It also contends that uncertainty about the exact magnitude of these ultimate price effects and slow adjustment of actual wages and prices create the opportunity for activist policies to have real effects in the short run.

The uncertainty arises because of the economy's complexity. People simply do not understand how the economy works with sufficient precision to be able to make consistently accurate forecasts of the effects of a given change in policy. For example, while people may realize that a tax cut will tend to increase the prices of certain consumption goods, they are likely to be unsure precisely how much these prices will rise, how much the increase will affect the price deflator they implicitly apply to their nominal wage, and hence how much to adjust their wage demands to maintain a constant real wage. The rational expectations view requires that people are able to make such calculations. In order to infer consistently the consequences of policy actions to within a random error on either side of the correct value and thus to offset immediately their intended real effects, people must know, or must act as if they know, the true structure of the economy.

Closely related to the issue of uncertainty is the issue of slow wage and price adjustment due to long-lasting contracts and other commitments. Contracts exist to reduce uncertainty. They are typically fulfilled even when the expectations upon which they were based turn out to have been incorrect. Thus, even if expectations adjust instantaneously upon the receipt of new information, wages and prices set by existing contracts may not.

The requirement that people know how the economy works extends also to how the monetary and fiscal authorities "work." That is, the public must be able to predict how the authorities will react to changes in the target variables such as GNP, employment, and inflation that the authorities are trying to control. This requires that the public be able to divine by observing the past relationship between changes in the target variables and subsequent changes in policy instruments — taxes, government expenditures, the money stock — the "reaction functions" of monetary and fiscal policy-makers. The public is encouraged to devote the resources necessary to uncover to the extent possible policy-makers' reaction functions because changes in policy instruments lead to changes in the demand for and the supply of those products and factor services relevant to profit-making. For this reason, it is in the public's own best interest to try to anticipate policy moves.

To illustrate why the public's forecasts of policy are important, suppose that people observe that the government increases spending above its trend rate of growth every time the unemployment rate exceeds, say, 8 percent.

Then should the unemployment rate exceed this figure, everyone will know that a fiscal stimulus program will soon be introduced, and they will plan for the future according to the implications this expected policy action is judged to have for prices, wages, rates of interest, the composition of total output, and so forth.[6] Because the changes in relative demands and supplies induced by the policy action are forecast without bias and immediately incorporated in individual behavior when expectations are rational, the short-run adjustment phase envisioned in the traditional activist view, during which real output and employment temporarily increase in response to the policy, occurs "instantaneously" in the rational expectations world. Hence, no predictable effects on these variables will result from the fiscal stimulus.

Since expectations play an important role in traditional analysis, the notion that individual behavior depends on anticipated events is not a proprietary contribution of the rational expectations school. Rather, the fundamental insight of this school is that anticipated policy changes (and for that matter any other anticipated event) cause people acting in their own self-interest to alter their behavior in such a way as to render the ultimate aggregate impact of the policies unpredictable.

An excellent example of this process is the cost of living clause in labor contracts. As people come to realize the consequences for prices and wages of stimulative activist policies they protect their real wages by insisting that nominal wages be automatically adjusted when prices rise; thus, activist policies that rely for their effectiveness on slow nominal wage adjustment will be rendered impotent because of this change in the structure of the economy induced

[6] The effect of activist fiscal policy in the rational expectations framework is analyzed in B.T. McCallum and J.K. Whitaker, "The Effectiveness of Fiscal Feedback Rules and Automatic Stabilizers Under Rational Expectations," *Journal of Monetary Economics* 5, April 1979, pp. 171-186.

by individuals' reaction to policy-makers' own past actions. Attempts to "fine tune" the economy by applying the policy prescriptions suggested by statistical analysis of the *average* historical relationships between policy instruments and ultimate policy objectives are doomed to failure because historical relationships are not stable.[7] Because the structure of the economy changes when policies change, policy-makers have no reason to expect anticipated changes in monetary or fiscal instruments to produce the reliable responses in real GNP and employment that would occur if people's behavior were in fact independent of that of the policy-makers themselves.

But if this is true — if people always act to offset the destabilizing influence of anticipated events — how can unemployment and production ever depart from their long-run equilibrium levels (as they so manifestly do)? The answer is that although anticipated events have no systematic aggregate impact, *unexpected* events invalidate people's plans and thus set in motion the kinds of adjustments described in the previous section. For example, suppose the monetary authority surprises everyone by suddenly and sharply reducing the rate of money growth below some previously generally expected rate. The ensuing weaker than expected demand for *all* products will, in the first instance, cause at least some people to believe mistakenly that demand has fallen only for *their* products; hence, they will reduce production and employment in the erroneous belief that the products they sell have fallen in value relative to other goods. In this way, the surprise in the money stock

produces a cumulative decline in real output and employment that will continue until expectations finally adjust.

The logic of the rational expectations view requires that if an event such as a sharp decline in the rate of money growth is foreseen, then inflation will decelerate immediately but there will be no short-term real effects. From the point of view of policy, then, a clear implication of the rational expectations hypothesis is that the inflation rate can be reduced — can in fact be made to equal any desired rate — if everyone is somehow convinced that the requisite monetary and fiscal actions are forthcoming. Under this view, a *credible* anti-inflation policy will indeed reduce the rate of inflation, and it will do so *costlessly* and quickly because rational economic agents act to insure there are no real effects from anticipated policy changes. If expectations are rational, there evidently is such a thing as a free lunch. Moreover, unless the authorities are capable of instituting policy changes in a totally unpredictable manner (and are willing to live with unexpected results if their actions turn out to have been at least partially foreseen), probably the best way to exploit the rationality of expectations is to provide a predictable policy regime. Hence, advocates of the rational expectations view prefer a stable money growth rule and other "nonactivist" policy formulas to activist, and often erratic and unpredictable, policy prescriptions.

III. What's Wrong with Rational Expectations?

Perhaps the most appealing feature of the rational expectations view is that its policy conclusions seem to depend only on the natural and rather flattering assumption that "the people cannot be fooled," at least not very often and certainly not systematically. But a careful analysis of the process through which expectational

[7] This point is originally due to Robert E. Lucas, Jr., "Econometric Policy Evaluation: A Critique," in Karl Brunner and Allan H. Meltzer, eds., *The Phillips Curve and Labor Markets*, Carnegie-Rochester Conferences on Public Policy Vol. 1, 1976, pp. 19-46. Also see papers by R.E. Lucas and T.J. Sargent, B. Friedman, R. Solow, and W. Poole in *After the Phillips Curve: Persistence of High Inflation and High Unemployment*, Conference Series No. 19, Federal Reserve Bank of Boston, June 1978.

adjustments offset the aggregate real effects of anticipated events reveals that this assumption is far less innocuous than it may first appear and that several even less appealing assumptions are also crucial for establishing the model's strikingly nontraditional results. To the extent that these assumptions are unpalatable, one is justified in questioning the validity of the policy impotence view despite the other undeniably endearing characteristics of the rational expectations theory.

One obvious criticism of the rational expectations approach is that it requires people to know more about the operation of the economy and about the data it continuously generates than is realistically possible. Just the fact that the doctrinal debate that is the subject of this paper has yet to be settled among professional economists suggests that the public is unlikely to understand the economy precisely enough for expectations to be strictly rational. Moreover, even if people could completely comprehend the economic structure as it currently exists if given enough time to study it, the structure clearly is subject to periodic, unpredictable alterations that render once well-understood historical relationships obsolete.[8]

The gathering and processing of the information required to monitor the evolving economy are costly, and the expense may easily outweigh the benefits that many people would perceive to flow from lowering the average forecast errors for those variables that guide their decision-making. Indeed, this line of argument suggests that simple "backward-looking" rules-of-thumb may provide the most efficient forecasts for the majority of market participants.[9] Nor does appeal to the strong evidence of rationality in the securities markets provide compelling evidence that *all* expectations are formulated in the data-intensive way required by the rational expectations theory.[10] The securities markets are highly centralized, trading is conducted for the most part on organized exchanges, transactions, storage, shipping and other costs are relatively low, and the goods being traded are fairly homogeneous — characteristics conducive to the rapid flow of information among all traders that is necessary if expectations are to be formulated rationally. Other markets are not so fortunate: most trading takes place in geographically dispersed locations (witness the markets for labor and new homes); transactions, storage, shipping, and other costs are relatively high (witness the markets for plant and equipment and other durable goods); the products being traded are heterogeneous (witness virtually any market other than the markets for money, securities, and agricultural commodities). For all of these reasons it is far from obvious that the expectations formation mechanism required by the rational expectations view is an accurate description of individual behavior in most markets.

The heterogeneity of products and factor services that characterizes the real world is the source of a second and probably a more damaging criticism of the rational expectations approach. The discussion in the previous section was intentionally vague about the nature of the adjustments to expected shifts in demands and supplies induced by anticipated events; recall that the argument was simply that the implied changes in relative prices lead people to undertake "appropriate" and "instantaneous" real output and employment adjustments. But unless all factors of production are suitable for producing all goods, unless labor and capital can be shifted from place to place costlessly and

---

[8] This criticism is developed in Benjamin Friedman, "Optimal Expectations and the Extreme Information Assumptions of 'Rational Expectations' Macromodels," *Journal of Monetary Economics* 5, January 1979, pp. 23-41.

[9] See McNees, "The Phillips Curve . . ."

[10] For a discussion of the theory and evidence of rationality in the stock market see Neil G. Berkman, "A Primer on Random Walks in the Stock Market," *New England Economic Review*, September/Ocotber 1978.

immediately, unless information flows between markets are completely unobstructed — that is, unless real adjustment costs are zero — how can this possibly happen?

Consider again the private sector's reaction to an anticipated increase in government spending. People anticipate an increase in the demand for "government goods" and because of the rise in interest rates a corresponding decline in investment goods demand (the extent of the decline in demand for investment goods of course depends on the strength of the crowding-out effect); similarly, the demand for factors of production skilled in producing government goods increases as the demand for factor inputs into investment goods production falls. But if real adjustment costs are not zero, the supply response may take quite some time to materialize. Production "in the pipeline" in investment goods industries may *slowly* decline as orders are cancelled and backlogs worked off, but numerous implicit and explicit contractual arrangements on both the input and the output side of this market make it expensive to reduce production immediately to the (perhaps) lower equilibrium level implied by the fiscal action. The increase in output in the government goods industries must for similar reasons occur only at the pace dictated by the costs of setting up new plants or preparing to increase capacity at existing ones. Thus, GNP and employment may for a time rise in response to the activist fiscal policy not because people are fooled or are behaving in any way "irrationally" but because economic and technological considerations dictate that real adjustments simply cannot occur instantaneously. For the same reasons, unless an anticipated monetary stimulus affects *all* prices equiproportionally (so that *no* relative price changes are expected to occur) systematic activist monetary policy can have real short-term effects (but not necessarily in the intended direction!).

A related criticism of the rational expectations model is that it apparently ignores the existence of contracts. Like the traditional monetarist school, the rational expectations view holds that relative price adjustments occur quickly in response to disturbances to demand and supply in particular markets. While this may be true in some markets — the securities and commodities markets, for example — it may not be true in those markets where prices are fixed by long-term contractual agreements.[11] Unless these contracts are subject to immediate renegotiation every time a change in the policy environment is imminent, or unless they are written with built-in escalator clauses that permit both upward and downward price changes in response to the *anticipated* price impact of anticipated events (in contrast to escalators based on *realized* price changes), the requisite relative price adjustments induced by expected activist policy can occur only slowly. Nor is the existence of contracts which do not contain these features inconsistent with the notion that expectations are formed rationally — far from it.[12] Relatively "risk averse" individuals may find it in their own best interest to enter into fixed-price contracts with other individuals or firms better suited to accept the risk of adverse price changes. Because agreements that limit the short-term flexibility of wages and prices prevent the relative price adjustments required to signal appropriate alterations in the pattern of real resource utilization, activist policies may produce their intended

[11] See Stanley Fisher, "Long-Term Contracts, Rational Expectations, and the Optimal Money Supply Rule," *Journal of Political Economy* 85, February 1977, pp. 191-206. The importance of the flexible price assumption in achieving the rational expectations results also is stressed in Martin Neil Baily, "Stabilization Policy and Private Economic Behavior," *Brookings Papers on Economic Activity* 1, 1978, pp. 11-50.
[12] See William Poole, "Rational Expectations in the Macro Model," *Brookings Papers on Economic Activity* 2, 1976, pp. 463-505.

effects in the short run even if expectations are rational.

Throughout this paper the presence or absence of an impact on *total* real output and employment has been the criterion used to determine whether or not activist policies "work" in the short run. But the *composition* of output may sometimes be as relevant a consideration for policy-makers as the size of the total. For example, in the interests of stimulating productivity growth the fiscal authority may introduce macroeconomic policies aimed at increasing the share of investment spending in total output. Even the strict version of the rational expectations model — with perfect price flexibility, zero real adjustment costs, and complete information — admits that activist policy can produce this outcome. Whatever the merits of the rational expectations argument that stabilization policy cannot influence total real output in the short run, this view does not imply that activist policy cannot be used to pursue other worthwhile macroeconomic objectives.

The potential for activist policy to change the composition if not the size of real GNP in the short run has implications for the economy's performance in the long run as well. For example, if the fiscal policy just mentioned — an acceleration of corporate depreciation allowances, say — succeeds in increasing the share of investment in total output (regardless of its effect on the size of the total), then the capital stock of the economy will be larger than it otherwise would have been in the absence of the policy change. Both the equilibrium real wage and the economy's potential long-run growth path increase accordingly. Alternatively, consider the long-run impact of an anticipated increase in the rate of growth of the money stock that causes a permanent increase in the rate of inflation but no immediate effects on total real GNP. The higher inflation rate tends to lower the demand for

nominal money balances at the expense of an increase in the demand for assets such as physical capital goods whose real value can be expected to rise or at least to remain stable as prices increase. This policy-induced shift in the composition of output also has important consequences for the behavior of the economy in the long run.[13] Even if the short-run policy implications of the rational expectations model are accepted completely (and there are good reasons not to do so), it does not follow that activist policies are also powerless to influence the economy in the long run.

IV. Conclusion: The Emerging Synthesis

The rational expectations model as widely interpreted implies that systematic and predictable activist stabilization policies have no impact on real output or employment in the short run. This paper explains why this conclusion depends on a set of highly restrictive assumptions that do not describe conditions in the real world. From a practical point of view, then, the rational expectations model does not establish a compelling case against the continued use of activist stabilization policies.

This is not to say that actual historical policies have been ideal or even desirable. In fact, only if the rational expectations view is *false* can one indict activist policy as destabilizing (unless activist policies have increased the magnitude of unanticipated policy shocks).[14] And even if true, the rational expectations model does not imply that *no* policy — including built-in stabilizers such as unemployment insurance and the progressive income tax — affects real output

---

[13] See Stanley Fisher, "Anticipations and the Non-Neutrality of Money," *Journal of Political Economy* 87, April 1979, pp. 229-52.

[14] Evidence that activist policies have contributed to economic stability in the postwar period is presented in M.N. Baily, "Stabilization Policy . . ."

and employment in the short run.[15] Thus, even on its own terms the conclusions of the rational expectations school must be interpreted with caution.

On the other hand, it is incorrect to argue that the rational expectations school has contributed nothing to our understanding of the channels through which policy actions influence the real economy or that the traditional rationales for activist policy have emerged unscathed from the rational expectations onslaught. The assumption that expectations are rational simply requires that in acting to further their own interests individuals anticipate the impact of expected policy changes on the wages, prices, and patterns of demand and supply of those goods and services important to them. This much seems unexceptionable, yet it carries with it the crucial implication that the estimated parameters that describe individual behavior in economic models used to generate activist policy prescriptions are dependent on the policies themselves. Under "ideal" conditions this interdependence between individual behavior and anticipated policy renders policy impotent. Under more realistic assumptions about information flows, real adjustment costs, and wage and price adjustment than are required to produce the strict rational expectations results, the model still implies that the impact of activist policy on real output and employment is substantially smaller than was previously believed to be the case.[16] While the presence of adjustment costs and other impediments to the frictionless flow of information and resources makes it impossible for individuals completely to offset anticipated events, their effort to do so up to the point justified by these costs reduces the impact of policy nonetheless.

To put this point another way, the traditional view summarized in this paper recognizes that activist policies have no effects in the long run but lead to predictable consequences in the short run. The rational expectations school argues that the length of the short run depends on the policy followed. What emerges is a synthesis in which activist policies still "work" for the traditional reason — that real adjustments cannot be made instantaneously — but work less powerfully and predictably than was customarily believed for a new reason — that stabilization policy is not a "game" against nature whose reactions do not alter in response to policy stimuli but a game against intelligent agents whose reactions depend on policy moves. This point, long understood instinctively by skilled practical policy-makers, rather than the extreme policy impotence position, is the important contribution to macroeconomic theory made by the rational expectations school.

---

[15] For a proof that built-in stabilizers are effective even under those conditions where activist policies are not, see B.T. McCallum and J.K. Whitaker, "The Effectiveness of Fiscal Feedback Rules . . ." The importance of tax parameters in influencing real behavior is also discussed in Ray C. Fair, "A Criticism of One Class of Macroeconomic Models with Rational Expectations," *Journal of Money, Credit and Banking* 10, November 1978, pp. 411-17.

[16] Empirical evidence in support of this position is provided in Ray C. Fair, "An Analysis of a Macro-Econometric Model with Rational Expectations in the Bond and Stock Markets," *American Economic Review* 69, September 1979, pp. 539-552. Fair concludes that in his model "anticipated policy actions are about one-fourth as effective (with respect to real output changes) when there are rational expectations in (the bond and stock) markets than when there are not."

LONG-TERM U. S. ECONOMIC OUTLOOK: ISSUES
AND METHODOLOGY

Arthur E. Rockwell, C.F.A.

Focus on the short-term economic, financial, and political outlook often leads to a failure to distinguish between temporary cyclical phenomena and underlying secular trends. Longer-term investment strategy requires both an ability to perceive and understand long-term economic trends as well as to forecast the potential economic environment over longer periods of time, such as five to ten years. The purpose of this article is to highlight the major issues involved in taking a longer-term view of the economy and to present some methodological approaches to it. Although a specific economic forecast is presented to the year 1985, the specifics of the forecast are inevitably dated. A forecast is no more than a conditional statement based on a given set of conditions and assumptions. Forecasting itself is an ongoing process of presenting plausible scenarios on which to base alternative investment strategies.

This article comprises six sections: (1) Summary; (2) 1985: The U.S. Economy; (3) Long-term Industry Outlook; (4) Demographics, Labor Force, and Employment; (5) The Productivity Dilemma; and (6) Energy and Inflation.

Section 2 presents the overall forecast through 1985 and discusses the major issues involved and the methodology of making a long-term forecast. Sections 4, 5, and 6 amplify some of the major issues developed in the overall discussion. However, a unique feature of this approach, from the investment point of view, is the integration of the long-term economic outlook with the industry forecast, which is presented in the third section. With the use of an input-output model of the United States economy, a specific forecast of real output, or final demands, and prices is presented for the economy at a detailed industry level, consistent within the framework of the overall macroeconomic forecast.

Although this approach has obvious limitations, e.g., specific industry profits cannot be forecast, it does provide a framework for a top-down economic approach through to specific industry categories. Final demand forecasts by industry are also a starting point for more detailed financial analysis of industries and companies. The methodology is viewed as a way in which economic forecasting and analysis can provide useful insights into the investment process.

---

*Reprinted from Security Pacific National Bank, *Economic Report,*
    March 1980, with an introduction.

Summary

The major theme of this report is the outlook for the United States economy through 1985. By 1985, the total annual value of output of the economy will have surpassed the staggering figure of $4 trillion! Unfortunately, much of this gain is ethereal as inflation will have accounted for most of it. A detailed analysis of labor force growth and productivity concludes that potential output will grow only on the order of a 2.7 percent average annual rate through 1985, below previous estimates, but seemingly realistic in light of changing demographic factors, the recent dismal history of productivity growth, and the energy outlook. Given the difficulties that the economy is likely to encounter in achieving full employment, real output over the 1979–1985 period is projected to grow at an annual trend rate of only 2.6 percent. The trend rate of inflation, as measured by the GNP deflator, is expected to be about 8.4 percent per annum over the forecast period. The net result is an annual trend growth rate in current, or nominal, dollars on the order of 11.2 percent.

The composition of real output is expected to change in a number of respects. Both nominal and real personal consumption expenditures will be squeezed by the competing demands of the other sectors. However, real spending on durables and services should maintain at least a rate of growth in line with projected real GNP. Real investment expenditure is forecast to increase its share of output modestly as business spends more on plant and equipment. The underlying demand for housing ensures a relatively constant share of real output devoted to this key sector. The sharpest change will occur in the government sector, which is projected to decline in the aggregate. But real federal expenditures on defense are likely to increase.

The real growth and inflation forecast contained in this report is somewhat more pessimistic than most official government forecasts of the economy, but appears realistic in terms of the near-term economic difficulties the United States is facing. Although inflation remains an intractable problem, progress is expected in this difficult battle, with the average inflation rate projected to decline to the 7.5 percent area by 1985. Interest rates, both long-term and short-term, are likely to remain high, declining only modestly over the forecast horizon.

Following this broad-brush picture of trends in the economy through 1985, a summary of a detailed industry forecast is presented. Based on the use of an inter-industry forecasting model, it summarizes and ranks the real growth prospects of a number of specific industries in the context of the long-term United States outlook presented herein.

An overview of the demographic factors affecting the economy in the 1980's is then presented, along with a detailed analysis and forecast of the size and composition of the labor force for the 1979–1985 and 1985–1990 periods. Specific industry employment forecasts for the 1979–1985 period are then presented.

The debate over the productivity dilemma is summarized along with an aggregate productivity forecast. In addition, a detailed look at productivity on an industry-by-industry basis, with a forecast, is presented.

The interrelated areas of energy and inflation are treated at a more detailed level. Specific inflation forecasts for the components of GNP and the industrial composition of wholesale prices are discussed.

1985: The United States Economy

FORECAST HIGHLIGHTS: 1979–1985

Although the United States economy in 1985 is not likely to be dramatically different from today's structure, a number of important trends that can be discerned today will, nevertheless, have a very real impact looking out over five years. These underlying trends will be analyzed in some detail in this report, but no attempt will be made to forecast the detailed path of the economy from 1979 to 1985. This year's long-term forecast differs in several key respects from last year's (1978–1984). Based upon the current inflationary experience, the changing demographic forces as we look further out into the 1980's, and a reevaluation of some basic assumptions, including defense spending, the new forecast anticipates slower real growth in Gross National Product, a higher inflation rate, and a change in sectoral shares.

The basic point of departure for a long-term forecast is an attempt to project the potential output of economy through time rather than a narrow concern with short-term shifts in aggregate demand. This report discusses the role of potential output in some detail and traces the sources of economic growth in the United States in the post-World War II era. The major input in the production of aggregate economic output is, of course, labor. Important trends in the labor force are underway with implications for the economy over the next five years quite different from the past five years' history. Since 1973 a major dilemma of the American economy has been the lag in labor's productivity growth. An attempt is made to explain this recent lag and to make some cautious assessments about its possible future path.

Once the underlying trend in potential output has been analyzed and forecast, the crucial step is to relate aggregate demand to potential. The critical issue in assessing the extent of any "gap" between actual and potential output is a determination of the rate of unemployment at which the labor force is considered fully employed. Having forecast the levels of both potential and actual output in the economy by 1985, the composition of this output is then analyzed in terms of the four major expenditure categories: personal consumption, gross private domestic investment, government purchases, and net exports.

No other single issue has occupied economists and policymakers in recent years as has inflation. An attempt is made to forecast the trend of inflation through 1985 and to differentiate inflation's impact upon the several sectors of the economy. The ability of the corporation to adjust to the underlying growth trend of the economy and to deal with the problem of inflation is a key determinant of aggregate corporate profits. These, along with the other major factors determining corporate profits, will be discussed as well as the outlook for dividend policy. The rate of inflation is also a key determinant in forecasting the average level of interest rates over this period.

Some of the risks to the forecast are briefly sketched to point out possibilities that, on the one hand, are a bit more optimistic and, on the other hand, more pessimistic in terms of the serious inflationary problems that the

Forecast Summary 1979-1985

- Slow, gradual unwinding of inflation with relatively sluggish real growth of the economy
- Cyclical recovery in the early 1980's following a downturn
- Gradual decline in the inflation rate to the 7.5% area by 1985
- Relatively restrictive monetary policy and a gradual reduction in the federal budget deficit
- Above-trend real growth of the investment sector
- Above-trend real growth of federal defense expeditures
- Interest rates to remain high, declining only modestly over the forecast horizon
- Corporate profits growth in line with the economy

FORECAST SUMMARY
1979–1985
(in billions)

Aggregate Demand	1973	1979P	1985F
Potential GNP (1972 $)	1219.9	1466.0	1720.0
Real GNP (1972 $)	1235.0	1431.1	1669.0
GNP Gap (%)	−1.2%	2.4%	3.0%
Unemployment Rate	4.9%	5.8%	7.0–7.5%
Nominal GNP (current $)	1306.6	2368.5	4481.0
Growth Trends	**1973–79**	**1979–85**	
Real GNP	2.5%	2.6%	
Inflation	7.7	8.4	
Nominal GNP	10.4	11.2	

economy faces over this period. This is discussed in the context of the constraints facing policymakers in the areas of fiscal, monetary, and "incomes" policies.

Finally, a brief epilogue on the 1985-1990 period indicates some further shifts in the economy that appear likely to occur by the end of the decade. The accompanying table briefly summarizes the highlights of the forecast from 1979 to 1985 and its quantitative dimensions are presented in the forecast summary.

THE ROLE OF POTENTIAL OUTPUT

The potential output path of the economy has generally tended to be a fairly smooth trend line, given the relatively stable trend growth of both the labor force and its productivity. It is also the trend path of full-employment output and gives the level of output that could be obtained with the unemployment rate at its so-called full-employment rate and labor productivity growth at its historical trend value. When actual GNP is below potential output, unemployment is above the full-employment unemployment rate (F.E.U.R.) and real output is lost. This difference between potential and actual real output is referred to as the GNP "gap." Conversely, when actual output is above potential, some additional output is temporarily gained, but only at the cost of a higher rate of price inflation. Thus, the potential output path does not represent an absolute physical maximum, but rather gives the level of output associated with a "full-employment" rate of unemployment and one that would be compatible with reasonable price stability.

A Moving Target

Evidence in recent years suggests that previous official estimates of the trend growth rate of potential output

have been overly optimistic. Given a post-war productivity trend on the order of 2 percent annually combined with rapid expansion of the labor force, most official calculations had potential output growing at a trend rate of at least 3.5 percent. However, since 1973, productivity growth in the economy has faltered, while the labor force has made unprecedented gains. Meanwhile, the economy has experienced severe inflationary pressures, and the ability to reach the hypothetical potential without aggravating inflationary pressures has been seriously questioned by most analysts inside and outside the government. Apparently heeding the call to reassess those potential output calculations, the Council of Economic Advisors in the *1979 Economic Report of the President* reevaluated the official estimates and revised them downward significantly. The revised estimates, from 1973 to 1978, imply that the trend growth of potential output over this period was only 3.0 percent, as follows: labor force growth, 2.5 percent; manhours per worker, −0.5 percent; and productivity, 1.0 percent. Furthermore, its projection of potential output from 1978 to 1983 was similarly 3.0 percent. However, the composition had a lower labor force growth and some anticipated rebound in productivity.

In the *1980 Economic Report of the President*, the Council has hedged its bets. It has "temporarily" lowered its potential output estimate from 3 to 2.5 percent during the three years beginning with the first quarter of 1979. This drop is attributed to the dismal near-term productivity outlook. Then the Council expects productivity to rebound to the 1.5 to 2.0 percent range, yielding a growth in potential output over the 1982–1985 period that is near 3 percent.

Estimating the Potential Path

However, recent work done by Security Pacific Bank, Data Resources, Inc., and others casts serious doubt on the CEA appraisal, viz., a "rebounding trend" back to the 3 percent per annum area for potential output. Security Pacific Bank now estimates potential GNP growth

CALCULATION OF POTENTIAL GNP GROWTH
Annual Trend Growth Rates

	SPNB Forecast 1979–85
Labor Force	1.8%
Manhours per Worker	−0.5
Productivity	1.4
	2.7%

SOURCES OF ECONOMIC GROWTH IN THE UNITED STATES
1950–1979
(Annual Trend Growth Rates)

Periods	Civilian Labor Force	Average Weekly Hours†	Productivity‡	Actual GNP	Potential GNP§
1950–79	1.8%	−0.4%	1.9%	3.5%	3.3%
1950–73	1.6	−0.3	2.3	3.7	3.3
1950–55	0.9	−0.1	2.1	4.2	2.3
1955–65	1.4	−0.2	2.6	3.5	3.5
1955–73	1.7	−0.4	2.3	3.6	3.6
1955–79	1.9	−0.4	1.9	3.3	3.5
1965–73	2.2	−0.6	2.0	3.7	3.8
1965–79	2.3	−0.6	1.3	3.2	3.5
1973–79	2.5	−0.5	0.5	2.5	3.1

†Total private nonagricultural
‡Output per hour, nonfarm business sector.
§Based on DRI est.

from 1979 to 1985 to average only 2.7 percent per year. Over this six-year period, growth in the labor force is expected to average 1.8 percent per year. Declines in manhours per worker should be on the order of 0.5 percent, giving a net labor input of 1.3 percent. Despite the recent dismal performance in productivity and a near-term expectation of very little improvement, it is anticipated that a rebound will occur in the early 1980's that will bring the average for the period to 1.4 percent.

SOURCES OF ECONOMIC GROWTH
In order to put today's difficulties and the longer-term forecast into proper perspective, it may be useful to review briefly the history of growth in the United States economy in the post-World War II era. From 1950 to 1979, the annual trend rate of growth in the economy has been about 3.5 percent in real terms. Over this long stretch, the labor force has grown at 1.8 percent, average weekly hours have declined 0.4 percent, and productivity has grown 1.9 percent. However, a closer look at the sub-periods summarized in the accompanying table illustrates that the pattern of growth has varied considerably. The rapid spurt in output from 1950 to 1965 was paced by rapid gains in productivity. In the Vietnam War era from 1965 to 1973, the trend rate of growth was a very strong 3.7 percent. Productivity gains remained fairly high at 2.0 percent, but the civilian labor force expanded at 2.2 percent rate. Tempering this rapid expansion of the labor force, however, was an accelerating

decline in average weekly hours. Nevertheless, this was a period of historically high growth of both potential and actual output. Since 1973, however, the trend in potential output dropped to only 3.1 percent. The major contribution to growth in this most recent era was the unprecedented expansion in the labor force as the "baby boom" children of the 1950's reached working age and the number of women entering the labor force accelerated rapidly. The labor force will again be the most significant factor contributing to potential output growth

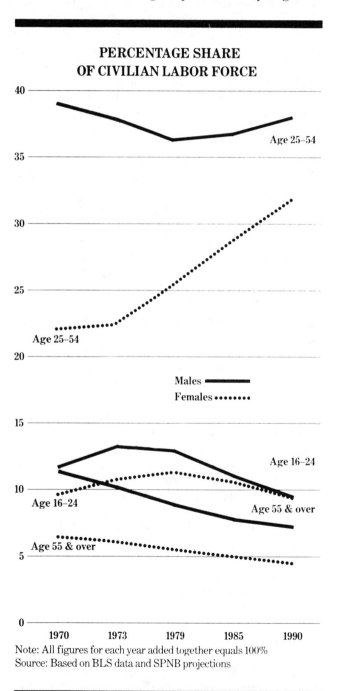

PERCENTAGE SHARE OF CIVILIAN LABOR FORCE

Age 25–54

Age 25–54

Males ▬▬▬
Females ••••••••

Age 16–24

Age 16–24

Age 55 & over

Age 55 & over

1970   1973   1979   1985   1990

Note: All figures for each year added together equals 100%
Source: Based on BLS data and SPNB projections

through the mid 1980's, but at a considerably slower rate than in the recent past. A more detailed assessment of these basic sources of growth is presented in the following sections.

THE CHANGING LABOR FORCE

No single factor in the determination of economic growth is more critical or as pervasive as the labor force. Labor is the primary input in the production of aggregate output and the income derived by labor is the major source of expenditures in the economy. Aggregate numbers on the civilian labor force only begin to tell the story. Even though with a known population base it would seem a very straightforward calculation, analysts have continually underestimated its growth. From 1950 to 1979, the total civilian labor force grew 1.8 percent per annum. Since 1973, however, it has grown at about a 2.5 percent rate, but a significant slowdown in the growth of the labor force is expected in the 1980's.

Determinants of the Labor Force

In any given period of time, a certain percentage of the total population is actively seeking employment in the monetized sector of the economy. This group constitutes the active labor force. The percentage of this group unable to find suitable employment is referred to as the unemployment rate. Thus, it is self-evident that the size of the population is a major determinant of the civilian labor force. From 1970 to 1979 the total population grew at a 1.8 percent annual trend rate. However, population trends in the 1980's are likely to be considerably different. From 1979 to 1985, total population will grow at only a 1.1 percent trend rate. From 1985 to 1990, civilian noninstitutional population growth will decelerate further to 0.8 percent.

One of the most troublesome variables to forecast in recent years has been the labor force participation rate. Most public as well as private forecasters estimate an increase in the participation rates among most population groups, but especially among women. The data presented in this report, although partly based on a revised set of projections from the Bureau of Labor Statistics, were revised upward in the light of more recent evidence. The overall civilian labor force participation rate is projected to rise from 63.7 percent in 1979 to 66.3 by 1985. The rate for all men is expected to remain flat over the period at 77.9 percent, and the rate for all women is expected to continue rising, from 51.0 percent in 1979 to 55.9 percent by 1985.

The accompanying graph illustrates the changing composition of the labor force over time. Men in the central age group, age 25 to 54, will experience a decline in its relative share of the labor force from 1970 to 1990, but will actually experience a slight recovery from 1979

to 1985. On the other hand, women in the central age group, age 25 to 54, will continue to expand its relative share, from 22.0 percent in 1970 to 31.8 percent by 1990.

The maturing of the labor force should lead to a more productive labor force. The greater productivity of a more experienced workforce should partially offset the slower labor force growth in the 1980's. The impact of more women in the labor force is ambiguous and will depend on the extent to which women with children will be able to work full time.

A separate section of this report is devoted to a more detailed analysis of the labor force.

The Declining Workweek

Another factor in the post-World War II period has been the declining trend in average weekly hours worked. In the total private nonagricultural sector, the workweek had declined from 39.8 hours in 1950 to an estimated 35.7 hours in 1979. The trend over this period has been an average annual decline of 0.4 percent. However, the long-term trend rate conceals some acceleration of the declining workweek. From 1950 to 1965 the annual de-

RECENT PRODUCTIVITY GROWTH
(Adjusted for Cyclical Variation)

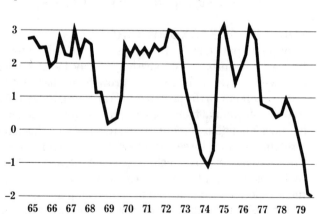

Note: Data are for private nonfarm business sector all persons
Source: Council of Economic Advisors

cline was only on the order of 0.2 percent. If measured from 1955 to the present, the decline was only on the order of 0.4 percent, but in more recent years, viz., since 1965, the decline has been on the order of 0.6 percent.

A number of factors have contributed to this trend of declining hours worked including: productivity growth, preference for leisure over work, the continuing shift from agriculture and industry into services, the increase of women and teenagers in the labor force, and the growing acceptance by many employers of more flexible scheduling and the use of part-time employees. Some easing of the trend of recent years is expected looking out to 1985, with the decline expected to average only 0.5 percent annually over the forecast period.

THE PRODUCTIVITY DILEMMA

As discussed above, productivity growth has been a key source of overall economic growth in the United States, both in the period following World War II and over an even longer historical horizon. However, the recent history of productivity has been quite dismal, and no immediate improvement is in sight. This lagging productivity is one of the root causes of our current inflationary problems and our balance-of-payments difficulties.

UNEMPLOYMENT BY AGE/SEX COMPOSITION

| | Historical Unemployment Rates | | | |
	1965	1973	1978	1979
Male				
16–19	14.1%	13.9%	15.7%	15.8%
20–24	6.3	7.3	9.1	8.6
25–34	3.0	3.3	4.3	4.2
35–44	2.6	2.0	2.8	2.9
45–54	2.5	2.1	2.8	2.7
55–64	3.3	2.4	2.7	2.7
65+	3.5	3.0	4.2	3.5
Men – 16 & over	4.0	4.1	5.2	5.1
Female				
16–19	15.7	15.2	17.0	16.4
20–24	7.3	8.4	10.1	9.6
25–34	5.5	5.8	6.7	6.4
35–44	4.6	3.9	5.0	4.6
45–54	3.2	3.2	4.0	3.9
55–64	2.8	2.8	3.2	3.2
65+	2.8	2.9	3.8	3.3
Women – 16 & over	5.5	6.0	7.2	6.8
Total	4.5%	4.9%	6.0%	5.8%
GNP Gap ($B)	–23.2	–15.1	25.3	34.9

UNEMPLOYMENT BY INDUSTRY

| | Unemployment Rates | |
	1973	1979
Agriculture	6.9%	9.1%
Nonagriculture	4.5	5.4
Mining	2.9	4.9
Construction	8.8	10.2
Manufacturing	4.3	5.5
Durable goods	3.9	5.0
Nondurable goods	4.9	6.4
Transportation, communication and public utilities	3.0	3.7
Wholesale and retail trade	5.6	6.5
Finance, insurance and real estate	2.7	3.0
Other services	4.8	5.4
Government	2.7	3.7
Total Civilian Unemployment Rate	4.9%	5.8%

Source: BLS

Why Productivity Has Lagged

Since 1973 productivity in the nonfarm business sector has averaged only 0.5 percent compared with a post-war trend of near 2.0 percent. A number of factors, some measurable but others more subtle, have accounted for this disappointing performance. The economic "boom-bust" cycle of the early 1970's, exacerbated by the Arab oil embargo of 1973, has discouraged capital investment in plant and equipment. The capital stock in relation to the labor force, i.e., the capital-labor ratio, has declined and is not expected to achieve its pre-1973 level in the foreseeable future. Another difficulty stems from the legislated environmental tradeoffs, which caused much of the actual capital investment to be put into such "non-productive" investment as pollution abatement and control equipment. The abrupt turnaround in the relative price of competing energy sources also required a significant investment just to accommodate this change.

Perhaps less obvious, but of a fundamental nature, has been the lag in research and development expenditure by private businesses and the federal government. During the 1960's, basic research was strongly supported by the government. However, in the late 1960's, Administration policies backed away from support of basic research, and, with the slowdown in the space program, private industry lost this favorable fallout.

The changing structure of the economy is also a major factor in the decline in productivity growth. The greatest productivity advances in output per manhour generally occur in high technology, manufacturing industries and traditionally, of course, American agriculture has been a major contributor to overall productivity growth. But the trend of recent decades toward a larger service sector economy makes it difficult to achieve the same rate of productivity advances of an economy in an earlier stage of industrial evolution. Advances in productivity in the highly labor-intensive service sector are difficult to achieve. A more detailed appraisal of the productivity problem, including specific industry data, is presented in a subsequent section of this report.

Guarded Optimism

There are no immediate signs of relief from the productivity slowdown the economy is currently experiencing. Certainly the near-term cyclical outlook is not encouraging. However, with a cyclical rebound, a slowdown in the rate of growth in the labor force, and some improvement in the investment area, the trend growth in productivity through 1985 should show a considerable improvement

over the recent past. There has been some pickup in both governmental and private business expenditures on research and development. This resurgence is critical if a sustained longer-term growth in productivity is to be achieved. Investment in producers' durable equipment by the private sector should help to improve the capital-labor and capital/output ratios by 1985. And, finally, the maturing of the workforce should contribute to productivity improvement.

UNEMPLOYMENT AND THE GAP

The relationship between the unemployment rate to the "gap" between actual and potential output, referred to as Okun's Law, has been a troublesome issue in the recent past as a method of forecasting the unemployment rate. But despite the instability of Okun's Law in today's inflationary environment, it appears unlikely that full employment can be achieved by 1985. The GNP gap may decline slightly from the 2.4 percent in 1979 by 1983 or 1984, but appears headed higher again by 1985 to around

LONG-TERM U.S. ECONOMIC OUTLOOK
1979–1985
(billions)

	(Current $)		(1972 $)	
	1979P	1985F	1979P	1985F
Gross National Product	2368.5	4481	1431.1	1669
Personal Consumption Expenditures	1509.8	2817	924.5	1069
Durable Goods	212.8	372	147.0	174
Autos and Parts	91.3	169	58.5	69
Except Autos and Parts	121.6	203	88.5	105
Nondurable Goods	597.0	1095	349.3	395
Services	700.0	1350	428.2	500
Gross Private Domestic Investment	386.2	762	214.8	254
Fixed Investment	367.8	732	204.6	244
Nonresidential	253.9	494	148.2	178
Producers' Durable Equipment	161.6	308	100.3	122
Structures	92.3	186	47.9	56
Residential	113.9	238	56.5	66
Change in Business Inventories	18.4	30	10.2	10
Government Purchases	476.1	912	274.1	316
Federal	166.3	333	99.2	121
Defense	108.3	226	64.7†	82
Nondefense	58.0	107	34.4†	39
State and Local	309.8	579	174.9	195
Net Exports	−3.5	−10	17.7	30

P = Preliminary   F = SPNB Forecast   † = Estimate

3.0 percent. The unemployment rate is likely to rise from the 5.8 percent average level in 1979 to the 7.0 to 7.5 percent range by 1985.

Full-Employment Unemployment Rate

There are many conceptual difficulties in trying to calculate a nominal unemployment rate that is, in effect, consistent with a fully-employed economy. In today's inflationary environment, most traditional estimates of the F.E.U.R. are deemed too low. The unemployment rate traditionally has been viewed as a measure of "slack" in the labor force. However, more recent concepts emphasize an F.E.U.R. that incorporates the concept of a "nonaccelerating inflation" rate of unemployment. This rate is clearly higher than most traditional estimates, but conceptually and empirically it is very difficult to use in making longer-term forecasts.

A simple method of calculation uses historical full-employment unemployment rates of the different sex-age categories and applies them to the forecasted labor force in 1985. This approach leads to an F.E.U.R. of 4.8–4.9 percent if 1965 and 1973 are considered the relevant full employment benchmarks. However, if the last two years are considered a more realistic benchmark, then an appropriate F.E.U.R. by 1985 is 5.7–5.9 percent.

Using unemployment rates by industrial employment categories and applying them to projected employment by industry in 1985 sheds little further light on the issue. The projected F.E.U.R. is 4.5 percent using 1973 rates, but climbs to 5.4 percent using the presumably more realistic 1979 unemployment rates.

Thus, an estimate for the full-employment rate of unemployment by 1985 is in the 5 to 6 percent area, with 5.5 percent a reasonable point estimate.

REAL OUTPUT AND INFLATION

Over the 1979–1985 period, the annual trend growth of the economy is forecast to be on the order of 11.2 percent. However, only 2.6 percent is accounted for by real growth and 8.4 percent is the result of inflation. From 1973 to 1979, nominal output grew at 10.4 percent andual rate, real GNP by 2.5 percent, and inflation at 7.7

GNP GROWTH & SECTORAL SHARES

	1979–85 Growth Trend		Share of GNP (Current $)		Share of GNP (1972 $)	
	(Current $)	(1972 $)	1979	1985	1979	1985
Gross National Product	11.2%	2.6 %	100.0%	100.0 %	100.0%	100.0%
Personal Consumption Expenditures	11.0	2.4	63.7	62.8	64.6	64.1
Durable Goods	9.8	2.9	9.0	8.3	10.3	10.4
Autos and Parts	10.8	2.8	3.9	3.8	4.1	4.1
Except Autos and Parts	8.9	2.9	5.1	4.5	6.2	6.3
Nondurable Goods	10.6	2.1	25.2	24.4	24.4	23.7
Services	11.6	2.6	29.6	30.1	29.9	30.0
Gross Private Domestic Investment	12.0	2.8	16.3	17.0	15.0	15.2
Fixed Investment	12.2	3.0	15.5	16.3	14.3	14.6
Nonresidential	11.7	3.1	10.7	11.0	10.4	10.7
Producers' Durable Equipment	11.3	3.3	6.8	6.9	7.1	7.3
Structures	12.4	2.6	3.9	4.1	3.3	3.4
Residential	13.1	2.6	4.8	5.3	3.9	4.0
Change in Business Inventories	8.5	–	0.8	0.7	0.7	0.6
Government Purchases	11.4	2.4	20.1	20.4	19.2	18.9
Federal	12.3	3.4	7.0	7.4	6.9	7.3
Defense	13.0	4.0	4.6	5.0	4.5	4.9
Nondefense	10.7	2.1	2.4	2.4	2.4	2.3
State and Local	11.0	1.8	13.1	12.9	12.2	11.7
Net Exports	–	9.2	-0.1	-0.2	1.2	1.8

percent. These numbers highlight the difficulties of achieving noninflationary growth in the foreseeable future. The accompanying tables provide a detailed forecast of the expenditure components of Gross National Product in nominal and real terms. GNP growth and sectoral shares, nominal and real, are also presented.

Personal Consumption: A Squeeze

Total personal consumption expenditures are expected to decline from 63.7 percent of nominal GNP in 1979 to 62.8 percent in 1985. In real terms, the share drops from 64.6 percent to 64.1 percent. The real growth in durable goods will be above trend for autos, household furnishings, and appliances. The growth of nondurables should be below trend as both food and fuel consumption decline as a result of inflationary pressures. The service sector is expected to continue its trend growth through 1985, with greater relative growth in such areas as health care and leisure and lesser growth in education.

Private Investment: Up a Little

Private investment is expected to grow somewhat above the GNP trend in real terms, but a full-fledged capital spending boom is not foreseen. A certain amount of catch-up is implicit in the real growth of producers' durable equipment as business seeks to increase productivity. Residential fixed investment, on trend in real terms, remains relatively strong despite cyclical problems. However, inflation accounts for much of the nominal increase. Tighter management control of inventories should maintain inventory investment at a fairly even keel over this period.

Government Purchases: Defense Rebounds

The real share of government purchases is expected to decline from 19.2 percent in 1979 to 18.9 percent by 1985. The decline in state and local spending, while reflecting some post-Proposition 13 influences, is primarily the result of demographic factors. Enrollment declines at the elementary and high school levels will mean much slower real growth in educational expenditures.

A major change in the forecast is at the federal level. Recent world developments have heightened the realization that real defense spending must increase sharply in the coming years to maintain a credible national defense posture. A real growth rate of 4 percent through 1985 will not be easy to achieve in the face of high inflation and the competition for scarce resources. However, even this above-trend growth of real defense expenditures will not bring its share of real output back to where it was in 1973. That sort of commitment would require real growth in excess of 6 percent annually.

The Foreign Sector

Net exports are expected to improve, in real terms, from $17.7 billion in 1979 to approximately $30 billion by 1985. Real export growth is expected to be on the order of 3.8 percent annually with real imports growing at a 2.7 percent rate. However, because of continuing price pressures from petroleum imports, the rate of inflation in the import sector will continue to exceed that of exports (10.0 percent versus 8.8 percent). The overall effect would be to increase the net export deficit in nominal dollars from $3.5 billion in 1979 to about $10 billion by 1985.

The accompanying graph illustrates the inexorable growth of the foreign sector's impact on the United States economy. Import prices are having a severe impact on domestic inflation and more real output must be devoted to exports to pay for higher priced imports.

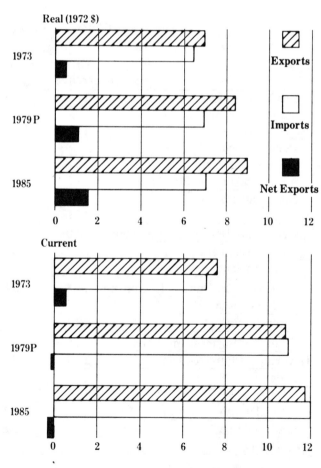

FOREIGN SECTOR OUTLOOK
(Percent Share of GNP)

INFLATION FORECAST
1979–1985
(Annual Trend Rates)

	1973–79	1979–85F
Personal Consumption Expenditures	7.6%	8.3%
Gross Private Domestic Investment	9.2	8.9
Government Purchases	8.5	8.8
Exports	10.8	8.8
Imports	13.7	10.0
Implicit Price Deflator (GNP)	7.7%	8.4%

Inflation

Inflation remains the major economic issue and the most difficult problem for policymakers and analysts to deal with. Energy is the key to the inflationary crisis both by its direct as well as indirect impacts. Near-term, there appears to be little hope for a slowdown in price pressures. However, the overall inflation forecast (GNP deflator) of 8.4 percent annual trend rate through 1985 assumes an easing of the inflation rate to the 7.5 percent area by the end of the forecast period. The accompanying table summarizes the expected inflation rates by major economic sectors. A separate section of this report provides a more detailed appraisal of the energy and inflation issues.

CORPORATE PROFITS

With a sluggish real growth rate of 2.6 percent and an inflation rate of 8.4 percent, corporations will be somewhat hard-pressed to maintain growth rates in profits, especially at the pretax level. However, compared to the difficulties in dealing with the unanticipated inflation in the early 1970's, it is assumed that corporations have learned to deal much more effectively in protecting their margins in today's inflationary environment. Capacity utilization rates in manufacturing are expected to improve gradually. Interest rates are expected to remain relatively high, both long-term and short-term, exerting further pressures on profits. But a key difficulty lies in the expected increase in unit labor costs, which are forecast to grow at an annual rate of 8.2 percent over the period.

Although pretax profits are expected to grow only at 9.3 percent, after-tax profits should grow at about 9.5 percent as a result of an expected lower effective corporate tax rate.

After-tax profits of nonfinancial corporations, however, should grow somewhat above trend, with relatively less favorable growth in the financial corporate sector. No significant change from recent trends is expected in dividend policies. The chances of achieving a higher dividend payout ratio appear slim in light of the fact that corporations will need to retain at least the same proportion of after-tax earnings if they are to

CORPORATE PROFITS OUTLOOK
1979–1985

	(Current $— billions) 1979P	1985F	Growth Trend 1973–79	1979–85F
Corporate profits w/IVA & CCA	178.4	291.0	10.3%	8.5%
Corporate profits before taxes	237.0	404.0	12.7	9.3
Corporate profits after taxes	144.7	250.0	13.7	9.5
Capital consumption allowance	131.0	270.0	10.0	12.8
Total CPAT & CCA	275.7	520.0	11.8	11.2
Dividends	52.8	97.5	11.3	10.8
Cash flow minus dividends	222.9	422.5	12.0	11.2
Retained Earnings	92.0	152.5	15.2	8.8
Capital consumption adjustment	−16.7	−58.0		
Inventory valuation adjustment	−41.9	−55.0		
Effective Tax Rate	38.9%	38.1%		
Dividend Payout Ratio	36.5%	39.0%		

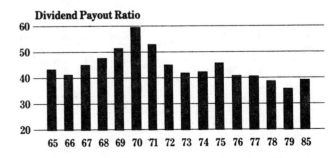

TRENDS IN DIVIDENDS 1965–1985F
(In Percent)

achieve expected investment levels. The high profit levels apparently achieved in 1979 and the concomitant drop in the dividend payout ratio is a cyclical phenomenon that makes the resulting earnings forecast from this base look a bit less favorable than it actually is.

INTEREST RATES

Forecasting the long-term trend in interest rates is hazardous at best. Needless to say, interest rates can be expected to be quite volatile over any period this long. The nominal long-term rate, as represented by the corporate bond rate, comprises the real rate of interest and the inflation rate. The real rate of return on capital has tended historically to be in the 2–2½ percent range, although since 1973 it seems to have dropped down to just over 1 percent. The primary reason for this recent discrepancy appears to be the miscalculation by long-term investors of the expected inflation outlook. Given our inflation assumption of about 8.4 percent and the expectation that the historical required real rate of return will begin to re-assert itself, average long-term rates should be on the order of 10⅝ percent as represented by the AAA corporate bond rate. However, we expect moderation of the inflation rate in the 1980's and a concomitant lowering of the bond rate.

Short-term rates are dependent on both monetary policy of the Federal Reserve as well as cyclical conditions in the economy. But, on average, we do not expect short-term rates to drop to previous historical norms in light of the higher built-in inflation in today's economy. The accompanying table presents the forecast of representative short-term and longer-term interest rates as average rates over the six-year forecast period.

INTEREST RATE OUTLOOK
1979–1985

	5-Year Average 1975–79	1979	SPNB Forecast 1980–85 Average
Short-Term			
Commercial Paper – 90 day – dealer	7.26	11.05	10½
Prime Rate	8.66	12.72	12⅛
Treasury Bills – 3 month	6.66	10.10	9¾
Treasury Bills – 12 month	7.57	10.78	10¼
Federal Funds	7.11	11.23	10⅝
Certificates of Deposit – 3 month	7.39	11.35	10¾
Longer-Term			
3–5 Year U.S. Governments	7.88	9.67	9⅞
New AAA Corporate Bonds	8.83	9.89	10⅝
New AA Utilities	9.16	10.26	11

POLICY CONSTRAINTS

Although the above forecast is viewed as realistic and most probable, many events can impinge upon the economy to cause this forecast to miss the mark. On the one hand, it is possible that near-term inflationary pressures are overestimated and thus the trend rate of inflation is overestimated. If so, somewhat more rapid real growth could be expected, and the economy would reach full employment by 1985. However, if the inflationary pressures are still being significantly underestimated, the risks to real growth are substantial. And if inflation continues to accelerate indefinitely into the future, at present still a low probability event, then the structure and ground rules of the economic system will have to undergo major changes.

Inflation and pressures from defense spending will make it difficult at best for the federal government to achieve a balanced budget by 1985. There is virtually no leeway for expanding non-defense federal expenditures at an above-trend rate. For much of the forecast period monetary policy will have to remain relatively restrictive, both to combat domestic inflation and to prevent any further deterioration in the international position of the dollar. Failure of fiscal and monetary policies to slow down inflation will lead to a much stronger "incomes" policy approach than the current voluntary wage-price guidelines, with comprehensive controls the final resort.

EPILOGUE: 1985-1990

Is there a happy ending to the austere scenario painted in this report? In many ways, things should be better in the second half of the decade. The economy will have made substantial progress in adjusting to high energy costs. The United States will be less dependent on foreign sources of energy, but this achievement will be extremely costly.

The growth of the labor force will decelerate further and productivity should improve. However, the potential output trend is still not likely to be any higher than the 2.7 percent annual trend rate forecast through 1985. Investment in residential construction should finally slow down after its long cyclical upswing and real personal consumption should make something of a comeback.

Long-Term Industry Outlook

SOME GENERAL CONCLUSIONS

The long-term forecast is reasonably optimistic on the outlook for the capital goods sector. Above-average growth can be expected in areas such as energy conservation, high technology, and automation. Recent tax reform should encourage business investment somewhat, but cost of capital considerations will tend to dampen any real capital spending boom.

Implications for the housing sector are also favorable with starts in the 1.5 to 2.2 million unit range during the 1979–1985 period and averaging a relatively high 1.9 to 2.0. After a near-term cyclical downturn, trend growth in housing should be more in line with GNP growth and multiple-unit dwellings should recover more rapidly in the post-1980 period.

The automobile outlook is less favorable. Real growth will be slightly above GNP trend. However, cyclical considerations, energy legislation, environmental pressures, rising labor costs, and foreign competition are all working to inhibit any increase in the domestic industry's share of personal consumption expenditures in current dollars. Replacement demand and considerations of fuel efficiency should help maintain auto sales in a range of 10.0 to 12.0 million units annually over the forecast period.

The expected increase in real defense expenditures will clearly bolster areas of the aerospace and electronics industries, but to some extent at the expense of real personal consumption.

Comparative Industry Growth

The accompanying table ranks 30 major industry categories, including government enterprises, by the expected trend growth of product shipments in producer prices to 1985. These have been classified according to relative growth prospects, viz., faster, moderate, or slower growth. Although the categories are somewhat arbitrary, they appear to fit reasonably well with generally held perceptions of these industries. These growth rates were computed with the aid of an interindustry forecasting model (INFORUM) based on an input-output approach to the economy. The forecast is consistent with the long-term aggregate forecast presented in the preceding section of the *Economic Report* and provides insights into relative growth prospects.

This industry forecast differs from last year's (1978–1984) in several key respects. First, the level of growth rates is lower, in line with the lower real GNP forecast. Secondly, as a result of changes in sectoral share estimates and relative prices, a number of relative rankings have shifted dramatically. For instance, communications, ordnance, leather, apparel, and textiles have risen considerably, whereas rubber and plastics, transportation, metals and metal products, government enterprises, food, and petroleum have dropped in the

COMPARATIVE INDUSTRY GROWTH
Product Shipments in Producer Prices
1979–1985

	Annual Trend Growth Rates
Faster Growth	
Communications	4.8%
Instruments	4.4
Electrical Machinery	4.4
Rubber and Plastics	4.2
Ordnance	4.0
Chemicals	4.0
Leather	3.8
Transportation Equipment	3.6
Non-electrical Machinery	3.5
Moderate Growth	
Trade	3.2
Apparel	3.1
Misc. Manufacturing	3.1
Textiles	3.0
Transportation	3.0
Financial Services	2.7
Metal Products	2.7
Furniture	2.7
Stone, Clay, Glass	2.7
Paper	2.7
Lumber	2.7
Metals	2.6
Slower Growth	
Printing and Publishing	2.3
Government Enterprises	2.1
Food	2.1
Construction	2.0
Agriculture	1.5
Tobacco	1.3
Mining	1.0
Utilities	0.9
Petroleum	−0.1

Source: SPNB forecast based on INFORUM Model.

rankings. Since growth of real product shipments is not necessarily correlated with profits, these results should not be misinterpreted as implying anything about future financial results.

In the faster growth category such industries as communications, instruments, electrical machinery, plastics, ordnance, and chemicals appear to have favorable prospects. Industries such as trade, transportation, financial services, paper, lumber, and metals are categorized as moderate growth, or roughly in line with the economy. Slower growth industries include such basic industries as construction, agriculture, mining, utilities, and petroleum.

Investment Sector Analysis

In the preceding section, 200 individual industries, defined in accordance with the Standard Industrial Classification (S.I.C.) codes, were aggregated into 30 major economic categories and then ranked in order of forecasted growth rates over the 1979–1985 period. In this section, however, a forecast is presented on the basis of categories that approximate the industrial breakdown of a broad stock market index, the Standard and Poor's 500 stock average. The specific S & P 500 industry categories are then grouped into ten functional groups according to past stock market behavior: consumer discretionary – durables; consumer discretionary – non-durables and services; consumer non-discretionary – non-durables; utilities; capital spending; technology; financial; energy; industrial commodity; and retail.

The accompanying table presents a forecast of real growth and prices for the ten investment groups and their major sub-groups of the 1979–1985 period. The right-hand column of the table indicates the relative weighting of each category in the S & P 500 as of December 31, 1979. Again, the results do not necessarily imply anything about relative profitability or market price performance for these industries.

In terms of real output growth, the groups expected to exceed the trend growth rate of real GNP include: technology; consumer discretionary – non-durables and services; capital spending; consumer discretionary – durables; and industrial commodity. Groups expected to grow in line with real national output include: financial; retail; and utilities. Lagging real growth of GNP are consumer non-discretionary – non-durables and energy.

However, there are some major differences within these broad groupings. For instance, drug & medical supplies, 4.7 percent, grows much faster than consumer non-discretionary – non-durables; telecommunications, 5.2 percent, exceeds utilities; aerospace, 5.0 percent, dominates capital spending; oil well machinery, 4.0 percent, far exceeds energy; and chemicals, 4.0 percent, leads industrial commodity.

INDUSTRY FORECAST BY INVESTMENT SECTORS
PERCENTAGE TREND GROWTH OF PRODUCT SHIPMENTS
1979–1985

	Real Growth (%)	Prices (%)	S&P 500 Weights 12/31/79
Consumer Discretionary—Durables	**3.1**	**8.7**	6.4%
Automobile	3.0	8.6	2.7
Automobile Parts	3.1	9.7	1.1
Building Materials	2.8	8.6	1.2
Household Appliances	4.2	7.4	.5
Textile & Apparel	3.1	9.2	.7
Tire & Rubber Goods	3.5	8.6	.3
Consumer Discretionary—Non-durables & Services	**3.3**	**8.4**	**7.5**
Brewers & Distillers	4.2	6.2	.8
Cosmetics & Toiletries	4.2	8.8	.9
Photography	5.4	8.8	1.2
Publishing	2.3	8.5	1.0
Soft Drinks	4.3	8.2	1.0
Air Transportation	4.0	8.8	.4
Hotel-Motel & Restaurants	4.3	7.8	.7
Leisure Time	1.6	8.9	1.5
Consumer Non-Discretionary—Non-durables	**2.2**	**9.4**	**11.7**
Containers—metal & glass	3.2	8.1	.4
Drug & Medical Supplies	4.7	7.7	5.8
Food & Allied Products	1.7	10.0	2.8
Soaps	4.2	8.8	1.4
Tobacco & Allied Products	1.3	7.7	1.4
Utilities	**2.5**	**8.8**	**11.9**
Telecommunications	5.2	6.1	6.0
Utilities—electric	2.2	9.3	3.6
Utilities—natural gas	−1.8	13.1	2.4
Capital Spending	**3.2**	**8.0**	**10.0**
Aerospace	5.0	7.2	2.6
Electrical Equipment	3.3	8.3	2.9
Machinery, General	3.3	8.3	2.8
Transportation	1.0	8.2	1.6
Technology	**5.2**	**7.7**	**10.7**
Electronics	5.6	7.6	1.9
Miscellaneous	–	–	1.0
Office Equipment	4.0	7.4	7.8
Financial	**2.6**	**9.0**	**5.8**
Banks and Finance Companies	2.6	8.3	3.5
Insurance	2.5	9.8	2.3
Energy	**.2**	**21.0**	**22.7**
Machinery—oil well	4.0	7.9	3.6
Oils—domestic & international	−.3	22.4	19.1
Industrial Commodity	**3.1**	**9.3**	**10.4**
Chemical & Allied Products	4.0	11.2	3.8
Forest Products	2.6	8.4	1.4
Metals & Mining	2.7	8.6	4.0
Paper & Paper Containers	2.7	8.2	1.2
Retail	**2.6**	**5.9**	3.0%
			100.0%

Demographics, Labor Force, and Employment

DEMOGRAPHIC OVERVIEW

The demographic aspects of economic growth are so basic and pervasive as to be sometimes overlooked. The rate of growth of population and its changing composition impact the labor force, housing, autos, and educational spending, just to mention a few areas. The forecasts on labor force and employment found in this report are based on the Bureau of the Census Series II population projection. This assumes that the fertility rate will return to its long-run replacement level of 2.1 from the current level of 1.7. Annual population growth has averaged 1.2 percent over the past 25 years. Since 1970 it has slowed to 0.8 percent. It is expected to accelerate moderately in the early 1980's and then return to about 0.8 percent by the end of the decade.

Baby Boom Influence

A dominant factor determining economic trends has been the influence of the population bulge known as the baby boom of the post-World War II period. As this large age group matured, a groundswell of demand was created – successively – for rattles, classrooms, and – currently – new homes. Assimilating this large age group is an important influence in today's economy. With the fast growth in the 25–34 age group during the recent past, the economy has witnessed strong demands for housing, for the goods to furnish these households, and for the credit to finance these purchases. By the mid-1980's the baby-boom age group will be swelling the 35–44 age group, traditionally a more conservative spending category of the population. This maturing should take some pressures off the housing market and durable goods spending.

LABOR FORCE OUTLOOK

In 1979 the average civilian labor force stood at 102.9 million persons. By 1985 the total is expected to reach 114.7 million, a net increase of 11.5 percent over the six-year period, or a 1.8 percent annual trend growth rate. This will represent a considerable slowing from the torrid 2.5 percent rate of the past decade, but is still a fairly healthy growth rate in the longer-term perspective of

CIVILIAN NONINSTITUTIONAL POPULATION
Annual Percent Changes

	1970–79	1979–85	1985–90
Male			
16–19	1.5%	−2.8%	−1.2%
20–24	3.7	−0.1	−2.8
25–34	3.9	2.3	0.6
35–44	1.0	4.0	3.2
45–54	−0.1	−0.3	2.4
55–64	1.5	0.7	−0.8
65 +	1.9	1.6	1.7
Men – 16 & over	1.9	1.1	0.8
Female			
16–19	1.2	−2.6	−1.2
20–24	2.1	−0.1	−2.7
25–34	3.7	2.2	0.6
35–44	1.0	3.7	3.1
45–54	−0.2	−0.4	2.4
55–64	1.4	0.5	−1.0
65 +	2.6	1.9	1.8
Women – 16 & over	1.8	1.1	0.8
Total	1.8%	1.1%	0.8%

Source: Based on BLS data.

United States history. From 1985 to 1990, the pace should slow further to about a 1.2 percent rate, bringing the total labor force to about 121.6 million persons at the end of the decade.

Population Growth

For any given period of time, a certain percentage of the total population is actively seeking employment in the monetized sector of the economy. This group constitutes the active labor force. The percentage of this group unable to find suitable employment is referred to as the unemployment rate. Thus, it is self-evident that the size of the population is a major determinant of the civilian labor force. From 1970 to 1979 the total civilian noninstitutional population grew at a 1.8 percent trend rate, with the largest growth occurring in the 20 to 34 age group. However, population trends in the 1980's are likely to be considerably different. From 1979 to 1985 the total civilian noninstitutional population will grow at only a 1.1 percent trend rate. The central age group, 35 to 44, will experience relatively larger growth, while the teenage and young adult groups will actually decline. From 1985 to 1990 civilian noninstitutional population growth will decelerate further to about 0.8 percent.

As a consequence of the birthrate drop of the 1960's, an important feature of the 1980's will be the sharp decline in the number of youths 16 to 24 years of age. The total civilian noninstitutional population, 16 years and over, should grow by an estimated 24.5 million, or 17.9 percent, from 1970 to 1979, but it is projected to grow by only 11.4 million, or 7.1 percent, from 1979 to 1985, and by 7.3 million, or 4.2 percent, from 1985 to 1990. While the teenage ranks will be thinner, population in the central age groups will be swollen by further aging of the many millions born in the post-World War II baby boom.

Participation Rates: The Critical Variable

One of the most troublesome variables to forecast in recent years has been the labor force participation rate. Most public as well as private forecasters estimate an increase in the participation rates among most population groups, but especially among women. The data presented in this report, although partly based on a revised set of projections from the Bureau of Labor Statistics, were revised upward by SPNB in the light of more recent evidence. A further rise in the participation rates of both male and female teenagers is expected due to a number of factors, including: decelerating college enrollments, greater economic pressures on households, and changing lifestyles. Further gains in labor force activity are also expected among women in the central age group. On the other hand, older workers, despite a lengthening of the mandatory retirement age to 70, are expected to opt for earlier retirement and leisure activities.

The overall civilian labor force participation rate is projected to rise from 63.7 percent in 1979 to 67.5 per-

CIVILIAN LABOR FORCE PARTICIPATION RATES
(Annual Averages, Percent of Population in Labor Force)

	1970	1979	SPNB Forecast 1985	1990
Male				
16–19	56.1%	61.7%	63.6%	64.8%
20–24	83.3	86.6	87.0	88.0
25–34	96.4	95.4	95.0	95.0
35–44	96.9	95.8	96.0	95.0
45–54	94.2	91.4	90.5	90.0
55–64	83.0	73.0	69.5	68.0
65 +	26.8	20.0	18.0	16.0
Men – 16 & over	79.7	77.9	77.9	77.5
Female				
16–19	44.0	54.5	62.0	65.0
20–24	57.7	69.1	78.0	82.0
25–34	45.0	63.8	74.0	80.0
35–44	51.1	63.6	71.0	76.0
45–54	54.4	58.4	60.0	62.0
55–64	43.0	41.9	41.0	40.0
65 +	9.7	8.3	7.2	6.6
Women – 16 & over	43.3	51.0	55.9	58.4
Total	60.4%	63.7%	66.3%	67.5%

Source: BLS; SPNB forecast

CIVILIAN LABOR FORCE
(millions)

	1970	1973	1979	SPNB Forecast 1985	1990
Male					
16–19	4.0	4.7	5.0	4.4	4.2
20–24	5.7	7.1	8.2	8.2	7.2
25–34	11.3	12.8	15.8	18.1	18.6
35–44	10.5	10.3	11.3	14.3	16.6
45–54	10.4	10.4	10.1	9.7	10.9
55–64	7.1	7.0	7.1	7.1	6.7
65 +	2.2	1.9	1.9	1.9	1.9
Men – 16 & over	51.2	54.2	59.5	63.7	66.1
Female					
16–19	3.2	3.8	4.5	4.4	4.3
20–24	4.9	5.6	7.0	7.9	7.2
25–34	5.7	7.2	11.2	14.8	16.5
35–44	6.0	6.1	8.1	11.3	14.1
45–54	6.5	6.6	6.9	6.9	8.0
55–64	4.2	4.2	4.6	4.6	4.3
65 +	1.1	1.1	1.1	1.1	1.1
Women – 16 & over	31.5	34.5	43.4	51.0	55.5
Total	82.7	88.7	102.9	114.7	121.6

Source: Bureau of Labor Statistics; SPNB forecast.

ANNUAL RATES OF CHANGE IN LABOR FORCE

	1970–79	1973–79	1979–85	1985–90
Male				
16–19	2.6%	1.3%	–2.2%	–0.9%
20–24	4.2	2.6	–	–2.6
25–34	3.8	3.5	2.3	0.5
35–44	0.9	1.7	4.0	3.0
45–54	–0.4	–0.6	–0.6	2.4
55–64	–	0.3	–	–1.2
65 +	–1.3	0.2	–	–
Men – 16 & over	1.7	1.6	1.1	0.7
Female				
16–19	3.7	2.8	–0.4	–0.5
20–24	4.2	3.9	2.0	–1.8
25–34	7.8	7.6	4.8	2.2
35–44	3.5	4.8	5.7	4.5
45–54	0.5	0.8	–	3.0
55–64	1.1	1.5	–	–1.3
65 +	0.9	1.4	–	–
Women – 16 & over	3.6	3.9	2.7	1.7
Total	2.5%	2.5%	1.8%	1.2%

The so-called "economic dependency ratio," i.e., the ratio of nonworkers to workers in the entire population, is expected to fall during the 1980's. In 1977 the ratio was 117.8, meaning there were 117.8 nonworkers for every 100 workers in the population. This ratio is expected to decline to below 100 by 1990. However, this ratio should reverse itself again after the year 2000, when post-World War II babies begin to reach retirement age.

EMPLOYMENT OUTLOOK

The difficulties that the economy seems likely to encounter in achieving full employment by 1985 were suggested in the long-term macroeconomic forecast earlier in this *Economic Report*. The full-employment unemployment rate (F.E.U.R.) was projected to be about 5.5 percent by 1985. However, it was assumed that the economy would be hard-pressed to achieve even this goal and that a more realistic range would be an actual unemployment rate in the 7.0–7.5 percent range.

cent by 1990. The rate for all men is expected to decline slightly over the period, and the rate for all women is expecteed to continue rising.

Changing Composition of the Labor Force

The accompanying tables illustrate the size of the projected labor force by 1985, annual rates of change for several sub-periods, and the changing composition of the labor force over time.

As a result of these expected changes, several general implications can be drawn. Some improvement is expected in the employment situation of youths. Because of the decline in this age category, there should be a lessening of competition for jobs and a narrowing in the relative gap in unemployment rates between teenagers and other groups. This decline, however, does not augur well for traditional youth market industries and will have a negative impact on college enrollments.

The maturing of the labor force should lead to a more productive labor force. The greater productivity of a more experienced workforce should partially offset the slower labor force growth in the 1980's. The impact of more women in the labor force is ambiguous and will depend on the extent to which women with children will be able to work full time.

COMPOSTION OF CIVILIAN LABOR FORCE
(Percentage Shares)

	1970	1973	1979	1985	1990
Male					
16–19	4.8%	5.3%	4.9%	3.8%	3.5%
20–24	6.9	8.0	8.0	7.1	5.9
25–34	13.7	14.5	15.3	15.8	15.3
35–44	12.7	11.6	11.0	12.5	13.7
45–54	12.6	11.8	9.8	8.5	9.0
55–64	8.6	7.9	6.9	6.2	5.5
65 +	2.6	2.2	1.9	1.7	1.6
Men – 16 & over	61.9	61.1	57.8	55.5	54.4
Female					
16–19	3.9	4.3	4.4	3.8	3.5
20–24	5.9	6.3	6.8	6.9	5.9
25–34	6.9	8.1	10.9	12.9	13.6
35–44	7.2	6.9	7.9	9.9	11.6
45–54	7.9	7.4	6.7	6.0	6.6
55–64	5.0	4.7	4.5	4.0	3.5
65 +	1.3	1.2	1.1	1.0	0.9
Women – 16 & over	38.1	38.9	42.2	44.5	45.6
Total	100.0%	100.0%	100.0%	100.0%	100.0%

Source: Based on BLS and SPNB projections.

Where Will the Jobs Be?

The accompanying table summarizes the historical growth trends of full-time employment in private industry by 29 broad industrial categories. It presents both a longer-term historical view of employment growth, 1958 to 1979, as well as the more recent and difficult 1973–1979 period. The major area that stands out in terms of both size and consistently strong growth is the area of finance and services.

The 1979–1985 employment forecast is based upon the long-term outlook presented in this report, with the aid of the INFORUM interindustry forecasting model. In terms of relative shares of full-time employment, finance and services will continue to expand. Ordnance is expected to rebound sharply over the forecast period.

Industries of declining shares of employment from 1979 to 1985 are expected to be agriculture, chemicals, transportation, utilities, and trade.

FULL-TIME EMPLOYMENT IN PRIVATE INDUSTRY
GROWTH AND COMPOSITION
1979–1985

	Annual Trend Growth Rates			Percentage Share	
	1958–79	1973–79	1979–85F	1979E	1985F
Agriculture	−2.3%	−0.6%	−1.5%	4.1%	3.4%
Mining	0.6	3.9	2.2	1.0	1.0
Construction	2.0	0.9	1.7	6.4	6.4
Ordnance	−1.0	−3.9	4.6	0.2	0.2
Food	−0.2	−0.1	0.9	2.1	2.0
Tobacco	−1.5	−1.7	−1.0	0.1	0.1
Textiles	−0.2	−2.4	1.8	0.9	0.9
Apparel	0.6	−1.4	0.6	1.9	1.8
Lumber	1.0	−0.3	0.6	0.8	0.8
Furniture	1.2	−0.8	2.5	0.7	0.7
Paper	1.0	−0.1	0.8	0.9	0.8
Printing and Publishing	1.5	1.6	0.7	1.5	1.4
Chemicals	1.6	1.8	0.2	1.4	1.2
Petroleum	−0.3	2.1	−0.2	0.3	0.2
Rubber and Plastics	4.2	2.2	2.5	1.0	1.0
Leather	−1.6	−2.6	3.0	0.3	0.4
Stone, Clay, Glass	1.2	0.4	0.9	0.9	0.8
Metals	0.7	−0.1	0.6	1.6	1.5
Metal Products	2.3	2.1	1.7	2.0	2.0
Non-electrical Machinery	2.7	2.0	1.4	3.0	2.9
Electrical Machinery	2.3	0.3	1.2	2.6	2.5
Transportation Equipment	0.6	1.3	0.5	2.5	2.3
Instruments	3.6	3.5	2.1	0.8	0.8
Misc. Manufacturing	1.1	1.6	−0.9	0.6	0.5
Transportation	0.6	0.7	0.4	3.9	3.6
Communications	1.8	0.8	0.5	1.5	1.4
Utilities	1.2	0.9	−0.6	1.0	0.8
Trade	1.5	1.8	0.8	26.2	24.7
Finance and Services	3.4	3.5	3.7	30.1	33.8
				100.0%	100.0%

E = INFORUM estimates   F = SPNB forecast

The Productivity Dilemma

THE PRODUCTIVITY LAG

From 1950 to 1979 the average annual growth rate of productivity, i.e., output per hour in the nonfarm business sector, was 1.9 percent. However, from 1950 to 1973, it averaged 2.3 percent, then dropped to 0.5 percent from 1973 to 1979. Because of the crucial importance of productivity as it affects our standard of living, real incomes, and the rate of inflation, the debates over the causes of the phenomenon have been intense.

The noted economist, Edward F. Denison, has attempted to measure the causes of the decline in productivity. However, the use of his production function approach in measuring the sources of economic growth has produced ambivalent results. The largest component of the negative net change in productivity is attributed to a residual category, "advances in knowledge and miscellaneous determinants." Thus, the most comprehensive attempt to measure the factors contributing to the decline ends up with a large "unexplained" residual.

The Major Causes of the Decline

Although it has proven extremely difficult to explicitly quantify the causes of the productivity lag, a number of contributing factors can be identified. Investment in plant and equipment by private business, for a host of reasons, has lagged the economy since 1973. Most measures of the capital stock imply a decline in the capital-labor ratio. Much of the investment that has occurred since the 1960's has been consumed by regulatory costs, pollution abatement and control equipment, and other such necessary but "nonproductive" investment. Plant and equipment conversion due to higher energy costs has further aggravated the situation since 1973.

The other major causes usually enumerated include: the lag in research and development expenditures since the late 1960's; the changing structure of the economy, viz., the shift into the lower productivity service sector out of higher productivity manufacturing; the rise of inexperienced women and youths in the labor force: the extremely severe cyclical pattern of the economy in the 1970's; and tax policies which have hampered saving and investment.

The Fundamental Reasons

The root causes of the phenomenon, however, appear to narrow down to three areas: marginal productivity of labor, energy cost increases, and unanticipated inflation. The traditional economic reasoning of marginal productivity theory sheds light on this issue which is often confused by discussing "average" productivity trends. With a given amount of capital and resource inputs, together with a relatively stable state of technology, additional inputs of labor will produce more output, but at a diminishing rate. It appears that, in recent years, the rapid growth of the labor force has led to a situation of small to perhaps negative marginal productivity of labor, which, in turn, has dragged down the average productivity of labor. Not only the size of the increment to the labor force, but its relative inexperience, i.e., women and youths, lends credence to the negative marginal productivity explanation.

The unexpected rapid rise in energy costs has led to a painful period of resource reallocation due to both short- and longer-term inelasticities, e.g., inelasticity of energy demand with respect to real GNP, supply inelasticities of alternative energy sources, and inelasticities of substitution between competing fuels. The net effect has been an obsolescence of a substantial part of the nation's capital stock. Furthermore, longer-term resource allocation decisions have been hampered by the fact that a comprehensive federal energy policy has been slow in developing.

Finally, the inflationary experience of the 1970's has created further distortions in the price system, thus hampering the market's response in handling resource reallocation efficiently. High interest rates have added greater uncertainty to the capital budgeting process in private industry and, of course, have substantially raised the nominal cost of capital to the firm.

PRODUCTIVITY OUTLOOK

Despite its dismal history since 1973 and even bleaker near-term outlook, productivity is expected to recover somewhat in the 1980's. Over the 1979–1985 forecast period, productivity growth should average about 1.4 percent annually. From 1985 to 1990, it should improve beyond that to perhaps closer to the 2.0 percent area.

The reasons for this guarded optimism are several. A cyclical recovery of the economy should bolster productivity from 1981 on. The expected slowdown in labor force growth should lead to some improvement in average productivity, via a reversal of the negative marginal productivity argument, and reinforced by the maturing of the labor force. There has been a recent pick-up in research and development spending and this trend should gain impetus from increased spending on aerospace and defense.

An above-trend growth in business spending on plant and equipment over the forecast period should gradually improve the capital-labor ratio. In addition, the share of investment dollars devoted to environmental, health, and safety expenditures by industry should be declining in the 1980's. Industrial adjustment to high energy costs since 1973 will begin to assert itself as newer, energy-efficient technologies become more widespread. There also appears to be much more political support for granting greater tax incentives for business investment as public policy seeks ways of overcoming the productivity dilemma.

Productivity Forecast by Industry

Although the productivity slowdown has been fairly widespread, it has not been universal. The accompanying table shows the productivity history for private industry classified into 29 industrial sectors. The longer-term history, 1958 to 1979, is presented, along with the more recent period, 1973 to 1979. Industries particularly hard hit include: mining; construction; rubber and plastics; stone, clay, glass; metals; metal prod-

ucts; trade; and services. Manufacturing industries have fared relatively better than nonmanufacturing.

The forecast for the 1979–1985 period is based on the long-term outlook, presented in this report, with the aid of the INFORUM interindustry model. Productivity is defined as output per employed person. Above-trend productivity industries include: agriculture; chemicals; electrical machinery; transportation equipment; and communications. Industries that are still expected to achieve negative productivity growth are: mining; ordnance; and finance and services.

PRODUCTIVITY OUTLOOK BY INDUSTRY
Output per Employed Person
(Annual Trend Growth Rates)

	1958–79	1973–79	1979–85F
Agriculture	4.4%	2.9%	3.0%
Mining	1.0	−5.6	−0.9
Construction	−	−3.1	0.2
Ordnance	1.8	2.0	−0.6
Food	2.6	2.6	1.3
Tobacco	2.5	2.1	2.3
Textiles	3.5	5.7	1.4
Apparel	3.0	2.5	2.7
Lumber	2.0	2.5	2.7
Furniture	2.4	1.1	0.2
Paper	2.7	1.6	1.9
Printing and Publishing	1.2	−0.3	1.7
Chemicals	4.2	1.0	3.8
Petroleum	3.6	2.3	0.1
Rubber and Plastics	1.9	−1.1	1.6
Leather	1.6	3.4	1.2
Stone, Clay, Glass	1.9	0.2	1.8
Metals	1.6	−1.1	2.1
Metal Products	1.3	−0.8	1.1
Non-electrical Machinery	2.3	0.7	2.4
Electrical Machinery	3.4	1.1	3.5
Transportation Equipment	3.0	0.5	3.5
Instruments	2.8	0.9	1.8
Misc. Manufacturing	2.7	0.3	3.9
Transportation	2.9	1.6	2.9
Communications	5.0	5.7	4.3
Utilities	3.2	1.4	1.4
Trade	2.5	0.9	2.4
Finance and Services	0.6	−0.4	−0.9

Source:
Based on INFORUM historical estimates and SPNB forecast.

Energy and Inflation

ENERGY POLICY ASSUMPTIONS

It now appears that United States energy policy is inexorably headed in the direction of allowing domestic energy prices to rise to world price levels. Government policy will attempt to partially offset some of the burdensome impacts on income distribution by means of tax policies, including the so-called "windfall profits" tax bill. By allowing prices to rise, competing energy sources will eventually become more attractive and the reliance on imported petroleum will diminish. However, the cost will be indeed great.

Data Resources, Inc. has estimated that the elasticity of energy demand with respect to real GNP is about 0.65. Over the 1979–1985 forecast period, a 2.6 percent real output growth rate implies about a 1.7 percent annual average rate of total energy demand. However, effective demand is likely to be somewhat below the 1.7 percent rate. OPEC marker crude appears likely to climb at about a 16.7 percent average rate over the period. Decontrolled domestic crude should climb at about a 24 percent average rate, composite wellhead price, through 1985. It is assumed that domestic crude's share of total consumption will remain about one half.

INFLATION OVERVIEW

The overall rate of inflation, as expressed by the deflator of Gross National Product, is expected to average about 8.4 percent through 1985, compared to the 7.7 percent average for the 1973–1979 period. The rate of increase in both 1980 and 1981 is expected to exceed 9 percent. By 1985 the rate of increase is forecasted to drop to about the 7.5 percent area. The accompanying table provides annual trend growth rates of inflation by detailed components of GNP, for the 1973–1979 period as well as the forecasted rates for 1979–1985. The differential impacts of inflation result in real personal consumption being squeezed by the other three sectors – investment, government, and net exports.

INFLATION OUTLOOK
GNP COMPONENT DEFLATORS
1979–1985

	Annual Trend Growth Rates	
	1973–79	1979–85F
Gross National Product	7.7%	8.4%
Personal Consumption Expenditures	7.6	8.3
Durable Goods	6.1	6.7
Autos and Parts	7.5	7.8
Except Autos and Parts	5.1	5.9
Nondurable Goods	8.0	8.4
Services	7.7	8.7
Gross Private Domestic Investment	9.2	8.9
Fixed Investment	9.2	8.9
Nonresidential	8.7	8.4
Producers' Durable Equipment	8.0	7.8
Structures	10.2	9.5
Residential	10.5	10.2
Change in Businesss Inventories	8.8	8.8
Government Purchases	8.5	8.8
Federal	8.0	8.6
State and Local	8.7	9.0
Exports	10.8	8.8
Imports	13.7	10.0

Major factors contributing to inflation over the 1979–1985 forecast period include energy costs, food and other commodity costs, sluggish productivity performance, increased federal expenditures on defense, unit labor costs (expected to grow at about an 8.2 percent rate), high import prices permeating the domestic economy, and a greater proportion of real output devoted to exports at the sacrifice of domestic consumption.

Other Inflation Indicators

Currently the most visible indicator of a rising price level in the economy is the Consumer Price Index, which has been rising at a faster rate than the GNP deflator. Using a market basket approach, it has been particularly sensitive to cost increases at the margin for food, fuels, and housing. This discrepancy between the CPI and the deflator is likely to persist for several years before converging again. Thus the average rate over the 1979–1985 period for the CPI is expected to be near 9 percent versus 8.4 percent for the GNP deflator.

Wholesale prices are also expected to increase at a faster rate than the GNP deflator, aggravated especially by the fuels component. Overall, the WPI is expected to increase at about a 9.7 percent annual average rate. The accompanying table provides estimates of expected wholesale price performance, over the 1979–1985 period, for 30 industrial sectors including government enterprises. Wholesale prices are led by petroleum, mining, agriculture, and utilities and are generally lower in manufacturing and trade.

An Appraisal

The risks to an inflation forecast are numerous. However, assuming reasonably firm monetary and fiscal policies and just a tolerable amount of external shocks over the 1979–1985 period, there is cause for some optimism that the base rate of inflation can be brought down to about the 7.5 percent area by 1985. Many of the factors contributing to the current inflationary surge should be easing or improving beyond 1981. Energy prices should ease somewhat and the nation's energy policy should begin to have more impact as we go further out in the 1980's. Food and commodity prices should be easing based on cyclical factors. But the major cause of improvement should come from the expected rebound in productivity. However, all favorable prospects dissipate if monetary and fiscal policies validate the inflation instead of pursuing restraint.

WHOLESALE PRICE OUTLOOK BY INDUSTRY
1979–1985

	Annual Trend Growth Rates
Agriculture	10.5%
Mining	11.6
Construction	7.3
Ordnance	8.8
Food	9.2
Tobacco	7.4
Textiles	9.5
Apparel	8.2
Lumber	7.9
Furniture	8.6
Paper	7.9
Printing and Publishing	8.1
Chemicals	9.9
Petroleum	18.1
Rubber and Plastics	9.7
Leather	7.1
Stone, Clay, Glass	7.9
Metals	8.0
Metal Products	8.3
Non-electrical Machinery	7.9
Electrical Machinery	7.7
Transportation Equipment	7.7
Instruments	8.6
Misc. Manufacturing	8.0
Transportation	8.3
Communications	6.3
Utitilities	10.4
Trade	5.8
Finance and Services	8.3
Government Enterprises	9.2

Source: SPNB forecast based on INFORUM Model.

TOTAL MONEY MANAGEMENT
with specific illustrations from the Bond Market

by Sidney Homer

Introduction

Last June Mr. William R. Salomon, the managing partner of Salomon Brothers, made a speech on "The Securities Markets in Transition." After discussing constructively the many changes that are taking place in Wall Street, he said:

"I also believe that the role of the institutional portfolio manager will broaden under the pressures of increasingly more dynamic markets. He will be obliged to alter his perspectives and responsibilities. He will have to manage funds on a *total money concept* instead of specializing in a particular area, such as stocks or bonds... This will present a great challenge as well as an opportunity..."

Since that talk was delivered, a great many institutional customers have asked for enlarged comments on the meaning of the "total money concept." This article is an attempt to provide an answer.

The dramatic changes which are underway in the structure of the securities markets have monopolized the headlines. In contrast, very little has been heard lately about new shifts in the pattern of institutional investing. After two decades of accelerating dynamics, are institutions settling down in a new established pattern? Did the violent market fluctuations and the liquidity problems of the last four years extinguish the pioneering spirit which marked the 1960's? I doubt it.

More likely we will see experimentation in wholly new institutional combinations and new investment programs. After all, the chief institutional dynamics of the last two decades were first a shift from bonds to stocks, and second a shift from blue chip stocks to less conventional equities. These were merely shifts within the area of conventional investment, i.e., stocks and bonds. In making these changes, institutions were following paths which had been well

trodden by private investors many decades earlier. The next changes are apt to be more novel. One novelty that will probably be much discussed is now being called *Total Money Management.*

What is it? It seems to mean different things to different people. It is being approached gingerly and in a variety of ways, some emphasizing one aspect, others another aspect, usually a step at a time. After all the word "total" is a big word. Can it be achieved? Can it be approached?

For the purposes of this article, I will select the broadest definition. It may never be completely achieved by institutions but it will be approached by some. *Total Money Management* has two aspects: First it requires a generalized overview of the whole universe of potential investment media—not just stocks, not just stocks or bonds, not just securities. Second, within the areas of investment that have been selected, it requires a totally flexible, sophisticated and forward-looking management. I will discuss these two aspects of *Total Money Management* in sequence.

THE OVERVIEW

The total money manager will not be confined to stocks and bonds. He will look beyond Wall Street and, indeed, beyond this continent. He will look beyond economics and beyond business statistics to worldwide social and political forces.

Table I provides an incomplete list of potential investment outlets which he will consider. They are not all, of course, suitable or attractive or legal or practical for every fund, but they are all suitable and legal and practical and *at times* attractive for certain funds. As such they all deserve the total manager's attention.

TABLE I
Some Potential Investment Outlets

Stocks—Large companies.
Stocks—Medium-sized companies.
Stocks—Small or new companies.
Stocks—Preferreds.
Bonds—High-grade.
Bonds—Medium-grade.
Bonds—Speculative and defaulted.
Private placements of long-term securities.
Loan commitments for a fee.
Convertible bonds and preferred stocks—high premium, stock equivalents.
Convertible bonds and preferred stocks—low premium, bond equivalents.
Loaning securities.
Warrants and other options.
Money market instruments—short-term, including repos.
Real estate mortgages—insured.
Real estate mortgages—conventional (with or without equity).
Mortgage backed instruments.
Real estate—unimproved.
Real estate—improved.
Real estate investment trusts.
Leases.
Direct loans to smaller companies.
Equity investments in small or privately held companies and venture capital.
Puts and calls and writing options.
Commodities.
Royalty agreements for natural resources.
Foreign currencies—money market instruments.*
Foreign dollar bonds.
Foreign currency bonds including Euro-dollar.*
Foreign equities.*
Equity investments in securities firms.
At present, limited by Federal regulations.

During recent decades, American long-term investing institutions with a choice, such as pension funds and retirement funds, have generally confined their basic investment policy decisions to the simple choice of stocks or bonds (sometimes mortgages). Twenty years ago a majority of such funds confined themselves to bonds. Then there set in a gradual shift to equities which became massive. Only recently, when high-grade bond yields reached 7–9%, was the question again raised—stocks or bonds? Only very few institutions gave serious consideration to the many other alternatives. However, since 1969 there have been times when both stocks and bonds turned in very shabby performances and inevitably the question was raised—what should we have done? Only a review of the unconventional alternatives would provide the answer.

The Shift to Equities

The institutional shift into equities has provided the dominant market dynamics of the last two decades. It has, however, long since reached the point where it is taken for granted and it has been reflected in the prices both of stocks and of bonds. The trend to equities will, no doubt, continue but this will provide few novelties. Also, the institutional shift from blue chip stocks into "white chip" stocks is a matter of history. These trends may from time-to-time cool off or warm up, but they will never again be novelties.

Heretofore the ultimate owners of investment funds have themselves answered the dominant conventional question "stocks or bonds?" by entrusting the management of their assets to bond experts or to stock experts. In recent years it has usually been the latter. These specialists have generally worked under the mandate given to them by their client and also tend to favor their own medium. Thus with a few exceptions the stock experts were not free to shift massively into bonds and the bond experts were not free to shift massively into stocks—without going back to the ultimate proprietors and asking for a change in mandate, which would rarely have been given. Few in fact, were given a mandate to go elsewhere than stocks or bonds.

Of course, many investment counsel firms and trust departments and insurance portfolio managers have been theoretically free to shift whole portfolios back and forth between stocks and bonds. They generally did not do so wholesale partly because of the risk of disaster if they were wrong, partly because at times neither field looked good (out of the frying pan, into the fire) and no doubt partly because the managers themselves were either bond experts or stock experts and did not feel comfortable moving massively into an unfamiliar and dangerous field. Another basic reason why some institutions neglected portfolio changes was a reluctance to realize book losses. Accounting practice often makes an artificial and dangerous distinction between book losses and realized losses. Since many institutional portfolios are carried at amortized cost these portfolios become frozen in bear markets.

Where Are the Generalists?

It is often said that the medical profession has too many specialists and too few generalists. Surely this is even more true of investment management. I am a bond man; perhaps you are a stock man, or an oil stock man, or a bank stock man, or a mortgage man. Where are the generalists?

There are of course top managers who seem to control overall investment policy, but look at them closely: this one has a stock market background, this one came up from the bond department. Of course, there always have been a few real generalists, wise men with long and balanced experience and a worldwide view of investment basics (I have known two or three), but very few. The institutional structure did not

demand that sort of management. I think it will. In England, Holland and Switzerland there has been semi-total money management for a long time—with an international perspective—but probably rarely so diversified among investment instruments as to deserve the strong term "total."

An attraction of *Total Money Management* is that the wide diversification of potential outlets permits the manager to avoid stampeding with the crowd. There are strong structural reasons why institutions tend to go one way or the other massively and almost in unison. They talk together. They know what the others are thinking and doing. They know their fellows can dominate near-term market trends. Furthermore, if their mistakes are shared with the best people in the biggest institutions, they are not censured as severely as if their mistakes arose from bucking a generally accepted opinion. The portfolio manager's job is perilous at best. Few can have the stature to survive eccentricities which go sour. The total money manager cannot avoid this risk. Indeed, he is employed to take it, but his much wider field permits him to avoid the "madness of crowds."

As of today, *Total Money Management*, as I define it here in extreme form, must remain a beautiful but unattainable mirage for the majority of American institutions. This is because laws, internal regulations, customers, liquidity requirements and accounting practices rule out many or most investments outside of the conventional sort. Laws and customs will change. This will permit steps toward more flexibility. But the process will be long and drawn out. There are, however, some funds which are today entirely free to invest in most of the media listed in Table I. And to the extent that they do so successfully they will be bound to attract more assets to themselves.

Another limitation should be considered: the traditional policy of matching assets to liabilities; for example, investing long-term funds only in long-term securities and short-term funds only in short-term securities; risk-averse funds only in high-grade securities; risk-seeking funds only in marginal securities, etc. This matching policy relieves the portfolio manager of a heavy burden. If he sticks to securities which match his liabilities, he can blame any shortfall in performance on this voluntary or legal strait-jacket. His job seems safe and his portfolio foolproof. But something is wrong with this word "foolproof." When we set up an important investment fund, we surely do not assume that the manager will be a fool.

In recent years many institutions have in fact invested long-term funds in short-term securities or vice versa and have refused to be limited by non-investment considerations. If well managed, they have benefited by their flexibility. Obviously the total money manager will have to keep a sharp eye on his liabilities, especially if his assets deliberately do not match, but he will have the freedom to adjust a large part of his investments for optimum performance.

Institutional Rigidities

During the past decade there has been a strong trend towards the cross-fertilization of our institutional structure. This will probably accelerate. Institutions are trying to get into each other's business either through merger or through changes in regulations. Only in cases where social programs would be helped has our government seemed to favor this trend. Our housing authorities would probably like to see every institution a mortgage buyer. Our states and municipalities would probably like to see every institution a buyer of municipal bonds. The institutions themselves have become aware that in our investment markets there is constant dynamic change, so that now one area of investment is outstandingly attractive and now another. They see that they are constantly thwarted by legal and conventional limitations which force them to confine themselves to only a few of the available outlets, often only the least attractive. Unfortunately these limitations are not apt to be liberalized soon except where social programs will be helped.

For example, the relative attraction of real estate mortgages and corporate bonds has swung massively several times during recent years: first in favor of mortgages, then in favor of bonds, etc., but many institutions such as Savings and Loan Associations have been unable to benefit much by these dramatic changes (see Table V). Furthermore, it is this rigidity of the institutional structure which has exacerbated and sustained some of these massive market maladjustments. This very rigidity and these consequent maladjustments are all to the advantage of the total money manager as long as he is free and is a small minority in the market. If everyone were entirely flexible, obvious opportunities would be few and far between—market maladjustments would be much rarer. There is, however, very little danger of everyone achieving such flexibility in our lifetimes.

An important first step is for each investing institution to identify its own rigidities and exemptions so as to try to minimize the former and exploit the latter. It should try to identify the rigidities of competing investing institutions so as to profit by them. Areas of the market which are forbidden to many institutions by law or custom are for that very reason often attractive to the fund which is free to invest. Areas which are open to every market participant are presumably usually less attractive. For example, the growing fund which does not have to produce maximum annual cash income can take advantage of that fact by concentrating on long-range principal performance while other funds are forced to concentrate on high-income securities. Again, the fund which does not need liquidity but nevertheless holds a mass of highly liquid assets is paying a large unnecessary price for liquidity unless it uses the liquidity profitably by a policy of making frequent portfolio improvements.

Taking an extreme view, there seems to be no investment reason (as distinguished from legal or practical reasons) why one good diversified well-managed portfolio could not support demand deposits, time deposits, life and property insurance policies, pensions and a variety of other liabilities all at the same time and could not hold at one time or another most of the assets listed in the table, of course with proper control of over-all risk. Our institutions are in fact distinguished from each other more by the services they render their beneficiaries than by the types of investments that are suitable for them.

INTENSIVE MANAGEMENT

Widening the area of investments is of course only one component of *Total Money Management*. Equally important is the intensive exploitation of each investment field in which funds are placed.

When the total money manager has selected his preferred fields for current investment, he presumably employs experts in each of those fields to manage those sub-portfolios intensively. This is almost as important as the selection of the best investment media. The good management of a poorly selected investment medium can often compensate for much of the unfortunate selection. For example, some actively managed bond portfolios, during the recent drastic bear bond market, did well as, no doubt, did some stock portfolios during bear markets. It is during bear markets in both stocks and bonds that the most obvious distortions occur providing rich opportunities. Distress blocks are freely available at disastrous concessions while other securities are often simultaneously saleable at fair market prices. The bear market presents many opportunities for the cool-headed investor to make

changes even though he makes no attempt to guess the bottom. But to profitably exploit a bear market, the portfolio manager must be free to ignore costs and other limitations and free to act quickly.

It is often argued that our markets are not large enough to permit large institutions to make desirable portfolio changes efficiently. This is at times true if the manager persistently follows the crowd and tries to sell or buy just when everybody else is doing the same thing. If he is aloof from mass impulse, however, he is apt to find surprisingly big markets. The bond market in particular has increased enormously in size and depth in recent years because of the vast volume of corporate bonds floated since 1965, the increase in yields, and the consequent wider clientele. I have seen entire nine figure corporate bond portfolios sold in the secondary market in less time than it took to write the tickets.

In spite of the many investment alternatives which I have listed above, stocks and bonds will always be potentially very important alternatives for the total money manager. The very size of these two markets and their importance to the economy assures each of them a basic role in the investment scene. They should not be the only alternatives, as they often are now, but they will always be important alternatives.

Investment Objectives

The manager of any securities portfolio has a choice of two objectives and a choice of two norms. His objective can be: 1) speculative (near-term performance), or 2) investment (long-term performance). His norm can be: 1) cash (absolute performance of principal and income figured against cost), or 2) the market (relative performance of principal and income figured against a fluctuating market average), combining these two options, he has four modus operandi. It is not appropriate to argue here for any one. They depend fundamentally on the temperament and skill of the portfolio manager, his terms of reference and his portfolio requirements. Every manager, however, should be entirely clear and consistent as to which modus operandi he is following. The fate of the speculator who becomes an investor in a bear market or of the investor who becomes a speculator in a bull market is too well known to require elaboration. The manager who can, by an opportunistic policy, consistently beat the market in which he is operating, is invaluable in bull markets and in bear markets. Such a relative standard frees him to make portfolio improvements which are valuable regardless of market trends.

It is not necessary here to comment on the advantages of a flexible and active management of a stock portfolio. That this can be done badly, and indeed has been done badly by some, is not a valid objection. All investment of any sort can be done badly. The word active management, as used here, need have no trading connotation. The world changes every week: as a result of last week's momentous events, have I the best portfolio within the range of my knowledge and wisdom? This is active management: active thinking, not necessarily active trading. History proves the great rewards which have accrued to investors who have held the right stocks persistently over long periods of years. It was not all luck.

With bonds, frequent portfolio changes are always appropriate. A case can be made that equities are handled best as long-term holdings while long-term bonds are handled best as short or medium-term holdings. This is because the values of large groups of bonds are tied together mathematically far more precisely than are the values of large groups of stocks. While relative bond *values* at a given rate of interest are fairly stable, relative bond *prices* are far from stable and it is this contrast which provides frequent opportunities for bond portfolio improvements at no risk or at modest risk. While most long-term bonds purchased should be appropriate for holding to maturity, none should be held to maturity. This is because the best bond values today will not be the best bond values next year and certainly will not continue to be the best bond values until maturity. Let me explore this point in some detail. Since I am a bond man, my discussion of intensive management from here on will be entirely concerned with bonds.

Relative Values Within the High-Grade Bond Market

In equity investment it is often correctly said that too much attention should not be given to trends of the market as a whole because it is individual stock issues which are held and they often or usually behave very differently from the market averages. It is not so widely recognized that the same is to some extent true of the bond market. While the general level of high-grade long-term bond yields and bond prices are usually rising or falling together and these general market fluctuations are of basic importance to any bond portfolio, the *size* of yield and price fluctuations in the various departments of the bond market and for individual bond issues are so far from uniform as to deserve major attention. While Bond A declines 10 points in the market, Bond B (same quality and maturity) declines 3 points. While Bond A rises 15 points in the market, Bond B rises 5 points. Occasionally Bond A and Bond B move in opposite directions. Furthermore, although general bond market trends are often unpredictable these relative performances are often or usually predictable. Why?

There are two causes of these performance differences which should be examined entirely separately although at times they overlap. They are: 1) changes in the yield spreads between different departments of the market or between a specific issue and other issues (a) and 2) differences in the mathematics of the price-yield relationship between different types of long-term bond contracts (for example, premium vs. discount bonds) whereby the same yield change will create very different price changes (b). Let me discuss these separately.

Changes in yield spreads can be fundamental or transitory. By fundamental I mean, for example, those caused by permanent or cyclical changes in the investment quality of an individual company and its bonds or of a whole class of companies (an industry) or changes caused by permanent changes in laws or in supply-demand relationships for a given type of bond. Much more frequent are transitory changes in spreads usually caused by temporary shifts in supply-demand relationships (i.e., a big new issue of a certain company or a congestion of new issues for a given class of companies) or by market psychology or by the leads and lags of a highly imperfect market. It is these more or less transitory changes in spreads which provide most of the opportunities to make frequent portfolio improvements. Especially in bear bond markets all sorts of large aberrations and distortions occur.

In illustrating such switch opportunities, the protagonist is tempted to use obvious easy foolproof switches the more easily to convince the most sceptical reader. However, the portfolio manager who does not consider himself a fool will seek more complex switches which are not foolproof, which involve risk and judgment, and which can give much higher rewards.

a. Yields and yield spreads, monthly, from 1945 through 1968 are listed, charted, and discussed at length in a book entitled *The Price of Money* which I wrote in collaboration with Richard Johannesen and which was published by the Rutgers University Press in 1968. Much of this monthly data is brought up to date in Salomon Brothers' publication *An Analytical Record of Yields and Yield Spreads.*

b. Structural and mathematical differences in yield-price relationships are discussed in detail in a new book called *Inside the Yield Book* in which I collaborated with Dr. Martin Leibowitz and which is being published jointly by Prentice-Hall, Inc. and the New York Institute of Finance.

Simple Bond Switches

An example of a "foolproof" switch is the sale of a seasoned 25-year 7½% bond at 100 to yield 7.50% and the substitution of a similar long-term 7½ at 98⅞ to yield 7.60%. Such opportunities occur in the market almost daily, usually involving a new issue. This is because similar seasoned issues do not adjust quickly and completely to a new new-issue level. If the discrepancy between these two twin issues is corrected in a year, the switch has increased the realized compound yield by about 118 basis points from 7.50% to 8.68% for that year. A continuing program of buying new issues at offering price, or better yet, after they have broken, and selling similar seasoned issues involves no risk of income loss or of permanent principal loss (provided the substitution is accurate) and can hardly fail to be profitable (see Table III).

Yet very few American institutions try for even this most elementary type of portfolio improvement. Many are so busy investing big new funds that there seems to be insufficient time to make constant portfolio changes. The total money manager will realize that his portfolio is much more important than his new money. If there literally is insufficient time to do both, he can sometimes profitably delay the permanent investing of the new money and make advantageous improvements. The main reason that so many wide yield spread distortions occur and at times persist and go beyond any possible rationale is that most institutions, large and small, fail to respond quickly even to big market changes. Many are following investment programs marked out in advance which have no niche for the new bargains. Others are frozen due to book losses. Many have so much new money that they do not want to sell overpriced holdings. At some point, of course, an obvious bargain will attract buyers, but there are long delays. Probably the best solution for the buyer who simply has insufficient time is to double up the size of his unit purchases. Most bond portfolios are over-diversified.

New Bond Issues

Suppose a large company floats a $150 million 25-year bond issue and they are 7½s offered at 100. Does this mean that this company's many other outstanding bond issues immediately adjust to this rate with differences only appropriate to differences in terms? Not at all. Such adjustments take perhaps two months or more. On the day of offering this company's old seasoned slightly shorter 7½s will probably come down in price to 101½ and their 7s will sell down to yield 7.25% and their 5s to yield perhaps 6.75%. Two months later these discrepancies will be reduced. They will not be eliminated because there are structural reasons why the low coupon bonds should always yield somewhat less than the high coupon bonds—but not by 75 basis points!

The market for seasoned bonds lags the new-issue market by weeks or months both on the upside and on the downside. It is this invariable lag which presents the most obvious opportunities for frequent easy portfolio improvements. Furthermore, it is by no means necessary to own a seasoned issue of the same company to make a good switch—relatively overpriced issues of any company will do as well.

Again the yield spread between the whole fields of new issues and of seasoned discount corporate bonds (of the same quality and maturity) frequently varies widely from week to week. Here are the yearly maximum and minimum spreads between the yields of new Aa utility bonds and the simultaneous yields of seasoned discount utility bonds of the same quality.

Some spread is always warranted by the lower coupon and better call protection of the discount issue, but the table shows that on frequent occasions an excessive yield pickup has been obtainable by switching into the new issue at yield gains of 60 to 100 basis points. At other times it would have

TABLE II

Yield Spreads of New Aa Utility Bond Issues and Simultaneous Yields of Discount Aa Utility Bonds (4⅛-⅜ Coupon) (in basis points)

	Minimum	Maximum
1968	+30	+ 63
1969	+35	+101
1970	+55	+ 95
1971	+27	+ 70

been profitable to switch back into the discount bonds if the yield loss were small, say, 25-35 basis points. This is because sooner or later wider spreads will permit a reversal at a profit (see below). Similar tables could be presented for industrial bonds or for medium discount corporate bonds with coupons of around 6% or for many other types of issues and they would show similar wide variations in spreads.

Yield spreads are much less, of course, between new issues and seasoned issues of about the same coupon. Such switches maintain the yield, however, and can be very worthwhile.

TABLE III

Yield Spreads of New Aa Utility Bond Issues Over the Simultaneous Yields of Current Coupon Seasoned Aa Utility Bonds (in basis points)

	Minimum	Maximum
1968	−7	+29
1969	−8	+38
1970	−8	+39
1971	0	+30

Agencies and Mortgages

Another illustration of the internal dynamics of the bond market can be derived from a comparison of the yields of Federal agencies and treasuries of the same maturity. The huge expansion of the agencies during recent years has at times overcrowded their market and created outsized yield advantages while at other times the yield spreads have been surprisingly narrow. This is shown in the following table.

TABLE IV

Yield Spreads of 10-Year Federal Agencies Over 10-Year Treasuries

	Minimum	Maximum
1968	+27	+ 67
1969	+38	+ 71
1970	+49	+ 96
1971	+52	+118

Again there are big swings in the spreads between long Governments and long prime corporate bonds. Since 1968 the spreads between Governments and prime discount Aa utilities has swung frequently between extremes of +40 basis points and +135 basis points, a change which is the equivalent of 10½ points in price. Obviously, it is worthwhile to pick up half this gain every now and then.

Again, since 1965 the spread between new high-grade corporate bond yields and long government yields has risen from 16 basis points to a maximum of 249 basis points. Not all of this was a swing; some good part was a trend. In 1971 alone, however, this spread ranged from 93 basis points up to 182 basis points, and in 1969 it ranged from 95 to 196 basis points.

While there are dozens of other useful spread swings which present transient opportunities for portfolio improvement, there are also more fundamental differentials between different major departments of the investment market which naturally attract the manager's constant attention although they do not lend themselves to the sort of two-way switching examined above. Here might be mentioned the spreads between prime bonds and low-rated bonds which vary dynamically; one such series has ranged from +280 basis points high to +35 basis points low since 1968.

Another good illustration of dynamic change between different departments of the investment market is to be found in a comparison of corporate bond yields and real estate mortgage yields. Mortgage yields over time can best be measured in terms of FHA mortgage yields. Table V below compares these with the simultaneous yields of new A utility bonds.

TABLE V

Yield Spreads of New A Utility Bond Issues Over the Simultaneous Yields in FHA Mortgages (in basis points)

	Minimum	Maximum
1968	+ 48	−51
1969	+126	−24
1970	+ 89	−19
1971	+124	−35

Obviously, if FHA mortgages had enjoyed a better secondary market and if the investor had been free to buy and sell at will, a program of switching back and forth between these two important markets would have raised the return from any fund far above the maximum yields of either medium.

The Mathematics of Bond Yields

In addition, attention should be directed to the complex mathematics of bond price-yield relationships. The traditional norm of "yield to maturity" is often very misleading as a guide to bond values. A thorough understanding of this subject has many investment implications. Such a study (as presented in our new book) shows, for example, that the prices of all bonds are much more volatile in a high yield market than they are in a low yield market when subjected to precisely the same percentage changes in yield. It shows furthermore, that discount bonds are more volatile up or down in any market than par bonds with the same yield change and that premium bonds are the least volatile of all. Thus, the portfolio manager who must hold long-term high-grade bonds can, if he is temporarily bearish, concentrate in premium bonds, or, if he is temporarily bullish, concentrate in discount bonds.

One reason why discount bonds fluctuate differently from par bonds which again fluctuate differently from premium bonds is to be found in the role of "interest on interest," which depends on the rate at which the fully compounding investor reinvests his coupons as they come due. This vitally affects his total realized compound yield from any dollar input. Table VI below shows the potential total returns from the purchase of a non-callable 20-year 8% bond at par. Yield to maturity is, of course, 8% but his fully compounded return can vary between 6.64% and 9.01% depending on whether the reinvestment rate is 5% or 10%.

TABLE VI

Total Return from an 8% Non-Callable 20-Year Bond Bought at 100

Assumed Reinvestment Rate	Amount of Interest on Interest	Coupon Income	Total Return	Realized Compound Yield
5%	$1,096	$1,600	$2,696	6.64%
7%	1,782	1,600	3,382	7.53
8%	2,200	1,600	3,800	8.00
10%	3,232	1,600	4,832	9.01

(From *Inside the Yield Book*, Table I)

It will be seen that interest-on-interest provides more than half of the total return when the reinvestment rate is high. In the case of low coupon discount bonds, however, the reinvestment rate of a smaller coupon stream is less important and that part of the yield provided by the discount is already compounding at the yield-to-maturity rate. Thus discount bonds enjoy partial protection against lower future reinvestment rates.

There is another mathematical difference between low coupon and high coupon bonds which is of great importance to the portfolio manager. A large part of the return from low coupon bonds comes at a distant date, i.e., maturity, while the return from high coupon bonds comes in much sooner in the form of large coupon payments. The distant date for low coupon bonds means that any change in the interest rate at which they are discounted in the market will create a much bigger change in the present value of the discount payment. Therefore, even at the same yield change, discount bonds are much more volatile in the market than are high coupon bonds. The following table shows the increase in bond price volatility as coupons decline.

TABLE VII

Increase in Price Volatility by Decrease in Coupon

Coupon	Price Decline if Yield Rises One Third from 7.11%; 20-Year Maturities
8	−20.64%
6	−21.76
4	−23.58
2	−27.07

(From *Inside the Yield Book*, Table 13)

Premium bonds are, of course, restrained by call price and therefore they usually yield much more than discount bonds. Also, their yields tend to fluctuate much less than the yields of discount bonds. The combination of this factor with their lower volatility per basis point change in yield makes for a high degree of price stability, especially when the premium is substantial. Thus the investor has the choice of maximum price volatility in discount bonds or maximum price stability in premium bonds.

Table VIII traces the total realized compound yield in one year following purchase of a premium bond, a par bond and a discount bond in a market (February 1971) when the going rate for new issues was 7% at date of purchase, and moves to 5% or 6%, or to 8% or 9%. In each case the contrast in performances is dramatic. This table should eliminate the widespread impression that usually all high-grade long-term bonds fluctuate together. To the total money manager, the conscious exercise of this choice will provide a very valuable tool for maximum bond performance.

TABLE VIII

Bond Performance According to Coupon; Interest Plus Principal; Changes in 1 Year

Coupon of 30-Yr. Bonds	Cost	Yield to Maturity at Cost	Total Realized Compound Yield if New Issue Rate Moves			
			7% to 9%	7% to 8%	7% to 6%	7% to 5%
8¾s*	109¼	7.94%	− .80	4.13	10.94	18.83
7s	100	7.00	− 4.16	1.24	13.18	21.19
4s	67.18	6.50	−12.14	−5.24	21.57	35.37

*Callable at 107 in 5 years.
(From *Inside the Yield Book*, Table 25)

Table IX compares a premium bond with a discount bond in recent markets. It shows simultaneous fluctuation since late 1970 of 30-year 8¾s and 30-year 6s based on the average yields of Aa 30-year utility bonds with these coupons.

TABLE IX

Premium and Discount Bond Price and Yield Fluctuations 30-Year Prime Utility 8¾s and 6s

	8¾s		6s	
	Yield Change	Price Change	Yield Change	Price Change
June 1970 to Feb. 1971	−114 b.p.	+13⅛%	−158 b.p.	+20½%
Feb. 1971 to Aug. 1971	+ 41	− 4½	+ 98	−11
Aug. 1971 to Jan. 1972	− 33	+ 3¾	− 77	+ 9⅝

Short-Term Money Market Instruments

For long-term investment funds, probably the most speculative and potentially profitable of all maneuvers is the accumulation, in expectation of a rise in yields, of a large portfolio of short-term money market instruments over and above the amounts needed for liquidity or other operating requirements. This can be tantamount to a short position in the bond and stock markets simultaneously. If either stock or bond market declines soon and substantially, the policy, if reversed in time, can be spectacularly profitable. If neither market declines substantially and soon, the policy can be costly to income and if they advance it can be a disaster. Furthermore, if either stocks or bonds declined and the holder of excess short securities failed to capitalize on this by switching from shorts into longs or equities, there is no gain at all from the short portfolio and probably a loss in yield. Just sitting pat with holdings of shorts and watching long markets first decline and then recover is an exercise in futility.

The potential profits and losses from temporary short holdings are very large indeed, overshadowing most options available to the bond portfolio manager. There have been many times when shorts did much better than both stocks and bonds. They are a key alternative which the total money manager must always keep before him. He is not forced to decide between stocks and bonds or other long-term outlets. However, for a short portfolio to work profitably for such a fund, timing is vital. The rate of return is usually against the shorts and in time this will offset their potential advantage. Therefore, an early decline in long-term markets is often required to justify the short holdings. Table X below illustrates the highly speculative nature of a policy of switching between very long bonds and very short paper and also the importance of timing. The table is calculated on the basis of fully compounded interest plus price change.

TABLE X

Profit and Loss from Maturity Swap (30-Year 7s at 100 into 1-Year Bills at 5%)

	Advantage of Bills	
If Future Bond Yields Are	One Year Hence	5 Years Hence
9%	+1,885 b.p.	+110 b.p
8%	+ 914	− 37
7%	− 200	−200
6%	−1,481	−381

(From *Inside the Yield Book*, Table 37)

Stating this point another way, the breakeven price of the long-term 7s compared with the 5% one-year bills is 97.94 at the end of one year (a market decline to this price would equate the overall return of the 7s to the 5s) while the breakeven price for the 7s at the end of 5 years would be 86.90; any higher price then would mean the 30-year 7s had given a higher total return than the bills. Maturity swaps, therefore, are not only highly speculative but depend on an early market response in the expected direction.

Medium Maturity Bonds

Some portfolio managers wishing to avoid judgments on the future of bond yields, settle on a compromise and buy medium maturities. Our study shows, however, how volatile medium maturity bonds can be, especially if they have low coupons. Table XI below shows the percent price changes for a variety of coupons and maturities if yields decline by 25% in a short period of time.

TABLE XI

Bond Price Volatility
(% Price Increases as Yields Decline 25% from 9.48%)

Coupon	1 Year	5 Years	10 Years	30 Years
3%	2.28%	11.11%	20.81%	37.36%
5%	2.27	10.63	19.06	32.86
7%	2.26	10.23	17.84	30.71
9%	2.25	9.90	16.94	29.46

(From *Inside the Yield Book*, Table 18)

Look at the 10-year 3s and compare their volatility with the 30-year 9s. They are not so very different. Then allow for the fact that 10-year yields usually swing much more than 30-year yields and you soon find that the medium-term 3s can be as volatile as the long 7s or 9s. They certainly don't represent a reasonable compromise between long and short for the man who fears a rise in interest rates. By the same token, low coupon mediums can be an excellent profit vehicle if they are bought at a time of tight money when medium-term interest rates are above long-term interest rates. A better compromise for the investor who must get his current income and who fears a rise in yields are the long high-coupon premium bonds discussed above.

Bond Swapping at a Loss in Yield

Many of the most advantageous bond swaps involve an immediate loss in yield in order to obtain a better principal performance and hence a higher total return. Such swaps, however, are overlooked or avoided by many institutions because of the intensive search for an immediate gain in income. To the total money manager better principal performance is exactly as desirable as better income. There are potentially large gains in many such swaps and of course there are risks if the manager's expectations do not materialize. The total money manager, however, will not avoid, as a matter of policy, these opportunities because of the associated risks. Indeed he will seek them.

One example of such a yield give-up swap is provided in the next table. Here the investor swaps a 7% bond selling to yield 7% into an otherwise similar 4% discount bond selling to yield 6.5%. The adverse yield spread is 50 basis points. In his opinion, this is too low and within a year should move at least to 60 basis points and perhaps to 100 basis points (just such a spread has been seen in the past). He may or may not base his spread expectations on a general decline in yields which would certainly widen the spread as the 7s become restrained by their call price.

Table XII shows the large potential profits or losses from this swap during the first year, compared with just holding the 7s. If there is no change in the 50 basis point spread he loses approximately the 50 basis point drop in yield. However, if the 50 basis point spread becomes just 60 basis points, the superior price performance of the 4s will turn the income loss into a 91 basis points net gain, that is to say his principal performance will pick up 140 basis points and thus much more than offset the yield loss. If the spread moves up to 90 basis points, a gain of 40, his overall gain from the swap that year will be 526 basis points, raising his effective yield from 7% to 12.26% that year. Of course, if the spread narrows (probably in a bear market), his losses would be even larger because he has given up yield and therefore time is against him. There are a great many other types of attractive swaps which involve an initial loss in yield but which offer large potential gains, for example, an opportune switch into shorts.

TABLE XII

Effect of Various Spread Changes on a Yield Give-Up Swap
(Sell 30-year 7s to Yield 7%, buy 30-year 4s to yield 6.5%)

If Spread in One Year Increases	Basis Point Gain or Loss from Swap
40 basis points	526
20	234
10	91
0	− 49
−10	−188
−20	−342
−40	−591

(From *Inside the Yield Book*, Table 34)

Finally, the following table shows the increase in price volatility of bonds as yields rise. Here the yield increases are all by one-third from various starting levels. This means that price opportunity and risk in the bond market are today much larger than they were in the past. Therefore, active bond portfolio management is now almost essential to the bond-holding institution.

TABLE XIII

Increase in Price Volatility as Yields Rise by One-Third

Starting Yield	Price Change of a 30-Year 3% Coupon	Price Change of a 30-Year 8% Coupon
2.25%	−14.01%	−11.78%
3.00	−17.38	−14.58
4.00	−21.00	−17.60
5.33	−24.48	−20.57
7.11	−27.20	−23.09

(From *Inside the Yield Book*, Table 14)

These illustrations are just samplings of the internal dynamics of the bond market. There are dozens of others. The total money manager will not confine himself to automatic unsophisticated switching from like to like and back. The bond he purchases need not be the twin brother of the bond he sells. Ideally he is constantly seeking to sell his most overpriced holding and to buy the best bargain that the market affords. While he may not often reach this ideal, he can approach it. Every issue he owns should always be for sale at a price, namely, that price which will permit him to replace it with a worthwhile advantage.

Finally, both his stock portfolio and his bond portfolio will benefit by the many other alternative investment outlets which are always available to him. When he sells a block of bonds, he does not have to buy another block of similar bonds or any sort of bonds and he does not have to put the proceeds into equities. He can go into shorts or elsewhere and he is by no means limited or even influenced in his purchase by the character of the item sold. Day by day he is forced to make the widest of investment judgments.

Total Money Management

Total Money Management, as described here, is essentially a combination of the nearly total freedom of choice which has always belonged to substantial private investors with the diversified expertise which is available to institutions. It is no accident that almost all great fortunes have been achieved by individuals and many of these have accrued from successful investment. Some of these, of course, were a result of accidental good luck but many were a result of good management.

Similarly, the S.E.C. study on institutional investment showed that the aggregate of private and miscellaneous investors consistently did better in stock investments than did any institutional category. While the data does not explain why private investors did better, it can be surmised that greater freedom of investment selection was one reason, less concentration in blue chips was another and most important, much less of a tendency to follow the crowd and rush into the latest investment fashion.

Most institutions will never have the freedom of selection that private investors have nor will they have the valuable privacy. Their fiduciary responsibilities, the nature of their liabilities, and their size puts them at a permanent disadvantage. Nevertheless some institutions, provided they have appropriate types of liabilities, can approach the freedom of private investors. They can thus achieve the opportunity to employ and exploit superior expertise in almost any investment media that they select.

Total Money Management does not necessarily imply an increase in risk taking or a policy of short-term speculation. It is adaptable to all sorts of investment objectives. Its worldwide diversification of potential investment media could in part reduce risk if this is the objective. Certainly the sort of active bond portfolio management that I have described for bonds would on balance greatly reduce the risk of a portfolio of long-term securities and greatly increase the yield. I have no doubt that the same could be said for most or all of the other types of investment media.

Institutional investment in the United States has traditionally been surrounded by taboos, laws, legal limitations and all sorts of voluntary and involuntary straitjackets. During the postwar years much has been done to loosen these restrictions, but many remain, especially those created by accounting considerations. The weakest aspect of institutional investment in the United States is probably its accounting and actuarial procedure. A sharp artificial distinction is often made between income and capital gain for tax-free funds. Profits and losses do not become profits or losses until realized. These artificialities mostly stem from the unfortunate system of valuing certain securities at amortized cost. The result has usually been that portfolios become frozen just when changes would be most profitable. Often managers are forced to accept lower yields because principal gains do not count as income. An essential first step on the road to effective investment is to eliminate all non-investment barriers to profitable portfolio improvements. In the case of tax-free funds, no accounting consideration should stand in the way of profitable and carefully considered investment changes.

Finally, it is not necessary to move all the way to free and uninhibited *Total Money Management* in order to obtain some of its benefits. An institution's list of potential investment media can be lengthened without including all or even most of those media listed in Table I. Frozen securities portfolios can be thawed out a bit by appropriate changes in accounting or policy limitations without being set entirely free for restructuring. Intensive management of a stock or bond portfolio is always possible and appropriate even though the manager has to live with some unfortunate limitations. I believe that during the next few years, our institutional investment market will see an important trend towards *Total Money Management*. As William R. Salomon said, "this will present a great challenge as well as an opportunity."

CASH FLOW CHARACTERISTICS OF MORTGAGE SECURITIES

Martin L. Leibowitz

General Partner and Manager,
Bond Portfolio Analysis Group, Salomon Brothers

In the short span of the past few years, a whole new universe of mortgage securities has exploded into the fixed income marketplace. These securities have become relevant as a potential alternative vehicle for virtually every bond portfolio manager. In fact, within some portfolios, the role of mortgage securities has grown from that of a sector within the bond portfolio to the magnitude of a distinct asset class unto itself.

Figure 1 illustrates the structure of the U.S. capital market. The sheer magnitude of mortgage debt commands attention. To this point, the primary institutional route for this market component has been through the various forms of mortgage pooling such as GNMA's, FHLMC's and conventional pass throughs. The volume of these pooled securities has grown enormously to the point where they now form an important sector of the fixed income markets. At the same time, it is clear that this pooling process has only begun to touch the tip of the overall mortgage iceberg.

For the bond portfolio manager, the very structure of mortgage securities presents a challenge. The typical bond portfolio manager has developed valuation standards based upon the simple and relatively assured cash flow patterns arising from the standard bond investment. The cash flow characteristics of mortgage securities depart from this basic pattern in two fundamental ways. First of all, the pattern of cash flow over time is far more complex than that associated with the simple bond. In fact, this complexity makes it difficult to even define what constitutes the long-term yield or the average life or effective maturity of the mortgage investment. The second problem that arises with most mortgage pools is that the cash flow is partially unknown, i.e., it will depend upon the prepayments and default experiences of the mortgages comprising a particular pool. Most bond portfolio managers have an almost innate aversion to such cash flow uncertainties.

These fundamental differences from the standard bond investment have posed a certain barrier to the full utilization of mortgage securities on a value-for-value basis within many bond portfolios. As always, that which constitutes a special problem for some investors will create a special opportunity for others. Over the past several years, this special opportunity in the mortgage securities market has often expressed itself in the very concrete form of a significant yield advantage.

To participate with confidence in this important market, the portfolio manager should first become comfortable with the cash flow characteristics of mortgage pools and understand the key factors determining investment life, long-term yield and short-term return.

F.A.F./I.C.F.A. Symposium, Boston, December 1979.

Figure 1

```
              OVERALL U.S. CAPITAL
              MARKET STRUCTURE

                    1/1/80


   Public Corporate            $   264Billion
   Private Corporate               143
   $-Pay Yankee/Canadian           45
   Convertible                     21
   U.S. Treasury                  535
   U.S. Agency                    145
   Non-pooled Mortgages         1,103
   Mortgage Pool                   80
   Common Stock                 1,095
   Preferred Stock                 41
```

Figure 2

```
              CASH FLOW PATTERNS


   *   STRAIGHT BOND

   *   SINKING FUND BOND

   *   SINGLE MORTGAGE WITHOUT PREPAY

   *   GRADUATED PAYMENT MORTGAGE

   *   MODEL MORTGAGE WITH LUMP-SUM PREPAY

   *   MORTGAGE SERVICING EFFECT

   *   MORTGAGE POOL WITH PRESCRIBED PREPAYS

   *   MORTGAGE POOL WITH VARIABLE PREPAYS
```

Patterns of Cash Flow

It will be useful to quickly review the cash flow patterns associated with various investments, starting with the simple bond and moving up to the more complex patterns of a mortgage pool with variable prepayments (Figure 2). The straight bond has a particularly simple and appealing cash flow pattern (Figure 3). The investor receives a fixed, semiannual flow of coupon payments throughout the life of the bond. At maturity, there is a balloon payment consisting of the original principal combined with the final coupon payment.

Actually, many bond investments violate this simple pattern, both in terms of complexity and uncertainty. For pro-rata sinking fund bonds, the mandatory retirement of principal over time leads to a cash flow pattern that is much more complex than generally recognized. In virtually all bond contracts, call features and/or optional payments inject some element of uncertainty as to the cash flow that will actually be received.

In contrast, a single mortgage, without a prepayment, actually represents the simplest of all cash flows (Figure 4). The total monthly payment is level throughout the mortgage's life. However, there is a certain intricacy in the way this level payment is apportioned between interest and principal. At the outset, the required interest payment consumes most of the total payment with relatively little available for repayment of principal. With the month-by-month repayment of principal, the interest due declines so that an increasing amount of the level payment becomes available for principal repayment. As is well known to any homeowner, the last payment consists almost totally of a repayment of the remaining principal, often accompanied by a certain glee.

A more recent variation on the level payment mortgage is the graduated payment mortgage (GPM). The underlying idea here is very appealing. The early years of home ownership are presumed to be the most difficult ones financially, with the homeowner's financial status normally improving with time and career growth. The GPM provides a cash flow schedule that is somewhat better tailored to this financial cycle (Figure 5). The early years consist of lower than normal payments, which do not suffice to fully pay all the interest due. As a result, increased levels of indebtedness are incurred during these early years. The mortgage payment increases each year over the first 6 years and then stays level for the remaining life of the mortgage contract. Since these later level payments must compensate for the smaller earlier payments, they are necessarily larger than those for a comparable standard mortgage that provides level payments throughout.

In the marketplace, the anticipated cash flow to a mortgage lender usually must take some consideration of the prospect of an early prepayment. For the standard level payment mortgage, the market convention takes the form shown in Figure 6. Prepayment is assumed to occur in one lump-sum payment at the end of the 12th year. (For older residential mortgages with short remaining lives, the estimated prepayment time is usually taken to be half the remaining life.)

Figure 3

BOND CASH FLOW

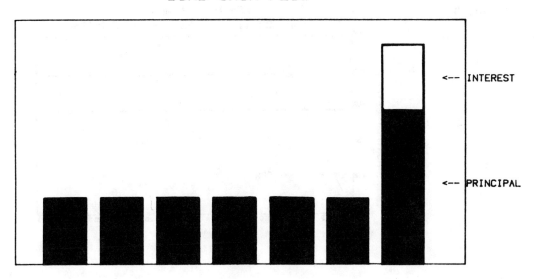

Figure 4

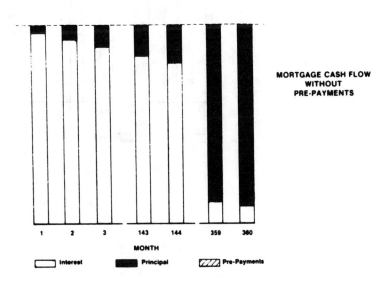

Figure 5

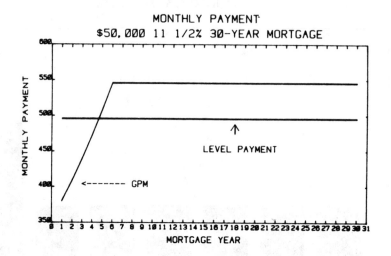

MONTHLY PAYMENT
$50,000 11 1/2% 30-YEAR MORTGAGE

LEVEL PAYMENT

<----- GPM

MONTHLY PAYMENT

MORTGAGE YEAR

Figure 6

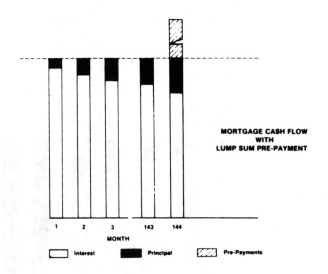

MORTGAGE CASH FLOW
WITH
LUMP SUM PRE-PAYMENT

MONTH

☐ Interest   ■ Principal   ▨ Pre-Payments

As mortgage pools were constructed and sold as pass-through securities, this lump-sum prepayment convention was adopted as a market standard for yield quotations. This was tantamount to viewing the entire pool, consisting of many different mortgages, as leading to one aggregate cash flow providing level payments throughout the first 12-year period and then prepaying all outstanding principal in the 12th year. The application of this idea of simultaneous lump-sum prepayment to a large pool of mortgages obviously leaves something to be desired in the way of realism. It conjures up an image of homeowners who reliably and quietly all meet their mortgage payments for an entire 12-year period and then suddenly the entire neighborhood rises up in unison and moves. The problem associated with this market convention will be discussed at greater length later in this article.

Another complication in the cash flow from mortgage pools is the "wedge" that arises from the service fee (Figure 7). Consider a pool of mortgages, each bearing a 9% interest rate. The institution which acts as a servicer for these mortgages extracts a certain fee, normally 1/2% of the remaining principal. This means that the investor in the pool will receive the equivalent of an 8 1/2% interest rate. As the years progress, the amortization of the principal balance reduces the magnitude of this servicing fee. Figure 7 illustrates this "wedge" effect for the case of a level payment mortgage without prepayments. The servicing effect is only a minor complication, but the investor in mortgage pass throughs should be aware of its presence.

A more serious problem in evaluating the cash flows from a mortgage pool arises from the estimation of prepayments. In reality, each of the underlying mortgages will have a life and death (i.e., a prepayment and/or default pattern) all its own. If he had perfect foresight and knew exactly when each mortgage would terminate, the investor would still find himself facing a highly complex cash flow (Figure 8). Prepayments in the early years would raise the total cash flow above the expected level. However, these same prepayments would act to reduce the outstanding principal. In turn, this would lower the regularly scheduled principal and interest payments for the subsequent periods. In general, one might expect to see a kind of peaking pattern shown schematically in Figure 8. The investor would expect to receive a larger cash flow in the early years which would be compensated for by a much skimpier cash flow in the later years. The precise pattern of this cash flow depends on the exact sequence of prepayments. The details of this cash flow pattern may have an overriding importance in determining the investment characteristics of a particular pass-through security.

In order to grasp the key role of the prepayment process in determining the cash flow from pass-through securities, it will be helpful to explore the impact of different prepayment rates using a simple prepayment model. The simplest possible prepayment model is one which treats prepayments in each period as being a constant percentage of the outstanding balance at the beginning of that period. Figure 9 shows the principal payments associated with a GNMA 8% pool at prepayment rates of 6% and 10%. Thus, for a 10% prepay rate, the first year's principal payments amount to approximately 11% of the original principal. This consists of 1% of

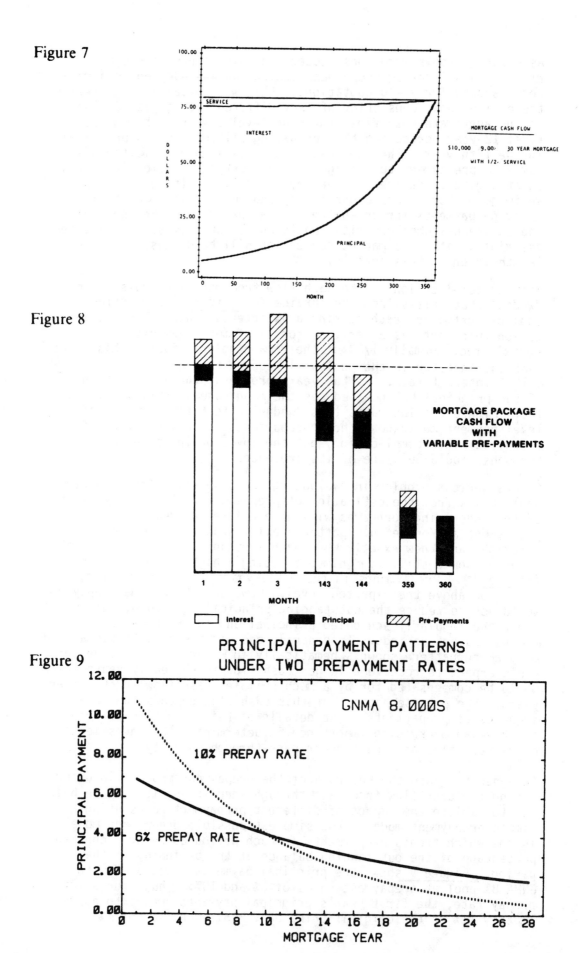

Figure 7

MORTGAGE CASH FLOW

$10,000   9.00%   30 YEAR MORTGAGE
WITH 1/2% SERVICE

Figure 8

MORTGAGE PACKAGE
CASH FLOW
WITH
VARIABLE PRE-PAYMENTS

☐ Interest   ■ Principal   ▨ Pre-Payments

PRINCIPAL PAYMENT PATTERNS
UNDER TWO PREPAYMENT RATES

Figure 9

GNMA 8.000S

10% PREPAY RATE

6% PREPAY RATE

PRINCIPAL PAYMENT

MORTGAGE YEAR

regularly scheduled principal amortization together with the 10%
assumed prepayment. These principal payments during the course of
the first year reduce the principal outstanding to approximately
89% of the initial balance. This new balance is then again subject
to a regularly scheduled payment together with a prepayment which
is 10% of this remaining 89%, i.e., roughly 9%. As a result of
these 10% percentage prepayments, the principal balance and hence
the dollar amount of the principal payments decline very rapidly
over the GNMA's life. The 6% prepayment rate obviously leads to
a more gradual decline.

However, the principal payments are only one component of the total
cash flow. Figure 10 illustrates the total cash flow of principal
and interest payments from this GNMA pool under the assumption that
the 10% prepayment rate is applicable. The scheduled principal and
prepayments are simply a reflection of the values shown earlier in
Figure 9. The interest payments are based on the stated rate of
8 percent of outstanding principal, and consequently decline as the
principal balance is reduced. The combination of these two effects
leads to an extremely rapid reduction in the total cash payments
received from the GNMA pool under this prepayment assumption. The
reduction is so rapid that the cash flow has fallen to less than
half of its initial value by the time the 8th year is reached.
This raises the interesting question as to whether GNMA investors
should perhaps retain this security only during the first eight
or so years of sizeable cash flow. By selling the security at that
point, they could then avoid the skimpier payments that would be
received in the later years.

This question must actually be answered in two parts. First of
all, the cash flow received in the early years is presumed to be
reinvested in other productive assets. This early cash flow is
thus embedded in a new investment process, and no longer bears
directly on the value of the remaining holding. The remaining
security itself obviously has a reduced principal balance as well
as a reduced cash flow. Hence, the second part of the question
is whether this residual holding provides a sufficient return to
justify a continued position in the portfolio. To gain some
insight into this issue, Figure 11 shows the same cash flow as
Figure 10, but now expressed in terms of a percentage of the
outstanding balance at the beginning of each year, i.e., as opposed
to the original balance used in Figure 10. In the first year, the
original and the outstanding balance coincide, so that both Figures
10 and 11 show the same total cash flow of approximately 18%. However, by the 8th year, the cash flow in Figure 10 had declined to
roughly 9% of the original balance. By that time, the principal
balance has shrunk as well. In fact, as shown in Figure 11, the
reduced cash flow for this 8th year still represents about 19%
of the then current level of the outstanding balance.

An interesting aspect of Figure 11 is that the cash flow actually
remains fairly constant as a percentage of the current balance
for as long as 15 years. After that point, it actually increases
as a percentage of the outstanding balance. This is exactly what
we would expect, upon a little reflection, since the last payment
must (by definition) fully repay the remaining principal as well
as the interest due. Returning to the original question of the

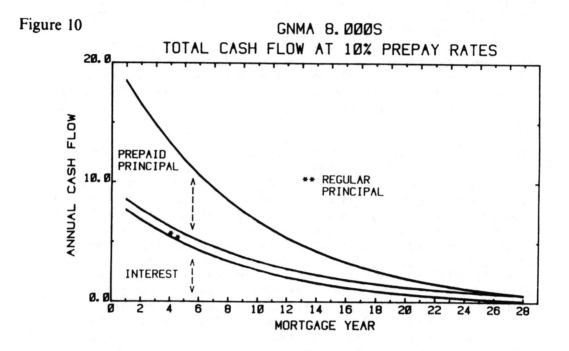

Figure 10

GNMA 8.000S
TOTAL CASH FLOW AT 10% PREPAY RATES

ANNUAL CASH FLOW

PREPAID PRINCIPAL

** REGULAR PRINCIPAL

INTEREST

MORTGAGE YEAR

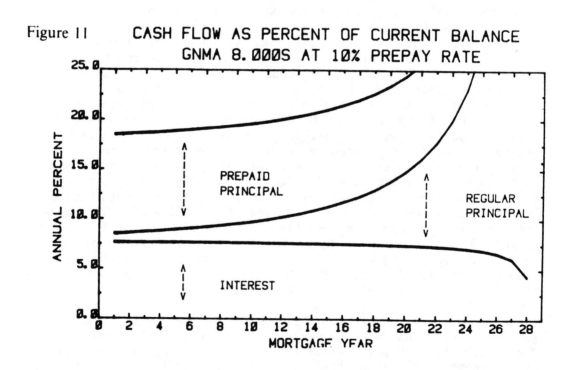

Figure 11

CASH FLOW AS PERCENT OF CURRENT BALANCE
GNMA 8.000S AT 10% PREPAY RATE

ANNUAL PERCENT

PREPAID PRINCIPAL

REGULAR PRINCIPAL

INTEREST

MORTGAGE YEAR

continued viability of the aging GNMA pool as a portfolio holding,
Figure 11 suggests that it will continue to provide a high level
of cash flow relative to the residual investment base that is represented by the then outstanding balance.

It is interesting to briefly examine the components of the cash
flow in Figure 11. For most of the period, the interest payments
remain constant at 8% of the monthly balance (or somewhat less
than 8% of the beginning-of-the-year balance shown in Figure 11).
The regular principal payments, on the other hand, constitute an
increasing percentage of the residual principal. The prepaid principal, on the other hand, constitutes, by definition, a fixed 10%
of the then monthly balance. The preceding is based upon the
simplest possible model relating to prepayment rates. Any reasonable projection of prepayment rates based upon historical experience
(or upon some refined analysis of historical experience) will naturally lead to a somewhat more complex pattern.

Figure 12 shows the prepayment rates that have been experienced on
FHA mortgages over the 1957-77 period. While we do not intend to
delve into the involved subject of models for projecting prepayment
rates, it may still be worth commenting on some of the problems associated with direct use of such raw historical data. For example,
the upsweep in payment rates in the 15th through 20th years is
largely a result of structural changes that have occurred in the
housing market over the past 20 years. Thus, this upsweep corresponds to data derived largely from the 1970's, a period when household mobility and mortgage turnover had reached levels far in excess
of that previously experienced. One should therefore be cautious
about viewing these higher prepayment rates as an intrinsic characteristic of the 15th to 20th years of a mortgage's life.

In fact, our studies seemed to suggest that the pattern for GNMA's
corresponds to a high level of relatively constant prepayments that
is reached after only a few years of initial aging. These same
studies seem to suggest that FHLMC pools may reach a somewhat higher
prepayment level with an even shorter period of aging. However, a
further discussion of prepayment rates would take us too far afield.
Once having made an assumption(s) regarding prepayment rates, one
can generate the cash flow pattern provided by a mortgage pool.
For the investor, this is only the raw material for an investment
decision. This complex cash flow is interesting in its own right,
but it is far from clear how to compare it against the standard
measures of investment value within the fixed income market. In
order to begin to achieve such comparisons, one must try to extract
the key characteristics of the cash flow. The first such characteristic which we will discuss is a measure of the "life" of the cash
flow.

Measures of Mortgage Life

There are many ways of characterizing the term or the life of a
mortgage (as indeed of any cash flow). The usual procedure that
is followed with straight bonds -- using the maturity representing
the date of the last principal payment -- is obviously inadequate
for mortgages and other fully amortized investments. In this section, a number of alternative characterizations of mortgage life
will be discussed (Figure 13).

Figure 12

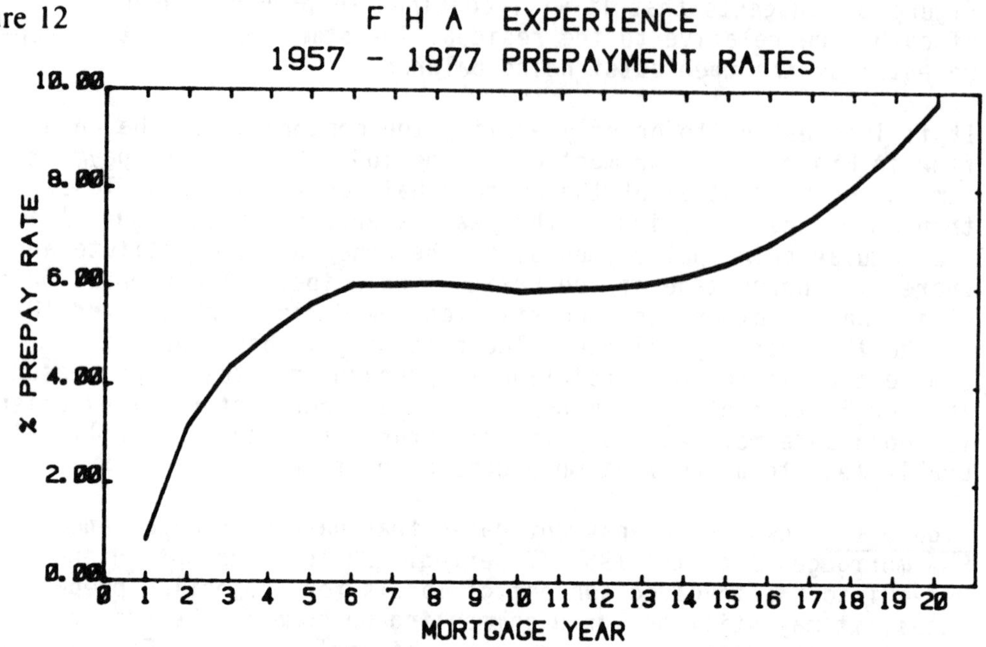

F H A EXPERIENCE
1957 - 1977 PREPAYMENT RATES

Figure 13

MEASURES OF MORTGAGE LIFE

* FINAL MATURITY

* MODEL LUMP-SUM PREPAY

* AVERAGE PRINCIPAL LIFE

* PRINCIPAL HALF-LIFE

* AVERAGE TERMINATION POINT

* MORTGAGE YIELD-BOOK-EQUIVALENT LIFE

* DURATION

* DURATION - EQUIVALENT BOND

* HORIZON VOLATILITY

The selection of a reasonable measure of mortgage life can be critical. Measures of investment life are used in several ways, both implicitly and explicitly, in the assessment of investment value:

1. The measure of investment life suggests the effective span of time during which a mortgage security provides a stated yield or return.

2. The measure of life suggests how to relate the mortgage security to other more familiar bond investments -- in particular, how to relate GNMA pass throughs to the Treasury yield curve.

3. The measure of life may well determine the volatility to interest rates that is associated with the investment.

Figure 14 shows how the principal balance of a GNMA declines with the passage of time. The top line represents the case of no pre-payments whatsoever. The conventional model of a 12-year lump-sum prepay corresponds to a principal balance following this top line for the first 12 years, and then immediately dropping to zero. This obviously unrealistic characterization is viewed within the market only as being a reasonable approximation to the actual, more complex process of statistical prepayments. The lower two lines in Figure 14 show the principal balances under the assumptions that prepayments follow a pattern corresponding to either 100% or 150% of the historical FHA prepayment experience.

The exact analogue of the "average life" concept that one usually encounters in the bond market can also be computed for a mortgage security with a specified prepayment pattern. In essence, this would involve determining the average time to each principal payment weighted by the relative magnitude of that payment. The resulting "average life" or "average principal life" corresponds to the bond-year technique used for serial and sinking fund bonds.

A simpler approach is the use of "the principal half life". This is the point at which the principal balance has been reduced to 50% of its original value. From Figure 14, it is immediately evident that this "half-life" point can vary radically with the prepayment assumption.

A more logical, but somewhat complex, approach for dealing with a mortgage pool is the "average termination point". A pool consists of many different mortgages, each of which pays a regularly scheduled payment up until the point where it either matures or makes a final prepayment. The average termination point is simply the average time of these final prepayments, weighted by the amount of mortgages prepaying at that point in time.

Mortgage Yield Books are based upon the model lump-sum prepayment technique. As noted earlier, the market convention employs a 12-year prepay, but most Yield Books display values for various prepayment dates. Another approach to the question of mortgage life is to first determine the "true yield" of the mortgage and then ask what lump-sum prepay date would lead to this yield value in the standard mortgage yield book. This date could be referred to as a "Mortgage Yield-Book-Equivalent Life". This procedure essentially traces the

Figure 14

PRINCIPAL BALANCES OVER TIME

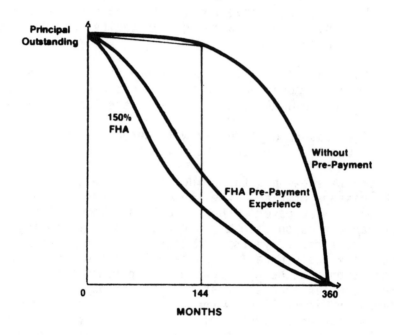

Figure 15 AVERAGE LIFE OF PAYMENT STREAM

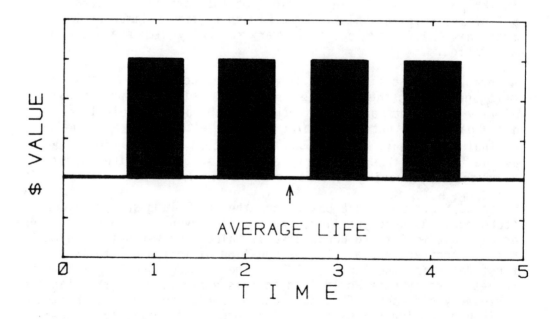

Figure 16

PRESENT VALUE OF PAYMENT STREAM
$ VALUE
CASH
FLOW
PRESENT
VALUE
Ø
1
2
3
4
5
6
T I M E

Figure 17

DURATION OF PAYMENT STREAM
$ VALUE
CASH
FLOW
PRESENT
VALUE
DURATION
Ø
1
2
3
4
5
6
T I M E

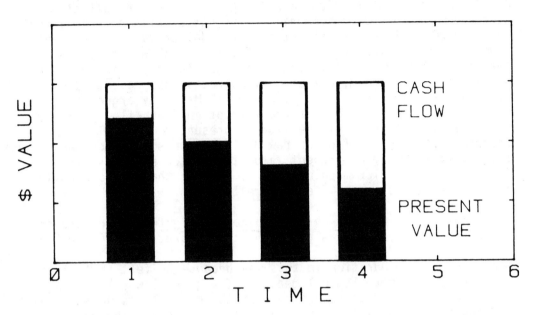

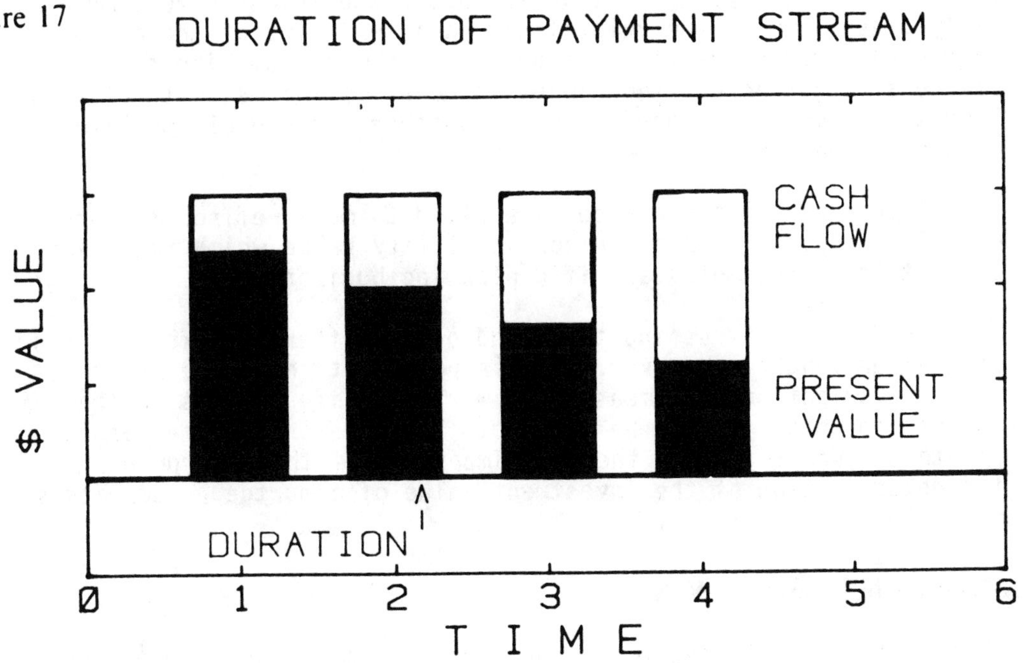

implications of the true yield value in terms of a life measure
that is commonly used in the marketplace. However, it suffers from
the backwards logic of viewing the life in terms of its significance
for the absolute yield value.

Duration is a concept which is being given increasing attention
within the fixed income community. Its basic definition is actually
quite simple. Figure 15 illustrates the dollar value of a level
payment stream. The average life of this stream would fall at
the simple fulcrum point indicated in the diagram. Figure 16 shows
a similar level stream, but also illustrates the present value of
each of the payments. In 1938, Frederick Macaulay argued that
a more appropriate measure of the life of any cash flow would be
the average time point of the flow of present values (i.e., as
opposed to simply the flow of raw dollar amounts). Since the earlier
payments have a higher present value than later payments, this
would lead to a fulcrum point that is shorter than the convention-
ally calculated average life (Figure 17).

This measure of the time to each payment, weighted by the present
value of that payment, was given the term "Duration" by Macaulay.

Macaulay defined Duration in this way because he felt that it represented a much more logical measure of a cash flow's life. At
the time, he failed to recognize that the cash flow's Duration also
had another, perhaps even more valuable, property. The Duration
value also represents the percentage price change associated with
an incremental yield move in the discount rate. The combination
of these properties enables one to use Duration to relate complex
cash flows to simple cash flows. For example, one can determine
the maturity of that par bond whose Duration is equal to that of
a given mortgage pool. This would enable the investor to immediately grasp some of the volatility characteristics of the mortgage pool through the association with the more familiar structure
of the straight bond. Thus, one can construe the maturity of this
"Duration-Equivalent Bond" as being another measure of the life
of the mortgage pool.

This same approach could also be applied to more refined measures
of volatility, e.g., the Horizon Volatility value which takes into
account the effect of a specific planning horizon.

One could go on discussing these and other different life measures
at greater length. However, at this point, it should be clear
that the selection of a measure of mortgage life depends on the
purpose to which it will be applied. It therefore becomes appropriate to turn to one of the most important of these purposes --
the determination of the investment value of a mortgage security's
cash flow.

Measures of Investment Value

As in all areas of investment, one must become familiar with the
conventional yardsticks of investment value that are being applied
in the marketplace. In addition, there may be considerable benefit
in asking whether these measures fully capture all the information
and judgments that a specific investor may wish to apply. The dis-

tinctions between general market yardsticks and the more refined, customized measures can sometimes, in themselves, provide a clear signal. This is particularly true when dealing with mortgage securities.

There are many measures of investment value that can be applied to mortgage securities (Figure 18). The most basic is the simple mortgage yield-to-maturity. This is the yield rate for a single mortgage under the assumption of no prepayments, i.e., that the original schedule of principal payments will be observed until the final maturity date. Apart from the common practice of basing this yield measure on the monthly compounding cycle that is consistent with the mortgage payment stream, this mortgage yield-to-maturity is identical in concept to the yield-to-maturity used in the bond market.

The very first thing that a bond manager must learn upon entering into the world of mortgage yields is the simple procedure for converting monthly compounded yield values to semiannual bond equivalents. As shown in Figure 19, this simple conversion leads to some astounding increments at the higher yield levels.

In dealing with mortgage pools, the basic marketplace convention is the yield-to-the-standard prepayment date. As discussed earlier, this standard prepayment assumption is normally 12 years or half the remaining life, whichever is shorter. This is often called "the mortgage yield". It is usually stated in terms of a monthly compounding basis, so that the conversions shown in Figure 19 are needed to obtain bond equivalent values.

The first departure from this market convention on the part of many investors is to replace the standard 12-year life with an estimated life based upon judgments regarding the prepayment prospects for the mortgage pool. This leads to a value which may be referred to as the "yield to an estimated average life".

In the preceding section, it was noted that there are a number of different measures of mortgage life that can be adapted to an estimated pattern of prepayments. By using these measures as the date of a lump-sum prepayment, one can construct yields to an estimated average life, half life, average termination point, etc. One can make an argument for each of these notions. However, in all such cases (including the conventional "mortgage yield"), one is essentially trying to artificially force a simple model cash flow to mimic the fundamental return characteristics of a very complex cash flow. The underlying cash flow for all these yield models is that of a mortgage providing level payments up to some prescribed prepayment date. At that point, all principal is repaid in one lump sum. In all such yield measures based upon this simplistic lump-sum prepay model, the idea is to achieve yield values that somehow reflect the more complicated cash flows that would result from the estimated pattern of prepayments.

This leads to the question as to whether there may not be a measure of investment value that can be applied directly to the estimated cash flow schedule. The answer is "yes". This yield value is usually referred to as "the cash flow yield". It is based upon an extension

Figure 18

MEASURES OF INVESTMENT VALUE

* YIELD TO STANDARD AVERAGE LIFE

* YIELD TO ESTIMATED AVERAGE LIFE

* YIELD TO OTHER "LIFE MEASURES"

* CASH FLOW YIELD

* REALIZED COMPOUND YIELD

* HORIZON RETURN

* HORIZON BOND EQUIVALENT

Figure 19

CONVERSION TABLE

MORTGAGE YIELD	BOND EQUIVALENT YIELD	INCREMENT
8.00	8.13	13 B.P.
9.00	9.17	17
10.00	10.21	21
11.00	11.26	26
12.00	12.30	30
13.00	13.36	36
14.00	14.41	41

of the same present value techniques that underlie the traditional yield-to-maturity concept for bonds. The cash flow yield concept is based upon consideration of every item of scheduled principal, interest, and prepaid principal that flows out of the mortgage investment. In Figure 20, we show how the present value of each of these payments can be added together to form the total present value of the payment stream. The magnitude of present value of each payment naturally depends on the discount rate that is used. At an 8% discount rate, the sum total of these present values may reach to the higher levels shown at the left in Figure 20. At a more stringent discounting rate of 10%, the value of future payments is reduced relative to the value of dollars in hand today, and the sum of present values of the future payment stream becomes smaller as shown schematically in the right side of Figure 20. (It is almost as if the discounting rate acts as a weight upon a coiled spring reflecting the present values of the payments. As the discount rate grows larger, the spring compresses under the increasing weight.)

As shown in Figure 20, at an 8% discount rate, the present value of the payment stream exceeds the market cost of the mortgage pool. In other words, under this 8% assumption, one can achieve an immediate increase in present value by paying out the market cost -- today's dollars -- and buying the cash flow stream at its higher present value. By the same token, at a 10% discounting rate, the market cost of the mortgage pool exceeds the present value of its future payments. In this case, the holder of the mortgage pool could increase the present value of his portfolio by selling the pool. At some discount rate in between these two levels, the present value of the payment stream will exactly equal its market cost. At this discount rate, the mortgage pool will represent a "fair value" in present value terms. This discount rate is shown in Figure 20 to be at the 9% level. This 9% rate is what we call "the cash flow yield". It is one application of the "internal rate-of-return" method that is used as a basic financial yield measure in all cases where one does not want to specify explicit reinvestment rates.

Figure 21 shows the interaction of various measures of investment value and mortgage life. The GNMA 8% pool consists of 2-year old mortgages each with a maturity of 28 years (excluding prepayments). Over this 28-year period, the most primitive yield measure is the mortgage yield-to-maturity having a value of 10.24%. As mentioned earlier, the first step for the bond portfolio manager is to translate every such measure into a semiannual equivalent value. This would raise the 10.24% to a 10.46% bond equivalent. The curve in Figure 21 essentially reflects the yield to a model lump-sum prepay at various dates ranging from 1 year to 28 years. The standard mortgage yield is based upon the 12-year prepay date. This leads to a value of 10.78% (in terms of monthly compounding or 11.03% in terms of semiannual equivalents). Using the assumption of a 10% prepayment rate, one can generate values for the various life measures that were discussed previously -- a weighted average life (WAL) of 7.8 years, a dollar half life (DHL) of 6 years, a Duration of 4.3 years, etc. For each of these life measures, the corresponding yield value can simply be read off the chart. However, this neglects the fact that the investor would actually receive a sequence of

Figure 20

CASH FLOW YIELD

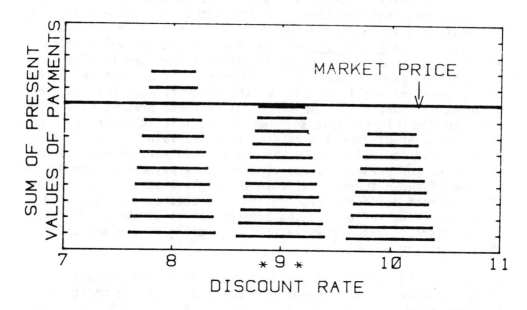

Figure 21

YIELD AND LIFE MEASURES

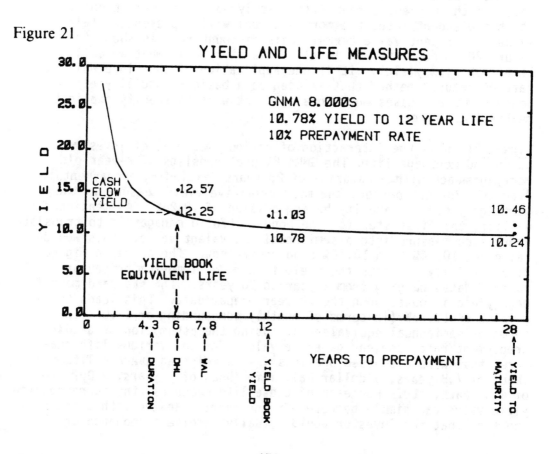

prepayments commencing with the first month's payments and extending
out to the very last maturity in the 28th year. In essence, each
prepayment could be viewed as one serial component of the total
cash flow. Return on those components that prepay early is high
-- on the order of 20-27%. However, the later prepayment dates.
provide yields which decrease until they reach the lower limit
of 10.24% at the final maturity date. The correct view for the
investor is to take into consideration all these elements of the
cash flow, as well as their respective timing. The cash flow
yield provides just such a comprehensive evaluation of the entire
stream of payments. As shown in Figure 21, the cash flow yield
has a value of 12.25% with a bond equivalent value of 12.57%.
It is worth noting that for this 10% prepayment assumption, the
cash flow yield exceeds the standard mortgage yield by more than
150 basis points.

Figure 21 also illustrates the previously discussed concept of Yield-
Book-Equivalent Life. Having determined the cash flow yield, one
can ask what prepayment date would generate this same yield value
using the standard mortgage yield book. The answer is slightly
greater than six years, a value which in this case turns out to
be close to the dollar half life. This example of the cash flow
yield was based upon the simple assumption of a uniform 10% prepayment rate. In practice, the judgment as to the level and time
pattern of payments is critical in the determination of the cash
flow yield. The prepayment rate plays a critical role in many
other ways as well.

The Key Role of the Prepayment

The pattern of prepayments from a mortgage pool determines its entire
cash flow (Figure 22). This impacts the cash flow that is received
over a short-term investment horizon as well as the residual cash
flow that can be obtained from the continued long-term holding of
the mortgage security. The prepayment pattern determines the long-
term yield received by the investor. In addition, by playing a
role in specifying the mortgage life, the prepayment pattern helps
to determine an appropriate location along the yield curve for
comparison with other securities, e.g., bonds with well-defined
maturities. The resulting yield curve placement leads directly to
an appropriate choice of benchmark issues to use in making yield
spread comparisons against other sectors of the marketplace. Such
yield spread comparisons are important for both short-term market
perceptions as well as the long-term relative value provided by
the security.

One of the problems involved in the estimation of a prepayment
pattern is the effect of changing rate levels on the prepayment
process itself. Ideally, the investor would prefer to have a
mortgage pool whose prepayment rate increased with higher interest
rate levels so that a greater cash flow could be put to work in
higher rate environments. Unfortunately, to the extent that the
mortgage holder is influenced by the availability of refinancing
at lower rates, the actual prepayment pattern will vary in just
the opposite way. The historical evidence to date reveals some
sensitivity to refinancing rates, housing cycle effects, etc.
However, any historical evidence must be carefully reviewed in

Figure 22

KEY ROLE OF PREPAYMENT RATE

* CASH FLOW DETERMINATION
    BOTH SHORT & LONG

* LONG TERM YIELD

* YIELD CURVE PLACEMENT

* YIELD SPREAD RELATIONSHIPS

* PREPAYMENT DEPENDENCE ON RATE LEVELS

* VOLATILITY RISK

* REINVESTMENT RISK

* UNCERTAINTY EFFECTS

* CHANGING ESTIMATES OF PREPAYMENT PROSPECTS

Figure 23

SALOMON BROTHERS MORTGAGE PASS THROUGH INDEX
DIMENSIONS AS OF JANUARY 1, 1979

Category	Number of Pools	Amount Issued	Amount Outst.	Avg. Pool Age	% of Index	Increase in Amount Outst. Over Year	% Growth
GNMA Pass Throughs	23,689	59.6	50.4	2.1	83	9.4	23
FHLMC PC's	75	11.1	9.7	1.1	16	4.7	93
Conventional Pass Throughs	13	1.0	0.9	0.7	1	0.7	316
TOTAL MORTGAGE PASS THROUGHS	23,777	71.7	61.0	1.9	100	14.8	32

Dollar Amounts in Billions

the new environment of 13% mortgage rates and with a whole new
generation of interest rate-sensitive consumers.

The prepayment pattern affects the volatility risk of a mortgage
pool in several important ways. Even if the standard "mortgage
yield" is used to value the pool at the end of a given investment
horizon, it will be the realized prepayments that determine how
much residual principal remains at risk. Thus, the greater the
prepayments, the lower the volatility risk relative to the original
investment base. Moreover, it is reasonable to expect that the
estimated prepayment process will influence the market judgments
over time, and that this will in turn impact the market's perceptions
of the security's remaining life. These perceptions could, in themselves, affect the security's market volatility.

The standard mortgage yield and even the cash flow yield measures
are based upon the assumption that all received payments may be
reinvested at the initial yield rate. To the extent that available
interest rates depart from this initial yield rate, the realized
return will vary accordingly. This creates a certain reinvestment
risk over any specified horizon. The magnitude of this reinvestment
risk will, of course, depend upon the prepayment pattern, with higher
levels of prepayments leading to more significant levels of risk.

The very uncertainty of the prepayment pattern creates a certain
problem for the highly risk-averse universe of fixed income portfolios. The fact that prepayments may depart greatly from any
estimate creates a certain hesitation among investors who wish to
at least count upon their cash flow (even if they cannot count on
their realized return because of the reinvestment risk). To the
extent that the prepayment patterns of a given class of mortgage
pools appear to lack predictability even within a certain reasonable
range, one may expect risk-averse investors to demand a correspondingly large yield premium.

Finally, at the end of an investment horizon, the value placed
upon the remaining principal in a mortgage pool will depend upon
the market's perception of the future prepayment process. Consequently, changing beliefs regarding this long-term prepayment process would have a significant effect on the short-term returns
realized by an investor.

Historical Returns

The subject of returns over short-term investment horizons can be
explored both from a historical and a prospective viewpoint. From
the historical viewpoint, the primary problems are to determine
the returns provided by various classes of mortgage pass-through
securities, to understand the components of this return behavior,
and to relate these returns to other sectors of the fixed income
market. In order to facilitate this analysis, Salomon Brothers
developed the Mortgage Pass-Through Rate-of-Return Index. Figure
23 shows the extent of the mortgage security universe covered by
this Index as of January 1, 1979.

Figure 24

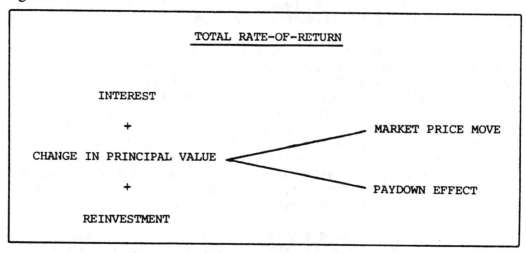

TOTAL RATE-OF-RETURN

INTEREST

+

CHANGE IN PRINCIPAL VALUE   MARKET PRICE MOVE

                      PAYDOWN EFFECT

+

REINVESTMENT

Figure 25

SUMMARY OF TOTAL RATE-OF-RETURN RESULTS FOR CALENDAR 1978

Sector	Percent Paydown	Pct. Price Move	+ Paydown Return	= Princ. Return	+ Interest Return	+ Reinv. Return	= Total Return
Total GNMA Pass Throughs	8.04	-6.86	0.96	-5.90	7.93	0.16	2.19
Total FHLMC PC's	10.69	-5.52	0.98	-4.54	8.24	0.27	3.97
Total Conv'tl. Pass Throughs	11.25	-7.90	0.97	-6.93	8.38	0.08	1.53
Total Mortgage Pass Throughs	8.43	-6.71	0.96	-5.76	7.98	0.17	2.39

Figure 26

HISTORICAL RETURNS
(JAN. 1, 1978 -- JAN. 1, 1979)

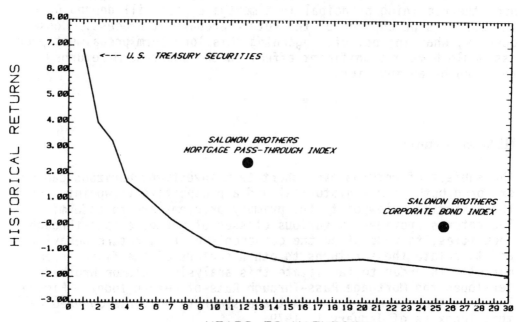

YEARS TO MATURITY

Figure 27

REALIZED HISTORICAL PERFORMANCE -- 1979

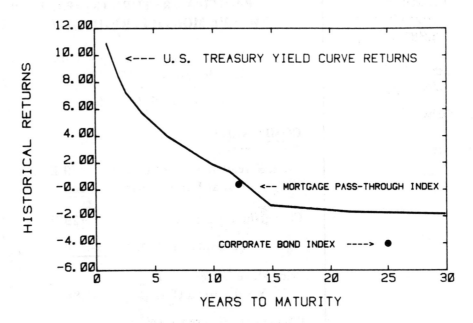

Figure 28

TOTAL RETURN COMPARISON OVER TWELVE MONTH PERIOD: 1/1/79 - 1/1/80		
Total Return GNMA 9's		+0.22%
Total Return US 8¾ '08		- 1.85
Difference in Total Returns		2.07%

COMPONENTS

Principal Return

Price Move	1.43	
Paydown Return	.44	
	1.87	1.87
Interest Return		.48
Reinvestment Return		- .28
		2.07%

Figure 29

```
┌─────────────────────────────────────────────────────────────┐
│              PRINCIPAL RETURN COMPARISON                      │
│          TWELVE MONTH PERIOD: 1/1/79-1//1/80                  │
│                                                              │
│        % Price Move Treasury 8¾ '08        -10.83%          │
│        % Price Move GNMA 9's               - 9.40           │
│                                                              │
│        Difference in % Price Move            1.43%          │
│                                                              │
│    COMPONENTS                                                 │
│    ─────────                                                  │
│                                                              │
│    Yield Spread at Start of Period      79 B.P.             │
│    Yield Spread at End of Period        108                 │
│                                                              │
│    Change in Yield Spread              +29 B.P.             │
│                                                              │
│    Horizon Volatility of GNMA          x-6.40              │
│                                                              │
│    Price Move Difference Due to                             │
│        Yield Spread Change             -1.86      -1.86    │
│                                                              │
│    Price Move Difference Due to                             │
│        General Rate Move and                                │
│        Volatility Difference                       3.29    │
│                                                              │
│                                                    1.43%   │
└─────────────────────────────────────────────────────────────┘
```

Figure 30

SELECTED MORTGAGE PASS THROUGH SECTORS		
TOTAL RATE-OF-RETURN		
	1978	1979
GNMA 7 1/2's	2.43	-0.10
8's	2.20	0.16
9's	0.56	0.22
FHLMC 8's	5.12	-1.15
10's		0.43
FFED 8 3/4's	2.11	0.51
BOA 9 1/2's		0.50

Over each historical period, the total return consists of coupon income, reinvestment of that income, and principal return. For amortizing securities such as mortgage pools, the principal return is a somewhat more involved concept than for a straight bond. One must include not only the impact of the change in market price, but also the return derived from the paydown received during the period (Figure 24). This Index takes the paydowns of nearly 24,000 mortgage pools on an individual month-by-month basis. After taking into consideration the effect of this paydown return, the calculation technique is totally consistent with that followed for the Salomon Brothers Long-Term Corporate Bond Index.

Figure 25 shows the components of the returns for the major sector groupings during calendar 1978. The total return of +2.39% for the overall mortgage universe appears to be a very unimpressive number in absolute terms. However, when compared against the disastrous returns provided by the corporate and Treasury markets in 1978 (Figure 26), the positive +2.39% mortgage return becomes considerably more impressive. Figure 27 shows the comparable results for calendar year 1979. During this period, widening spreads in the corporate and mortgage markets resulted in both areas doing more poorly relative to Treasuries than in 1978. However, relative to the long-term corporate market, the Mortgage Index showed an advantage of over 400 basis points.

This historical analysis can be further refined in terms of the sources of the realized returns. For example, in Figure 28, the total return from GNMA 9's is contrasted with that from a long Treasury bond. The GNMA's return advantage of 207 basis points is then further refined in terms of four components of return. The price move component of principal return comprises 143 basis points of this return advantage. This price move can itself be further analyzed in terms of the basic forces at work in the marketplace. Thus, in Figure 29, we see that these 143 basis points represent the net result of two contrasting larger effects. The first effect is a 29 basis point widening in spread of the GNMA's over the Treasuries which would have led by itself to a 1.86% disadvantage for the GNMA's. However, this was compensated by the reduced volatility of the GNMA in a year when the market underwent a significant increase in rates. This reduced volatility "saves" the GNMA from 3.29% in incremental principal loss relative to the long Treasuries. The net result of these two effects was the 143 basis point advantage for the GNMA's. Such analyses of the sources of return can provide valuable insights into what has really happened in the marketplace over a given period.

Another application of this Index is to examine the different returns by various classes within the mortgage universe. Figure 30 shows that in 1978, the lower coupon GNMA's outperformed the higher coupon GNMA's. This may well have been due to a lack of an appreciation of the true yield characteristics of the discount GNMA's and to a subsequent correction of that viewpoint. In contrast, in 1979, all of the coupon categories seem to have performed almost equally badly, perhaps suggesting that there had been a stabilization in the market perception of these coupon spreads.

Figure 31

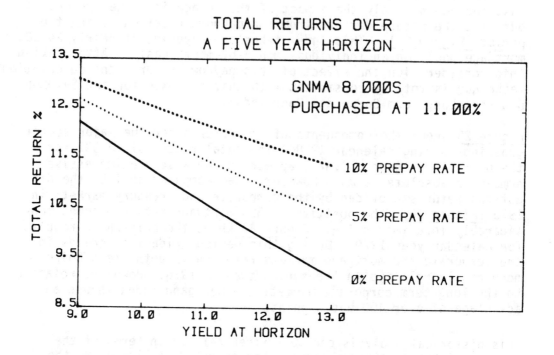

TOTAL RETURNS OVER
A FIVE YEAR HORIZON

GNMA 8.000S
PURCHASED AT 11.00%

10% PREPAY RATE

5% PREPAY RATE

0% PREPAY RATE

Figure 32

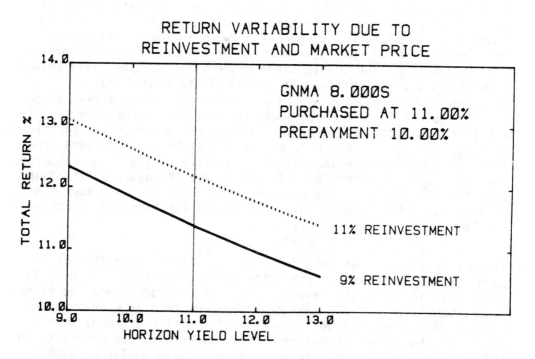

RETURN VARIABILITY DUE TO
REINVESTMENT AND MARKET PRICE

GNMA 8.000S
PURCHASED AT 11.00%
PREPAYMENT 10.00%

11% REINVESTMENT

9% REINVESTMENT

Prospective Horizon Returns

The study of historical performance is important and intriguing. However, its ultimate purpose is to help provide insights that can be usefully applied to the future. In attempting to evaluate the prospective return from a given mortgage security, one must consider how this return can be affected by all the factors which we have discussed.

In Figure 31, the prospective return patterns are shown for GNMA 8's over a 5-year horizon. In this diagram, reinvestment is assumed to take place at the initial mortgage yield rate of 11%. The total return then depends primarily on the mortgage yield assigned to the pool at the end of the investment horizon. A secondary effect is the impact of the prepayments received over the horizon period. For the range of yields depicted in the diagram, the mortgage pool will remain a discount instrument, i.e., priced below par. Consequently, higher prepayment rates lead to greater total returns. The magnitude of this prepayment effect depends upon the level of the discount. Thus, the prepayment rate has a larger and larger effect with increasing yield levels at the horizon.

In the preceding Figure, the reinvestment rate was assumed to be constant throughout the horizon period. In dealing with strongly amortizing securities, such as mortgage pools, this seemingly modest assumption can hide a sizeable variability in returns. Figure 32 shows the realized returns with reinvestment at a 9% and an 11% level over the 5-year period. Prepayment is assumed to occur at the 10% rate. Because of the larger cash flow generated at this prepayment level, the reinvestment effect is seen to be sizeable. In this diagram, the reinvestment process has been greatly simplified through the assumption of a single uniform reinvestment rate, no matter what yield level is reached at the end of the horizon.

More refined treatment of the reinvestment process would require a detailed model of rate movements within the horizon period. While this can easily lead to more complications than anyone wants, the key point is that the investor should recognize that amortizing mortgage pools have a substantially greater reinvestment risk than straight bonds.

There is one interesting facet of this reinvestment effect which emerges when a linkage is assumed between the reinvestment rate and the level of yields reached at the horizon. In Figure 33, a particularly simple version of this linkage is illustrated. All interim cash flows are presumed to be reinvested at a rate corresponding to either 1) the original 11% purchase yield shown in the earlier figures, 2) the final yield level reached at the horizon, or 3) a value midway between the original 11% yield and the horizon yield. In the latter two cases, there is a certain compensation between the reinvestment rates and the price moves associated with the changing yield levels. For example, a yield level of 13% leads to a substantial price loss, but reinvestment at the higher than expected 13% level provides an almost complete off-set to this price loss. As a result, the total return curve in Figure 33 is virtually flat when reinvestment takes place at the horizon yield level. These types of compensating offsets can be

Figure 33

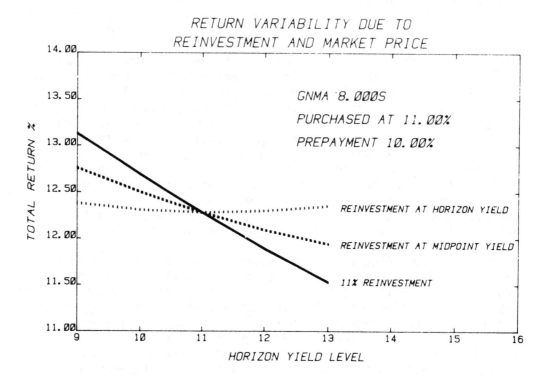

RETURN VARIABILITY DUE TO
REINVESTMENT AND MARKET PRICE

GNMA ·8.000S
PURCHASED AT 11.00%
PREPAYMENT 10.00%

REINVESTMENT AT HORIZON YIELD

REINVESTMENT AT MIDPOINT YIELD

11% REINVESTMENT

Figure 34

HORIZON PREMIUM BOND AND 12-YEAR PREPAY MODEL

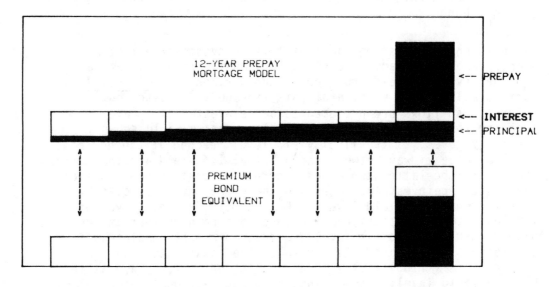

extremely important for investors who are concerned with minimizing variability of return over specified planning periods. In particular, it points to the possibility of a very special role for mortgage securities in certain types of immunization plans, Guaranteed Investment Contracts, etc.

In reality, the impact of reinvestment will depend critically upon the actual procedures for investing coupons and prepayments, as well as the pattern traced by interest rates throughout the period. Since the analyses underlying Figures 32 and 33 were based upon very simple models of the reinvestment process, one should be careful in using these results to make generalizations about the reinvestment effect.

Bond Equivalencies

An understanding of mortgage cash flow characteristics and the forces that shape them are essential for any bond portfolio manager who wishes to become an informed participant in the mortgage securities market. However, once such understanding is attained, there still remains the need to render simple judgments in familiar terms. For many bond portfolio managers, assessment of the investment value of a mortgage security would be greatly facilitated if it could be related to the yield-to-maturity characteristics of the more familiar bond market. In fact, there are a number of ways in which one can determine bond equivalents that reflect the judgments needed to evaluate a mortgage pool. As a simple (although not terribly useful) example of this equivalence procedure, consider the case of a single mortgage that actually does prepay its 12th year. As shown in Figure 34, this would lead to a level cash flow over the first 12 years followed by the balloon prepayment at the end of the 12th year. However, if we neglect the structure of this cash flow in terms of interest, scheduled principal, and prepayment, then the overall stream of payments is virtually identical to that from a simple bond. The coupon payments represent level flows throughout the life of the bond. At maturity, the principal prepayment together with the last coupon constitutes a final balloon payment. In this fashion, the simple standard mortgage model can be related to a 12-year bond with a yield-to-maturity that matches the mortgage yield (after adjusting for the monthly compounding effect). Since the mortgage's annual cash flow arises from the combined payment of interest and principal, it will generally require a higher coupon rate on the equivalent bond to match these annual payments. Moreover, the lump-sum payment is only a reduced portion of the mortgage's original principal amount. These two effects combine to make the mortgage's annual cash flow become a significantly larger percentage of the lump-sum balloon payment than for a straight bond having the same nominal interest rate. Consequently, the simple bond equivalent of a par mortgage will be a premium bond under this lump-sum payment model. For example, an 11% mortgage is equivalent to a premium bond consisting of a 12-year 13.08% coupon bond priced to yield 11.26% (on the standard semiannual basis).

This approach can be extended to consideration of more complex prepayment patterns and investment situations. With these equivalencies in hand, the portfolio manager can then render his investment judgments in the more familiar context of the bond portfolio.

Conclusion

The market of pooled mortgage securities constitutes a major challenge for the traditional bond portfolio manager. Its size, its liquidity, its uniformity, and its enormous growth command attention, both as a sector within the bond markets as well as a possibly separate asset class unto itself. As the bond manager first ventures into the mortgage world, he may understandably be dismayed by the complexity and the underlying uncertainty associated with the cash flow characteristics of these instruments. As he struggles to grasp the implications of these characteristics and to relate them to more comfortable gauges of investment value, he may often wonder whether the mortgage market is worth all the trouble and extra effort that it demands. During these periods of momentary discouragement, he should reflect on the fact that it is these very complexities and unfamiliarities which, in part, keep the mortgage market from being totally integrated into the larger institutional bond market. He will then realize that it is just this "trouble" that creates the special opportunity that the mortgage security market so often represents.

THE DEVELOPMENT OF MORTGAGE-RELATED SECURITIES: A REVOLUTION IN FIXED INCOME PORTFOLIO MANAGEMENT

Edward H. Ladd, C.F.A.

President, Standish, Ayer & Wood, Inc.

It is my role to examine the portfolio management implications of mortgage-related instruments. I have divided this discussion into four sections:

1. An examination of whether the investment environment is conducive to usage of mortgage-related securities.

2. A review of the advantages and risks of such securities compared to other fixed income alternatives.

3. The assessment of the compatability of mortgage type instruments with the objectives and requirements of different types of investors.

4. A discussion of portfolio management tactics that may be employed for mortgage-related securities.

While this first step—the examination of the investment environment—may strike you as a diversion, it is apparent that no security instrument exists for all seasons or economic conditions. For example, if one anticipates a major reduction in inflation, a pronounced decline in interest rates, and a business environment with major credit risk, I would argue that one should be heavily invested in very long-term, call-protected government bonds. In that environment, intermediate maturity mortgage-backed bonds or pass-through instruments with heavy future cash flow that must be invested at lower interest rates are obviously undesirable instruments. It is my belief, however, that the odds are small that we will experience a major and prolonged decline in interest rates. To the contrary, I suggest that the critical features of the next five to ten years will be a generally high level of interest rates, an exceptionally volatile market, and the development of serious credit problems. If I am right on these

F.A.F./I.C.F.A. Symposium, Boston, December 1979.

predictions, the environment will be reasonably constructive for most mortgage-related securities. Let me describe the basis of my assumptions for the future.

As we all know, the United States has been in an exceptionally long bear market for bonds. Interest rates have been rising on a secular trend. While sharp cyclical fluctuations have come in the interim, the yields at the peak and trough of each cycle have been higher than in the preceding cycle. As a result, present interest rates are the highest in the history of the United States.

The former peak in short-term rates came in the early days of the Civil War. The records are a little unclear, but it appears that the government had to pay in the area of 10 percent to 12 percent to finance the initial war effort. The recent Treasury bill and note financings have exceeded these yields by a substantial margin.

Perhaps more important, we have determined that the previous peak in yields on long-term government bonds occurred in 1814 as a result of the War of 1812. It is a little unclear in retrospect as to why the War of 1812 took place at all. The American population was evidently feeling bellicose, with some debate as to whether we should fight France or England. It was apparently decided that the British represented a better target, but for the initial years of the war, the British were occupied with subduing Napoleon.

In 1814, Britian had progressed in its first objective, at least temporarily, by sending troops to the United States to attack the East Coast cities. The initial target was Washington. In the face of this threat, President Madison called up 95,000 troops and, unfortunately for the U.S., only about 7,000 responded. After 66 casualties, the remaining troops fled in panic, and the British advanced on Washington virtually unopposed. President Madison fled in such haste that the British arrived at the White House in time to eat the remains of his warm supper.

The British then proceeded to burn the White House and the Treasury, creating such panic in the countryside that the currency was being discounted. The reports are quite vague, but most suggest that the paper money was generally discounted to about 85 cents on the dollar. While it is a little difficult for us to conceive of this discounting in a modern context, it suggests that the value of the dollar depreciated so quickly that it was easier to mark down the value of the dollar than to mark up the price of goods that could be acquired for dollars.

It was under those circumstances that the famous 6's of 1790 (which had been issued under the auspices of Alexander Hamilton with no maturity but callable "at the pleasure of the government") fell to a low of $65, which produced a yield of 9.22 percent. Until 1979, the yield of 9.22 percent represented a high-water mark in the history of the United States. That level was breached early in 1979. Yields went to the 10 percent level in early October.

I would argue that the predominant reason for the rise in past rates and the key to future interest rates is the level of inflation. Historically, a rough relationship has existed between inflation and interest rates, and this is logical. Inflation adds directly and immediately to the volume of credit required to finance the economy, whether it be the cost of new plant and equipment, the required level of working capital, or the funds required to finance housing transactions. At the same time, inflation does not add directly to the supply of capital. In recent years personal savings appear to have been discouraged as inflation has eroded real rates of return. It is a natural and reasonable phenomenon for lenders and investors to expect a positive real rate of return. In this context, the key to future interest rates is future inflation. The preponderance of evidence suggests that high inflation will persist.

If I am right in my assessment of the underlying momentum of inflation (and the resulting relatively high level of interest rates), inflation will represent the premier investment risk of the next decade. The existence of this risk will have a dramatic impact on the securities markets and particularly on the structure and characteristics of fixed income securities. The implications include a much greater emphasis on intermediate issues and amortizing securities with regular cash flow.

Another key feature of the future will probably be continued extreme volatility of interest rates. This volatility stems in part from the fact that so many historical precedents have been broken. We are operating in uncharted waters with an accelerating change of pace. Earlier in the postwar era, both internationally and domestically, many of the sources of stability, protective features, and margins of safety had been weakened or eradicated. In the markets, the speed of communication and the sophistication of the participants add to the volatility. As frosting on the cake, the Federal Reserve has told us that its emphasis on monetary aggregates rather than Federal funds rates will mean much broader swings in yields.

With the increase in market volatility, still greater advantages will accrue to successful interest rate forecasters. While we are all struggling to predict yields, interest rate forecasting is a high risk, zero sum game. The evidence suggests that it is harder to forecast than it might seem. I have been less kind to test the consensus of forecasts of a group of leading money market experts, and I have found them correct in predicting the direction of rates (forget the magnitude of the change!)

almost 50 percent of the time. Some persuasive evidence suggests that markets are reasonably efficient and, of all markets, the highly liquid U.S. bond market—with exceptional communications between informed professionals—should be among the most efficient. I am not suggesting that the market is totally efficient nor that interest rate forecasting is impossible; it is, however, difficult and substantial advantages can be realized in holding amortizing assets such as many mortgage-related securities, with a regular return of capital that facilitates periodic reinvestment.

Lastly, I would contend that one of the distinguishing characteristics of the debt markets during the next decade will be a rise in the incidence of quality problems and credit losses. Although the postwar era has had few credit difficulties, a new development is an exceptionally rapid buildup in debt and this has accelerated in recent years. In both the consumer and corporate sectors, the margins of protection and debt coverage have narrowed dramatically. I vaguely remember when many electric utilities were rated AAA, when pretax interest coverage for a utility was five times, when commercial banks had no debt and maintained equity capital of 10 percent of deposits, when earnings were not bloated by inflation-induced inventory profits and underdepreciation, and when the 36-month auto loan was perceived as creating a major risk. In virtually every sector, the margins of safety are smaller and the quality of credit is lower.

I am aware of historical studies that over long periods of time lower grade bonds provide a sufficient incremental yield to offset the defaults and credit losses. To me, that analysis seems analogous to extrapolating future stock prices from the vantage point of September 1929. I contend that we are in a period of increasing concern about credit quality, and that yield differentials between high grade and lower grade debt are often not compensatory for the risk. While mortgage-related securities are not uniform in quality, the vast majority of issues outstanding are of exceptionally high quality.

In this perspective, we can examine in more detail the attraction of mortgage-related instruments. In a generally high, but volatile, interest rate environment, the flexibility of intermediate rather than long-term maturities has a major advantage. The mortgage-backed bonds have typically carried final maturities of five to ten years. Most single-family pass-through instruments appear to have average lives of seven to ten years. Regular cash flow available for reinvestment provides a dollar averaging opportunity for those investors who hesitate to place major bets on interest rate forecasting.

The mortgage-related instruments stand in marked contrast to the traditional long-term corporate bond. With a 30- (or in the case of telephone, 40-) year maturity, the long bond is an inflexible, fixed income vehicle that suffers severe erosion in value in a period of accelerating inflation and rising interest rates. If I have learned well only one thing in almost 20 years as a bond manager, it is that long bonds mature very slowly. It takes many years to heal the wounds of badly timed purchases. To add insult to injury, the typical long corporate provides only a limited period of protection against call and only a modest call premium relative to the potential downside risk. Even that protection has been brought into question by some of the methods employed to weaken the protection against refunding (the celebrated case of the Florida Power & Light 10-1/8's) or by the recent effort by the Bell System companies to reduce the call premium. Thus, the long bond represents an instrument with limited appreciation potential but substantial depreciation risk, a contract heavily rigged against the investor. The United States capital market is virtually the only market that continues to condone very long-term bonds as a traditional financing instrument. I regard the long bond as an anachronism in an inflation-prone, capital-short society, and I expect that the next decade will produce a rising investor interest in more flexible shorter-term and intermediate-term issues, such as the typical mortgage-related instrument.

With regard to quality, the mortgage-related instruments generally rank quite high compared with corporate issues. Certainly GNMAs with the FHA/VA collateral, as well as the government guarantee, have exceptional credit strength. The mortgage-backed bonds secured by FHA/VA loans or GNMAs are also of very high quality. While the conventional loan pools guaranteed by the Federal Home Loan Mortgage Corporation must rank somewhat lower in credit strength, these securities also represent high grade obligations in view of their Federal Agency related status.

The quality of mortgage-backed bonds issued by savings and loans or savings banks and secured by conventional mortgages are of more questionable quality. In looking at such issues, I personally am much more impressed by the value of the collateral than by the strength of the issuer. Thrift institutions have suffered from rising interest rates and their credit strength has eroded. As a result, capital ratios have declined, deposit outflows have accelerated, liquidity has weakened, and more importantly earnings have deteriorated. During the past few decades, thrift institutions have operated under the critical assumptions that interest rates would fluctuate within a tolerable band, depositors would remain reasonably loyal, and Regulation Q ceilings would protect thrift institutions from unfettered competition. In this environment, they borrowed short and lent long, and they have been caught in the act. All of the critical assumptions now appear seriously flawed. Interest rates have risen dramatically, and increasingly sophisticated depositors are aware of the yield differentials between thrift institutions and alternatives such as commercial banks, money market mutual funds, and direct purchases of bonds. Regulation Q is leaking like a sieve (as evidenced by the Money Market Certificate). At the very least, those ceilings are going to be raised sharply in forthcoming years, and it would not be too surprising if the ceilings were effectively removed altogether.

In this environment, thrift institutions find themselves caught with a rapidly rising cost of deposits, a heavy burden of inflexible, old lower yielding assets, and a limited flow of new money to invest at today's high interest rates. Federal regulatory authorities have announced that they are preparing contingency plans to ensure the viability of thrift institutions. In view of the intractable problem of the old assets and the political pressures forcing up the Regulation Q ceilings, even the best managed thrifts have only limited flexibility. I suspect we will witness a rising volume of forced mergers and consolidations and perhaps some emergency steps to prevent individual thrifts from failing. This is not an environment that would leave me particularly comfortable with subordinated, unsecured obligations of thrift institutions.

Fortunately, the mortgage-backed bonds issued by thrift institutions are secured and, in fact, are heavily overcollateralized. In many instances these mortgage-backed bonds are collateralized by conventional loans, and the value of that collateral might be questionable. Real estate prices have soared in recent years, abetted by ample cheap financing, a rising tide of speculative activity, and a preference for tangible assets such as residential real estate. In recent months mortgage rates have risen dramatically, and many thrifts, faced with disintermediation, have become hesitant to lend at almost any rate. As housing transactions are virtually all financed with mortgage money, I anticipate at a minimum a considerable slowing in the pace of housing inflation, a slower turnover of unsold houses, and perhaps a material puncturing in housing price speculation. Reports are increasing that housing prices have declined in recent months.

I find it hard to believe that the resulting weakness in real estate prices will seriously undermine the quality of mortgage-backed bonds that are heavily overcollateralized. Nonetheless, only the perception, not necessarily the actuality, of a credit problem can adversely affect the market performance of a security. Under current circumstances, with worries about both the credit quality of selected thrift institutions and the value of conventional mortgage collateral, one should be hesitant to pursue conventionally-backed, mortgage-backed bonds without receiving a significant yield advantage over other high grade issues to compensate for the greater risk. To avoid or mitigate these risks, happily many mortgage-backed bonds are overcollateralized by FHA/VA loans, thus enhancing quality and providing ample protection.

Unlike mortgage-backed bonds, the conventional pass-through mortgages are neither overcollateralized nor the obligation of the issuer. With regard to the latter, I have a vague worry that not all the investors in such instruments are aware of the limited role of the issuer, and it is possible that some of the opprobrium may be attached to the issuer if serious credit problems develop with the mortgages. In any case, the conventional mortgage pass-throughs also have private mortgage insurance that offers protection on at least a portion of the collateral. With this exception, the investor has all the pleasures and pains of the underlying mortgages. With concern about perception, if not actuality, of credit difficulties on conventional mortgages, one should hesitate to invest in such issues under today's circumstances when yield differential over GNMAs or FHLMCs appears small relative to risk.

Thus far in our analysis, most of the higher quality mortgage-related securities provide substantial opportunities for investors. The yields are also very attractive. GNMA 10's with an estimated ten-year average life are currently providing a bond equivalent yield 11.46 percent (before adjustment for faster recoupment of the discount), compared with yields of 10.29 percent on ten-year Treasuries and 11-5/8 percent on 30-year Aa-rated electric utility bonds, the latter obviously having considerably greater maturity and credit risk. FHLMC 10's with an estimated eight-year average life provide a bond-equivalent yield of 11.62 percent versus 8-year Agencies of 10.75 percent, and FHA/VA overcollateralized, seven-year mortgage-backed bonds with a yield of 11.30 percent, versus 10.90 percent on seven-year industrials. In a performance-oriented, fixed income universe, the mortgage-related instruments provide a substantial yield advantage. It is readily apparent that the high returns and favorable characteristics provide portfolio managers with an exceptionally desirable instrument compared to many bonds.

Even with their attractive features and yield advantages, mortgage-related securities have a number of disadvantages. One significant disadvantage is the uncertainty and unpredictability of the cash flow from pools of mortgages. In spite of regular amortization, prepayments, and proceeds from foreclosures, the timing of prepayments (whether due to relocation or refinancing) and foreclosures is unknown. We have enough history on GNMAs to conclude that to date repayment has been considerably faster than the 12-year prepayment assumption used for pricing of GNMAs, and that higher coupon mortgages have greater prepayments, and thus a resulting shorter life than lower-coupon mortgages.

We do not have enough history to be sure about correlation between GNMA cash flow and interest rates. For example, during the next 12 months I would expect an increase in foreclosures but a significant reduction in payoffs due to relocation and a drastic reduction in refinancing, as interest rates are at historically high levels and mortgage money will not be easy to obtain at any price. Because of somewhat greater difficulty in refinancing FHA/VA loans than conventionals, GNMAs are less exposed to these problems than FHLMCs. Due to the lack of significant prepayment penalties on conventional loans, FHLMCs, in particular, lack call protection. Nonetheless, it is quite possible that mortgage pass-through securities may suffer from adverse selection through a deceleration in cash flow when interest rates are highest and the reinvestment opportunities are greatest. If one adds the uncertainty of cash flow timing to the importance of interest on interest as a component of total return, the future return from pass-through securities is quite unpredictable. As Marty Leibowitz has pointed out, pass-throughs are, for better or worse, extremely interest rate sensitive.

While general inflation/interest rate levels and earnings pressures on thrift institutions should mitigate any significant decline in mortgage rates, it should be emphasized that only a short period of lower rates is necessary to create refinancing risks. In this context, pass-through securities, particularly FHLMCs, share some of the call risk of many corporate bonds. This analysis suggests that, all other things being equal, discount pass-throughs with pools of lower coupon mortgages are preferable to current coupons or premiums.

Another possible drawback of pass-through securities is the gradual erosion of marketability as amortization reduces the outstanding principal. With a round lot defined as effectively a $1 million piece, by the end of 10 years at a 200 percent FHA factor, the original principal on a GNMA 9 percent will have been paid down to only $330,000. After 20 years, the original principal will be down to tag ends. The problem may be compounded if persistence of inflation results in a rise in the size of a round lot. The result will be a gradual deterioration in the marketability over the life of the issue. A need may arise for some variety of repackaging pools or prerefunding by investors to preserve marketability. While small lots may produce future marketability problems, I am pleased and impressed that definitions of good delivery have already been changed to a more accommodating policy. Furthermore, with imagination and computer technology, I suspect methods will arise to mitigate loss of marketability on odd lots.

A more serious potential difficulty is the price vulnerability of pass-through instruments in periods of high interest rates. One would ordinarily expect that the defensive nature of the instrument would result in below-average price volatility compared to intermediate-term bonds; however, during the 1973-1974 period of high interest rates, a heavy concentration of GNMA ownership had developed among thrift institutions. As these institutions experienced disintermediation, and therefore slowed the rate of acquisition of GNMAs, or in some instances liquidated the securities, yield spreads between GNMAs and intermediate-term bonds widened. During the past few years, the ownership of GNMAs and more recently FHLMCs has broadened, and proportionate ownership of thrift instituions has decreased. I am not aware of major liquidation of mortgage-related assets by thrift institutions during 1979 with the resultant market impact. Thus, I am hopeful that the future price volatility of pass-through securities will not be accentuated by the ownership by thrifts.

In 1979, another series of problems have contributed to adverse price performance and marketability of pass-throughs. These problems include inability or unwillingness of mortgage bankers to carry inventories of mortgages in a period of rising short-term interest rates, thus resulting in an accelerated flow of GNMA sales and some market congestion. A further problem may have been created by speculation on the part of some institutions who evidently committed to buy more GNMAs in the forward market than they could pay for. Rumors suggest that some dealers may have suffered substantial losses. This problem is expected to result in a further tightening of dealer standards to require that customers have financial strength to honor their commitments.

These problems, while significant in the very short term, are primarily technical in nature and should wash out over the longer run. The more serious long-term problem is the continuing very large supply of mortgage-related instruments. Some observers argue that the supply of new instruments will contract. They cite the facts that, in the past, either regulatory pressure and/or thrift management miscalculation produced a policy at thrifts whereby borrowers have been favored relative to savers, with the resulting artificially low mortgage rates. The resulting cheap mortgage money, the flight to tangible assets, as well as other government programs designed to favor homeownership, have resulted in a national overcommitment to housing. The statistics are staggering. The annual volume of new residential mortgage loans, even when adjusted to exclude inflation, increased by one and a half times from the late 1960's to the late 1970's, even with no significant increase in the volume of housing starts. The mortgage debt outstanding has grown from less than $200 billion in 1959 to about $440 billion in 1969, and to $1.3 trillion in 1979. The volume of mortgage formation has been exacerbated by substantial mortgage borrowing for non-housing purposes. As an example, the Federal Reserve Bank of New York has estimated that in both 1977 and 1978, mortgage financing in excess of residential requirements represented about $40 billion per year. The argument then runs that new pressure to establish equitable deposit rates for small savers, earnings pressures on thrifts, a general rise in interest rates, and rapidly rising cost of homeownership will puncture the speculation, curtail residential construction, and slow borrowing. Furthermore, household formations headed by persons 25 to 34 years old, and averaging 700,000 per year during the last half of the 1970's, may be only 540,000 per year in the early 1980's, and at only 340,000 per year by the late 1980's according to Census Bureau projections. These projections may well prove optimistic as the Bureau is merely extrapolating trends of the past 15 years. As it is during the 25- to 34-year age period that households make the greatest shift away from rental housing toward homeownership, some have argued that this bodes ill for housing.

While this thesis may have some merit, it is also true that the passing of the population bulge into the 35- to 44-age group, while not adding significantly to housing demand, may affect the mix of demand as families expand and income levels rise. I suspect, therefore, that turnover of the existing house stock will remain at a high level, that home prices will continue to rise over the longer term and, as a result, the volume of mortgage creation will grow considerably during the next decade. Moreover, for better or for worse, the national commitment to homeownership remains strong. In addition to government support, the past general inflation in housing adds substantially to future mortgage requirements. I also anticipate much more active usage of government programs, such as GNMA or FHLMC, to lend guarantees to mortgage-related instruments. While one could argue the government's willingness to guarantee vast volumes of debt (on the theory that the contingent liability costs the government nothing) adds to inflation, little is being done to curtail such guarantees.

All these factors suggest that the volume of mortgage financing will probably remain reasonably heavy; however, by far the most important factor for the supply of mortgages is the structural changes I foresee for thrift institutions. These institutions, savings banks, and savings and loan associations hold about 50 percent of all residential mortgages (with commercial banks and life insurance companies accounting for the bulk of the remainder). As previously mentioned, thrift instituions are in major disarray as a result of suffering the penalties of borrowing short and lending long in a rising interest rate environment. Since June 1, 1978, their problems have been compounded by the rapid growth of the six-month Money Market Certificate. After only 18 months, thrifts find that over 20 percent of deposits are already derived from Money Market Certificates—the proportion is growing rapidly and virtually all new money is coming from this source.

The growth of these short-term deposits may well accelerate if Congressional proposals to reduce the minimum from $10,000 to $5,000 or $1,000 are implemented. Other changes in Regulation Q would intensify the deposit cost problems. Thrift managements anxiously analyze the vulnerability of their remaining passbook savings paying 5½ percent where many institutions still find that half of their dollar volume of passbook savings are in accounts of $10,000 or more. It does not seem a major overstatement to contend that the thrift institutions are alive today only because a substantial number of passbook depositors are either exceptionally stupid or lethargic.

In this environment, I suggest that we are at the early stages of a profound strategic reevaluation and structural change for thrift institutions. Their managements are asking themselves how long can they continue accepting six-month deposits and investing the funds in 30-year mortgages. In reviewing the past unhappy policy of placing an increasingly short-term volatile deposit base in long-term assets, thrift managements are beginning to embrace the principle of an asset/liability match. This match, a linking of asset lives to deposit lives, is a strategy followed by thrift institutions in virtually all developed countries outside the United States.

With an increasing proportion of short-term liabilities, this strategy suggests the U.S. thrift institutions have little or no appetite to acquire additional long-term fixed rate mortgages. In spite of increasing interest in short-term mortgages with variable rate features, the VRM in most areas of the country has yet to win wide borrower support. Furthermore, until very recently they have faced regulatory and Congressional opposition. In many cases, lenders that have introduced VRM's have had to price them at an unacceptably large discount in rate from fixed rate mortgages. No signs have been seen yet of a good secondary market developing in VRM's. I am a warm supporter of the VRM concept, but I am becoming discouraged by the limited market acceptance and regulatory roadblocks. Incidentally, the much heralded introduction of the graduated payment mortgage (GPM) may be popular with borrowers but does little to solve the thrift institution problems, because the GPM involves a longer, rather than a shorter, fixed price contract.

I do not foresee that thrift institutions can abandon their role of mortgage originators. Substantial political and regulatory pressures exist for them to continue their historic role. The Community Reinvestment Act implemented in early 1979 exerts additional pressure on lenders to meet community financial needs. Faced with this dilemma and with the difficulties of the VRM, I visualize that thrifts will adopt a new strategy; namely, originating mortgages but then selling off the long-term mortgages through GNMA, FHLMC, or private mortgage insured pass-throughs to institutions that can better tolerate long-term assets. This process has already begun, and I see it accelerating in the period ahead, resulting in thrift institutions gradually converting to mortgage bankers, thereby deriving profits from origination and service fees rather than from interest margin between asset yields and deposit costs.

I am suggesting that we are in the early stages of a profound transformation in the process of mortgage formation in the United States. Unless the VRM concept takes hold, the result will be a massive flow of additional mortgages sold through the pass-through mechanism to permit mortgage originators that cannot absorb the risk of holding long-term assets to transfer mortgages to other institutions who can absorb that risk.

In the interim, the Federal government is contemplating emergency measures to assist problem thrifts through the difficult earnings transition. One of the major proposals (and in my judgment the only proposal sufficiently powerful to do the job in the short run) would be the acquisition by GNMA of low yielding mortgages (7½ percent coupon or less) at par from problem thrifts. I do not know whether GNMA will elect to retain such mortgages and, if so, what source of funds GNMA will use to accomplish the purchase or whether GNMA will eat the loss (with the resultant deficit and inflationary implications) and sell the low coupon mortgages to private investors at prevailing market prices. This program will funnel new money into thrifts who will then relend at prevailing market rates. The result may be no new net supply of mortgage assets but rather an increasing flow to the market of lower coupon mortgages. This could create an opportunity for investors, as more attractive discount coupons might become available when interest rates are high and discounts are most valuable.

In any case, the volume of mortgage-related securities seems likely to grow at a rapid pace. In my judgment, the continuing supply of these instruments is their greatest drawback. While the prospective volume of mortgage-related issues is enormous, some consolation, at least in a relative sense, is that the prospective volume of other fixed income securities is also vast. Consider Treasury financing requirements, financing of new electric generating units, funding of short-term corporate loans, etc. Before one becomes too gloomy about the yield consequences on mortgage assets of the heavy supply, it is appropriate to ask whether the supply of mortgages, high yields on such mortgages, and increasing competition between mortgages and bonds will drag the entire fixed income market lower in price and higher in yield. Who will buy all those bonds at yields significantly lower than high grade pass-through mortgages? Another question is whether the pressure from the mortgage market will force a change in the nature of the corporate bond instrument, such as shorter final maturities, larger sinking funds, and/or improved call protection.

I suspect the volume of mortgage-backed bonds is less awesome, in part because of the hesitancy of thrifts to issue such bonds in periods of high interest rates, and in part because, if a thrift wishes to employ a substantial volume of debt, it is cheaper to borrow directly from the Federal Home Loan Bank than to use the mortgage-backed bond. In any case, the characteristics of the mortgage-related issues are desirable and their yields are attractive, but I predict they will remain relatively cheap in order to accommodate the continuing volume of new mortgage financing. It requires an imagination more vivid than mine to contemplate a shortage of mortgages or a buying panic of mortgage-related instruments.

In view of this volume of sales of mortgages, it becomes appropriate to ask the question as to who will buy. Which types of investors can or should own mortgage-related securities in view of their objectives and the characteristics of the instruments? We can start with thrift institutions. I have already suggested that they will be originating and selling mortgages, but will they also buy? I suspect that thrifts will absorb some pass-through securities but probably not too many, as even the shortest average life instruments will appear long relative to the short deposit structure of thrifts.

The incentive for thrift purchases of such securities include their understanding and traditional preference for mortgages and amortizing assets. Some thrifts may have legal or tax reasons (the need for qualifying assets) that may spur mortgage instruments. Finally, some areas of the country may have conventional mortgage yields below the national average, thereby prompting thrifts to buy mortgage-related issues rather than to originate. In those instances, the limited costs of managing mortgage-related instruments and the potential benefits from active management may make marketable mortgage securities competitive with whole loans. These same considerations probably apply to retail or regional commercial banks that heretofore have been traditional mortgage holders.

Life insurance ownership of mortgage-related instruments appears to have considerably greater potential. The life insurance companies command a very large pool of capital and have relatively long-term liabilities. In recent decades, life companies have traditionally invested the bulk of their assets in intermediate and long-term private placements and commercial mortgages. Many life companies have stretched for yield by foregoing marketability and by a willingness to accept some credit risk. The life companies in recent decades have reduced their proportionate exposure to residential mortgages, but we hear reports of a recent revival of interest in mortgage-related securities, as well as some accelerated acquisition of whole residential loans. This renewed interest in residential mortgages reflects the rise in yields of such instruments relative to returns on private placements and income producing property mortgages, as well as the sheer volume of cash flow available for reinvestment at life companies.

The principal disadvantage of mortgage-related securities in the asset structure of a life company is the relatively short life and high degree of interest rate sensitivity versus relatively long-term liabilities. The length of life company liabilities stands in marked contrast to the shortness of thrift institution liabilities. Life companies have traditionally attempted to immunize their risks with long assets, but I detect some willingness to shorten assets by insisting on sinking funds, amortization, and shorter final maturities. This shortening may be a belated response to the pain life companies have endured by holding a heavy commitment in very long-term assets during a period of rapidly rising interest rates. More important, it is also a reflection of the gradual shift in life company mix of business toward shorter life term insurance and particularly guaranteed insurance contracts that are very interest rate sensitive. Also, some life companies may have been motivated to shorten assets because of the policy loan risk.

This context indicates room for an increasing volume of mortgage-related assets in life company portfolios. The maturity, while relatively short, is acceptable and returns are attractive. Furthermore, if my fears about credit problems are justified, it would not be surprising to find life companies becoming more quality conscious, thus upgrading their asset structure. In some instances, life companies may by-pass the mortgage-related securities and seek somewhat greater returns (and risk) through acquisition of whole loans.

Other major sources of capital are the endowment and pension funds, the latter including governmental as well as corporate funds. Their assets are growing at a rapid pace and liquidity requirements are generally limited, if not non-existent. As a reflection of adverse experience with common stocks, pension funds have recently allocated a greater proportion of their assets to fixed income securities. Furthermore, pension trusts have typically had a high quality bias and, with generally limited inhibitions about realizing losses, have engaged in active management by using marketable securities.

It is possible that pension funds, as well as other institutional investors, may be encouraged by regulatory authorities to expand their mortgage holdings as socially responsible assets. While such governmental pressure to allocate credit would be deplorable, it is certainly not inconceivable.

With this background, I visualize that pension funds will continue to be major purchasers of mortgage-related instruments. Such securities offer significant advantages over long corporates. Mortgage assets are also increasingly competitive with guaranteed insurance contracts. The GICs have been very popular in recent years but often suffer from a variety of defects including inflexibility, penalties to the investor in the event of withdrawal, and difficulty in assessing quality. With insurance companies turning to mortgage assets to cover their guaranteed insurance contracts, it would not be surprising if pension funds short-circuited the process through direct purchases of mortgage-related securities that provide superior quality, marketability, and flexibility for roughly equivalent returns.

Thus, pension funds are natural buyers of such instruments and can be expected to take on increasingly large volumes of mortgage-related assets. In fact, mortgage-related securities, with their maturity, quality, and return, appear so desirable for pension purposes that it would not be surprising to find such issues as a "core holding." Some funds may prefer usage of GNMAs or FHLMCs in a passive fund as a specialized and segregated, but perhaps substantial portion, of the total fixed income portfolio.

While I can understand the usage of mortgage instruments as a passive core holding, active management can enhance the total return to the investor with limited incremental risk. To improve their return, portfolio managers have a variety of tactics that are particularly adaptable to mortgage-related assets in view of the generally favorable marketability and the existence of a current as well as a forward and a futures market, a feature that does not exist for the typical corporate bond. Such tactics include:

— arbitraging mortgage-related instruments with bonds.

— arbitraging between various GNMAs, FHLMCs and conventional pass-throughs with the disparities in yields and different risk levels.

- arbitraging between conventional loan collaterialized mortgage-backed bonds versus bonds secured by FHA/VA loans or GNMAs.

- adjusting maturity preference within the mortgage-related area. While we have not dwelt upon them today, specialized instruments range in average life from 5 years (GNMA mobiles) to 18 years (FHA project loans).

- taking advantage of disparities among the current, forward, and futures market.

- working with characteristics of different pools by switching from slower paying to faster paying pools.

- emphasizing somewhat older pools which may be at a faster paying stage of their life cycle (significant changes in the cash flow exist at different periods during the life of a mortgage).

- arbitraging different coupons to obtain greater returns through faster recoupment of discounts.

- adjusting coupons to dampen or to induce the market volatility.

- anticipating market or regulatory developments which would increase or shrink the supply of various coupons or types of issues.

This list is not exhaustive but rather indicates the panoply of opportunities for active management of mortgage-related securities. In fact, I would argue that the variety and flexibility of mortgage-related assets provide a greater array of possibilities for active portfolio management than any other fixed income market. As an example, contemplate the range of maturity on the short-term instruments, such as FHA construction loans with an average life of 6 to 18 months or GNMA mobile home loans with lives of 5 to 12 years, or long-term instruments, such as various GNMA or FHA project loans with an average life of 18 to 20 years. Quasi-mortgage-related assets include fully insured SBA participations that do not have mortgage backing but have a government guarantee and monthly amortization characteristics that might be included as a mortgage-related asset with short maturities.

In addition to the variety of maturities, these issues offer coupon selection from 4½ percent to 12½ percent and wide diversification of function, issuer, and quality. From a portfolio manager's perspective, this means that if rates are expected to rise over the near term, one could sell longer maturity, lower coupon issues and move into higher coupon, shorter issues. In addition, the type of security function should be considered (i.e., multifamily project loans have relatively little reason for principal prepayments except default or exhaustion of depreciation). Neither of these events is likely to occur without some ability to analyze or anticipate. Hence, in the assumed rise in rates, the multifamily projects would be relatively unattractive versus shorter, higher coupons or faster prepayers. Conversely, SBA participation certificates are relatively unattractive in a falling rate environment, because the underlying loans have no prepayment penalties (i.e., an instant par call). These are examples of portfolio flexibility, all within the mortgage-related assets category.

We have discussed only one dimension of this market—the cash market. A unique aspect of these assets is the cash forward market, which is active, sizable, and again flexible. Virtually no other fixed income market has this opportunity for creative portfolio management. A portfolio manager who knows he will be getting contributions can lock up today's rates without having the cash today, gradually through the drawdown schedule of an FHA construction loan or in one shot with a GNMA or FHLMC purchase out to six months. The above contributions need not be cash—they could be amortization from other mortgage-related assets or a bond maturity on which a significant loss exists (which precludes sale prior to maturity).

Another example of the use of forward markets is the so-called roll. These arbitrages involve analysis of cost-of-carry versus market prices. In other words, if short-term rates are higher than the adjusted current yield on GNMAs or FHLMCs, the bonds are sold for immediate delivery and repurchased simultaneously (no market risk if guaranteed coupon) for a forward month. Conversely, if short-term rates are lower than adjusted current yield, then it is often possible to sell for immediate delivery and repurchase simultaneously for a forward month at a price low enough to more than offset interest lost.

To those who wish to engage in active management, I would suggest that the field of mortgage-related assets is sufficiently new and complex that the market may be less efficient than is the case in traditional bonds, thereby creating for investors unusual opportunities to enhance returns in mortgage-related assets.

In conclusion, I think it is obvious that the day of the mortgage-related instrument has arrived. These issues offer some major advantages including amortization and cash flow of pass-through securities, intermediate maturities of mortgage-backed bonds at a time when intermediate issues appear increasingly attractive, generally high quality, favorable and improving marketability, and more importantly a yield that compares very favorably to bonds, particularly on a quality and maturity risk-adjusted basis.

Significant disadvantages also exist. The mortgage-related asset category includes some lower quality issues. The cash flow, while providing flexibility, also results in unpredictability. Most important is the likelihood of a continuing heavy supply of mortgage-related instruments offered in the markets.

Despite these drawbacks, mortgage-related assets appear to be appropriate and attractive to a broad array of institutional investors. Many of these instruments are conducive to active management, thereby offering investors a significant increment in return over passive investment. Last but not least, mortgage-related instruments offer a new challenge for fixed income portfolio managers. Moving from bonds to mortgage-related instruments is analogous to switching from two dimensional to three dimensional tic-tac-toe. Once you have made the transition, it is boring to go back. So I contend that the mortgage-related asset opens a new and exciting opportunity, not only for investors but also for portfolio managers.

by Lee N. Price

Growth or Yield: The Choice Depends on Your Tax Rate

▶ The personal income tax on dividends is generally higher than that on capital gains. This differential will presumably lead high-income individuals to prefer, hence bid up, the shares of companies that emphasize capital gains rather than current dividend yield. And it is indeed the prospect of capital gain, rather than growing dividends, that justifies this emphasis; on the basis of accumulating dividends, many growth stocks won't catch up with income stocks for 20 or 30 years.

One can always calculate the annual appreciation rate necessary to justify the purchase of any stock over the alternative investment offering the best after-tax return. But investment decisions between yield and growth stocks should be based, not merely on a stock's appreciation rate, but on the spread between the appreciation rate and the company's expected growth rate—on the rate of change, in other words, in P/E multiple.

Charts based on a 10-year holding period (the apparent average for individual investors) permit an investor to use his own assumptions about dividend growth rates and P/E multiple risk to gauge the relative appeal of growth and risk under differing tax rates. The charts are also handy for analyzing the effects of changes in discount and tax rates. ▶

THE INVESTOR who has wistfully watched his favorite growth stocks of the 1960s fall to historically low price-earnings multiples in the last five years may be forgiven for feeling that the present emphasis on yield is overdone. Earnings per share for Johnson & Johnson, for example, have risen from $1.50 to an estimated $4.17 at a fairly consistent rate between 1970 and 1977; yet the share price has fallen from $130 to $70.

Investment theory over the last 30 years has assumed that rational investors with equal information and equal objectives will assign rational weights to earnings growth relative to dividend yield. The effect of differences in tax rates between individuals, corporations and institutions has received frequent, but only

peripheral, attention. This article reviews the prior research on the implications of differential tax rates for equity valuation and provides a graphical method of comparing any two or more stocks with different yield-growth characteristics. It also examines the potential impact on both growth and yield stock return of the proposed elimination of preferential capital gains treatment and reduction of taxes on dividends.

Effect of Differential Taxation on Investors

Miller and Modigliani's classic paper postulated that, in a perfect capital market, the value of a company is independent of its dividend policy.[1] Thus, since the personal income tax rate on dividends is generally higher than that levied on capital gains, the optimum dividend policy should be one of zero dividends.[2] But corporations do, in fact, pay dividends. Obviously, there must be imperfections in capital markets that partially override the effect of differential taxation.

Benjamin Graham suggested that investors have more confidence in dividends received now than in future capital gains based on dividends reinvested.[3] Others have suggested that investors prefer different dividend payout ratios depending upon their willingness to bear risk.[4] Past research has presumed that differential taxation leads high-income individual investors to prefer, and therefore bid up, the shares of companies that emphasize growth and capital gains rather than current dividend yield.[5]

Evidence on current investor holdings poses a potential problem for this theory. Even after the recent four-year trend away from growth stocks, institutional equity portfolios remain heavily underweighted in

1. Footnotes appear at end of article.

Lee Price is a general partner of Rosenberg Capital Management of San Francisco and has primary responsibility for quantitative disciplines used in equity valuation, portfolio diversification and economic forecasting.

such high yield, mature, low beta areas as telephone and electrical utility issues.[6] On the other hand, individual trust accounts managed by bank custodians appear to be heavily overweighted in these high yield issues.[7] This seemingly contradictory behavior could be explained by:

1. A difference in risk-aversion and time horizon between the two groups of investors. Elderly individuals may prefer the stability of low beta stocks, despite the higher tax rate on their dividends (and may be averse to buying long-term bonds or waiting for long-term capital appreciation). Institutional portfolio managers may prefer the open-ended, long-term potential of higher growth.
2. Dual trust obligations stipulating that current income go to one beneficiary while principal is eventually inherited by remaindermen. Since capital gains cannot be paid out to the initial beneficiary, high yield stocks provide a convenient combination of income, capital preservation and some inflation protection.

Evidence nevertheless suggests that there are a substantial number of individual investors who are very much aware of the impact of differential tax rates on investment returns and who bias their selection be-

tween growth and yield stocks accordingly. The following sections develop a graphical presentation of why these investors should behave as they apparently do. Portfolio managers with identical growth and yield expectations may select very different portfolios depending upon their recognition of the implications of tax rates.

Putting Growth and Yield in Perspective

How should the investor compare two stocks of equal risk but different growth and dividend yield characteristics? The yield advocate can clearly point to higher immediate income. Growth advocates frequently counter that, after some crossover point, growth stocks will actually yield more on cost than present yield stocks. The number of years to "dividend crossover" gained brief currency as a measure of risk in the early 1970s; it was felt that most investors would not want to wait more than 10 years for equal dividends.[8]

But dividend crossover does not necessarily imply equal total dividends. Consider Figure A. In 17 years, a two per cent yield, 10 per cent growth electronics company (Stock B) will produce the same *annual* div-

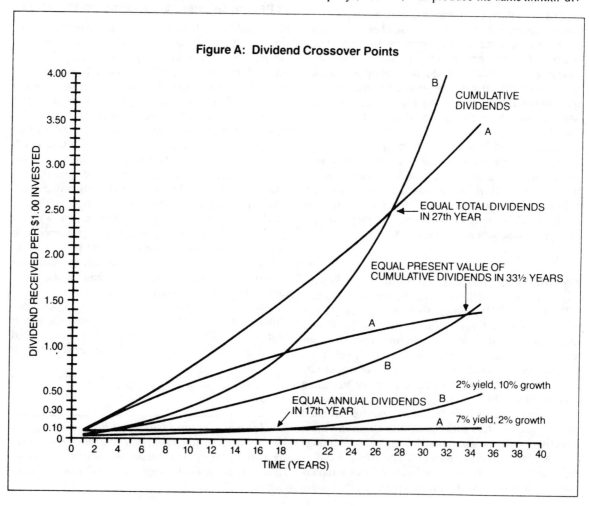

Figure A: Dividend Crossover Points

idends as a seven per cent yield, two per cent growth utility (Stock A). But it will take Stock B *an additional 10 years* to equal the total *cumulative* dividends of Stock A. Furthermore, dividends received from the yield stock can be reinvested immediately and compounded thereafter. The true present value crossover of cumulative dividends is thus six years longer still—a total of 33 years.

Unless investors are willing to wait 20 to 30 years for equal dividend income, the dividend crossover approach seems unlikely to generate much support for growth stocks. Price appreciation—and the accompanying capital gains taxes—must rationally be the major expectation of growth stock investors. Indeed, the lower the stock's current yield and the higher the investor's dividend tax rate, the more important the capital gains portion of his expectation becomes.

How Much Price Appreciation is Needed?

Individual investors appear to hold equities for an average of 10 years.[9] This average may camouflage a bimodal distribution, with inactive investors and trustee accounts having a much longer holding period and very active individuals a much shorter one. However, the shorter the holding period, the less opportunity for dividend growth to play a factor in total return, and the more important capital gains.

The high-income investor, who appears likely to be the swing factor in the historical emphasis on growth stocks over current yield stocks, must continually estimate the tradeoff between the equity market and alternative investments. Given his current 70 per cent tax rate on unearned income, his best alternative appears to be municipal bonds, which if held to 10-year maturity might provide a current yield of five per cent. Figure B shows the cash flow from $1,000 invested in such a municipal bond: Each year the investor will receive $50.00 in income and after 10 years, his original principal of $1,000. There are no federal taxes involved. Theoretically, at least, since the stock market is more risky, the investor should demand a considerably higher return from an equity investment.

If the high-income investor opts for the stock market, he is faced with a 70 per cent tax on dividends received and, including preference taxes, a 42 per cent tax on capital gains. With state income taxes, the actual rates are often higher. The second half of Figure B shows the expected cash flow from an investment in a two per cent yield, 10 per cent growth stock assuming current tax rates. For the same $1,000 investment, the initial after-tax return from the stock is clearly much lower than the return from the municipal bond. After 10 years, the reported growth stock dividend will have increased from $20.00 to $51.90. But the investor will receive only $15.60 after taxes.

Since the cash flow from the equity investment is at no time equal to that from the municipal bond investment, the price received from the equity after 10 years, P_{10}, must clearly be higher than the $1,000 invested, particularly since 42 per cent of the capital gain will be taxed away. Since P_{10} is the only unknown, it is possible to compute its value directly, assuming that the municipal bond rate of five per cent is the best after-tax reinvestment rate and, therefore, the appropriate discount rate. The formula for computing P_{10} for any combination of current yield, projected growth, discount rate, dividend tax and capital gains tax is developed in the appendix.

Given the required target sale price, it is a straightforward matter to determine the annual percentage capital appreciation necessary to justify the purchase of any given stock over the alternative investment offering the best after-tax return. Table I illustrates required annual appreciation rates for different combinations of yield and growth as they should rationally be viewed by the high-income investor. A stock with seven per cent yield and two per cent growth (our Stock A) requires 4.7 per cent annual appreciation, while a stock with two per cent yield and 10 per cent growth (Stock B) requires 6.4 per cent annual appreciation.

At first glance, the high-income investor might conclude that Stock A is a better investment than Stock B, since it requires less capital appreciation. His ultimate choice, however, will depend heavily on his view of market efficiency. If the market is efficient in valuing all stocks at any point in time, a company with constant 10 per cent growth and no disappointments or surprises to affect investors' growth and risk expectations should maintain its present price-earnings multiple, or at least its multiple relative to the market (whatever that is). It should show 10 per cent annual capital appreciation.

The tradeoff between yield and growth should therefore be based not only on the absolute appreciation required, but on the spread between the price appreciation and the company's expected growth rate—i.e., on the annual change in P/E multiple required to justify the investment. Stock A requires 4.7 per cent annual appreciation with only two per cent growth; it thus requires a 2.7 per cent annual increase in P/E. The growth stock, on the other hand, although it requires a higher (6.4 per cent) appreciation, offers 10 per cent expected earnings growth; it can actually incur a 3.3 per cent annual decline in P/E and still equal the after-tax return on the best alternative.

Lines of Equal P/E Multiple Risk

If a portfolio manager can confidently project constant price-earnings multiples, the above analysis would clearly point to growth stocks as the best alternative. The problem is that, whether or not they are willing to admit it, most investors appear wary of such confidence. In a risk-averse environment, the doubt that past growth rates can be sustained leads to the suspicion that growth has traditionally been overvalued. If so, there is a substantial risk of P/E decline. (To be sure, these suspicions are strongly influenced by the recent history of capital losses in growth stocks.)

How much would P/E have to decline before the yield-growth tradeoff favors yield? Figure C plots lines of equal multiple risk for the high-income investor (see the appendix for their derivation). The line farthest to

the left shows equivalent yield-growth tradeoffs assuming no decline in P/E (a high risk assumption): A one per cent yield, seven per cent growth stock will provide exactly the same after-tax total return to the high-income investor as an eight per cent yield, four per cent growth stock—if both P/Es remain unchanged. Lines further to the right show equivalent tradeoffs assuming three, six, nine, 12 and 15 per cent annual declines in P/E. Assuming that the market is fairly efficient, a price-earnings decline of 15 per cent

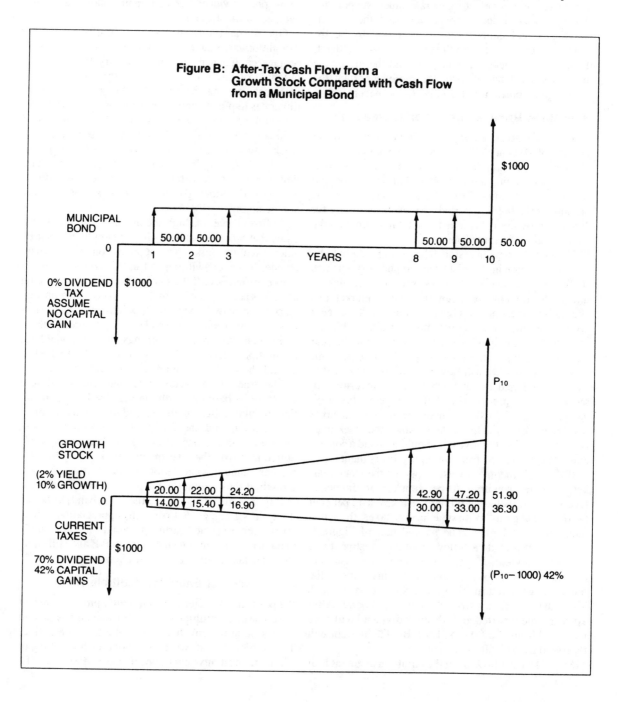

Figure B: After-Tax Cash Flow from a Growth Stock Compared with Cash Flow from a Municipal Bond

MUNICIPAL BOND

50.00 50.00   50.00 50.00 50.00

0   1   2   3   YEARS   8   9   10

0% DIVIDEND TAX ASSUME NO CAPITAL GAIN

$1000

$1000

P_{10}

GROWTH STOCK

(2% YIELD 10% GROWTH)

20.00 22.00 24.20   42.90 47.20 51.90
14.00 15.40 16.90   30.00 33.00 36.30

0

CURRENT TAXES

$1000

70% DIVIDEND 42% CAPITAL GAINS

$(P_{10} - 1000)\ 42\%$

each year for the next 10 years seems unlikely. This line thus represents a relatively conservative assumption.

Assuming a 7.5 per cent growth rate for the Standard & Poor's 500 index, and given its current five per cent yield, the market appears to offer the high-income individual a total return superior to a bond's after-tax five per cent—as long as absolute P/E does not fall more than 2.5 per cent a year for the next 10 years. Growth Stock B from our previous example falls to the right of the second line, and therefore represents a return superior to that of the municipal bond's if its P/E falls less than four per cent a year and a return superior to the market's if its relative P/E falls less than 1.5 per cent a year. The high yield alternative, Stock A, falls far to the left of the left-most line and is therefore considerably more risky in terms of price-earnings multiple; its multiple must actually increase for its return to even equal the municipal bond's return.

Using equal multiple risk lines such as those in Figure C, an investor can position his stocks using *his own* assumptions of dividend growth and risk. He can project growth using historical data, sustainable reinvestment rate or even gut feeling. If he thinks that Stock C, with four per cent yield and eight per cent growth, should have roughly the same multiple risk as Stock B, he can plot the two and note that Stock C would actually have to fall in price by 25 per cent and produce a yield of 5.5 per cent before equalling the return on Stock B.

The investor can also use his own assumptions of market growth to plot the S&P 500 and interpret the position of his other stocks in terms of relative P/E multiple risk. Even the tax-exempt institutional investor can benefit from these curves. It is presumably those individual investors who find a given yield-growth combination most attractive who establish the marginal trades, hence the equilibrium price. The institutional investor who undertakes to appraise investment values from their viewpoint will have a better picture of stock value.

Different Stocks for Different Tax Rates and Different Interest Rates

Once a group of stocks is plotted in terms of expected growth relative to current yield, overlay lines for different tax rates clearly point out the relative advantages of different stocks for different investors. For the high-income investor, the lines of equal multiple risk are almost vertical (as in Figure C). In the case of 100 per cent dividend taxation, the lines would be perfectly vertical, there being no difference between a two per cent and a 12 per cent yield.

A pension plan with a zero tax rate on both dividends and capital gains would have much flatter curves, all of which would be shifted to account for the best alternative investment being the after-tax return on a taxable, 10-year corporate bond at roughly eight per cent (Figure D). To the tax-exempt investor, both extremes of growth and yield (Stocks A and B) appear more risky than the overall market, but Stock B is more attractive than Stock A.

TABLE I: Annual 10-Year Appreciation Needed to Justify Various Yield-Growth Combinations
Given Dividend Tax Rate = 70.0%
Capital Gains Rate = 42.0%
After-Tax Reinvestment Rate = 5.0%

Yield	Growth Rate												
	−4	−2	0	2	4	6	8	10	12	14	16	18	20
0.5	7.5	7.5	7.5	7.4	7.4	7.4	7.4	7.3	7.3	7.3	7.2	7.2	7.1
1.0	7.3	7.3	7.3	7.2	7.2	7.2	7.1	7.0	7.0	6.9	6.8	6.7	6.6
1.5	7.2	7.2	7.1	7.0	7.0	6.9	6.8	6.7	6.6	6.5	6.4	6.2	6.1
2.0	7.1	7.0	6.9	6.9	6.8	6.7	6.6	6.4	6.3	6.1	5.9	5.7	5.5
2.5	6.9	6.8	6.7	6.7	6.5	6.4	6.3	6.1	5.9	5.7	5.5	5.2	4.9
3.0	6.8	6.7	6.6	6.4	6.3	6.2	6.0	5.8	5.6	5.3	5.0	4.7	4.3
3.5	6.6	6.5	6.4	6.2	6.1	5.9	5.7	5.4	5.2	4.9	4.5	4.1	3.6
4.0	6.5	6.3	6.2	6.0	5.8	5.6	5.4	5.1	4.8	4.4	4.0	3.5	2.9
4.5	6.3	6.2	6.0	5.8	5.6	5.4	5.1	4.7	4.4	3.9	3.4	2.8	2.1
5.0	6.2	6.0	5.8	5.6	5.4	5.1	4.8	4.4	4.0	3.4	2.9	2.2	1.3
5.5	6.0	5.8	5.6	5.4	5.1	4.8	4.4	4.0	3.5	2.9	2.3	1.4	0.4
6.0	5.8	5.6	5.4	5.1	4.8	4.5	4.1	3.6	3.1	2.4	1.6	0.7	−0.5
6.5	5.7	5.5	5.2	4.9	4.6	4.2	3.7	3.2	2.6	1.8	0.9	−0.2	−1.5
7.0	5.5	5.3	5.0	4.7	4.3	3.9	3.4	2.8	2.1	1.2	0.2	−1.1	−2.7
7.5	5.4	5.1	4.8	4.4	4.0	3.6	3.0	2.3	1.6	0.6	−0.6	−2.0	−4.0
8.0	5.2	4.9	4.6	4.2	3.7	3.2	2.6	1.9	1.0	−0.1	−1.4	−3.1	−5.4
8.5	5.0	4.7	4.4	3.9	3.5	2.9	2.2	1.4	0.4	−0.8	−2.3	−4.3	−7.1
9.0	4.8	4.5	4.1	3.7	3.2	2.5	1.8	0.9	−0.2	−1.5	−3.3	−5.6	−9.0
9.5	4.7	4.3	3.9	3.4	2.9	2.2	1.4	0.4	−0.8	−2.3	−4.3	−7.1	−9.0
10.0	4.5	4.1	3.7	3.1	2.5	1.8	0.9	−0.1	−1.5	−3.2	−5.5	−8.9	−9.0

The lines of multiple risk for the corporate holding company with an extremely low tax rate on dividends (7 to 15 per cent) but higher capital gains taxes (34 per cent) would be even flatter (Figure E). Since yield is more important than growth to such a corporation, Stock A is actually equal to growth Stock B. If its growth were four per cent, instead of two per cent, Stock A would offer a return superior to both the market's and the growth stock's.

Even if the portfolio manager is concerned with only a single tax rate (say, for tax-exempt pension funds), he can still use a series of overlays to plot changing risk-reward relations under different interest rate environments. A high reinvestment rate (corporate bond rate) will always make current yield appear more attractive than future growth, since the investor is giving up more reinvestment income with the latter. Conversely, low interest rates will make growth stocks relatively more attractive to all investors, since the reinvestment interest on current dividends becomes less important. These considerations go a long way toward explaining why high market risk (beta) is frequently associated with high growth and low yield.

Implications of Potential Tax Changes

The Carter Administration has been considering a far-reaching package of tax reform legislation. Among the proposals are three changes that would directly affect stock market valuation:

1. ending the preferential tax treatment of capital gains by requiring all non-exempt investors to treat such gains as ordinary income;
2. reducing the maximum individual tax rate on unearned income from 70 to 50 per cent; and
3. ending the double taxation of corporate dividends by allowing investors to "gross up," paying only that percentage of their ordinary tax rate that has not, in effect, already been paid by corporations.

While the first change would clearly disadvantage equity investors, the latter two offer some advantages. Economists have predicted both positive and negative market response to such a tax package, depending on

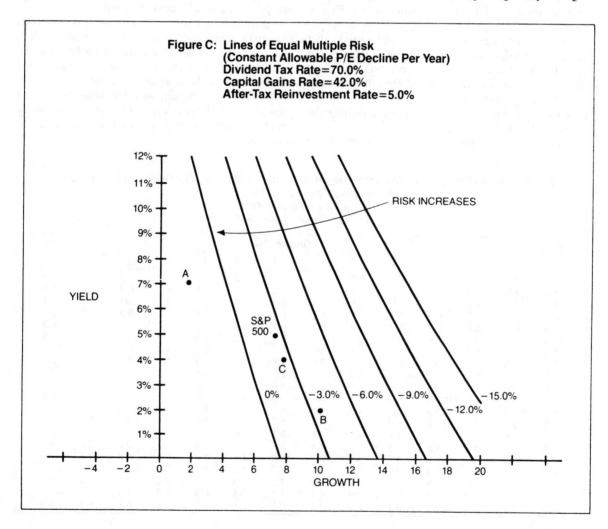

Figure C: Lines of Equal Multiple Risk
(Constant Allowable P/E Decline Per Year)
Dividend Tax Rate=70.0%
Capital Gains Rate=42.0%
After-Tax Reinvestment Rate=5.0%

how investors change their trading patterns, whether the changes would apply to all income levels, and how gradually they would be implemented.[10] The implications of "grossing up"—which favors companies that pay a high current tax rate—have also received wide coverage by brokerage reports.[11] Lost in the discussion about market and economic effects has been the intramarket readjustment that would occur for all individual investors, regardless of their tax rates. The lines of equal multiple risk developed here offer a convenient methodology for comparing revised yield-growth tradeoffs for investors of different tax levels.

If the maximum ordinary tax rate is reduced to 50 per cent, taxable corporate bonds will still offer high-income investors a relatively unattractive after-tax yield of four per cent. Municipal bonds would remain the best alternative to equities. However, at all corporate tax rates above zero, the tax rate on dividends to all investors would be less than the tax rate on capital gains. Since the effective average corporate tax rate was close to 25 per cent in 1976, the high-income

investor's average dividend tax rate might drop from 70 to 33 per cent.[12] Whereas the average investor may now pay a 40 per cent tax on dividend income and a 20 per cent tax on capital gains, under the proposed tax package he would pay 40 per cent on capital gains and 20 per cent on dividends.

Figure F shows the set of equal multiple risk curves used in Figure C (applicable to the high-income investor) overlaid by a set reflecting a dividend tax rate of 30 per cent and a capital gains tax rate of 50 per cent. It is immediately apparent that the overall market becomes more attractive. The S&P 500 yield could decline from five to 2.5 per cent and still offer the high-income investor the same −1.5 per cent per year multiple risk it does now. Of course, market prices are not entirely determined by high-income investors, and tax-exempt institutions would not experience the same incentives to invest. However, there does appear to be reason to expect renewed public participation in the market.

It is also apparent from Figure F that stocks that currently appear attractive to the individual investor

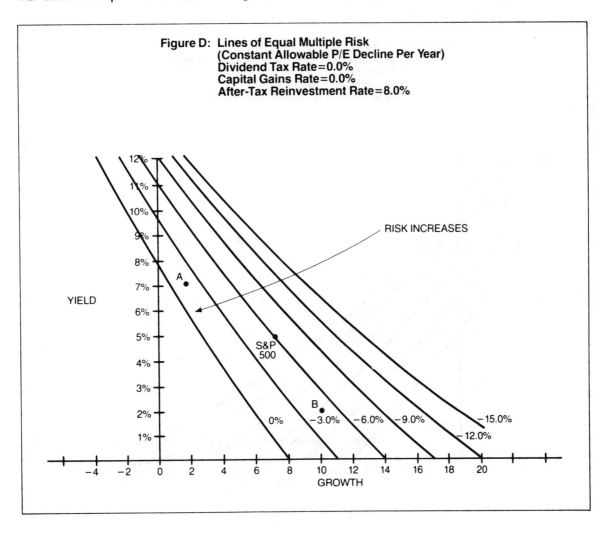

Figure D: Lines of Equal Multiple Risk
(Constant Allowable P/E Decline Per Year)
Dividend Tax Rate=0.0%
Capital Gains Rate=0.0%
After-Tax Reinvestment Rate=8.0%

because of their low relative multiple risk would, under the new tax rates, appear relatively unattractive, or at least not as attractive as high yield securities.

Assuming that growth expectations remain unchanged for all stocks, and that individual investors have been largely responsible for supporting growth stocks in the past, new tax legislation could either cause high yield securities to rise in value to the point where their yields dropped by two percentage points, or growth stocks to drop in value to the point where their yields increased by two percentage points. For example, McGraw Edison (MGR) currently sells at a 6.4 per cent yield and is apparently viewed by the market as having approximately the same P/E multiple risk as Black and Decker (BDK). Both lie along a line that allows for a four to five per cent P/E decline per year. (Note that the actual P/Es are widely disparate—roughly 6.4 for MGR and 9.7 for BDK on projected 12-month earnings. Only the P/E risk is the same.) As the result of tax rate changes alone, either MGR's yield should drop to five per cent or BDK's

should increase to five per cent in order to maintain the same relative P/E risk relation.

In any case, to the extent that individuals react to differential taxation, a change in tax policy should affect the relative attractiveness of growth stocks relative to yield stocks. ∎

Footnotes

1. M.H. Miller and F. Modigliani, "Dividend Policy, Growth and the Valuation of Shares," *Journal of Business,* October 1961, pp. 411-433.
2. D.E. Farrar and L.L. Selwyn, "Taxes, Corporate Financial Policy and Return to Investors," *National Tax Journal,* December 1967, pp. 444-454.
3. The corporation's ability to manipulate reported earnings is legend. Investors may well view declared dividends as a more reliable indicator of true earning power than earnings per share. In an imperfect capital market with uncertainty, a dividend "speaks louder than a thousand words." See E. Solomon, *The Theory of Financial Management* (New York: Columbia University Press, 1963).

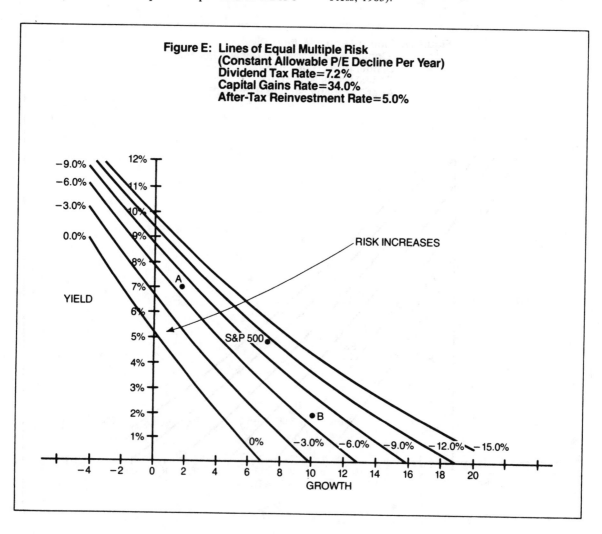

Figure E: Lines of Equal Multiple Risk (Constant Allowable P/E Decline Per Year) Dividend Tax Rate=7.2% Capital Gains Rate=34.0% After-Tax Reinvestment Rate=5.0%

4. See F.D. Arditti, et al., "Taxes, Uncertainty and Optimal Dividend Policy," *Financial Management,* Spring 1976, pp. 46-52.

5. Implications of this so-called "clientele effect" include the hypothesis that high growth, low yield stocks (which generally have high betas) should show risk-adjusted returns that are historically lower than comparable returns on higher yield, lower beta stocks. Black and Scholes' original test of this hypothesis concluded that the effect was negligible. However, more recent work with adjusted betas does seem to show a statistically significant impact.

The test for a curved security market line due to the clientele effect is usually performed as a regression of excess historical return against divergences of risk (beta), variance and yield from the market norm. Michael Brennan has projected a theoretical coefficient for yield of 0.4, but Black and Scholes found a value of 0.23, with a standard error of 0.24. Barr Rosenberg's unpublished analysis of prices from 1931 to 1966 indicates a coefficient of 0.56, with error of 0.24. The clientele effect may have been stronger in this period, since individual maximum tax rates were 91 per cent on

ordinary income, versus 25 per cent on capital gains until 1968. However, the low interest rates during the Treasury Accord would have abnormally swayed investors to high yield stocks, a balancing bias. See M.J. Brennan, "Taxes, Market Valuation and Corporate Financial Policy," *National Tax Journal* No. 23, 1970, pp. 417-427; F. Black and M. Scholes, "The Effects of Dividend Yield and Dividend Policy on Common Stock Prices and Returns," *Journal of Financial Economics* No. 1, 1974, pp. 1-22.

6. As of December 1976, banks and investment companies held only 48 per cent of the S&P 500 market weighting in American Telephone, 66 per cent in electric utilities, and 74 per cent in natural gas utilities. See H.C. Mackin, "Institutional Ownership Monitor" (White, Weld & Co., April 20, 1977), pp. 4-5.

7. Personal communication from D.B. Van Dusen, Vice President–Pension Portfolio Manager, United States Trust Company (September 13, 1977), whose statement was unanimously accepted by other portfolio managers in attendance. IRS sample data show that of $20.0 million dividends declared in 1973, $18.8 million, or 94 per cent, were on taxable individual, rather than tax-exempt

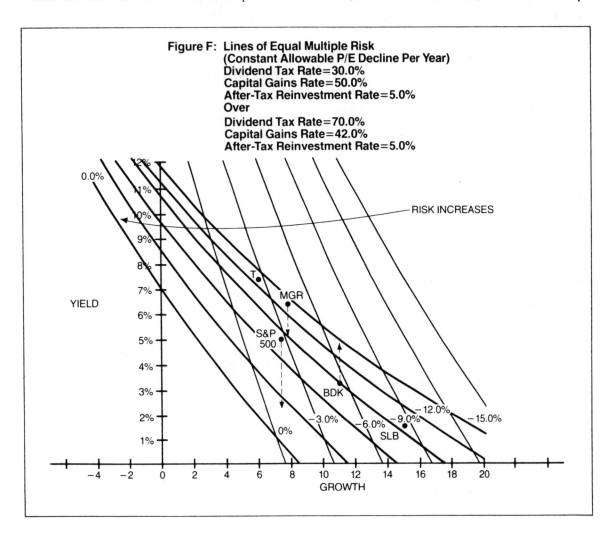

Figure F: Lines of Equal Multiple Risk
(Constant Allowable P/E Decline Per Year)
Dividend Tax Rate=30.0%
Capital Gains Rate=50.0%
After-Tax Reinvestment Rate=5.0%
Over
Dividend Tax Rate=70.0%
Capital Gains Rate=42.0%
After-Tax Reinvestment Rate=5.0%

institutional, returns. Internal Revenue Service, "Statistics of Income—1973, Individual Tax Returns," (Washington, D.C., 1976), p. 25.

8. See R.M. Baylis and S.L. Bhirud, "Growth Stock Analysis: A New Approach," *Financial Analysts Journal,* July/August 1974, pp. 63-70.

9. Average holding period for an individual is determined as the total value of public individual holdings divided by the value of individual trades per year or, equivalently, the value of individual holdings as a percentage of total NYSE market value divided by the value of individual trades as a percentage of total NYSE trading divided by market percentage turnover. For 1975, this was roughly 10.1 years (70%/30% ÷ 23%). See T.T. Murphy, editor, *1977 Fact Book* (New York Stock Exchange, June 1977), pp. 7, 17, 53, 55.

10. See M.S. Feldstein, "Tax Reform and The Investor," *The Data Resources Review of the U.S. Economy* (Data Resources, Inc., September, 1977), pp. 1.11-1.20 or G.A. Smith and D.J. Peters, "Investment Implications of the Proposed Tax Package," *Strategy Planning* (E.F. Hutton, September 1977), pp. 1-11.

11. For example, the computer screens prepared by N. Weinger, Oppenheimer and Co. Inc.

12. The increase in after-tax dividends to the investor under "grossing-up" is equal to the corporate tax rate/(one − corporate tax rate). The investor's new effective dividend tax rate (as a percentage) is:

100 − (1 + increase in after-tax dividend) × (100 − present dividend tax rate).

E.g., a corporation with a 25 per cent tax rate would show a 33 per cent increase in after-tax dividends to all of its investors. Those investors, whose new maximum tax rate is 50 per cent, would be taxed at a new rate of:

100 − (1 + 0.33) × (100 − 50) = 33%.

Appendix

A. Total price appreciation needed for an equity investment to provide an after-tax return equal to the best alternative

The total return from an equity investment will equal the best alternative after-tax return, R, if the present value of all after-tax cash flows from dividends and capital gains, discounted at the rate R, is equal to the current security price, P. The present value of a cash dividend in year i equals the actual dividend reduced by the applicable tax rate, TD, and discounted back to present value using an appropriate after-tax reinvestment rate, R (about five per cent for 10-year tax-free municipal bonds trading at par):

$$\text{PV of Dividend}_i = \frac{\text{Dividend}_i\,(1-TD)}{(1+R)^i} \quad . \qquad (1)$$

Assuming constant dividend growth at a rate, G (which could be less than or greater than projected earnings growth, depending on changes in payout ratio), the actual dividend in year i will be:

$$\text{Dividend}_i = \text{Current Dividend} \times (1+G)^i \quad . \qquad (2)$$

The present value of proceeds from eventual sale of the stock in year N (e.g., 10th year) is the price at that time (P_N), less applicable capital gains taxes (at rate TC), discounted back to present value using the same reinvestment rate, R:

$$\text{PV of sale} = \frac{P_N - (P_N - P)TC}{(1+R)^N} \quad . \qquad (3)$$

The price paid now, P, must equal the sum of the present value of all future dividends up to the time of sale plus the present value of the sale proceeds in order for the reinvestment return to equal that of the best alternative:

$$P = \frac{\text{Current Dividend}\,(1-TD)\,(1+G)}{1+R} + \frac{\text{Current Dividend}\,(1-TD)\,(1+G)^2}{(1+R)^2} + \cdots$$

$$+ \frac{\text{Current Dividend}\,(1-TD)\,(1+G)^N}{(1+R)^N} + \frac{P_N - (P_N - P)TC}{(1+R)^N} \quad . \tag{4}$$

Dividing both sides of Equation 4 by the current price and using a summation sign, this equation can be rewritten as:

$$1 = \text{Current Yield}\,(1-TD)\sum_{i=1}^{N}\left(\frac{1+G}{1+R}\right)^i$$

$$+ \frac{TC + \frac{P_N}{P}(1-TC)}{(1+R)^N} \quad . \tag{5}$$

Finally, Equation 5 can be rearranged to calculate the percentage capital appreciation necessary:

$$\left\{\frac{P_N}{P} - 1\right\} \times 100 \tag{6}$$

$$= \left\{ \frac{\left[1 - \text{Current Yield}\,(1-TD)\sum_{i=1}^{N}\left(\frac{1+G}{1+R}\right)^i\right](1+R)^N - TC}{1-TC} - 1 \right\} \times 100.$$

Note that there are no "theoretical" valuation assumptions embodied in Equation 6 except the presumption that dividends increase at a constant rate and that the investor will reinvest them when received at the best alternative rate, R.

B. Annual price appreciation and constant multiple risk lines

For any given time period, N, the percentage price increase from Equation 6 can be annualized as:

Annual Percentage Appreciation =

$$\left(\sqrt[N]{P_N/P - 1}\right) \times 100 \quad . \tag{7}$$

This necessary price appreciation can then be compared with the projected growth of the company. If payout ratios are constant, earnings growth equals dividend growth equals G. Constant market valuation in terms of P/E ratios would then mean:

$$P_N/P = E_N/E = \frac{\text{Dividend}_N}{\text{Current Dividend}} = (1+G)^N \ , \qquad (8)$$

or an annual appreciation of G per cent.

The set of current yield and growth values that satisfies Equations 6 and 8 for the specified tax and reinvestment rates TD, TC, and R makes up the left-most ''equal multiple risk'' line in Figures C and D—i.e., price-earnings multiples are assumed to remain constant. Lines to the right on these figures are determined by inserting an allowable annual P/E decline factor, F, into Equation 8:

$$P_N/P = \frac{E_N}{E} (1-F)_N$$

$$= \frac{\text{Dividend}_N}{\text{Current Dividend}} (1-F)^N$$

$$= (1+G)^N (1-F)^N \ , \qquad (9)$$

where F = 0.03, 0.06, 0.09, 0.12 and 0.15, respectively. If the assumed dividend growth rate, G, included a change in payout ratio, then Equations 8 and 9 would hold only for dividend growth and the ''equal multiple risk'' refer only to price-dividend multiples. Otherwise, the lines refer to both P/E and P/D multiple risk.

How to win at the Loser's Game

*Financial analysis can outperform random selection —
but only in one direction!*

Edward M. Miller, Jr.

Recently, the very idea of security analysis has been under attack: the stock market is such an efficient processor of information that it is virtually impossible to do better than the market averages and money spent on attempting to do so is simply wasted.

While the logic behind the random walk theory is unimpeachable, the necessary conditions to apply it to the New York Stock Exchange simply are not met. Nevertheless, the random walk theory can be modified to fit American institutions, and the modified theory does have implications for investment strategy.

THE LOGIC BEHIND RANDOM WALK

There are two ways to argue that all available information is promptly incorporated into stock prices. One is to argue that all investors are supermen, each of whom is capable of completely digesting and analyzing the full range of available information without ever making a mistake. The other is to argue that the market itself incorporates some mechanism that prevents particular stocks from being either over or undervalued.

Since all investors are not supermen, any realistic theory will have to allow for the existence of different types of investors, some knowledgeable and some uninformed. While obviously there is a smooth gradation of knowledge and ability among investors, this paper will assume only two types. (The author has discussed the case where there are many opinions about a stock elsewhere).[11]

One type will be assumed to be highly rational and aware of the publicly available information. We hope that most institutions will fall into this category. The remainder of investors will be assumed to be less well-informed, and to be at times ignorant of available information to which their attention has not been drawn. Many individual investors, untrained in se-

curity analysis, and with little time to devote to their investments, will be in this category.

THE MARKET AS SUPER-COMPUTER

If we reject the idea of all investors being supermen, support for the efficient market hypothesis must rest on the ability of the well-informed investors to keep market prices at levels where they fully incorporate all available information.[1] Given that ability, there cannot be undervalued securities, because the informed investors would have spotted the opportunities and bid the prices up until the securities were no longer undervalued. Likewise, there cannot be overvalued securities, because the informed investors would sell these stocks (going short if necessary), driving the price down to where the security was no longer overvalued. Thus, if securities can be neither undervalued nor overvalued, it follows that they must be correctly valued. Furthermore, if securities are always correctly valued, there would appear to be no role for security analysis (other than to select a portfolio that is diversified and provides the desired level of risk).

Before accepting this surprising conclusion, let us look more closely at the necessary conditions for such an efficient market. When this has been done, we will find that, although competition among informed investors eliminates opportunities to earn more than a "competitive" return, *this does not imply that securities must be correctly valued at all times,* or that such a competitive return can be earned without detailed and skilled security analysis.

We should accept the argument that there are unlikely to be undervalued securities promising more than a competitive return. Several million investors are looking for good buying opportunities, including a

1. Footnotes appear at the end of the article.

large number of institutional investors with full time managers. In addition, major brokerage firms with large staffs are also looking for undervalued securities. Company managements usually have a strong interest in a high stock price and can be expected to publicize any favorable information about the firm. Thus, the argument that competition will have eliminated the opportunity to earn returns above the competitive level can be accepted.

The other part of the argument is that selling by informed investors will prevent stocks from being bid up above their proper value. Yet, long selling by informed investors can be a restraint on the price of a stock only as long as these investors have stock to sell. Indeed, there are substantial numbers of stocks that the better informed investors do not hold; for example, the American Stock Exchange thought it worthy of note that more than half of the issues traded on their exchange were held by at least one institutional investor.[1] Obviously, selling by institutions cannot prevent a run up in the remaining stocks.

If the uninformed keep buying, there will eventually come a time when the better informed investors have "bought out" the others. Once this has happened, only short selling can keep the uninformed from bidding prices up to clearly unreasonable levels. Thus, it is necessary to look closely at how short sales are actually conducted. Once this has been done, it will appear that short selling as practiced in America is not the type of short selling that is needed for efficient security markets.

WHY THERE IS INEFFICIENCY ON THE SHORT SIDE

By definition, a short sale occurs when someone sells a stock he does not own (i.e., is short of). How can one sell what one does not have? Simple; one's brokerage firm borrows the stock certificate in order to make delivery to the buyer. Eventually, the short seller will close out the short sale by buying the stock and using the purchased stock certificate to repay the loan. Stock certificates are valuable pieces of paper, however, and owners are reluctant to lend them out without adequate security. To provide such security, the proceeds of the sale of the stock are deposited with the owner-lender, depriving the short seller of use of these funds. In current United States practice, the short seller does not even receive interest on the funds deposited with the lender of the stock.

Here, the real world differs from that assumed in the academic literature, whose short sellers are assumed to receive use of the proceeds of a short sale. Such an assumption is necessary to make sales of borrowed stock completely symmetrical with sales of owned stock. This "imperfection" in the short selling

process is why real world markets need not be as efficient as predicted by academic theory.

When the lender of a stock certificate transfers it to the borrower for a short sale, he deprives himself of the dividends on the stock. Naturally, he is willing to do this only if the short seller reimburses him for the lost dividends. Thus, short sellers must pay dividends on the stock they sell short until they cover their positions.

A short sale of a dividend paying stock can only be profitable if the expected rate of return on the stock is below zero. To see this, imagine a stock with an annual dividend of d% of its selling price. Since someone selling the stock short will have to pay this dividend, he can show a profit only if the stock declines over the year more than d%. A stock declining in value at d% per year and paying a dividend of d% would have a total return of zero. Thus, short sellers can show a profit by selling an overvalued stock only if stock is so overvalued that its expected return is negative.

THE LIMITS TO AN EFFICIENT MARKET

So far, we have accepted the argument that well-informed investors will bid stocks up to the point where they promise no more than a competitive return (here called C). Keep in mind the additional argument that, by short selling, they will force overvalued stocks down in price until they promise a return of 0%. In both cases, the effects of risk are abstracted from. (They will be discussed later.) Thus, it appears that the actions of well-informed investors will limit the expected returns on stocks to the range 0 to C percent. Within this range, it is likely that most stocks will have expected returns of C, but, given the large number of part time and uninformed investors, there are likely to be some stocks with expected returns lower than C. These are stocks that badly-informed speculators have driven up in price causing well-informed investors to drop them from their portfolios.

In a market where some stocks have expected earnings of less than C, the average of the expected earnings of all stocks must be less than C. In particular, an index fund or broadly based stock average should show earnings of less than C. A well-informed investor should be able to avoid investing in stocks with a subnormal expected return, leaving him with a portfolio with an expected return of C. *Thus, investors doing good security analysis should be able to beat both the averages and the index funds.* The presence of extremely large numbers of very well-qualified analysts does not make above average performance impossible, contrary to the assertion of the proponents of the efficient market hypotheses. Such above average returns are made possible by the presence in the market of a large number of investors investing on either the basis of no security analysis or bad security analysis, and hence earning below average returns.

Since an investor can expect to earn average returns by random selection, it may be wondered what type of investment strategy will give below average returns. Diagram 1 shows how the expected return varies with the level of analysis. The lowest returns are earned by those who use naive analysis, such as buying the stock with the highest dividend rate or the lowest price/earnings ratio without understanding the reason why other investors are avoiding these stocks. Better results are obtained by those who use either random selection (or something close to it), or who employ very sophisticated analysis, trying to avoid holding the losers. Those at the low point of the curve, who consistently buy apparently undervalued stocks only to watch them decline further, are likely to change their strategy, moving towards one extreme or another. Thus, investors tend to separate themselves into two groups, those who are very well-informed, and those who are not. This provides a theoretical rationale for the assumption made at the beginning of the paper, namely that there were two classes of investors, knowledgeable and uninformed.

DIAGRAM 1

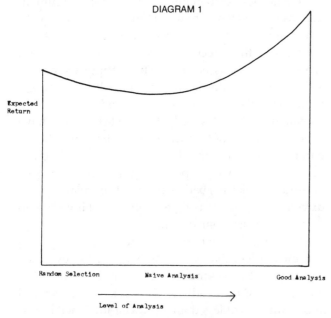

Of course, many who are not themselves able to do good analysis (typically because of lack of time) will attempt to purchase good analysis through advisory services, investment counselors, and mutual funds. Unfortunately, the investor who is unable to analyse individual companies in order to pick the best values may not be able to pick mutual funds or investment management firms any better.

Transactions costs of one form or the other may prevent investors from obtaining good analysis. For instance, in buying a mutual fund, the investor loses the opportunity to time his purchases and sales of individual issues for maximum tax advantage. The investor with a number of different issues in his portfolio, some with gains and some with losses, has a variety of tax techniques available to him. By selective selling of those stocks with losses, he can reduce his ordinary income by up to $3000 per year. Stocks with gains can either be held to retirement, given to charity, given to relatives in lower tax brackets, or sold during years when income is unusually low. Losses can be taken while they are still short term, while gains can be held until they become long term. Since a mutual fund normally pools gains and losses, its after tax return is likely to be lower than the before tax return of an investor taking advantage of the tax laws. Those that rely on investment counselors or purchased advice will have substantial fees to pay, and the improvement in performance may not cover these.

The question is sometimes asked, "If security analysts or investment advisors are so good, why aren't they rich, instead of living off selling their advice."[11] The previous analysis provides the answer. With large numbers of competent advisors around (plus some that are not so competent), the best that can be hoped for is a return that is only somewhat above average. The increase in rate of return possible is enough to justify paying for advice if large sums are to be managed, but not enough to permit the advisor to parlay his small personal grubstroke into a fortune. Thus, good investment analysts, like the rest of us, must work for a living.

THE ROLE OF THE SECURITY ANALYST

Under the assumption previously discussed, there will be a large number of properly valued stocks, and a smaller number of overvalued stocks. In such a market, the role of the security analyst is not to search for undervalued stocks that promise returns above the competitive level (for the competition is likely to be such that such securities will not exist), but to detect and avoid overvalued securities. As a practical matter, this means that the security analyst will spend his time looking for negative facts about particular stocks that are either not known to less informed investors, or whose significance has not been fully realized.

The previous argument has implications for how the security analyst goes about his business. With the traditional goal of looking for a few winners among many potential losers, a large number of stocks are given a quick analysis in the hope of finding the one stock that will double. Once it is realized that the goal is to avoid holding a bad stock, it becomes clear that having to examine large numbers of stocks requires that the examination of each one must be cursory. Such cursory examinations increase the probability of a mistake being made and an overvalued stock being included in the portfolio.

The optimal procedure for the security analyst starts with deciding how many stocks are required in the final portfolio to assure adequate diversification without incurring unnecessary transactions costs. A somewhat larger (but still small) sample of stocks is chosen for extensive analysis prior to inclusion in the portfolio. The initial selection of stocks could be random, but a better procedure would start by excluding stocks unsuited for the portfolio on the grounds of the wrong level of risk, or a dividend rate that was not suited for the tax status of the purchaser. A stratified sampling procedure (such as one stock from each industry) might then be used to assure the desired degree of diversification.

The preliminary set of stocks would then be subject to extensive analysis to determine if any were overvalued. The overvalued stocks would be dropped, and the remainder would be included in the portfolio after a final check to insure adequate diversification still existed. Such a strategy is designed to minimize the risk of purchasing a low total return stock while assuring adequate diversification and avoiding unnecessary expenses for analysis.

Once the portfolio had been selected, most of the manager's attention would be devoted to keeping it under review. From time to time there might be a speculative surge in the price of a stock, causing it to become overvalued. The stock would be sold. A tentative replacement would be selected based on maintaining the desired level of risk, and remaining diversified (i.e., the expected return of the new stock should have as little covariance with the expected return of the rest of the portfolio as practical). The proposed addition to the portfolio would be subjected to intensive analysis and would be bought if not overvalued. From time to time, other stocks might be sold to maintain the desired level of systematic risk, to reduce the proportion of the portfolio exposed to a particular risk (including a decline in one company or industry), or to eliminate securities no longer suited to the tax status of the portfolio owner.

IMPLICATIONS FOR INVESTOR PROTECTION

Only a small number of individuals need be overoptimistic about a stock for it to be bid up to an excessive price. Suppose the average naive investor who believes a story about a company with a million shares outstanding buys one thousand shares. It will be necessary for only a thousand investors, out of the millions that exist, to be deceived for the stock to be bid

up. Even if negative information is readily available, there are likely to be a thousand who have not taken the time to inform themselves.

This is the flaw in our current approach to investor protection through full disclosure. Even if the facts are readily available and known to the vast majority, the uninformed will still be numerous enough to bid stock up to unreasonable levels. An alternative approach would be to try to so organize the market that short selling prevented stocks from being bid to excessive heights. This would require establishing an institutional structure in which a short seller receives a market return on the proceeds from selling stocks short. One possibility would be to provide for him to receive interest at the market rate on the funds left with the lender of the certificate borrowed.

There are several reasons for believing a reasonably competent analyst should be able to uncover enough situations where stocks are overvalued to pay his salary. Most important, overvaluation can readily occur (as previously described) even where only a minority of investors are unaware of readily available information. While favorable information about a particular company is usually given wide distribution by the management of that company, unfavorable information will normally either be left unmentioned, or relegated to a footnote in the annual report. Although brokers spend much time distributing information about candidates for purchase, they devote very little attention to potentially overvalued companies that might be candidates for sale: any customer may generate commissions by buying a recommended stock but only those who already own a stock can respond to a sell recommendation (leaving aside the small minority who would consider a short sale). In addition, putting out sell recommendations could deprive an analyst of access to the information sources inside a company he needs to do his job and maintain his reputation, or could antagonize underwriting customers of his firm. Finally, in certain cases, sell recommendations could invite libel suits. (XYZ company should be sold because its President is a crook or a fool.)

R. E. Diefenbach,[4] in an article in the *Financial Analysts Journal*, reported that his mutual fund received 1,209 buy recommendations from 24 brokerage firms between November 17, 1967, and May 23, 1969 but only 46 sell recommendations. His experience was consistent with what would be expected from theory. Most of the sell recommendations proved profitable, showing that analysts can recognize an overvalued stock. On the other hand, only 47% of the buy recommendations outperformed the Standard and Poor's 425 Industrial Stock Average. While theory suggests that these recommendations would have done slightly better than average, the poor results are consistent with a market in which it is difficult to do appreciably better than the averages.

As additional evidence that it is possible to identify underperformers, Professor Fabozzi [15] has shown that 74% of the stocks criticized by one service ("The Quality of Earnings Report") for poor accounting subsequently underperformed the market. Presumably other close readers of corporate reports could also identify future underperformers.

More impressive confirmation of the inability of informed investors to select potential winners, combined with an ability to spot losers, was recently provided by Klemosky [8] He examined the price behavior during 1963 to 1972 of stocks that were subject to net buying or selling by institutions (presumably the better informed investors). He found that heavy institutional buying of a stock was typically followed by declines in the price of that stock. Stocks of which institutions were large net buyers typically declined (relative to the market) after the quarter in which the buying occurred. However, heavy sales of stocks by institutions were typically followed by declines in price, indicating that the institutions were able to spot (and sell) overvalued securities. An ability to spot losers but not winners is precisely what is predicted by the theory set out in this paper.

IMPLICATIONS FOR RANDOM WALK THEORY

If buying and selling by well-informed investors will limit the anticipated return on stocks to the range of 0% to C%, with most stocks expected to yield the competitive rate of C%, this implies that upper and lower limits will exist for the price of each stock, with the majority of stocks priced at the lower limit.

An illustration may make the argument clear. Suppose there is a mining company paying a dividend equal to 5% of its stock's selling price (a peculiar dividend policy that facilitates exposition) whose largest mine will be exhausted in ten years. This fact is in the public domain, but has not been given much publicity. The stock is held only by less informed investors who are not aware of this negative factor. The better informed investors have estimated that the value of the stock after exhaustion of the mine will be V.

Suppose the competitive rate of return is 10%, and the company is expected to pay a 5% dividend till then. To achieve the required 10% return from holding the stock, the investors will buy the stock only if its price can be expected to rise at 5% per year or more. Thus, in years before exhaustion of the mine, the lower limit to the price will be $(1.05)^{-n}V$. In the jargon of the technical analysts, this is the support price.

Since the stock pays a 5% dividend, it won't be profitable to sell the stock short unless its price is expected to decline at 5% per year or more. Thus, there will be an upper limit to the price which is $(1.05)^{n}V$. This might be referred to as the resistance level. In between the upper and lower levels, a well-informed long-term investor will find it profitable to neither buy nor sell the stock. Between these limits, the price of the stock is free to fluctuate up and down with the buying and selling of the stock by less informed investors. Ten years before exhaustion of the mine, this range of prices is from 61% of the value ten years hence to 163% of the value ten years hence (or, for a stock expected to sell at $10 in a decade, the current price can fluctuate from 6⅛ to 16¼, a quite respectable range.)

The standard argument for the random walk theory is that, if the price of a stock displays any pattern other than a random walk, it will be possible for investors aware of the pattern to make money by buying or selling the stock. In turn, their buying or selling will raise or lower the price sufficiently to eliminate the non-random pattern. Although such an argument is valid where the seller immediately receives use of the proceeds of his sale, this condition is not met for the United States security market.

This can be seen by considering our mining stock. Suppose that if the stock rises during January, it will continue to rise at an annual rate of 4% per year for the next year. If it falls during January, it will decline for the next year at 4% per year. It is rather easy to construct a profitable trading rule: buy the stock if it rises during January and hold for a year; if it falls in January, don't buy the stock. Such a policy promises a return of 9% (4% in capital gains, and 5% in dividends) whenever the stock is bought.

Yet, a rational man upon being informed of this profit making opportunity would choose to ignore it. The reason? The 9% return promised is less than the 10% promised elsewhere. Since it is possible for profitable trading rules to exist but for investors to decline to take advantage of them, there is no theoretical reason for the price of a stock yielding a return between 0 and C to follow a random walk. There are a large number of non-random patterns of price movements whose existence is quite consistent with there being a large number of well-informed investors. (Of course, it is necessary for there to be some less informed investors in the stock, but a shortage of such individuals is not expected.)

Diagram 2 shows the price ranges within which such a stock may fluctuate. Whenever the price of the stock reaches either the upper or lower limit, further price changes are restrained by either buying or short selling by knowledgeable investors. A possible out-

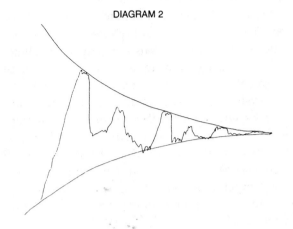

DIAGRAM 2

come would be for the stock to act as if it were restrained between "reflecting barriers."[3]

One strategy would be to buy stocks that were near their lower limit, arguing that a major decline would be prevented by smart investors buying on the fundamentals, while a surge of speculative interest could result in a large rise. A possible way to detect such situations would be to inspect charts of stock prices over time looking for resistance levels in volatile stocks. This provides a rationale for "technical analysis," which has frequently been regarded by academic writers as having no theoretical rationale. Of course, to actually detect "resistance" levels from charts, the fundamentals must stay put long enough for the lower limits to become apparent. In the real world this may not happen too often. (In fact, theory suggests that upper and lower levels should shift over time following a random walk with a trend.) An alternative strategy using fundamental analysis is to look for stocks that are properly priced based on their fundamentals, but that just might have a sudden run up based on speculative considerations.

INCLUSION OF RISK

For simplicity in presentation, risk has been ignored up to this point, with the result that for all stocks the upper limit on the expected rate of return is the same, C. Of course, investors will demand a higher expected return from the riskier stocks than they require from the less risky stocks. Thus, the competitive limit of C will depend on the risk of the stock. If investors are able to diversify their portfolios, the capital asset pricing model[14] can be extended to argue that the upper competitive limit on the rate of return should be a linear function of the systematic risk, such that the competitive limit is equal to the sum of the risk-free interest rate and the product of the beta coefficient of the stock and the price of systematic risk. However, as the author has pointed out elsewhere[13], the systematic risk of a stock depends on its covariance with the level of national income as well as its covariance with the stock market.

Investors will normally attempt to hold a well-diversified portfolio. This should not be a difficult task, since there will be a large number of stocks promising a competitive return from which to choose. One minor complication does exist. Investors might well attempt to have every major stock group represented in their portfolio in proportion to its total value on the stock exchange (attempting to approximate a market portfolio). Within each group, investors would concentrate on those stocks that promised a competitive return, avoiding those which had been bid up by less informed investors to unreasonable levels. One can conceive of a situation where most members of a popular speculative group (computers say) were overpriced. In order to obtain the diversification benefits of participation in this group, well-informed investors might be willing to pay a slight premium over the price that would be required by its expected return and beta. Thus, the price of particular securities would depend somewhat on industry group and other factors besides expected return and systematic risk.

The lower limit on the return, set by the possibility of short selling, would also depend on the risk. Because short selling is a way to hedge against a decline in the market, investors might very well accept a negative expected return from short selling in order to obtain the insurance value. Since the insurance value of a short position will depend on the systematic risk of that stock when held long, the minimum rate of return will be equal to the beta of the stock multiplied by the amount by which the market discounts price per unit of beta.

Let r be the interest rate of risk-free obligations
         b be the beta of a stock
and p be the reduction in price per unit of beta
         C be the upper limit on competitive returns
         L be the lower limit on competitive returns

Then $C = r + pb$ and $L = pb$ Thus, $C-L = r$

In other words, the width of the band within which the return on the stock fluctuates is equal to r, the rate of return on riskless investments and is independent of the systematic risk of the stock.

There remain several complications to be noted. The opportunities for selling stocks short profitably are much fewer than the opportunities for going long. This means that, if there are imperfections in the market such that individuals differ in their willingness to pay for insurance against a market decline, the price of systematic risk in the "short" market will be set by those willing to pay the most for insurance. This may make price of systematic risk in the "short" market higher than the value estimated in the long market.

THE ROLE OF SHORT SELLING

In the security markets, there is an asymmetry

between short and long sales, arising from the need to borrow certificates before they can be sold, and from the institutional arrangements for doing so. In markets for commodity futures and stock options, what is being traded are not items already in existence but contracts to make future delivery. Such contracts are as easily written on the long side as on the short side. Thus, it would appear that the institutional arrangements in the commodity and options markets would permit these markets to be efficient if there are sufficient numbers of well-informed speculators. Prices on such efficient markets would be expected to follow a random walk.

There is one important exception to the rule that the short seller does not receive use of the funds from the short sale, or even interest on them. If a brokerage firm, trading for its own account, takes a short position in a stock and is able to borrow the stock from the account of a client of the firm, the brokerage firm does have use of the proceeds of the sale. It can use these funds to reduce the amount that it needs to borrow from a bank to carry its customers' margin accounts. Because of this, a brokerage firm can show a profit from a short sale of a stock that rises in price but at a rate less than the rate of interest at which it borrows. Brokerage firms have a substantial advantage over other investors in their ability to profit from short selling. Thus, it is not surprising that brokers do a disproportionate amount of the short selling that is done. However, the total financial resources available to brokers are sufficiently small that this exception to the rule that short sellers do not receive use of the proceeds should not affect the validity of the argument of this paper.

The argument so far has been developed on the assumption that investors are just as willing to sell short as to buy long. This is probably not so. Most institutions, including pension funds, other trust funds, and mutual funds, cannot sell short as a matter of law. Large individual investors legally can go short, but there is a sufficient prejudice against doing so that such short sales are relatively rare. As noted earlier, brokers seldom put out sell recommendations, forcing the potential short seller to do his own analysis.

When an investor sells a stock short, he incurs a nonsystematic risk. The stock he sold short just may go up sharply giving him substantial losses. In theory this can be diversified against through holding a large number of long and short positions. Currently, short selling is a technique used primarily by individuals. Many individual portfolios are too small to completely diversify away the non-systematic risk incurred by going short. This will limit the extent to which such individuals take advantage of the insurance option provided by short sellings and may cause the floor to

be lower than it otherwise would be.

Because of the scarcity of potential short sellers, it is possible that there are unexploited opportunities for better than normal returns through short selling. The effect of this would be to decrease the lower limit on return below the product of a stock's beta and the price of systematic risk. A paucity of potential short sellers does not eliminate the concept of a competitively set lower limit to the return on a stock, it just lowers this limit. Whatever short sellers there are will presumably look for the most attractive opportunities, and by competing among themselves eliminate any opportunities for better than competitive returns on short sales.

AN EXPLANATION FOR MERGERS

Because of legal restrictions and investor prejudice, an increase in the price of stock frequently does not call forth an increase in the supply through short selling. However, the company itself may take advantage of this situation through issuing new stock since, unlike short sellers, it receives the proceeds of the sale. Sometimes this is done through selling new stock for cash which can then be invested in the business. This approach has the disadvantage that the additional stock may force the price down, and this result may not be in the interest of the company (or its owners, the original stockholders). Thus, as a rational monopolist, a company may be reluctant to take advantage of an overvalued stock by making additional stock sales.

Instead, many companies seek to discriminate in the market for their stock by using their overvalued stocks to purchase other companies. This minimizes the impact on a company's stock price by putting the additional stock in the hands of individuals who probably would not have normally considered purchasing the company's stock. Once they have received the stock as part of an exchange, they will frequently hold it through inertia, a desire to avoid brokerage commissions, or a desire to avoid capital gains taxes (where the stock exchanged in a tax free exchange had a tax basis far below the market price of the new stock). Purchases of companies with stock provide a way to dispose of overvalued stock with a minimal effect on the market for the stock. Thus, limitations on short selling are probably one of the major reasons for many of the mergers and takeovers that have been seen in recent years.

THE RATIONALITY OF INDEX FUNDS IN AN EFFICIENT MARKET

So far in this paper it has been argued that index funds are poor investments for pension funds because the stock markets are inefficient. However, should the stock market prove to be efficient, this logically implies pension funds should not invest in index funds or endeavor to assemble a portfolio that contained stocks in the same proportion as they were represented on the stock exchange. (Such a strategy has been described as trying to hold the "market basket" of securities.)

If investors properly utilized all publicly available information, they would take the difference in tax rates between capital gains and ordinary income into account. Individuals are taxed at only half of the normal rate (with some complications because of the minimum tax) on capital gains. Thus, rational tax paying investors should give preference in their portfolios to the securities expected to yield their return in the form of capital gain. In an efficient market, these will be the stocks paying either low dividends, or no dividends. Efforts by tax paying investors to acquire these stocks will raise their price, resulting in lower expected total returns before tax than can be earned on dividend paying stocks of a similar degree of risk. Investors not subject to the income tax, notably pension funds, would find that their best returns were achieved by investing primarily in high dividend paying stocks. Such a strategy should give an appreciably better return than a random sample of all stocks or index funds.

The possibility of increasing the dividend yield of a portfolio without incurring excessive market or non-market risk has been shown by Sharpe and Sosin.[19] Thus, if it is believed that the stock markets are efficient, managers of pension funds should avoid index funds,[2] choosing instead to invest preferentially in the dividend paying stocks avoided by individual investors in the higher tax brackets.

It is interesting that the banks managing the large pension funds appear to have been the greatest proponents of investing in the low dividend paying growth stocks expected to yield large capital gains. This is evidence that they at least do not believe the stock markets to be efficient.

---

[1] See Malkiel [10], Lorie and Hamilton [9], Black [2], Posner [16], Vasicek and McQuown [21].

[2] See Good, Ferguson, and Treynor [6] and Miller [12].

[3] See Jensen [7], Williamson [20], Friend, Blume, and Crockett [5], and Sharpe [18].

REFERENCES

1. American Stock Exchange, "162 Amex Issues Held by Ten or More Institutional Investors," *American Investor*, April, 1974.

2. Fischer Black, "Implications of the Random Walk Hypothesis for Portfolio Management," *Financial Analysts Journal*, Vol. 27 (March/April, 1971), No. 2, pp. 16-22.

3. Paul H. Cootner, "Stock Prices: Random vs. Systematic Changes," in Paul H. Cootner, Editor, *The Random Character of Stock Market Prices* (Cambridge, Massachusetts, MIT Press, 1964).

4. R. E. Diefenbach, "How Good is Institutional Brokerage Research," *Financial Analysts Journal*, January/February, 1972, pp. 54-60.

5. Irwin Friend, Marshall Blume, and Jean Crockett, *Mutual Funds and Other Institutional Investors, A New Perspective: A Twentieth Century Fund Study* (New York: McGraw-Hill Book Co., 1970).

6. Walter R. Good, Robert Ferguson, and Jack Treynor "An Investor's Guide to the Index Fund Controversy," *Financial Analysts Journal* (November/December, 1976), pp. 27-36.

7. Michael C. Jensen, "Risk, the Performance of Mutual Funds in the Period 1945-1964," *Journal of Finance*, Vol. 23 (May, 1968), No. 2, pp. 389-416.

8. Robert C. Klemosky, "The Impact and Efficiency of Institutional Net Trading Imbalances," *Journal of Finance*, March, 1977, pp. 79-86.

9. James H. Lorie and Mary T. Hamilton, *The Stock Market: Theories and Evidence* (Homewood, Illinois, Richard D. Irwin), pp. 70-112.

10. Burton Malkiel, *A Random Walk Down Wall Street* (New York, W. W. Norton & Co.), pp. 167-170.

11. Edward Miller, "Risk, Uncertainty, and Diversity of Opinion," *Journal of Finance*, September, 1977, pp. 1151-1168.

12. ——, "Index Fund Argument is Illogical: Market Averages Can Be Beaten," *Pensions and Investments*, June 5, 1975, p. 25.

13. ——, "Portfolio Selection in a Fluctuating Economy," *Financial Analysts Journal*, May/June, 1978, pp. 77-83.

14. ——, "A Simple Counter Example to the Random Walk Theory," forthcoming, *Financial Analysts Journal*.

15. Frank J. Fabozzi, "Quality of Earnings A Test of Market Efficiency," *Journal of Portfolio Management*, Fall, 1978.

16. Richard A. Posner, "The Prudent Investor's Powers and Obligations in an Age of Market (index) Funds," *Journal of Contempory Business*, Summer, 1976.

17. William F. Sharpe, "Capital Asset Prices: A Theory of Market Equilibrium Under Conditions of Risk," *Journal of Finance*, Vol. 19 (September, 1964), pp. 425-442.

18. ——, "Mutual Fund Performance" in *Security Prices: A Supplement, Journal of Business*, Vol. 39 (January, 1966), No. 1, Part 2, pp. 119-138.

19. ——, and Howard B. Sosin, "Risk Return and Yield: New York Stock Exchange Common Stocks, 1928-1969," *Financial Analysts Journal*, March/April, 1976.

20. Peter J. Williamson, "Measuring Mutual Fund Performance in the Period 1945-1964," *Journal of Finance* (November/December, 1972), pp. 78-82.

21. Oldrich A. Vasicek and John A. McQuown, "The Efficient Market Model," *Financial Analysts Journal*, Vol. 28 (September/October, 1972), No. 5, pp. 71-84.

The dividend puzzle

"The harder we look at the dividend picture, the more it seems like a puzzle, with pieces that just don't fit together."

Fischer Black

Why do corporations pay dividends? Why do investors pay attention to dividends? Perhaps the answers to these questions are obvious. Perhaps dividends represent the return to the investor who put his money at risk in the corporation. Perhaps corporations pay dividends to reward existing shareholders and to encourage others to buy new issues of common stock at high prices. Perhaps investors pay attention to dividends because only through dividends or the prospect of dividends do they receive a return on their investment or the chance to sell their shares at a higher price in the future.

Or perhaps the answers are not so obvious. Perhaps a corporation that pays no dividends is demonstrating confidence that it has attractive investment opportunities that might be missed if it paid dividends. If it makes these investments, it may increase the value of the shares by more than the amount of the lost dividends. If that happens, its shareholders may be doubly better off. They end up with capital appreciation greater than the dividends they missed out on, and they find they are taxed at lower effective rates on capital appreciation than on dividends.

In fact, I claim that the answers to these questions are not obvious at all. The harder we look at the dividend picture, the more it seems like a puzzle, with pieces that just don't fit together.

THE MILLER-MODIGLIANI THEOREM

Suppose you are offered the following choice. You may have $2 today, and a 50-50 chance of $54 or $50 tomorrow. Or you may have nothing today, and a 50-50 chance of $56 or $52 tomorrow. Would you prefer one of these gambles to the other?

Probably you would not. Ignoring such factors as the cost of holding the $2 and one day's interest on $2, you would be indifferent between these two gambles.

The choice between a common stock that pays a dividend and a stock that pays no dividend is similar, at least if we ignore such things as transaction costs and taxes. The price of the dividend-paying stock drops on the ex-dividend date by about the amount of the dividend. The dividend just drops the whole range of possible stock prices by that amount. The investor who gets a $2 dividend finds himself with shares worth about $2 less than they would have been worth if the dividend hadn't been paid, in all possible circumstances.

This, in essence, is the Miller-Modigliani theorem.[1] It says that the dividends a corporation pays do not affect the value of its shares or the returns to investors, because the higher the dividend, the less the investor receives in capital appreciation, no matter how the corporation's business decisions turn out.

When we say this, we are assuming that the dividend paid does not influence the corporation's business decisions. Paying the dividend either reduces the amount of cash equivalents held by the corporation, or increases the amount of money raised by issuing securities.

IF A FIRM PAYS NO DIVIDENDS

If this theorem is correct, then a firm that pays a regular dividend equal to about half of its normal earnings will be worth the same as an otherwise similar firm that pays no dividends and will never pay any dividends. Can that be true? How can a firm that will never pay dividends be worth anything at all?

Actually, there are many ways for the stockholders of a firm to take cash out without receiving dividends. The most obvious is that the firm can buy back some of its shares. This has the advantage that most investors are not taxed as heavily on shares sold as they are on dividends received.

If the firm is closely held, it can give money to its shareholders by giving them jobs at inflated salaries, or by ordering goods from other firms owned by the shareholders at inflated prices.

If the firm is not closely held, then another firm or individual can make a tender offer which will have the effect of making it closely held. Then the same methods for taking cash out of the firm can be used.

Under the assumptions of the Modigliani-Miller theorem, a firm has value even if it pays no dividends. Indeed, it has the same value it would have if it paid dividends.

TAXES

In a world where dividends are taxed more heavily (for most investors) than capital gains, and where capital gains are not taxed until realized, a corporation that pays no dividends will be more attractive to taxable individual investors than a similar corporation that pays dividends. This will tend to increase the price of the non-dividend-paying corporation's stock. Many corporations will be tempted to eliminate dividend payments.

Of course, corporate investors are taxed more heavily on realized capital gains than on dividends. And tax-exempt investors are taxed on neither. But it is hard to believe that these groups have enough impact on the market to outweigh the effects of taxable individuals.

Also, the IRS has a special tax that it likes to apply to companies that retain earnings to avoid the personal taxation of dividends. But there are many ways to avoid this tax. A corporation that is making investments in its business usually doesn't have to pay the tax, especially if it is issuing securities to help pay for these investments.

If a corporation insists on paying out cash, it is better off replacing some of its common stock with bonds. A shareholder who keeps his proportionate share of the new securities will receive taxable interest but at least the interest will be deductible to the corporation. Dividends are not deductible.

With taxes, investors and corporations are no longer indifferent to the level of dividends. They prefer smaller dividends or no dividends at all.

TRANSACTION COSTS

An investor who holds a non-dividend-paying stock will generally sell some of his shares if he needs to raise cash. In some circumstances, he can borrow against his shares. Either of these transactions can be costly, especially if small amounts of money are involved. So an investor might want to have dividend income instead.

But this argument doesn't have much substance. If investors are concerned about transaction costs, the corporation that pays no dividends can arrange for automatic share repurchase plans, much like the automatic dividend reinvestment plans that now exist. A shareholder would keep his stock in trust, and the trustee would periodically sell shares back to the corporation, including fractional shares if necessary. The shareholder could even choose the amounts he wants to receive and the timing of the payments. An automated system would probably cost about as much as a system for paying dividends.

If the IRS objected to the corporation's buying back its own shares, then the trustee could simply sell blocks of shares on the open market. Again, the cost would be low.

Thus transaction costs don't tell us much about why corporations pay dividends.

WHAT DO DIVIDEND CHANGES TELL US?

The managers of most corporations have a tendency to give out good news quickly, but to give out bad news slowly. Thus investors are somewhat suspicious of what the managers have to say.

Dividend policy, though, may say things the managers don't say explicitly. For one reason or another, managers and directors do not like to cut the dividend. So they will raise the dividend only if they feel the company's prospects are good enough to support the higher dividend for some time. And they will cut the dividend only if they think the prospects for a quick recovery are poor.

This means that dividend changes, or the fact that the dividend doesn't change, may tell investors more about what the managers really think than they can find out from other sources. Assuming that the managers' forecasts are somewhat reliable, dividend policy conveys information.

Thus the announcement of a dividend cut often leads to a drop in the company's stock price. And the announcement of a dividend increase often leads to an increase in the company's stock price. These stock price changes are permanent if the company in fact does as badly, or as well, as the dividend changes indicated.

If the dividend changes are not due to forecasts of the company's prospects, then any stock price changes that occur will normally be temporary. If a corporation eliminates its dividend because it wants to save taxes for its shareholders, then the stock price might decline at first. But it would eventually go back to the level it would have had if the dividend had not been cut, or higher.

Thus the fact that dividend changes often tell us things about the corporations making them does not explain why corporations pay dividends.

HOW TO HURT THE CREDITORS

When a company has debt outstanding, the indenture will almost always limit the dividends the company can pay. And for good reason. There is no easier way for a company to escape the burden of a debt than to pay out all of its assets in the form of a dividend, and leave the creditors holding an empty shell.[2]

While this is an extreme example, any increase in the dividend that is not offset by an increase in external financing will hurt the company's creditors. A dollar paid out in dividends is a dollar that is not available to the creditors if trouble develops.

If an increase in the dividend will hurt the creditors, then a cut in the dividend will help the creditors. Since the firm is only worth so much, what helps the creditors will hurt the stockholders. The stockholders would certainly rather have $2 in dividends than $2 invested in assets that may end up in the hands of the creditors. Perhaps we have finally found a reason why firms pay dividends.

Alas, this explanation doesn't go very far. In many cases, the changes in the values of the stock and bonds caused by a change in dividend policy would be so small they would not be detectable. And if the effects are large, the company can negotiate with the creditors. If the company agrees not to pay any dividends at all, the creditors would presumably agree to give better terms on the company's credit. This would eliminate the negative effects of cutting the dividend on the position of the stockholders relative to the creditors.

DIVIDENDS AS A SOURCE OF CAPITAL

A company that pays dividends might instead have invested the money in its operations. This is especially true when the company goes to the markets frequently for new capital. Cutting the dividend, if there are no special reasons for paying dividends, has to be one of the lowest cost sources of funds available to the company.

The underwriting cost of a new debt or equity issue is normally several percent of the amount of money raised. There are no comparable costs for money raised by cutting the dividend.

Perhaps a company that has no profitable investment projects and that is not raising money externally should keep its dividend. If the dividend is cut,

the managers may lose the money through unwise investment projects. In these special cases, there may be a reason to keep the dividend. But surely these cases are relatively rare.

In the typical case, the fact that cutting the dividend is a low cost way to raise money is another reason to expect corporations not to pay dividends. So why do they continue?

DO INVESTORS DEMAND DIVIDENDS?

It is possible that many, many individual investors believe that stocks that don't pay dividends should not be held, or should be held only at prices lower than the prices of similar stocks that do pay dividends. This belief is not rational, so far as I can tell. But it may be there nonetheless.

Add these investors to the trustees who believe it is not prudent to hold stocks that pay no dividends, and to the corporations that have tax reasons for preferring dividend-paying stocks, and you may have a substantial part of the market. More important, you may have a part of the market that strongly influences the pricing of corporate shares. Perhaps the best evidence of this is the dominance of this view in investment advisory publications.

On the other hand, investors also seem acutely aware of the tax consequences of dividends. Investors in high tax brackets seem to hold low dividend stocks, and investors in low tax brackets seem to hold high dividend stocks.[3]

Furthermore, the best empirical tests that I can think of are unable to show whether investors who prefer dividends or investors who avoid dividends have a stronger effect on the pricing of securities.[4]

If investors do demand dividends, then corporations should not eliminate all dividends. But it is difficult or impossible to tell whether investors demand dividends or not. So it is hard for a corporation to decide whether to eliminate its dividends or not.

PORTFOLIO IMPLICATIONS

Corporations can't tell what dividend policy to choose, because they don't know how many irrational investors there are. But perhaps a rational investor can choose a dividend policy for his portfolio that will maximize his after-tax expected return for a given level of risk. Perhaps a taxable investor, especially one who is in a high tax bracket, should emphasize low dividend stocks. And perhaps a tax-exempt investor should emphasize high dividend stocks.

One problem with this strategy is that an investor who emphasizes a certain kind of stock in his portfolio is likely to end up with a less well-diversified portfolio than he would otherwise have. So he will probably increase the risk of his portfolio.

The other problem is that we can't tell if or how much an investor will increase his expected return by doing this. If investors demanding dividends dominate the market, then high dividend stocks will have low expected returns. Even tax-exempt investors, if they are rational, should buy low dividend stocks.

On the other hand, it seems that rational investors in high brackets will do better in low dividend stocks no matter who dominates the market. But how much should they emphasize low dividend stocks? At what point will the loss of diversification offset the increase in expected return?

It is even conceivable that investors overemphasize tax factors, and bid low dividend stocks up so high that they are unattractive even for investors in the highest brackets.

Thus the portfolio implications of the theory are no clearer than its implications for corporate dividend policy.

What should the individual investor do about dividends in his portfolio? We don't know.

What should the corporation do about dividend policy? We don't know.

[1] See Merton H. Miller and Franco Modigliani, "Dividend Policy, Growth, and the Valuation of Shares." *Journal of Business* 34 (October, 1961): 411-433. Also Franco Modigliani and Merton H. Miller, "The Cost of Capital, Corporation Finance, and the Theory of Investment: Reply." *American Economic Review* 49 (September, 1959): 655-669.

[2] This issue is discussed in more detail in Fischer Black and Myron Scholes, "The Pricing of Options and Corporate Liabilities." *Journal of Political Economy* 81 (May/June, 1973): 637-654.

[3] See Marshall E. Blume, Jean Crockett, and Irwin Friend, "Stockownership in the United States: Characteristics and Trends." *Survey of Current Business* 54 (November, 1974): 16-40.

[4] See Fischer Black and Myron Scholes, "The Effects of Dividend Yield and Dividend Policy on Common Stock Prices and Returns." *Journal of Financial Economics* 1 (May, 1974): 1-22.

CONCEPTUAL FOUNDATIONS OF
TECHNICAL ANALYSIS*

Robert A. Levy

The stock market fundamentalist relies upon economic and financial statistics and information. He investigates corporate income statements, balance sheets, dividend records, management policies, sales growth, managerial ability, plant capacity, and competitive forces. He looks to the daily press for evidence of future business conditions. He analyzes bank reports and the voluminous statistical compilations of the various government agencies. Taking all these factors into account, he projects corporate earnings and applies a satisfactory earnings multiplier (price-earnings ratio, capitalization rate) to arrive at the intrinsic value of the security under observation. He then compares this intrinsic value to the existing market price and, if the former is sufficiently higher, he regards the stock as a purchase candidate.[1]

The term "technical" in its application to the stock market means something quite different than its ordinary dictionary definition. It refers to the study of the market itself as opposed to the external factors reflected in the market. Technical analysis is, in essence, the recording of the actual history of trading (including both price movement and the volume of transactions) for one stock or a group of equities, and deducing the future trend from this historical analysis.[2]

Various tools of technical analysis have evolved over the years. Time and space preclude a discussion of these numerous tools; rather, they will simply be identified. The interested reader is encouraged to consult one or more of the cited publications for more complete information.[3] The precursor of all technical principles was the Dow Theory, which evolved

---

* Reprinted by permission of the *Financial Analysts Journal* (July/August 1966).

[1] Robert D. Edwards and John Magee, *Technical Analysis of Stock Trends* (Springfield, Mass.: John Magee, 1958), p. 3.

[2] *Ibid.*, p. 5.

[3] See particu'arly: *Encyclopedia of Stock Market Techniques*, Investors Intelligence, Inc., Larchmont, N.Y., 1963; Garfield A. Drew, *New Methods for Profit in the Stock Market* (Boston: The Metcalf Press, 1954); and Joseph E. Granville, *A Strategy of Daily Stock Market Timing for Maximum Profit* (Englewood Cliffs, N.J.: Prentice-Hall, Inc., 1960).

as a result of the work of Charles H. Dow, editor of *The Wall Street Journal* from 1889 to 1902, and his followers. Other technical tools or indicators include the Elliott Wave Principle, Barron's Confidence Index, odd lot statistics, short interest ratios, breadth (advance—decline) indexes, statistics on new highs and lows, upside-downside volume data, bar charts and point-and-figure charts (which picture price and volume movements), moving average trend-lines, relative strength measures, and statistics on debits and credits of brokerage balances—to name a few of the more important ones.

Technical theory can be summarized as follows:

1. Market value is determined solely by the interaction of supply and demand.

2. Supply and demand are governed by numerous factors, both rational and irrational. Included in these factors are those that are relied upon by the fundamentalists, as well as opinions, moods, guesses, and blind necessities. The market weighs all of these factors continually and automatically.

3. Disregarding minor fluctuations in the market, stock prices tend to move in trends which persist for an appreciable length of time.

4. Changes in trend are caused by the shifts in supply and demand relationships. These shifts, no matter why they occur, can be detected sooner or later in the action of the market itself.[4]

The basic assumption of technical theorists is that history tends to repeat itself. In other words, past patterns of market behavior will recur in the future and can thus be used for predictive purposes. In statistical terminology, the stock market technician relies upon the dependence of successive price changes.

The assumption of the fundamental analyst is quite different. He believes that each security has an intrinsic value which depends upon its earning potential, and that actual market prices tend to move toward intrinsic values. If his belief is correct, then determining the intrinsic value of a security by capitalizing future earnings is equivalent to predicting the security's future price.[5]

THE CASE FOR TECHNICAL ANALYSIS

Robert D. Edwards and John Magee, two outspoken advocates of the technical school, argue that:

It is futile to assign an intrinsic value to a stock certificate. One share of United States Steel, for example, was worth $261 in the early Fall of 1929, but you could buy it for only $22 in June of 1932! By March 1937, it was selling for $126 and just one year later for $38. . . . This sort of thing, this wide divergence between presumed value and actual value, is not the exception; it

---

[4] Edwards and Magee, *op. cit.*, p. 86.

[5] Eugene F. Fama, "Random Walks in Stock Market Prices," *Financial Analysts Journal*, XXI, No. 5 (September–October 1965), p. 55.

is the rule; it is going on all the time. The fact is that the real value of a share of U.S. Steel common is determined at any given time solely, definitely, and inexorably by supply and demand, which are accurately reflected in the transactions consummated on the floor of the New York Stock Exchange.

Of course, the statistics which the fundamentalists study play a part in the supply-demand equation—that is freely admitted. But there are many other factors affecting it. The market price reflects not only the differing value opinions of many orthodox security appraisers but also all the hopes and fears and guesses and moods, rational and irrational, of hundreds of potential buyers and sellers, as well as their needs and their resources—in total, factors which defy analysis and for which no statistics are obtainable, but which are nevertheless all synthesized, weighed, and finally expressed in the one precise figure at which a buyer and seller get together and make a deal (through their agents, their respective brokers). This is the only figure that counts.

. . . In brief, the going price as established by the market itself comprehends all the fundamental information which the statistical analyst can hope to learn (plus some which is perhaps secret from him, known only to a few insiders) and much else besides of equal or even greater importance.

All of which, admitting its truth, would be of little significance were it not for the fact, which no one of experience doubts, that *prices move in trends* and trends tend to continue until something happens to change the supply-demand balance.[6]

The technical analyst justifies his activities in several ways. First, he contends that short-term market fluctuations are more important than long-term trends, where importance is judged by the profit potential in trading. Certainly the trader who buys at the bottom of each short-term movement and sells at the top will realize greater profits than the investor who benefits only from the major trend. Second, the technician contends that information on fundamental conditions comes too late for maximum profit. The fundamentalist is forced to wait for statistics on sales, orders, earnings, dividends, and similar factors. By the time information of this sort is made publicly available, the market may have already discounted its effect and commenced a substantial upward or downward move. The technical trader, however, can act instantaneously on any change in stock prices whether or not the news underlying the change has been made public. The technician believes that the movement of the market precedes the movement of other economic series, rather than vice versa.[7] (In this regard, he has the support of the National Bureau of Economic Research which, in its study of business cycles, has listed stock market prices as one of 12 leading indicators.)[8]

It is admitted by technicians that some fundamental analysts may be able to forecast the trend of business quite accurately; they may even

---

[6] Edwards and Magee, *op. cit.*, pp. 5–6.

[7] George L. Leffler and Loring C. Farwell, *The Stock Market* (New York: The Ronald Press Company, 1963), p. 574.

[8] Julius Shiskin, "Business Cycle Indicators: The Known and the Unknown," *Business Cycle Developments* (Washington: U.S. Department of Commerce, Bureau of the Census, September 1963), Appendix H.

know exactly what present economic conditions are, and what future conditions will be; moreover, they may be absolutely correct in their earnings projections for a given company. Yet, even assuming all of this to be true, their projections of stock market action could be grossly in error.[9] It is only technical analysis which can detect the buying and selling pressures caused by psychological and emotional, rather than economic and financial, factors. Only the market action itself reflects the existence of inside information not made publicly available. This important fact has been relied upon by all technicians, and written about by George A. Chestnutt, Jr., the manager of a mutual fund which depends heavily on technical methods.

There are so many factors, each having its own effect on the price fluctuations of any individual stock, that it is practically impossible to analyze them *separately* and give each its proper weight in an attempt to estimate the stock's future market action. Often the essential information is known only to insiders. It is not released to the public until it is too late to act upon it.

Fortunately, we do not need to know *why* one stock is stronger than another in order to act profitably upon the knowledge of the fact. The market itself is continually weighing and recording the effects of all the bullish information and all the bearish information about every stock. No one in possession of inside information can profit from it unless he buys or sells the stock. The moment he does, his buy or sell orders have their effect upon the price. That effect is revealed in the market action of the stock.[10]

The argument of the technical analyst, in a nutshell, is that stock price moves are caused by the interaction of supply and demand, and that the flow of funds into and out of various securities is first detected by the various technical market indicators, not by the analysis of fundamental economic and financial statistics.[11]

A Critique of the Intrinsic Value Approach

Technicians agree that trends and patterns evolve, for the most part, as a result of market action taken by those persons who have, or think they have, some superior knowledge of underlying fundamental factors. The obvious corollary, which fundamentalists are quick to point out, is that the possessors of this superior knowledge are in the best position to maximize their profits from stock market transactions. Since fundamental knowledge, so the argument goes, is the "stuff" which even technical analysts must ultimately rely upon to produce the trends and patterns which they study, so it must therefore be a better foundation for security appraisal.

---

[9] Joseph E. Granville, *New Key to Stock Market Profits* (Englewood Cliffs, N.J.: Prentice-Hall, Inc., 1963), p. 20.

[10] George A. Chestnutt, Jr., *Stock Market Analysis: Facts and Principles* (Larchmont, N.Y.: American Investors Corporation, 1965), p. 19.

[11] Joseph E. Granville, *A Strategy of Daily Stock Market Timing for Maximum Profit, op. cit.,* p. 9.

In fact, *there is little justification for denying that properly performed fundamental analysis is superior to technical analysis.* The technician must wait until those persons who have critical information, which others do not have, make their move in the market. Even though the technical analyst may be able to act before critical information is publicly available, nevertheless he will be later in his actions than will be the "insiders" who are first aware of the underlying fundamental factors. The conclusion must be, therefore, that investment analysis will be most successful when the analyst is among the first to gain and correctly evaluate the necessary superior knowledge.

But the technician still has a strong argument. First, it is possible that properly performed fundamental analysis could lead to unsatisfactory investment results. The opinion of the fundamentalist regarding the intrinsic value of a given security, even if correct, must be shared by other investors who control substantial financial resources and are willing to place these resources in the market place. Only when opinions are converted into action, and only when a sufficient amount of capital is involved, will the market price move toward intrinsic value. Thus, the fundamental analyst may find himself heavily invested in a security for a considerable length of time before market support develops. Of course, this lowers his rate of return by tying up funds which could have been invested elsewhere. The technician, however, purports to avoid this potential problem by delaying his investment until market support for a particular stock has already appeared. It is conceivable that the sacrifice in profits resulting from late selection is no greater than the opportunity cost of unproductive capital arising from early selection.

Second, and of greater importance, how many investors are able to successfully engage in fundamental analysis? How many are capable of being among the first to recognize and evaluate critical information? How many have the necessary nonmonetary resources (primarily time and reliable statistical information)?

Assume, for the sake of argument, that all investors are capable, and that they have sufficient time to analyze the economic and financial factors affecting any given security. These investors will then attempt to project the earnings of a particular company and capitalize these earnings in order to arrive at some estimate of intrinsic value. The most important of the statistical data upon which the investors will rely are the company's financial statements. Under these circumstances, how successful will the fundamentalist be in his analysis? The question could be posed in a more direct manner: How complete and reliable are the corporate financial reports which are the major source of information for the fundamental analyst?

The purpose of published annual reports is to convey information to present and prospective stockholders about the operations of the corporate entity. This information should include all that is relevant (both qualitative and quantitative) to enable the investor to make a rational and informed judgment as to the investment worth of the company. Consequently, published annual reports should be designed for the use of the skilled financial analyst. Only then can they possibly include information in sufficient volume and detail as to provide for an efficient allocation of capital resources through investment selection.

The Securities and Exchange Commission, through Regulation S-X, has prescribed the form and content of financial reports filed with the SEC. The Securities Acts Amendments of 1964 extended these filing requirements to most over-the-counter companies, thereby matching the requirements which theretofore had been imposed only upon listed firms. Prior to 1964 the SEC's filing requirements had only an indirect effect (through public pressure) on the form and content of published annual reports to stockholders. The published reports could, and often did, differ from the Form 10-K annual reports filed with the SEC. Differences were both as to dollar amounts and as to the extent of the information provided. However, in May 1964 the SEC adopted Rule 14a–3 which prescribed, among other things, that any material differences between the methods of reporting to the SEC and the methods of reporting to stockholders must be noted in the published annual report along with a reconciliation of the differences. Consequently, subsequent to 1964, published annual reports did not differ in dollar amount from the Form 10Ks. Nevertheless, there are still considerable differences in the extent and volume of information in the two reports. Many corporations publish no more than a summary balance sheet, income statement, and statement of retained earnings for a one-year, or perhaps two-year period. Needless to say, this is unsatisfactory to the fundamental analyst.

Some of the information which is badly needed in published reports, but which is seldom available, includes: (1) production in units; (2) sales in units; (3) rate of capacity operated; (4) breakdown of operations as between domestic and foreign; (5) division of sales as between intercompany and outsiders; (6) wages, wage rates, hours worked, and number of employees; (7) state and local taxes paid; (8) amount and details of selling and general expenses; (9) amount and details of maintenance expenditures; (10) details of capital expenditures; (11) details of inventories; (12) details of properties owned; (13) number of stockholders; (14) sales by product line and by consuming industry; (15) research and development costs; (16) details of long-term lease arrangements; (17) details of stock option and pension plans; (18) more complete disclosure of depreciation policies; and (19) orders booked and unfilled orders.[12] And this is by no means an all-inclusive list.

The American Institute of Certified Public Accountants has com-

---

[12] Benjamin Graham, David L. Dodd and Sidney Cottle, *Security Analysis* (New York: McGraw-Hill Book Company, Inc., 1962), pp. 80–82.

mented extensively upon the adequacy of information in published reports. Of particular importance are the remarks appearing in three of the *Accounting Research Studies*, covering the accounting ramifications of financial leases, business combinations, and pensions, respectively.[13] In these studies, investigations of annual reports revealed gross inadequacy of information.

The sparse quantity of information is only one of the problems of the fundamentalists, however. Of equal importance is the question of reliability. Presumably, when the financial statements of a company are accompanied by the unqualified approval of an independent certified public accountant, investors and creditors may be assured of the fairness and integrity of the reports. The auditor's report indicates whether he feels that the financial position of the company and the results of its operations are presented fairly, in conformity with generally accepted accounting principles. The audit supposedly eliminates, or at least discloses, unintentional errors by corporate accountants, bias on the part of corporate management, deviations from generally accepted accounting principles, and deliberate falsification. The audit also determines whether the financial statements have been prepared on a basis consistent with that of the prior year and whether they fully disclose all material facts.[14]

In practice, there are many reasons why the auditor's certificate is of less-than-desirable significance. First, the auditor's examination is limited to a program of tests which are not infallible in detecting errors. Second, such concepts as "fairness," "materiality," "full disclosure," and "consistency" are subjective in nature and cannot be objectively verified.[15] Third, and fortunately least frequent in occurrence, there may be outright dishonesty by the independent auditor or collusion between the accounting firm and its corporate client. Fourth, and of greatest importance, there are no truly generally accepted accounting principles. The accounting profession is in a state of flux. In some cases, there are a multiplicity of acceptable procedures, while in other cases, those principles which have been applied for so many years are now being subjected to serious reanalysis and skeptical reevaluation.

Questions as to both fairness and objectivity of financial reporting were raised in five of the *Accounting Research Studies*.[16] The specific

---

[13] John H. Myers, "Reporting of Leases in Financial Statements," *Accounting Research Study No. 4* (New York: American Institute of Certified Public Accountants, 1962); Arthur R. Wyatt, "A Critical Study of Accounting for Business Combination," *Accounting Research Study No. 5* (New York: American Institute of Certified Public Accountants, 1963); and Ernest L. Hicks, "Accounting for the Cost of Pension Plans," *Accounting Research Study No. 8* (New York: American Institute of Certified Public Accountants, 1965).

[14] Walter B. Meigs, *Principles of Auditing* (Homewood, Ill.: Richard D. Irwin, Inc., 1959), pp. 1–2.

[15] *Ibid.*, pp. 14–17.

[16] Robert T. Sprouse and Maurice Moonitz, "A Tentative Set of Broad Accounting Principles for Business Enterprises," *Accounting Research Study No. 3* (New York:

problems included asset valuation, treatment of leases, business combinations, adjustments for changes in price level, and pensions. In each of these areas there is considerable doubt as to the propriety of presently employed accounting principles (particularly as to the appropriateness of historical cost valuations).

Additional accounting problems exist in the following areas: (1) matching revenues and expenses (e.g., direct versus absorption costing, installment sales, long-term construction contracts, stock options, depreciation, the investment credit, and deferred taxes); (2) distinguishing between several acceptable accounting methods and determining the effect of using one as opposed to another (e.g., depreciation, the investment credit, and inventory valuation); and (3) estimating various factors which are relevant to the accounting process (e.g., depreciable lives and bad debt expense).

Financial ratios, while potentially useful to the fundamentalist, can be no better than the figures from which they are derived. And these figures, in turn, are only as good as the underlying accounting principles. Year-to-year comparisons and trends are suspect because the flexibility of accounting procedures permits manipulation of the financial data. Inter-company comparisons are also unreliable because of the wide choice of permissible accounting methods.

The end-result is that the analyst, using publicly available information, has an extremely difficult task in trying to reconstruct a corporation's financial statements in order to get some picture of the company's earning power.

Nor does the analyst's problems terminate upon the evaluation of recent financial statements. This only provides him with an approximation of current and historical earnings. Now he must project these into the future. Moreover, a one-year projection is not adequate. As stated in a widely respected text on fundamental analysis:

> Typically, these . . . studies rest on a careful but too abbreviated forecast of probable future earnings for a company—covering generally only the next 12 months or less.
> . . . While such a measurement is important, it is hardly sufficient for an investment recommendation, since value cannot soundly be established on the basis of earnings shown over a short period of time.[17]

And that isn't all of the fundamentalist's trials and tribulations. Determining current and historical earnings is a difficult task indeed. Projecting these earnings for a number of years into the future is even more difficult. But now comes the most difficult job of all: selecting an appropriate

---

American Institute of Certified Public Accountants, 1962); Myers, *op. cit.*; Wyatt, *op cit.*; Accounting Research Division, "Reporting the Financial Effects of Price-Level Changes," *Accounting Research Study No. 6* (New York: American Institute of Certified Public Accountants, 1963); and Hicks, *op. cit.*

[17] Graham, Dodd and Cottle, *op. cit.*, p. 434.

price-earnings multiple (or capitalization rate). The problems inherent in this last step are reflected in the following statement by Graham, Dodd and Cottle, commenting upon a 1953 estimate by the Value Line Investment Survey of the 1956–1958 prices of the stocks in the Dow Jones Industrial Average.

> . . . although the earnings estimates were wide of the mark in several instances . . . the aggregate earnings estimate for the 29 stocks was very close to the actual. . . . By contrast, the aggregate market value estimate for 1956–1958 was significantly less accurate—missing by more than 22 percent the three-year mean price. . . . This tends to confirm our view that earnings can be predicted with more confidence than can the capitalization rate or multiplier, which to a major degree will reflect the market psychology existing at the time.[18]

Reference to the historical relationship between market price and *current* earnings is to no avail. Graham, Dodd and Cottle compared, over the 25–year period, 1935–1959, the quarterly earnings (on an annualized basis and seasonally adjusted) of Standard and Poor's 500 Composite stock group with the quarterly average stock-price index. They found that in 46 out of the 100 quarters stock prices moved counter to the change in earnings (i.e., earnings increased while prices declined, or vice versa).[19]

Granville emphasized this same important point by demonstrating the lack of correlation between prices and earnings as uncovered in his examination of hundreds of stocks. He found that price-earnings ratios fluctuated widely and that this fluctuation "dilutes the widely held belief that good earnings are a necessary accompaniment to advancing stock prices."[20]

With all of these difficulties (determining current earnings, projecting future earnings, and selecting an appropriate capitalization rate) it might be expected that even the best fundamental analysts can be far wide of the mark. This expectation would be justified by the facts. The 1965 range of the Dow Jones Industrial Average was 840.59 to 969.26, and the average of the 1963–1965 DJIA annual high-lows was 813.60.[21] But in March of 1961 Naess and Thomas projected the 1965 Average at 688; and Value Line, in January of 1961, suggested that the mean for 1963–1965 would be 705.[22] Errors of this size are not unusual. Graham, Dodd and Cottle, in the 1962 edition of their book, *Security Analysis,* stated that "careful consideration of this problem . . . led us to increase our 1951 valuation standards by an arbitrary 50 percent."[23] Such arbitrariness certainly bespeaks unreliability.

---

[18] *Ibid.,* p. 439.

[19] *Ibid.,* p. 719.

[20] Granville, *New Keys to Stock Market Profits, op. cit.,* p. 21.

[21] "Statistical Section," *Barron's,* XLVI, No. 24 (June 13, 1966), p. 57.

[22] Graham, Dodd and Cottle, *op. cit.,* p. 418.

[23] *Ibid.,* p. 421.

It is clear that fundamental analysis, even when performed by so-called experts, can be quite inaccurate. The question remains as to whether technical analysis offers any better possibilities. At least one prominent author believes that it does.

There have been frequent occasions when technical analysis was the *only* thing that could possibly have given the correct answer to the future trend of the market. This was true, for example, in the spring of 1946. If any investor had then possessed a crystal ball which would have shown him what corporate earnings were to be a year later, he could only have concluded that stock prices would be considerably higher. Instead, they were substantially lower in the face of record earnings and dividends.

There was nothing in the "fundamentals"—either in 1946 or 1947—to explain why prices had collapsed in the meantime. But there was considerable evidence of a weak *technical* situation in the market beforehand. . . . The investor who acted on technical grounds did not need to concern himself with *why* the market should seem to be acting irrationally, whereas the analyst of business facts and probabilities—unable to find a "reason"—was forced to conclude that the market could not do what it actually did.

* * * * *

In a broad sense, the experience of the past 10 years has very clearly demonstrated that the price-to-earnings ratio is a much more important factor than the actual level and/or trend of earnings themselves. Since the ratio is determined by investment psychology, the study of technical market action has, on the whole, been more fruitful than fundamental analysis.[24]

MAJOR CRITICISMS OF TECHNICAL ANALYSIS

There are at least four major criticisms of technical analysis. The first three are closely interrelated. First, it is contended that the behavior of the stock market in the past may not be indicative of its behavior in the years to come. That is to say, even assuming that technical analysis would have been successful over the last decade, there is no guarantee that it will be successful over the next decade. Typical of the response to this criticism is the following denial by Edwards and Magee.

. . . all the new controls and regulations of the past several years, the new taxes which have placed a heavy handicap on successful investors, the greatly augmented and improved facilities for acquiring dependable information on securities, even the quite radical changes in certain portions of our basic economy, have not much altered the "pattern" of the stock market.[25]

The second contention of the critics is that technical traders acting on the results of their studies tend to create the very patterns and trends which they claim have predictive significance. In other words, the market action may be a reflection of the chart action instead of the reverse. Technicians recognize that this possibility exists. However, they argue that the habits and evaluative methods of individuals are so deeply ingrained that the same kinds of events continually produce the same kinds

---

[24] Drew, *op. cit.*, pp. 242–244.
[25] Edwards and Magee, *op. cit.*, p. 1.

of market responses. Since these habits and methods are extremely durable, and since fundamental analysts greatly outnumber the technicians, it is unlikely that technical trading alters the response of the fundamentalists to external factors; and hence the actions of technicians probably do not have a major influence on the behavior of a competitive market.[26]

This second criticism inevitably leads to a third—that, if technical analysis is continually successful, an influx of technical traders will neutralize whatever profit potential exists. An analogy can be offered in the field of horse racing. If someone were to perfect a system of wagering on horses, and if he were to publicize this system so as to make it available for everyone's use, the amount of betting on the highest rated horses would change the odds sufficiently to offset the profitability of the system. There are several reasons why this criticism is not fatal to the art of technical analysis. First, it is quite possible that extremely successful technical "systems" have been developed but, for this very reason, have not been publicized or made available for general use. Second, it is likely that those who are not engaged in technical analysis would be reluctant to believe the claims of successful technicians. Third, to the extent that technical analysis may depend in part upon the use of electronic computers and sophisticated mathematical techniques, both the expense and the requisite training and knowledge will prevent its exploitation by the majority of the investing public. Fourth, and most important, is the following argument given by Granville:

> There is no danger that the revelation of new techniques will so enlighten the masses as to render them (the techniques) useless. The application of such things requires time and work, and human nature is such that most people will neither have the time, patience, or desire to do the work necessary to achieve the results which might be had when these things are done.[27]

Finally, the fourth major criticism of technical analysis is its subjectivity. Advocates of the technical school contend that their methods preclude the somewhat arbitrary determinations which accompany fundamental analysis (e.g., selection of a capitalization rate). Critics, however, maintain that the technician's favorite tool, the chart of stock price movements, is subject to a wide variety of interpretations. Without debating the validity of this criticism, it may be noted that the recent use of the computer for purposes of analyzing price and volume movements would tend to reduce the subjectivity which might otherwise be inherent in technical analysis.

IMPLICATIONS OF THE RANDOM WALK THEORY

The most critical indictment of technical analysis, thereby giving indirect support to the fundamentalists' side of the debate, is the random

---

[26] *Ibid.*, pp. 391–392.

[27] Granville, *New Key to Stock Market Profits, op. cit.*, p. 11.

walk theory. This theory restates the above-mentioned criticisms in slightly different context. It argues that the activities of chart readers, if successful, would help to produce the independence of successive stock price changes. But this independence, once established, renders chart reading an unprofitable activity. On the other hand, fundamentalists who consistently evaluate the effect of new information on intrinsic values will be able to realize larger profits than those who can not.[28]

There is nothing . . . which suggests that superior fundamental or intrinsic value analysis is useless in a random walk-efficient market. In fact, the analyst will do better than the investor who follows a simple buy-and-hold policy as long as he can more quickly identify situations where there are non-negligible discrepancies between actual price and intrinsic values than other analysts and investors, and if he is better able to predict the occurrence of important events and evaluate their effects on intrinsic values.

If there are many analysts who are pretty good at this sort of thing, however, and if they have considerable resources at their disposal, they help narrow discrepancies between actual prices and intrinsic values and cause actual prices, on the average, to adjust "instantaneously" to changes in intrinsic values.[29]

The random walk theory, while refuting the concepts of technical analysis and neither proving nor disproving those of fundamental analysis, presents an empirical challenge to both schools of thought. The challenge to the technician is a direct one. If the random walk model is valid, as suggested by empirical evidence to date, then future price movements cannot be predicted by studying the history of past price movements alone. Consequently, the work of the chartist may be useless. To vindicate himself, the technician should not restrict himself to verbalizing about trends and patterns; rather, he should demonstrate their predictive significance empirically. The challenge to the fundamentalist, while still empirical, is indirect. The random walk theory is based on the premise of an "efficient" market where actual stock prices at any given time are likely to be close approximations of intrinsic values. The fundamental analyst must therefore demonstrate that his methods consistently result in the detection of discrepancies between actual prices and intrinsic values when these discrepancies exist.[30]

Conclusions

The analysis of financial and economic fundamentals must ultimately be the underlying foundation for security appraisal. Market prices will, in the long run, tend to move toward intrinsic values. Thus, the determination of value is the critical factor in investment selection. The criticisms of fundamental analysis presented in this paper are directed at practicabil-

---

[28] Eugene F. Fama, "The Behavior of Stock Market Prices," *The Journal of Business*, XXXVIII, No. 1 (January 1965), p. 39.

[29] Fama, "Random Walks in Stock Market Prices," *op. cit.*, p. 58.

[30] *Ibid.*, p. 59.

ity rather than theory. It is the inability of most investors to *properly apply* fundamental techniques which is the basis for skepticism. As the art of fundamental analysis is further developed and properly applied, it will provide a sounder basis for investment evaluation.

Nevertheless, there is conceptual justification for contending that, except for the most sophisticated of the professional analysts, technical stock analysis may be as satisfactory, or perhaps more satisfactory, than fundamental analysis. Moreover, there is conceptual support for recommending technical analysis as a supplement to fundamental analysis for even the top professionals.

However, conceptual reasoning is not enough. There is a vast amount of empirical evidence which supports the random walk model of stock market behavior and thus denies the value of technical analysis. In order to attain recognition from serious students of the stock market, technicians must combine existing conceptual support with empirical evidence which has been heretofore lacking.

by Franco Modigliani and Gerald A. Pogue

An Introduction to Risk and Return

Concepts and Evidence

1. Introduction

Portfolio theory deals with the selection of optimal portfolios by rational risk-averse investors: that is, by investors who attempt to maximize their expected portfolio returns consistent with individually acceptable levels of portfolio risk. Capital markets theory deals with the implications for security prices of the decisions made by these investors: that is, what relationship should exist between security returns and risk if investors behave in this optimal fashion. Together, portfolio and capital markets theories provide a framework for the specification and measurement of investment risk, for developing relationships between expected security return and risk, and for measuring the performance of managed portfolios such as mutual funds and pension funds.

The purpose of this article is to present a non-technical introduction to portfolio and capital markets theories. Our hope is to provide a wide class of readers with an understanding of the foundation upon which the modern risk and performance measures are based, by presenting the main elements of the theory along with the results of some of the more important empirical tests. We are attempting to present not an exhaustive survey of the theoretical and empirical literature, but rather the main thread of the subject leading the reader from the most basic concepts to the more sophisticated but practically useful results of the theory.

2. Investment Return

Measuring historical rates of return is a relatively straightforward matter. We will begin by showing how investment return during a single interval can be measured, and then present three commonly used measures of average return over a series of such intervals.

The return on an investor's portfolio during a given interval is equal to the change in value of the portfolio plus any distributions received from the portfolio expressed as a fraction of the initial portfolio value. It is important that any capital or income distributions made to the investor be included, or else the measure of return will be deficient. Equivalently, the return can be thought of as the amount (expressed as a fraction of the initial portfolio value) that can be withdrawn at the end of the interval while maintaining the principal intact. The return on the investor's portfolio, designated R_P, is given by

$$R_P = \frac{V_1 - V_0 + D_1}{V_0}, \qquad (1a)$$

where

V_1 = the portfolio market value at the end of the interval

V_0 = the portfolio market value at the beginning of the interval

D_1 = cash distributions to the investor during the interval.

The calculation assumes that any interest or dividend income received on the portfolio securities and not distributed to the investor is reinvested in the portfolio (and thus reflected in V_1). Furthermore, the calculation assumes that any

Reprinted by permission of the
Financial Analysts Journal (March/April 1974).

distributions occur at the end of the interval, or are held in the form of cash until the end of the interval. If the distributions were reinvested prior to the end of the interval, the calculation would have to be modified to consider the gains or losses on the amount reinvested. The formula also assumes no capital inflows during the interval. Otherwise, the calculation would have to be modified to reflect the increased investment base. Capital inflows at the end of the interval, however, can be treated as just the reverse of distributions in the return calculation.

Thus given the beginning and ending portfolio values, plus any contributions from or distributions to the investor (assumed to occur at the end of the interval), we can compute the investor's return using Equation (1a). For example, if the XYZ pension fund had a market value of $100,000 at the end of June, capital contributions of $10,000, benefit payments of $5,000 (both at the end of July), and an end-of-July market value of $95,000, the return for the month is a loss of 10 per cent.

The arithmetic average return is an unweighted average of the returns achieved during a series of such measurement intervals. For example, if the portfolio returns [as measured by Equation (1a)] were -10 per cent, 20 per cent, and 5 per cent in July, August, and September respectively, the average monthly return is 5 per cent. The general formula is

$$R_A = \frac{R_{P1} + R_{P2} + \ldots + R_{PN}}{N}, \quad (1b)$$

where

R_A = the arithmetic average return
R_{PK} = the portfolio return in interval k, k=1, ..., N
N = the number of intervals in the performance-evaluation period.

The arithmetic average can be thought of as the mean value of the withdrawals (expressed as a fraction of the initial portfolio value) that can be made at the end of each interval while maintaining the principal intact. In the above example, the investor must add 10 per cent of the principal at the end of the first interval and can withdraw 20 per cent and 5 per cent at the end of the second and third, for a mean withdrawal of 5 per cent of the initial value per period.

The time-weighted return measures the compound rate of growth of the initial portfolio during the performance-evaluation period, assuming that all cash distributions are reinvested in the port-folio. It is also commonly referred to as the "geometric" rate of return. It is computed by taking the geometric average of the portfolio returns computed from Equation (1a). For example, let us assume the portfolio returns were -10 per cent, 20 per cent, and 5 per cent in July, August, and September, as in the example above. The time-weighted rate of return is 4.3 per cent per month. Thus one dollar invested in the portfolio at the end of June would have grown at a rate of 4.3 per cent per month during the three-month period. The general formula is

$$R_T = [(1 + R_{P1})(1 + R_{P2}) \ldots$$
$$(1 + R_{PN})]^{1/N} -1, \quad (1c)$$

where

R_T = the time-weighted rate of return
R_{PK} = the portfolio return during the interval k, k=1, ..., N
N = the number of intervals in the performance-evaluation period.

In general, the arithmetic and time-weighted average returns do not coincide. This is because, in computing the arithmetic average, the amount invested is assumed to be maintained (through additions or withdrawals) at its initial value. The time-weighted return, on the other hand, is the return on a portfolio that varies in size because of the assumption that all proceeds are reinvested. The failure of the two averages to coincide is illustrated in the following example: Consider a portfolio with a $100 market value at the end of 1972, a $200 value at the end of 1973, and a $100 value at the end of 1974. The annual returns are 100 per cent and -50 per cent. The arithmetic and time-weighted average returns are 25 per cent and zero per cent respectively. The arithmetic average return consists of the average of $100 withdrawn at the end of Period 1, and $50 replaced at the end of Period 2. The compound rate of return is clearly zero, the 100 per cent return in the first period being exactly offset by the 50 per cent loss in the second period on the larger asset base. In this example the arithmetic average exceeded the time-weighted average return. This always proves to be true, except in the special situation where the returns in each interval are the same, in which case the averages are identical.

The dollar-weighted return measures the average rate of growth of all funds invested in the portfolio during the performance-evaluation period—that is, the initial value plus any contributions less any distributions. As such, the rate is influenced by the timing and magnitude of the contributions and distributions to and from the portfolio. The measure is also commonly referred to as the "internal rate of return." It is important to corporations, for example, for comparison with the actuarial rates of portfolio growth assumed when funding their employee pension plans.

The dollar-weighted return is computed in exactly the same way that the yield to maturity on a bond is determined. For example, consider a portfolio with market value of $100,000 at the end of 1973 (V_0), capital withdrawals of $5,000 at the end of 1974, 1975, and 1976 (C_1, C_2, and C_3), and a market value of $110,000 at the end of 1976 (V_3). Using compound interest tables, the dollar-weighted rate of return is found by trial and error to be 8.1 per cent per year during the three-year period. Thus each dollar in the fund grew at an average rate of 8.1 per cent per year. The formula used is

$$V_0 = \frac{C_1}{(1+R_D)} + \frac{C_2}{(1+R_D)^2} + \frac{C_3}{(1+R_D)^3} + \frac{V_3}{(1+R_D)^3} ,$$ (1d)

where

R_D = the dollar-weighted rate of return.

What is the relationship between the dollar-weighted return (internal rate of return) and the previously defined time-weighted rate of return? It is easy to show that under certain special conditions both rates of return are the same. Consider, for example, a portfolio with initial total value V_0. No further additions or withdrawals occur and all dividends are reinvested. Under these special circumstances all of the C's in Equation (1d) are zero so that

$$V_0 = \frac{V_0(1+R_{P1})(1+R_{P2})(1+R_{P3})}{(1+R_D)^3} ,$$

where R_P's are the single-period returns. The numerator of the expression on the right is just the value of the initial investment at the end of the three periods (V_3). Solving for R_D we find

$$R = [(1+R_{P1})(1+R_{P2})(1+R_{P3})]^{1/3} - 1 ,$$

which is the same as the time-weighted rate of return R_T given by Equation (1c). However, when contributions or withdrawals to the portfolio occur, the two rates of return are not the same.

Because the dollar-weighted return (unlike the time-weighted return) is affected by the magnitude and timing of portfolio contributions and distributions (which are typically beyond the portfolio manager's control), it is not useful for measuring the investment performance of the manager. For example, consider two identical portfolios (designated A and B) with year-end 1973 market values of $100,000. During 1974 each portfolio has a 20 per cent return. At the end of 1974, portfolio A has a capital contribution of $50,000 and portfolio B a withdrawal of $50,000. During 1975, both portfolios suffer a 10 per cent loss resulting in year-end market values of $153,000 and $63,000 respectively. Now, both portfolio managers performed equally well, earning 20 per cent in 1974 and -10 per cent in 1975, for a time-weighted average return of 3.9 per cent per year. The dollar-weighted returns are not the same, however, due to the different asset bases for 1975, equaling 1.2 per cent and 8.2 per cent for portfolios A and B respectively. The owners of portfolio B, unlike those of A, made a fortuitous decision to reduce their investment prior to the 1975 decline.

In the remainder of this article, when we mention rate of return, we will generally be referring to the single interval measure given by Equation (1a). However, from time to time we will refer to the arithmetic and geometric averages of these returns.

3. Portfolio Risk

The definition of investment risk leads us into much less well explored territory. Not everyone agrees on how to define risk, let alone how to measure it. Nevertheless, there are some attributes of risk which are reasonably well accepted.

If an investor holds a portfolio of treasury bonds, he faces no uncertainty about monetary outcome. The value of the portfolio at maturity of the notes will be identical with the predicted value. In this case the investor bears no monetary risk. However, if he has a portfolio composed of common stocks, it will be impossible to exactly predict the value of the portfolio as of any future date. The best he can do is to make a best guess or most-likely estimate, qualified by statements about the range and likelihood of other values. In this case, the investor does bear risk.

One measure of risk is the extent to which the *future* portfolio values are likely to diverge from the expected or predicted value. More specifically, risk for most investors is related to the chance that future portfolio values will be less than expected.

Thus if the investor's portfolio has a current value of $100,000, and an expected value of $110,000 at the end of the next year, he will be concerned about the probability of achieving values less than $110,000.

Before proceeding to the quantification of risk, it is convenient to shift our attention from the terminal value of the portfolio to the portfolio rate of return, R_p, since the increase in portfolio value is directly related to R_p.[1]

A particularly useful way to quantify the uncertainty about the portfolio return is to specify the probability associated with each of the possible future returns. Assume, for example, that an investor has identified five possible outcomes for his portfolio return during the next year. Associated with each return is a subjectively determined probability, or relative chance of occurrence. The five possible outcomes are:

Possible Return	Subjective Probability
50%	0.1
30%	0.2
10%	0.4
-10%	0.2
-30%	0.1
	1.00

Note that the probabilities sum to 1.00 so that the actual portfolio return is confined to take one of the five possible values. Given this probability distribution, we can measure the expected return and risk for the portfolio.

The expected return is simply the weighted average of possible outcomes, where the weights are the relative chances of occurrence. The expected return on the portfolio is 10 per cent, given by

$$E(R_p) = \sum_{j=1}^{5} P_j \ R_j$$
$$= \ 0.1 (50.0) + 0.2 (30.0) + 0.4 (10.0)$$
$$+ \ 0.2 (-10.0) + 0.2 (-30.0)$$
$$= \ 10\%, \qquad (2)$$

where the R_j's are the possible returns and the P_j's the associated probabilities.

If risk is defined as the chance of achieving returns less than expected, it would seem to be logical to measure risk by the dispersion of the possible returns below the expected value. However, risk measures based on below-the-mean variability are difficult to work with and are ac-

---

1. Footnotes appear at end of article.

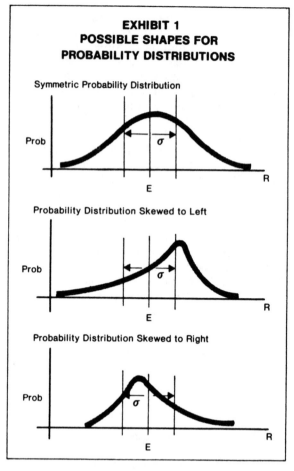

**EXHIBIT 1
POSSIBLE SHAPES FOR
PROBABILITY DISTRIBUTIONS**

Symmetric Probability Distribution

Probability Distribution Skewed to Left

Probability Distribution Skewed to Right

tually unnecessary as long as the distribution of future return is reasonably symmetric about the expected value.[2] Exhibit 1 shows three probability distributions: the first symmetric, the second skewed to the left, and the third skewed to the right. For a symmetric distribution, the dispersion of returns on one side of the expected return is the same as the dispersion on the other side.

Empirical studies of realized rates of return on diversified portfolios show that skewness is not a significant problem.[3] If future distributions are shaped like historical distributions, then it makes little difference whether we measure variability of returns on one or both sides of the expected return. If the probability distribution is symmetric, measures of the total variability of return will be twice as large as measures of the portfolio's variability below the expected return. Thus if total variability is used as a risk surrogate, the risk rankings for a group of portfolios will be the same as when variability below the expected return is used. It is for this reason that total variability of

EXHIBIT 2
RATE OF RETURN DISTRIBUTION FOR A PORTFOLIO OF 100 SECURITIES
(EQUALLY WEIGHTED)

January 1945 – June 1970

	RANGE		FREQ.	1, , ,5, , , ,10, , , ,15, , ,20, , ,25, , ,30, , ,35, , ,40, , ,45, , ,50,
1	-13.6210	-12.2685	1	*
2	-12.2685	-10.9160	2	**
3	-10.9160	-9.5635	2	**
4	-9.5635	-8.2110	3	8**
5	-8.2110	-6.8585	8	8******
6	-6.8585	-5.5060	9	********
7	-5.5060	-4.1535	17	8***************
8	-4.1535	-2.8010	18	******************
9	-2.8010	-1.4485	27	***************************
10	-1.4485	-0.0960	28	8***************************
11	-0.0960	1.2565	30	******************************
12	1.2565	2.6090	50	**
13	2.6090	3.9615	35	***********************************
14	3.9615	5.3140	33	*********************************
15	5.3140	6.6665	18	8*****************
16	6.6665	8.0190	14	**************
17	8.0190	9.3715	4	****
18	9.3715	10.7240	2	**
19	10.7240	12.0765	2	8*
20	12.0765	13.4290	3	***

SCALING FACTOR = 1

Average Return = 0.91% per month
Standard Deviation = 4.45% per month
Number of Observations = 306

returns has been so widely used as a surrogate for risk.

It now remains to choose a specific measure of total variability of returns. The measures most commonly used are the variance and standard deviation of returns.

The variance of return is a weighted sum of the squared deviations from the expected return. Squaring the deviations ensures that deviations above and below the expected value contribute equally to the measure of variability, regardless of sign. The variance, designated σ_p^2 for the portfolio in the previous example is given by

$$\sigma_p^2 = \sum_{j=1}^{5} P_j \left(R_j - E(R_p) \right)^2$$

$$= 0.1(50.0 - 10.0)^2 + 0.2(30.0 - 10.0)^2$$
$$+ 0.4(10.0 - 10.0)^2 + 0.2(-10.0 - 10.0)^2$$
$$+ 0.1(-30.0 - 10.0)^2$$

$$= 480 \text{ per cent squared.} \tag{3}$$

The standard deviation (σ_p) is defined as the square root of the variance. It is equal to 22 per cent. The larger the variance or standard deviation, the greater the possible dispersion of future realized values around the expected value, and the larger the investor's uncertainty. As a rule of thumb for symmetric distributions, it is often suggested that roughly two-thirds of the possible returns will lie within one standard deviation either side of the expected value, and that 95 per cent will be within two standard deviations.

Exhibit 2 shows the historical return distributions for a diversified portfolio. The portfolio is composed of approximately 100 securities, with each security having equal weight. The month-by-month returns cover the period from January 1945 to June 1970. Note that the distribution is approximately, but not perfectly, symmetric. The arithmetic average return for the 306-month period is 0.91 per cent per month. The standard deviation about this average is 4.45 per cent per month.

EXHIBIT 3
RATE OF RETURN DISTRIBUTION FOR NATIONAL DEPARTMENT STORES

January 1945 – June 1970

	RANGE		FREQ.	1				5				10				15				20				25				30				35				40				45				50
1	-32.3670	-29.4168	1	8
2	-29.4168	-26.4666	0	
3	-26.4666	-23.5163	0	
4	-23.5163	-20.5661	1	8
5	-20.5661	-17.6159	1	8
6	-17.6159	-14.6657	3	8 **
7	-14.6657	-11.7155	13	8 ***********
8	-11.7155	-8.7653	11	8 *********
9	-8.7653	-5.8151	39	8 *************************************
10	-5.8151	-2.8649	47	8 ***
11	-2.8649	0.0853	45	8 ***
12	0.0853	3.0355	34	8 ********************************
13	3.0355	5.9857	28	8 **************************
14	5.9857	8.9359	25	8 ***********************
15	8.9359	11.8861	17	8 ***************
16	11.8861	14.8363	17	8 ***************
17	14.8363	17.7865	9	8 *******
18	17.7865	20.7366	8	8 *******
19	20.7366	23.6868	5	8 ****
20	23.6868	26.6370	2	8 *

SCALING FACTOR = 1

Average Return = 0.81% per month
Standard Deviation = 9.02% per month
Number of Observations = 306

Exhibit 3 gives the same data for a single security, National Department Stores. Note that the distribution is highly skewed. The arithmetic average return is 0.81 per cent per month over the 306-month period. The most interesting aspect, however, is the standard deviation of month-by-month returns—9.02 per cent per month, more than double that for the diversified portfolio. This result will be discussed further in the next section.

Thus far our discussion of portfolio risk has been confined to a single-period investment horizon such as the next year; that is, the portfolio is held unchanged and evaluated at the end of the year. An obvious question relates to the effect of holding the portfolio for several periods—say for the next 20 years: Will the one-year risks tend to cancel out over time? Given the random-walk nature of security prices, the answer to this question is no. If the risk level (standard deviation) is maintained during each year, the portfolio risk for longer horizons will increase with the horizon length. The standard deviation of possible terminal portfolio values after N years is equal to $\sqrt{N}$ times the standard deviation after one year.[4] Thus the investor cannot rely on the "long run" to reduce his risk of loss.

A final remark should be made before leaving portfolio risk measures. We have implicitly assumed that investors are risk averse, i.e., that they seek to minimize risk for a given level of return. This assumption appears to be valid for most investors in most situations. The entire theory of portfolio selection and capital asset pricing is based on the belief that investors *on the average* are risk averse.

4. Diversification

When one compares the distribution of historical returns for the 100-stock portfolio (Exhibit 2) with the distribution for National Department Stores (Exhibit 3), he discovers a curious relationship. While the standard deviation of returns for the security is double that of the portfolio, its average return is less. Is the market so imperfect that over a long period of time (25 years) it rewarded substantially higher risk with lower average return?

Not so. As we shall now show, not all of the security's risk is relevant. Much of the total risk (standard deviation of return) of National Department Stores was diversifiable. That is, if it had been combined with other securities, a portion of the variation in its returns could have been smoothed out or cancelled by complementary variation in the other securities. The same portfolio diversification effect accounts for the low standard deviation of return for the 100-stock portfolio. In fact, the portfolio standard deviation was less than that of the typical security in the portfolio. Much of the total risk of the component securities had been eliminated by diversification. Since much of the total risk could be eliminated simply by holding a stock in a portfolio, there was no economic requirement for the return earned to be in line with the total risk. Instead, we should expect realized returns to be related to that portion of security risk which cannot be eliminated by portfolio combination.

Diversification results from combining securities having less than perfect correlation (dependence) among their returns in order to reduce portfolio risk. The portfolio return, being simply a weighted average of the individual security returns, is not diminished by diversification. In general, the lower the correlation among security returns, the greater the impact of diversification. This is true regardless of how risky the securities of the portfolio are when considered in isolation.

Ideally, if we could find sufficient securities with uncorrelated returns, we could completely eliminate portfolio risk. This situation is unfortunately not typical in real securities markets where returns are positively correlated to a considerable degree. Thus while portfolio risk can be substantially reduced by diversification, it cannot be entirely eliminated. This can be demonstrated very clearly by measuring the standard deviations of randomly selected portfolios containing various numbers of securities.

In a study of the impact of portfolio diversification on risk, Wagner and Lau [27]* divided a sample of 200 NYSE stocks into six subgroups based on the Standard and Poor's Stock Quality Ratings as of June 1960. The highest quality ratings (A+) formed the first group, the second highest ratings (A) the next group, and so on. Randomly selected portfolios were formed from each of the subgroups, containing from 1 to 20 securities. The month-by-month portfolio returns for the 10-year period through May 1970 were then computed for each portfolio (portfolio composition remaining unchanged). The exercise was repeated ten times to reduce the dependence on single samples, and the values for the ten trials were then averaged.

Table 1 shows the average return and standard deviation for portfolios from the first subgroup (A+ quality stocks). The average return is unrelated to the number of issues in the portfolio. On the other hand, the standard deviation of return declines as the number of holdings increases. On the average, approximately 40 per cent of the single security risk is eliminated by forming randomly selected portfolios of 20 stocks.

---

* References appear at end of article.

TABLE 1. RISK VERSUS DIVERSIFICATION FOR RANDOMLY SELECTED PORTFOLIOS OF A+ QUALITY SECURITIES

June 1960—May 1970

Number of Securities in Portfolio	Average Return (%/month)	Std. Deviation of Return (%/month)	Correlation with Market	
			R	R²
1	0.88	7.0	0.54	0.29
2	0.69	5.0	0.63	0.40
3	0.74	4.8	0.75	0.56
4	0.65	4.6	0.77	0.59
5	0.71	4.6	0.79	0.62
10	0.68	4.2	0.85	0.72
15	0.69	4.0	0.88	0.77
20	0.67	3.9	0.89	0.80

Source: Wagner and Lau [27], Table C, p. 53.

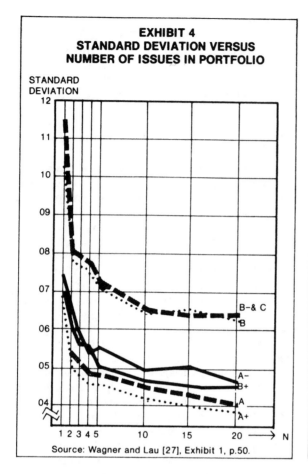

**EXHIBIT 4
STANDARD DEVIATION VERSUS
NUMBER OF ISSUES IN PORTFOLIO**

Source: Wagner and Lau [27], Exhibit 1, p.50.

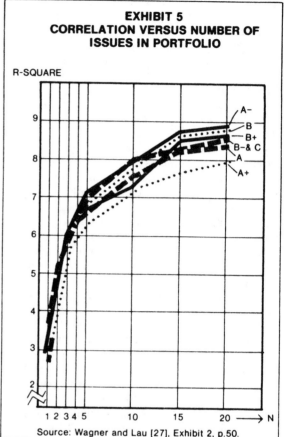

**EXHIBIT 5
CORRELATION VERSUS NUMBER OF
ISSUES IN PORTFOLIO**

Source: Wagner and Lau [27], Exhibit 2, p.50.

However, it is also evident that additional diversification yields rapidly diminishing reduction in risk. The improvement is slight when the number of securities held is increased beyond, say, 10. Exhibit 4 shows the results for all six quality groups. The figure shows the rapid decline in total portfolio risk as the portfolios are expanded from 1 to 10 securities.

Returning to Table 1, we note from the next to last column in the table that the return on a diversified portfolio follows the market very closely. The degree of association is measured by the correlation coefficient (R) of each portfolio with an unweighted index of all NYSE stocks (perfect positive correlation results in a correlation coefficient of 1.0).[5] The 20-security portfolio has a correlation of 0.89 with the market. The implication is that the risk remaining in the 20-stock portfolio is predominantly a reflection of uncertainty about the performance of the stock market in general. Exhibit 5 shows the results for the six quality groups.

Correlation in Exhibit 5 is represented by the correlation coefficient squared, R^2 (possible values range from 0 to 1.0). The R^2 coefficient has a useful interpretation: it measures the proportion of variability in portfolio return that is attributable to variability in market returns. The remaining variability is risk, which is unique to the portfolio and, as Exhibit 4 shows, can be eliminated by proper diversification of the portfolio. Thus, R^2 measures the degree of portfolio diversification. A poorly diversified portfolio will have a small R^2 (0.30 - 0.40). A well diversified portfolio will have a much higher R^2 (0.85 - 0.95). A perfectly diversified portfolio will have an R^2 of 1.0; that is, all the risk in such a portfolio is a reflection of market risk. Exhibit 5 shows the rapid gain in diversification as the portfolio is expanded from 1 to 2 securities and up to 10 securities. Beyond 10 securities the gains tend to be smaller. Note that increasing the number of issues tends to be less efficient at achieving diversification for the highest quality A + issues. Apparently the companies comprising this group are more homogeneous than the companies grouped under the other quality codes.

The results show that while some risks can be eliminated via diversification, others cannot. Thus we are led to distinguish between a security's "unsystematic" risk, which can be washed away by mixing the security with other securities in a diversified portfolio, and its "systematic" risk, which cannot be eliminated by diversification. This proposition is illustrated in Exhibit 6. It shows total portfolio risk declining as the number of holdings increases. Increasing diversification gradually tends to eliminate the unsystematic risk, leaving only systematic, i.e., market-related risk. The remaining variability results from the fact that the return on nearly every security depends to some degree on the overall performance of the market. Consequently, the return on a well diversified portfolio is highly correlated with the market, and its variability or uncertainty is basically the uncertainty of the market as a whole. Investors are exposed to market uncertainty no matter how many stocks they hold.

5. The Risk of Individual Securities

In the previous section we concluded that the systematic risk of an individual security is that portion of its total risk (standard deviation of return) which cannot be eliminated by combining it with other securities in a well diversified portfolio. We now need a way of quantifying the systematic risk of a security and relating the systematic risk of a portfolio to that of its component securities. This can be accomplished by dividing security return into two parts: one dependent (i.e., perfectly correlated), and a second independent (i.e., uncorrelated) of market return. The first component of return is usually referred to as "systematic", the second as "unsystematic" return. Thus we have

Security Return = Systematic Return
  + Unsystematic Return.   (4)

Since the systematic return is perfectly correlated with the market return, it can be expressed as a factor, designated beta (β), times the market return, R_m. The beta factor is a market sensitivity index, indicating how sensitive the security return is to changes in the market level. The unsystematic return, which is independent of market returns, is usually represented by a factor epsilon (ε'). Thus the security return, R, may be expressed

$$R = \beta R_m + \varepsilon' .   (5)$$

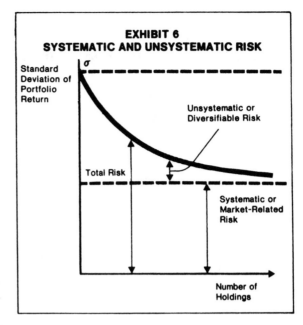

EXHIBIT 6
SYSTEMATIC AND UNSYSTEMATIC RISK

For example, if a security had a β factor of 2.0 (e.g., an airline stock), then a 10 per cent market return would generate a systematic return for the stock of 20 per cent. The security return for the period would be the 20 per cent plus the unsystematic component. The unsystematic component depends on factors unique to the company, such as labor difficulties, higher than expected sales, etc.

The security returns model given by Equation (5) is usually written in a way such that the average value of the residual term, ε', is zero. This is accomplished by adding a factor, alpha (α), to the model to represent the average value of the unsystematic returns over time. That is, we set $\varepsilon' = \alpha + \varepsilon$ so that

$$R = \alpha + \beta R_m + \varepsilon ,   (6)$$

where the average ε over time is equal to zero.

The model for security returns given by Equation (6) is usually referred to as the "market model". Graphically, the model can be depicted as a line fitted to a plot of security returns against rates of return on the market index. This is shown in Exhibit 7 for a hypothetical security.

The beta factor can be thought of as the slope of the line. It gives the expected increase in security return for a one per cent increase in market return. In Exhibit 7, the security has a beta of 1.0. Thus, a ten per cent market return will result, on the average, in a ten per cent security return. The

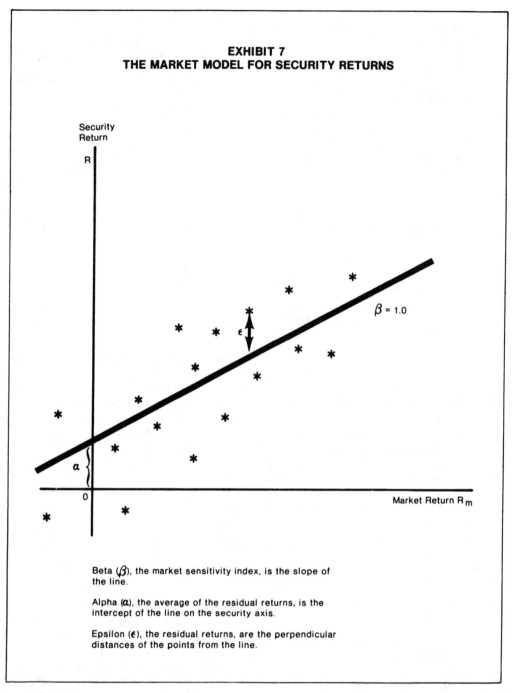

EXHIBIT 7
THE MARKET MODEL FOR SECURITY RETURNS

Security Return

R

β = 1.0

ϵ

α

0

Market Return R$_m$

Beta (β), the market sensitivity index, is the slope of the line.

Alpha (α), the average of the residual returns, is the intercept of the line on the security axis.

Epsilon (ϵ), the residual returns, are the perpendicular distances of the points from the line.

market-weighted average beta for all stocks is 1.0 by definition.

The alpha factor is represented by the intercept of the line on the vertical security return axis. It is equal to the average value over time of the unsystematic returns (ϵ') on the stock. For most stocks, the alpha factor tends to be small and un-

stable. (We shall return to alpha later.)

Using the definition of security return given by the market model, the specification of systematic and unsystematic risk is straightforward—they are simply the standard deviations of the two return components.[6]

The systematic risk of a security is equal to β

times the standard deviation of the market return:

$$\text{Systematic Risk} = \beta\,\sigma_m . \qquad (7)$$

The unsystematic risk equals the standard deviation of the residual return factor ε:

$$\text{Unsystematic Risk} = \sigma_\varepsilon . \qquad (8)$$

Given measures of individual security systematic risk, we can now compute the systematic risk of portfolio. It is equal to the beta factor for the portfolio, β_p, times the risk of the market index, σ_m:

$$\text{Portfolio Systematic Risk} = \beta_p\,\sigma_m . \qquad (9)$$

The portfolio beta factor in turn can be shown to be simply an average of the individual security betas, weighted by the proportion of each security in the portfolio, or

$$\beta_p = \sum_{j=1}^{N} X_j\,\beta_j . \qquad (10)$$

where

X_j = the proportion of portfolio market value represented by security j

N = the number of securities.

Thus the systematic risk of the portfolio is simply a weighted average of the systematic risk of the individual securities. If the portfolio is composed of an equal dollar investment in each stock (as was the case for the 100-security portfolio of Exhibit 2), the β_p is simply an unweighted average of the component security betas.

The unsystematic risk of the portfolio is also a function of the unsystematic security risks, but the form is more complex.[7] The important point is that

with increasing diversification this risk can be reduced toward zero.

With these results for portfolio risk, it is useful to return to Exhibit 4. The figure shows the decline in portfolio risk with increasing diversification for each of the six quality groups. However, the portfolio standard deviations for each of the six groups are decreasing toward different limits because the average risks (β) of the groups differ.

Table 2 shows a comparison of the standard deviations for the 20-stock portfolios with the predicted lower limits based on average security systematic risks. The lower limit is equal to the average beta for the quality group ($\bar{\beta}$) times the standard deviation of the market return (σ_m). The standard deviations in all cases are close to the predicted values. These results support the contention that portfolio systematic risk equals the average systematic risks of the component securities.

The main results of this section can be summarized as follows: First, as seen from Exhibit 4, roughly 40 to 50 per cent of total security risk can be eliminated by diversification. Second, the remaining systematic risk is equal to the security β times market risk. Third, portfolio systematic risk is a weighted average of security systematic risks.

The implications of these results are substantial. First, we would expect realized rates of return over substantial periods of time to be related to the systematic as opposed to total risk of securities. Since the unsystematic risk is relatively easily eliminated, we should not expect the market to offer a risk premium for bearing it. Second, since

TABLE 2. STANDARD DEVIATIONS OF 20-STOCK PORTFOLIOS AND PREDICTED LOWER LIMITS

June 1960—May 1970

(1) Stock Quality Group	(2) Standard Deviation of 20-Stock Portfolios $\sigma \cdot \%/\text{mo}$	(3) Average Beta Value for Quality Group $\bar{\beta}$	(4) Lower Limit* $\bar{\beta} \cdot \sigma_m$ $\%/\text{mo}$
A+	3.94	0.74	3.51
A	4.17	0.80	3.80
A-	4.52	0.89	4.22
B+	4.45	0.87	4.13
B	6.27	1.24	5.89
B- & C	6.32	1.23	5.84

* $\sigma_m = 4.75\%$ per month.

Source: Wagner and Lau [27], p. 52, and Table C, p. 53

security systematic risk is equal to the security beta times σ_m (which is common to all securities), beta is useful as a *relative* risk measure. The β gives the systematic risk of a security (or portfolio) relative to the risk of the market index. Thus it is often convenient to speak of systematic risk in relative terms (i.e., in terms of beta rather than beta times σ_m). ∎

The remainder of "An Introduction to Risk and Return: Concepts and Evidence" will appear in the May/June issue.

Footnotes

1. The transformation changes nothing of substance since

$$\widetilde{M}_T = (1 + \widetilde{R}_P)\, M_0$$
$$= M_0 + M_0 \widetilde{R}_P \,,$$

where

$\widetilde{M}_T$ = terminal portfolio value

$\widetilde{R}_P$ = portfolio return.

Since $\widetilde{M}_T$ is a linear function of $\widetilde{R}_P$, any risk measures developed for the portfolio return will apply equally to the terminal market value.

2. Risk measures based on below-the-average variation are analytically difficult to deal with. H. Markowitz, in Chapter 9 of [18], develops a semivariance statistic which measures variability below the mean and compares it with the more commonly used variance calculation.

3. See for example M. E. Blume [2].

4. This result can be illustrated as follows. The portfolio market value after N years, $\widetilde{M}_N$, is equal to

$$\widetilde{M}_N = M_0 [(1 + \widetilde{R}_{P1})(1 + \widetilde{R}_{P2}) \ldots (1 + \widetilde{R}_{PN})]\,,$$

where M_0 is the initial value, and $\widetilde{R}_{pt}$ (t = 1, ..., N) is the return during year t [as given by Equation (1a)]. For reasonably small values of the annual returns, the above expression can be approximated by

$$\widetilde{M}_N = M_0 [1 + \widetilde{R}_{P1} + \widetilde{R}_{P2} + \ldots + \widetilde{R}_{PN}]\,.$$

Now, if the annual returns, $\widetilde{R}_{pt}$ are independently and identically distributed with variance σ^2, the variance of $\widetilde{M}_N$ will equal $(M_0)^2\, N \sigma^2$, or N times the variance after one year. Therefore, the standard deviation of the terminal value will equal $\sqrt{N}$ times the standard deviation after one year. The key assumption of independence of portfolio returns over time is realistic, since security returns appear to follow a random walk through time.

A similar result could be obtained without the restriction on the size of the $\widetilde{R}_{pt}$ if we had dealt with continuously, as opposed to annually, compounded rates of return. However, the analysis would be more complicated.

5. Two securities with perfectly correlated return patterns will have a correlation coefficient of 1.0. Conversely, if the return patterns are perfectly negative correlated, the correlation coefficient will equal -1. Two securities with uncorrelated (i.e., statistically unrelated returns will have a correlation coefficient of zero. The average correlation coefficient between returns for NYSE securities and the S&P 500 Stock Index during the 1945-1970 period was approximately 0.5.

6. The relationship between the risk components is given by

$$\sigma^2 = \beta^2\, \sigma_m^2 + \sigma_\varepsilon^2$$

This follows directly from Equation (5) and the assumption of statistical independence of R_m and ε'. The R^2 term previously discussed is the ratio of systematic to total risk (both measured in terms of variance):

$$R^2 = \frac{\beta^2\, \sigma_m^2}{\sigma^2}\,.$$

Note also that the R^2 is the square of the correlation coefficient between security and market returns.

7. Assuming the unsystematic returns (ε_j') of securities to be uncorrelated (reasonably true in practice), the unsystematic portfolio risk is given by

$$\sigma^2(\varepsilon_p') = \sum_{j=1}^{N} X_j^2\, \sigma^2(\varepsilon_j')\,,$$

where $\sigma^2(\varepsilon_j')$ is the unsystematic risk for stock j. Assume the portfolio is made up of equal investment in each security and $\bar{\sigma}^2(\varepsilon')$ is the average value of the $\sigma^2(\varepsilon_j')$. Then, $X_i = 1/N$ and

$$\sigma^2(\varepsilon_p') = \frac{1}{N}\, \bar{\sigma}^2(\varepsilon')\,,$$

which (assuming $\bar{\sigma}^2(\varepsilon')$ is finite) obviously approaches zero as the number of issues in the portfolio increases.

References

[1] Black, Fischer, Jensen, Michael C., and Scholes, Myron S. "The Capital Asset Pricing Model: Some Empirical Tests." Published in *Studies in the Theory of Capital Markets*, edited by Michael Jensen. (New York: Praeger, 1972), pp. 79-121.

[2] Blume, Marshall E. "Portfolio Theory: A Step Toward Its Practical Application." *Journal of Business*, Vol. 43 (April 1970), pp. 152-173.

[3] Blume, Marshall E., and Friend, Irwin. "A New Look at the Capital Asset Pricing Model." *Journal of Finance*, Vol. XXVIII (March 1973), pp. 19-33.

[4] Brealey, Richard A. *An Introduction to Risk and Return from Common Stocks*. (Cambridge, Mass.: MIT Press, 1969.)

[5] Fama, Eugene F. "Components of Investment Performance." *The Journal of Finance*, Vol. XXVII (June 1972), pp. 551-567.

[6] Fama, Eugene F., and MacBeth, James D. "Risk, Return and Equilibrium: Empirical Tests." Unpublished Working Paper No. 7237, University of Chicago, Graduate School of Business, August 1972.

[7] Francis, Jack C. *Investment Analysis and Management*. (New York: McGraw-Hill, 1972.)

[8] Friend, Irwin, and Blume, Marshall E. "Risk and the Long Run Rate of Return on NYSE Common Stocks." Working Paper No. 18-72, Wharton School of Commerce and Finance, Rodney L. White Center for Financial Research.

[9] Jacob, Nancy. "The Measurement of Systematic Risk for Securities and Portfolios: Some Empirical Results." *Journal of Financial and Quantitative Analysis*, Vol. VI (March 1971), pp. 815-834.

[10] Jensen, Michael C. "The Performance of Mutual Funds in the Period 1945-1964." *Journal of Finance*, Vol. XXIII (May 1968), pp. 389-416.

[11] Jensen, Michael C. "Risk, the Pricing of Capital Assets, and the Evaluation of Investment Portfolios." *Journal of Business*, Vol. 42 (April 1969), pp. 167-247.

[12] Jensen, Michael C. "Capital Markets: Theory and Evidence." *The Bell Journal of Economics and Management Science*, Vol. 3 (Autumn 1972), pp. 357-398.

[13] Levy, Robert A. "On the Short Term Stationarity of Beta Coefficients." *Financial Analysts Journal*, Vol. 27 (November-December 1971), pp. 55-62.

[14] Lintner, John. "The Valuation of Risk Assets and the Selection of Risky Investments in Stock Portfolios and Capital Budgets." *Review of Economics and Statistics*, Vol. XLVII (February 1965), pp. 13-37.

[15] Lintner, John. "Security Prices, Risk, and Maximal Gains from Diversification." *Journal of Finance*, Vol. XX (December 1965), pp. 587-616.

[16] Mains, Norman E. "Are Mutual Fund Beta Coefficients Stationary?" Unpublished Working Paper, Investment Company Institute, Washington, D.C., October 1972.

[17] Markowitz, Harry M. "Portfolio Selection." *Journal of Finance*, Vol. VII (March 1952), pp. 77-91.

[18] Markowitz, Harry M. *Portfolio Selection: Efficient Diversification of Investments*. (New York: John Wiley and Sons, 1959.)

[19] Miller, Merton H., and Scholes, Myron S. "Rates of Returns in Relation to Risk: A Reexamination of Recent Findings." Published in *Studies in the Theory of Capital Markets*, edited by Michael Jensen. (New York: Praeger, 1972), pp. 47-78.

[20] Modigliani, Franco, and Pogue, Gerald A. *A Study of Investment Performance Fees*. (Lexington, Mass.: Heath-Lexington Books, Forthcoming 1974.)

[21] Pogue, Gerald A., and Conway, Walter. "On the Stability of Mutual Fund Beta Values." Unpublished Working Paper, MIT, Sloan School of Management, June 1972.

[22] Securities and Exchange Commission, *Institutional Investor Study Report of the Securities and Exchange Commission*, Chapter 4, "Investment Advisory Complexes", pp. 325-347. (Washington, D.C.: U.S. Government Printing Office, 1971.)

[23] Sharpe, William F. "Capital Asset Prices: A Theory of Market Equilibrium under Conditions of Risk." *Journal of Finance*, Vol. XIX (September 1964), pp. 425-442.

[24] Sharpe, William F. *Portfolio Theory and Capital Markets*. (New York: McGraw-Hill, 1970.)

[25] Treynor, Jack L. "How to Rate the Management of Investment Funds." *Harvard Business Review*, Vol. XLIII (January-February 1965), pp. 63-75.

[26] Treynor, Jack L. "The Performance of Mutual Funds in the Period 1945-1964: Discussion." *Journal of Finance*, Vol. XXIII (May 1968), pp. 418-419.

[27] Wagner, Wayne H., and Lau, Sheila. "The Effect of Diversification on Risk." *Financial Analysts Journal*, Vol. 26 (November-December 1971), pp. 48-53.

by Charles D. Ellis

The Loser's Game

Disagreeable data are streaming out of the computers of Becker Securities and Merrill Lynch and all the other performance measurement firms. Over and over and over again, these facts and figures inform us that investment managers are failing to perform. Not only are the nation's leading portfolio managers failing to produce positive absolute rates of return (after all, it's been a long, long bear market) but they are also failing to produce positive *relative* rates of return. Contrary to their oft articulated goal of outperforming the market averages, investment managers are not beating the market: The market is beating them.

Faced with information that contradicts what they believe, human beings tend to respond in one of two ways. Some will assimilate the information, changing it—as oysters cover an obnoxious grain of silica with nacre—so they can ignore the new knowledge and hold on to their former beliefs; and others will accept the validity of the new information. Instead of changing the meaning of the new data to fit their old concept of reality, they adjust their perception of reality to accommodate the information and then they put it to use.

Psychologists advise us that the more important the old concept of reality is to a person—the more important it is to his sense of self-esteem and sense of inner worth—the more tenaciously he will hold on to the old concept and the more insistently he will assimilate, ignore or reject new evidence that conflicts with his old and familiar concept of the world. This behavior is particularly common among very bright people because they can so easily develop and articulate self-persuasive logic to justify the conclusions they want to keep.

For example, most institutional investment managers continue to believe, or at least say they believe, that they can and soon will again "outper-

Charles D. Ellis is President of Greenwich Research Associates, Incorporated.

Reprinted by permission of *Financial Analysts Journal* (July/August 1975).

form the market." They won't and they can't. And the purpose of this article is to explain why not.

My experience with very bright and articulate investment managers is that their skills at analysis and logical extrapolation are very good, often superb, but that their brilliance in extending logical extrapolation draws their own attention far away from the sometimes erroneous basic assumptions upon which their schemes are based. Major errors in reasoning and exposition are rarely found in the logical development of this analysis, but instead lie within the premise itself. This is what worried Martin Luther. It's what *The Best and The Brightest* is all about. It's what lifted LTV above $100; why the Emperor went for days without clothes; and why comedians and science fiction writers are so careful first to establish the "premise" and then quickly divert our attention from it so they can elaborate the persuasive details of developing "logic."

The investment management business (it should be a profession but is not) is built upon a simple and basic belief: Professional money managers can beat the market. That premise appears to be false.

If the premise that it is feasible to outperform the market were accepted, deciding how to go about achieving success would be a matter of straightforward logic. First, the market can be represented by an index, such as the S&P 500. Since this is a passive and public listing, the successful manager need only rearrange his bets differently from those of the S&P "shill." He can be an activist in either stock selection or market timing, or both. Since the manager will want his "bets" to be right most of the time, he will assemble a group of bright, well educated, highly motivated, hard working young people, and their collective purpose will be to beat the market by "betting against the house" with a "good batting average."

The belief that active managers can beat the market is based on two assumptions: (1) liquidity offered in the stock market is an advantage, and (2) institutional investing is a Winner's Game.

The unhappy thesis of this article can be briefly stated: Owing to important changes in the past ten years, these basic assumptions are no longer true. On the contrary, market liquidity is a *liability* rather than an *asset,* and institutional investors will, over the long term, *under*perform the market because money management has become a Loser's Game.

Before demonstrating with mathematical evidence why money management has become a Loser's Game, we should close off the one path of escape for those who will try to assimilate the facts. They may argue that this analysis is unfair because so much of the data on performance comes from bear market experience, giving an adverse bias to an evaluation of the long-term capabilities of managers who have portfolio beta's above 1.0. "Of course," they will concede with dripping innuendo, "these interesting analyses may have less to say about dynamic fund managers operating in a decent market." Perhaps, but can they present us with evidence to support their hopes? Can they shoulder the burden of proof? After many hours of discussion with protesting money managers all over America and in Canada and Europe, I have heard no new evidence or persuasive appeal from the hard judgment that follows the evidence presented below. In brief, the "problem" is not a cyclical aberration; it is a long-term secular trend.

The basic characteristics of the environment within which institutional investors must operate have changed greatly in the past decade. The most significant change is that institutional investors have become, and will continue to be, the dominant feature of their own environment. This change has impacted greatly upon all the major features of the investment field. In particular, institutional dominance has converted market liquidity from a source of *profits* to a source of *costs,* and this is the main reason behind the transformation of money management from a Winner's Game to a Loser's Game.

Before analyzing what happened to convert institutional investing from a Winner's Game to a Loser's Game, we should explore the profound difference between these two kinds of "games." In making the conceptual distinction, I will use the writings of an eminent scientist, a distinguished historian, and a reknowned educator. They are, respectively, Dr. Simon Ramo of TRW; naval historian, Admiral Samuel Elliot Morrison; and professional golf instructor, Tommy Armour.

Simon Ramo identified the crucial difference between a Winner's Game and a Loser's Game in his excellent book on playing strategy, *Extraordinary Tennis for the Ordinary Tennis Player.* Over a period of many years, he observed that tennis was not *one* game but *two.* One game of tennis is

---

For the ten years ending December 31, 1974, the funds in the Becker Securities sample had a median rate of return of 0.0 per cent. The S & P total rate of return over the same period was 1.2 per cent per annum. (Within the Becker sample, the high fund's annual rate of return was 4.5 per cent, the first quartile fund's return was 1.1 per cent, the median 0.0 per cent, the third quartile 1.1 per cent and the low fund's annual rate of return 5.6 per cent.)

Unfortunately, the relative performance of institutionally managed portfolios appears to be getting worse. Measuring returns from trough to trough in the market, the institutionally managed funds in the Becker sample are falling farther and farther behind the market as represented by the S & P 500 Average. It appears that the *costs* of active management are going up and that the *rewards* from active management are going down.

	S&P 500 Average	Becker Median	Institutional Shortfall
Last Three Market Cycles (9/30/62 to 12/31/74)	5.3%	4.1%	(0.8%)
Last Two Market Cycles (12/31/66 to 12/31/74)	2.1%	0.4%	(1.7%)
Last Single Market Cycle (9/30/70 to 12/31/74)	2.2%	(0.3%)	(2.5%)

Data: Becker Securities 1974 Institutional Funds Evaluation Service.

played by professionals and a very few gifted amateurs; the other is played by all the rest of us.

Although players in both games use the same equipment, dress, rules and scoring, and conform to the same etiquette and customs, the basic natures of their two games are almost entirely different. After extensive scientific and statistical analysis, Dr. Ramo summed it up this way: Professionals *win* points; amateurs *lose* points. Professional tennis players stroke the ball with strong, well aimed shots, through long and often exciting rallies, until one player is able to drive the ball just beyond the reach of his opponent. Errors are seldom made by these splendid players.

Expert tennis is what I call a Winner's Game because the ultimate outcome is determined by the actions of the *winner*. Victory is due to *winning more points than the opponent wins*—not, as we shall see in a moment, simply to getting a higher score than the opponent, but getting that higher score by *winning* points.

Amateur tennis, Ramo found, is almost entirely different. Brilliant shots, long and exciting rallies, and seemingly miraculous recoveries are few and far between. On the other hand, the ball is fairly often hit into the net or out of bounds, and double faults at service are not uncommon. The amateur duffer seldom *beats* his opponent, but he beats himself all the time. The victor in this game of tennis gets a higher score than the opponent, but he gets that higher score *because his opponent is losing even more points*.

As a scientist and statistician, Dr. Ramo gathered data to test his hypothesis. And he did it in a very clever way. Instead of keeping conventional game scores—"Love," "Fifteen All," "Thirty-Fifteen," etc.—Ramo simply counted points *won* versus points *lost*. And here is what he found. In expert tennis, about 80 per cent of the points are won; in amateur tennis, about 80 per cent of the points are *lost*. In other words, professional tennis is a Winner's Game—the final outcome is determined by the activities of the *winner*—and amateur tennis is a Loser's Game—the final outcome is determined by the activities of the *loser*. The two games are, in their fundamental characteristic, not at all the same. They are opposites.

From this discovery of the two kinds of tennis, Dr. Ramo builds a complete strategy by which ordinary tennis players can win games, sets and matches again and again by following the simple strategem of losing less, and letting the opponent defeat himself.

Dr. Ramo explains that if you choose to win at tennis—as opposed to having a good time—the strategy for winning is to avoid mistakes. The way to avoid mistakes is to be conservative and keep the ball in play, letting the other fellow have plenty of room in which to blunder his way to defeat, because he, being an amateur (and probably not having read Ramo's book) will play a losing game and not know it.

He will make errors. He will make too many errors. Once in a while he may hit a serve you cannot possibly handle, but much more frequently he will double fault. Occasionally, he may volley balls past you at the net, but more often than not they will sail far out of bounds. He will slam balls into the net from the front court and from the back court. His game will be a routine catalogue of gaffs, goofs and grief.

He will try to beat you by winning, but he is not good enough to overcome the many inherent adversities of the game itself. The situation does not allow him to win with an activist strategy and he will instead lose. His efforts to win more points will, unfortunately for him, only increase his error rate. As Ramo instructs us in his book, the strategy for winning in a loser's game is to lose less. Avoid trying too hard. By keeping the ball in play, give the opponent as many opportunities as possible to make mistakes and blunder his way to defeat. In brief, by losing less become the victor.

In his thoughtful treatise on military science, *Strategy and Compromise,* Admiral Morrison makes the following point: "In warfare, mistakes are inevitable. Military decisons are based on estimates of the enemy's strengths and intentions that are usually faulty, and on intelligence that is never complete and often misleading." (This sounds a great deal like the investment business.) "Other things being equal," concludes Morrison, "the side that makes the fewest strategic errors wins the war."

War, as we all know, is the ultimate Loser's Game. As General Patton said: "Let the other poor dumb bastard lose his life for his country." Golf is another Loser's Game. Tommy Armour, in his great book *How to Play Your Best Golf All the Time,* says: "The way to win is by making fewer bad shots."

Gambling in a casino where the house takes at least 20 per cent of every pot is obviously a Loser's Game. Stud poker is a Loser's Game but Night Baseball with deuces, trays and one-eyed Jacks "wild" is a Winner's Game.

Campaigning for elected office is a Loser's Game: The electorate seldom votes *for* one of the candidates but rather *against* the other candidate. Professional politicians advise their candidates: "Help the voters find a way to vote *against* the other guy, and you'll get elected."

Recent studies of professional football have found that the most effective defensive platoon members play an open, ad hoc, enterprising, risk-taking style—the proper strategy for a Winner's Game—while the best offensive players play a careful, "by the book" style that concentrates on avoiding errors and eliminating uncertainty, which is the requisite game plan for a Loser's Game. "Keep it simple," said Vincent Lombardi.

There are many other Loser's Games. Some, like institutional investing, used to be Winner's Games in the past, but have changed with the passage of time into *Loser's Games*. For example, 50 years ago, only very brave, very athletic, very strong willed young people with good eyesight had the nerve to try flying an airplane. In those glorious days, flying was a Winner's Game. But times have changed and so has flying. If you got into a 747 today, and the pilot came aboard wearing a 50-mission hat with a long, white silk scarf around his neck, you'd get off. Those people do not belong in airplanes any longer because flying an airplane today is a Loser's Game. Today, there's only one way to fly an airplane. It's simple: Don't make any mistakes.

Prize fighting starts out as a Winner's Game and becomes a Loser's Game as the fight progresses. In the first three or four rounds, a really strong puncher tries for a knockout. Thereafter, prize fighting is a gruelling contest of endurance to see who can survive the most punishment, while the other fellow gets so worn out that he literally drops to defeat.

Expert card players know that after several rounds of play, games like Gin Rummy go through a "phase change" after which discards no longer improve the relative position of the discarding player. During this latter phase, discards tend to add more strength to the opponent's hand than they remove weakness from the hand of the discarder. This changes long hands of Gin Rummy into a Loser's Game, and the correct strategy in this latter phase of the game is to evaluate discards not in terms of how much good they will do for your hand to get rid of them, but rather how much good they may do for your opponent.

Many other examples could be given, but these will suffice to make the distinction between Winner's Games and Loser's Games, to explain why the requisite player strategy is very different for the two kinds of games, and to show that the fundamental nature of a game can change and that Winner's Games can and sometimes do become Loser's Games. And that's what has happened to the Money Game.

The Money Game was a phenomenal Winner's Game in the mid-1920's when John J. Raskob, a prominent business executive, could write an article for a popular magazine with the encouraging title "Everybody Can Be Rich." The article gave a cookbook recipe that anybody could, theoretically, follow to riches beyond the dreams of avarice. The Great Crash abruptly reversed the situation, and made investing a Loser's Game for nearly two decades.

It was during these decades of the thirties and forties that preservation of capital, emphasis on the safety of bonds, and sobersided conventional wisdom came to dominance and the foundation was laid for the renaissance of the Winner's Game. The bull market of the 1950's gave dramatic and compelling evidence that the situation had changed, that big money could be made in the market. And this news attracted people who like to make big money—people who like to win.

The people who came to Wall Street in the 1960's had always been—and expected always to be—winners. They had been presidents of their high school classes, varsity team captains, and honor students. They were bright, attractive, outgoing and ambitious. They were willing to work hard and take chances because our society had given them many and frequent rewards for such behavior. They had gone to Yale and the Marines and Harvard Business School. And they were quick to recognize that the big Winner's Game was being played in Wall Street.

It was a glorious, wonderful, euphoric time. It was a time when almost anybody who was smart and willing to work hard could win. And almost all of us did.

The trouble with Winner's Games is that they tend to self-destruct because they attract too much attention and too many players—all of whom want to win. (That's why gold rushes finish ugly.) But in the short run, the rushing in of more and more players seeking to win expands the apparent reward. And that's what happened in Wall Street during the 1960's. Riding the tide of a bull market, institutional investors obtained such splendid rates of return in equities that more and more money was turned over to them—particularly in mutual funds and pension funds—which fueled the continuation of their own bull market. Institutional investing was a Winner's Game and the winners knew that by playing it faster, they would increase the rate of winnings. But in the process, a basic change occurred in the investment environment; the market came to be dominated by the institutions.

In just ten years, the market activities of the investing institutions have gone from only 30 per cent of total public transactions to a whopping 70 per cent. And that has made all the difference. No longer are the "New Breed on Wall Street" in the minority; they are now the majority. The professional money manager isn't competing any longer with amateurs who are out of touch with the market; now he competes with other experts.

It's an impressive group of competitors. There are 150 major institutional investors and another 600 small and medium sized institutions operating in the market all day, every day, in the most intensely competitive way. And in the past decade, these institutions have become more active, have developed larger in-house research staffs, and have tapped into the central source of market information and fundamental research provided by institutional brokers. Ten years ago, many institutions were still far out of the mainstream of intensive management; today such an institution, if any exists, would be a rare collector's item.

Competitively active institutional investing has resulted in sharply higher portfolio turnover. The typical equity portfolio turnover has gone from 10 to 30 per cent. As we've already seen, this acceleration in portfolio activity plus the growth in institutional assets and the shift of pension funds toward equities have increased the proportion of market transactions of institutions from 30 to 70 per cent which has, in turn, produced the basic "phase change" that has transformed portfolio activity from a source of incremental profits to a major cost, and that transformation has switched institutional investing from a Winner's Game to a Loser's Game.

The new "rules of the game" can be set out in a simple but distressing equation. The elements are these:

(a) Assume equities will return an average nine per cent rate of return.[1]
(b) Assume average turnover of 30 per cent per annum.
(c) Assume average costs—dealer spreads plus commissions—on institutional transactions are three per cent of the principal value involved.[2]

---

1. Use of nine per cent is for convenience only, and is an accommodation to its conventional acceptance. If time permitted, I'd prefer to justify and then use a figure of, perhaps, 12 per cent for the next decade which would reflect the market's reflection of expected inflation.

2. This estimate was made by the senior trading partner of a major institutional block trading firm. Other experts indicate this estimate may be low.

(d) Assume management and custody fees total 0.20 per cent.
(e) Assume the goal of the manager is to outperform the averages by 20 per cent.

Solve for "X": $(X \cdot 9) - [30 \cdot (3+3)] - (0.20) = (120 \cdot 9)$

$$X = \frac{[30 \cdot (3+3)] + (0.20) + (120 \cdot 9)}{9}$$

$$X = \frac{1.8 + 0.20 + 10.8}{9}$$

$$X = \frac{12.8}{9}$$

$$X = 142\%.$$

In plain language, the manager who intends to deliver *net* returns 20 per cent better than the market must earn a gross return before fees and transactions costs (liquidity tolls) that is more than 40 per cent better than the market. If this sounds absurd, the same equation can be solved to show that the active manager must beat the market *gross* by 22 per cent just to come out even with the market *net*.

In other words, for the institutional investor to perform as well as, *but no better than,* the S&P 500, he must be sufficiently astute and skillful to "outdo" the market by 22 per cent. But how can institutional investors hope to outperform the market by such a magnitude when, in effect, they *are* the market today? Which managers are so well staffed and organized in their operations, or so prescient in their investment policies that they can honestly expect to beat the other professionals by so much on a sustained basis?

The disagreeable numbers from the performance measurement firms say there are *no* managers whose past performance promises that they will outperform the market in the future. Looking backward, the evidence is deeply disturbing: 85 per cent of professionally managed funds underperformed the S&P 500 during the past 10 years. And the median fund's rate of return was only 5.4 per cent—about 10 per cent *below* the S&P 500.

Most money managers have been losing the Money Game. And they know it, even if they cannot admit it publicly. Expectations and promises have come down substantially since the mid-1960's. Almost nobody still talks in terms of beating the market by 20 per cent compounded annually. And nobody listens to those who do.

In times like these, the burden of proof is on the person who says, "I am a winner. I can win the Money Game." Because only a sucker backs a "winner" in a Loser's Game, we have a right to expect him to explain exactly what he is going to do and why it is going to work so very well. This is not very often done in the investment management business.

Does the evidence necessarily lead to an entirely passive or index portfolio? No, it doesn't necessarily lead in that direction. Not quite. But the "null" hypothesis is hard to beat in a situation like this. At the risk of over-simplifying, the null hypothesis says there is nothing there if you cannot find statistically significant evidence of its presence. This would suggest to investment managers, "Don't do anything because when you try to do something, it is on average a mistake." And if you can't beat the market, you certainly should consider joining it. An index fund is one way. The data from the performance measurement firms show that an index fund would have outperformed most money managers.

For those who are determined to try to win the Loser's Game, however, here are a few specific things they might consider.

First, be sure you are playing your own game. Know your policies very well and play according to them all the time. Admiral Morrison, citing the *Concise Oxford Dictionary,* says: "Impose upon the enemy the time and place and conditions for fighting preferred by oneself." Simon Ramo suggests: "Give the other fellow as many opportunities as possible to make mistakes, and he will do so."

Second, keep it simple. Tommy Armour, talking about golf, says: "Play the shot you've got the greatest chance of playing well." Ramo says: "Every game boils down to doing the things you do best, and doing them over and over again." Armour again: "Simplicity, concentration, and economy of time and effort have been the distinguishing features of the great players' methods, while others lost their way to glory by wandering in a maze of details." Mies Van der Rohe, the architect, suggests, "Less is more." Why not bring turnover down as a deliberate, conscientious practice? Make fewer and perhaps better investment decisions. Simplify the professional investment management problem. Try to do a few things unusually well.

Third, concentrate on your defenses. Almost all of the information in the investment management business is oriented toward purchase decisions. The competition in making purchase decisions is too good. It's too hard to outperform the other fellow in buying. Concentrate on selling instead. In a Winner's Game, 90 per cent of all research effort should be spent on making purchase decisions; in a Loser's Game, most researchers should spend most of their time making sell decisions. Almost all of the really big trouble that you're going to experience in the next year is in your portfolio right now; if you could reduce some of those really big problems, you might come out the winner in the Loser's Game.

Fourth, don't take it personally. Most of the people in the investment business are "winners" who have won all their lives by being bright, articulate, disciplined and willing to work hard. They are so accustomed to succeeding by trying harder and are so used to believing that failure to succeed is the failure's own fault that they may take it personally when they see that the average professionally managed fund cannot keep pace with the market any more than John Henry could beat the steam drill.

There is a class of diseases which are called "iatrogenic" meaning they are doctor-caused. The Chinese finger cage and the modern straightjacket most tightly grip the person who struggles to break free. Ironically, the reason institutional investing has become the Loser's Game is that in the complex problem each manager is trying to solve, his efforts to find a solution—and the efforts of his many urgent competitors—have become the dominant variables. And their efforts to beat the market are no longer the most important part of the solution; they are the most important part of the problem. ■

EVOLUTION OF MODERN PORTFOLIO THEORY

PROFESSOR WILLIAM F. SHARPE*

In this paper, I will do a sweep of the theory of finance as it applies to investment management. I will note quite a bit about the past, a bit about the present and somewhat less about the future, and I will speculate some as to where we may be going in terms of investment theory. I will also mention some ways in which newer elements of theory have been put into practice.

KEY INGREDIENTS

I will indicate first the things that I consider the key ingredients in the development of investment theory. We will start in the 1900's with Irving Fisher. He published over a number of years and was the first to put together in a methodical way the ideas of discounting, interest rate determination, and present value. There were many precursors, but Fisher really put together the way in which the society's time preference (peoples' preferences for goods over time) interacts with productive opportunities to determine interest rates—and the way in which present value is related to future prospects via discounting. This was an elegant view of the world, although it was thought to apply primarily to bonds and instruments where the payoffs were known with certainty, and usually where the payments were level up to maturity, with a par payment at the end.

In 1938 John Burr Williams published a superb book, *The Theory of Investment Value*. The appendix has some of the finest security analysis you will ever see. Dr. Williams took the Fisherian view and applied it to stocks. He was the first really to deal with the valuation of growth stocks and, in general, with instruments whose payments were not level followed by a par payment. So he was the first to give us a theory of investment value for equity instruments, although this theory also dealt primarily with investment instruments where you could predict with some certainty the streams of payments.

Unfortunately, this book was not very influential in its day. People in the industry were caught up in Graham & Dodd, which took a somewhat different view of the world, and did not have a rigorous theoretical underpinning. People in the academy were not very interested in investments to the extent that they were concentrated primarily on bonds. The Williams' book did not really come into its own until perhaps twenty years later. This, by the way, was the inspiration for the dividend discount model (now called DDM in the industry), which is the bedrock for several modern valuation systems. The idea that present value is the value of future prospects discounted at an appropriate rate is now standard in virtually every finance course. In Williams' time the question of the appropriate rate was a little obscure. A notion existed that the riskier the investment, the greater should be the discount rate, but with no detailed specification as to how one ought to view risk or the relationship between the discount rate and risk.

---

*Dr. Sharpe is Timken Professor of Finance at Stanford University's Graduate School of Business. In addition to his academic involvement, he has had extensive experience as a consultant to the investment management community and as an advisor to institutional portfolio managers. This paper is based on a talk given at Wells Fargo Bank on June 18, 1979.

The next date in my chronology is 1952—truly a watershed year. It was then that Harry Markowitz published his first article on portfolio analysis. For the first time, rigorous theory dealt with risk. Before, there had been an understanding that there was risk in the world, and that people didn't like it. Somehow, one ought to value something as being worth less (other things being equal), the riskier it was. This was about the level of sophistication at the time. With Markowitz's portfolio theory in 1952 we had a major breakthrough! We had the other side of the risk/return combination. This approach was *normative*; that is, *prescriptive*. Markowitz was addressing the issue of how you *should* manage a portfolio, how you *should* take into account risk versus return. We shall see that this differs from some of the later work.

The next ingredient came from a paper by Tobin in 1958. Tobin observed that the ability to borrow and lend allows one to dichotomize the portfolio selection process into the selection of a good combination of say, equities, with leverage being used to tailor the mix to the client's attitude towards risk. At this stage we were still in a normative context, concentrating on what one should do, without much analysis as to where the numbers came from or the state of the world in which one does such things.

The next phase, beginning in the 1960's, dealt with efficient markets and equilibrium theory. This was *positive,* or *descriptive* analysis—an attempt to model using simplifications and abstractions of what the world is really like. What *is* the relationship between risk and return in actual markets? This approach really has two rather different strands. The first was basically empirical—the so-called random walk literature. People observed that stock prices and prices of commodity futures seemed to follow no predictable patterns. The allusion was made that the track a stock price makes on a chart is very similar to a path a drunk would make staggering across a field if you looked down from a helicopter. "There is no sense in the stock market," is one way it was put. But on reflection, it was pointed out that this is the way it ought to be. If the price of a stock reflects everything that is now known about the future, then the only thing that will cause a major change in the price will be new information, and new information by definition involves surprise. A surprise (by definition) is as likely to be a happy surprise as it is to be a depressing one. Anything that you now know about what is coming in the future will already be incorporated in the price. This leads to the notion that in an efficient market, a market in which prices reflect future prospects as they are now known, you should expect price behavior that is essentially random.

This approach suggests that the *intrinsic value* of a stock ought to follow a kind of random walk. But it still begs the question because it doesn't specify what value is. To know what is meant by saying price will equal value and value will follow a random walk, you have to have some notion as to what value is. What *is* the relationship between present value and future prospects, taking risk into account? This was the task undertaken by the *Capital Asset Pricing Model*—a model of the relationship between risk and return in a market that is efficient, in which knowledge is widely available and incorporated efficiently into stock prices. We will look at this and some of its extensions.

The late 1960's through the mid-1970's was a period of confrontation in which there were, in effect, warring camps. People in the academy were saying, "We have looked at all of these models and we have figured out that the market is efficient. This suggests that the best way to own a portfolio is to buy the S&P's 500, or something like it, and then sit on it. Furthermore, all the activity going on, or at least 98% of the activity going on in investment management organizations, is superfluous at best and a waste of money at worst. Therefore, you all ought to go out of business or go into highly passive management." Those were not the words being used then, but that is how it would be said today.

People in the investment industry found this a difficult pill to swallow and took a different position. "We will search for the chink in the armor. If we can find just one little place where the market is not efficient, or find some assumptions in the theory that are really far too extreme, we will just ignore everything the academics are saying."

Both sides took extreme positions. People on the industry side could not bring themselves to take what was good from the equilibrium theory and use that as a context in which to operate. On the other side, the academics, being classical statisticians, took as a prior belief the idea that the market is perfectly efficient, and refused to change their beliefs unless presented with overwhelming evidence of inefficiency. This kind of hard-headedness on both sides was most unfortunate.

As one would expect, there had to be a happy ending. It came in the 1970's Modern Portfolio Theory (a term which *Institutional Investor* has given to us). I do not know what *Institutional Investor* means by Modern Portfolio Theory, but I am going to give you my definition of the term.

Here, too, are two strands. The first involves *expanded equilibrium theories;* in other words, bringing in more aspects from the real world. An example of this would be considering tax effects and their implications for security prices and then expanding the basic theory as to the nature of the world to see what an efficient market with some of these complications might look like. Most of the work along these lines is being done by academics.

The other strand of Modern Portfolio Theory might best be characterized as *portfolio management in a nearly efficient market.* Another variation is portfolio management in an efficient market. If the market is efficient, but more complicated than we used to think it was, there is work to be done—difficult and sophisticated work. If the market is not perfectly efficient, even more work needs to be done. Note that here we are back in a normative or prescriptive mode. We are asking, as Markowitz did earlier, what *should* you do? How *should* you manage money? The difference is that it is now being done in the context of an efficient, or nearly efficient, market. In other words, we are putting together our understanding of the world as it is with techniques for operating efficiently in that world. So, we have come full circle; we are back to a prescriptive mode while taking advantage of what we have learned over the past 20 years concerning the environment in which we operate.

MARKOWITZ'S PORTFOLIO THEORY

Let us now consider the major ingredients. Much of this will be familiar, but it is helpful to see it again in sequence, because sometimes we tend to lose sight of the interrelationships among the pieces. Let us begin with Markowitz (1952). The first observation that Markowitz made was that you should think of a portfolio in terms of its return *and* its risk. It is important to understand that all of this theory is *forward-looking.* What return do you expect in the future? What risk do you assess looking forward? In the investment business we have tended to rely to a major extent on past behavior for estimating most aspects of risk. This is a procedure that works well in some cases and not so well in others. The theory has to do with forward-looking risk and forward-looking return. These should be estimated as best one can, using everything available—past data, computer runs, judgment, industry knowledge, etc. It is important not to associate the theory with some of the implementation, which has relied (perhaps slavishly) on past relationships for projection into the future, as the two are separable.

A portfolio has a return and a risk and lots of portfolios exist. If we plotted enough of them, the circumscribed area in Figure 1 would be full of dots. Markowitz's observation was: given the portfolios that one might consider with the same risk, clearly the best one in that risk category is the one with the highest return. This is the notion of an *efficient portfolio,* one that gives the highest return for a given level of total portfolio risk. In general, many portfolios are efficient, plotting along the curve at the top of the area in Figure 1.

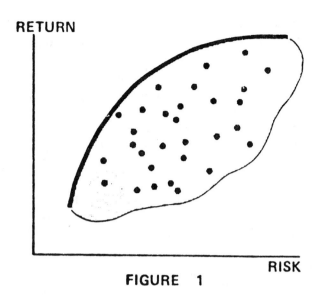

FIGURE 1

The task of investment management (after estimating all the risk and returns) is to limit consideration to efficient portfolios--in other words, to weed out the inefficient combinations in order to concentrate on the efficient ones. Markowitz noted that to do this you have to use mathematical programming, a complicated—and, at the time, expensive—procedure. While other procedures may get you close, to get all the way to efficiency you have to use very sophisticated procedures that have to be done by computers. It is unreasonable to assume that even smart, hard-working, dedicated human beings can routinely deal with this very complicated problem and get all the way to the efficient frontier. It is a matter of conjecture as to how close human beings can get, but the argument made then (and now by myself and others) is that there is no reason not to use these procedures to get all the way there. And, of course, since 1952 the cost of these procedures has come down dramatically. Computer costs are miniscule now compared to 1952, and we are also much more clever now about procedures for doing this job.

The other observation Markowitz made was: of the efficient portfolios, the best for a given client depends on that client's attitude toward risk versus return. One can plausibly assume that nobody likes risk and everybody likes return, but the question is how much risk one is willing to tolerate in order to get more return. As you consider portfolios moving along the frontier in Figure 1 (from left to right), you are taking on more risk in order to get more return. The question is where on that tradeoff should a particular account be? The idea is that an investment manager should tailor the account so that the highly risk-tolerant client, not very averse to risk, should be given a portfolio on the upper right-hand portion of the frontier portfolio, and the one who is very risk-averse would be given one on the lower left-hand portion.

TOBIN'S SEPARATION THEOREM

In 1958 Tobin noted that something was left out of Markowitz's analysis. Markowitz told us to concentrate on the portfolios that fell along an efficient frontier like that in Figure 1. If, in fact, the only portfolios available were portfolios that were risky, then that is right. But what if something is available like a Treasury bill—something with a fixed return so it is known for certain that you are going to earn a given amount in nominal terms over the next year? That changes the picture. For example, if you take the portfolio that plots at point A in Figure 2 and the Treasury bill that plots at point T and split your money, putting half in one and half in the other, you will end up with a risk and a return that will plot precisely half way between the two points. If you take portfolio B and do the same thing, you will end up with a risk and return half way between points B and T. By changing the mix between B and Treasury bills, you can find a combination of risk and return anywhere along the line between T and B. Moreover, if you could borrow at the Treasury bill rate, then by leveraging portfolio B you could get to a point where you would have more return on your assets (because you are borrowing at a lower rate than you expect to make) and also more risk (because you are leveraged). If you make the rather strong assumption that a client can borrow or lend at the same rate, then the whole picture changes and you are led to the conclusion that there is one *optimal combination of risky assets* (point M in Figure 2), and the risky portion of every portfolio should be put in that particular portfolio mixed with Treasury bills and/or leveraging to taste. The idea is that you have a single optimal portfolio that, given your estimates of risk and return, is the best mix of, say, equities; you deal with the tailoring aspect by adjusting the bond/stock mix.

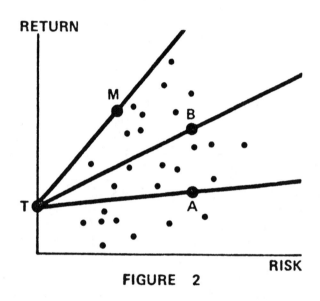

FIGURE 2

THE CAPITAL ASSET PRICING MODEL

Tobin's separation theorem leads directly to the Capital Asset Pricing Model. I am always a little embarrassed showing how simple the basic ideas behind the Capital Asset Pricing Model are, with not very much to it, if you strip it down to its bare bones. First, let us assume a pool of information is available in the society about the future and that this information is fairly widely known, fairly widely understood, and fairly widely analyzed. Further, let's assume that the people who make the market—that is, who really determine the prices—are either explicitly or implicitly doing what Markowitz said they ought to do. These are very strong assumptions. But, as with other exercises in economic analysis, one does not ask, "Are the assumptions rigorously plausible?" because, of course, they are not. Rather, the question is, "Do the implications accord reasonably with reality?" As we will see, the implications do accord rather well.

Having made these assumptions and recognizing what Markowitz and Tobin said, one is led very rapidly to the following conclusion. First, everybody will draw the same picture, because everyone is doing the same analysis, running the same computer programs, etc. Second, everybody is going to come to the same conclusions about the best mix of stocks. But how can all investment managers agree on the best mix of stocks? They cannot, unless that mix happens to be the *market portfolio*—a portfolio of all stocks in market value proportions. If everyone were led to the conclusion that some other mix was better, everyone would try to buy this mix. But it is impossible for everyone to hold something other than the market and, therefore, prices would have to adjust. The first big implication of the Capital Asset Pricing Model is that under these very strong assumptions the only efficient combination of risky securities would be the market portfolio. Any combination that does not look like the market portfolio would be inefficient. The market portfolio would be the best risky portfolio, and anything that diverges significantly from the market portfolio would be inferior exante and, over the long run would be inferior ex-post.

This was the basis for the index fund. Of course the S&P's 500 is not the market portfolio, it is a piece of the market portfolio—a large piece, but not the entire piece. The Capital Asset Pricing Model, however, was the logical foundation for the index fund. The implication was that the market portfolio over time would beat most non-market portfolios—that is, portfolios that diverge significantly from the market. In fact, the S&P's 500 (which is not even the market portfolio in its entirety) has done exceedingly well compared to most actively-managed funds, so this is one implication that holds up pretty well.

Another implication is that the smart investment managers, in fact, will hold portfolios that look like the market. One may argue as to the intelligence of some of one's colleagues in the business, but we know that most pension funds (if one thinks of the funds as a whole) and most other large institutionalized funds are highly related to the market. Something like 95 percent or more of what happens to a given fund can be attributed to movements in the market as a whole. Most large institutionalized funds are at the moment very close to market surrogates (indeed, they are very close to the S&P's 500). So this implication also stands up well when compared with the real world.

Another big message from the Capital Asset Pricing Model is summed up in Figure 3. On the vertical axis is return and on the horizontal axis is *beta*. Beta is a measure of the sensitivity of a

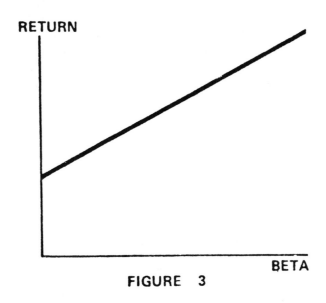

FIGURE 3

security to moves in the market. A security with a beta of 1.00 moves on average about 1 for 1 with market moves. A security with a beta of 1.5 (like an airline) is aggressive—it tends to move 50% more than the market in a market move. A security with a beta of 0.5 is defensive—it tends to move 50% as much. The Capital Asset Pricing Model says beta is the thing you ought to focus on when you think about risk. Why? First, because the model suggests a portfolio view. One is not interested in the risk of a security per se, one is interested in the contribution that security will make to the risk of a portfolio. But what portfolio? An efficient one; and the Capital Asset Pricing Model says that smart people hold portfolios that look a lot like the market.

Beta, thus, measures the contribution of a security to the risk of an efficient portfolio. It deals with the kind of risk that is related to the market, and that remains even in a highly diversified portfolio. Other components of risk (non-market risk) tend to wash out through the diversification process. Although market risk is a small part of the risk of an individual security (somewhere about 25 percent on average), it is an exceedingly large part of the risk of an efficient portfolio and of almost every large institutional portfolio. It is this kind of risk that is relevant in a portfolio context. If the market is efficient, this is the kind of risk that will be rewarded. The Security Market Line in Figure 3 summarizes this relationship. It says that if the market is sensible, securities will be priced so that those with high betas will have high expected returns, and vice versa—a very plausible notion. Many variations concern the magnitude of the slope, whether or not it is perfectly linear or maybe curved a little bit, etc. But the basic idea is simply that the most important measure of risk for a security is one that captures its contribution to the risk of an efficient portfolio. Beta is such a measure. In an efficient market, securities will be priced so that bad news (more risk) is accompanied by good news (more return).

EXPANDED CAPITAL ASSET PRICING MODELS

The Security Market Line, as part of an ongoing valuation element in the investment management process, is now being used by many investment management firms. The first major expansion was based on some work done by Brennan in 1970 having to do with the fact that people pay taxes, and usually pay more taxes on dividends than on capital gains. One might therefore surmise that, in the market, securities that pay more of their return in the form of yield are, other things being equal, not as desirable for investment by tax-paying entities as those that pay more of their return in the form of capital gains.

Figure 4 shows the implications of this complication; the front face shows the familiar Security Market Line. In an efficient market, securities with higher betas, other things being equal, will be priced to provide higher expected returns. The side face shows that securities with higher yields (that pay more of their return in the form of taxable dividends) should be priced to provide higher total returns. In other words, they should provide a higher *before-tax* return so that *after-tax,* the "typical" (taxable) investor will end up even. The hypothesis is that there is a Security Market Plane relating return to beta *and* yield, and that in a perfectly efficient market every security would plot on such a plane.

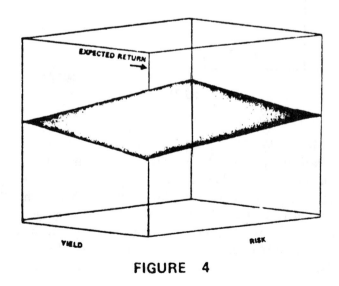

EXPECTED RETURN

YIELD   RISK

FIGURE 4

As an empirical issue, what does that plane look like? How steep is it with respect to beta? How steep is it with respect to yield? The idea goes back to 1970, but was not seriously considered until quite recently. Only recently have sophisticated-enough empirical procedures been applied to historical data to convince at least some people that this phenomenon really exists. Securities with higher yields on average have done better before taxes. Some questions still exist about the precise nature of this relationship, but it seems prudent to acknowledge it and incorporate it in the investment process.

Other extensions have been made. For example, if people care more about purchasing power than about nominal dollar value, securities that are better hedges against inflation would be more desirable. If the market is efficient, however, such securities would be priced to provide lower returns. The idea is that an efficient market has no free lunch. The good news is that a given stock is a better hedge against inflation; the bad news is that you can expect to do a little worse because of this desirable property. It is a very straightforward matter to put this in a model.

Other extensions are seen. Stocks that are more liquid should presumably be more appealing and, therefore, should be priced to provide somewhat lower expected returns. As a practical matter, one needs to be able to predict in advance which stocks are the better inflation hedges or will be more liquid in order to use this in an ongoing investment mangement process. Thus far, we have not been able to do a good enough job predicting some of the other factors that are undoubtedly important in the abstract but that, because of lack of predictability, may not be reflected in security prices. The yield effect is one about which we feel strongly that we have crossed the threshold. It is predictable enough, and it is something that can and should be incorporated in the investment management process. We have not given up hope on some of the other ideas, but they have yet to be proven as practical.

It is important to understand that, even if the market were perfectly efficient with every security plotting right on the plane, the investment management process would still require sophisticated procedures. In particular, it would require the tailoring of portfolios to meet clients' attitudes toward risk and clients' attitudes toward yield vis-a-vis gains. For example, a tax-exempt client should be given a portfolio that has an above-average yield in order to get the reward in higher before-tax return that the market is offering. Clients in very high tax brackets should be given portfolios that have below-average yields. Only the client whose tax bracket is in a sense "typical" of the tax bracket impounded in the market should be given a broadly represented market portfolio. Whereas the earlier Capital Asset Pricing Model suggested that the market portfolio would be fine for everybody, this extension suggests that it is not the best portfolio for the tax-exempt client. The yield-tilted passive funds recently making their appearance represent the first implementation of this idea.

PORTFOLIO MANAGEMENT IN A NEARLY EFFICIENT MARKET

That is the efficient market story. Now let us consider the other part of Modern Portfolio Theory—portfolio managment in a nearly efficient market. In a sense, the investment management process has always been intended to find securities whose prices depart from value. The whole business of active management is one of finding "mispriced" securities. But people often lose sight of the fact that you cannot talk about a security being mispriced unless you have some fairly fixed notion about what it means to say a security is correctly priced. To say that you have a notion of what correct pricing means is to say that you have a valuation model. You cannot escape the problem of selecting a valuation model if you are going to be in active management and operate in any logical manner.

Let me illustrate in terms of the Security Market Plane. In an efficient market everything would be priced to plot on the Security Market Plane. To say that someone has made a mistake is to say that a security is priced so that it does not plot on the plane. For example, looking forward you might observe a security priced so that, given your predictions, its expected return is 17%, whereas the plane says that a security of that risk and yield so priced will return 2% per year more than it should. It is clearly underpriced if your estimate is right. This is summarized with *alpha*—the other Greek letter that we use often. Alpha means simply the extent to which you think the security is going to return more (if it is positive) or less (if it is negative) than it ought to, given your estimation of the valuation relationship as it exists in the market today.

The trick of investment management is, first to come up with good estimates of alpha and, second to trade them off against risk. This is also true in the yield-tilt business. when you decide that you are going to tilt a portfolio away from the market yield, you still must determine how far to go because, as you go away from market proportions, you take on non-market risk. One has to balance additional return with the additional risk. In the case of active managemment, to the extent that you are right about your alphas, you want to overload the portfolio with positive alphas. You want to hold more of each of them than you would normally hold in a passive portfolio, because you think they are underpriced. But as you concentrate on fewer and fewer securities, portfolio risk builds because you are losing diversification. How do you trade these aspects off? To do so you need two things: a very good set of risk estimates, and mathematical programming—a procedure that can perform the very delicate act of balancing off the return against the risk. Inside some organizations, it looks as though the security analysis process does turn up cases of mispricing, but the portfolio managment process manages to take all the good out of the system, so the portfolios do not beat the market after costs. Several explanations are possible. One worthy of serious consideration is that the balancing of risk versus return is so delicate that it cannot be done effectively by a traditional investment management organization. The hope is that organizations that first implement effective procedures, such as mathematical programming, will be able to outperform those that do so later. Of course, when everybody does it, the game will be lost, but that day will not come for awhile.

Another piece of this process is often lost sight of. It is important to recognize that what is important is not what you think is going to happen, but what is likely to happen when you think what you think. Let us say that General Motors looks from the Security Market Plane as though it is priced so that it will return 17% per year for many years when it ought to return 15%. You assign what might be called an "over-time" or *slow game alpha* of 2% to General Motors. What you really care about is what you think General Motors will do next year. Will General Motors do better or worse than it ought to? In particular, what is the relationship between the slow game alpha and what might be called the "next-year" or *fast game alpha*—the best estimate of the extent to which a security is going to do better or worse than it should over the next twelve months? Two things can happen. First, let us say that you are right and over the next year the market will realize that you were right. The market is going to revalue that stock so that over the next twelve months you are not going to make 2%. Instead you will make 10% or 20% or 30%. This would lead you to expect that the actual abnormal return over the next twelve months might be considerably larger than the 2% obtained from the valuation process. On the other hand, maybe the market was right and you were wrong; maybe what you saw was just an error in your predictions or your Security Market Plane or maybe you were just a little right. If so, while you expected an abnormal return of 2%, the actual magnitude might be, say, ½ of 1%.

What is most likely to happen over the next twelve months may, thus, differ in either direction from what you expect, so it is imperative to estimate your *predictive accuracy*—the relationship between whatever you are predicting (be it alphas, earnings, or whatever) and what is really likely to happen in terms of abnormal performance over some reasonable forthcoming holding period.

It is remarkable how few organizations do this. How can you possibly be in the active management business without having any notion concerning the accuracy of your predictions? If your predictions are superb, you ought to buy very few stocks; if they are poor, you ought to buy a great many; if they are in between, you ought to do something in between. But, if you do not know how good you are, you run one of two risks: either you will think you are better than you are, become too concentrated, take on too much risk, and make your client worse off; or you will not think you are as good as you are, you will not concentrate enough, and your client will not get the good out of your predictions. It is a delicate balancing act, and you not only need to know how to do it, but you also need all the ingredients. Predictive accuracy is one of the major ingredients.

One organization I am familiar with has worked very hard to understand the relationship between its alphas, as predicted at the beginning of the year, and actual abnormal performance over subsequent periods. The good news is that, by and large, the fast game alphas are larger than the slow game alphas, so it looks as though the market catches up with the organization's predictions, outweighing the effects of wrong predictions.

Many other things go on in the Modern Portfolio Theory area. One important part of this exercise is finding out what the client is all about—where one client differs from another. This involves all kinds of things for personal trust accounts. For institutional accounts, it requires an attempt to really understand a client's attitude towards risk, yield, etc. Generally one cannot go to a client, even a sophisticated one, and say, "Here is our current tradeoff between return and risk. Where on that tradeoff would you like to be?" The client will say, "What do you mean by return?" You might say, "Well, we expect 10%." "What do you mean by risk?" "Well, a standard deviation of 18.3%." Alternatively, you could say to the client, "Here is a probability distribution of rate of return and here is another one; which one do you prefer?" From this you can infer something about the client's risk aversion. What you have got to do is put the problem in a context the client can understand, using the kinds of numbers the client deals with.

In this connection the industry has gone quite far in the pension fund area because enough money is available to pay for sophisticated analysis. For example, we can use "Monte Carlo" procedures that draw balls out of urns inside the computer. You say to the client, "Here are eleven different bond/stock mixes—all bonds, 90% bonds, and so on down to 0% bonds, with the rest in stocks. For each one, here is a picture of the impact on your pension fund. If we use all bonds, then given your actuarial procedures, etc., our estimate is that ten years from now you are going to be, most likely, about 90% funded; but if things turn out badly you could be, say, 80% funded; and if things turn out well you could be 100% funded. In contrast, if we use all stocks, our best estimate is that ten years from now you will be 100% funded and you will not have to be contributing much. Again, however, if things do not go well you are going to be 30% funded and your contributions will be large."

This theme has variations, but the idea is to embed our understanding of the risk/return tradeoff in the context of the client's own personal or institutional situation. Characterizing the situation as a choice between different bond/stock mixes gives us two things. First, we get a strategic bond/stock mix; we know where that client ought to be positioned in terms of bonds and stocks under normal circumstances. Second, we get an inside look into the client's attitude towards risk and return, which can then be used as part of the ongoing management process, both in altering the bond/stock mix as markets change, and in stock selection. At present much remains to be done in the personal account area along these lines.

Another aspect of Modern Portfolio Theory is performance measurement. We now have procedures that not only tell you what you have done, but also help to identify why you have done what you have done. What are you good at? What are you bad at? We still have challenges, however, and the statistical problems are very great. In a sense, by the time you have enough data on the investment management organization to know really what it is good at, all the people have either died or gone to another organization. But the situation is far from hopeless and careful performance measurement can provide relevant information for decision making.

CURRENT AND FUTURE RESEARCH

Let me briefly identify where I think research is going. I will focus on academic research because that is an area I am closer to. Much of the current research in finance deals with the pricing of instruments such as options and commodity futures. Quite a bit of research also deals with the pricing of instruments such as bonds, where a lot of attention is paid to the fact that money is paid over different periods. Most of the work that we have talked about concentrates on a single period view. In other words, it focuses on risk and sweeps under the rug the multi-period nature of the instrument. This assumption appears to be satisfactory, given the way stock prices behave, but not so satisfactory given the way bond prices behave.

One of the strands of research (the one I consider the most important) is an attempt to derive a single, generalized theory of value that, at a satisfactory level of rigor, will incorporate both the time dimension and the risk dimension. At the moment we have two very rigorous theories and a practical marriage between them. One deals very elegantly with time (the Fisherian analysis and its extensions), one deals elegantly with risk (the Capital Asset Pricing Model and its extensions); the marriage of the two works fairly well, but is not quite as elegant as we would like it to be. A potential breakthrough in this area has been made by Douglas Breeden. He has found that under plausible conditions the longer, multi-period problem collapses to something that looks very much like the Capital Asset Pricing Model. The major difference is that betas are measured not relative to the market portfolio but, rather, relative to a measure of the unanticipated change in the level of consumption in the economy. It is too early to tell whether we are going to be able to implement this idea, but initial tests suggest that what we have been doing may be a good surrogate for this broader approach. It may well be that this will provide a theoretical foundation which will give us solace that what we have been doing all along is perfectly all right.

I look for continuing efforts to obtain an integrated generalized theory that will have many of the attributes of the theories we now use in practice. The development of specialized models will continue for valuation of particular instruments, such as convertible bonds, certain kinds of variable-rate mortgages, commodities futures, options, etc. I think most of the research in Modern Portfolio Theory (in the sense that I have used the term here) will be done in investment management organizations themselves and to a much lesser extent in the academic environment. This is partly because it involves a lot of work and partly because academics are still much more interested in models of efficient markets than they are in ways in which one might exploit inefficiencies, if found. I do not think that this is bad but I am a little depressed that my colleagues do not do more research on portfolio management per se.

I have only scratched the surface of this subject. I hope that this paper has provided a context within which one can fit some of the pieces of the approach, and that it will help to furnish a larger view of the available material.

THE DESIGN AND CONTROL OF LARGE PORTFOLIOS

JAMES R. VERTIN, C.F.A.

This panel is concerned with a very neatly stated challenge: "the design and control of large portfolios to achieve explicit investment objectives in changing market and economic conditions." This description captures completely what the asset management business is all about: the efficient creation and systematic maintenance of portfolios that directly and continuously relate to objectively-stated client goals. I would call this the "ABC's" of investment management. (For you fellow travelers, those "ABC's" are, of course, Alpha, Beta and Sigma!). The description also captures the sense of dynamics that pervades our business, the fact of continuous change in the social, political, economic and psychological environment, against which we must pit our methods and our judgments day in and day out. In all, an illuminating description of a challenge worthy of our most serious attention and our most enterprising ingenuity.

The focus of my paper is the pension portfolio, at once both the "cleanest" of account types and the most demanding. And, I'm assuming that the portfolio will be actively, not passively, managed. In the introduction to a 1977 article in the *Financial Analysts Journal* by Sidney Cottle, the pension management future is described (in part) as follows: "With the passage of ERISA, setting explicit portfolio objectives (has become) a critical task. Objectives must match the pension sponsor's needs with what the money manager can reasonably attain in the expected investment environment, balancing risk against return. Pension executives are now beginning to appraise both risk and return within a systematic framework and to specify them in quantitative terms. In response, we can expect pronounced changes in the way money managers organize the investment decision-making process ....'While they may not come about quickly or easily, (these) changes are inevitable. The management of pension portfolios will become more and more a discipline and less and less an art."

These observations add dimension to the challenge of this panel. We are no longer alone with the money; we are still the managers, but the plan sponsor has joined us as an active planning and process participant. Objectives must now relate to the matching of future resources with future liabilities, more and more frequently defined quantitatively, not subjectively. Risk and return are to be explicitly appraised and balanced, again in objective terms. A systematic, disciplined framework for decision-making is suggested and, surely, a new approach and focus for our efforts is implied. All of this, of course, to take place within a dynamic environment, for high stakes, and in an uncertain world! Impossible? No. But open minds, broader understanding, new knowledge and new methods are required for success.

In our own attempts to prepare for the future, we at Wells Fargo began some time ago to construct the systematic, disciplined framework and the new decision-making process that our analysis had led us to conclude were needed. At the same time, we evolved a philosophy concerning portfolio management and an approach to its execution that allowed us to mesh style and substance in what we felt was a forward-looking manner, combining newer ideas from capital market and portfolio theory with fundamental concepts from classical financial theory to provide an improved methodology with which to progress. Today, we see ourselves as problem solvers broadly engaged in the customer satisfaction business, with the total portfolio as our management focus. It is from this perspective on the world that my comments flow.

Paper presented at May 1978 Annual Conference of The Financial Analysts Federation.

We regard the process of structuring large portfolios as involving a set of three major, separate but inter-related decisions. Of these, the first and most important is the *asset allocation* decision: how much exposure to the capital markets in what form of investment media. Through this decision, which determines the portfolio's diversification across alternative asset classes, the manager has his largest impact on the probable distribution of future portfolio returns and on their relationship to customer requirements. It is the decision that matches customer needs and preferences (expressed as objectives) with the investment risk and return trade-offs that are expected to exist in the market. In order to make this decision with any real hope of having future plan resources match up with future plan liabilities, an imposing array of essential questions must be answered—not the least of which is resolution of the conflicting goals that bedevil the plan sponsor itself.

This problem is stated in both general and specific terms on <u>Page 1</u> of the attachment. It will yield to rational analysis, however, and from its solution come several of the crucial inputs to the asset allocation decision: the sponsor's time horizon, the sponsor's utility function or tolerance for risk, and some fix on the true return requirements of the plan. Other inputs are generated by us as asset manager: the expected returns on both stocks and bonds as asset classes, and the expected variability and co-variability of those returns.

<u>Page 2</u> of the attachment describes these information requirements, which are all ultimately stated in quantified terms. To gain perspective on the problem, assumptions can be varied and a variety of expected wealth distributions can be generated for comparison with the customer's requirements and preferences to obtain, before the fact, agreement on the asset mix which offers the best set of probable outcomes relative to the stated objectives. With such agreement in hand, the customer knows what his risks are and what distribution of returns he has a right to expect, while the manager knows the degree to which both systematic and residual risk must be controlled through time. The progress of the portfolio can be monitored in relation to these performance objectives set before the fact and, through systematic adjustment, the portfolio can continuously reflect an appropriate mix of assets as conditions change, maximizing the probability that the manager will satisfy the agreed-upon requirements.

<u>Page 3</u> of the attachment shows two such simulations, one done in a five-year and one in a ten-year time frame, where the required rate of return was set at eight percent per year and the customer's risk aversion was high. In the five-year case, the optimal trade-off between risk and return in the context of an eight percent return requirement occurred with an asset mix of 70 percent equities/30 percent bonds. Several higher stock proportions provided a higher expected median portfolio return at the same probability level, but each of these gave away too much downside protection and involved too much variability of returns relative to the added return to be acceptable to this customer. In the ten-year case, the optimal mix turned out to be 100 percent stocks, a solution which met all the customer's explicitly-stated constraints and requirements but which was, nevertheless, modified by him on grounds of general prudence. Incidently, while these simulations involved only stocks and bonds as asset alternatives, other simulators are available that are "open-ended" and can handle additional alternatives such as cash or real estate.

Leaving the asset allocation area now, the next major decision area is that of *risk control*. By controlling both the systematic (market-related) and the specific (non-market-related) elements of total risk, a manager can govern the distribution of probable returns within a consistent framework. In my opinion, it is the absence of disciplined, rigorous processes for risk control that more than anything else explains the erratic and sometimes astonishing outcomes that money managers have all too often dished up to their customers. It doesn't *have* to be that way! But, if we are to control risk, we must be able to manage it. To manage it, we must have some systematic way to identify, quantify, monitor, measure and adjust it in an ongoing manner. On the fixed-income side, conventional means will suffice. We simply specify the proportions to be held in each of three more-or-less independent cross-sectional dimensions of the bond portfolio: maturity, quality, and type.

Control of equity portfolio risk is a much more complicated problem, however, and here we bring to bear notions from capital market and portfolio theory for assistance. Market-related risk is controlled by managing to a specified portfolio beta. But market-related risk, the nondiversifiable risk which manifests itself in relative-to-market portfolio volatility, is only one aspect of total risk. We must also concern ourselves with residual risk, the diversifiable risk element that manifests itself in non-market-related variability and is measured by sigma. The *complete* risk control decision, then, involves specification of two management targets: the beta coefficient which controls the on-average response of the equity portfolio to changes in the market level (i.e., its relative volatility based on systematic risk considerations); and sigma, which controls the degree of variability of the portfolio return around the market return by specifying the permitted level of residual, non-market-related risk to be assumed. Taken together, beta and sigma are positive, powerful means for risk control and, thus, for risk management. They are easily quantified, implemented, monitored and adjusted in the light of changes in expectations or forecasts. Of overriding importance, they work.

To summarize to this point, Page 4 of the attachment—a generalized set of specifications relating to what we call a "Growth" objective, one common among large pension accounts—sets forth nearly everything we think is needed to structure a portfolio effectively. The control dimensions are: the asset mix, including cash proportions; the equity segment's market-related risk level as specified by the beta target; and the *spread* of risk across the equity risk spectrum (i.e., the Risk Sector targets), and across the other dimensions of the market captured in our Economic/Market Sector targets, which are sort of super-industry categories. In our process, these targets are instructions to portfolio managers concerning the composition of portfolios. They are generated by the organization's policy group (made up of its senior investment professionals), communicated through a policy statement updated monthly, and monitored for compliance through a management information system with exception reporting. Operationally, then, this is our control framework, through which portfolios are structured, managed, and adjusted.

The final decision area to be discussed is that of *security selection*: the choice of specific issues with which to populate the portfolio and through which to meet its target specifications. Since, at present, our selection techniques in the fixed-income area are probably very much the same as other investment managers, relying primarily on traditional concepts and methods, I will focus here on *stock selection* where we employ a non-traditional approach and process. The area of stock selection, of course, is the principal place where one seeks to find the alpha, that most elusive of the "ABC" elements of portfolio management. And find them we must for, unless the portfolio produces an excess return over and above the market rate of return (which is easily captured for equities by an index fund), or a positive alpha, if you will, how can we hold out our judgmental capabilities as having value for our customers? This is the heart of the active versus passive management controversy.

We start our stock valuation and selection activities from the following base: what is being priced out there in the market place is the consensus judgment about future returns, suitably differentiated by relative riskiness and relative liquidity, two factors that we believe to systematically affect equity pricing. These expected returns (for both bonds and stocks and, in fact, for any form of investment asset) are represented by expected future cash flows to the investor, discounted at some rate that reflects the relative degree of certainty (or uncertainty) that the investor has about receiving them. Our working universe of some 370 stocks is divided into five risk Sectors, with Sector 1 (the lowest-risk issues) at one end and Sector 5 (the highest-risk issues) at the other. Stocks are placed in one or another sector by our analysts, who are guided by a beta measure. So, we end up with all the issues in our universe sorted by relative riskiness, lowest to highest. We follow a similar course in assigning securities to one of five Liquidity sectors.

Every night you can look in the paper and observe the consensus price that investors agreed upon for each of these issues at the close of trading. Price, then, is given. Another given is our analyst's estimates of the future growth rate of earnings and dividends for each company, not just for the current quarter or year, but looking out five years, and ten years, and more. The fact that these estimates cannot be precise is assuredly a problem, but it is a problem shared by all forecasters together and, in fact, could be a source of opportunity if you have reason to believe that your forecasts are in some way superior. Investment decision-making is an exercise in decision-making under conditions of uncertainty much like that faced by corporate officers in making their capital budgeting decisions, for example. We approach the problem of deriving the necessary cash flow estimates by using the same discounted cash flow format that they use. Given current prices, our estimates of earnings and payout, and the resulting divided flows, we solve for the discount rate implicit in these numbers and re-sort our stocks *within each risk sector* from highest expected return to lowest expected return.

To digress a moment, when we plot all the expected returns from the 370 stocks in our universe and put a line of best fit through the resulting "cloud" of points, we get a very useful tool which, with acknowledgment to William Sharpe at Stanford who invented the term in a slightly different context, we call the Security Market Line. This Line moves around in both slope and position, as illustrated on <u>Page 5</u> of attachment. It represents the trade-off between risk and expected return across the equity spectrum represented by our stock universe, and is in many respects analogous to a fixed-income yield curve. When it is relatively flat, as in 1972, the added expected payoff for assuming higher risk is small and, as in 1974 at the top of the page, vice versa when it is steep. Typically, also, the Line will be high in position when the expected return spread in favor of stocks over bonds is large (nearly 600 basis points at the end of March, 1978) and low in position when the spread is small (less than 200 basis points in June, 1972).

Our experience is that definite information is contained in this "expected return" approach to stock valuation and selection. Therefore, we require the resulting codings to be extensively present in our portfolios. I know that this sounds like a cliche', but how many organizations literally waste their security analysts' efforts, either by overriding them through committee screens or by permitting portfolio managers to pick and choose depending on their personal feelings about the analysts' analyses? We give a coding weight of five to stocks appearing to be most undervalued based on risk- and liquidity-adjusted expected return comparisons (these would be the P-1 issues in the lower left graphic on <u>Page 6</u> of attachment, and a weight of one to those appearing most overvalued (the N-2 issues in the same graphic).

We require portfolio managers to maintain an average equity portfolio coding score of 3.8 on this 1-to-5 scale, which means an average coding level in the undervalued area. If a portfolio falls below this score, the fact is reported as an exception by our monitoring and must be adjusted upward. Of course, any adjustment of one policy or target factor is undertaken in the context of all policy and target factors across the total portfolio so as to minimize the costs of transacting. That is, we want any one transaction to produce as many improvements in policy/strategy/target compliance as possible—two, three, or even four helpful shifts in composition. Since this is essentially a numbers-crunching problem, balancing off the changes in one control dimension against changes in the others until the optimum set of trade-offs is obtained, we provide computer assistance to portfolio managers for its accomplishment. Utilizing portfolio optimization computer programs, a portfolio manager can quickly and accurately determine which trade or trades will maximize the codings and produce other desired portfolio characteristics at minimum transaction expense.

In brief, then, that's the Wells Fargo approach to the design and composition of large portfolios. Through our process, we can effectively translate customer requirements into quantified statements for control and management purposes, efficiently implement our internal forecasts and judgments, quickly adjust to changes in the external environment, and systematically maintain our portfolios in line with agreed-upon constraints and objectives. The process is highly structured, highly disciplined, and highly manageable. It serves us well and, we believe, also serves our customers well.

Working with the described approach, we have found that the role of our security analysts has changed very little, while a new role is emerging for that class of investment professionals called "portfolio managers." Since this approach involves the organization in many areas of decision-making that were formerly the province of the portfolio manager and since it is explicitly client-oriented to a degree not present in the past, a better current description for our portfolio managers might be "Client Service Officers." The professionalism of these individuals is no less valuable, but it is directed far more extensively to the total portfolio than to the individual issues, and far more extensively to the total relationship rather than to the portfolio in isolation. In effect, the Client Service Officer represents us to the customer and represents the customer back to us, focusing our resources on the customer's particular problems and preferences and assisting broadly in finding solutions to those problems, in a manner consistent with those preferences.

At the portfolio itself, the organization—in cooperation with the CSO and other support personnel—is producing the inputs and adjustments required to make these solutions operational and to keep them tuned to changing circumstances in the context of the customer's specific situation. This new role is still evolving at Wells Fargo, but it is well enough established for us to know that it is a development having many interesting implications for the future structure of our firm.

Thus, we find that the creation of a systematic framework for investment management and change in the decision-making process in turn induces structural change within the management organization itself. We have found ourselves becoming more manageable, more flexible, and more productive. And, certainly, we have become more competitive. But—at least in the context of this panel—these are side issues. The central point is that we believe very strongly that we have enhanced the quality of our professional practice—which is what we started out to do in the first place, looking to the future. With an open mind and a willingness to consider change, your own methods for structuring portfolios can be made responsive to that interest. It seems a worthwhile thing to explore!

THE PENSION FUND PROBLEM

Conflicting goals of:
- Plan Participants
- Stockholders
- Corporate Officers and Directors

PLAN PARTICIPANTS' GOALS

- Successful Funding of Plan
- Continued Viability of Company

Investment Objectives

- Low Risk — Certainty of Returns
- Long Planning Horizon

STOCKHOLDERS' GOAL

Maximize Value of his Stock by Reducing Costs of Pension Benefits

Investment Objectives

- High Risk — High Return
- Long Planning Horizon

MANAGEMENTS' GOAL

Control total risk of the Company by Managing the Impact of Pension Costs on Company Earnings

Investment Objectives

- Low Risk — Certainty of Returns
- Short Planning Horizon

THE PROBLEM:

What Beta (.9, 1.0, 1.1, 1.2) do I want?

What Alpha (-2.0, -1.0, 0, 1.0, 2.0) can I expect?

What specific risk (0.1, 2.0, 4.0, 6.0, 8.0) is appropriate?

What time horizon (3, 5, 10, 20 years) should I consider?

What return (6, 7, 8, 9%) do I need?

Whose utility (shareholders, investment officers, pensioners) should I maximize?

ASSET ALLOCATION INFORMATION REQUIREMENTS

- Plan Requirements
- Capital Market Assumptions
- Manager Evaluation

PLAN REQUIREMENTS

- Actuarial Assumption
- Planning Horizon
- Risk Aversion

CAPITAL MARKET ASSUMPTIONS

- Expected Return — Stocks, Bonds
- Risk — Stocks, Bonds
- Correlation — Stocks with Bonds
- Spread High vs. Low Risk Stock
- Spread High vs. Low Quality Bonds
- Short or Intermediate Change in Spreads

MANAGER EVALUATION

- Equity Portfolio Beta
- Equity Portfolio Diversification
- Quality Fixed Income Portfolio
- Security Selection Skill (Alpha)
- Market Timing Skill
- Managerial Costs — Fees, Transaction costs, etc.

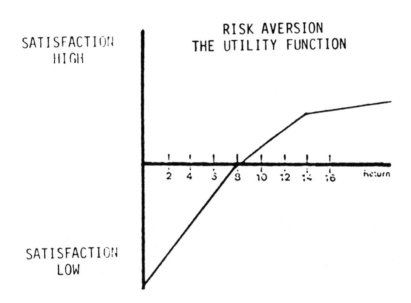

RISK AVERSION
THE UTILITY FUNCTION

SATISFACTION HIGH

SATISFACTION LOW

return

ASSET ALLOCATION PROGRAM INPUTS

Return Stocks (.14)

Risk Stocks (.20)

Correlation Stocks, Bonds (.5)

Return Bonds (.08)

Risk Bonds (.06)

Investment Horizon (5 years; 10 years)

Minimum Required Return (.08)

Risk Aversion (five to one)

EXPECTED RETURNS DISTRIBUTIONS
5 YEAR INVESTMENT HORIZON
(Annual Rate of Return Compounded Annually)

PORTFOLIO MIX		MEAN	STANDARD DEVIATION	5%	25%	50%	75%	95%	PROBABILITY OF 8% RETURN	UTILITY RANK
STOCKS	BONDS									
100%	0%	14.0	8.8	−1.2	6.5	12.3	18.3	27.6	69	7
90	10	13.4	8.1	−0.5	6.7	12.0	17.5	26.0	69	5
80	20	12.8	7.3	0.2	6.8	11.6	16.6	24.3	69	3
70	30	12.2	6.6	0.9	6.8	11.2	15.8	22.6	69	1
60	40	11.6	5.9	1.5	6.9	10.8	14.9	21.0	68	2
50	50	11.0	5.2	2.1	6.9	10.4	14.0	19.3	68	4
40	60	10.4	4.6	2.7	6.9	9.9	13.1	17.7	66	6
30	70	9.8	4.0	3.1	6.8	9.4	12.1	16.1	64	8
20	80	9.2	3.4	3.5	6.7	8.9	11.3	14.7	61	9
10	90	8.6	3.0	3.6	6.4	8.4	10.4	13.4	55	10
0	100	8.0	2.7	3.5	6.0	7.8	9.7	12.3	48	11

EXPECTED RETURNS DISTRIBUTIONS
10 YEAR INVESTMENT HORIZON
(Annual Rate of Return Compounded Annually)

PORTFOLIO MIX		MEAN	STANDARD DEVIATION	5%	25%	50%	75%	95%	PROBABILITY OF 8% RETURN	UTILITY RANK
STOCKS	BONDS									
100%	0%	14.0	6.2	2.6	8.2	12.3	16.5	22.9	76	1
90	10	13.4	5.7	3.0	8.2	12.0	15.8	21.7	76	2
80	20	12.8	5.2	3.4	8.2	11.6	15.1	20.4	76	3
70	30	12.2	4.7	3.8	8.1	11.2	14.4	19.2	76	4
60	40	11.6	4.2	4.1	8.0	10.8	13.7	17.9	75	5
50	50	11.0	3.7	4.5	7.9	10.4	12.9	16.6	74	6
40	60	10.4	3.2	4.7	7.8	9.9	12.1	15.4	73	7
30	70	9.8	2.8	4.9	7.6	9.4	11.3	14.1	70	8
20	80	9.2	2.4	5.0	7.3	8.9	10.6	13.0	65	9
10	90	8.6	2.1	5.0	7.0	8.4	9.8	11.9	58	10
0	100	8.0	1.9	4.8	6.6	7.8	9.1	11.0	46	11

POLICY GUIDANCE STATEMENT
GROWTH OBJECTIVE

1. TOTAL PORTFOLIO - ASSET MIX (a)

	CURRENT GUIDELINE	PRIOR MONTH GUIDELINE
EQUITY PORTION	70%	70%
CASH EQUIVALENTS (% OF EQUITY PORTION)	0%	0%
BOND PORTION	30%	30%
CASH EQUIVALENTS (% OF BONDS)	5%	5%

2. EQUITY INVESTMENT STRATEGY

	S&P 500	GUIDANCE RANGE	CURRENT TARGET	PRIOR MONTH TARGET
EQUITY RISK LEVEL (b)	1.00	1.00-1.04	1.02*	1.04
RISK SECTORS				
1 (LOW)	59%	53-61%	55%	56%
2	15	12-20	18 *	15
3	13	11-19	17	17
4	10	4-12	6	6
5 (HIGH)	3	0-7	4 *	6
ECONOMIC/MARKET SECTORS				
MANUFACTURING-PROCESSING	9%	7-15%	13%	13%
CAPITAL GOODS	18	12-20	14	14
PETROLEUM	18	16-24	22	22
GENERAL BUSINESS	1	0-5	1 *	2
TRANSPORTATION	2	0-6	0 *	1
CONSUMER-BASIC	12	9-17	15 *	11
CONSUMER-DISCRETIONARY	17	11-19	13 *	15
FINANCE	6	4-12	10	10
SHELTER	3	0-7	2	2
UTILITIES	14	8-16	10	10

(a) GENERAL SOLUTION FOR POOLED FUND PARTICIPANT

(b) PORTFOLIOS HOLDING EQUITIES VALUED AT $1 MILLION OR MORE SHOULD HOLD AT LEAST THE EQUIVALENT OF 40 EQUAL-DOLLAR-WEIGHTED ISSUES; AT VALUES LESS THAN $1 MILLION AT LEAST THE EQUIVALENT OF 30 EQUAL-DOLLAR-WEIGHTED ISSUES SHOULD BE HELD.

* JUDGMENTAL CHANGE

SECURITY MARKET LINE

HISTORICAL HIGH AND LOW (1972-1978)

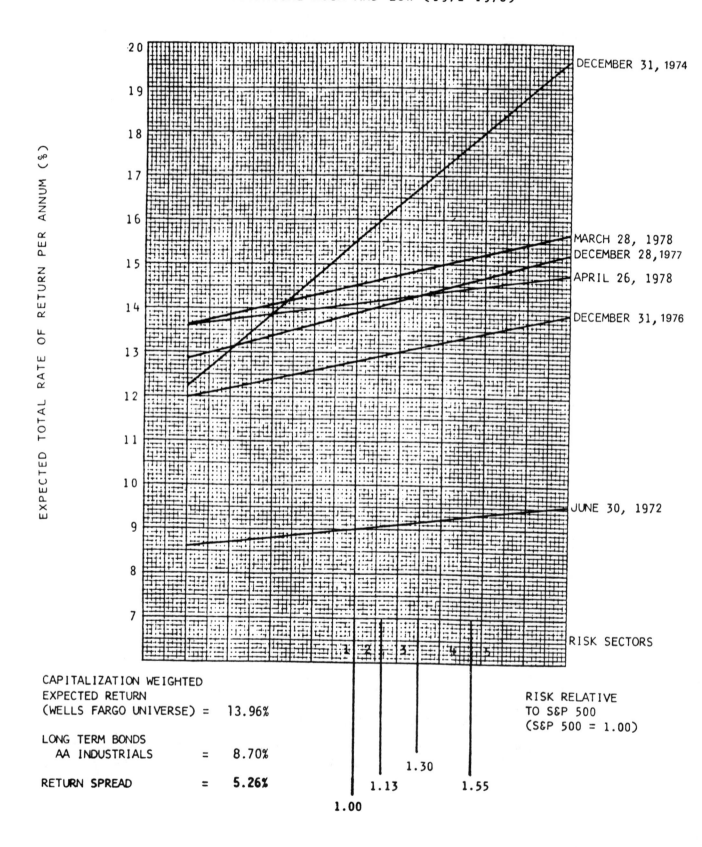

CAPITALIZATION WEIGHTED
EXPECTED RETURN
(WELLS FARGO UNIVERSE) =   13.96%

LONG TERM BONDS
  AA INDUSTRIALS   =   8.70%

RETURN SPREAD   =   5.26%

RISK RELATIVE
TO S&P 500
(S&P 500 = 1.00)

Expected
Return %

If we plot hundreds of securities we obtain the following graph:

20 —
19 —
18 —
17 —
16 —
15 —
14 —
13 —
12 —
11 —

.5   .75   1.0   1.25   1.5   Risk

Security Market Line

The line mathematically represents the average relationship
between risk and return at this time. It is called the
current Security Market Line.

WELLS FARGO STOCK
Coding Process*

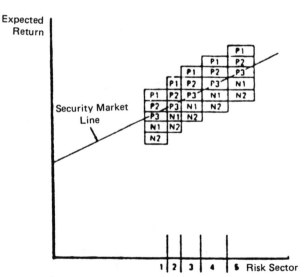

Expected
Return

Security Market
Line

P1
P1 P2
P1 P2 P3
P1 P2 P3 N1
P1 P2 P3 N1 N2
P2 P3 N1 N2
P3 N1 N2
N1 N2
N2

1 2 3 4 5 Risk Sector

*Stocks are coded by Risk Sector. The top 20% in
each Risk Sector are coded P1, the next 20%, P2, etc.

PERFORMANCE OF STOCK VALUATION MODEL*
December 31, 1974 – December 31, 1977

	Price Appreciation Total Period
10% Most Attractive	231%
15% Next Most Attractive	117
25% Next Most Attractive	76
30% Next Most Attractive	41
20% Least Attractive	16

*Does not include transactions costs or dividend income

Financial Analysts Journal, May/June 1978—all rights reserved
Copyright © The Financial Analysts Federation, 1978

by Fischer Black

The Ins and Outs of Foreign Investment

▶ Other things equal, an increase in a country's residents' investment in foreign countries means an equal increase in foreigners' investment in their country. In effect, residents exchange assets within their country for assets outside their country.

Because investors will shift assets between countries in anticipation of any changes in rate of return, we will tend to see no particular correlation between asset flows and rates of return among countries. Instead, countries with attractive investment opportunities will show up as countries attracting investment of physical capital.

In the absence of special information advantages, all investors should own a piece of the same world portfolio. In reality, investors tend to concentrate their holdings in domestic assets because they are familiar. This effect is probably stronger than it should be. Because trading of domestic investors will cause stock prices to reflect all available information, foreign investors can safely buy domestic shares even if they don't have much information about them.

Foreign investment and changes in foreign investment can have a big effect on a country's trade balance. A rich country that consumes its return on large outward foreign investment will tend to show a trade deficit. Conversely, a poor country with large inward foreign investment may show a trade surplus. If a country raises its taxes on capital, driving capital goods out of the country, it will tend to show a surplus in its balance of trade.

The balance of payments is an even more

Fischer Black is Professor of Finance at the Alfred P. Sloan School of Management, Massachusetts Institute of Technology. This article was written as part of a project for R. Shriver Associates, under a contract with the U.S. Treasury Department, to study foreign portfolio investment in the United States.

mysterious concept. We do not even know how to define it meaningfully, let alone measure it. For every proposed definition it is uncertain whether we would rather have a surplus, a deficit, or neither. ▶

THIS article attempts to lay out the basic economic influences on investment across national boundaries. It assumes throughout that investors and corporate managers attempt to take advantage of any profit opportunities they see: They attempt to maximize the value of and income from the portfolios and firms they own or control, net of any taxes they must pay, and taking account of any government controls or possible expropriation.

The approach it takes could be called neoclassical economics. It also draws heavily on the modern theory of finance, which assumes that investors choose their portfolios in the light of both risk and expected return. It contrasts with the kind of analysis that assumes supply and demand for goods or labor can be out of balance because prices don't move fast enough to bring them into line. Prices are unlikely to move slowly (except by government edict) with profit-maximizing investors and managers around.

Why Foreign Investment Exists

Why do investors hold assets in other countries? They may have saved more than they can invest profitably at home. Or their governments may tax capital heavily or threaten to take it way. Perhaps they want the advantages of international diversification or feel more optimistic about the prospects for foreign assets than foreigners are. A more relevant question might be, "Why don't investors hold more assets in other countries?"

The Distribution of Wealth

If a country's residents are wealthier than the country, they will hold assets in other countries. Suppose that the residents of country A are worth $150 billion, but that investments in country A are worth only $100 billion. The residents of country B, however, are worth only $50 billion, while investments in country B are worth $100 billion.

If A and B are the only countries in the world, there is bound to be foreign investment. In general, the residents of A must hold $50 billion of B's assets, plus an added amount equal to the value of assets in A held by residents of B. If residents of B hold $10 billion of A's assets, the residents of A must hold $60 billion of B's assets, since they have $150 billion in assets, only $90 billion of which is invested within their own country. (We define assets broadly, as including real assets, financial assets, deposits and money held by individuals.)

Other things being equal, the thriftier a country's residents, the more they are likely to own of other countries' assets. Conversely, when a country's residents spend more than they earn, they are likely to find that foreign ownership of their assets increases. Thus increasing foreign investment can be sign of changes in the spending habits of a country's citizens, rather than a sign of any change in foreigners' investment preferences.

The fact that an uneven distribution of wealth may lie behind much foreign investment may go unnoticed by investors or even by the countries receiving the foreign investment. Any single investor of country A is unlikely to feel the constraints that necessitate $50 billion of his country's wealth being invested in Country B. He feels free to invest his whole portfolio in A, or to invest his whole portfolio in B, or to divide it in any way between A and B. He may even be able to sell short some of A's securities, or borrow in A, and invest an amount in A or B greater than the value of his portfolio.

It may also go unnoticed that an increase in foreign investment in one country means, if nothing else has changed, an equal increase in that country's residents' investments outside the country. If a resident of B, deciding to invest in A, sells an asset in B and buys an asset in B, and if no assets move from A to B or from B to A, then a resident of A must simultaneously decide or agree to invest in B. In this situation, we can say that, for every investment by B's residents in A, there is a simultaneous investment by A's residents in B. The residents of B, as a group, exchange ownership of assets in B for ownership of assets in A with the residents of A, as a group. Gross foreign investment increases, but net foreign investment stays the same.

When a foreigner invests in the U.S., he must give something up. Normally, either he gives up a claim on a foreign asset or he imports goods or services. To understand one side of the transaction, we must understand the other. Most increases in gross foreign investment in the U.S. are accompanied by increases in gross U.S. investment abroad.

The Distribution of Investment Opportunities

We have assumed that assets change hands without changing locations. In fact, however, real assets can move between countries. This section assumes that the assets moving between countries are investment goods—machines, tools, industrial and agricultural chemicals and the like.

The owner of an investment good will place it where it will earn the highest rental (net of taxes and other government levies). When he transfers the asset to another country, foreign investment in that country will go up. Thus a country that has improved investment opportunities (or that lowers its taxes on capital or investment goods) will find that foreign investment in the country is higher than it would otherwise have been.

For example, suppose that the residents of our countries A and B have the same wealth—each group owns $100 billion in assets. If investment opportunities are greater in B, the assets will be distributed unevenly: There will be, say, $150 billion of assets in B and only $50 billion of assets in A.

The fact that investment opportunities are greater in B than in A will not show up in the form of a higher interest rate or higher expected return on assets in B. If investors are on their toes, they will shift assets between countries in anticipation of any changes in interest rates or expected return. Sometimes they will shift too much or too soon, and assets will flow into the country that turns out to have the lower interest rate or expected return. Since this is about as likely to happen as the reverse, we should see no particular correlation between asset flows and the pattern of interest rates and expected returns among countries. The fact that expected returns on risky assets are not observable creates another obstacle to seeing a correlation between differences in expected return and flows of physical capital.

Similarly, the specific sectors within a country that have more attractive investment opportunities will not show up as sectors with higher returns to investors. They will show up as sectors attracting investment of physical capital. But the flows of physical capital into these sectors will keep the returns to investors at about the same levels as, sometimes higher and sometimes lower than, the returns to investors in other sectors.

Taxes and the Threat of Expropriation

Taxes and other government levies can have an important effect on investment between countries. If one country increases its taxes on capital (the corporate income tax, for example), and other countries do not, then capital goods will leave the country with the higher tax rate. If a country reduces its taxes on capital, then capital goods will come in and net foreign investment in the country will increase. Similarly, if a country has a habit of expropriating capital goods without compensation at market value (by nationalizing certain industries, for example) or if there is a threat of such expropriation in the future, then capital goods will leave the country and net foreign investment in the country will decline.

A change in taxes on foreign investors or foreign investments will affect the ownership of assets in different locations and the locations of the assets. If the government of A or the government of B imposes a tax on the holdings of A's residents in B, residents of A will want to do one of two things—transfer capital goods from B to A, or exchange ownership of assets in B for ownership of assets in A. If they transfer capital goods to A, the return on assets in A will fall, and residents of B who own assets in A will transfer some of them back to B. The net effect will be reduced foreign investment by residents of A in B, reduced foreign investment by residents of B in A, and a flow of capital goods into A.

Changes in the likelihood of expropriation of foreign investments will have similar effects. Expropriation can take various forms. When a country imposes interest rate ceilings on bank deposits, the depositors may view the act as expropriation. Limits on the freedom of an investor to transfer assets out of the country are a form of expropriation. A new government that takes away some of the wealth of members of the old government, or of groups that prospered under the old government, is, in effect, expropriating that wealth.

If country B changes to a government that favors taking assets within country B away from residents of other countries, capital goods will be transferred out of country B and both inward and outward foreign investment will decline. Residents of B will reduce their holdings of assets outside B because assets inside B will become more attractive as residents of other countries reduce their holdings of them.

Thus an increase in taxes on foreign investment or in the likelihood of expropriation of foreign investment will tend to reduce both gross and net foreign investment in a country. An increase in taxes on capital or in the likelihood of expropriation of capital without regard for who owns it will tend to reduce net inward foreign investment, while increasing gross outward foreign investment: Even the residents of the country will tend to shift the capital they own to other countries.

Although all kinds of taxes and controls will affect both net and gross foreign investment, lower taxes are not necessarily better than higher taxes, as we will see.

Internation Diversification

Suppose that both country A and country B have assets worth $100 billion, partly because investment opportunities are the same in both. Suppose further that both the residents of A and the residents of B

own $100 billion in assets. Finally, suppose that the taxes on residents of A are just like the taxes on residents of B. In this situation, the residents of A may own only assets in A, while the residents of B may own only assets in B. But it will almost always be better for the residents of A to own some assets in B and for the residents of B to own some assets in A because of the benefits of international diversification.

The benefits to an investor of diversifying his portfolio across assets in different countries are similar to the benefits of diversifying his portfolio across assets in different industries within a country. A decline in the value of assets in one country may be offset by an increase in the value of assets in another country. For a given level of expected return, an investor who diversifies across countries will find that he has less risk than an investor who diversifies only within his own country.

We are not talking here about the investor's ability to concentrate his portfolio in a country that is likely to do better than other countries in the short run, and to switch his holdings successfully from one country to another as his expectations change. There is no evidence that investors are able to do this, and investors as a group can't switch their portfolios from one country to another because all assets in each country must always be held by someone.

We are talking about keeping a portfolio invested in assets of different countries. Normally, this strategy implies that an investor will not sell his investments in a given country to buy assets in another country. He may sell them to get money to spend, or to avoid or take advantage of a change in tax laws. But he does not have to have high turnover in his investment portfolio to get the benefits of international diversification.

In fact, in the absence of special taxes on investment across national boundaries and of the threat of expropriation, if investors agree on the prospects for investments in each country they should hold a piece of the same portfolio—the world market portfolio of risky assets. The world market portfolio contains all risky assets in every country. If the U.S. has risky assets worth 10 times as much as the risky assets in Japan, then both a U.S. investor and a Japanese investor would have 10 times as much invested in U.S. risky assets as in Japanese risky assets. The Japanese investor would invest much more abroad than at home.

In practice, of course, there are many reasons why an investor will not hold a share of the world market portfolio. Many countries have taxes or controls that restrict inward or outward foreign investment. And many assets, such as personal property and claims on an individual's future income, are not for sale.

Nevertheless, the amount of international investment we would expect in an unrestricted world is enormous. To get the benefits of international diversification, most investors would keep most of their wealth in foreign risky assets. This is why we say that, what we have to understand is not why foreign investment occurs, but why it isn't much more common.

The Distribution of Information

Investors may not agree about the prospects for assets in different countries.* In particular, there may be systematic differences between investors within a country and investors outside the country.

For example, at a given point in time investors outside the U.S. may think U.S. assets are going to do better than other assets, while investors within the U.S. think other assets are going to do better than U.S. assets. Thus foreigners will hold an unusually large share of U.S. assets, while U.S. residents will hold an unusually large share of foreign assets. In other words, gross foreign investment, both inward and outward, will be higher than usual. Similarly, if foreigners think the relative prospects for U.S. assets are worse than U.S. residents think they are, gross foreign investment will be reduced. Either way, there will be no obvious effect on net foreign investment.

Of course, it is not possible for everyone to think that the prospects for U.S. assets are infinitely better than the prospects for foreign assets. The price of U.S. assets would rise and the price of foreign assets would fall until investors were willing to hold all of both kinds of assets.

One important factor affecting systematic differences between investors is the distribution of information. Residents are generally more familiar with assets inside their country than with assets outside their country. Investors tend to concentrate their holdings in assets they are familiar with. Thus U.S. residents tend to hold more U.S. assets, and U.K. residents tend to hold more U.K. assets.

Ignorance about assets in other countries acts like a tax on investment in other countries: It tends to reduce both gross and net foreign investment. This effect is probably stronger than it should be. Since investors within a country usually have all available information about a company that operates in that country, their trading will cause the stock price to reflect all of the available information. Investors outside of the country can safely buy the stock; even if they don't have much information on the company, they can rely on those investors who do to keep the price fair.

So long as investors insist on buying the stock of familiar companies, they will benefit less than they should from international diversification (and from other kinds of diversification as well).

---

* We assume that investors judge investments in terms of both expected return and risk. When we say the prospects for a country's assets are better than the prospects for another country's assets, we mean the expected return compares more favorably with the return commensurate with the assets' risk levels.

Willingness To Bear Risk

If investors in country A are more willing to bear risk than investors in country B, the former may hold most of the risky assets in both countries. We may find investors in A borrowing to buy risky assets and investors in B lending so they won't have to hold risky assets. In effect investors in A will borrow from investors in B, directly or indirectly, and will use the money to buy risky assets in B.

This in itself will have no obvious effect on net investment between A and B. It will, however, affect gross foreign investment and the composition of foreign investment in both countries. The existence of differences in willingness to bear risk will tend to increase gross foreign investment: The countries more tolerant of risk will tend to hold foreign equity assets, while the countries more averse to risk will tend to hold foreign debt assets.

If this tendency is extreme, the residents of B may hold short-term notes issued by the government of A, while the residents of A make direct investments in B and hold common stock of companies in B. Such a pattern implies nothing more nor less than differences in willingness to tolerate risk; the fact that equity investments may be classed as "long term" while government bills are classed as "short term" has no significance. The only broad economic effect this pattern will have is that residents of A will gain in wealth relative to residents of B in good times, while residents of B will gain in wealth relative to residents of A in bad times. Investors choosing between debt and equity assets, between direct and portfolio investment, or between various sectors of an economy are in effect exercising choices of taste that have no other identifiable economic consequences.

The fact that residents of A may be more willing to bear risk than residents of B does not mean they will do it for free. It merely means the expected return needed to induce residents of A to hold assets with a given amount of risk is lower than the expected return needed to induce residents of B to hold the same assets.

Should Foreign Investment Be Constrained?

The biggest question of broad economic significance related to foreign investment is the choice between the benefits of free international investment and trade and the benefits of the government revenues derived from taxing inward or outward foreign investment and imports or exports. Sometimes constraints—in the form of direct or indirect taxation, expropriation or outright banning of foreign investment—will benefit a country's economy. At other times, the country that imposes constraints will find itself their victim.

Foreign Investment and the Trade Balance

Suppose that an American oil billionaire retires to an island off the coast of France. All the food, jewels and other things that he buys are imported to the island. Since he continues to hold his wealth, which is located entirely outside of the island, he is a large outward foreign investor. Since goods and services flow into the island, but rarely flow out, the island shows a large trade deficit. Will he worry about this trade deficit? Probably not.

Foreign investment and changes in foreign investment are closely tied in with a country's trade balance. A country that holds large net outward foreign investments and consumes the return from these investments will tend to show a trade deficit. But since this deficit occurs because the country is so wealthy, it is hardly cause for alarm. Similarly, a country with large inward foreign investment may find itself with a large trade surplus. Since this is a result of the fact that the country is poorer than other countries, it is nothing to be pleased about.

Changes in foreign investment may also affect the trade balance. If a country raises its taxes on capital, capital goods will tend to flow out of the country, leading to a trade surplus. If a country's residents go through a period during which they save much more than residents of other countries, they will tend to export more (because they consume less of what they produce) and import less. This too will lead to a trade surplus. This surplus may turn to a deficit, however, when the country starts consuming the fruits of its foreign investment.

In general, when a resident of A acquires ownership of an asset in B, he must give up something in exchange. If he gives up a claim on an asset in A, then there is a change in gross foreign investment, but not in net foreign investment. This is true whether the claim he gives up is a common stock, a government bill or a claim on a demand deposit in one of A's banks. If he gives up goods or services, however, there will be a change in net foreign investment, and the transaction will form part of the trade balance. His country will have more of a surplus or less of a deficit than otherwise.

Free Trade and Investment

The benefits of free foreign investment into or out of a country are like the benefits of free trade—often illusory. The potential benefits are there, if most countries negotiate a balanced reduction in barriers to free trade and investment. But if a single country unilaterally reduces its barriers to trade or investment, other countries may gain more than all the benefits: The country that made the move may end up worse off.

A country can profit from such trade restrictions as taxing foreign investment or expropriating property. The clearest example of this is the oil exporting nations. Until recently, they had relatively free trade and investment, and they were poor. Now they have heavy export taxes and have discouraged inward for-

eign investment by expropriating foreign property without adequate compensation. And they are rich.

How can we induce them to lower their barriers to free trade and investment? We can't because we have nothing to offer in exchange, except perhaps outright cash grants. To be in a position to negotiate, we must set up barriers ourselves. The most direct way to do that is to start taxing imports of oil. (While it would be nice to tax investments in oil exporting countries, it would be impossible because these investments can be made indirectly.)

If we put a tax on imports of oil equal to the export tax imposed by the producing countries, we will have something to bargain with. If other consuming countries impose a similar tax, we would have a good collective bargaining position. he tax would hurt some individuals and some sectors of the economy, but would permit general tax cuts that would benefit most individuals and most sectors.

The natural countermeasure to someone else's tax is a tax of your own on exactly the same transaction. If France taxes exports of wine, the U.S. can tax imports of wine. If Canada taxes investments by U.S. residents in Canada, the U.S. can tax the same investments. Countertaxing, by increasing the damage done by taxation, should make it easier to negotiate reductions in both taxes. You can't win a tariff war by refusing to fight. If someone else imposes a tax in spite of your warnings, you must impose one too, (or threaten to do so) to show you mean business. Only then can you negotiate a general reduction in taxes on international transactions.

If another country subsidizes foreign investment or exports, however, you should not retaliate: You should rejoice and pretend not to notice. If it bans certain types of foreign investment, you will not have to impose a tax or a ban of your own to have a basis for negotiation. A ban will not, as a tax does, yield any direct benefits for the country imposing it.

Taxation of international trade and investment causes distortions but, then, any taxation causes distortions. It is not obvious that modest levels of taxation of international transactions are always worse than low or no taxes.

Employment, Inflation and the Balance of Payments

Employment, inflation and the balance of payments are three subjects generally irrelevant to discussions of foreign investment. We don't know enough about the relation between these factors and foreign investment to be able to take them into account.

We can make a few partial statements about employment. If, by imposing a tax on capital, a country drives physical capital out, thus reducing net inward foreign investment, it will probably reduce wages and employment. The less capital per worker, the less certain his employment and the lower his wages are likely to be. Offsetting this effect, however, will be the proceeds of the tax on capital. It may be hard to say which of these effects is more important.

Since we don't know what causes increases or decreases i the rate of inflation, we don't know how foreign investment fits into the picture. All existing theories of inflation violate the assumption that investors constantly try to take advantage of any profit opportunities they see. Furthermore, it is not at all clear what harm inflation does, or what harm changes in the rate of inflation do. We know that some people gain at the expense of others, but that is common to all economic phenomena. We don't know if there are any general gains from better control of inflation, in the sense that there are general gains from free trade and investment.

The balance of payments is the most mysterious concept of all. We don't even know how to define it meaningfully, let alone how to measure it. And for every proposed definition, we are uncertain about whether we would rather have a surplus, a deficit or neither. If accumulation of gold represents a balance of payments surplus, is that good? Do we want to hold gold rather than productive assets? If we don't have gold, can we settle our international accounts? Should we count foreign securities of some sort as reserves along with gold? If so, where do we draw the line, and why? Why not include all foreign securities? Why not domestic securities, too? Why not the ability to issue domestic securities in the future? The list of questions is endless.

Objectives of Direct versus Portfolio Investment

In a world where investors try to maximize the returns on their investments, the objectives of direct and portfolio investment will be the same. An investor will want to maximize the value of the enterprise in which he holds shares, whether he holds two shares or all shares.

If foreigners gain control of a U.S. company and then try to hurt U.S. residents by interfering in some way with the operations of the company, thy will almost always hurt themselves more than they hurt the company's customers. The customers can go to a competitor, but the value of the company will decline sharply, costing the foreigners much of the value of their investment.

If foreigners gain control of a U.S. company and move some of its operations abroad, despite the fact that those operations can be done at lower cost in the U.S., the foreigners will again be the biggest losers. The company will lose sales to its competitors, and the value of its shares will decline.

On the other hand, if some of the company's operations can be done at lower cost abroad, and the previous managers did nothing about it, then both the company's customers and its owners will be better off if the shifts are made. A transfer of ownership to foreigners may have the same benefits any transfer of ownership may have. When old ways are thrown out and new ways brought in, the company, its customers and its competitors' customers sometimes gain.

Of course, it is possible that foreign owners will try to appropriate some of the company's assets to their own benefit; this will hurt the company and the other shareholders. But this is a problem common to any company with minority shareholders who do not share in effective control of the company. The law provides solutions, at least in part, to problems of this kind. And foreign owners of shares in a U.S. company cannot usually escape U.S. law.

It is sometimes claimed that foreign investors take their profits home rather than reinvesting them. Whether they do or not depends on whether net inward foreign investment is increasing or decreasing. If it is increasing, profits are being reinvested. The more relevant point is that, with all foreign investment, foreigners *own* their profits. Even if they reinvest them, they continue to own them and the further profits they earn on them.. But there is no difference between direct and portfolio investment in this respect. Foreign investors own their profits whether they come from majority or minority ownership of a firm.

Investment in Specific Sectors

Foreign investment will often be concentrated in certain industries or sectors of an economy, partly because foreigners will be more familiar with certain sectors and partly because they may be more optimistic about certain sectors. This concentration of foreign investment will tend to displace U.S. investment in those sectors but, if investors act sensibly, it will not increase the total amount invested in any sector.

Concentration of foreign investment within a sector does not have any apparent consequences. It is similar in its impact to concentration of investment in the shares of a single company. Foreigners can disrupt the sector in which they have large investments if they have sufficient control over the companies involved, but in doing so they will hurt themselves more than they hurt us.

For example, if they acquire control over all the companies that produce burglar alarms abroad, they will drive down the foreign price and drive up the domestic price. Since they will not be maximizing profits, they will lose the value of some of their investment. Other companies will start producing burglar alarms for the domestic market and will make extra profits because prices will be high. On balance, U.S. residents gain at the expense of foreigners.

Only where an industry is vital to our defense does there seem to be reason to restrict foreign investments. There are no obvious economic reasons for restricting the extent of foreign investments in most sectors. ∎

INTERPRETING THE NEW PRUDENT MAN
STANDARD INTRODUCED BY ERISA

ROBERT W. MURPHY

The lawyer's world is peopled with fictitious characters but the measurement of our conduct against the imagined conduct of these fictitious characters creates very real consequences. The bona fide purchaser, the reasonably prudent man in a negligence case, the good judge enforcing due process, the wise director exercising business judgment—all these are examples of fictitious characters each with broadly conceptualized qualities and abilities against whom our conduct is to be judged. Frank Cummings,[1] in discussing this "unmanageable criterion" of the "prudent man" before the American Bar Association National Institute on Fiduciary Responsibilities under the Pension Reform Act, suggested that, following the analogy of the broad brush requirement of the National Labor Relations Act that an employer bargain in good faith, the courts will eventually develop a series of tight little cubbyholes (he called "fiduciary torts") that will then create a clearer and more workable definition of imprudent conduct.[2] The difficulty is that the alert investing fiduciary cannot wait for what Mr. Cummings terms a judicial gloss on the term "prudence" that will create specific identifiable courses of conduct deemed to be "imprudent."

The analogy to the National Labor Relations Act is indeed pertinent. The law contains only a vague, generalized obligation to bargain in good faith, but this term now has been clarified by specific decisions as to what is not deemed to be good faith bargaining—for example, insisting to point of impasse on an agreement as to subjects that do not fall within the mandatory subjects of wages, hours and terms and conditions of employment (known as the Borg-Warner rule), refusal to divulge necessary information, demanding a bond, etc.

It might help in an attempt to prophesy what so-called fiduciary torts may be identified by future court decisions and what conduct may not meet the new Federal "prudent man" standard, if we should first anticipate the circumstances under which a trustee might be charged with failure to act with the care, skill, prudence and diligence required to meet the prudent man standard.

Generally, a trustee might find himself subject to criticism and even litigation charging lack of prudence in three specific circumstances:

1.   If there is a material loss to the trust by reason of a particular investment going sour.

2.   If a trustee has not anticipated the financial needs of the pension fund so that there are not funds available when required without an untimely and premature sale of investments the market for which may be depressed.

Source: Proceedings of a I.C.F.A. et al. Seminar on ERISA, January 1976.

3.   *Possibly,* and I emphasize this as only a possibility, if in the comparisons between pension fund performance made by the various rating agencies such as investment firms, actuaries and corporate treasurers, the performance of a particular pension fund in total return including appreciation is at or near the bottom of the list even though the fund may not actually have suffered a loss. I have personally sat in directors meetings over the years and reviewed comparisons between the various pension funds of one company for so-called relevant periods. The difficulty was always to know (1) what period was in fact relevant, (2) were the limitations on permitted investments in the trust instrument and investment philosophies conveyed to the trustee identical, and (3) what kind of period we were then in, and when would we find an appropriate terminal point so we could make the most critical comparison of all. That is to say, if any period of time is to be used as a relevant basis for comparing fund performance, it must, at the very least, be of sufficient length and be sufficiently representative to include both the upside and downside of a cycle. What we might call a "go-go" type of fund will look better in a bull market and a more conservative fund may come off better if compared in a bear market. Generally speaking prudence will be tested under one of these three situations.

In stating these three primary situations for creating liability, however, I recognize that there may be others. For example, in a leading federal case that arose under the now preempted Illinois trust statute and its prudent man rule, *Santarelli v. Katz* (1959), 270 F. 2d 762, the liability arose because the trustee failed to exercise preemptive rights in two new stock issues. However, the thrust of this case was primarily conflict of interest since by failing to take advantage of preemptive rights, the trustee's wife enhanced the value of her share interest in the company.

If these three situations are those most likely to touch off liability, it seems to me we should find it easier to plan protection against liability by considering how each could arise.

As to the first situation when an investment goes sour, prudence would be tested by whether there were obvious straws in the wind, published reports, even prevalent rumors, and other data available that the trustee ignored. It is also possible that certain securities will be found by the courts to be unacceptable for pension fund investment under any circumstances and regardless of degree of diversification. I should hope the courts would not develop a list of proscribed investments, e.g , possibly REITS or arbitrage transactions, where they impose a strict liability on a theory that some kinds of investment are *per se* imprudent. However, we cannot be certain until we have some court decisions under the federal prudent man rule. Also, investing fiduciaries are of course necessarily prophets. No investment is made except on the postulate of certain conditions the trustee prophesies will happen. One badge of imprudence would be to ignore that there is always more than one possibility. There may be clear signs of an upsurging market but there is always the possibility that this prophecy will not come true or that it will be long-delayed, short lived or will not occur at all. Therefore the prudent trustee must consider more than one possibility and what will happen if what he believes to be the most likely course of events does not come about. Here it is most important that the trustee document the rationale of his investment decisions.

As to the second type of happening that would create a charge of imprudence—failure to anticipate the cash needs of the fund—it would seem this should be avoided by reason of the fact that the Act now requires that the trustee be given a statement of funding policy.[3] The funding policy should estimate the number of retirees each year and their estimated pensions and forecast employer contributions. It should give an indication of the rate of growth of the eligible group. But of course there will be contingencies it cannot forecast—market conditions, or for example the sudden closing of a plant employing a comparatively younger work force. The funding plan, and growing out of it but quite different from it, the investment policy, must expect the unexpected.

As to the third type of liability—a failure to keep up with the outstanding performance of the best pension trust managers—while it might be a good way to lose an account, it seems to me very questionable, short of outrageously poor performance almost to the point of gross negligence, that this would create a legal liability. The difficulty of determining a representative period for comparison should of itself make this a dubious basis for imposing legal liability. The answer, "Wait and see—the final returns are not yet in," would make it difficult ever to prove that damages have accrued. However, the Act permits suits in federal courts with no jurisdictional dollar minimum as required when federal jurisdiction is founded on diversity of citizenship. This facilitates class suits under Federal Rule 23 that in the past have been deterred because each claim of each member of the class was required in most cases to be above the jurisdictional amount for federal suit. What lawyer can guarantee that there will not be such suits, particularly involving fixed contribution plans, based only on very poor portfolio performance, nor, if there are such suits, how the federal courts will decide them?

Since an obvious correlation exists between risk and high return, we have always had the issue of prudent stewardship. A whole body of common law going back to *Harvard College v. Amory,* 26 Mass. (9 Pick.),446, 461 (1830), and before, define the responsibility of the trustee in his exercise of judgment to preserve the trust and at the same time to obtain a reasonable return and "to observe how men of prudence, discretion and intelligence manage their own affairs, not in regard to speculation, but in regard to the permanent disposition of their funds, considering the possible income as well as the probable safety of the capital to be invested" (this being the precise language of the Massachusetts court).

Every law school class in trusts studies such cases as *ex parte Cathorpe,* decided by the British Court of Chancery in 1785, (1 Cox Eq. Cases 182), involving a proposed mortgage of three thousand pounds, which the Lord Chancellor refused to permit although he admitted there were several orders permitting similar investments which "had been made in this very lunacy."

In 1890 in the case of *Dickinson, Appellant,* (152 Mass. 184), the Massachusetts Supreme Court condemned an investment in Union Pacific stock on the grounds that the Union Pacific "ran through a new and comparatively unsettled country" and with all those Indians it would be taking "a considerable risk to invest any part of a trust fund in stock of such a road." I cite these historic antecedents not because they do much to illumine your concept of "prudent investment," but because they prove the problem is definitely not new and the judges have been brought up to consider these precedents in judging prudent investment.

In the past, in many states, the matter of trust investments has been regulated by state statute, but at least for any trust involving employees of a company in interstate commerce or where the trust investments are made in or affect interstate commerce, federal law now supersedes any state statute, whether statute law or decision law.

How does it change the trustee's duty?

1.   First of all, it defines a fiduciary somewhat more broadly than the definitions to which we have been accustomed. It permits suits against him in federal courts without the usual jurisdictional requirements and he must be bonded.

2.   In the second place, the new rules preempt state laws on the same subject and adopt a federal prudent man rule that the fiduciary must act "with the care, skill, prudence and diligence under the circumstances then prevailing that a prudent man acting in like capacity and familiar with such matters would use in conducting an enterprise of like character and like aims." This differs from the Restatement of Trusts, Sec. 174, stating the prudent man standard as "that of a man of ordinary prudence in dealing with his own property." The reason for stating the rule in

this new manner was apparently not the objection in a famous case decided by the House of Lords in 1888 *(Knox v. Mackinnon,* 13 App. Cas. 743, 766) that this might require "a trustee to shew that he was a stupid fellow, careless in money matters. . ." and who therefore had indeed used the same prudence that he, a prudent man, had used in handling his affairs, but rather that Congress intended to focus on the "special nature and purpose of employee benefit plans." (Conference Committee Report). In other words, the touchstone for comparison is now not what a prudent private investor would do with his own investments, but what the well-managed pension trustee would do under like circumstances.

However, the more things change the more they remain the same. Congressman Dent twice made an identical statement on the floor of the House about fiduciary responsibilities.[4] He said:

"All plans will be subject to the new Federal trust standards which will delineate the rights and responsibilities of those who are covered by and those who deal with pension plans. These standards, *embodying existing trust concepts,* will prevent abuses of the special responsibilities borne by those dealing with plans."

Therefore, much that we have learned as to prudent trusteeship in still valid law. For example, the Restatement of Trusts, Sec. 174, tells us that if the trustee has greater skill, or advertises greater skill, than that of a man of ordinary prudence, the trustee is obligated to utilize his higher skill. The comments on this section of the Restatement also suggest that a prudent man will not be deemed to have used proper care unless he acquaints himself with the terms of the trust and with the *nature and circumstances* of the trust property. How similar is the new expression of the prudent man rule advertising to "an enterprise of *like character* and *like aims.*" [emphasis added]

In this connection it must be pointed out under the long-standing Internal Revenue Code provisions, qualified retirement plans must be "for the exclusive benefit of the employees and their beneficiaries" and to carry out this requirement, the Internal Revenue Service has developed general rules governing investment of plan assets, including the requirement that cost must not exceed fair market value at time of purchase, that there must be a fair return commensurate with prevailing rate, sufficient liquidity to permit distributions, and the safeguards and the diversity that a prudent investor would adhere to. The Conference Report again adverts to these long-standing standards.

3.   The Act provides us with specific rules as to diversification. Somewhat baffling language requires fiduciaries to diversify plan assets to minimize the risk of large losses "unless under the circumstances it is clearly prudent not to do so." The Conference Report states that this word "clearly" is meant to put a burden of proof on the trustee once the plaintiff meets the initial burden of demonstrating that there was failure to diversify and a loss occurred.

When it comes to the employer's own stock or real estate, there are hard and fast rules as to diversification. Unless the plan is an "eligible individual account plan" defined as a profit sharing, stock bonus, thrift or savings plan, an employee stock ownership plan or a money purchase plan in existence on the date of enactment, it will eventually have to reduce the employer securities and employer real property to 10 percent and even an eligible individual account plan must provide specifically for investment in employer securities in excess of the 10 percent limit. It should be noted that unless the securities are "qualifying employer securities" or the real estate is "qualifying employer real property," with minor exceptions a trustee cannot hold employer investments or employer real estate, regardless of the plan. "Qualifying employer real estate" is further strictly defined to require geographic dispersement—itself a mandate to diversify.

But suppose an eligible individual account plan does provide that all of the assets of the plan may be invested in the stock or other securities of the employer company. And suppose a certain percentage is mandatory. Is the trustee then relieved of a fiduciary duty in connection with such securities? Section 404 (a) (ii) states that, in the case of such an individual account plan, the diversification requirement and the prudence requirement *"only to the extent that it requires diversification"* is not violated by acquisition or holding of the qualifying employer securities. What fiduciary obligations remain? In the Committee Report as to Sec. 407, it is stated that in the case of other types of plans where the 10 percent rule applies, if prudence requires that less than 10 percent of the assets be held in employer securities and employer real property, the lower limit should then apply. If a higher percentage is merely discretionary should not the same rule apply? However, some plans will state, for example, that at least 50 percent of the plan assets or another percentage *must* be invested in employer securities or that all of the *company contribution* in a contributing stock ownership plan must be so invested. There may be an employee relations advantage in thus tying the employee's financial future to the financial health of the company where he works, not offset by an employee relations disadvantage when the employee's stake in the trust is tied to the employer's stock in a declining market.

The definition of fiduciary is framed in terms of having discretionary authority or discretionary control over either the plan management or the plan assets. If the terms of the plan take away from the trustee such discretionary authority and discretionary control, it would then seem in this connection he is not acting as a fiduciary under the strict terms of this definition. Nevertheless, ERISA requires that the trustee have exclusive management and control of the trust assets and even the terms of the plan give the trustee protection only if consistent with ERISA (404 (a) (1) (D)).

Section 404 (a) (ii) is rather precise in relieving the trustee of the prudence requirement *"only to the extent that it requires diversification."* Suppose certain factors in the industry and the economy as a whole cause the trustee to believe very strongly that it is not prudent to place any part of the fund assets in the stock of the company. It would seem under the co-fiduciary rules that the trustee might have some obligation to raise the issue and to bring whatever knowledge he has to the attention of his co-fiduciaries and of the company.

The same problem exists where the investments are either designated by the Company or by a co-fiduciary. The trustee is again placed in a most difficult and compromising position. But he nevertheless retains certain duties to be prudent as a co-fiduciary and to exercise the investment powers he alone possesses under the Act.

I would suggest, as to every other situation, that is, except for these rigid rules as to employer investments, the standards the Conference Report sets out for judging adequate diversification will give fund managers only a small degree of guidance. These are: (1) the purposes of the plan, (2) the amount of the plan assets, (3) financial and industrial conditions, (4) the type of investment, whether mortgages, bonds, shares of stock or otherwise, (5) distribution as to geographic location, (6) distribution as to industries, and (7) the dates of maturity. For example, does the reference to type of investment—mortgages, bonds or stocks—merely mean that with high-risk investments more diversification is needed, or does it imply that an all-stock portfolio or even an all-bond portfolio is insufficiently diversified? I would read this as merely a factor for consideration.

Needless to say a simple reading of the last four items listed in the Committee Report might indicate only that one should diversify in every possible way—as between equities and fixed return investments, as between real estate and securities, as between short-term and long-term bonds, as to geographic location, as to industry, and so on. One of the rules of life engraved over the door of the temple in Delphi was "nothing too much." The famous French statesman,

Talleyrand, often repeated the same rule, "Rien de trop" that means the same thing. Reading of the Committee Report, it appears that may be exactly what Congress meant to tell us as to investment policy. Life being so uncertain and economic forces so confused, there can only be one good rule, "nothing too much." Never too much of any one kind of investment. But this interpretation would rule out the judgmental factors demanded by our existing precedents and the language of the act, "unless it is clearly prudent not to do so."

In any case, these standards in the Conference Committee Report are indeed elementary and simplistic compared with the techniques investment analysts have developed for structuring a portfolio to achieve adequate return and minimize the degree of risk. A study at the University of Chicago by Fisher and Lorie entitled "Some Studies of Variability of Returns on Investments in Common Stock," 43 J. Bus. 99, 109-34 (1970), demonstrated that after a rather small amount of diversification, the resulting reduction in portfolio risk attributable to each additional security becomes negligible. This 1970 study with respect to the New York Stock Exchange revealed that two stocks yielded 40 percent of the benefits of maximum diversification, eight stocks produced 80 percent of the maximum, 90 percent was achieved by holding 16 stocks, 95 percent by holding 32 stocks, and 99 percent by holding 128 stocks. It has been pointed out on numerous occasions that to the extent transaction costs increase according to the number of holdings, the cost of diversification can quickly outweigh the reduction of risk.

What if anything is accomplished by giving such emphasis to diversification and by listing in the Conference Report these standards for diversification?

1.   The reference to dates of maturity can be read with the requirements of Section 402 (b) (1) that from now on every employee benefit plan must describe a procedure under the plan establishing and carrying out a "funding policy and method consistent with the objectives of the plan." As explained in the Conference Report, funding policy requires the plan's sponsor to determine the plan's short- and long-run financial needs, and communicate them to the persons responsible for investments. This should, of course, provide some guidance for the trustee's investment policy.

2.   Whatever sophisticated means a trust develops for determining prudent diversification, if sued, in defending the policies it should be able to hang its defense on some category from the long list in the Conference Report, making relevant the evidence as to the procedures in fact used.

3.   The extensive emphasis on diversification should help to develop in the court decisions support for judging prudent investment on a total portfolio basis rather than on an individual investment basis.

If diversification is indeed so important, a trustee who had not met expectations on one investment should certainly be able to set off the profits which he made on other investments due to his sound diversification policies. Some confusion has come about because the leading case of *Deare v. Deare,* decided in 1895 by the High Court of Justice, (11 TRL 183), laid down a clear rule that a trustee cannot set off a profit derived from one breach of trust against the loss resulting from another. Only last year, the New York Court of Appeals in an unfortunate case of *Bank of New York v. Spitzer,* (364 N.Y.S. 2d 164), in *dicta* applied this rule as a basis for stating that "total return concept" of fiduciary liability—in which an imprudent investment in one security might be offset by an overall gain in all investments held by the fund—cannot be accepted. In this case, in the mandated accounting period, the Bank of New York showed losses with respect to four securities, and in the same period gain from other securities of the same trust fund that far exceeded the losses. Actually, the Court did not find the Bank liable, but took the occasion to state:

> "The fact that the portfolio showed substantial overall increase in total value during the accounting period does not insulate the trustee from responsibility for imprudence with respect to individual requirements for which it would otherwise be surcharged. . . . The focus of inquiry, however, is nonetheless on the individual security as such."

If this be the rule, one might ask why the Federal Act places so much stress on diversification. However, in *Bank of New York v. Spitzer* they were there applying New York State trust law and the court in this very case admitted that:

> "The record of any individual investment is not to be viewed exclusively, of course, as though it were in its own water-tight compartment, since to some extent individual investment decisions may properly be affected by a consideration of the performance of the fund as an entity. . . ."

While the rule has been established at common law that the loss from one breach of trust cannot be set off against the profit from another, quite a different legal question is involved in whether the total investment policy does indeed involve a breach of trust at all. Certainly there are cases where a carefully defined plan of investment includes a clear policy to invest in certain few areas with obvious risk, but a very high return, with the assumption that the growth and high rate of return justifies setting up a reserve against the predictable losses.

We come now to the third case where a trustee's alleged lack of prudence might incur liability. There is no dramatic loss of assets and no failure to produce funds at the time needed but simply a situation where the trustee, possibly by overly conservative management, has invested only in very safe securities with low return. He has fragmentized the trust, causing undue transaction costs and has avoided anything with a reasonably high return in favor of the very safe and the most conservative. The result is that he has no capital loss but when his performance is compared by the rating services, his trust goes to the very bottom of the list, measured in income or appreciation of assets. When will such a trustee, if allowed to continue by the employing company, incur lack-of-prudence liability?

In today's inflationary economy, prudence demands that an attempt be made as much as possible to safeguard the purchasing power of capital as well as its original dollar value. What then of this situation where lack of prudence might be charged—no significant loss, no stocks or bonds gone sour, but simply a relatively poor portfolio performance? In an article in the *New York Law Journal* in 1968, Breen, "Legal Aspects of Substituting Common Stocks for Fixed-Income Securities under the Prudent Man Rule," 159 N.Y.L.J., No. 125, p. 4 (June 27, 1968), it was stated:

> "Probably the risk to be minimized in the original concept of prudence was the risk of dollar loss. But in today's atmosphere of seemingly inevitable inflation and of actual pressure on the dollar from outside sources and the possibility of actual devaluation, the risk to be minimized might well be the risk of only having maintained the actual dollar value of trust principal."

I am not sure this language is as pertinent in 1976 as it appeared in 1968. The author noted that while no court has yet surcharged a trustee for failure to seek the appreciation of a trust res, the possibility of such a ruling is by no means remote.

Those of you who may have attended certain Sunday Schools in your youth, may have been exposed to a so-called parable related in both the Gospel of Matthew and the Gospel of Luke, sometimes called Parable of the Talents, which was in fact a parable of three trustees. The settlor of the trust was about to leave on a journey to a far country. To one trustee he entrusted $5,000, to another $2,000, and to a third only $1,000. The first two trustees were highly speculative in their investments, obtained high rates of interest, and by reason of their investment policies doubled the trust res. The third trustee—unduly concerned with the prudent-man rule and with the obvious requirement as stated by the Executive Committee of the Trust Division of the American Bankers Association that the trustee is "primarily a conserver"—decided that the only prudent way to invest the money was to bury it in the ground. The settlor of the trustee returned, according to the parable, and was highly pleased with the performance of the first two trustees, but as to the latter was highly displeased to the extent that there was weeping and gnashing of teeth, and the trust investment was taken away from that trustee and given to the first more speculative trust.

This ancient parable is cited only to show you that the prudent-man rule is not at all of recent vintage and probably goes back literally to the year one. Furthermore, it illustrates that there has always been an obvious dilemma in balancing the proper desire for the best possible return against preserving the trust res. In an inflationary economy, some overly prudent investments may be equivalent to burying the capital in the ground.

I am not of course suggesting for one moment that there might not wisely be a preponderance of bonds instead of equities in the portfolio, properly diversified as to maturity dates and presumably with no maturity date extending beyond a reasonable term. We must always recall, in making comparisons, that a qualified plan achieves tax exemption on its entire income. A nine percent return, therefore, on a corporate bond would compare with income to an individual of possibly double this amount. The distinction between capital gains and ordinary income for such a pension trust simply does not exist.

4.   Repeatedly, the Conference Report has emphasized that regardless of any rules as to diversification, expressed as a percentage or otherwise, the degree of diversification and the allocation of the portfolio must meet the overall standard of prudence. (See Conference Committee Comments on Sec. 407.)

The statisticians have a rule—used by all quality control departments—that the size of the sample required depends upon predictability and uniformity of the mass. An analogous rule might apply as to diversification. Where there is uniformity—that is clear predictability of performance—less diversification is required than with securities involving less uniform predictability and higher risks.

Many other factors of prudence are equally as important as diversification. These include industry studies, technical studies, detailed current knowledge of an issuer, and the characteristics of its management. It is indeed fortunate, therefore, that the prudent man rule has been phrased in terms of prudence "in the conduct of an enterprise of like character and with like aims." In other words, the standard will now presumably be the standard of a well-managed benefit fund. This obviously differs from the standards of one's personal investment policy or of a testamentary trust with tax questions and the diverse interests of life tenants and remaindermen. It turns the limelight on a basis of comparison—handling a pension fund by knowledgeable people using the highest techniques of money management applicable to pension funds.

A distinction may be made in investment decisions relating to a defined contribution plan and a defined benefit plan. See 88 Har. L. R., 974-979 (1975). In a defined contribution plan, the employee wants the highest possible return and rate of growth, but is also directly affected if there is poor portfolio performance. In a defined benefit plan, risk-taking primarily affects the employer's cost; the employee gets no immediate benefit from a high return, but may suffer from investment failure only if the employer fails or goes out of business. With the defined contribution plan where the employee's benefit is directly related to successful investment policy, there is an obvious trust exposure. On the other hand, where the plan is of the defined benefit type, two opposite reactions have been expressed. One is that so long as the company is still in business, the employee has no interest or concern and the trustee can follow the employer's direction. On the other hand, just the opposite opinion has also been expressed, that since only the employer gains by a higher return, the employees have a right to demand that the fund be invested solely in no-risk securities. It seems to me the answer is to treat this situation no differently than any other problem of prudent trusteeship.

I now will comment on a special problem bearing on fiduciary liabilities, the possible liability for misconduct of co-fiduciaries—a vital concern with the enlarged definition of fiduciary, creating a large and uncontrollable cadre of those labeled "fiduciaries" with the contagion they represent to the other fiduciaries. How can you keep your co-fiduciaries from getting you into trouble and how can you isolate yourself from their derelictions?

ERISA provides four ways trustees may avoid liability for co-fiduciary investment decisions:

(a) The plan may provide that the trustees are subject to the direction of a named fiduciary who is not a named trustee such as an investment committee and in that case the trustee may follow "the proper directions" of such fiduciary made in accordance with the terms of the plan and not contrary to the Act. The term "proper directions" thus implies a duty to review these designations.

(b) There can be an agreement provided it is authorized by the plan parceling out specific responsibilities among trustees in which case the trustee to whom the responsibilities are not allocated are generally not liable.

(c) A named fiduciary other than the trustee may appoint an investment manager or managers and here Sec. 405 provides that no trustee shall be liable for the acts or omissions of such investment manager or be under an obligation to invest or manage an asset which is subject to the management of such investment manager. The investment manager is defined in terms that require that he be delegated power to manage, acquire or dispose of any asset, be registered as an investment adviser under the Investment Advisers Act of 1940, or be a qualified bank or insurance company. Furthermore, this investment manager must acknowledge in writing that he is a fiduciary with respect to the plan.

(d) A plan participant may, pursuant to regulations issued by the Secretary of Labor, pick his own investments. The Act permits a participant or beneficiary to control the assets attributable to his share of the fund in an individual account plan if the plan so authorizes. In such a case, neither he nor any plan fiduciary will be liable for breach of fiduciary standards resulting from exercise of that control. Sec. 404(c)(1)(2). Under such an administrative arrangement, the participants would bear responsibility for the amount of the benefits they ultimately receive by choosing the level of risk to be assumed and particular investments to be made. One may well question how broad a choice can be permitted and still maintain efficient management in an individual account plan and if a broad choice is not permitted whether liability can arise by limiting the choice. We must await regulations. (See 88 Har. L.R., at 975 (1975).)

In defining the liability that one fiduciary will have for the breach of a co-fiduciary in the first three situations, Sec. 405 of the Act begins by stating three rules: first, a fiduciary is his co-fiduciary's keeper where there is knowing participation or knowing concealment of his co-fiduciary's breach; second, if the fiduciary violates the prudent man rule of Sec. 404 in the administration of his fiduciary responsibilities and thus enables another fiduciary to commit a breach; and third, if he has knowledge of a breach by another fiduciary unless he makes reasonable effort under the circumstances to remedy the breach. These rules apply to the first two situations where one fiduciary is subject to designations of another and where the fiduciaries have divided responsibilities by agreement. However, when one comes to Sec. 405(d) providing for investment managers, the Act reduces the liability for the acts of another by eliminating items (2) and (3), as to the prudent man rule and the knowledge of the breach. Unless the co-fiduciaries therefore are *participating* knowingly or are knowingly *concealing* the breach of trust by the investment manager, it would appear no trustee shall be liable for the acts or omissions of such investment manager or have any investment obligations if he reports breaches of which he has knowledge so he is not knowingly concealing the breach. Appointment of an investment manager thus appears to give substantial protection to the trustee.

The Conference Report, however, in referring to the protection from having an investment manager even here qualifies the protection with the words: ". . . as long as the named fiduciary had chosen and retained the investment manager prudentially, the named fiduciary would not be liable for acts of omissions of the manager." One can well ask if the manager is retained prudentially after the reports of the manager repeatedly indicate investments in which a prudent trustee would obviously not invest. Furthermore, it is not clear if a trustee has knowledge of a breach and is therefore knowingly concealing it when he has knowledge of the facts which were later held to constitute the breach. Section 406 (a) as to prohibited transactions uses the language "if he knows or should know." It would seem the omission of "should have known" as to the breach of co-fiduciary, plus the express deletion of the paragraph as to knowledge in reference to investment managers, thus means actual knowledgeable participation or concealment must be present.[5]

Cases where one trustee has been held liable under the present trust law for failure to supervise the conduct of the co-trustee are generally cases of almost shocking lack of care. For example, in *Adams' Estate*, 1908, 70 A. 436, 221 Pa. 77, trustee A allowed trustee B to have sole access to a safety deposit box and after co-trustee B had embezzled the contents, but been required to put them back, A still continued to let B have sole access to the box. Obviously, when a second embezzlement occurred, it appeared this was getting to be a habit and the co-trustee was held liable.

Two of the available insurance policies that insure fiduciaries against potential liability under ERISA contain language that the fiduciary is not insured if he had knowledge of a breach by his co-fiduciary. Here again, what is knowledge of a breach? Must the co-fiduciary have clear knowledge that the violation is occurring or is he violating the Act if he knows of facts, which facts were later held to constitute a breach? For example, does he have knowledge of a breach if he receives copies of the investment report and it later comes to light that one of the investments was clearly unduly speculative and otherwise less than prudent?

It is difficult enough to pick out a course of investment strategy that the courts will find prudent. The situation worsens when one enters a finger-pointing exercise to prove that one is not responsible for imprudence of one's co-fiduciaries.

In opening, in New York in 1975, the American Bar Association National Institute on "Fiduciary Responsibilities Under the Pension Reform Act," Mr Mendes Hershman, chairman of the American Bar Association Section of Corporation, Banking and Business Law, stated[6] that in his opinion the courts will more likely follow corporate director precedents in reviewing complaints of mismanagement of plan funds than they will trustee precedents.

In addition to the similarity in the insurance policies insuring both risks, I would suggest two parallel rules that should apply to both areas of law:

First, if the cases challenging the conduct of corporate directors give us guidance in this area, it is to be found in the perfectly obvious fact that any fiduciary director or trustee must be diligent in seeking out the facts. Just as a wise director will faithfully attend board meetings, review the material that is available to aid him in reaching a correct decision, and not ignore any obvious trends or danger signs of which he should be aware, it would seem to me that the investing fiduciary primarily must be diligent in seeking out the investment facts. This is his first duty as a prudent man.[7]

Second, corporate directors have been shielded by a so-called "business judgment" rule. Things may not always turn out as planned, but if the directors, after carefully weighing alternatives, exercise a bonafide business judgment, the courts will not normally, by hindsight, substitute their own judgment. Are not trustees entitled to the protection of a similar business judgment rule? If a trustee, after carefully weighing alternatives, and documenting his rationale, exercises business judgment as to portfolio selection, a court should respect that business judgment and not by hindsight vision substitute its own.

But until there are court decisions, we will all continue to guess what this fictitious prudent man is really like. Is there only one prudent man or different prudent men for different kinds of trusts? How can this prudent fellow monitor his less than prudent co-fiduciaries? And what *is* being "prudent"?

One may only hope that the court decisions will develop some synonyms for "prudent" that include not simply the words "cautious" and "conservative," but also words such as "shrewd," "wise," "knowledgeable," and "farsighted." But until we have such decisions, we should err on the conservative side. But not too conservative. Even here, remember—nothing too much. Not even of conservatism.

REFERENCES

1. Of the law firm of Gall, Lane and Powell in Washington; Senator Javits' Chief of Staff and principal draftsman of Senator Javits' Pension Reform Bill.

2. *The Business Lawyer,* special issue, October, 1975, page 26.

3. Sec. 402(b) (1).

4. On February 26, 1974 when the House passed HR2, and again on August 20, when the House approved the Conference Committee Report.

5. *Words and Phrases,* (Vol. 23A, p. 481) cites literally dozens of cases where under widely divergent situations knowledge includes constructive knowledge. None of the decisions seem to cover a situation where a trustee is held to have constructive knowledge of derelictions of the co-trustee. A federal case has held that in maritime situations "knowledge" means not only personal cognizance, but also means knowledge of which a captain is bound to avail himself of conditions likely to produce or contribute to loss unless appropriate means are adopted to prevent it. *(Tebbs v. Baker-Whiteley Towing Co.,* D. C., Md., 271 F. Supp. 529, 538.) Substitute the word "trustee" for "Captain" and the similarity between a trustee's prudent conduct and that of a ship captain's is not as remote as it might at first seem.

6. Proceedings of the ABA National Institute, Special Issue of *The Business Lawyer,* October, 1975, page 12.

7. See complaint filed by Teachers' Retirement System of the City of New York vs. United States Trust Company, Supreme Court, State of New York, County of New York No. 11528-75 where the basis of the action is so stated as to failure to sell Penn-Life and Singer Stock.

Reprinted from Financial Analysts Journal, March/April 1978—all rights reserved

by Henry C. Wallich

Investment Income During Inflation

▶ There is no disputing the failure of equities to protect the investor against inflation in recent years: The value of corporate equity holdings of U.S. households dropped from 144 per cent of disposable income in 1968 to 59 per cent in 1976. But this experience lends no plausibility whatever to the argument that bonds are a better hedge against inflation merely because their current yield is twice that of stocks.

According to Irving Fisher, expectations of future price increases should generate a premium over and above the real interest rate equal to the expected inflation rate. Because the inflation premium is taxable, however, high nominal bond yields by no means solve the problem of conserving capital during inflation.

Nor is it correct, in an inflationary environment, to refer to bonds as "riskless." Good bonds are riskless, or nearly so, only with respect to default risk. They are exposed to market risk from changes in interest rates and to purchasing power risk from changes in the inflation rate. If, on the other hand, inflation is brought under control, and interest rates fall, it will no longer be possible to reinvest coupon income at the rate of interest prevailing when the bonds were originally purchased. But the rise in bond prices will be limited by call features and sinking funds that reduce their effective maturity.

Adequate equity prices are an essential condition of continued growth in output and employment—our major economic objectives. In the euphoria that preceded the present gloom, some investors believed the stock market would outperform the economy forever. Today the opposite belief—that the market will always underperform the economy—seems to have taken hold. That belief has implications that go far beyond the question of investment performance. ▶

INVESTMENT income during inflation is of concern, not only to the Federal Reserve, but to all Americans, whether they currently own significant amounts of capital or not. Inflation drives a wedge between nominal and real values, making it difficult to measure accurately the value of assets and the return on them. Inflation, while tending to increase the nominal rate of return, often reduces the real value of assets. Failure to see this, known among economists as money illusion, may leave the investor unaware of what is happening to him. He sustains this illusion at his peril because the consequences may be very real. This holds equally true for the nation as a whole.

One way of avoiding money illusion is to compute wealth data, not in dollar terms, but as a percentage of income. This takes account of both the rise in prices and the rise in the real income of households. Presumably people's behavior and degree of satisfaction with their asset position depends, not on the level of wealth—even when it is computed in constant dollars—but on wealth in relation to income and living standards.

The financial assets of American households reached a high of over four times disposable income in 1968. By 1976, they had fallen to a little over three times disposable income. This was primarily the result of a drop in household corporate equity holdings from 144.4 per cent of disposable income at year-end 1968 to 59.0 per cent at year-end 1976. At current stock market prices, the ratios for both

Henry Wallich is a Member of the Board of Governors of the Federal Reserve System. This article is adapted from his presentation to the Fall 1977 Seminar of the Institute for Quantitative Research in Finance.

total financial assets and the equity component are bound to be substantially less. Since household total liabilities as a percentage of disposable income remained virtually unchanged over this period (73.4 per cent in 1968, 72.8 per cent in 1976), net financial assets after debt declined just as much as gross financial assets.

The experience of American households with real estate has undoubtedly been better than their experience with stocks. Precisely how much better is hard to say—inflation-adjusted data for real estate holdings of households leave something to be desired. According to the statistics, land and residential structures rose from 110.2 per cent of disposable personal income in 1968 to 113.4 per cent in 1976 (again, year-end data). Accordingly, statistics that show the net worth of households declining from 505.3 per cent of disposable personal income in 1968 to 419.1 per cent in 1976 probably paint too dark a picture of the degree of impoverishment.

For many households, gains from real estate undoubtedly exceeded losses on equities. Moreover, since there are many more families owning homes than there are families owning stocks, it seems probable that there has been some redistribution of wealth in the direction of greater equality as a result of these developments.

Bond Investment

In the face of the foregoing evidence, analysts and investors have shifted away from equities and toward bonds and, within the equity field, from growth stocks to dividend stocks. One analyst, writing in this journal, foresees that "the great task of security analysis during the next decade will be to develop an acceptable rationale for equity investing in a period of high, riskless, fixed investment opportunities. If you can get eight to 10 per cent on high-grade bonds, why buy equities?" He observes, "Perhaps the high-bracket investor would be better off enhancing his capital at the rate of five to six per cent a year (a handsome accumulation rate) with tax-free bonds, and not bothering with equities at all."*

No one would dispute the failure of equities in recent years to protect the investor against inflation. Unfortunately the unquestionable fact does not lend plausibility to the assumption that bonds are better, even if their current yield is twice that of stocks.

The behavior of bond returns during inflation rests on a theory developed over 80 years ago by Irving Fisher. Fisher found empirically that interest rates moved with inflation. He demonstrated theoretically that expectation of future price increases should generate a premium, over and above the real interest rate, equal to the expected inflation rate.

Fisher's view has become so nearly axiomatic that the apparent premium contained in today's bond yields is often regarded as a measure of expected inflation. Independent forecasts of the inflation rate over the next five years—forecasts such as those of the National Association of Business Economists—agree with the five to six per cent inflation forecast implicit in the present eight to nine per cent bond rate, allowing for a real rate of three per cent and a risk premium of perhaps one per cent.

I might point out that there is no obvious mechanism enabling an investor to "demand" payment of an inflation premium so long as there is no alternative investment that would better protect him and to which he could shift if he could not obtain the premium he desired. I might further note that periods of high inflation, such as the late 1940's and the early 1950's, did not generate premiums remotely commensurate with the rates of inflation realized, perhaps because inflation then—correctly—was not expected to continue.

More significant yet for the individual investor is the fact that the inflation premium is taxable. The implications for the real rate he will receive after taxes are obvious.

Today's high nominal bond yields, therefore, by no means solve the problem of conservation of capital during inflation. If an investor expected a five per cent rate of inflation to prevail indefinitely, he could conserve his principal only by adding to it at the rate of five per cent per year. He might have to save—out of other income—enough to make up for any after-tax deficiency in the premium. He could not consume any part of his interest unless his top tax bracket were very modest.

Pretty much the same applies to the investor who owns tax-exempts yielding five to six per cent. An investment adviser who provides his client with the standard rates of return available today on long-term investment has by no means solved the investor's inflation problem.

From the point of view of the borrower, the inflation premium is in effect a repayment of principal. The private borrower is favored by the tax system, since that premium, as well as the real interest rate, is tax-deductible. Logically, the investor should treat it in the same way—i.e., as part of his capital. Inflation in effect turns bonds into annuities or serial bonds. By the time a 30-year bond matures, a five per cent rate of inflation will have reduced its purchasing power to about 25 cents on the dollar, a six per cent

---

* Mendon W. Smith, "New Rationalizations," *Financial Analysts Journal* (July/August 1976), pp. 17-18, 19.

rate to less than 20 cents.

My personal view is that we must and will get inflation under control, and that these computations will remain academic. But I have found no strong evidence that investors and investment advisers universally share tis belief. Neither, however, am I aware that investors and their advisers widely follow the practices (described earlier) that are necessary to conserve capital, given their own inflation expectations.

The problem becomes particularly acute in the case of a trust with a lifetime beneficiary and a remainderman. The law governing trusts lays down the rights of the respective parties. So deeply are its concepts ingrained in everyday speech that we have derived the word "windfall" from the good fortune of the life tenant of an entailed estate who, because of the consequences of a heavy storm, is allowed to sell off more timber than he would otherwise be allowed to cut. Inflation is, in fact, a continuing windfall that allows the life tenant to consume the estate to the detriment of his successor. This is true even of inflation correctly anticipated by the participants, if it is not anticipated by the law.

Inflation thus creates a serious problem for the trustee, who has a fiduciary responsibility toward both parties. He gets little help from the Uniform Principal and Income Act, which my legal friends tell me is valid in 39 jurisdictions in the United States. Interest is therein defined as income and thus must be paid to the beneficiary. There seems to be no easy way to keep the corpus intact in real terms if it is totally invested in fixed interest claims. Even if it is partly invested in equities, these equities would have to turn in a remarkable performance, far beyond maintaining their own value against inflation, in order to compensate for attrition of the bond component. I must confess that I have been surprised, in talking to investment advisers and trustees, to find them paying no great attention to this range of problems.

In addition, referring to bonds as "riskless" seems to indicate a serious misconception about the total nature of risk in bond investment during inflation. Good bonds are riskless, or almost so, only with respect to default risk. They are exposed to market risk from changes in interest rates and to purchasing power risk from changes in the inflation rate. Unfortunately, the probability distribution of both risks is skewed in a manner adverse to the investor.

If, as I expect, inflation is brought under control, interest rates will fall and bond prices will rise. Their rise, however, will be limited by the call feature or, in its absence, by approaching maturity. In addition, industrial corporation bonds have sinking funds that reduce the average maturity of the issues. Moreover,

if interest rates do fall, the investor's return on bonds will be overstated by the yield to maturity concept because the latter assumes that all income payments from the obligation are reinvested at the rate of interest prevailing at the time of purchase. Meanwhile, individual company credit risk may mount as some firms find themselves caught with long-term high interest obligations while their competitors are able to refinance more cheaply.

If inflation or expectations of inflation were to accelerate, on the other hand, investors' losses could escalate. What market risk can do to a bond is epitomized by a quotation for British 2-1/2 per cent consols, which had a market price at one point lower than their yield. And what inflation can do to the purchasing power of bonds is illustrated, however remotely, by the fate of German bonds following the two world wars. After World War I, bonds were practically wiped out and were only revalued by law to at best 25 per cent. After World War II, German bonds were devalued to 6-1/2 per cent. Investment advisers who speak of bonds as being riskless should take note of history.

Nothing can make me believe this could happen in the United States. But what is happening right now is a gradual attrition of the purchasing power of bonds. Except in the not very likely event of a falling price level, these losses can never be retrieved.

Equities

The *real* value of the Standard & Poor's 500 Index — i.e. its value adjusted for inflation—stands today at about the level of 1956. Twenty years' worth of profits plowed back, for many companies surely adding up to more than the 1956 value of the stock have contributed nothing to market value. Household holdings of equities, in constant dollars, likewise are worth little more today than they were in 1956.

Why have stocks behaved so poorly? The answer may be in the minds of men, hence unobservable. But two observations stand out. Profits, correctly computed, are low compared with the past, and price-earnings ratios, which capitalize these profits, have shrunk severely. The low level of profits is reflected in the diminished share of corporate profits in the GNP, after proper correction for inventory valuation and underdepreciation, both due to inflation. It can likewise be seen in the historically low rate of return on the net worth of corporations, computing this return, as it should be computed, at replacement cost rather than book value.

Whether shrinking price-earnings ratios reflect lower expectations of future growth or simply a higher risk factor could perhaps be established by examining the work of security analysts. I would be inclined to fault analysts more severely for errors in evaluating future growth of enterprises than for being wrong about price-earnings ratios. The latter, after all, are determined by the stock market and not by the underlying business facts.

What has been the role of inflation in this debacle? Is it responsible for the course that profits have taken? Or are there more fundamental reasons for their behavior, such as a lasting decline in the productivity of capital? I shall comment briefly on only the first of these two possibilities.

Inflation has apparently deceived many businessmen about the true level of their operating profits. Only about half the large firms, and fewer of the small firms, use LIFO for inventory accounting. Few, if any, seem to take into account replacement costs of plant and equipment. This is reflected in the difficulty firms have in generating new investment projects with an adequate return, where current prices of plant and equipment must be taken into account. The market, however, seems not to have been deceived by the often seemingly good but actually illusory profits reported to stockholders—as both research done on the effect of particular accounting methods on stock prices and the low level of stock prices actually prevailing would indicate. There may be some question whether the market has given adequate weight to the reduction in the real value of corporate debt, which in the long run should enhance debt capacity and benefit equity prices, even though it creates no immediate cash flow.

We have no means of knowing whether the downtrend in profits, which has been going on with interruptions since the mid-1960's, will continue or not. At present we are enjoying a recovery, but one far from complete. We can diagnose, however, the consequences for our economy, for growth and for employment if profits fail to retain some semblance of their past share in the GNP. Low profits and low stock prices generally mean that investment does not pay. They mean that the return on capital is low relative to its cost. Low profits, especially when combined with low price-earnings ratios, cause the market's valuation of a company to fall below the replacement cost of its assets. Thus it becomes less profitable for a firm to invest in new plant and equipment than to buy another firm whose stock likewise is selling below replacement cost, or even to buy back its own shares.

It would be wrong to say that an economy in that condition cannot continue because it cannot finance investment by traditional methods. Other forms of financing could be developed. In countries where conditions of this sort have prevailed, government has found itself driven to subsidize investment that was not justified by profits. But I doubt that this is the route our country will want to go.

A more likely sequence seems to me the reestablishment of equilibrium between return and cost of capital through market forces. Inadequate investment, which we are already experiencing, will bring pressure on capacity. Over time, that should lead to more adequate profit margins, even though in the short run such pressures could have adverse consequences that might endanger the continued expansion of the economy.

In a very real sense, adequate equity prices are an essential condition of continued investment and growth. Failure to achieve such prices will damage not only investors. It will slow down economic growth, raise unemployment and frustrate our major national economic objectives. It will, in the end, lead to fundamental changes in our economy.

If these considerations have validity, there is a need to reevaluate the current view that equities cannot keep up with inflation. In the euphoric phase that preceded the present gloom of security analysts, everyone thought the stock market would outperform the economy forever. The market was discounting, not only the future, but the hereafter. Today the opposite view seems to have taken hold— people expect the market to *underperform* the economy forever. This view, as I have tried to show, has implications that go far beyond the humble question of investment performance. ∎

by Michael E. Porter

Industry Structure and Competitive Strategy: Keys to Profitability

The intensity of competition in an industry determines the degree to which investment inflows drive returns to the free market level, hence the ability of firms in the industry to sustain above average returns. Intensity of competition is not a matter of luck. The underlying economic and technological characteristics of the industry determine the strength of the five basic competitive forces—threat of new entrants, bargaining power of buyers, rivalry between existing competitors, threat of substitute products and bargaining power of suppliers. These forces range from intense in industries like tires, paper and steel, where no firm earns spectacular returns, to mild in industries such as oil field equipment and services, cosmetics and toiletries, where high returns are common.

The goal of competitive strategy for a company is to find a position in its industry where these competitive forces will do it the most good or the least harm. A company may take a defensive posture, positioning itself so that its capabilities provide the best defense against the existing array of competitive forces. Alternatively, it can take an offensive approach by developing strategies designed to influence the balance of existing forces or to exploit a change in the competitive balance before rivals recognize it.

The first step in structural analysis is an assessment of the competitive environment in which the company operates—the basic competitive forces and the strength of each in shaping industry structure. The second is an assessment of the company's own strategy—of how well it has positioned itself to prosper in this environment. Taken together, these steps are the key to forecasting a company's earning power.

THE success of a company's competitive strategy depends on how it relates to its environment. Although the relevant environment is very broad, encompassing social as well as economic forces, the key aspect of the company's environment is the industry or industries in which it operates. Industry structure has a strong influence in defining the rules of the competitive game as well as the strategies potentially available to the company.

The intensity of competition in an industry is not a matter of luck. Rather, competition is rooted in underlying industry economics and

goes well beyond the established competitors. Not all industries have equal potential. They differ fundamentally in their ultimate profit potential as the collective strength of the forces of com-

This is an adapted version of Chapter 1 in the forthcoming Free Press publication entitled *COMPETITIVE STRATEGY: TECHNIQUES FOR ANALYZING INDUSTRIES AND COMPETITORS* by Michael E. Porter. Copyright © 1980 by The Free Press, a Division of Macmillan Publishing Co., Inc. By permission of the author and publisher.

Michael Porter is Associate Professor at the Harvard Business School.

Figure I Forces Driving Industry Competition

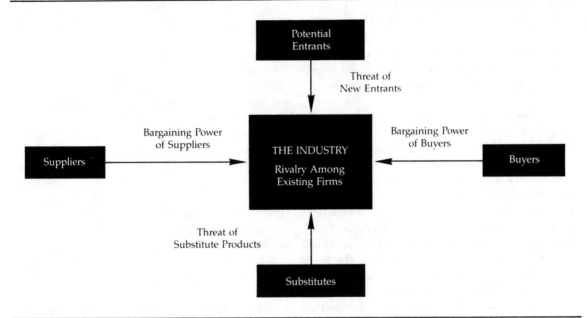

petition differs; the forces range from intense in industries like tires, paper and steel, where no firm earns spectacular returns, to relatively mild in industries such as oil field equipment and services, cosmetics and toiletries, where high returns are common.

The essence of competitive strategy for a company is to find a position in its industry where it can best cope with these competitive forces or can influence them in its favor. Knowledge of the underlying sources of competitive pressure can reveal the basic attractiveness of an industry, highlight the critical strengths and weaknesses of a company, clarify the areas where strategic changes may yield the greatest payoff and pinpoint the industry trends that promise the greatest significance as either opportunities or threats.

Structural Determinants of Competition
Competition in an industry continually works to drive down the rate of return on invested capital toward the competitive floor rate of return, or the return that would be earned by the economist's "perfectly competitive" industry. This competitive floor, or "free market," return is approximated by the yield on long-term government securities adjusted upward by the risk of capital loss. Investors will not tolerate returns below this rate for very long before switching their investment to other vehicles, and firms habitually earning less than this return will eventually go out of business.

The presence of rates of return higher than the adjusted free market return serves to stimulate the inflow of capital into an industry either through new entry or through additional investment by existing competitors. The strength of the competitive forces in an industry determines the degree to which this inflow of investment drives the return down to the free market level, hence the ability of firms to sustain above-average returns.

The state of competition in an industry depends on five basic competitive forces, illustrated in Figure I. The collective strength of these forces determines the ultimate profit potential in the industry, where profit potential is measured in terms of return on invested capital. As Figure I demonstrates, competition extends well beyond the established players. Customers, suppliers, substitutes and potential entrants are all competitors and may be more or less prominent depending on the particular circumstances.

All five competitive forces jointly determine the intensity of industry competition and profitability, but the strongest force or forces become crucial from the point of view of strategy formulation. For example, even a company with a very strong market position in an industry where potential entrants are no threat will earn low returns if it faces a superior, lower cost substitute. Even with no substitutes and blocked entry, intense rivalry between existing competitors will limit potential returns.

Different forces take on prominence, of

course, in shaping competition in each industry. In the ocean-going tanker industry the key force is probably the buyers (the major oil companies), while in tires it is powerful original equipment market buyers coupled with tough competitors. In the steel industry, the key forces are rivalry with foreign competitors and substitute materials.

The underlying *structure* of an industry, reflected in the strength of its five competitive forces, should be distinguished from the many short-run factors that can affect competition and profitability in a transient way. Fluctuations in economic conditions over the business cycle can influence the short-run profitability of nearly all firms in an industry, as can material shortages, strikes, spurts in demand and the like. While such factors have tactical significance, the focus of structural analysis is on identifying the stable, underlying characteristics of an industry—its economic and technological structure—that shape the arena in which competitive strategy must be set.

Industry structure can shift gradually over time, and firms will have unique strengths and weaknesses in dealing with structure. Yet understanding industry structure must be the starting point for strategy analysis. The key economic and technological characteristics critical to the strength of each competitive force are discussed below.

Threat of Entry

New entrants to an industry bring new capacity, the desire to gain market share and often substantial resources. They can bid down prices or inflate costs, reducing profitability. Companies diversifying through acquisition into an industry from other markets often apply their resources to cause a shake-up, as Philip Morris did with Miller beer. Thus acquisition into an industry with intent to build position should probably be viewed as entry, even if it doesn't add a competitor in the literal sense.

Most often, the decision whether or not to enter or diversify into an industry will depend on the *entry deterring price*. The entry deterring price is that which, adjusted for product quality and service, just balances the potential rewards from entry (forecast by the potential entrant) against the expected costs. Of course, incumbent firms may eliminate the threat of entry by pricing below the hypothetical entry deterring price. If they price above it, gains in terms of profitability may be short-lived, since potential entrants will forecast above-average profits from entry, and

will enter.

The cost of entry into an industry will depend in part on the *probable reaction from existing competitors*. If a potential entrant expects the incumbents to respond forcefully to make its stay in the industry a costly and unpleasant one, it may well decide not to enter. If the industry has a history of vigorous retaliation to entrants, if the incumbent firms have substantial resources to fight back (including excess cash and unused borrowing capacity, excess productive capacity or great leverage with distribution channels or customers), or if the industry's growth is sufficiently slow that entry of a new competitor would depress the sales and financial performance of established firms, then potential entrants are likely to meet strong retaliation from incumbents.

The cost of entry will also depend importantly on *barriers to entry* into the industry. Entry barriers are features of an industry that give incumbents inherent advantages over potential entrants. A number of industry characteristics commonly lead to such barriers.

The *need to invest large financial resources in order to compete* creates a barrier to entry, whether those resources must be raised in the capital markets or not. While today's major corporations have the financial resources to enter almost any industry, the huge capital requirements in fields like computers and mineral extraction limit the pool of likely entrants. Capital may be required not only for production facilities, but also for things like customer credit, inventories or covering start-up losses. Xerox created a major barrier to entry in copiers, for example, when it chose to rent copiers rather than sell them outright.

Potential entrants will generally be at a disadvantage in the *capital markets*. Unless a company is entering an industry through diversification, the newcomer is in an inherently riskier position than the established firms, and this will be reflected in the risk premiums it will have to pay to attract capital.

A potential entrant will face barriers if the industry is characterized by *economies of scale*— declines in unit costs of a product (or operation or function that goes into producing a product) as the absolute volume produced per period increases.[1] Scale economies deter entry by forcing the entrant either to come in at large scale and risk strong reaction from existing firms or to accept a cost disadvantage, both undesirable options. Scale economies can be present in nearly every function of a business—production, research and development, marketing, service

1. Footnotes appear at the end of article.

– 302 –

network, sales force utilization or distribution. For example, scale economies in production, research, marketing and service are probably the key barriers to entry in the mainframe computer industry, as Xerox and GE sadly discovered.

Scale economies may relate to an entire functional area, as in the case of a sales force, or they may stem from particular operations or activities. In television set manufacturing, economies of scale are large in color tube production but less significant in cabinetmaking and set assembly. Each component of costs must be examined separately to determine the extent of economies of scale.

Scale economies may form a particularly significant entry barrier if the companies in an industry are generally diversified or vertically integrated. A company that is part of a multibusiness firm may be able to achieve scale economies if it is able to *share operations or functions* subject to economies of scale with other companies in the firm. Consider, for example, a company that manufactures small electric motors that go into industrial fans, hairdryers and cooling systems for electronic equipment assembled by other divisions of the firm. If its economies of scale in motor manufacturing extend beyond the number of motors needed in any one market, it will reap economies in motor manufacturing that exceed those available if it only manufactured motors for use in, say, hairdryers. Thus related diversification around common operations or functions can remove restraints imposed by limited volume of a given market.[2] The prospective entrant must be appropriately diversified or face a cost disadvantage.

The benefits of sharing are particularly potent when a company can incur *joint costs*. Joint costs occur where a firm producing product A (or an operation or function that is part of producing A) must inherently produce product B. For example, technological constraints limit the amount of space airline passenger services can devote to passengers, but make available cargo space and payload capacity. Since it can spread the cost of putting the plane into the air over both passengers and freight, the firm that competes in both passenger and freight may have a substantial advantage over the firm competing in only one market. A similar advantage accrues to businesses whose manufacturing processes result in by-products. The entrant that cannot capture the highest incremental revenue from the by-products will face a disadvantage if incumbent firms can.

The potential entrant also faces the possibility of foreclosure of inputs or markets for its product if most established competitors in the industry are *integrated* (operate in successive stages of production or distribution). In such cases, incumbents purchase from in-house units or sell their inputs in-house. The unintegrated entrant will face a difficult time getting comparable prices and may get "squeezed" if integrated competitors offer it different terms from those offered their captive units.

Entry can be deterred by an entrant's need to secure *distribution channels* for its products. Existing competitors may have ties with channels based on long relations, high quality service or even exclusive contracts whereby the channel is solely identified with a particular manufacturer. To the extent that logical distribution channels for the product are served by established firms, the newcomer must persuade the channels to accept its product, using price breaks, cooperative advertising allowances and other measures that generally cut into profits. A new food product, for example, must displace others from the fiercely competitive supermarket shelf via promotions, intense selling efforts or heavy advertising to create consumer pull. Sometimes this barrier to entry is so high that, to surmount it, a new firm must create an entirely new distribution channel in order to get into the industry.

Newcomers will find it particularly difficult to compete with established firms for distribution channels and buyers if the industry is characterized by *product differentiation*. Product differentiation means that established firms have brand identification and customer loyalties stemming from past advertising, customer service and product differences. Not infrequently, these firms can benefit from economies of scale as a result. The cost of creating a brand name, for instance, need only be borne once; the name may then be freely applied to other products of the company, subject only to any costs of modification. A newcomer, on the other hand, must spend heavily to overcome existing distributor and customer loyalties. Investments in building a brand name are particularly risky, since they are unrecoverable.

Product differentiation is perhaps the most important entry barrier in baby care products, over-the-counter drugs, cosmetics, investment banking and public accounting. In the brewing industry, product differentiation is coupled with economies of scale in production, marketing and distribution to create high barriers.

Entry can also be deterred if *switching costs* are high. Switching costs are one-time costs of switching brands or switching from one supplier's product to another's. Switching costs may include such things as employee retraining costs, the cost of new ancillary equipment, the cost and time needed to test or qualify a new source or to redesign a product or even the psychic costs of severing a relationship. If such costs are high, the entrant must offer a major improvement in cost or performance to induce the buyer to switch. For example, suppliers of intravenous solutions and kits for use in hospitals have different procedures for attaching solutions to patients, and the hardware for hanging the solution bottles are not compatible. This industry is characterized by relatively high returns.

Government policy may also represent a substantial entry barrier in some industries. Government can consciously or unconsciously limit or even foreclose entry into industries, using such controls as licensing requirements or limits on access to raw materials (e.g., coal lands or mountains suitable for ski areas). Government regulation restricts entry to such industries as trucking, railroads, liquor retailing, broadcasting and freight forwarding.

More subtle restrictions on entry can stem from government subsidies to incumbents or from governmental controls such as air and water pollution standards or product safety and efficacy regulations. Pollution control requirements can raise capital needed for entry and can increase required technological sophistication and even optimal scale of facilities. Standards for product testing, common in industries like food and other health-related products, can impose substantial lead times on getting into an industry, not only raising the cost of entry but giving established firms ample notice of impending entry and, sometimes, full knowledge of competitor products. Government policy in such areas certainly may have social benefits, but it often has second-order consequences for entry that go unrecognized.

While the barriers mentioned so far can perhaps be surmounted by entrants willing to invest the capital, established firms may have other *cost advantages* not replicable by potential entrants no matter what their size and attained economies of scale. For instance, some industries are characterized by *proprietary product technology*—know-how or techniques that are kept proprietary through patents or secrecy. In others, the established firms may have locked up the most *favorable raw material sources*, or tied up foreseeable raw material needs early at prices reflecting a lower demand for them than cur-

rently exists. For example, Frasch sulphur firms like Texas Gulf Sulphur gained control of some very favorable salt dome sulphur deposits many years ago, before mineral right holders were aware of their value as a result of the Frasch mining technology. Discoverers of sulphur deposits were often disappointed oil companies exploring for oil. Similarly, established firms in some industries may have cornered *favorable locations* before market forces bid up prices to capture their full value. Potential newcomers will enter at a permanent competitive disadvantage.

Experience Curve

Another important factor that creates cost advantages is the *experience curve*. In some businesses, unit costs tend to decline as the firm gains more cumulative experience in production. Experience is just a name for certain kinds of technological change. Workers become more efficient (the classic learning curve), layout improves, equipment and processes become specialized. Changes in product design techniques and operations control make manufacturing easier.

Cost declines with experience seem to be most significant in businesses involving a high labor content and/or complex assembly operations (aircraft, shipbuilding). They are nearly always greatest in the early and growth phases of a product's development, diminishing in later phases.

In some ways, cost declines with experience operate in the same manner as scale economies. Experience can lower costs in marketing, distribution and other areas as well as production or operations within production, and each component of costs must be examined for experience effects. Diversification can enhance cost declines due to experience, since diversified firms can share operations or functions subject to experience cost declines and units in diversified firms can benefit from the experience gained by other related units. In the case where an activity like raw material fabrication is shared by multiple business units, experience obviously accumulates faster than it would if the activity were used solely to meet the needs of one company.

Economies of scale are often cited as one of the reasons costs decline with experience. But economies of scale are dependent on volume per period, not cumulative volume, and are very different analytically from cost declines with experience. Economies of scale and experience also have very different properties as entry barriers. The presence of economies of scale *always* leads to a cost advantage for the large-scale or properly diversified firm over the small-scale or undiversified firm, presupposing that the large firm has the most efficient facilities, distribution systems, service organizations and other functional units for its size.

Experience is a more ethereal entry barrier than scale. The mere presence of an experience curve does not ensure an entry barrier. The experience must be proprietary—i.e., not available to competitors and potential entrants through (1) copying, (2) hiring competitors' employees or (3) purchasing the latest machinery from equipment suppliers or the relevant know-how from consultants or others.

If the experience curve can be kept proprietary by established firms, then they can erect an entry barrier. Newly started firms, with no experience, will have inherently higher costs than established firms and will have to incur heavy start-up losses from below or near-cost pricing before they can gain the experience requisite to cost parity with established firms. Because of their lower costs, established firms (particularly the market share leader) will have higher cash flows to invest in new equipment and technique. New entrants will never catch up. A number of firms (notably Texas Instruments, Black and Decker and Emerson Electric) have built successful strategies based on the experience curve through aggressive investments to build cumulative volume early in the development of their industries, often by pricing in anticipation of future cost declines.

Many times, however, experience cannot be kept proprietary. Even when it can, it may accumulate more rapidly for the second and third firms in the market than it did for the pioneer. The later firms can observe some aspects of the pioneer's operations. In situations where experience cannot be kept proprietary, new entrants may actually have an advantage if they can buy the latest equipment or adapt to new methods unencumbered by having operated the old way in the past.

An experience barrier can be nullified by product or process innovations leading to a substantially new technology that creates an entirely new experience curve.[3] New entrants can leapfrog the industry leaders and alight on the new experience curve, to which the leaders may be poorly positioned to jump. Similarly, technological change may penalize the large-scale firm if facilities designed to reap economies of scale are specialized, hence less flexible in adapting to new technologies.

Commitment either to achieving scale economies or to reducing costs through experience has some potential risks. It may cloud the perception of new technological possibilities, or of other ways of competing less dependent on scale or experience. Emphasis on scale over other valuable entry barriers such as product differentiation may work against image or responsive service. Hewlett-Packard has erected substantial barriers based on technological progressiveness in industries like calculators and minicomputers, where other firms are following strategies based on experience and scale.

Properties of Entry Barriers

All entry barriers can and do change as conditions in the industry change. The expiration of Polaroid's basic patents on instant photography, for instance, greatly reduced its absolute cost entry barrier built by proprietary technology; it is not surprising that Kodak plunged into the market. Product differentiation in the magazine printing industry has all but disappeared, reducing barriers. Conversely, in the auto industry economies of scale increased enormously with postwar automation and vertical integration, virtually stopping successful new entry.

While entry barriers sometimes change for reasons largely outside a company's control, company strategic decisions can have a major impact on entry barriers. In the 1960s, many U.S. wine producers stepped up product introductions, raised advertising levels and expanded distribution nationally, increasing entry barriers by raising economies of scale and product differentiation and making access to distribution channels more difficult. Similarly, decisions by members of the recreational vehicle industry to integrate vertically have greatly increased the economies of scale there.

Finally, some firms may possess resources or skills that allow them to overcome entry barriers into an industry more cheaply than most other firms. Gillette, with well developed distribution channels for razors and blades, faced lower costs of entry into disposable lighters than many other potential entrants would have faced.

Rivalry Between Existing Competitors

Rivalry between existing competitors takes the familiar form of jockeying for position—using tactics like price competition, advertising battles, product introductions and increased customer service or warranties. Rivalry occurs because one or more competitors either feel pressured or see the opportunity to improve position. In most industries, competitive moves by one firm have noticeable effects on its competitors and thus may incite retaliation. Firms are consequently *mutually dependent*.

A sequence of actions and reactions may or may not leave the initiating firm and the industry as a whole better off. If moves and countermoves escalate, then all firms in the industry may suffer and be worse off than before. Some forms of competition (notably price competition) are highly unstable and likely to leave the entire industry worse off from a profitability standpoint. Price cuts are quickly and easily matched by rivals and, once matched, lower revenues for all firms unless industry price elasticity of demand is very great. Advertising battles, on the other hand, may well expand demand or raise the level of product differentiation in the industry, to the benefit of all firms.

Rivalry in some industries is characterized by such phrases as "warlike," "bitter" or "cutthroat," while in other industries it is termed "polite" or "gentlemanly." The intensity of rivalry can be traced to the presence of a number of interacting structural factors.

When the *competitors in an industry are numerous*, the likelihood of mavericks that will touch off rivalry is great, since some firms may believe they can make moves without being noticed. Even if there are relatively few firms, if they are *relatively balanced* in terms of the resources for sustained and vigorous retaliation, they may be prone to take each other on. On the other hand, when an industry is highly concentrated or dominated by one or a few firms, relative power will be stable and apparent to everyone, and the leader or leaders will be able to impose discipline through devices like price leadership.

Slow industry growth is generally a destabilizing force for rivalry, since it can turn competition into a market share game for firms seeking expansion. When industry growth is rapid, firms can improve results just by keeping up with the industry; in fact, all their financial and managerial resources may be consumed by expanding with the industry.

High fixed costs create strong pressures for all firms to fill capacity, which often leads to rapidly escalating price cutting. Many basic materials like paper and aluminum suffer from this problem. The key is fixed costs relative to value added, rather than the absolute level of fixed costs. Firms purchasing a high proportion of costs in outside inputs (low value added) may feel enormous pressures to fill capacity to break even, even if the absolute proportion of fixed

costs is low. A similar situation faces industries whose products are very difficult or costly to store. Here firms will be vulnerable to temptations to shade prices in order to ensure sales. This sort of pressure keeps profits low in lobster fishing and in industries that manufacture certain hazardous chemicals.

When the industry *product is perceived as a commodity or near-commodity*, buyer choice will largely be dictated by price and service, creating strong pressures for price and service competition. Differentiation, on the other hand, creates layers of insulation against competitive warfare because buyers have preferences and loyalties to particular sellers. Similar insulation against rivalry is provided by *switching costs* (defined earlier).

Rivalry is increased by pressures that lead to *chronic overcapacity*. For example, where economics dictate that capacity can be augmented only in large increments, capacity additions can be chronically disruptive to the industry supply-demand balance, particularly when there is a risk of bunching of capacity additions. The industry may face chronic periods of the kind of overcapacity and price cutting that afflict chlorine, vinyl chloride and ammonium fertilizer.

Competitors that are diverse in strategies, origins, personalities and relationships to their parent companies create volatile rivalry because they have differing goals and differing ideas about how to compete and are continually colliding head-on in the process. They have a hard time accurately reading each others' intentions and agreeing on the rules of the game for the industry. Strategic choices "right" for one competitor will be "wrong" for the others.

Foreign competitors often add a great deal of diversity to industries because of their differing circumstances and often differing goals. Owner-operators of small manufacturing or service firms may be willing to accept subnormal rates of return on their investment capital in exchange for independence; such low returns may appear unacceptable or irrational to a large publicly held competitor. In such an industry, the posture of the small firms may limit the profitability of the larger concern. Similarly, firms viewing a market as a dumping outlet for excess capacity will adopt policies contrary to those of firms that view the market as their main business.

Differences in the way companies competing in an industry relate to their corporate parents is another important source of diversity. A company that is one part of a vertical chain of busi-

Figure II Exit and Entry Barriers Combine

ENTRY BARRIERS	EXIT BARRIERS: Low	EXIT BARRIERS: High
Low	Low Returns	Worst Case
High	Best Case	High Returns But Risky

nesses within its corporate organization may well adopt goals very different from those of a free-standing company competing in the same industry. A company that represents a "cash cow" in its parent company's portfolio of businesses will behave differently from one being developed for long-run growth.

Industry rivalry becomes even more volatile if a number of firms in the industry have *high stakes in achieving success.* For example, a diversified firm may place great importance on achieving success in a particular industry in order to further its overall corporate strategy. Or a foreign firm like Bosch, Sony or Philips may perceive a strong need to establish a solid position in the U.S. market in order to build global prestige or technological credibility. Such firms may be willing to sacrifice profitability for the sake of expansion.

Finally, industry rivalry can be volatile when an industry faces high *exit barriers*—factors that keep companies competing in businesses even though they may be earning low or even negative returns on investment. Excess capacity does not leave the industry, and companies that lose the competitive battle do not give up. Rather, they hang on grimly and, because of their weakness, sometimes resort to extreme tactics that can destroy the profitability of the entire industry.

Exit barriers may be high when assets are highly specialized to a particular business or location, hence difficult to liquidate; when labor agreements, resettlement costs or spare parts maintenance create fixed costs of exit; when interrelationships between one company and others in a multibusiness firm in terms of image, marketing ability, access to financial markets, shared facilities and so on lend the business broader strategic importance; when government denies or discourages exit because of job loss and regional economic effects (particularly common outside the U.S.); or when managements are unwilling to make economically justified exit decisions because of loyalty to employees, fear of the consequences for their own careers, pride or other emotional reasons.

While exit barriers and entry barriers are conceptually separate, their combination is an important aspect of the analysis of an industry. Exit and entry barriers often rise and fall together. The presence of substantial economies of scale in production, for example, usually implies specialized assets, as does the presence of proprietary technology. Figure II illustrates the possible combinations. The best case from the viewpoint of industry profits is where entry barriers are high but exit barriers are low. Here entry will be deterred and unsuccessful competitors will leave the industry. Where both entry and exit barriers are high, profit potential is high but is usually accompanied by more risk. Although entry is deterred, unsuccessful firms will stay and fight in the industry.

While the case of low entry and exit barriers is unexciting from a profitability standpoint, the worst case is where entry barriers are low and exit barriers are high. Here entrants will be attracted by upturns in economic conditions or other temporary windfalls. They will not leave the industry, however, when results deteriorate. As a result, industry capacity will stack up and profitability will usually be chronically poor.

Shifting Rivalry

Industry features that determine the intensity of competitive rivalry can and do change. As an industry matures, its growth rate declines, resulting in intensified rivalry, declining profits and (often) a shakeout. In the booming recreational vehicle industry of the early 1970s, nearly every producer did well; but slow growth since then has eliminated the high returns to all except the strongest members. The same story has been played out in industry after industry—snowmobiles, aerosol packaging and sports equipment, to name a few.

Rivalry can also shift when an acquisition introduces a very different personality into an industry. This has been the case with Philip Morris' acquisition of Miller Beer and Procter & Gamble's acquisition of Charmin Paper Company. Also, technological innovation can boost the level of fixed costs in the production process and raise the volatility of rivalry, as it did in the shift from batch to continuous-line photofinishing in the 1960s.

While a company must live with many of the factors determining the intensity of industry rivalry that are built into industry economics, it may have some latitude to influence rivalry through its choice of strategy. A company may try to raise buyers' switching costs by designing its product into its customers' operations or by making its customers dependent for technical advice. A company can attempt to raise product differentiation through new kinds of service, marketing innovations or product changes. Focusing selling efforts on the fastest growing segments of the industry or on market areas with the lowest fixed costs can reduce the impact of industry rivalry. If it is feasible, a company can try to avoid confrontation with competitors having high exit barriers, thus sidestepping involvement in bitter price cutting.

Pressure from Substitute Products

All firms in an industry are competing, in a broad sense, with industries producing substitute products. Substitutes limit the profit potential of an industry by placing a ceiling on the prices firms in the industry can charge. The more attractive the price-performance tradeoff offered by substitutes, the tighter the lid on industry profits. Sugar producers confronted with the large-scale commercialization of high fructose corn syrup, a sugar substitute, are learning this lesson today, as are producers of acetylene and rayon, who face tough competition from lower cost alternatives.

Substitutes not only limit profits in normal times, but also reduce the bonanza an industry can reap in boom times. In 1978, the producers of fiberglass insulation enjoyed unprecedented demand as a result of high energy costs and severe winter weather. But the industry's ability to raise prices was tempered by the plethora of insulation substitutes, including cellulose, rock wool and styrofoam. These substitutes are bound to become an even stronger force once the current round of plant additions by fiberglass insulation producers has boosted capacity enough to meet demand (and then some).

Identifying substitute products entails searching for other products that can perform the same *function* as the product of the industry. Sometimes this can be a subtle task, one that takes the analyst into businesses seemingly far removed from the industry in question. Securities, for example, face increasing competition from alternative investments such as real estate, insurance and money market funds.

Government regulations, subsidies and tax policies should also be considered in the search for substitutes. The U.S. government is currently promoting solar heating, for example, using tax incentives and research grants. Government de-

control of natural gas is quickly eliminating acetylene as a chemical feedstock. Safety and pollution standards also affect relative cost and quality of substitutes.

Attention should focus on substitute products that (a) are enjoying steady improvement in price-performance tradeoff with the industry's product, (b) would entail minimal switching costs for prospective buyers or (c) are produced by industries earning high profits. In the latter case, substitutes often come rapidly into play if some development increases competition in their industries and causes price reduction or performance improvement.

Effective defense against substitute products may require *collective industry action*. While advertising by one firm in an industry does little to bolster the industry's position against a substitute, heavy and sustained advertising by all industry participants may well improve the industry's collective position against the substitute. Similar arguments apply to collective industry response through industry groups and other means in areas such as product quality improvement, marketing efforts and product distribution.

Trend analysis can be important in deciding whether company strategy should be directed toward heading off a substitute strategically or accepting the substitute as a key competitive force. Electronic alarm systems, for example, represent a potent substitute in the security guard industry. Electronic systems can only become more important as a substitute since labor-intensive guard services face inevitable cost escalation, while electronic systems are highly likely to improve in performance and decline in cost. Here the appropriate response of security guard firms is probably to offer packages of guards and electronic systems, with the security guard redefined as a skilled operator, rather than attempt to compete against electronic systems with a traditional guard service.

Bargaining Power of Buyers

Buyers represent a competitive force because they can bid down prices, demand higher quality or more services, and play competitors off against each other—all at the expense of industry profitability. The power of each important buyer group depends on a number of characteristics of its market situation and on the relative importance of its purchases from the industry compared with the industry's overall business.

A buyer group will be powerful if it *purchases large volumes relative to seller sales*, so that retaining its business is financially important to the seller. Large volume buyers are particularly potent forces if heavy fixed costs characterize the industry (as in corn refining and bulk chemicals) and raise the stakes to keep capacity occupied.

Buyer power is enhanced if the products purchased from the industry *represent a significant fraction of total purchases*. In this case, the buyer will be prone to expend the resources necessary to shop for a favorable price and to purchase selectively. If the product sold by the industry is a small fraction of the buyer's costs, the buyer will usually be much less price sensitive. Similarly, a buyer suffering from *low profits* has great incentive to lower purchasing costs. Suppliers to Chrysler, for example, are complaining that they are being pressed for superior terms. Highly profitable buyers are generally less price sensitive and more concerned about the long-run health of their suppliers (that is, unless the purchase represents a large fraction of their costs). Buyer power is also increased if buyers have a lot of *information* about market conditions, supplier costs and offers to other buyers.

If buyers are either already partially integrated or *pose a strong threat of backward integration*, they are in a position to demand bargaining concessions. Major automobile producers like General Motors and Ford frequently use this bargaining lever. They engage in the practice of *tapered integration*, or producing some of their needs for a given component in-house and purchasing the rest from outside suppliers. Not only is their threat of further integration particularly credible, but partial manufacture in-house gives them detailed knowledge of costs, which is a great aid in negotiation. Buyer power can be partially neutralized when firms in the industry offer a threat of forward integration into the buyer's industry.

Finally, the *impact of the supplier's product* on the buyer's business will help determine the bargaining power of purchasers. If the quality of the buyer's product is very much affected by the quality of the industry's product, the buyer will generally be less price sensitive. In oil field equipment, for instance, a malfunction can lead to large losses (as witness the enormous cost of the recent failure of a blowout preventer in a Mexican offshore oil well); the quality of enclosures for electronic medical and test instruments can greatly influence the user's impression about the quality of the equipment inside.

Finally, *switching costs* (defined earlier) lock the buyer to particular sellers and mitigate buyer power. On the other hand, if the industry's products are standard or undifferentiated, buyers, sure that they can always find alternative suppliers, may play one company against another, as they do in aluminum extrusion.

Most sources of buyer power apply to consumer as well as to industrial and commercial buyers. For example, consumers tend to be more price sensitive if they are purchasing products that are undifferentiated or expensive relative to their incomes.

The power of wholesalers and retailers is determined by the same rules, with one important addition. Retailers can gain significant bargaining power over manufacturers if they can *influence consumers' purchasing decisions*, as they do in audio components, jewelry, appliances and sporting goods. Similarly, wholesalers can gain bargaining power if they can influence the decisions of the retailers or other firms to which they sell.

Altering Buying Power

The power of buyers can rise or fall as the underlying factors creating buyer power change with time or as a result of a company's strategic decisions. In the ready-to-wear clothing industry, for example, the buyers (department stores and clothing stores) have become more concentrated and control has passed to large chains; as a result, the industry has come under increasing buyer pressure and suffered falling profit margins. So far the industry has been unable to differentiate its products or to engender switching costs that would lock its buyers in sufficiently to neutralize these trends.

A company's choice of the buyer group it sells to is a crucial strategic decision. A company can improve its strategic posture by finding buyers who possess the least power to influence it adversely—in other words, by *buyer selection*. Rarely do all the buyer groups a company sells to enjoy equal power. Even if a company sells to a single industry, there are usually segments within that industry that exercise less power (and that are less price sensitive) than others. For example, the replacement market for most products is less price sensitive than the original equipment market.

Bargaining Power of Suppliers

Suppliers can exert a competitive force in an industry by raising prices or reducing the quality of the goods they sell. Such price increases can squeeze profitability out of an industry unable to recover cost increases in its own prices. By raising their prices, for example, chemical companies have contributed to the erosion of profitability of contract aerosol packagers because the packagers, facing intense competition from self-manufacture by their customers, have limited freedom to raise their prices.

The conditions making suppliers powerful are largely the inverse of those making buyers powerful. If a supplier group is *dominated by a few companies and more concentrated than the industry it sells to*, it will be able to exert considerable influence on prices, quality and terms. On the other hand, the power of even large, powerful suppliers can be checked if they have to compete with *substitutes*. Industries producing alternative sweeteners, for example, compete sharply for many applications even though individual suppliers are large relative to individual customers.

If suppliers sell to a number of industries, so that one particular *industry does not represent a significant fraction of sales*, they will be much more prone to exert pricing pressure. If the industry is an important customer, suppliers' fortunes will be closely tied to the industry, and suppliers will want to protect the industry through reasonable pricing and assistance in activities like research and development and lobbying.

Differentiation and switching costs cut off buyers' options in playing one supplier off against another and raise supplier power. And a *credible threat of forward integration* provides a check against an industry's ability to improve the terms on which it purchases.

It is important to recognize *labor* as a supplier, and one that exerts great power in many industries. There is substantial empirical evidence that scarce, highly skilled employees (e.g., engineers and scientists) and/or tightly unionized labor can bargain away a significant fraction of potential profits in an industry. The features that determine the potential power of employees as a supplier include those outlined above plus labor's *degree of organization* and the ability of the supply of scarce varieties of employees to *expand*. Where labor is strongly organized and supply of scarce employees constrained from expansion, they can be a factor in competition.

Government, which has been discussed primarily in terms of its possible impact on entry barriers, must also be recognized as a potentially powerful buyer and supplier. In these roles, government can often influence industry competition by the policies it adopts. Government plays a crucial role as a buyer of defense-related products and as a supplier of timber through the Forest Service's control of vast timber reserves in the western United States. Many times government's role as a supplier or buyer is determined more by political factors than by economic circumstances, and this is probably a fact of life.

The conditions determining supplier power are frequently beyond a company's control. However, as with buyer power, the firm can sometimes improve its situation through strategy. It can promote a threat of backward integration, seek to eliminate switching costs and the like.

Structural Analysis and Competitive Strategy

Once the forces affecting competition in an industry and their underlying causes have been diagnosed, a company is in a position to identify its strengths and weaknesses relative to the industry. The crucial strengths and weaknesses from a strategic standpoint are the company's posture vis à vis the underlying causes of each competitive force. Where does it stand against substitutes? Against the sources of entry barriers? In coping with rivalry from established competitors?

Competitive strategy is taking offensive or defensive action in order to strengthen a company's position in relation to the five competitive forces—positioning the company so that its capabilities provide the best defense against the existing array of competitive forces, influencing the balance of forces through strategic moves that improve the company's relative position or anticipating shifts in the factors underlying the forces and responding so as to exploit change by choosing a strategy appropriate to the new competitive balance before rivals recognize it.

A *positioning strategy* takes the structure of the industry as given and matches the company's strengths and weaknesses to it, building defenses against the competitive forces or finding positions in the industry where the forces are weakest. Knowledge of the company's capabilities and of the causes of the competitive forces will highlight the areas where the company should confront competition and where it should avoid competition. If the company is a low cost producer, for example, it may choose to confront powerful buyers while it takes care to sell them only products not vulnerable to competition from substitutes.

Alternatively, a company can take an offensive approach by developing *strategies designed to influence the balance of competitive forces*. Innovations in marketing can raise brand identification or otherwise differentiate the company's product.

Capital investments in large-scale facilities or vertical integration can bolster entry barriers. Structural analysis can be used to identify the factors driving competition that will be most susceptible to strategic action.

Industry evolution is important strategically because evolution can present opportunities to *exploit changes in the sources of competition.* In the familiar product life cycle pattern of industry development, for example, growth rates change as the business matures, advertising declines and companies tend to integrate vertically.

These trends are not so important in themselves; what is critical is whether they affect the structural sources of competition. For example, extensive vertical integration, both in manufacturing and in software development, is taking place in the maturing minicomputer industry. This very significant trend has greatly increased economies of scale as well as the amount of capital necessary to compete in the industry. This in turn has raised entry barriers and threatens to drive some smaller competitors out of the industry.

Obviously, the trends carrying the highest priority from a strategic standpoint are those that affect the most important sources of competition in the industry and those that elevate new structural factors to the forefront. In contract aerosol packaging, for instance, the dominant trend toward less product differentiation has increased the power of buyers, lowered the barriers to entry and intensified competition.

The task of structural analysis in the long run is to examine each competitive force, forecast the magnitude of each underlying cause and construct a composite picture of the likely profit potential of the industry. Of course, this picture may differ considerably from present realities. Today, the solar heating business is populated by dozens and perhaps hundreds of companies, none with a major market position. Entry is easy and competitors are battling to establish solar heating as a superior substitute for conventional heating methods.

The potential of solar heating will depend largely on the shape of future barriers to entry, the improvement of the industry's position relative to substitutes, the ultimate intensity of competition and the power that will be captured by buyers and suppliers. These characteristics will, in turn, be influenced by such factors as the establishment of brand identities, the creation of significant economies of scale or experience curves in equipment manufacture, the ultimate capital costs and the eventual importance of fixed costs in production.

Of course, no structural analysis can be complete without a diagnosis of how present and future government policy, at all levels, may affect competitive conditions. For purposes of strategic analysis it is usually more illuminating to consider how government affects competition through the five competitive forces than to consider it as a force in and of itself. However, strategy may well involve treating government as a factor to be influenced.

Structural Analysis and Diversification

The framework for analyzing industry competition is obviously useful in setting diversification strategy, since it provides a guide for answering the extremely difficult question inherent in diversification decisions: What is the potential of this business? The framework may allow a company to spot an industry with a good future before this potential is reflected in the prices of acquisition candidates. It will also help a company identify industries where its strengths will allow it to overcome entry barriers more cheaply than other firms. And the framework can help in identifying acquisitions that can take advantage of existing operations—for example, acquisitions that would allow a firm to overcome key entry barriers by providing shared functions or preexisting relations with distribution channels. ∎

Footnotes

1. To avoid needless repetition, the term "product," rather than "product or service," is used throughout to refer to the output of an industry. The principles of structural analysis will apply equally to product and service businesses. They also apply to industry competition in any country or international market, although some of the institutional circumstances may differ.

2. For this entry barrier to be significant, it is crucial that the shared operation or function be subject to economies of scale that extend beyond the size of any one market. If this is not the case, cost savings of sharing can be illusory. A company may see its costs decline after entering a related business as overhead is spread, but this depends solely on the presence of excess capacity in the operation or function in the base business. Such economies are short run, and once capacity is fully utilized the true cost of the shared operation will become apparent.

3. For an example of this drawn from the history of the automobile industry, see William J. Abernathy and Kenneth Wayne, "The Limits of the Learning Curve," *Harvard Business Review*, September-October 1974, p. 109.

**Then
and now**

A particularly
unhappy anniversary

Why didn't things turn out better?

James H. Lorie

Usually, an anniversary of a disaster creates ambivalence; the unhappiness of the memory is somewhat offset by the consolation that things aren't as bad as they used to be. On this 50th anniversary of the Great Crash of 1929-32 (GC I), the consolation is missing. Things *are* as bad as they used to be. The performance of the stock market in recent years has been in some ways worse than in GC I, and the causes of the recent "crash" (GC II) seem more intractable. This essay compares the two crashes and discusses the causes of the recent (current?) disaster.

THE TWO CRASHES COMPARED

There are scores of reasonable ways to compare the severity of the two crashes. One can compare highest days to lowest days; highest months to lowest months; highest year-ends to lowest year-ends. One can consider all stocks, only stocks on the New York Stock Exchange, or changes in the levels of various indices. One can compare rates of return with different assumptions about investment policies, uses of dividends, and the tax status of the investor. One can base measurements on current dollars or constant dollars, and current dollars can be converted to constant dollars in various ways. One can compare the speed of declines as well as their duration.

To achieve tolerable brevity and clarity, this essay contains only a few of the many reasonable comparisons. The conclusions have not been seriously affected by the choice of measurements, with one exception — the choice of measurements based on constant rather than current dollars. One's impression of the severity of GC I is enhanced when measurements are in current dollars, since the Consumer Price Index

declined by about 20% from 1929 to 1932. In contrast, measurements in current dollars of changes in stock prices during GC II would tend to conceal the severity of the decline. For example, the CPI rose about 90% between 1968 and 1978 and 18% between 1972 and 1974, the period of most dramatic decline. Since the more meaningful comparison is between changes in the value of stocks rather than between changes in prices, the measurements given below will be based on constant dollars, unless otherwise indicated.

Between the end of 1929 and the end of 1932, prices of stocks on the New York Stock Exchange declined on the average by 63%, in constant dollars. The comparable figure for the period from the end of 1972 to the end of 1974 was 53%.[1] During the period of the most rapid and almost continuous decline, GC I was somewhat more severe.

If one focuses somewhat arbitrarily on the decades following the year-ends in 1929 and 1968, GC II was more severe. During the earlier decade, the decline in the dollar value of stocks on the New York Stock Exchange was 49%; during the later decade, 54%. During the earlier decade, the average annual rate of return for the tax-exempt investor who invested in every common stock on the New York Stock Exchange in proportion to its value was +2.0%; during the decade 1968-78, the return was between −2.0 and −3.0%. For the investor in a relatively high tax bracket, the relative severity of GC II was even greater. The average annual rate of return during GC I was between +1.5 and +1.8%; during GC II, the return was about −5.0%.

1. Footnotes appear at the end of the article.

Perhaps enough has been said to indicate that GC II has been a major disaster for investors, comparable to and in some ways more severe than GC I. The bodies have not fallen from high windows so frequently in recent years, in part, perhaps, because the initial shock in GC II was not nearly as severe. The long decline that began about the end of 1968 was neither understood nor expected at the beginning. Nor was GC II accompanied by a general economic collapse as was GC I. Between 1929 and 1932, GNP in constant dollars declined by about 30%. Even by 1939, GNP was only about 4% higher than in 1929, an average annual rate of expansion of less than one-half of 1%. In 1932, employment was down about 20% from 1929. The rate of unemployment rose from less than 4% in 1929 to almost 25%, and averaged about 18% for a decade.

In contrast, in the ten years (so far) of GC II, GNP rose about 37%. Employment rose about 24%; unemployment was more than 8% for only one calendar year, and averaged less than 6%.

The proximate cause of GC I was the worst depression in this country's history. The cause of GC II is more mysterious, occurring as it did during a period of substantial economic expansion. The causes will always be somewhat mysterious, but there are some leading candidates. They will be discussed after some general remarks about inflation, which is itself a cause.

INFLATION

In this country, inflation has occurred almost exclusively during and immediately after wars. The main exception has been the inflation that began in the late 1960's and continues today. When inflations were believed to be brief martial aberrations, they did not receive the careful study that they are currently receiving. Common stocks were widely considered to be good "hedges" against inflation. Their value and associated rates of return were thought to be relatively immune to inflation. Yet, investors who correctly anticipated in 1968 that the price level would almost double in the next ten years would not have predicted that rates of return on T-bills would be greater than on common stocks during that decade. Surprises such as these have led to a reexamination of old beliefs about the effects of inflation and have spawned some new conjectures.

One ancient belief which has been reexamined is a generalization of Irving Fisher's "law" that expected nominal rates of return on debt instruments are the sum of the expected real rate and the expected rate of inflation. This idea seems sensible and consistent with economic theory and empirical work.

Fisher's "law" was casually generalized to common stocks. In other words, the expected nominal rate of return on stocks is the expected real rate plus the expected rate of inflation. Over the past 50 years, the average annual real rate of return on common stocks on the New York Stock Exchange has been about 7%. If investors expect that rate to continue and if the expected annual rate of inflation is between 6–7%, the implied expected annual rate of return on common stocks would be between 13–14%.

Can Fisher's "law" be reconciled with recent experience? The average annual rate of inflation over the past decade has been about 7% and the average annual rate of return on common stocks has been about 2% in current dollars and has been negative when deflated by the Consumer Price Index. At first glance, this experience of the last decade seems to repudiate Fisher's "law"; at second glance, however, the "law" still holds.

Interest rates on bonds have risen as inflation and expected inflation rose during the past decade, as implied by the "law." Investors, being risk-averse, will hold common stocks in preference to bonds only if expected rates of return on stocks are higher than on bonds, since stocks are riskier. Perhaps, the dramatic decline in the value of common stocks during the past decade has been the mechanism by which the expected return on common stocks has been raised to provide the necessary risk premium on stocks.

Expected nominal rates of return on common stocks (and bonds) must rise when increased rates of inflation are expected. There are only three mechanisms by which that increase in rates of return can be achieved: (1) an increase in the present value of expected corporate profits (before taxes to investors); (2) a reduction in tax rates on property income; or (3) a decline in stock prices. An explanation of the negative real return on common stocks during the past decade is to be found in an analysis of three modes of adjustment to the imperative that expected nominal rates of return be increased. Fisher's "law" holds, but in the past decade the process by which it has worked has been traumatic for investors.

PROFITS

Corporate profits after taxes and before adjustments rose from $48 billion in 1968 to $118 billion in 1978.

Almost everyone agrees that reported profits — the numbers just cited — are not a correct measure of "economic" profits, the profits of importance to investors. The two standard adjustments are for the understatement of costs of inventory and capital consumption during periods of inflation such as 1968-78.

Department of Commerce figures for these adjustments cause adjusted profits to be $46 billion and $76 billion for 1968 and 1978, respectively. With these adjustments, profits rose about 65% while prices were rising about 90%.

A further adjustment is appropriate to allow for the effect of inflation on the real burden of net corporate indebtedness. Corporations are net debtors, so the effect of this adjustment is to raise "economic" profits relative to reported profits. Net corporate indebtedness rose substantially from 1968 to 1978 as did the rate of inflation. Thus, the effect of this adjustment would be to increase the percentage increase in profits from 1968 to 1978. On the basis of the inadequate data available for making the necessary calculation, one can reasonably, if not confidently, conclude that fully adjusted profits grew somewhat less rapidly than the general price level between 1968 and 1978.

This small discrepancy might seem only moderately disappointing until one realizes that corporations each year made net investments in assets of many billions of dollars. Indeed, even though assets employed and book values increased substantially, there was a small decrease in profits, measured in constant dollars. The behavior of profits was, therefore, unfortunate for investors. There may be many causes, but increased costs of complying with Federal regulation is undoubtedly a major one, as is discussed below.

In GC I, there was a general economic collapse. In 1933, total corporate profits were actually negative. The decline in profits in itself could explain the decline in the market. In GC II, adjusted profits failed to keep pace with the rise in prices and the return on assets fell sharply, but the change in profits is not the sole explanation of a real decline of about 50% in the market value of American corporations.

THE VALUATION OF PROFITS

The value of common stocks is the present value to the investor of expected future profits. As indicated above, the profits of American corporations were disappointing during GC II, but the performance of profits did not in itself explain the decline of about half in the market value of corporations. Also, investors have decided to value profits less highly.

There are two possible explanations: (1) an increase in the perceived riskiness of investing in common stocks; and (2) increased rates of taxation on returns from investments, particularly returns in the form of capital gains. If investors believe that investing in common stocks has become riskier, they will discount expected profits at higher rates and thereby reduce their present value — that is, the prices of stocks.

Similarly, if investors are subjected to higher rates of taxation on returns from common stock, those returns become less valuable and prices of common stocks are correspondingly reduced.

When one discusses perceptions of risk, one abandons measurement and resorts to conjecture. Nevertheless, it is certainly plausible to conjecture that the rapidly increasing governmental intervention in economic processes, the high and widely fluctuating rate of inflation, and the growing severity of the "energy crisis" since the OPEC oil embargo of 1973-74 have increased the uncertainties and risks of doing business.

There are various dramatic, simple indications of the growth of Federal intervention, though they understate the increase in governmental disruption of economic life. For example, it has been estimated that about 25,000 additional Federal regulations are currently being issued annually and are published in the 60,000 pages of the *Federal Register*. The *Code of Federal Regulations* is currently about 73,000 pages and growing at the rate of about 5,000 pages annually. There have been efforts to estimate the current, annual, direct costs to business of complying with Federal regulation and, according to these estimates, current annual costs are about $100 billion. And, these costs have almost certainly more than doubled since 1968.

The point, however, in discussing the causes of GC II is not primarily that costs of regulation are large and growing rapidly; it is also important to note that Federal regulation adds greatly to the uncertainties and risks of doing business. Will a proposed nuclear powered generator be delayed several years by Federal regulators or Federal courts? Will regulators require that children's pajamas be made of fabrics impregnated with flame retardant, or will flame retardants be prohibited because eating them is bad for the health? Will hiring practices that are not discriminatory be sufficiently "affirmative"? Will Federal allocations of oil make its use wise or impossible in a proposed plant? Will changes in taxes make the expected return on a major investment unsatisfactory?

The number of such questions could be extended greatly. The existence of these questions has undoubtedly increased the risks of doing business. The confidence with which investors can forecast profits has been diminished, and, in a world of risk-averse investors, the result has been to reduce the value of stocks.

Inflation itself has been a cause of greater uncertainty. From 1953 to the mid-1960's, the rate of inflation was low and fluctuations in annual rates from year to year were almost always less than 1 percentage point. Since 1968, fluctuations have increased dramatically along with the rate. These changes have enhanced the difficulties and hazards of contracting for future goods and services and, consequently, have increased the uncertainties of future returns on investments by businesses or in businesses. Of especial importance is the disruption caused by price and wage controls or the threat of such controls.

Finally, there are the uncertainties caused by the energy crisis. The disruption of oil supplies from the OPEC countries in 1973-74, the severalfold increase in the price of oil and other fuels, and the efforts of the United States government to cope with and disguise these facts by price controls, allocations of supplies, and other devices have added enormously to the uncertainties of economic life.

These three sources of increased uncertainty have caused stocks to be valued less highly.

TAXES

Common stocks, like other financial assets, are valued for their returns to the investor, after the government takes its cut. Unfortunately for investors in common stocks, and also for those who benefit from jobs and increased productivity, Federal taxes on property income (interest, dividends, capital gains, etc.) rose sharply between 1968 and 1978. Taxes rose for two reasons. First, rates were raised by statute in 1969 and 1976. Second, inflation caused an increase in effective rates.

Historically, capital gains have provided more than half the total return from investing in common stocks. Prior to 1970, the maximum Federal tax rate on long-term capital gains was 25%. In 1969, the "Tax Reform" Act raised the maximum tax over a period of several years. The story is a bit complicated, because the total tax consisted of an "alternative" tax plus an additional tax of 10% on half of capital gains in excess of $30,000.

Between 1970 and 1976, the maximum "alternative" tax increased from 25% to 35%. The additional tax caused the maximum tax to be between 44-45%. In 1976, the rate was raised again. The additional tax rate was raised to 15%, and it applied to half of capital gains in excess of $10,000. The theoretical maximum rate of Federal taxation rose to slightly over 49%, and the rate was reached at lower levels of property income.

The deliberate increases by statute were substantial, but not as great as the inadvertent increases because of inflation. For example, if the prices of stocks doubled during an interval when the general price level doubled, the owners of stocks would have had no gain in the value of their stocks and, yet, would have been subject to heavy taxation if the stocks were sold.

The tax would have been an expropriation of capital under the guise of a tax on capital gains.

Such results were not merely hypothetical. In a recent study, Feldstein and Slemrod estimated the effective rates of taxation on capital gains for investors in 1973.[2] In that year, investors paid taxes on $4.6 billion in nominal capital gains. After adjusting for inflation, the stocks which were sold were worth about $1 billion less than they cost. On the average, the effective rate of taxation was approximately doubled. The rate was more than 100% for many investors. Such confiscatory rates make stocks less valuable.

There have been no statutory changes in tax rates on dividends since 1968, but inflation has raised the effective rates just as it has for capital gains. Stockholders are taxed at rates determined by the level of dividends in current dollars. During periods such as 1968-78, the dividends in current dollars rise, as do taxes and tax rates, even while inflation may have made the dividends less valuable.[3]

CONCLUSION

In the decade after 1968, the value of common stocks on the New York Stock Exchange fell by about 50%, a crash comparable in severity to the Great Crash of 1929-32, whose 50th anniversary this *Journal* is commemorating in this issue. The Great Crash of 1929-32 was accompanied and largely caused by the severest depression in this country's history. The recent "great Crash" occurred during a period of substantial economic expansion.

During 1968-78, the Consumer Price Index rose by about 90%. During such a period, expected nominal rates of return on common stocks must rise. There are only three ways in which such an increase can be effected: (1) an increase in the present value of expected corporate profits (before taxes on property income); (2) a reduction in tax rates on property income; and (3) a fall in stock prices. Unfortunately for investors, only the third mode of adjustment was possible, given government policies, and the result was the second "Great Crash."

Profits have been disappointing and profits have been valued less highly. The value of stocks is determined by the future, not by history. Expected profits are valued more highly if they can be confidently forecast than if the future seems especially murky. Three factors have greatly increased the perceived riskiness of investing in common stocks: (1) inflation; (2) massive governmental intervention in economic affairs; and (3) the energy "crisis". Rates of inflation and fluctuations in rates have risen, thus increasing the uncertainties in contracting to buy or sell goods and services. The government — especially the

Federal government — has intervened massively in economic life, increasing the costs and uncertainties of doing business. The thousands of new regulations which are issued each year initially have ambiguities which are often cleared up only after years of uncertain progress through the bureaucracy and the courts. The cost of energy has increased enormously as has the uncertainty of continuous supply, a new source of risk made worse by government control of prices and allocations of supply. The result of all of these uncertainties has been to increase the risk of investing in and to reduce the value of common stocks.

Finally, tax rates on capital gains and dividends have risen sharply, in part because of statutory changes and in part because of inflation. The rates are very high and in some instances, over 100%.

In retrospect, it is not surprising that the value of American corporations has fallen sharply. What makes the decline especially regrettable is that much of it has been the result of governmental policies — policies which created inflation, disrupted markets,

and taxed property incomes at extraordinarily high rates. These policies may have produced benefits but they also impoverished investors and reduced the general economic welfare. The sharp increase in the cost of capital to corporations, which has been caused by the decline in the market, has reduced the rate of corporate investment, the rate of improvement in productivity, and the rate of economic growth of the entire economy.

[1] The decline from the end of September 1929 to the end of December 1932 was 69%. In current dollars, the decline was 85%.

[2] Martin Feldstein & Joel Slemrod, "Inflation and the Excess Taxation of Capital Gains on Corporate Stock", Working Paper, National Bureau of Economic Research, February 1978.

[3] In 1978, the maximum tax rate on long-term capital gains realized after 1978, was reduced to 28%. Accelerating inflation has probably caused effective rates to continue to rise.

Reprint from *Southern Economic Journal*
Volume 44   Number 4   April 1978

Revolutions in Economic Theory

DUDLEY DILLARD
University of Maryland

I. Introduction

By revolutions in economic theory I mean breakthroughs that result in far-reaching changes in the main body of economic theory, commonly referred to as the principles of economics. Specific reference will be to the British experience from 1776 to the present during which the revolutionaries have been Adam Smith, David Ricardo, John Stuart Mill, Alfred Marshall, and John Maynard Keynes. My purpose is to examine these five revolutions in order to discern the anatomy of revolutions in economic theory. The background material is familiar to all professional economists, but the interpretation differs from the usual one. Disagreement is one of the characteristics for which economics as a discipline is noted, although the optimal amount of disagreement has probably been exceeded. My paper may contribute to agreement on things about which economists disagree.

Smith, Ricardo, Mill, Marshall, and Keynes have been chosen because they rank among the greatest economists in nearly any hall of fame. In the mainstream of classical-neoclassical economics they are the giants whose works have been the centerpieces of the principles of economics from generation to generation for the past two centuries. They are not necessarily the only revolutionary economic theorists, but confining the choice to one country simplifies the analysis without unduly limiting the significance of the conclusions. Historically the British economy has been in the vanguard of modern capitalist development, and consequently turning points in capitalism have come earlier there than elsewhere. The United Kingdom is the classical home of economic theory because it is the classical home of modern capitalism. Major innovations in economic theory have been intimately connected with historical crises and the related innovations in policy growing out of those crises.

II. Thesis

My thesis is that revolutions in economic theory have emerged in close association with arguments for social reform [20]. The predicate form used to state the thesis may be varied to say that these theories are arguments for reform; or that the theories can be understood as arguments for reform; or that the theories may be interpreted as arguments for reform. The relation of theory to policy (reform) stands as a hypothesis to be tested in each case by reference to the evidence. Like any scientific hypothesis, this one could be wrong. The degree of confirmation varies from case to case, but the general finding is that the hypothesis is overwhelmingly confirmed.

This thesis does not require that the revolutionary economists themselves thought of their innovative theories as arguments for policies. Some were more conscious of their purposes than others. Typically reform programs are not explicit in the theoretical treatises of economists. One must look into their pamphlets and correspondence to ascertain their views on policy and reform. For example, Ricardo says little about Corn Law repeal in his *Principles of Political Economy* [19], but one has only to look into his 1815 pamphlet on profits [17] to understand the historical and empirical reference of his theory of value and distribution in the *Principles*.

The essence of revolutions in economic theory lies in their substance rather than in the invention of new techniques of analysis. Without techniques there can be no economic theory, but economics is more, much more, than techniques. The selection of tools and the manner of their use depend on the purpose for which they are intended. All the breakthrough theorists were great technicians even though their tools were sometimes left with rough edges to be polished by their successors.

III. Anatomy of Revolutions in Economic Theory

The Five Revolutions

Adam Smith. Adam Smith's economic theory in the *Wealth of Nations* constitutes an argument for a policy of laissez-faire. At no one place in the *Wealth of Nations* does Smith draw up a list of measures to be used to achieve laissez-faire, but neither does he attempt to conceal his dislike for the existing order. He inveighs against primogeniture and entail [24, 361–62], which impeded the natural course of opulence in agriculture. He advocated elimination of the exclusive privileges of guilds, repealing the Statute of Apprentices and the law of settlement [24, 437]. By explicit condemnation and by implication, the deficiencies of the mercantile system leap at the reader from every chapter. Mercantile restrictions not only violated the liberties of the people, but they impeded the mobility of labor and contributed to an inefficient employment of labor. His positive appeal was for "the obvious and simple system of natural liberty" [24, 651].

Despite the pin-making machine, Smith's pragmatic perspective was more attuned to capital accumulation than to technological innovation. Capital not only sets labor to work but the division of labor associated with innovation is extended by the accumulation of capital. Smith's dichotomy between productive and unproductive labor takes on meaning in relation to capital accumulation. Productive labor is that which contributes to accumulation, and unproductive labor is that which does not contribute to accumulation. This is clear from the full title of the chapter, "Of the Accumulation of Capital, or of Productive and Unproductive Labour" [24, 314–32].

Smith's chapter "Of the Different Employment of Capitals" [24, 341–55] is perhaps the one most strategic for his theory as a whole. It is a puzzling chapter if read in isolation from the rest of Smith's theory, but as a piece of the main argument its meaning is quite clear. In saying that labor employed in agriculture is more productive than labor employed in manufacturing, that labor in manufacturing is more productive than labor in domestic trade, and that labor in domestic trade is more productive than labor in foreign trade, Smith was standing mercantilist theory on its head. Foreign trade, which Thomas Mun argued enjoyed top priority as a contributor to England's "treasure," comes last in Smith's priorities. Only after capital has been allocated to appropriate uses will "the surplus capital disgorge(s) itself into the carrying trade, which is a symptom rather than a cause of great national wealth" [24, 354]. This view of capital allocation drives the final nail into the mercantilist coffin. The invisible hand appears in a chapter on mercantilism in a paragraph devoted to the "natural" preference for domestic over foreign trade [24, 423]. Smith's practical aim was to abolish mercantilistic barriers impeding the efficient allocation of resources and to argue the case for laissez-faire. His theory as a whole can be understood as an argument for this policy.

Ricardo. Ricardo's is one of the clearest cases of a theory that emerged from a preoccupation with policy. Repeal of the British Corn Laws was, of course, that issue. Ricardo's great insight was to see at the close of the Napoleonic Wars that Britain's continued industrial leadership depended on the free import of inexpensive food. In 1815 he published a pamphlet entitled *An Essay on the Influence of a Low Price of Corn on the Profits of Stock* [17], in which he argued that a low price of food grain would lead to high profits in all sectors of the British economy. Two years later Ricardo published his great treatise *On the Principles of Political Economy and Taxation* [19], which developed more fully the theoretical model of the earlier pamphlet and added a theory of value. Wesley Mitchell expressed the close relation between Ricardo's theory and policy as follows: "The practical problem was whether the power of the state should be used to maintain the high incomes of the farmers and landlords, or whether the import duties should be reduced to safeguard the incomes of manufacturers and merchants. The theoretical problem was: what determines the proportions in which the national dividend is shared between landlords, capitalists, and laborers" [14, 5–6]?

Diminishing returns in agriculture was the strategic concept in Ricardo's argument that inexpensive food was necessary to prolong British industrial leadership. With the Corn Laws in effect, the cost of growing food at the margin rose sharply because of the limited supply of fertile land in the United Kingdom. In order for workers to maintain a subsistence income, their labor-embodied wages had to rise sharply under agricultural protection. When wages rose, profits fell—the most axiomatic of Ricardian principles. A fall in profits reduced the incentive to accumulate and to invest domestically. An early stationary state, with all its attendant evils, would be the consequence of continuing the protective Corn Laws. Repeal of the Corn Laws, on the other hand, would lower labor-embodied wages, raise profits, stimulate capital accumulation, and greatly prolong Britain's industrial dominance. Ricardo's architectonics provided the rationale for a policy that was to become the basis for the grand design of a British century.

Ricardo's pragmatic bent carried him beyond a theoretical argument for a new economic policy. He entered Parliament, where he championed the cause of parliamentary reform, which was a prerequisite to repealing the Corn Laws. Ricardo's spirit as architect of Britain's golden age is seen in the Great Reform Act of 1832, which brought parliamentary representation to the formerly excluded industrial regions and broke the political power of the landed interests. Parliamentary reform, in turn, led in 1846 to repeal of the Corn Laws. Ironically, repeal of the Corn Laws rendered Ricardo's *Principles* partially obsolete in the sense that diminishing returns became less strategic under free trade. New economic issues came to the fore and called for a new principles of political economy.

Mill. In the Preface of his treatise on political economy, John Stuart Mill says its most characteristic quality ". . . is that it invariably associates the principles with their applications" [13, xxvii]. Evidence in support of Mill's characterization of his work is the full title, *Principles of Political Economy with Some of Their Applications to Social Philosophy.* Mill professed to be a faithful Ricardian, but his stated objective was to write a new *Wealth of Nations.* He was careful to point out that while his object was practical, he had not sacrificed scientific reasoning [13, xxviii].

Although Mill was respectful of his great predecessors, Smith and Ricardo, he marched to the beat of a different drummer. Mill lived in an age of an increasingly self-conscious but disappointed working class that had lived through the Industrial Revolution and aspired to share in its fruits. Mill was an ardent reformer, and he argued passionately in his *Principles* for the welfare of the wage-earning and peasant classes.

Mill visited Paris in 1830, the year in which the July monarchy came to office as a result of a revolution. Social unrest was less marked in England than on the Continent, but Mill witnessed the sensational rise and sudden collapse of Robert Owen's Grand National Consolidated Trades Union in 1834. The English Chartist Movement became active in the late 1830s, and its champions marched into London to present the Great Petition to Queen Victoria in 1848, only to be dispersed by armed forces under the command of the old Duke of Wellington.

Concurrent publication of Smith's *Wealth of Nations* and the signing of the American Declaration of Independence in 1776 has frequently been pointed to by way of showing that both events were related to the currents of history, namely, the decline of mercantilism. Importance should also be attached to the concurrent publication of Mill's *Principles* and Marx's *Communist Manifesto* in the same year, 1848, in which social revolutions rocked the capitals of western Europe. All three of these 1848 events were responses to the unsatisfied and rising aspirations of the working classes of Europe and England.

Mill expressed strong sympathy for the French revolution of 1848, which attempted under Louis Blanc to establish a mild form of socialism (cooperative workshops financed with government capital) in France. In socialism Mill saw the future hope of mankind, but for his own day he felt people were not ready for such far-reaching changes in social institutions. Mill's reforms were directed toward improvements within the system of private property. He championed workers' cooperatives, trade unions, peasant proprietorship, land reform, colonization, birth control, and more education for the children of the laboring classes.

The linchpin of Mill's "new-fashioned economics" was his distinction between the laws of production and the laws of distribution. The former partake of the nature of physical truths and are not subject to change. The laws of distribution, on the contrary, are provisional and depend upon the customs of society [13, 199–201]. Why did Mill devise this crucial distinction? It is not present in his predecessor Ricardo nor is it to be found in his successor Marshall. Neither did Marx give credence to this distinction, at least not so long as the means of production are privately owned. After the advent of collective ownership, however, Marx would agree with Mill that distribution of the social product among the comrades is subject to many options. Clearly Mill found the distinction between the laws of production and the laws of distribution strategic for linking the principles of economics with far-reaching social reform, and ultimately with socialism.

Mill was much more than a readable Ricardo. In Ricardo the economic struggle focuses on landlords against factory owners. Wage earners are relegated to the sidelines as observers of contesting property owners. In Mill, the laboring classes occupy the central arena, and property owners are expected to accommodate their interests to assist in promoting the welfare of wage earners and small farmers. Mill's new staging of the social drama is facilitated by differentiating the laws of distribution from those of production.

In his attitude toward the stationary state, Mill differs sharply from his predecessors. Ricardo paints deeply pessimistic hues to future economic development in the stationary state when profits fall to the minimum and accumulation ceases. Mill's stationary state is infused with optimism, especially with reference to "the futurity of the labouring classes" [13, 752–94].

Between 1848 and 1871 Mill's *Principles of Political Economy* went through seven editions. During his lifetime it was accepted as the definitive work in political economy and continued in wide use as a general textbook well into the twentieth century. Simplified versions were published, among which Henry Fawcett's was most notable in England [23, 533]. In the United States Professor J. Laurence Laughlin issued a bowdlerized edition that deleted many of Mill's "dangerous thoughts" [8]. Between Ricardo and Marshall, Mill clearly dominated Anglo-Saxon economics.

Marshall. A prophetic reviewer wrote in 1890 that Alfred Marshall's *Principles of Economics* ". . . will serve to restore the shaken credit of political economy, and will probably become for the present generation what Mill's *Principles* was for the last" [3, 221]. This prophecy was more than fulfilled. Marshall's *Principles* stands as a landmark in the history of economic analysis. When published in 1890, it was probably the most masterful work ever written in economics, and in some respects it remains the greatest treatise of all time in economics. Whereas Mill wrote his *Principles* in eighteen months, Marshall devoted a lifetime to the development of economics as a separate science with standards comparable to those of the physical and biological sciences [3, 250–51]. Keynes contrasts the impatient Jevons with the deliberate Marshall: "Jevons saw the kettle boil and cried out with the delighted voice of a child; Marshall too had seen the kettle boil and sat down silently to build an engine" [3, 188].

Marshall describes his reason for going into economics in the following passage:

> From Metaphysics I went to Ethics, and thought that the justification of the existing condition of society was not easy. . . . I had doubts as to the propriety of inequalities of *opportunity*, rather than of material comfort. Then, in my vacations I visited the poorest quarters of several cities . . . looking at the faces of the poorest people. Next, I resolved to make as thorough a study as I could of Political Economy [3, 165–66].

In the opening chapter of the *Principles*, Marshall says the problem of poverty ". . . gives to economic studies their chief and their highest interest" [11, 4]. Throughout his writings runs a moral tone that reflects his ethical impulse to do good, to improve the well-being of humanity, ". . . to open up to all the material means of a refined and noble life" [16, 174]. Keynes speaks of

Marshall's two views, that of a pastor and that of a scientist, and says that Marshall gave preeminence to the pastor aspect [3, 169]. As between the cool head and the warm heart of Cambridge men, the latter prevailed in Marshall [16, 174]. He fits the case of "The heart knows reasons that reason cannot know."

Professor A. C. Pigou, Marshall's pupil and successor in the chair at Cambridge, said Marshall was convinced that the chief value of economics was as a "handmaid to practice."[1]

> Starting out then with the firm view that economic science is chiefly valuable, neither as an intellectual gymnastic nor even as a means of winning truth for its own sake, but as a handmaid of ethics and a servant of practice, Marshall resolutely set himself to mould his work along lines conforming to that ideal [16, 84].

As in the case of the four other revolutionary economists, Marshall's purpose was to show that gradual reform within the framework of private enterprise could raise the poor above the poverty level to a fuller and nobler life. His motto, "Natura non facit saltum" was the key to his position as a theorist and as a reformer. The revolutionary drums that stirred Mill had faded, and Marshall represented the voice of a society confident that it could reconcile class conflict through gradualist measures for uplifting the multitude. Marshall flirted with socialism for many years but abandoned it as a bad mistress:

> For more than a decade, I remained under the conviction that the suggestions, which are associated with the word "socialism," were the most important subject of study, if not in the world, yet at all events for me. But the writings of socialists generally repelled me, almost as much as they attracted me. . . . I decided to say little on the matter, till I had thought much longer [9, vii].

Marshall's *Principles* may be understood as an alternative to socialism for the purpose of eliminating poverty in a capitalistic society.

In addition to viewing public expenditures on education as a "national investment" [11, 216, 716–18], Marshall appealed to what he called the "latent chivalry in business life" [16, 330, 342; 11, 719, 721] in the war against poverty.[2] Marshall was eager to communicate with businessmen, and even in the *Principles* he went to great pains to write at a level intelligible to men of affairs. He deliberately avoided complex analysis, relied on short chains of reasoning,

---

1. Pigou repeats the expression "handmaid to practice" on page 85 and uses the phrase "handmaid to ethics" on page 82. The main theme of Pigou's "In Memoriam" essay [16, 81–90] is that Marshall's scientific work was subordinate to ethical and practical considerations.

2. Here the expression *"war* on poverty" seems appropriate. See Marshall's essay "Social Possibilities of Economic Chivalry" (1907), especially the section entitled "Chivalry in War and Chivalry in Business" [16, 323–46]. In order to combat poverty Marshall urged that industrial society appeal to the same motives that characterized the chivalrous behavior of medieval knights. "I want to suggest that there is much latent chivalry in business life, and that there would be a great deal more of it if we sought it out and honoured it as men honoured the mediaeval chivalry of war" [16, 330].

and wrote in simple prose. Some of his complex mathematical papers he never published because he felt they were too far removed from the conditions of real life and might be misleading. His preference for the particular equilibrium rather than the more elegant and mathematically complex general equilibrium rested on a desire to remain closer to actual experience. Although Marshall was a powerful mathematician, he used mathematics sparingly, and in the *Principles* it is relegated to an appendix and geometry to footnotes to the text. Edgeworth says that Marshall ". . . deferred to the prejudices of those whom he wished to persuade" [16, 67]. In appealing to the chivalry of businessmen, Marshall differed sharply from Mill, who repudiated upper-class philanthropy in favor of autonomous working-class movements for achieving reform.

Keynes. Keynes's revolutionary work, *The General Theory of Employment, Interest and Money,* is addressed to professional economists and makes only occasional reference to economic policy. The central theoretical argument is that the aggregate volume of employment and output depend on the level of effective demand, which is determined by the schedule of the propensity to consume and the magnitude of investment. Keynes stressed that his theory was general in the sense of being applicable to all levels of employment in contrast with the prevailing special theory of equilibrium only at full employment. He criticized this special theory as ". . . misleading and disastrous if we attempt to apply it to the facts of experience" [4, 3]. In the decades since it was published Keynes's *General Theory* has become synonymous with the terms "Keynesian Revolution" and "The New Economics."

What quality of Keynes's *General Theory* created the sole revolution in economic theory in the twentieth century to date? The answer is that his theory was addressed to the central issue of his generation and was based on an insight that saw a workable resolution of the problem, which reached crisis proportions during the Great Depression. As early as 1919 in the *Economic Consequences of the Peace,* Keynes expressed skepticism concerning the stability and rationality of capitalism. He had no faith in laissez-faire, and during the 1920s he proposed monetary remedies for economic instability. The onset of the great crisis in 1929 sharpened Keynes's heretical vision of the capitalist process. He reasoned that if there are deficiencies in total spending (demand) in the private sector, the economy may be balanced with increased spending in the public sector. In order not just to transfer spending from the private to the public sector through taxation, Keynes recommended government spending financed through borrowing, that is, deficit spending. In a pamphlet entitled *The Means to Prosperity,* Keynes verbalized his insight concerning the stimulation of effective demand through loan-expenditure. This 1933 pamphlet contained the insight and a program but very little theory. What remained in order to create a revolution was to construct a.system of analysis that would elaborate the insight and justify the program. In 1936 came the argument for the policy in the guise of the *General Theory*. Primarily it is a theory explaining how laissez-faire capitalism works and why mass unemployment results from a deficiency of effective demand. The theory is presented in a manner designed to show how unemployment, instability, and other faults of laissez-faire capitalism can be rectified.

The program Keynes associated with his general theory is not limited to indirect governmental measures such as fiscal and monetary policies. He saw the need for governments to take an increasing role in directly stabilizing the economy at high employment. At the close of the chapter on long-term expectations, Keynes wrote:

> I expect to see the State, which is in a position to calculate the marginal efficiency of capital-goods on long views and on the basis of the general social advantage, taking an ever greater responsibility for directly organising investment; since it seems likely that the fluctuations in the market estimation of the marginal efficiency of different types of capital, calculated on the principles I have described above, will be too great to be offset by any practicable changes in the rate of interest" [4, 164].

In summarizing the general theory, Keynes wrote: "Our final task might be to select those variables which can be deliberately controlled or managed by central authority in the kind of system in which we actually live" [4, 247]. No statement could show more clearly the manner in which the selection of variables in the theory is influenced by the program of action.

Common Elements in the Five Revolutions

Theories Oriented to Issues of a Practical Kind. What are the common elements in the five revolutions described above? In every case the theories are oriented to issues of an essentially practical kind. Typically these were burning issues of the generation. Each economist had an insight or vision [23, 41–42, 892–93, 1171–72] into how the problems could be resolved. These problems were for Smith, mercantilist restrictions on private enterprise; for Ricardo, high labor costs and low profits associated with import restrictions on food; for Mill, frustrations of the laboring classes in an age of rising aspirations and threatened revolution; for Marshall, persistent poverty of workers in an age of rising living standards; for Keynes, massive unemployment and the near collapse of the capitalist system. The solutions were for Smith, laissez-faire in domestic and international economic relations; for Ricardo, repeal of the Corn Laws; for Mill, cooperative workshops, peasant proprietorship, trade unions, emigration, and ultimately socialism; for Marshall, elimination of poverty gradually through education and the chivalry of businessmen; for Keynes, increased public spending to offset deficiencies in private spending. The strategic concepts were, respectively, the natural progress of opulence, diminishing returns in agriculture, distinction between the laws of production and distribution, the principle of continuity, and effective demand. In each case the theory may be understood, may be interpreted, as an argument for the program offered to solve the problem to which the theory is oriented.

Smith and Mill combined in single treatises their theories and the applications. Ricardo, Marshall, and Keynes made only passing references to policy in their treatises, but an examination of their other writings makes clear the intimate relation between their theories and their policies. In all cases the authors viewed their treatises as statements of fundamental laws or principles. Otherwise they would not qualify as scientific treatises. Some were more open than others in acknowledging the relation of theory to policy in their treatises or elsewhere. The purpose of this paper is not to defend the close connection between theory and practice as sound economic science. It is only being reported.

Periodicity of Economic Revolutions. Using dates of publication of major treatises as the criterion, revolutions in economic theory occurred in 1776, 1817, 1848, 1890, and 1936. The intervals are 41, 31, 42, and 46 years, respectively, or an average of exactly 40 years. If my thesis is correct, the spacing of these revolutions at fairly regular intervals is not fortuitous. As responses to once-a-generation problems, revolutionary theories occur once a generation. By definition, fundamental problems remain unsolved for some time, but they do not last forever. After a new theory has been created to resolve the basic problem in the economic structure of economic society, some time must elapse before another maladjustment in institutions arises and attains a condition in which it can be solved. The economic environment changes continually, but not so rapidly as to call forth continuous revolution. That would be a contradiction in terms.

Obsolescence of Economic Theory. The principles of economics are always on the road to obsolescence. They become decreasingly relevant to new problems that emerge with the passage of time. Techniques may be improved, and epicycles may be built upon epicycles, but sooner or later the old theory becomes irrelevant to the major issue of the new day. Then the situation is ripe for a revolution. Changes in economic theory are episodic and discontinuous, in contrast with the more or less continual change in the environment to which any given economic theory has relevance. A new system of theory cannot be built on the one it succeeds because they are addressed to different problems. The old theory is not wrong so much as it becomes obsolete or irrelevant to the new problem. In a sense, a successful theory helps to induce its own obsolescence by providing a solution to a major problem, which in time is replaced by a different problem that requires a different theory. We have noted this especially in the case of Ricardo.

Continuity in Techniques of Analysis. Elements of continuity exist from generation to generation despite the episodic nature of changes in economic theory. Future revolutionaries begin by learning the old economics. They master the tools of the trade and carry some of the techniques over into their new theory. Ricardo came to economics by reading Adam Smith but shifted the central problem to distribution, for which Smith's value theory was very inadequate. John Stuart Mill was brought up on Ricardo and was in some respects his disciple. In fact, one of Mill's chief faults arose from retaining too much of Ricardo's theory for serving purposes that differed greatly from Ricardo's. When the young Marshall was told to study political economy if he wanted to be realistic about social ethics, he began reading Mill's *Principles*. Keynes's father was a colleague of Marshall's, and the young Keynes learned his early economics from Marshall. Continuity among these five economists was increased by intergenerational overlaps among fellow countrymen, personal associations, and the continuity in institutions to which they oriented their theories.

Creativity may be dulled by being steeped in old doctrines. Mill's experience of attempting to apply Ricardian techniques in a different setting for different purposes is not unique. In the Preface to the *General Theory*, Keynes tells of the intellectual obstacles he encountered in sloughing off old ideas before arriving at his new and revolutionary conception of theory [4, vi–vii]. The difficulty of breaking new ground is heightened by the temptation to follow familiar paths. A tabula rasa of economics, however, would not be an optimal staging ground for revolutions in economic theory even if it were possible. Some continuity is inevitable.

Recognition of Revolutions. In any age there are competing solutions to insistent problems. Who is right and who is wrong may not be immediately evident. Sir James Steuart's massive treatise on the *Principles of Political Economy*, endorsing mercantilist policies, was published less than a decade before Smith's *Wealth of Nations*. Steuart's work sank quickly into oblivion in Britain while Smith's won increasing acclaim. Malthus contested Ricardo's theory and policy at every step. He opposed repeal of the Corn Laws and wrote a *Principles of Political Economy* in answer to Ricardo's *Principles*. Malthus's *Political Economy* was largely forgotten while Ricardo's became the foundation of nineteenth-century classical economics. Mill and Marshall seem to have won immediate recognition as great contributors. Marshall's *Principles* was a technical triumph, and the reforms advocated were of a gradualist nature and not likely to arouse animosity.

Keynes's *General Theory* stirred unprecedented controversy and met strong resistance, perhaps because the theory represented a sharp break with tradition and the policies flew in the face of the conventional wisdom extending as far back as Adam Smith. By Keynes's time economics had become an established discipline with many practitioners and numerous professional journals. Opposition to Keynes was much stronger among the older than among the younger generation of economists. As economics becomes more organized as a normal science in Kuhn's sense [7], revolutions may be more difficult to achieve. The established professionals in a science are typically the last to recognize the need for a revolution in their discipline and the last to accept it once it occurs. Keynes's senior colleagues in Britain held out for years before conceding revolutionary significance to the *General Theory*. A few never did accept the idea of a Keynesian revolution.

Personal Qualities. Not surprisingly the men who made breakthroughs in economic theory during the past two centuries were highly intelligent. John Stuart Mill has been called the greatest mind of the nineteenth century. Any test that measures his mental achievements as a child against others of his chronological age will place his IQ among the highest in history. Bertrand Russell said, "Keynes's intellect was the sharpest and clearest I have ever known" [21, 97]. Keynes said, "Ricardo was the greatest mind that found economics worthy of its powers," and Harrod asks if we should not substitute the word Keynes for the word Ricardo in that sentence [2, 467]. Marshall was a second wrangler in Mathematics at Cambridge University in a class in which the first wrangler was the future Lord Rayleigh, the great mathematical physicist (1842–1919). Smith's achievement as the founder of modern economic theory was of a somewhat different kind. His insights into history and human nature were penetrating even though his logical precision may not have equaled that of his fellow revolutionaries [2, 466].

Age at Breakthrough. At the time of publication of their major economic work all five revolutionary economists were men of considerable worldly maturity yet young enough to be at the height of their intellectual prowess. The average age at publication was 48, with a range from 42 for Mill to 53 for Smith. Ricardo was 45, Marshall 48, and Keynes 52. And at age 42 Mill had been a practicing professional scholar at the highest level for nearly a quarter of a century; he was never young!

Unlike mathematicians, whose intellectual breakthroughs often come in their twenties and thirties, these revolutionary economists had lived long enough to gain insights into the workings of economic society. For mathematicians, exposure to the real world is unnecessary and may even be a disadvantage because it distracts from their abstract world of pure mathematics. Only association with other mathematicians is important in the maturing of mathematical genius. In the social sciences, however, worldly maturity is essential for breakthrough achievements of the kind that form the subject of this paper. An economist who aspires to this level of achievement cannot afford the mathematicians' option of analytical elegance for its own sake. Insight into the complexities of the economic world takes considerable time to be of a quality that can see solutions to economic problems of historic dimensions.[3]

3. For Keynes's statement of the qualities required for a great economist, see his biographical essay on Marshall [3, 150–266]. ". . . the master-economist must possess a rare *combination* of gifts" [3, 170]. About Marshall, Keynes wrote, ". . . his mixed training and divided nature furnished him with the most essential and fundamental of the economist's necessary gifts—he was conspicuously historian and mathematician . . ." [3, 170–71].

IV. Validity of Economic Theories

According to the foregoing discussion, the principles of economics change episodically from time to time because the principles oriented to the strategic problems of one generation are not relevant to the strategic problems of another generation. This means that the principles of economics have contingent rather than universal validity. What can be said about the validity of the five theories reviewed above?

Testing the validity of an economic theory involves three steps, which will be referred to as validity I, validity II, and validity III [1]. Validity I relates to the logical consistency of the concepts and propositions that make up the theory as a whole. Validity II answers the question: How good is the theory as a whole for the purpose for which it was intended? In relation to the above discussion, this translates into the question: How valid is the theory as an argument for the program implicit or explicit in the theorist's system of thought? Validity III tests the feasibility and workability of the program in the historical context for which it was proposed.

Systematic application of these criteria of validity would require an entire volume or perhaps five volumes. A few observations and illustrations must suffice here. Attention will be focused on Ricardo and Marshall as two somewhat different types of cases, with briefer reference to the other three.

As one has a right to expect from a sometime professor of logic, Adam Smith tied his theory together well if not impeccably. Charges of inconsistency on value, rent, and productive and unproductive labor can be resolved in the light of the major purpose of his theory. Certainly Smith's theory as a whole argues persuasively against mercantilism and in favor of laissez-faire. The social indignation expressed so forthrightly by Smith, the liberal reformer, echoed a rising tide of contemporary protest against the old order. The significance of his theory and the realization of his laissez-faire reforms arose precisely because he spoke for an idea whose time had come. His practical program, for which his theory argued persuasively, was historically relevant and workable at the time it was offered. It was realistic and not utopian.

Although Smith was generally correct, he was not right in every respect. He claimed more than was justified for his theory and for his program. The British case was, in fact, a special one, and Smith failed to realize—at least he did not acknowledge—the limitations of laissez-faire. As an admirer of Newton, he overdid the natural order as applied to economic institutions. The absolute and universal terms in which he argued the case for the obvious and simple system of natural liberty imparted rigidity into his theory. Consequently, when the empirical and historical justification of laissez-faire weakened with the rise of mass production, giant corporations, and the growth of business monopoly arising from destructive competition, Smith's theory changed from one of liberal reform to one easily used to justify the status quo.

What made his theory more persuasive at the time made it less valid in the long run. He did political economy a disfavor by claiming universal validity for his ideas. If Smith had been more insightful into the future course of economic development, he might have made a greater contribution to economics.

Despite limitations on Smith's prevision of history and the excessive claims of generality for his theory, his work served quite well the intention for which it was devised. It stands as a valid even if a vulnerable theory.

Ricardo was a powerful logician and scores well on validity I. The logical relations among wages, profits, and rent are bound together by the theory of value, which he called the "sheet anchor" of his system. Ricardo simplified the determination of distributive shares by isolating the analysis at the margin where there is no rent. Wages are determined by the subsistence of workers, and at the margin the residual product goes to profit. Rent on superior land is the difference between its produce and the produce on marginal land, with equal applications of labor and capital.

On validity II, Ricardo's theory of value and distribution argues well the case for inexpensive food through free trade. As part of the argument for reform, the labor theory of value is more strategic in relation to diminishing returns than as a basis for determining the exchange value of commodities. Diminishing returns in agriculture cause labor inputs for subsistence to rise and consequently wages must rise, in manufacturing as well as in agriculture. The theory as a whole makes a persuasive case for free trade in food through repeal of the Corn Laws.

For validity III, the feasibility of Ricardo's program was demonstrated by events in England during the three decades from 1817 to 1846 and its workability by English economic history after 1846. As the Industrial Revolution shifted the balance of power away from the landed interests to the industrial classes, Parliament was reformed and the Corn Laws repealed.

Ricardo, like other economists, argued the case for free trade as being in the public interest. Clearly free trade in food helped to prolong British industrial leadership. Even British agriculture did not suffer in the manner opponents of Ricardo had contended. British agriculture remained prosperous after 1846 until the onset of the crisis of 1873.

Ricardo, as did Adam Smith before him, inferred too much generality and too wide applicability for his theory and policy. He failed to recognize that Britain was a special case and that free trade might have severe limitations for public policy in differently situated countries such as Germany and the United States during the nineteenth century. Ricardo's political economy was so heavily oriented to diminishing returns that it was not very helpful after diminishing returns ceased to be an important practical issue. Nor was Ricardo's theory very useful with respect to other major problems such as economic instability and business cycles, which dated from his era. The monographic nature of Ricardo's *Principles* probably gave his theory greater impact for a few decades but hastened its obsolescence in the longer period.

John Stuart Mill's weakness lies with validity II. His theory remained too Ricardian to make a convincing case for his non-Ricardian program. Although Mill wrote after the Corn Laws had been repealed, he reasserted the Ricardian maxim that the law of diminishing returns in agriculture ". . . is the most important proposition in political economy" [13, 177]. He should have recognized, as Marshall did, that "The Law of Diminishing Return is almost inoperative in Britain . . ." [16, 326]. Mill's longest step toward theoretical argument for working-class reform came with the non-Ricardian distinction between the laws of production and distribution. If Mill had gone further in creating a new set of principles in conformity with his views on reform, he might have saved himself the frustration typified in the following sentence in a chapter on Remedies for Low Wages: "Can political economy do nothing, but only object to everything, and demonstrate that nothing can be done?" [13, 373]. Ricardo's free trade argument was a poor guide for Mill's militant interventionism. Among the five economists under review, Mill makes the least convincing case for his program. In general stature as a political economist, he ranks below the other four.

Unlike Smith, Ricardo, Mill, and Keynes, Marshall was not an explicit political economist. He self-consciously changed the name of the discipline from "political economy" to "economics" in order to give his work a more "scientific" character. Consequently, one must look carefully at Marshall outside the *Principles*, at his papers and his correspondence, to understand fully his dedication to forging tools of analysis, an "economic organon," that would be useful for solving fairly specific problems. In the closing paragraph of the *Principles*, Marshall says, "We have reached very few practical conclusions" [11, 722].

Smith and Ricardo were laissez-fairests fighting to overcome existing mercantilistic barriers, including the Corn Laws. Once laissez-faire became accepted policy, say by the middle of the nineteenth century, making a case for it became primarily a matter of defending the status quo. Jevons, for example, presumed to do this with his marginal utility doctrine that the subjective preferences of individuals correspond to the objective structure of prices in a free market. Marshall was not a laissez-fairest, but he was closer to being one than Keynes or Mill. So among the five economists, Marshall was the one best suited to make his case with modest positive reforms. He is the one who could most easily maintain the "scientific dignity of ethical neutrality" and still argue for what he thought was desirable economic policy.

In terms of validity I, Marshall's logical consistency is of the highest caliber. Better than anyone else before him, he forged a symmetrical system of supply and demand relations, including cost and utility, into an integrated theory of value. He applied the theory of value to the factors of production to get a theory of distribution. Marshall seems to have thought of everything by way of anticipating criticisms of the logical consistency of his theory. In price theory he explicitly assumes the marginal utility of money is constant in order to focus on substitution effects and to set aside the income effects associated with changes in relative prices [11, 95]. In discussing distribution he explicitly warned that marginal productivity analysis does not constitute a theory of wages.

With reference to validity II, Marshall's theory as a whole provides a good argument for his program of gradual reform within the confines of private enterprise. His devotion to marginal analysis meshes with his motto "Natura non facit saltum." Marshall has been criticized for carrying his analysis to the subjective level of utilitarian sacrifices and satisfactions, in contrast to his objective level based on money costs and revenues. The subjective level of analysis detracts from the sharp, scientific focus of most of his theory. This may be explained in terms of Marshall the reformer wanting to say something meaningful about peoples' real (subjective) feelings, e.g., the boy eating blackberries. If Marshall had been less concerned with reforms leading to a noble life for everyone, he need not have diluted his professional reputation to say things that are not easily defended as "scientific" economics.

With respect to validity III, Marshall's gradualism and moralizing tone suited the spirit of late Victorian England. The elimination of poverty by means of education and business chivalry was compatible with the liberal-progressive tempo of Marshall's generation prior to World War I. However, his high expectations for business chivalry for uplifting the poor and the Residium seem utopian and was not compatible with realistic expectations.

Marshall recognized but failed to incorporate into the principles of economics some of the emerging problems of his day. He placed in an appendix of the *Principles* the disturbing thought that the term "margin" has no significance "in relation to commodities the cost of production of which diminishes with a gradual increase in output" [11, 805]. He relegated to a separate, nontheoretical volume the problems associated with large-scale enterprise and the concentration of business power. Marginal analysis, which tells what happens when not very much happens, was ill designed to deal with problems of economic instability, mass unemployment, and capitalist development. Marshall's *Principles* was not very helpful in casting light on the causes and remedies of the Great Depression of the 1930s. At that time Keynes took up the task of guiding economic theory out of the valley of irrelevance.

The validity of Keynes's *General Theory* can be summed up very briefly as follows. The author of *A Treatise on Probability* was an excellent logician (validity I), and the author of *Essays in Persuasion* knew how to use theory to argue his case for reform. The general workability and acceptability of Keynes's program are demonstrated by the history of economic policies in western democracies in the three decades after World War II. There is much to justify referring to this generation of economics as the Age of Keynes.

V. The Coming Revolution in Economic Theory

A full generation has passed since the most recent (Keynesian) revolution in economic theory. For more than a decade dissatisfaction with economics has been growing because of its seeming inability to reconcile the unsatisfactory course of economic events, featured by simultaneous inflation and recession, with the principles of the discipline. Measured rates of unemployment have grown secularly higher, and previously unacceptable rates of inflation have become normal. Superimposed on the old problems of unemployment and inflation have come new problems related to ecology, energy, and scarcity of natural resources. These newer problems have created doubts whether economic growth, which is the key to successful functioning of a capitalist economy, is even desirable. All these signs suggest that the situation is ripening for another revolution in economic theory.

The setting for a possible coming revolution may be put in terms of a problem, a program, and a theory.

Problem

Surely the problem addressed by the new revolutionary theory will be related to the current unsatisfactory performance of the economy. In addition to the problems enumerated in the preceding paragraph, other basic concerns include microeconomic externalities, income distribution, quality as distinguished from quantity of production, and others. Mere enumeration of problems, however, is not helpful because we need to know which problems can be solved in the foreseeable future within the framework of democratic political institutions and existing social values. In order to meet the criteria of validity III, a program for which a theory is an argument must be feasible and workable in the historical setting in which it is proposed. History in retrospect does not bestow revolutionary significance on brilliant theories which relate to problems that cannot be solved. The insight and prescience that characterize the genius of breakthrough theorists is not available to ordinary mortals, and consequently the content of revolutions in economics is basically unpredictable. Ordinary mortals are free, however, to speculate about the possible characteristics of future economic revolutions.

Program

Broad types of economic policies may be classified as laissez-faire, interventionism, and economic planning. The policy to which the new theory is oriented will not be laissez-faire because history does not run backwards. Recent policies in western democracies have been interventionist, combining indirect monetary and fiscal controls with a large dose of direct regulation of private enterprise. Keynes's program was much more interventionist than those of

Mill and Marshall. Keynes highlighted fiscal and monetary policy and flirted with economic planning in the form of socialization of investment. Perhaps the new revolution will place much more emphasis on economic planning relative to fiscal and monetary policies, but with less direct regulation than at present. Economic planning is distinguished from other policies by its wider scope of conscious calculation; it may be defined as a system in which decisions concerning the employment and allocation of resources are made in terms of economy-wide accounting for costs and revenues. The conscious application of economy-wide accounting should, logically, eliminate troublesome discrepancies between social and private costs, which are the subject of much present regulation, as in the environmental field. Economy-wide accounting as the basis for decision-making should eliminate involuntary unemployment since society at large gains from the employment of anyone who produces something more than nothing. The problem is to devise institutional arrangements for putting this principle into effect. We lack a clear vision of how that can be done, and the function of the new economics is to furnish that vision.

Indicative planning is one form of general economic planning that is consistent with political democracy and private enterprise. It may be conceived as an information system designed to reduce institutional uncertainty [12, 3]. Because information is a public good, indicative planning requires close cooperation between business and government. Economics will need a positive theory of government to replace the negative theory that has characterized it since Adam Smith. Economists will need to replace knee-jerk opposition to bureaucracy with a serious study of it in both the private and the public sectors. Bureaucracy is a function of large-scale organizations, which is here to stay because of technological imperatives.

Theory

The integration of micro- and macroeconomics is a probable aspect of the new revolution in economic theory. What is needed on the micro side is a model of the behavior of an economy in which the firms in a typical industry are characteristically large in size and small in number. An astonishing fact of economic theory is the persistence of the small-scale, competitive, self-regulating model after a century of the age of mass production. This is the problem that Marshall, the father of modern microeconomics, shunted out of the *Principles* into *Industry and Trade*. Keynes did not challenge Marshallian micro theory. Abandoning the competitive model will bring power relations to the center of economic analysis. In a system of planning, the market mechanism will not be sacrificed but will be socialized in the sense that it be made to work in a manner that reflects social costs and social benefits.Public authority can use marketlike incentives to harness private interests to public goals and thus eliminate a great deal of direct regulation, along the lines suggested by Charles Schultze in the 1976 Godkin lectures [22]. Thus a possible configuration of the coming revolution in economics is one in which microeconomics will be transformed and integrated with macroeconomics within a framework of economic planning.

VI. Summary and Conclusion

Our finding is that the five revolutions have in each case been products of great individual talent with insight into the leading issues of a generation and a capacity to formulate intellectual constructions with logical consistency and historical relevancy. From these findings we have proposed the thesis that revolutionary economic theories emerge in close association with reform. Some economists may not be pleased with this thesis. This may be one of those situations in which each individual finding is accepted because of overwhelming evidence but the general thesis is rejected because it conflicts with preconceptions about the nature of economic science. Economic science is presupposed to be positive, ethically neutral, and subject to unbroken cumulative progress rather than episodic turnarounds. The positive-normative dualism is not helpful. Economics is positive in the sense that the validity of its theories is tested by an appeal to facts, but the appeal is indirect through action that necessarily involves normative values [20, 5–6]. Ethical neutrality has not been characteristic of innovative economic theories. What needs to be done about ethical judgments is to make them explicit rather than to pretend they do not or should not exist in a manner that bears upon the content of economic theory. Economics is a moral science.

The thesis propounded in this paper has been applied only to revolutionary theorists and does not necessarily apply to others. Moreover, what has been valid about revolutionary theories during the past two centuries will not necessarily hold in the future. The relation between theory and practice could change. The most acclaimed theories of the future may turn out to be those of greatest analytical and mathematical elegance, without reference to pressing problems of economic life. The circumstances most congenial to this latter condition would be a world in which economic problems cease to be matters of large public concern. Such a state of economic bliss does not seem likely in the foreseeable future. Meanwhile, a reasonable expectation is that the new breakthroughs in economic theory will follow the pattern of those described in this paper.

References

1. Dillard, Dudley, "A Note on Methodology in Modern Economic Theory." *American Economic Review*, December 1944, 856–62 and September 1945, 665–67.

2. Harrod, Roy F. *The Life of John Maynard Keynes*. New York: Harcourt, Brace and Company, 1951.

3. Keynes, John Maynard. *Essays in Biography*. London: Macmillan and Co., 1933.

4. _____. *The General Theory of Employment, Interest and Money*. New York: Harcourt, Brace and Company, 1936.

5. _____. *The Means to Prosperity*, in *The Collected Writings of John Maynard Keynes*, IX, 335–66. Cambridge: Cambridge University Press, 1972.

6. Krupp, Sherman Roy, ed. *The Structure of Economic Science*. Englewood Cliffs, New Jersey: Prentice-Hall, Inc., 1966.

7. Kuhn, Thomas S. *The Structure of Scientific Revolutions*. Second enlarged edition. Chicago: University of Chicago Press, 1970.

8. Laughlin, J. Laurence. *Principles of Political Economy of John Stuart Mill*, abridged. New York: D. Appleton and Co., 1888.

9. Marshall, Alfred. *Industry and Trade*. London: Macmillan and Co., 1919.

10. _____. *Money, Credit and Commerce*. London: Macmillan and Co., 1923.

11. _____. *Principles of Economics*, 8th ed. London: Macmillan and Co., 1930.

12. Meade, James E. *The Theory of Indicative Planning*. Manchester: Manchester University Press, 1970.

13. Mill, John Stuart. *Principles of Political Economy with Some of Their Applications to Social Philosophy*. London: Longmans, Green and Co., 1929.

14. Mitchell, Wesley C., "The Prospects of Economics," in *The Trend of Economics*, edited by Rexford G. Tugwell. New York: Alfred A. Knopf, 1924.

15. _____. *Types of Economic Theory*, edited by Joseph Dorfman. New York: Augustus M. Kelley, 1969.

16. Pigou, A. C., ed. *Memorials of Alfred Marshall*. London: Macmillan and Co., 1925.

17. Ricardo, David. *An Essay on the Influence of a Low Price of Corn on the Profits of Stock, Shewing the Inexpediency of Restrictions on Importation*, in *Works and Correspondence of David Ricardo*, edited by Piero Sraffa, IX, 9–41. Cambridge: Cambridge University Press, 1951.

18. _____. *Notes on Malthus's Principles of Political Economy*, in *Works and Correspondence of David Ricardo*, edited by Piero Sraffa, II. Cambridge: Cambridge University Press, 1951.

19. _____. *On the Principles of Political Economy and Taxation*, in *Works and Correspondence of David Ricardo*, edited by Piero Sraffa, I. Cambridge: Cambridge University Press, 1951.

20. Rogin, Leo. *The Meaning and Validity of Economic Theory*. New York: Harper & Brothers, 1956.

21. Russell, Bertrand. *The Autobiography of Bertrand Russell, 1872–1914*. Boston: Little, Brown and Co., 1951.

22. Schultze, Charles L. *The Public Use of Private Interest*. Washington: The Brookings Institution, 1977.

23. Schumpeter, Joseph A. *History of Economic Analysis*, edited by Elizabeth Boody Schumpeter. New York: Oxford University Press, 1954.

24. Smith, Adam. *An Inquiry into the Nature and the Causes of the Wealth of Nations*, edited by Edwin Cannan. New York: The Modern Library, 1937.

25. Ward, Benjamin. *What's Wrong with Economics?* New York: Basic Books, Inc., 1972.

The Future of American Capitalism

R. JOSEPH MONSEN

What is the future of American capitalism? Before World War I there were no socialist or communist governments, yet today the world is covered by communist systems that encompass more than a third of the world's population. When socialist nations are added to the list, one sees that the face of Western Europe and Africa is rapidly changing and entering the non-captialist world. What other political or economic change of comparable importance has occurred in the twentieth century?

After the turn of the century (in that great period just prior to World War I often referred to as *"la belle époque"*), capitalism and its step child, colonialism, covered most of the globe. By the end of the 1980s, some observers predict, there will be only three major industrial capitalist governments: the United States, Japan, and West Germany. Indeed, there is cause to worry whether even these three will survive, for both Japan and West Germany could well become socialist systems in more than name.

How much has American capitalism changed in this century—or merely in the past fifty years? In many ways, it has changed considerably. The Great Depression of the 1930s, preceded by the stock market crash, ushered in the New Deal and with it the beginning of vastly changed relations between government and business. Regulation of business increasingly replaced laissez faire as the philosophy of government-business relations. With the great increase in environmental and affirmative action laws, this regulative surge has continued during the past decade. The locus of decision-making power has been shifting continually during the past fifty years from private hands to those of government bureaucrats. At the same time, government expenditures rose from 10 percent of the gross national product (GNP) in 1929 to 23 percent in 1976.[1]

Thus, the role and cost of government have changed American capitalism dramatically. It can be argued, of course, that this change has saved the system from far more drastic change. Others argue that this change has created the profit squeeze, high rates of inflation, high unemployment, and the severe drop in real terms in the stock market of the past decade. This long-run major shift in the government's share of society's national product is troubling to most advocates of capitalism in the United States. It is too suggestive of trends occurring in Great Britain or Italy—and concomitant economic chaos.

Income taxes in this past half-century have made

it difficult for anyone not in oil or real estate (where special tax advantages have existed) to join the ranks of the great rich who made their money before the advent of high tax rates. Despite high inheritance taxes, however, the great fortunes of the past have still been passed on with the ingenuity of skillful tax lawyers. For the middle class in the United States most, if not all, real increases in the standard of living (indeed, if there have actually been any at all) in the past decade have come about by a working spouse. Since the cost of housing has been significantly outrunning income gains in recent years, we have witnessed a situation in which only a third or a fourth of all families in the United States can afford to purchase homes—a significant drop from a half or more a decade ago. This change alone raises questions as to whether an increase in the standard of living has taken place for most of the population in recent years. Further, the full impact of the energy crunch has not yet been felt by the U.S. populace.

Despite these difficulties of the past decade, real progress for those on the lower half of the income scale has occurred since the grim days of the 1930s. While a negative income tax, in name, has yet to be passed, food stamps, welfare programs, and social security benefits raised the floor of poverty in this country considerably above the basic standard of living in such countries as Great Britain even under a socialist government. The list of changes in education, health care, and other major programs could also be enumerated. These may have come more as the result of economic growth, however, than any particular government policy. We cannot second-guess how American capitalism might have been with a lesser role of government; we can only note the changes that have occurred and are occurring and the basic direction of those changes.

R. Joseph Monsen is Professor and Chairman of the Department of Business, Government, and Society in the Schools of Business Administration, University of Washington. His teaching interests lie in corporate social responsibility, theories of the firm, and theories of capitalism. He has published extensively, and serves as trustee of the Seattle Art Museum and a founder-trustee emeritus of the Seattle Opera.

The bulk of the population in the United States still enjoys the world's highest standard of living coupled with as many freedoms as any mass society has ever achieved in world history. The obvious concern is whether this standard of living can continue, or indeed if it can resume its growth in real terms in the future, and whether basic freedoms that have persisted for the past two centuries can be maintained. The major dangers to American capitalism are seen both as external threats from war, terrorists, or resource blackmail and as internal dangers from a growing role of government in the society and hostile interest groups.

Literature on the Future of Capitalism

Since Adam Smith, two centuries ago, nearly every great economist has been concerned with the question: "What is the future of capitalism?" Adam Smith considered the system, later to be called capitalism, as basically a utopian system. His *Wealth of Nations*[2] can be viewed as outlining an early utopia. Adam Smith's initial concern and fear was that the role of government would be too large and would interfere with the operation of his system. This fear, it should be noted, has continued to exist for the past two centuries and in recent years has increased in intensity as the role of government has, in fact, substantially expanded.

Marx and Keynes, despite being basic antagonists, did agree on one thing: that the decreasing rate of return on capital would result eventually in the demise of capitalism. Unlike Marx, Keynes, in his *General Theory*,[3] set out to rectify this flaw. By increasing the role that government played in the economy, Keynes visualized that capitalism could be saved. He was therefore both an apologist and a doctor for the ailing capitalist systems of the 1930s. To the Marxists, the pressure upon the capitalist nations to counteract this declining rate of return explains imperialism, colonialism, and most modern wars. But many modern economists worry that Keynes, in his efforts to save capitalism, may have let loose an incurable virus in the form of increasing government deficits and power that will stifle capitalism eventually, anyway. So the debate rages today.

Of all the theorists who have written on capitalism in this century, Schumpeter may be the most thorough and the most brilliant. In his now classic book, *Socialism, Capitalism and Democracy*,[4] Schumpeter discusses five basic reasons why capitalism will fail. Despite the fact that Schumpeter is an ardent, even passionate, supporter of capitalism, he had little hope that it would survive as an economic system. Schumpeter's pessimism rested upon his reluctant acceptance of the following arguments.

1. Inflation would inevitably result from a high level of employment. The collaboration between union leadership and government leadership would under these conditions spell perennial inflation. This, in turn, would create the conditions for further government controls, which, coupled with the redistribution of wealth under inflationary circumstances, destroys the middle class and the very fiber of capitalism.

2. Entrepreneurship declines as government controls proliferate, making the entrepreneur's role increasingly difficult, and in the process sapping the strength from the motivating force of capitalism itself.

3. Capitalist values decline as a result of the very success of capitalism. The traditional capitalist values (outlined best by Ben Franklin) of thrift, industry, reliability, and utilizing saving not in consumption but in investment are being replaced by modern drives for consumption, security, equality, and regulation. Thus, the scheme of values of capitalist society blows away in the secular winds created by the very economic success of capitalism.

4. Loyalty to capitalism as a system is destroyed by the spirit of rationalism which capitalism creates. Such mystical feelings and values as loyalty to the traditional assumptions of capitalism—private property, a free market, competition, entrepreneurship, and the capitalist value system—wither before the critical gaze of rationalism. The modern drive toward rationalizing the firm and the business process creates a bureaucracy which replaces the family firm and the entrepreneur.

5. The alienation of the intellectuals is fostered, even created, by capitalism. Capitalism tends to create, educate, and subsidize a vested interest in social unrest. The intellectuals cannot help nibbling, even attacking, the foundation of capital-

ism, since they live on criticism and "their whole position depends on criticism that stings." The capitalist order is unable to effectively control the intellectual sector. Indeed, in the very process of expanding the educational apparatus and the facilities for higher education, capitalism further expends and creates the demand for the very group who is "digging its own grave." Thus, the intellectuals, perhaps more than anything else, are destroying capitalism as a system.

Baran and Sweezy, in their now-famous book, *Monopoly Capital*,[5] attempted to analyze American capitalism from a neo-Marxist point of view. Since they are not orthodox Marxists, their analysis does not lead them to the traditional conclusion that capitalism will fail because its rate of return on capital is falling and therefore the capitalists are forced to squeeze the workers more and more until the workers finally rebel and overthrow the system. Quite the opposite, Baran and Sweezy find that monopoly capitalism creates an "economic surplus." This, in turn, creates problems for the system to absorb this surplus. But since the system generates more surplus than it can effectively utilize, which leads to depressions, the government must aid in wasting the surplus, and wars are a major method of waste.

Nonetheless, if monopoly capitalism is to fall, it will have to come about through some other nontraditional Marxist route. At the very end of their book, Baran and Sweezy prophesy that the "prospect of effective revolutionary action to overthrow the system is slim." What they see as the more likely course is the continuation of the present process of decay until the compulsions of the system affect human nature so severely that the increasing rate of psychic disorders will lead to the "impairment and eventual breakdown of the system's ability to function even on its own terms." Thus, Baran and Sweezy rely on an essentially noneconomic, nonpolitical argument to accomplish the demise of capitalism. It is interesting that since they base the book on an economic analysis, their final hope for the collapse of the system must lie outside the main thrust of their argument.

Two radically opposite analysts of capitalism, who nonetheless share a common belief that the government policy of deficit spending may ultimately destroy capitalism are Marxist James O'Connor (author of the *Fiscal Crisis of the State*)[6] and famous libertarian Milton Friedman (author of *Capitalism and Freedom*).[7] Strange bedfellows indeed! O'Connor is pessimistic about the future of American capitalism because he sees the monopolist firms taking all the profits from the system but the government absorbing all the costs (that is, socializing the monopolist's costs), particularly of various externalities and welfare to keep the society functioning. Since the government is taking in less in taxes than its various programs are costing, the deficits mount, with important consequences. (1) Increasing inefficiency in the system, which often results in further government programs and costs (a Catch-22 situation). (2) The organization of government workers, because they are being squeezed since the government's finances are in the red, particularly state and local government workers in education, police and similar sectors. This will lead to increasing agitation and breakdown of the government sector as strikes in the public sector occur more and more frequently. (3) A malaise gradually settles upon the society because of increasing social costs. (4) Finally, the government, following deficit financing, will create inflation and make those workers in the competitive sector (as opposed to those working for the monopoly firms that are taken care of) more dependent upon the state programs to survive. This in turn increases further deficits and ultimately creates the "fiscal crisis of the state." This argument might be labeled "a radical conservative analysis of the future of American capitalism."

Milton Friedman, the best-known conservative economist in America, simply argues that the use of deficit spending and other Keynesian fiscal policies only result in destabilizing the economy and increasing the total economic uncertainty. Friedman argues that the effects of deficit spending are uncertain. But increasing uncertainty increases chances of business cutbacks in investment and consumer cutbacks in spending. Thus, the very opposite result (a depression) can occur from Keynesian fiscal policies that were designed to create growth and stability. Above all else, Friedman feels, business and consumers hate uncertainty and they will hedge themselves to protect against it. Friedman therefore argues

that what is needed is a steady and acknowledged growth rate of the money supply.

In this regard Friedman is a believer that capitalism can be saved by the "right" economic manipulation—those monetary policies that will reduce uncertainty. O'Connor, of course, is basically a Marxist determinist whose analysis leads to only one eventual conclusion—the demise of capitalism. Yet both see the use of fiscal deficits as a factor which is inherently destructive to the capitalist system.

The long-wave (fifty-year) business cycle has recently come to attention again in the work of the Belgian Marxian economist Ernest Mandel. His book, *Late Capitalism*,[8] is one of the most influential discussions of capitalism that has been written in post-World War II Europe. Baran and Sweezy, in *Monopoly Capital*, argued the evidence for the "Kondratieff cycle," so called because Shumpeter named it after the Russian economist who first claimed to have discovered a cycle of some fifty years' duration, was weak and "unconvincing." Nonetheless, the long business cycle has recently received considerable attention as a model to explain the severe depression in the stock market in real terms and the high levels of unemployment in the past decade in capitalist nations.

No very convincing explanation of these recent events has yet won much of a following. Yet the Kondratieff cycle is beginning to gain adherents among both the followers of Mandel and, more recently, of the well-know economist from the Johnson era, Walt Rostow.[9] Rostow recently argues "that the world has entered—for the fifth time in 200 years—a new phase of the Kondratieff cycle. The beginning of each phase is marked by accelerated inflation, high interest rates, and shifts of income to producers of food and energy."

Paradoxically, we now have well-known anti-Marxists as well as Marxists accepting the controversial Kondratieff cycle. To the Marxists, of course, the cycle is simply another characteristic inherent in the framework of the capitalist mode of production. To Mandel the entire "Capitalist industrial cycle thus appears to be the consequence of accelerated capital accumulation, over-accumulation, decelerated capital accumulation and under-investment. The rise, fall and revitalization of the rate of profit both correspond to, and command, the successive movements of capital accumulation."[10] The result from a Marxist standpoint, of course, is that these very cycles eventually result in a revolution of the working class that will overthrow capitalism. To a non-Marxist, such as Rostow, the end is not so determanistic. Rather, the economy can be manipulated by Keynesian policies and by the addition of a private-public partnership to overcome the difficulties created by business cycles. Thus, once again we have the Marxians sure that the future of capitalism is collapse while the non-Marxians are still considrably more optimistic about capitalism's future.

Sociologist Daniel Bell, in *The Cultural Contradiction of Capitalism*,[11] argues that a crisis besets contemporary capitalism that may be fatal. That is, American capitalism has lost its traditional base for its legitimacy—namely its Protestant ethic sancitification of work. Without this moral system of rewards which justifies work and the basic values of traditional capitalism, it has nothing to support a rationalistic capitalist system. The substitution of a form of modern hedonism, which Bell feels promises material ease and luxury and yet shies away from the social permissiveness and libertarianism which hedonism implies, only further accentuates this crisis. That crisis, which Bell sees as a rational technocratic system of decision making requiring meritorious rewards to function efficiently, is faced instead with a culture that is fostering antirational modes of behavior that are contradictory to the functioning of capitalism.

Bell sees this cultural contradiction as the basic challenge to contemporary capitalism. Modern capitalism, as he sees it, has lost its religion and with it the ultimate sources of religious feeling that justified the social structure and made people operate in a rational "Capitalist" mode—even if unintentionally. The very success of capitalism breeds an antireligious, antirational mode of behavior.

Bell is very much in the Schumpeterian and Weberian tradition in his mode of analysis, for he looks at capitalism as an economic system in which private property traditionally is the backbone of a bourgeois society. His argument is that "the ultimate support for any social system is the acceptance by the population of moral justification of authority." Since capitalism, in losing its religion, has also lost its support system for private property, it has lost its chief defense for the basic assumption of capitalism itself.

Ernest Van Den Hagg argues a somewhat similar thesis.[12] He contends that religion was the stabilizing system that by promising eternal rewards and punishments acted to offset temporal injustice in this world. The wrongs of capitalism could be forgiven and forgotten by the justice that was sure to come in the next world. Efficiency was gained in this world through market capitalism, and justice was promised in the next through religion. This gave temporal stability to capitalism as an economic system. But with the disappearance of belief and the rise of secularism and particularly of socialism as a belief system, the future of capitalism is in doubt. As socialism promises justice and equality in this world, Van Den Hagg argues, the result will not necessarily be more justice, and certianly not more freedom, but rather merely the passing of power, income, and prestige from the entrepreneurs to the bureaucrats. The latter group, he argues, and not the intellectuals or paraintellectuals, will be the great "new class"—the beneficiaries of socialism. This line of argument, stemming from Bell, Weber, and Schumpeter, ultimately leads to the rise of a new bureaucratic society with a new religion called socialism.

Robert Heilbroner has been analyzing capitalism for several decades. In his earlier writing he had felt that capitalism was sufficiently stable that this century in America would see little fundamental change in its economic system. More recently he has become well known for his predictions of chaos, war, and collapse. His environmental scenario has pollution creating havoc with the atmosphere and climate.

Before war and pollution loomed so large in his concern for the future of America and, indeed, the world, Heilbroner, in *The Limits of American Capitalism*,[13] had argued, that "In the end capitalism is weighed in the scale of science and found wanting, not alone as a system but as a philosophy." Indeed, he has claimed that "capitalism as an ideal has never garnered much enthusiasm. The acquisitive behavior on which it is perforce based has suffered all through history from the moral ambivalence in which it has been held." In talking about the last third of this century, Heilbroner asserts that the broad limits are drawn and are unlikely to change. Namely, it is beyond the present limits of capitalism to replace the guiding principle of production for profit. It is beyond the present limits of capitalism in the U.S. to nationalize the great corporations or the private ownership of the means of communication. It is impossible to end the concentration of private wealth. Thus, Heilbroner sees little possibility of changing the present structure of privilege or to displace the present social order with a new one.

The Limits of American Capitalism was written in 1965; today some of these limits seem less impregnable. Yet we see no immediate storming of the bastions in this country to totally change these basic assumptions of the society. Heilbroner's concern over war and environmental collapse presents risks of a different nature. Wars seem more assured in probabilistic terms—the question is *what kind* and *where* as to their potential impact on American capitalism.

The Issues Raised

What is tne effect, or potential effect, on the future of capitalism in this country of the issues raised by these scholars? Let us review what effects these issues may have upon our society.

War. Obviously a total nuclear war could destroy most civilized life on the planet. If we assume a most optimistic mode, however, it will not be unlikely to expect three to six limited wars between now and the turn of the century—based upon experience since 1900. The *World Almanac* lists thirty-seven American military actions between 1900 and 1973. Further, since the end of World War II, the United States has threatened to unleash some form of military might on no fewer than 215 occasions. All this suggests that if we are able to avoid major military conflict over the next quarter century, which is by no means certain, the society and economy will probably be subjected to the pressures of limited military involvements several more times in this century. The implication for social and economic disruptions caused by more "Korean wars" for example, are horrible to con-

sider, but the probabilities nonetheless remain high—given our historical experience. Indeed, this is a most optimistic forecast given our experience in the past seventy-five years.

Inflation. War has been the most frequent initial cause for major inflationary eras in U.S. economic history. At times inflation has been curtailed shortly after the cessation of hostilities. More recently, following Vietnam, inflationary runs have been harder to control—particularly when occurring with other factors of resource scarcity such as oil monopolies. Given the probabilities of war and scarcities during the next twenty-five years, bouts of inflation are to be expected. I assume, however, that the United States will not experience a runaway inflation in the next quarter century. While we may expect periods of high inflation rates, they will not be either permanent or so high as to cause major social upheaval.

Unemployment. It is remarkable that our unemployment rate has not been vastly higher than it is, given three facts: the baby boom of the fifties and sixties, which brought so many new people into the labor market in recent years; the major social change of women wanting to enter the labor market and doing so in huge numbers; and the fact that the economy in the seventies has had a number of recessions. Thus, many economists might have expected unemployment rates in the U.S. to have been considerably higher than they have been. This observation is unsatisfying to those without jobs, but to economists looking at the major trends of supply, women workers, and the state of the economy and job market, the U.S. economy has been remarkably resilient to have weathered this problem as successfully as it has. The rest of this century should have more favorable factors to reduce unemployment rates—as the result of lower birth rates and with the initial influx of married women workers absorbed. Therefore, I am basically optimistic about long-run employment trends in the U.S. during the rest of the century.

Business cycle—do long waves exist? This is obviously a very controversial issue among economists. If they do exist, as many Marxist[14] and non-Marxist[15] economists now agree, the implications may be that a long-term turn-up of twenty to twenty-five years will begin in the last part of the 1980s and continue well into the next century. If so, then we are at least halfway through (and probably near the bottom of) a long-wave economic cycle that last bottomed out in the Great Depression of the 1930s. Many Marxists, including Mandel, are less optimistic about the ability of capitalism to weather these long waves. They argue that world capitalism has reached the end of an era. "The expansionary phase of the postwar long wave is over and we are entering an indefinite period of stagnation; industrial cycles will continue to occur, but booms will be shorter and slumps longer. . . ."[16]

Rostow and most capitalist economists would not agree. It is a sign of viability of the system to have survived a stock market drop in real terms not seen since since the early 1930s. Evidence of the decline in the stock market is seen by the fact that if the market had continued to grow during the past decade at the same rate it did from 1926 to 1965, yielding a real return of 7.2 percent a year over that long period, it should today be at a level of around 2,500 on the Dow Jones Industrial Average. If the total market value of publicly held companies in the United States over the ten-year period from 1965 to 1975 is computed, it becomes evident that in real terms, accounting for inflation, the value of these companies fell nearly 50 percent during this period. Also those teenagers who, particularly, have had difficulty getting employment can attest with investors that the recent years have not been universally prosperous—even though, unlike the 1930s, there was not a major collapse of the economy. Thus, there is some attestation that, for whatever reason—government interference or the long Kondratieff business cycle—the seventies will not be noted as a period of economic euphoria.

The latter years of this century, to some of the followers of the Kondratieff cycle, look far more promising. Therefore, the economic future of American capitalism depends very much on the model from which it is viewed. Most optimistically, one might add, even if the long cycles do exist they have not created conditions in the United States yet that make us ripe for revolution. The most that could be said is that adverse economic conditions have furthered the enlarged role of government regulation within the economy—perhaps an insidious, but not a dramatic, turn of events.

The change in values in American society. Can changing values destroy capitalism? A number of scholars seems to think so. Further, it is not hard to see how the ideas of Fabian socialism have changed the British economic system from one of capitalism to one based increasingly upon socialist norms and values. The decline in great Britain's economic fortunes seems to have occurred as socialist values have spread and gained political acceptance. Not that such a correlation may be entirely fair—but it is nonetheless suspicious to hard headed businessmen. If it is true that the Puritan work ethic is being replaced in America by an increasingly hedonistic-centered set of values, this may be a partial explanation to what appears to be a declining productivity trend in this country. Not only is productivity, and with it the standard of living, susceptible to change under the onslaught of changing values, but so are the very fabric and laws of our economic and political system. If those who see a change occurring in our value system are correct and this change is taking the economy further from the basic postulates of capitalism, such a claim is serious.

It would be foolhardy to ignore such analysis just because the data are soft and difficult to tabulate empirically. Certainly there are threads of egalitarianism, which deTocqueville[17] noted as characteristic of this nation on his trip to America in 1830. Politicians exploit such issues successfully today. Such threads can be used to develop an American form of a "people's capitalism," which by the turn of the century could present some basic changes in the economy—at least in the distribution of income and living standards for some groups.

Populist egalitarianism therefore is an old but still strong idea in American politics and could spell substantial changes in our system before the year 2000. One must remember that "tax reforms" are basically income redistribution schemes, all of which are value-laden in nature and political in specifics. The change in work values, the desire for security, for our government to play a larger role in the economy, the expectation of a rising standard of living, and particularly the values that place the blame upon certain groups or issues all are at work presently, creating a changing and evolving economy. One need only think back to the generation of one's parents to remember that personal consumer debt (with the possible exception of a home mortgage) was considered "bad." Much more recently, the changes in sexual mores have affected both the economy and our way of living. Values and mores continue to change and in our post-industrial society the rate of change is often hard to assimilate. The question is not whether capitalism is changing in America, but whether the society's values and ideas are changing in such a way that the basic structure of capitalism as we know it will disappear and evolve into something quite new and different.

Technological change. Modern capitalism is the child of the industrial revolution. Indeed, to Schumpeter innovation and technological change explain the basic features of the business cycles. To Heilbroner it is the engine of change pulling the whole society and economy into new worlds—with both good and disastrous consequences. The spectre of environmental catastrophe, the burning of the world if not its nuclear destruction, can be traced to consequences of new technology. The world has seen more basic change in the past century and a half than in the whole millennium before. Looking down the road to the turn of the century, technological changes that are quite possible (at least according to Herman Kahn of the Hudson Institute), will be quite capable of not only destroying all life but also of creating and growing new plants and animals and genetically altering man— perhaps into even another species.

Any such technological changes that can send man to the moon, establish space colonies, death rays, and change man's longevity can also likely change democratic capitalism—through the creation of almost full central information and power or to a more dangerous form of despotism that such new technology makes possible. Since a form of chemical bliss is also to be expected, in the form of a Huxley-like "soma," we may apparently not mind such changes. Given such potential alternatives, it is indeed hard to predict the consequences upon capitalism of further technological change. It seems safest to assume, therefore, that despite the pos-

siblities of breath-taking innovations, the government and business institutions will attempt to keep them under control so that the framework of our system may not be fundamentally altered in the near future.

Resources. The risks in making forecasts are exemplified in the work of Herman Kahn, our best-known futurist. For example, in his book *The Year 2000,*[18] Kahn does not mention the possibility of oil and resource scarcities or of world cartels' controlling scarce resources among his many forecasts. Yet the OPEC nations have had a major and disastrous effect upon the stability of many Western governments. Obviously the scarcity of energy at low prices or the controlling of other resources by cartels can lead to greater government controls, nationalization, and even to the overthrow of governments.

Despite Kahn's failure to consider such a scenario, it does seem likely that the rest of this century will see national governments regulating and controlling the price and supply of many natural resources. In the U.S., the main result is not apt to be the shift of power from the two main center parties but merely the growth in power of the executive branch of government in controlling and regulating the economy—thus the rise of a "Command President" becomes more likely under any conditions of crisis.

Environmental pollution. Two arguments suggest that capitalism can be destroyed by such non-market-controlled problems as pollution. Such externalities are handled in our economy largely by government regulation. The result of such regulation is to increase the cost of consumer goods (thereby tending to lower the overall material standard of living of the consumer) and to take more and more decisions out of the hands of business managers and in the process decrease the firm's efficiency. As such regulatory bureaucracies grow in decision-making power, the drag upon the economy becomes substantially larger. The net effect is to make capitalism less viable and indeed less of an operational system. On the other hand, Heilbroner has argued that environmental pollution may eventually destroy the earth by drastically altering the earth's climate. That would destroy capitalism along with the rest of the world.

Despite these two pessimistic scenarios it is more

likely, I suspect, that American capitalism can survive better because the political repercussions of uncontrolled externalities may be abated and the rising costs of bureaucratic regulation may become more noticeable to both the politicians and the public.

Government spending. One of the most pervasive trends in the past quarter-century in all Western capitalist countries has been the continual expansion of the share of GNP spent by the government—particularly the civil government. While military expenditures have varied in relation to the Korean and Vietnamese conflicts, going up and down over this period, the civil expenditures of capitalist governments have largely done nothing but expand. Thus, some economists, including even Marxist ones, have argued that this has been a major factor in the profit squeeze most non-oil firms have felt during the past decade. The civil segment of state expenditures has grown rapidly for a number of reasons, in particular the following: political pressure by special-interest groups for benefits; a low level of productivity generally, but particularly in the expanding service activities sponsored by the state (administration, health, education); and increasing regulatory costs in new areas such as the environment.

Indeed, all of the capitalist countries' share of GNP spent by government, except that of Japan, where the most exceptionally rapid economic growth has occurred, have long since passed Colin Clark's magic number of twenty-five percent. Clark theorized that once a government passed this mark the drag on the economy would substantially affect businesses' ability to grow and remain profitable. The nation's growth rate would slow down perceptibly. Whether or not this theory is correct, it may well be that the increasing share of government-spent GNP is adversely affecting management morale and expectations. In so doing the increasing role of the government in the economy (and along with it the higher costs of doing business as controls and regulations have escalated) has had a less than salutary effect upon the private business sector—which has in capitalist systems been the sustaining growth sector.

Whether or not this expansion can be halted or reduced is extremely difficult to forsee. There would be little cause for optimism except that in California both governors Reagan and Brown have made relatively successful attempts to slow the growing expansion of state expenditures. Further, California has also enacted a referendum to roll back property tax levels. If these movements spread, it is possible that the total share of local, state, and government expenditures might yet level off. Indeed, in the past few years the most rapid growth in government spending has been at the state and local levels, where now the taxpayers' revolts are occurring. Thus, there is some cause for cautious optimism.

Alternative Scenarios

Market capitalism. This version might best be called "roll back the clock." Is it possible to return to an era not seen in the U.S. since before the 1930s, when the market was king? It seems an unlikely possibility. Certainly if under conservative Presidents, Nixon and Ford, the system was not returned perceptibly to greater reliance on market forces and decentralized decision making, does the future hold any more likely possibility? Yet, at times more liberal administrations can be more conservative than the conservatives themselves. The fact that there is currently talk of deregulating certain highly regulated industries, such as the airlines, gives hope that the appreciation of the market is not totally dead. Thus, the possibility of market capitalism —operating in specific areas of our economy now regulated—cannot be dismissed. One scenario might therefore predict that by the end of the century the effective use of market capitalism might be better understood than in recent years and that a dual economy could exist-- private capialism and a public or regulated sector. Therefore a dual economy, in which market capitalism was allowed to be a vigorous enforcer of competition for the public good, can be envisioned. This could be spurred by disillusionment with other alternatives of regulation and nationalization. It would not likely be a total market capitalism but a dual or triple sector one in which market capitalism was allowed to operate in specific industries for specific purpose of increasing the production of public goods (privately) at the lowest prices (or at least lower than possible under regulated alternatives).

Regulated capitalism. If a "more of the same" or "wind up the clock" scenario were used as a straight-line projection for the next twenty-five years, what would our economy look like by the turn of the century? Easy as a straigh-line projection appears, the past quarter-century, as did its predecessors, has had its share of major crises. This approach suggests that wars, shortages, inflation, and recessions would be part of the scenario. The result of these crises or stresses upon the system will quite probably be to increase the government's role in decision making in the economy. Corporate managers will make their decisions within relatively narrow parameters. A continuing high level of regulative legislation will mean that guidelines and government approval will be required for almost all business decision. Business decisions regarding prices, wages, rent, energy controls, and so forth, if not set outright (as the next scenario suggests), will be sufficiently constrained so that profit returns will be lower than we have been used to in the first half of this century and therefore capital shortages may be common among businesses. Business, however, will be considerably more "responsible" because of laws, guidelines, and public expectations.

This projection suggests that a new form of "regulated" or "bureaucratic capitalism" may have evolved by the turn of the century without any drastic changes occurring—merely the extrapolation of the past quarter-century into the future. What does this mean for the average individual? Namely, that security will be at an even higher level in the society but that the incentives and opportunities to become Edisons, Fords, or Lands, will be slim indeed.

Planned capitalism. This scenario might be called "speeding up the clock." It assumes that our political system remains unchanged but that regulations eventually move to outright planning of the economy in terms of growth, regional development, employment, inflation, wages, rents, and profit margins. All of these planning examples have prototypes in Western Europe in the postwar period. Further, the United States itself, under a conservative President, has engaged in various wage and price controls in efforts to meet "planned inflationary rates." The Labor government in Great Britain recently asked Parliament for "permanent" wage, price,

and profit controls. France's successful economic growth after World War II has been attributed by some to "indicative planning."

Whether planned capitalism, which we assume would also be a highly regulated capitalism, would also adopt such common European forms as state-owned (nationalized) firms is hard to predict. A possible scenario is that the economic problems of energy, inflation, scarce natural resources, unemployment, regional development, and bankruptcy might force our government to take over such individual firms as Lockheed, or such industries as the railroads, oil, or the airlines. These changes could be initiated by public demand for continuation of services (affecting transportation), governmental needs for military security (affecting the Merchant Marine or defense companies), or the continued decrease in public trust and confidence in certain businesses (as has affected the oil industry). Indeed, all these factors are present now; it would take only a confluence of circumstances and the 'right' mix of politicians to promote them to change the system to a form of mixed socialism. All this could be done by a reluctant Congress or president who could suggest no other alternative.

While there is a strong antinationalization bias in this country, circumstances could create further government firms. I do not see this, however, as a rampant trend similar to the large-scale nationalizations that exist in Europe. The American approach has always been to regulate, not nationalize. Nonetheless, as Amtrak points out clearly, there are occasions where the public sector assumes control however unwillingly. So we may expect some but not rampant nationalization to occur in the U.S. during the next quarter-century.

Another scenario for the future of business is that this country could be increasing direct partnership between business and government as in the case of Comsat, a communication satellite created through a partnership between American Telephone and the government. In Europe, of course, there are many examples of the government owning stock in private firms—in Great Britain the National Enterprise Board has been given funds to buy stock in firms who need capital for expansion or who might go bankrupt without help. This process has not been tried in the United States, but Sweden has pioneered such attempts to aid businesses in need and at the same time to gain government representatives on more boards. This partnership between business and government (particularly in new ventures) would be more ideologically acceptable in this country presently than outright total government ownership.

There are numerous other vehicles by which government can participate, direct, control, or plan business beyond what is now commonly practiced. Other new ideas will undoubtedly appear and become popular during the next twenty years. It should be expected that such changes and new ventures would still have to be ideologically compatible with our present dominant centrist ideology.

While there has been strong traditional opposition to planning in this country, in recent years a growing number of important businessmen such as Henry Ford II, Irwin Miller, and Michael Blumenthal have come out favoring some form of national planning. The so-called Humphrey-Hawkins and Humphrey-Javits bills have presented Congress for the first time with some consideration of the planning issue. Hence, it would be foolhardy to forecast the next quarter-century without at least considering the probability of a planning mechanism in some guise as part of our government system. What would be the effect on business? If carried out on a cooperative basis as is typical of Japan or earlier of French indicative planning, big business might indeed find it beneficial. It could reduce uncertainty in the government sector and make it possible for firms to plan more rationally. The real danger would be whether the relationship between the planners and business would be developed along cooperative or adversary lines.

Command capitalism ("throw away the clock"). The previous scenarios all assumed that the political movement will remain unchanged during the rest of this century. There is obviously the possibility of change in our political environment and in the structure of our government. While there is, of course, the chance of a military coup or of electing a president who is a demagogue, I perfer to trace another scenario that I believe has a higher probability of occurring by the end of the century. That is of a shift to what I call "Command" capitalism.

Command capitalism is essentially a version of our present system with the major exception that the President has assumed the prominant role of an active Commander-in-Chief in both peace and wartime— with all that implies. Essentially it can be thought of as close to wartime capitalism. Of the three branches of government, the executive branch becomes permanently the major and dominant power. This transition has been occurring in this century. The President and his bureaucracy have continued to increase in power dramatically. Congress, by contrast, has been too often stalemated by conflicting interest groups. Indeed, one can predict that if interest group stalemate continues to plague the legislative branch severely during the rest of this century, crises in both foreign and domestic affairs will force the President, by default, to become a Command President.

The country has suffered through interest-group stalemates before, and the powers of a Mediatory Presidency have usually been sufficient to resolve them. But, as interest groups have become more vigorous and with more public disclosure of positions via the media, their leaders have been less able to compromise, trade votes, and longroll to make legislation possible. The traditional role of the President as a mediator becomes impossible when the major interest groups refuse to compromise. Indeed, we predict the role of a Mediatory Presidency will become more and more ineffectual. Crises in both foreign and domestic affairs necessitate actions and this pressure in turn can compel the emergence of a "Command Presidency." It can be argued that this is already occurring with the powers presently available to the President in his capacity as Commander-in-Chief. During war or extraordinary circumstances, a President has specific and implied command power that enable shim to cut through traditional restraints on executive power. This is precisely the power needed to overcome interest-group stalemate in Congress.

What will be the effect on the economic system? As we have already observed, the direction of economic affairs over the past fifty years has steadily gravitated to the Presidency. This trend would accelerate under a Command Presidency.

Thus, the President would increasingly direct national economic planning (even if only indicative) in order to guarantee economic well-being at home, but also to insure that public-sector and private-sector programs will be harmoniously interrelated. Further, controls (especially wage and price controls) on a permanent basis would seem to be inevitable under such a model. While the precedents for such programs are rooted in crisis (inflation, unemployment, wars, energy and resource shortages), as crisis becomes more acute or occurs in clusters, the Command Presidency model, ostensibly to rescue private enterprise, would intrude into the private sector more deeply than in any of the previous models.

Just as Rome evolved from the Republic into the Empire under Caesar, so certainly are there pressures for the transformation of democracies under crisis to move to more centralized and peak power dominated forms of government—not necessarily through choice but through expediency.

Coda

We have looked at several alternative scenarios for the future of American capitalism. Granted, totally unexpected turns of events may occur (indeed we may expect they will), but since they are impossible to predict it seems best to start with those alternatives that at this moment appear most likely. Despite the possibilities of "Command" capitalism, I remain cautiously optimistic that both democracy and bureaucratic capitalism will survive this century in the United States. I am, however, considerably less sanguine about the prospects for their survival elsewhere in the world.

REFERENCES

1. *Economic Report of the President, January 1977* (Washington, D.C.: Government Printing Office, 1977), p. 196.

2. Adam Smith, *Wealth of Nations,* 2 vols. (New York: Dutton, 1776).

3. J. M. Keynes, *General Theory of Employment, Interest, and Money* (London: Macmillan, 1936).

4. J. A. Schumpeter, *Capitalism, Socialism, and Democrary,* 3rd ed. (New York: Harper & Brothers, 1950).

5. P. A. Baran and P. M. Sweezy, *Monopoly Capital* (New York: Monthly Review Press, Modern Reader, 1966).

6. James O'Connor, *The Fiscal Crises of the State* (New York: St. Martin's Press, 1973).

7. Milton Friedman, *Capitalism and Freedom* (Chicago: University of Chicago Press, 1962).

8. Ernest Mandel, *Late Capitalism* (London: NLB, 1975).

9. W. W. Rostow, *The World Economy* (Austin: University of Texas Press, 1978).

10. Mandel, op. cit., pp. 109-110.

11. Daniel Bell, *The Cultural Contradictions of Capitalism* (New York; Basic Books, 1976).

12. Ernest Van Den Hagg, "Economics Is Not Enough—Notes On the Anticapitalist Spirit," *Public Interest* (Fall 1976).

13. R. L. Heilbroner, *The Limits of American Capitalism* (New York: Harper Torchbooks, 1966).

14. Mandel, op. cit.

15. Rostow, op. cit.

16. B. Tauthorn, "Mandel's 'Late Capitalism,' " *New Left Review* (July/August 1976).

17. Alexis de Tocqueville, *Democracy in America* (New York: Vintage Books, 1945).

18. Herman Kahn and A. J. Wiener, *The Year 2000* (New York: Macmillan, 1967).